S0-AFC-507

Manual Communication

*to those interested in helping
deaf people to communicate*

All proceeds from the sale of this book will be deposited into the Ohio University Fund in the name of The School of Hearing and Speech Sciences. All monies so deposited will be used solely for the purpose of financing the provision of services to hearing-impaired persons in appropriate Ohio University programs.

MANUAL COMMUNICATION

A Basic Text and Workbook with Practical Exercises

by
Dean A. Christopher, Ph.D.
Associate Professor
School of Hearing and Speech Sciences
Ohio University

Illustrated by
William R. Edwards

Administrative Assistant
Sherry K. Edwards

University Park Press
Baltimore • London • Tokyo

UNIVERSITY PARK PRESS
International Publishers in Science and Medicine
Chamber of Commerce Building
Baltimore, Maryland 21202

Copyright © 1976 by University Park Press

Typeset by The Composing Room of Michigan, Inc.
Manufactured in the United States of America
by Universal Lithographers, Inc.

All rights, inlcuding that of translation into other languages,
reserved. Photomechanical reproduction (photocopy, microcopy) of
this book or parts thereof without special permission of the
publisher is prohibited.

Library of Congress Cataloging in Publication Data
Christopher, Dean A   1940-
Manual communication.

Includes bibliographical references and index.
1. Deaf--Means of communication. 2. Sign language.
I. Title. [DNLM: 1. Manual communication. HV2474
C556m]
HV2471.C5   419   75-38884
ISBN 0-8391-0811-7

Table of Contents

MASS ACLD INC.
1296 WORCESTER ROAD
FRAMINGHAM CTR MASS 01701

Chapter 3 Manual Communication Applied To Hearing, Speech, and Language Evaluation 513

Introduction

According to Dr. William Stokoe ("CAL Conference on Sign Languages," **The Linguistic Reporter,** Vol. 12, No. 2, April 1970), five separate modes are subsumed under the term "Manual Communication:" 1) Sign Language, 2) Fingerspelling, 3) Signed English, 4) Manual English, and 5) Simultaneous Method. These five are characterized as follows:

1. *Sign Language:* A language composed of largely arbitrarily formed signs or sign phrases. The signs are not universally shared nor, for that matter, universally understood. Various investigations into the nature of sign language seem to suggest that it possesses its own distinctive properties of word formation, meaning, and grammar. For example, one finds syntactic orders such as "Me school go now" or "Girl happy." In short, American Sign Language has a structure that is quite different from English.

2. *Fingerspelling:* This mode of communication employs the fingers of either hand in various configurations representing the twenty-six letters of the American alphabet in order to formulate words, phrases, and sentences.

3. *Signed English:* An approach which makes use of the American Sign Language in order to communicate a thought. The message is encoded and expressed in accordance with the syntactical rules governing the English language, although there is a tendency to omit inflections. For example, "He want some cookie."

4. *Manual English:* An approach which fuses fingerspelling, signs based on the American Sign Language, and invented sign forms relating to the morphemic aspects of the English language; for example, "ing" (present progressive), "s" (pluralization), "ed" (past tense of regular verbs), etc. These invented forms are grafted onto the signs. The message is encoded and transmitted in accordance with the grammatical rules governing the English language. For example, if one were using Manual English to say "I watched the boy riding the horse," the word "I" would be signed, the word "watched" would be signed as "watch" plus "ed," "the" may be fingerspelled or it may be signed (depending on the region, since a common sign is not used for this word throughout the United States), "boy" would be signed, "riding" would be signed as "ride" plus "ing," "the" would be signed or fingerspelled, and "horse" would be signed. Also, with certain words, it is permissible to sign part of the word and fingerspell the rest of it. For example, "slowly" could be signed as "slow" with the "ly" fingerspelled.

5. *Simultaneous Method:* An approach which attempts to coordinate the product of lip movements, accompanied by the presence or absence of voice, with manual communication. As Stokoe points out, the user of the Simultaneous Method may employ one of the modes to explain the other. For example, in the sentence "The man hit the ball," the addresser may use the sign "hit" and fingerspell the word "hit" in order further to clarify the desired meaning since the sign ("hit") may stand for other synonyms like "strike," etc.

Toward a Philosophy of (Re) Habilitation

Generally, individuals suffering from impaired hearing encounter varying degrees of difficulty relating to academic success and linguistic development, as well as in social and emotional adjustment. At the core of these problems rests a breakdown in the process of communication. Language, viewed as a structured system of signs or symbols including the rules that stipulate how they may be used, provides the vehicle for communication. To the extent that impaired hearing diminishes or precludes the acquisition of linguistic information, the communication process is proportionately affected. Thus, an objective of (re)habilitation is to help these individuals become more communicatively able by increasing their "linguistic pool" of information.

The preferred use of the Simultaneous Method (defined here as the synchronization of speech and Manual English) as part of the Total Communication approach, especially within an educational setting, may be viewed as potentially providing the aurally handicapped individual with an improved model for communication based on multimodality involvement. Thus, with the spoken aspect of a given message providing both aural and oral cues and clues that a person may be able to profit from through the use of amplification and speechreading, in close synchronization with the use of corresponding signs and/or fingerspelling which are transmitted within the syntactic and grammatical structure of the English language (Manual English), the hearing-impaired individual then may be exposed to a richer and more viable educational experience aimed at helping him become more able to communicate with his hearing peers.

Total Communication

Recently, Dr. David M. Denton, Superintendent of the Maryland School for the Deaf, advanced a definition of "Total Communication":

> By Total Communication is meant the right of a deaf child to learn to use all forms of communication available to develop language competence at the earliest possible age. This implies introduction to a reliable receptive-expressive symbol system in the preschool years between the ages of one and five. Total Communication includes the full spectrum of language modes: child devised gestures, formal sign language, speech, speechreading, fingerspelling, reading, and writing. Every deaf child must have the opportunity to develop any remnant of residual hearing for the enhancement of speech and speechreading skills through the use of individual and/or high fidelity group amplification systems.

Consonant with the above statement and pursuant to the central theme that an acoustically impaired individual needs, among other things, to develop and/or improve upon a form of communication, manual communication has been introduced to the hearing and speech curriculum at Ohio University. The professional hearing and speech clinician must not only diagnose but also prescribe therapy for a hearing-impaired person. Acquiring skill in manual communication as well as using it appropriately may be viewed as an asset to a clinician attempting to fulfill a professional obligation to those hearing-impaired individuals who are less able to communicate.

Organization of the Book

This book presents a total of forty-eight lessons aimed toward the dual objectives of helping the student both acquire and apply the skill of manual communication. The first forty-four lessons relate to the former objective, and the remaining four lessons relate to the latter. Each of the first forty-four lessons presents the following:

1. A visual illustration of a given letter or sign
2. A written description associated with a particular letter or sign
3. Practice material involving both encoding and decoding processes with answers provided for the latter

The last four lessons help the student apply the material in the preceding lessons to the areas of hearing, speech, and language.

The forty-eight lessons are disproportionately divided into three chapters. The first chapter contains two lessons: The first lesson introduces the American Manual Alphabet, and the second lesson presents basic number concepts. Lessons three through forty-four are subsumed under chapter two and present the building blocks (basic vocabulary) needed to communicate in sign language. The remaining four lessons, chapter three, involve the application of manual communication to hearing, speech, and language evaluation.

To further reinforce the learning process, frequent review sections covering the first forty-four lessons of the text are presented elsewhere in a separate workbook. This material may be used by the instructor and/or student to further evaluate the extent to which previously presented content has been mastered, or to structure further self learning tasks.

A large number of the signs presented in each of the lessons in chapter two has been based on the system of signs traditionally used by deaf people in America (American Sign Language, or ASL). However, it should be kept in mind that there exist regional differences in signs akin to regional dialects in speech. Accordingly, the student is cautioned not to view this system of signs as absolute. Added to this list are newly developed signs invented both to represent various morphemic aspects relating to the English language as well as to depict words with related meaning as proposed under the concept of Seeing Essential English. For convenience to those using the text in an educational setting, each lesson contains twenty signs. These are not in any alphabetical order. Rather, both "content" and "function" words are presented together, the aim being to enable the student to formulate and communicate in sentence form as early as possible. Also, those signs relating to some of the morphemic elements of our language are presented early in the chapter to help the student implement the skill of communicating in the Simultaneous Method as previously discussed. Finally, some signs such as "name" and "train" (noun) are frequently confused, possibly because the hands execute "subtle" movements. These and other such words are presented in different lessons in the hope that the student first will learn and stabilize the given sign before comparing and contrasting signs.

The author does not purport that this material has not been presented elsewhere in different forms; nor does he impugn the countless contributions of the many educators of the deaf in various foundations and school programs to the development of manual communication. The material contained in this book is reorganized and presented here in a form designed to facilitate learning of the skill.

How to "Decode" an Illustrated Sign

Although each of the signs presented in this book is accompanied by a description aimed at helping the reader interpret the illustrated sign, an attempt has been made to make each picture as descriptive as possible. However, the student should pay particular attention to certain visual cues that are used to "define" a sign. These cues are illustrated and explained below:

1. Look first for the presence of a basic configuration that will speed up the encoding or decoding process. For instance, you will note that for the sign "car" both hands first assume the configuration of the finger-spelled letter *S* while for the sign "drive" both hands first adopt the configuration of the letter *D*.

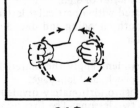 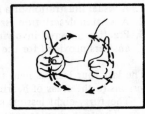

CAR DRIVE

2. The starting point for a given hand movement also is significant. Look at the illustrated signs for "keep" and "save." In the sign "keep," the right hand, in the configuration of the letter *V*, first is positioned approximately three to four inches in front of the left hand (closer to the viewer); then, the right hand is moved toward and establishes contact with the left hand. In the sign "save," the right hand, in the configuration of the letter *V*, first is positioned approximately three to four inches below the left hand; then, the right hand is moved up from below and touches the left hand.

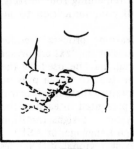 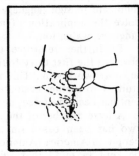

KEEP SAVE

3. The direction of movement of either or both hand(s) is another important cue that helps to identify and distinguish one sign from another. For example, you will note that for the sign "borrow" both hands are moved toward the signer while for the sign "loan" both hands are moved in a forward direction (away from the signer) as suggested by the broken arrows.

BORROW LOAN

4. You will note that many signs are marked with an asterisk (*). This means that the particular motion should be repeated several times. For instance, in the sign "play," both hands, in the configuration of the letter *Y*, repeat the basic motion several times. A word of caution: For some signs, the repeated motion serves to signify a change in meaning. For example, the sign for "spring" is made similarly to the sign for "grow," except that the motion is repeated several times.

 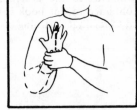

PLAY * GROW, SPRING*

5. Certain signs are executed in two steps. For example, in the sign "brother-in-law," the sign for "brother" is executed first, followed by the sign for "law." In the sign "hand," first the left hand remains stationary while the right hand executes a motion. Then the hands exchange spatial positions and the right hand remains stationary while the left hand performs a motion.

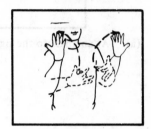

BROTHER-IN-LAW   **HAND**

6. Be sure to note the ending point of a sign. Some signs just terminate or "disappear," but other signs end in a definite and different configuration than when they started. For instance, in the sign "chocolate" (*), the dotted C hand starts where the dot is marked and makes several circular movements and returns to its original starting point. In the sign "thrill," the dotted hands indicate where the sign begins while the solid hands show where the sign ends.

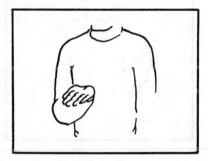
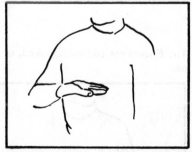

CHOCOLATE*   **THRILL**

Certain descriptions appear frequently in this text. These are listed and illustrated below:

The hand, with the thumb and fingers extended and joined, is held with the fingertips pointing to the viewer:

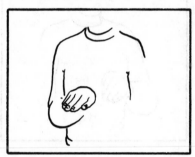

(a) The palmar side is facing up (or the back is facing down)

(b) The palmar side is facing down (or the back is facing up)

The hand, with the thumb and fingers extended and joined, is held with the fingers:

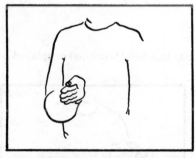
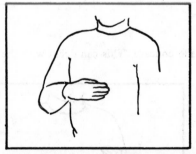

(a) Pointing toward the viewer with the back facing to the right

(b) Pointing to the left with the back facing the viewer

(c) Pointing to the left with the back facing down

(Please note the "fingers pointing" actually refers to the entire hand. If *just* the fingers are pointing, some reference will be made to flexion or bending of the fingers.)

The hand, with the thumb and fingers extended and joined, is pointing to (or past) the viewer:

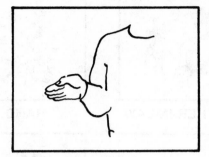

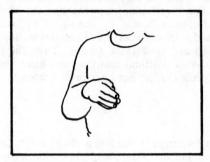

(a)   At an angle to the right   (b)   At an angle to the left

The hand, with the fingers extended and joined, is held with the fingers pointing:

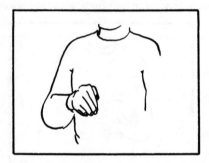

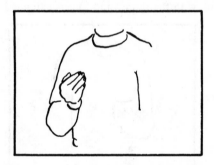

(a)   Downward at approximately a 45-degree angle   (b)   Upward at approximately a 45-degree angle

This is a flexing of the fingers at the third joint (nearest the palm). If the hand is pointing at a 45-degree angle, then the fingers remain straight while the wrist flexes up or down.

The fingers are curved, crooked, or made concave. This can occur with the fingers together (touching) or splayed apart:

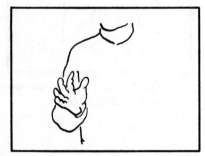

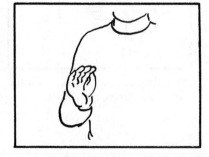

(a)   Curved apart   (b)   Curved together   (c)   Crooked apart

The middle finger is flexed at about a 45-degree angle (remaining fingers and thumb are extended and apart):

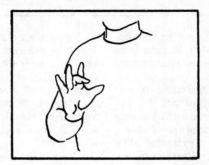

The hand, with only the index finger extended (remaining fingers and thumb are contracted):

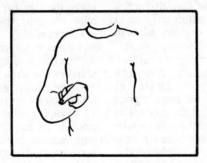

Some Suggestions on How to Use this Book

Listed below are some suggestions on how to best use this book so that you may begin to establish your mastery of manual communication. Further suggestions are presented in chapters one and two.

This book is designed to help the beginning student master the skill of manual communication with the support of a classroom instructor. To enhance the learning process, a rather complete verbal description of how a given sign typically should be made is presented. The rationale for this approach is twofold: First, since any given sign can be illustrated only from a limited number of perspectives,* frequently the movements that serve to "define" the sign, — for example, the initial and terminal positions of the hand(s), direction of movement, etc. — are not always lucid to the beginning student. Hence, a detailed verbal description may serve to further help the reader interpret the illustrated sign. Second, a detailed verbal description aids the learning process in that the student is freed from taking copious notes in the classroom. This should result in affording the student with additional time to concentrate on the instructor who may be demonstrating and/or using a given sign or a series of signs. Outside the classroom, the student has a reliable description of each sign for correct practice. This obviates the need on the part of the student to devise his/her own system of mnemonic devices aimed at separating or otherwise preserving the identity of a specific sign or a given number of signs. Additionally, for those students who may have only an occasional need to use this skill in a professional setting, a detailed verbal description of the signs can serve as a reliable memory aid in preserving and retrieving important information.

2. You are encouraged to make a list of frequently used words or expressions. Practice saying them while fingerspelling and/or signing them. Remember not to be overly concerned about speed. Go slowly at first. Speed comes with frequent practice. Remember to concentrate more on clean, well formed fingerspelled letters and signs. If you take pride in speaking well (articulating clearly), then be equally careful when expressing yourself manually.

3. For hearing people, verbal communication is enriched by such suprasegmental elements as rhythm, inflections, intonational patterns, etc. The manual communicator also can supplement the meaning conveyed by a given sign. For example, the speed with which a given motion is executed coupled with an appropriate facial expression can capture many a "mood." For instance, if you make the sign for "cross", look angry — don't smile! As with speaking, manual communication is woven into your personality. What kind of personality do you project when you speak?

4. Practice signing and fingerspelling the material provided in the encoding section at the end of each lesson. You are encouraged to change parts of the sentences as well as create sentences of your own.

5. Obviously, sincere interest and desire as well as ample practice are required if you intend to become a competent manual communicator. Practice with someone at every available opportunity. The more you think and express yourself in the Simultaneous Method, the greater your chances of enhancing and stabilizing your newly acquired skill.

1. The preferred mode of manual communication used in this book is the *Simultaneous Method* (speech and Manual English). This means that from the start you should establish the habit of speaking while signing and fingerspelling. At first, sign and/or fingerspell words while saying them. Next, move to phrases and whole sentences. Remember that telegraphic signing or fingerspelling will not facilitate the skill. Moreover, if you should happen to apply this method to the (re)habilitation process later on, you may encounter limitations.

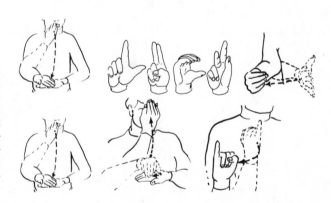

---

* For example, the perspective used in this book to depict the sign for the letter *A* may not be familiar to some readers. The following sign for *A*:   is another view of the same manual action for clarification. The reader is also referred to the verbal description for *A* in the text.

CHAPTER 1

INTRODUCTION TO MANUAL COMMUNICATION: FINGERSPELLING

The first lesson contained in this chapter introduces the student to one aspect of Manual Communication: FINGERSPELLING, a way of formulating a message by employing the fingers of either hand to execute a series of configurations, each associated with one of the twenty-six letters of the American alphabet. The second lesson presents some basic concepts involving numbers.

1

THE AMERICAN MANUAL ALPHABET

As a mode of communication, The American Manual Alphabet involves the use of either hand (in contrast with the British system which involves both hands) in formulating twenty-six configurations, each representing a letter of the American alphabet. Below is a view of the American Manual Alphabet, illustrating how the letters would appear to the viewer.

A	B	C	D	E	F
G	H	I	J	K	L
M	N	O	P	Q	R
S	T	U	V	W	X
		Y	Z		

lesson one
The American Manual Alphabet

This lesson presents the twenty-six letters of the American alphabet. The letters are illustrated as they would appear to the viewer. Although the right hand is used here, either hand may be used to formulate the letters. The spatial positioning of the hand, for all the finger-spelled letters, is that presented in the illustration below. Look at the illustration and read the description of how each of the fingerspelled letters should be made. Then, try to imitate the illustration.

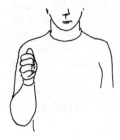

The right hand, in the configuration of the fingerspelled letter *A*, is positioned approximately six to eight inches in front of and to the right side of the signer's body at chest level. This spatial positioning is used for all of the remaining letters.

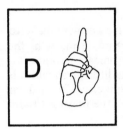

This letter is made with the wrist slightly flexed upward, with the index finger half flexed and with the thumb flexed inward to touch the fingertips. The palmar surface is toward the viewer.

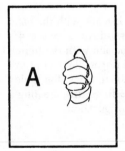

This letter is made with a compact hand (the fingers are contracted and clasped to the palm), with the thumb resting on the index finger. The hand, with the wrist flexed upward at about a 45-degree angle, is positioned approximately six inches in front of and to the right side of the body at chest level.

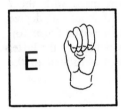

This letter is made with the wrist flexed upward at about a 45-degree angle, with the fingers and thumb contracted, and with the side of the thumb touching all four fingertips. The palmar surface is toward the viewer.

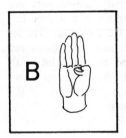

Make this letter with the wrist flexed upward, the fingers extended upward and together, with the thumb flexed against the palm. The palmar surface of the hand faces the viewer.

Make this letter with the wrist flexed upward and with the index finger half flexed, while the other fingers are extended and together. The thumb is curved inward to touch the side of the flexed index finger. The palmar surface is toward the viewer.

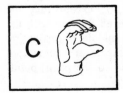

This letter is made with the thumb and fingers curved so as to resemble the letter *C*. The wrist flexes the hand to about a 45-degree angle with the joined fingers pointing to the left.

Make this letter by aligning the thumb and index finger in a parallel (but not touching) manner horizontally, while the remaining fingers are contracted and clasped to the palm. Point the thumb and index finger toward the viewer.

3

 This letter is made with the index and middle fingers extended and joined, and with the remaining fingers contracted and clasped to the palm. The thumb is flexed inward and touches the back of the third finger. The index and second fingertips are pointing to the viewer, with the backside of the hand facing to the right.

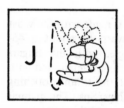 This letter is made with the wrist flexed upward, and with the hand in a compact position, except for the little finger which is extended vertically. The palmar side of the little finger is toward the viewer.

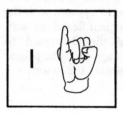 This letter is made with the *I* hand flexed at about a 45-degree angle; next, the little finger formulates the outline of the letter *J* as the hand is rotated to the right.

 This letter is made with the hand flexed upward, with the index and middle fingers extended and apart. The remaining fingers are contracted and clasped to the palm, with the thumb extended and touching the side of the index finger. The back side of the hand is facing the signer.

 Make this letter with the wrist flexed at about a 45-degree angle upward and with the index finger and thumb extended and apart to form a right angle. The remaining fingers are contracted and clasped to the palm. The back of the hand is toward the signer.

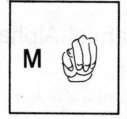 This letter is made with the wrist flexed slightly upward and with the thumb flexed inward and positioned under the third finger. The first three fingers are bent over the thumb, creating an outline of this letter, while the little finger is clasped to the palm.

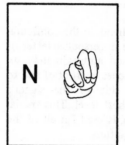 This letter is made similarly to the previous letter (*M*), except that the thumb is contracted inward and placed under the second finger, with the first two fingers bending over the thumb to create an outline of this letter. The remaining fingers are contracted and clasped to the palm.

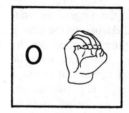 This letter is made with the hand flexed upward to about a 45-degree angle and with the thumb and joined fingers flexed inward. The thumb touches the index and middle fingertips, creating a circular configuration.

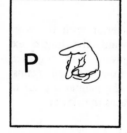 Make this letter with the hand flexed slightly downward, and with the index and middle fingers extended and apart. The remaining fingers are contracted and clasped to the palm, with the thumb flexed inward and touching the palmar side of the middle finger.

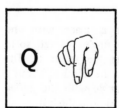 This letter is made similarly to the letter *G*, except that the hand is flexed forward with the index and middle fingertips (remaining fingers are contracted and clasped to the palm) pointing downward.

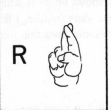 **R** This letter is made with the hand flexed upward at about a 45-degree angle, with the second finger crossed over the index finger while remaining fingers are contracted and clasped to the palm with the thumb resting on the third finger.

 **W** This letter is made similarly to the letter *V*, except that the third finger also is elevated. The three fingers are suggestive of the letter *W*.

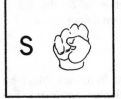 **S** Make this letter with the wrist flexed slightly upward and with the fingers contracted and clasped to the palm with the thumb resting on the second and third fingers. The back side of the fist hand is facing the signer.

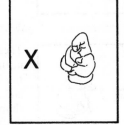 **X** This letter is made with the wrist flexed upward to about a 45-degree angle and with the index finger bent into a hook form, while the remaining fingers are contracted and clasped to the palm, with the thumb contracted inward and touching the fingers.

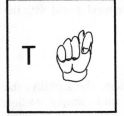 **T** This letter is made with the wrist flexed slightly upward and with the thumb positioned between the index and second fingers, with the index finger bent over the thumb. The remaining fingers are contracted and clasped to the palm.

 **U** Make this letter with the wrist flexed upward, the index and middle fingers extended and joined. The remaining fingers are contracted and clasped to the palm, and the thumb is contracted inward and touching the third finger.

 **Y** Make this letter with the wrist flexed upward to about a 45-degree angle, with the thumb and little finger extended and pointing upward. The remaining fingers are contracted and clasped to the palm.

 **V** This letter is made similarly to the previous one (*U*), except that the index and middle fingers are split apart to form a "victory" sign.

 **Z** Make this letter with the wrist flexed slightly upward and with the index finger extended (remaining fingers are contracted and clasped to the palm, with the thumb flexed inward and touching the fingers). Then, the hand makes the motion of a *Z* pattern while moving from top to bottom the way this letter is written.

SOME FREQUENTLY CONFUSED FINGERSPELLED LETTERS

For beginning students, the following fingerspelled letters often are a source of constant confusion. The difficulty, especially under faster rates, shows up more when decoding (receiving) than when encoding (sending) fingerspelled messages. Listed here are some clues that may help you.

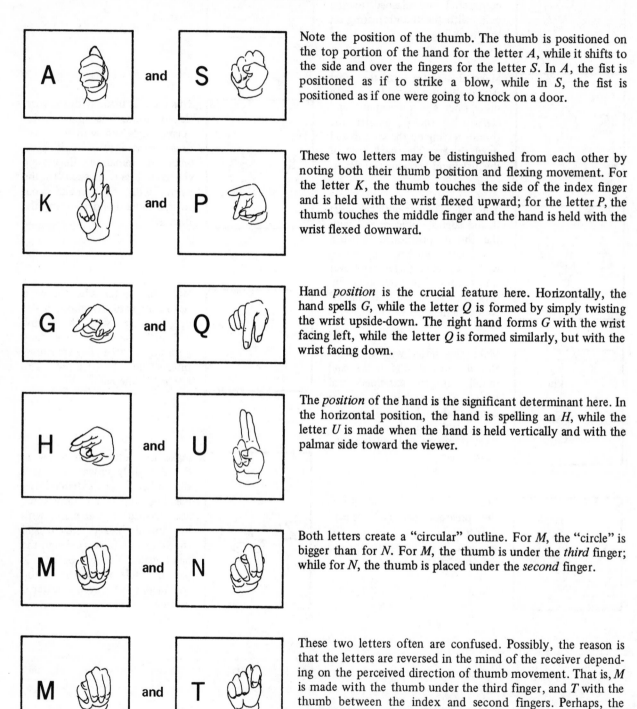

Note the position of the thumb. The thumb is positioned on the top portion of the hand for the letter *A*, while it shifts to the side and over the fingers for the letter *S*. In *A*, the fist is positioned as if to strike a blow, while in *S*, the fist is positioned as if one were going to knock on a door.

These two letters may be distinguished from each other by noting both their thumb position and flexing movement. For the letter *K*, the thumb touches the side of the index finger and is held with the wrist flexed upward; for the letter *P*, the thumb touches the middle finger and the hand is held with the wrist flexed downward.

Hand *position* is the crucial feature here. Horizontally, the hand spells *G*, while the letter *Q* is formed by simply twisting the wrist upside-down. The right hand forms *G* with the wrist facing left, while the letter *Q* is formed similarly, but with the wrist facing down.

The *position* of the hand is the significant determinant here. In the horizontal position, the hand is spelling an *H*, while the letter *U* is made when the hand is held vertically and with the palmar side toward the viewer.

Both letters create a "circular" outline. For *M*, the "circle" is bigger than for *N*. For *M*, the thumb is under the *third* finger; while for *N*, the thumb is placed under the *second* finger.

These two letters often are confused. Possibly, the reason is that the letters are reversed in the mind of the receiver depending on the perceived direction of thumb movement. That is, *M* is made with the thumb under the third finger, and *T* with the thumb between the index and second fingers. Perhaps, the confusion stems from viewing *M* as being made with the last three fingers instead of the first three. Always note the *position* of the *thumb* for these two letters.

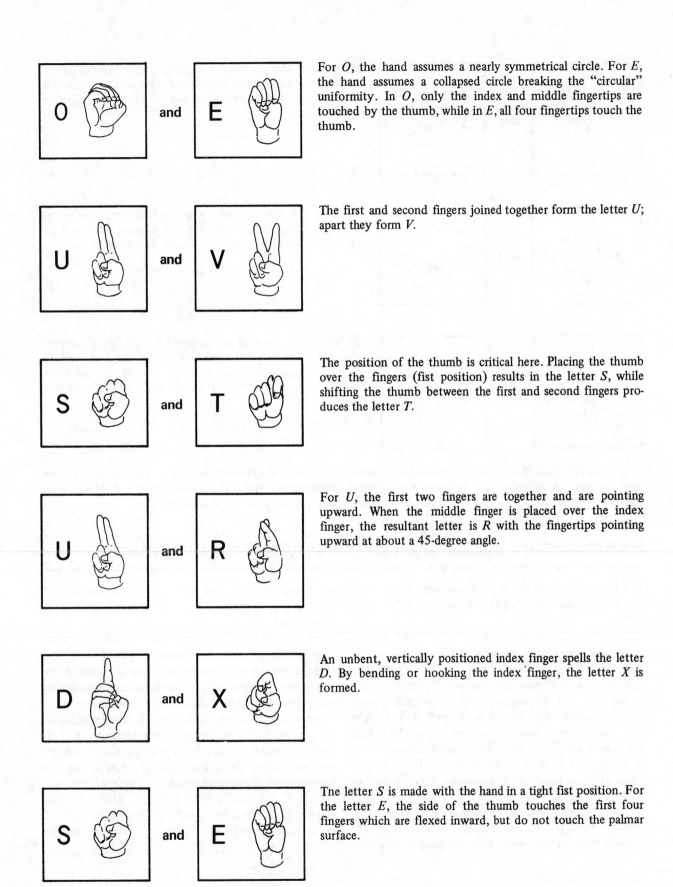

For *O*, the hand assumes a nearly symmetrical circle. For *E*, the hand assumes a collapsed circle breaking the "circular" uniformity. In *O*, only the index and middle fingertips are touched by the thumb, while in *E*, all four fingertips touch the thumb.

The first and second fingers joined together form the letter *U*; apart they form *V*.

The position of the thumb is critical here. Placing the thumb over the fingers (fist position) results in the letter *S*, while shifting the thumb between the first and second fingers produces the letter *T*.

For *U*, the first two fingers are together and are pointing upward. When the middle finger is placed over the index finger, the resultant letter is *R* with the fingertips pointing upward at about a 45-degree angle.

An unbent, vertically positioned index finger spells the letter *D*. By bending or hooking the index finger, the letter *X* is formed.

The letter *S* is made with the hand in a tight fist position. For the letter *E*, the side of the thumb touches the first four fingers which are flexed inward, but do not touch the palmar surface.

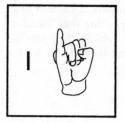 and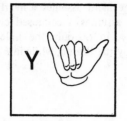

The *position* of the *thumb* is important here. For the letter *I*, the thumb is contracted inward and rests on the backside of the first two fingers, while for the letter *Y*, the thumb is extended fully.

 and

The letter *J* is always made with the *little* finger, while the letter *Z* is always made with the *index* finger starting at the top and moving down (the way you would write it).

 and

The letter *L* is made with the thumb and index finger extended so that a right angle is formed. (Be careful *not* to extend the remaining fingers.) For the letter *G*, the thumb and index finger are flexed and form a parallel line along a horizontal plane.

It is suggested, first, that the signer practice these confusion pairs to be sure that the differences are formed distinctly. Secondly, it is suggested that precise, accurate signs are the equivalent of precise articulation of speech. Sloppiness in either can not only make a bad impression, but can also lead to misunderstanding.

Exercises in Encoding (Expressive) Fingerspelling

In learning to encode and express messages in fingerspelling, the beginning student should keep the following in mind:

1. Initially, speed should not be a major concern to you. Speed will come with intensive and extensive practice. More importantly, concentrate on *good letter formation* and *smoothness* of transition from one fingerspelled letter to the next. Jerking your hand while fingerspelling tends to cause undue visual fatigue on the part of the receiver and may seriously impair reception or decoding. Practicing in front of a mirror may be helpful to you.

2. Fingerspell shorter words at first and longer ones later. Think in *syllables*. With practice, you will soon be able to fingerspell whole words.

3. The preferred mode of communication is the *Simultaneous Method*. Accordingly, try to coordinate the spoken form of the word with the fingerspelled one, *syllabically* at first, and as whole words later on. Let your fingers dictate how fast you should speak. Slow down if need be.

4. Fingerspell with your hand held approximately six to eight inches in front of and slightly to the side of your body at chest level. Holding your hand as suggested may be of help to those who try to garnish information by alternately monitoring both your hand and lips.

Again, it is important that you practice synchronizing the product of lip movement, accompanied by the presence or absence of voice, with what your hand is fingerspelling. Spelling by *syllables* will help you do this. The two modes ought to be in phase.

Practice fingerspelling the following series of orthographic (not phonetic) symbols. Remember, you are encouraged to use these syllables and make up your own words.

Practice fingerspelling the following series of orthographic (not phonetic) symbols.

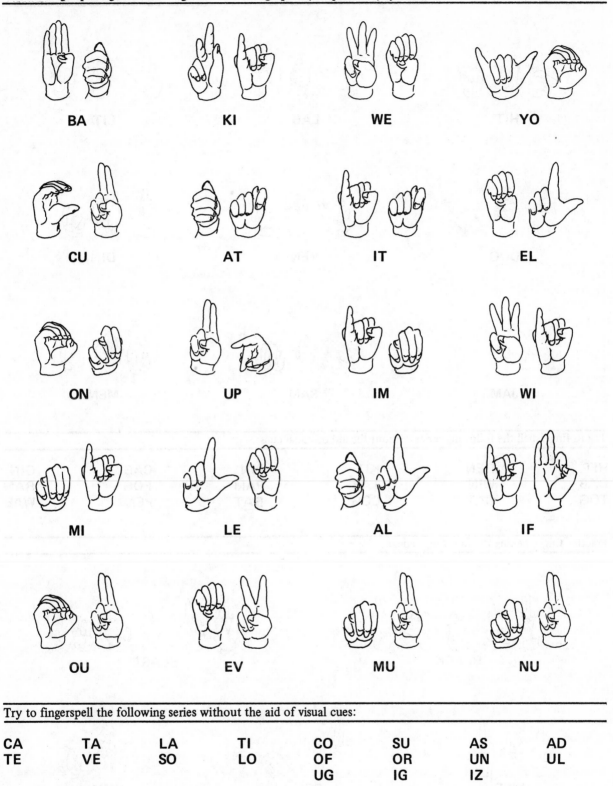

BA	KI	WE	YO
CU	AT	IT	EL
ON	UP	IM	WI
MI	LE	AL	IF
OU	EV	MU	NU

Try to fingerspell the following series without the aid of visual cues:

CA	TA	LA	TI	CO	SU	AS	AD
TE	VE	SO	LO	OF	OR	UN	UL
				UG	IG	IZ	

Practice fingerspelling the following series:

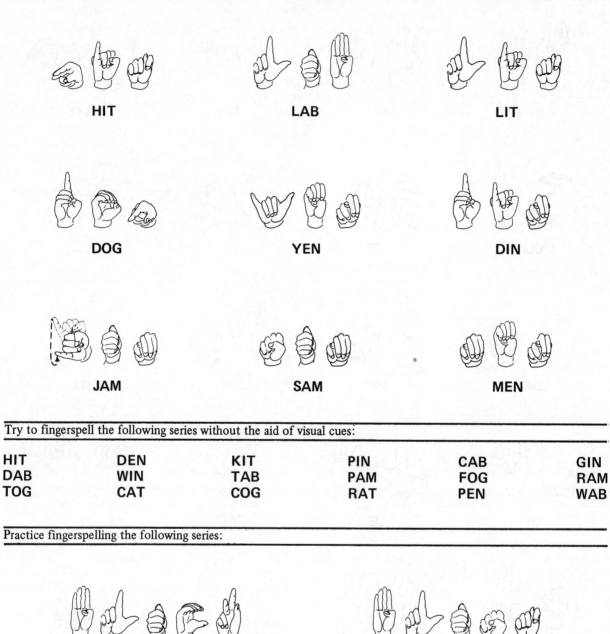

HIT   LAB   LIT

DOG   YEN   DIN

JAM   SAM   MEN

Try to fingerspell the following series without the aid of visual cues:

HIT	DEN	KIT	PIN	CAB	GIN
DAB	WIN	TAB	PAM	FOG	RAM
TOG	CAT	COG	RAT	PEN	WAB

Practice fingerspelling the following series:

BLACK   BLAST

WED   BEG   HIM

Remember: DON'T FINGERSPELL PHONETICALLY!

Practice fingerspelling in sentence form. Initially, try pausing slightly (one or two seconds) between words, thus cueing the viewer that you are ready to make the transition to a new word. This is accompanied by hold- ing the fingerspelled configuration of the last letter of a given word a bit longer before moving on. When you encounter double letters, repeat the given letter.

THEY HOPE TO FIND THE ROPE.
WE FEAR THAT THE EAR CAN HEAR.
WHAT IS YOUR NAME?
CAN WE HELP YOU NOW?
SHOW HIM THE DOG.
THE CAT TOOK A NAP.
WHERE DOES HE LIVE?
WHAT TIME DO YOU HAVE?
MAKE US SOME COFFEE AND TEA.
IT CAME AGAIN.
HERE IS A DIME FOR YOUR TIME.
HOW OLD ARE YOU?
TIM SAYS TRIM THE TREE.
THE OLD SCOUT CAN SCOLD.
SEE THE GLASS ON THE GRASS.
WHY TRY TO FRY THIS FLY?
MAY WE HAVE THE GRAY HAY?
FLIP THE FLAG FOR THE TRIP.
SHE LOST MY RING IN THE SPRING.
FIND THE FEET IN THE FOG.
THE ANT IS IN THE PLANT.
THE AIR CHASED THE CHEAP CHAIR.
HOPE WILL SHAPE THE SHELL IN THE SHIP.
ICE IS TWICE AS NICE.
THE FAT CAT SAT WITH THE BAT.

THE CAR MAY HIT THE BAR.
KAY AND FAY MAY STAY.
THE BAD LAD WAS MAD.
THE OX HIT THE FOX WITH A BOX.
TELL THE BELL NOT TO YELL.
WE ATE NEAR THE GATE.
DASH AFTER YOU CATCH THE ASH.
THE DOOR WAS OPEN.
THE DOME WILL COME DOWN.
THERE IS SHOCK NEAR THE DOCK.
WHERE IS THE RED BALL?
SHOW US YOUR NOSE.
THIS IS A ZEBRA.
THE INK CAN SINK IN THE WATER.
WHERE IS THE OLD COPY?
SHE IS IN IT.
PAY US WHEN YOU CAN.
SHOW ME THE SLOW SHIP.
WE CAN SIT IN THE SINK.
THE TOY IS ON THE BOY.
CHOP THE CHAIR WHEN YOU CAN.
DROP THE DRUM IN THE SLUM.
DRAW WITH THE RAW STRAW.
PRAY FOR RAY AND KAY.
THE BIRD CAN TRY TO FLY IN THE SKY.

Try to fingerspell the following series without the aid of visual cues:

DWARF	TEACH	BLINK	PLACE	THINK	PLANT	BAY
BLAME	WAY	DWELL	BEACH	DRINK	EACH	THING
PLATE	STAY	BLADE	SWAY	BRIGHT	LEACH	PINK

Practice fingerspelling the following series:

PHONE

SWAT

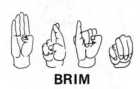

BRIM

GRIP

Try to fingerspell the following series without the aid of visual cues:

DRONE	STATE	SCREAM	SLATE	SWELL	DRIP	SWIM
CLIP	SLIM	CRONE	TIM	SKETCH	BLADE	SCRAP
SKATE	SWEET	SLIP	BRIM	PRONE	TRIM	SCROLL

Practice fingerspelling the following series:

SWAT

BLINK

Try to fingerspell the following series without the aid of visual cues:

STAVE	LIKE	SAVE	BIKE	WIPE	HALL
WIDE	BALL	FORE	CALL	FORK	MALL
WELD	DEAL	WELL	VEAL	WILL	MEAL

Practice fingerspelling the following series:

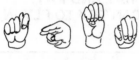

THEM

THREW

SHOE

SLEW

Try to fingerspell the following series without the aid of visual cues:

WHEN	PRY	THE	CHAP	SHOE	SWING
THEN	CHIP	SHE	SLING	THREW	FLEW
THEM	SLOT	DREW	BOTH	FRY	
BREW	WORM	CRY	WHO	CHOP	
DREW	WHY	CLAP	HE	SLAP	

Try to fingerspell the following series without the aid of visual cues:

CHAP	LAKE	CHAR	BOAT	HIDE	BOOT
HIVE	WARM	LAZY	WORK	LADY	WORTH

Practice fingerspelling the following series:

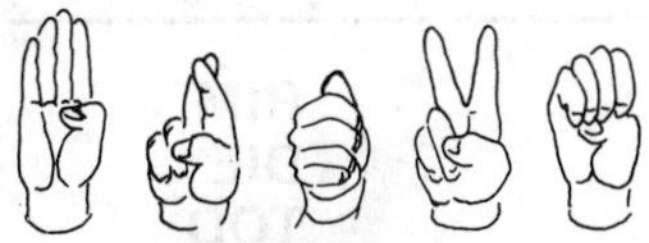

BRAVE

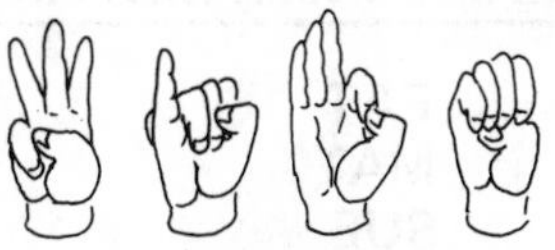

WIFE

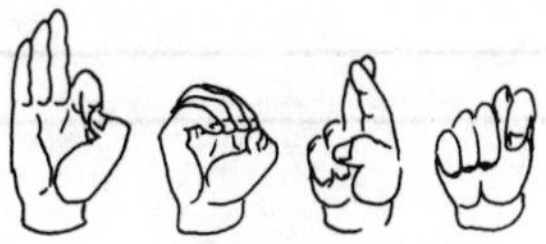

FORT

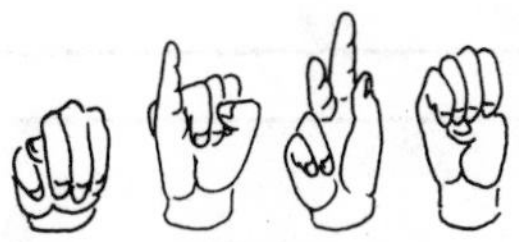

MIKE

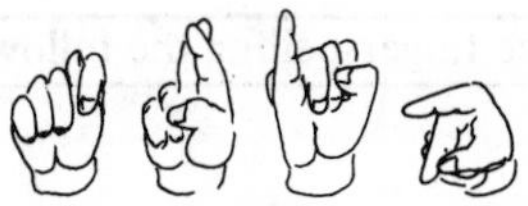

TRIP

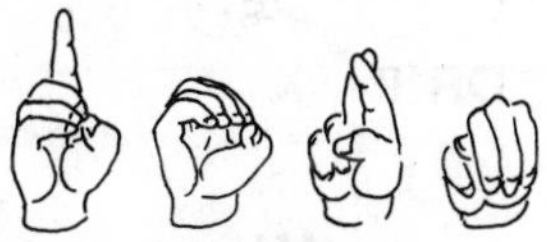

DORM

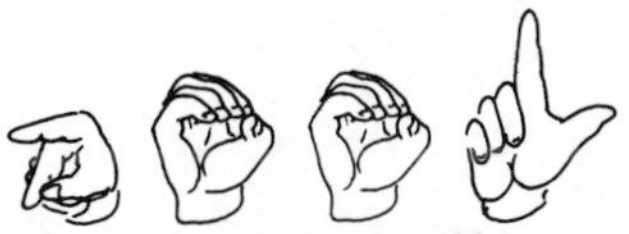

POOL

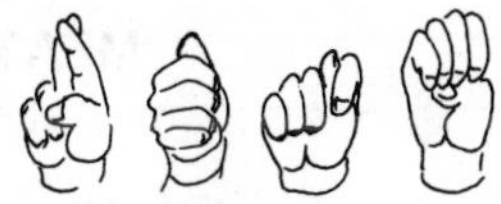

RATE

Try to fingerspell the following series without the aid of visual cues:

COOL	RIPE	DORM	BEAT	MATE
NORM	CLIP	HATE	FORM	WIPE
WEED	TOOL	RIPE	DEED	NEAT

Practice fingerspelling the following series:

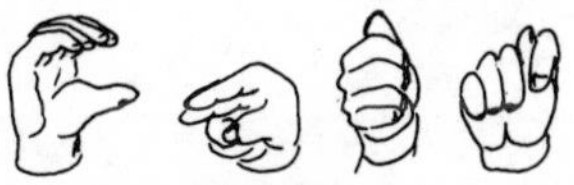

CHAT

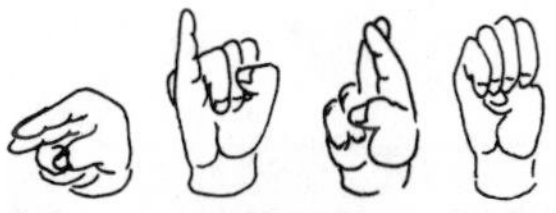

HIRE

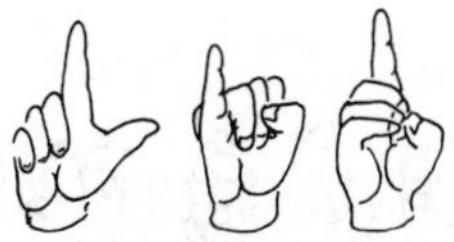

LID

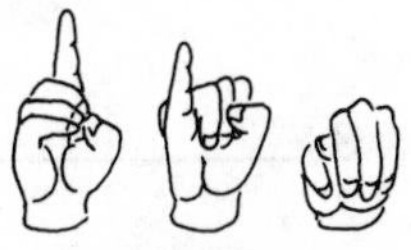

DIM

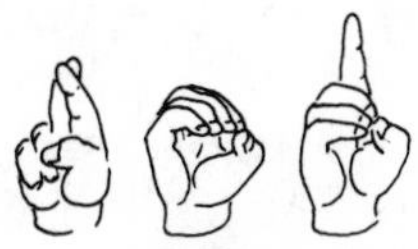

ROD

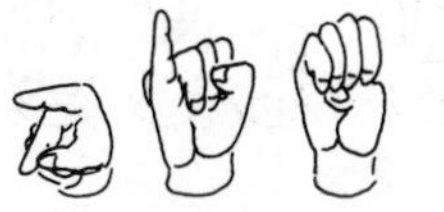

PIE

TIM

KEG

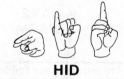

HID

Try to fingerspell the following series without the aid of visual cues:

LED	FAT	MEG	CUE	RIM	MUG
LEG	MAT	DID	HUE	DIE	RUG
LID	SUE	LIE	TUG	TOD	
TIE	LUG	GOD	NED	CAT	
MOD	RED	RAT	KID	DUE	

Practice fingerspelling the following series:

MEAT

DRIP

Exercises in Decoding (Receptive) Fingerspelling

The beginning student is encouraged to practice sending and receiving fingerspelled messages with someone. Use of a mirror also may help you to see how the words look.

These sections are designed for self-instruction. Look at each fingerspelled word and write beside it what you think is the correct answer. Having responded, turn to the answer section at the end of the lesson for the correct answer.

1. 　　　　　　　　1. _____

2. 　　　　　　　　2. _____

3. 　　　　　　　　3. _____

4. _____   **4.** _____

5. _____   **5.** _____

6. _____   **6.** _____

7. _____   **7.** _____

8. _____   **8.** _____

9. _____   **9.** _____

10. _____   **10.** _____

11. _____   **11.** _____

12. _____   **12.** _____

13. _____   **13.** _____

14.   14. _____

15.   15. _____

16.   16. _____

17.   17. _____

18.   18. _____

19.   19. _____

20.   20. _____

21.   21. _____

22.   22. _____

23.   23. _____

24. _____

25. _____

26. _____

27. _____

28. _____

29. _____

30. _____

31 _____

32. _____

33. _____

34. _____

35. _____

36. _____

37. _____

38. _____

39. _____

40. _____

41. _____

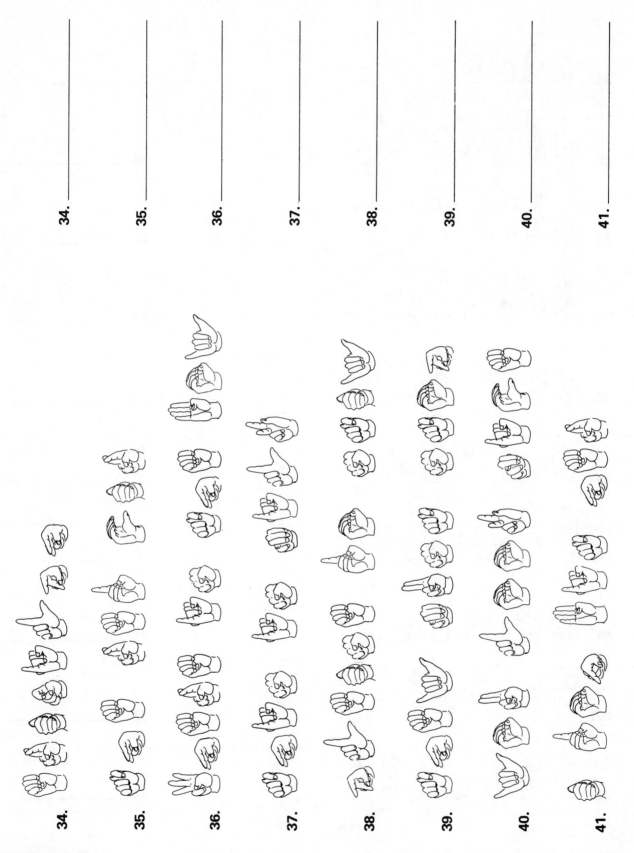

34. 35. 36. 37. 38. 39. 40. 41.

42. _____

43. _____

44. _____

45. _____

46. _____

47. _____

48. _____

49. _____

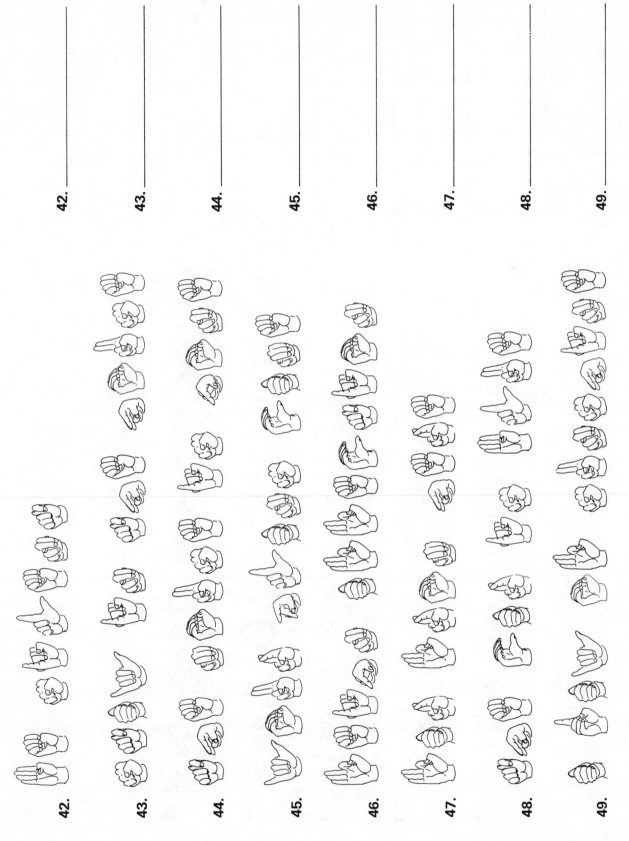

42.

43.

44.

45.

46.

47.

48.

49.

50. _____

51. _____

52. _____

53. _____

54. _____

55. _____

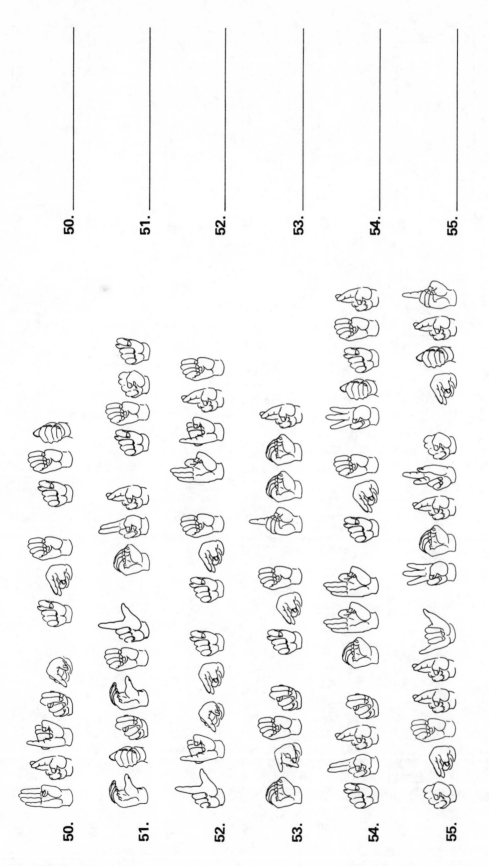

50.

51.

52.

53.

54.

55.

Pick the appropriate answers to form a complete sentence:

56. THE BOYS ARE ____________________.

a) 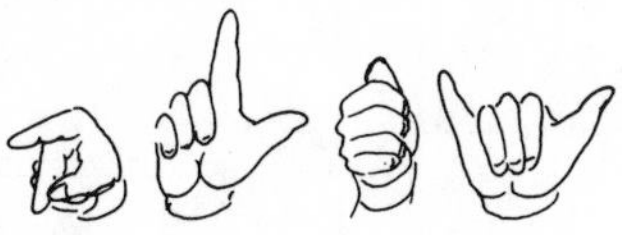 b) 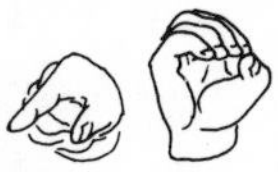 c) 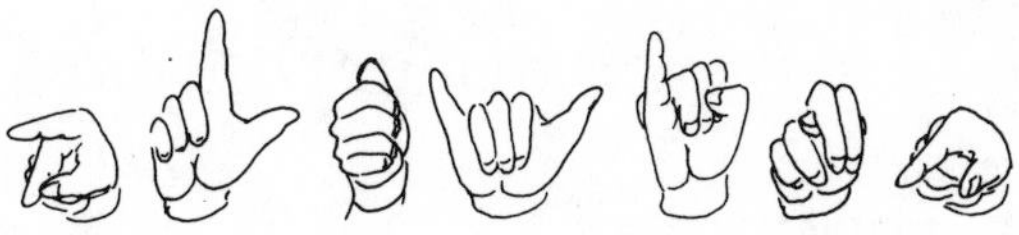

57. MARY WANTS TO____________________.

a) 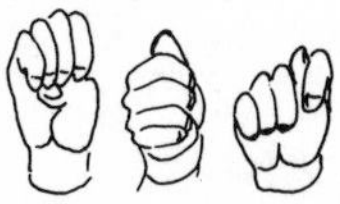 b) 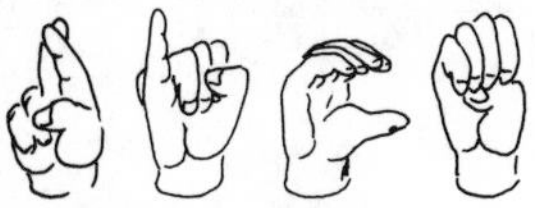 c) 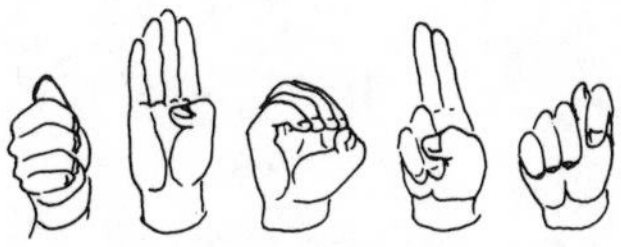

58. THIS BOOK IS____________________.

a) 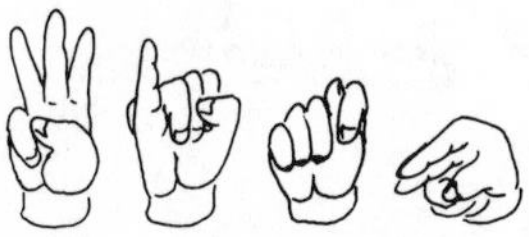 b) 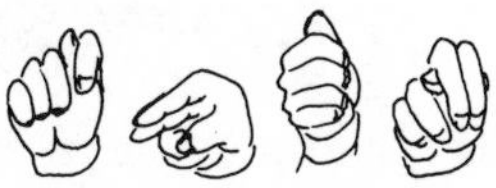 c) 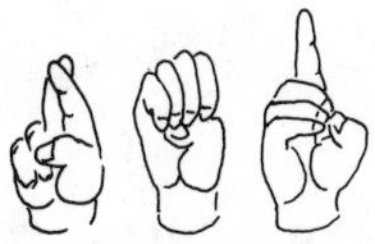

59. YOU STOLE MY____________________.

a) 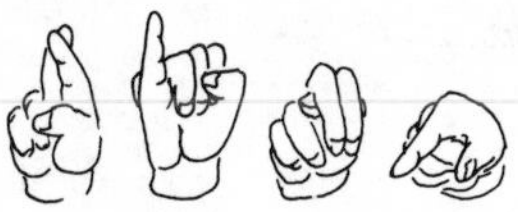 b) 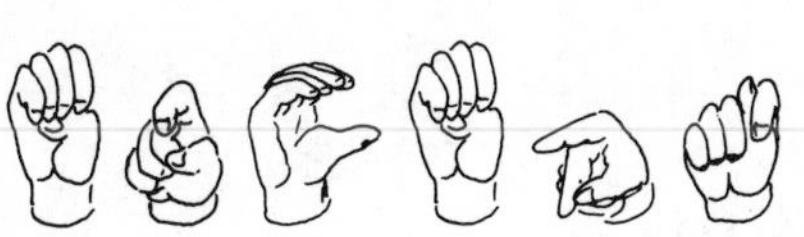 c) 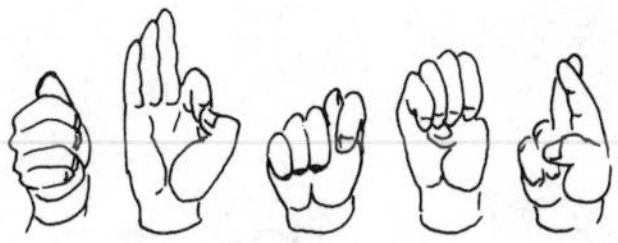

60. TODAY IT IS____________________.

a) 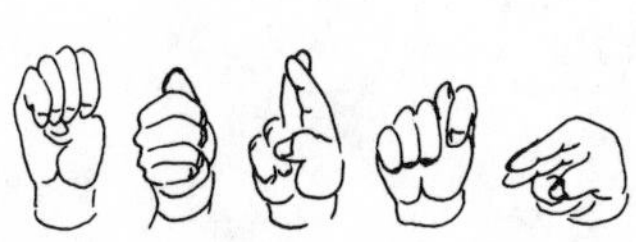 b) 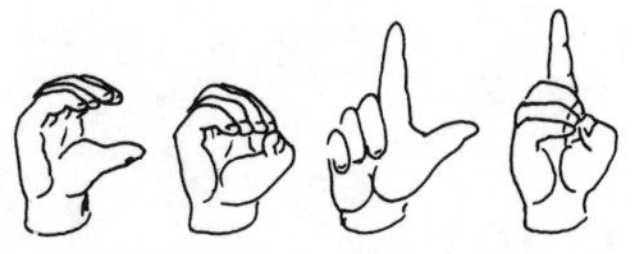 c) 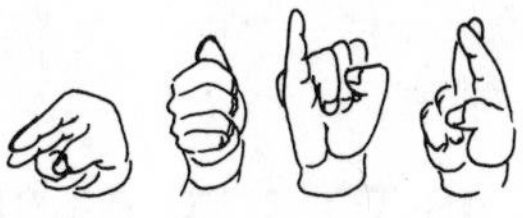

61. THE CAR IS____________________.

a) 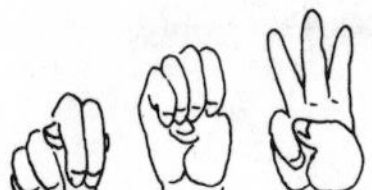 b) 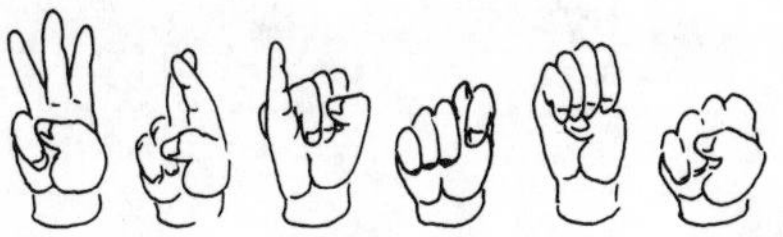 c) 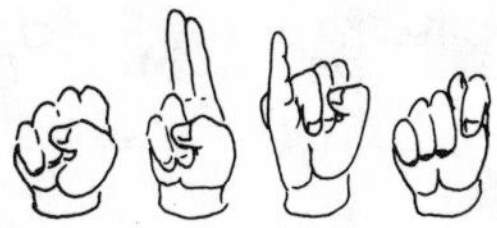

62. YOU HAVE_____EYES.

a) 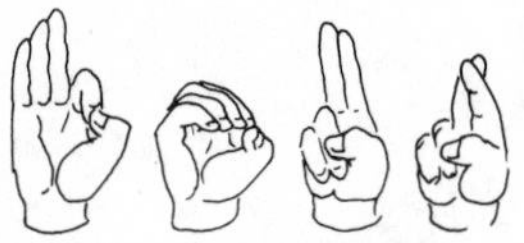   b)    c)

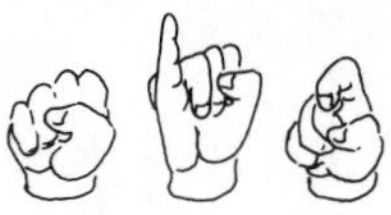

63. WE BREATHE_____.

a) 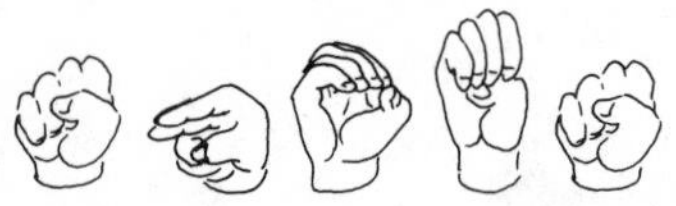   b) 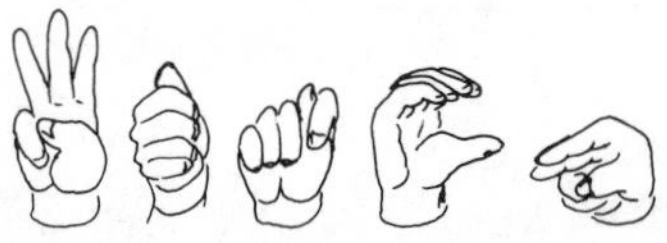   c)

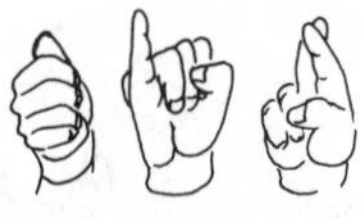

64. FOOT IS TO TOE AS HAND IS TO_____.

a)    b) 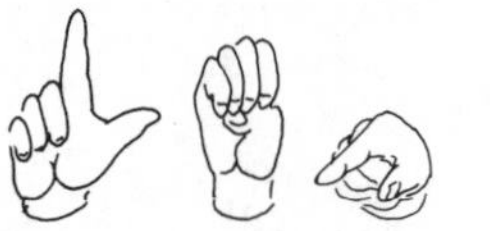   c)

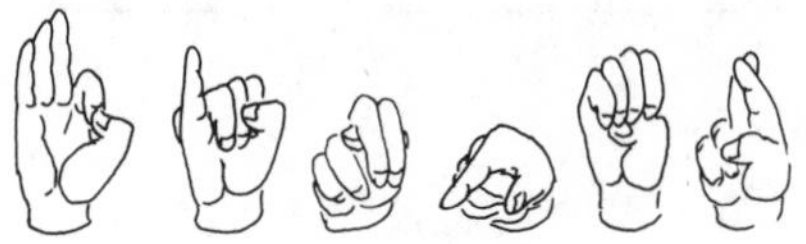

65. SLAVE IS TO BOND AS KING IS TO_____.

a)    b) 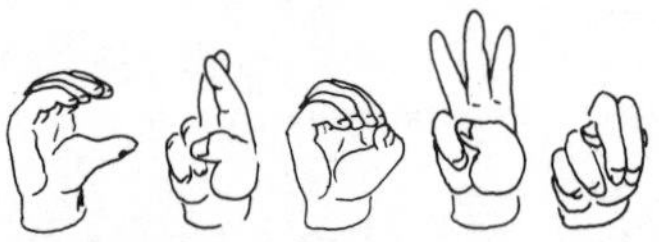   c)

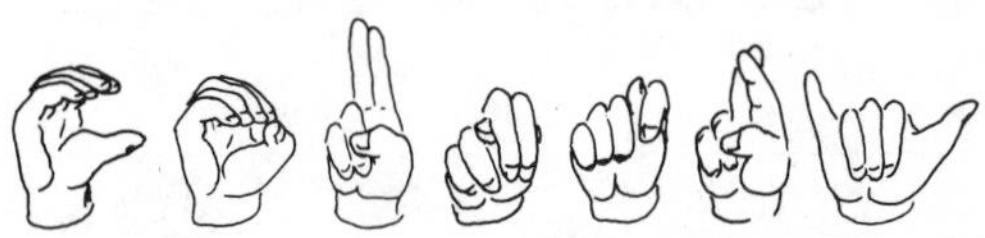

66. SEE IS TO LOOK AS TOUCH IS TO_____.

a) 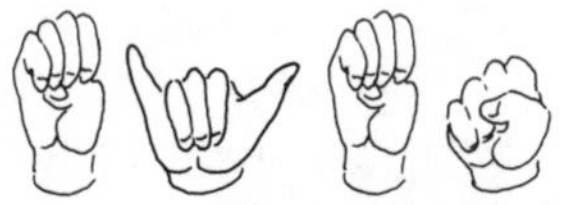   b) 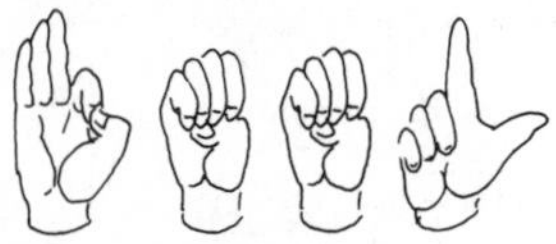   c)

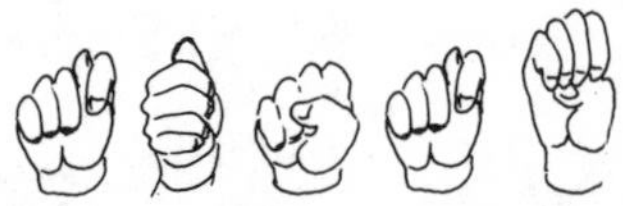

67. PHONE IS TO RING AS CLOCK IS TO_____.

a)    b) 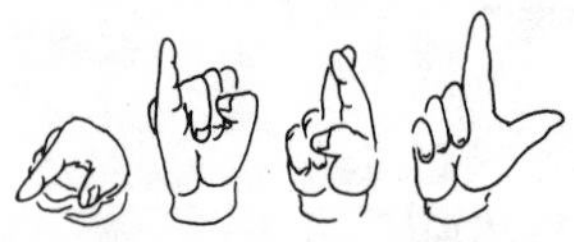   c)

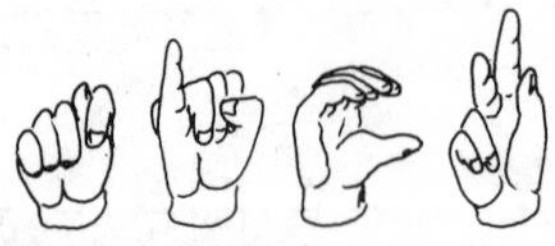

THE DESK IS TOO LARGE.
OUR BOOKS ARE NEW.
WE SAW THE CAR ACCIDENT.
THERE ARE MANY ANIMALS IN THE ZOO.
THIS IS A PERFECT PICTURE.
PLACE THE POT ON THE BURNER.
SHOW THEM THE GUEST ROOM.
THE ICE IS MELTING.
PRINTERS ARE ALWAYS BUSY.
WE WANT MORE SNOW.

WE WERE LATE FOR CLASS.
MY TIE IS SOILED.
SOME DOGS CAN BARK.
MY HUSBAND IS SICK.
THE FLOOR NEEDS CLEANING.
TELL ME THE TRUTH.
OUR BOY IS GONE.
THE SCISSORS CAN CUT.
HE WANTS MONEY.
THE PONY RAN AWAY.

Answers for Practice Exercises in Decoding (Receptive) Fingerspelling, Lesson 1

1. BOYS
2. TRACE
3. THEM
4. WHEN
5. DECIDE
6. ZEBRA
7. XENOPHOBIA
8. PEACE
9. THOUGHT
10. ABE
11. DANCE
12. KINDLY
13. FIBER
14. BITTER
15. SILENT
16. PLACID
17. DEAF
18. TRICK
19. AVOID
20. VANITY
21. ARID
22. YOUTH
23. HEARING
24. PANE
25. SKIP
26. MUJA
27. KRUBUL
28. XYLOPE
29. KHRESH
30. BUHANJ
31. GOJEG
32. BRUBRU
33. DEPHSEL
34. ERAXILPH

35. THE RED CAR.
36. WHERE IS THE BOY?
37. THIS IS MILK.
38. PLEASE DO STAY.
39. THEY MUST STOP.
40. YOU LOOK NICE.
41. A DOG BIT HER.
42. BE SILENT.
43. STAY IN THE HOUSE.
44. THE MOUSE IS GONE.
45. YOUR PLANS CAME.
46. FEIGN AFFECTION.
47. FAR FROM HERE.
48. THE CAR IS BLUE.
49. A DAY OF SUNSHINE.
50. BRING THE TEA.
51. CANCEL OUR TEST.
52. LIGHT THE FIRE.
53. OPEN THE DOOR.
54. TURN OFF THE WATER.
55. SHERRY WORKS HARD!
56. c) PLAYING
57. a) EAT
58. c) RED
59. a) RING
60. b) COLD
61. a) NEW
62. b) TWO
63. c) AIR
64. c) FINGER
65. b) CROWN
66. b) FEEL
67. c) TICK

lesson two
Number Concepts

This lesson presents concepts relating to numbers. For most of the numbers, the spatial positioning of the hand is that presented in the first illustration below. However, certain numbers do require the hand to assume a different spatial positioning, and some even involve the other hand.

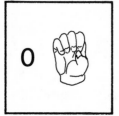

The right hand, in the configuration of the fingerspelled letter *O* (also zero), is positioned approximately six to eight inches in front of and to the right side of the body at chest level.

3 This number is made with the wrist flexed upward and with the thumb, index and middle fingers extended and apart. The remaining fingers are contracted and clasped to the palm. The palmar side of the hand faces the viewer.

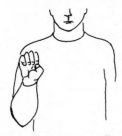

0 This number is made with the wrist flexed upward at about a 45-degree angle and with the thumb and joined fingers flexed inward. The thumb touches the index and middle finger tips, creating a circular (fingerspelled letter *O*) configuration.

4 This number is made with the wrist flexed upward and with the fingers extended and apart, while the thumb is flexed inward and pressed against the palm. The palmar side of the hand faces the viewer.

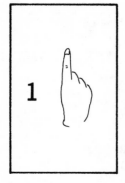

1 This number is made with the wrist flexed upward at an angle, with the index finger extended and pointing vertically. The remaining fingers are contracted and clasped to the palm, with the thumb flexed inward and touching the fingers. The back side of the hand is facing the viewer. Thus, this number should not be confused with the letter *D*.

5 This number is made with the wrist flexed upward and with the thumb and fingers extended and apart. The palmar side of the hand faces the viewer.

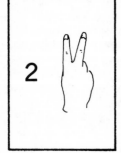

2 This number is made with the wrist flexed upward, the index and middle fingers extended and apart. The remaining fingers are contracted and clasped to the palm, with the thumb contracted inward and touching the third finger. The back side of the hand is facing the viewer. Thus, this number should not be confused with the letter *V*.

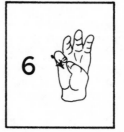

6 This number is made with the wrist flexed upward at about a 45-degree angle, with the thumb and little finger flexed inward and touching each other. The other fingers are extended, apart and slightly curved. The palmar side of the hand faces the viewer.

24

7

This number is made with the wrist flexed upward at about a 45-degree angle, with the thumb and third finger flexed inward and touching each other. The other fingers are extended, apart and slightly curved. The palmar side of the hand faces the viewer.

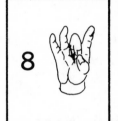

8

This number is made with the wrist flexed upward at about a 45-degree angle, with the thumb and middle finger flexed inward and touching each other. The other fingers are extended, apart and slightly curved. The palmar side of the hand faces the viewer.

9

This number is made with the wrist flexed upward at about a 45-degree angle, with the thumb and index finger flexed inward and touching each other. The other fingers are extended, apart and slightly curved. The palmar side of the hand faces the viewer.

10

This number is made with the wrist in a horizontal position, with the thumb extended and pointing upward (remaining fingers are contracted and clasped to the palm). The back side of the hand faces to the right. Next, with the configuration maintained, the hand is quickly rotated to the right and left several times.

11

This number is made with the wrist flexed upward at about a 45-degree angle and with the fingers contracted and clasped to the palm. The thumb is contracted inward and rests on the first and second fingers; then, the index finger quickly is extended vertically. The palmar side of the index finger faces the viewer.

12

This number is made with the wrist flexed upward at about a 45-degree angle and with the fingers contracted and clasped to the palm. The thumb is contracted inward and rests on the first and second fingers; then, the index and middle fingers quickly are extended vertically. The fingers are apart with the palmar side toward the viewer.

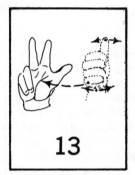

13

This number is made by combining the numbers "ten" and "three." First, the number "ten" is made, followed by the number "three" as the hand is moved slightly to the right.

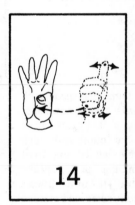

14

This number is made by combining the numbers "ten" and "four." First, the number "ten" is made, followed by the number "four" as the hand is moved slightly to the right.

NOTE: The numbers fifteen through nineteen are made by simply combining "ten" plus "five" for fifteen, "ten" plus "six" for sixteen, etc.

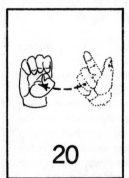

20

This number is made with the wrist flexed upward at about a 45-degree angle and with the thumb and index finger extended and apart (resembling an *L* configuration). The other fingers are contracted and clasped to the palm. Next, the sign for "zero" is made as the hand is moved slightly to the right. The palmar side of the hand faces the viewer.

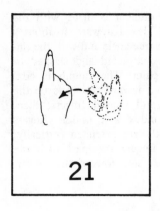

21

This number is made similarly to the number twenty, except the second step (sign for zero) is replaced by the sign for the number one.

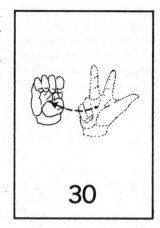

30

This number is made by combining the number "three," followed by "zero" as the hand is moved slightly to the right.

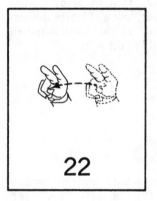

22

This number is made with the wrist in a horizontal position and with the index and second fingers extended, apart and pointing to the viewer (the palmar side of the fingers facing down). Next, with the configuration maintained, the hand is moved slightly to the right.

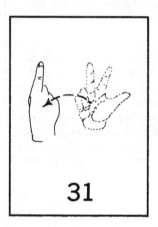

31

This number is made by combining the number "three," followed by "one" as the hand is moved slightly to the right.

NOTE: The numbers thirty-two through ninety-nine are made similarly, with the first step each time being the formation of the sign "four" for "forty," "seven" for "seventy," etc. and followed by a slight movement to the right, with the hand ending in the added number.

23

This number is made with the wrist flexed upward at about a 45-degree angle with the thumb and index finger extended and apart (resembling an *L* configuration). The other fingers are contracted and clasped to the palm. Next, the sign for the number three is made as the hand is moved slightly to the right.

NOTE: The numbers twenty-four through twenty-nine are made similarly, with the first step each time being the formation of the letter *L*, followed by a slight movement to the right, and ending in the added number.

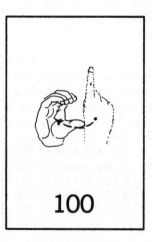

100

This number is made by combining the number "one," followed by the hand fingerspelling the letter *C* as it is moved slightly to the right. Thus, "one-hundred" is represented as "one centennial."

NOTE: The numbers "two hundred," "three-hundred," "eight-hundred" etc. are made similarly with the number changing each time, being followed by the *C* sign.

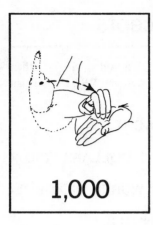

1,000

This number is made with both hands being involved. The left hand, with the thumb and fingers extended and joined, is positioned in front of the body with the fingertips pointing to the viewer at an angle and with its back side facing down. The right hand first mades the number "one." Then, the right hand is rotated to the left as the fingerspelled letter *M* is being made. Next, the right *M* hand is moved downward and touches the left palm with its fingertips. (The back side of the right hand is facing up.)

NOTE: This sign represents one thousand as "one millenniun." Also, "two thousand," "six thousand," etc. are made similarly with the number changing each time, being followed by the hand, in the configuration of the letter *M*, touching the palm of the opposite hand.

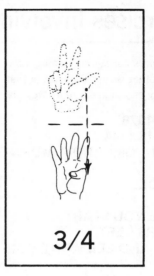

3/4

For fractions, the hand goes through a motion suggestive of how the fraction is written. First, the hand makes the number "three." Then, without flexing the wrist, the hand is moved three or four inches straight downward (as the arrow suggests) and makes the numfer "four."

NOTE: The downward movement of the hand is suggestive of the imaginary dividing line separating the numerator from the denominator. Other fractions are made similarly, with the numerator always signed first, followed by the downward movement, and ending in the number of the denominator.

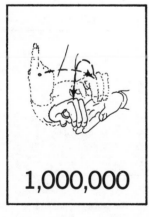

1,000,000

This number is done similarly to the previous one (one thousand), except that the right *M* hand touches the left palm *twice*. That is, the right *M* hand first touches the left palm. Next, with the configuration maintained, the right *M* hand makes a small arc movement forward and retouches the left hand near the fingertips.

NOTE: This latter motion is suggestive of three additional zeroes. That is, "one million" is represented as "one thousand times one thousand."

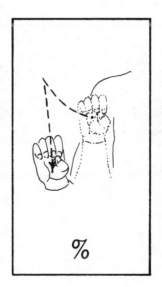

%

The right hand, in the configuration of the letter *O*, is held with the wrist flexed upward at about a 45-degree angle and with the back side of the hand facing the signer. Next, with the configuration maintained, the right *O* hand first is swung to the right and upward. Then, it is brought straight down. The back side of the *O* hand is facing the signer.

NOTE: This sign is imitative of the way this symbol would be written.

Encoding Exercises Involving Number Concepts

Encode the following sentences containing number concepts. Fingerspell all of the other words. Please note that *digits are signed the way they are spoken, not as they are written*. For example, if "1972" is said as "19-72", then sign it as "19" and "72." Do not say "19-72" and sign "1 - 9 - 7 - 2."

NEXT YEAR WILL BE 1976.
THE HOUSE NUMBER IS 1144.
CALL ME BEFORE 8 TOMORROW MORN-
    ING.
HE HAS A SIZE 16 NECK.
HIS SHOE SIZE IS 10½.
COUNT TO 12 BEFORE YOU START.
WE HAVE 100 DOLLARS LEFT.
MULTIPLY 7 TIMES 8 AND SEE WHAT YOU
    GET.
SHE IS 40 YEARS OLD.
THIS IS ROUTE 77.
THREE-FOURTHS (3/4) OF YOU WILL PASS.
WE HAVE 1000 DOLLARS.
LEND ME 95 CENTS, PLEASE.
MY CAR COST ME 400 DOLLARS.

BEDTIME IS AT 11 TONIGHT.
THE EXTENSION IS 216.
THE BILL WAS FOR 10 DOLLARS AND 3
    CENTS.
THE MOTOR BIKE IS WORTH 3000 DOL-
    LARS.
GIVE ME SIX MORE MINUTES.
TODAY IS MY LUCKY DAY TO WIN THE
    FOUR BETS.
EIGHT TIMES FIVE IS FORTY.
MY TELEPHONE NUMBER IS 614-594-2332.
SHE HAS 2000 PENNIES.
WE WANT 50%.
THIS IS ONLY 10%.
GIVE US 22%.

Decoding Exercises Involving Fingerspelling and Number Concepts

Decode the following illustrated material:

1.  1. _____

2.

 2. _____

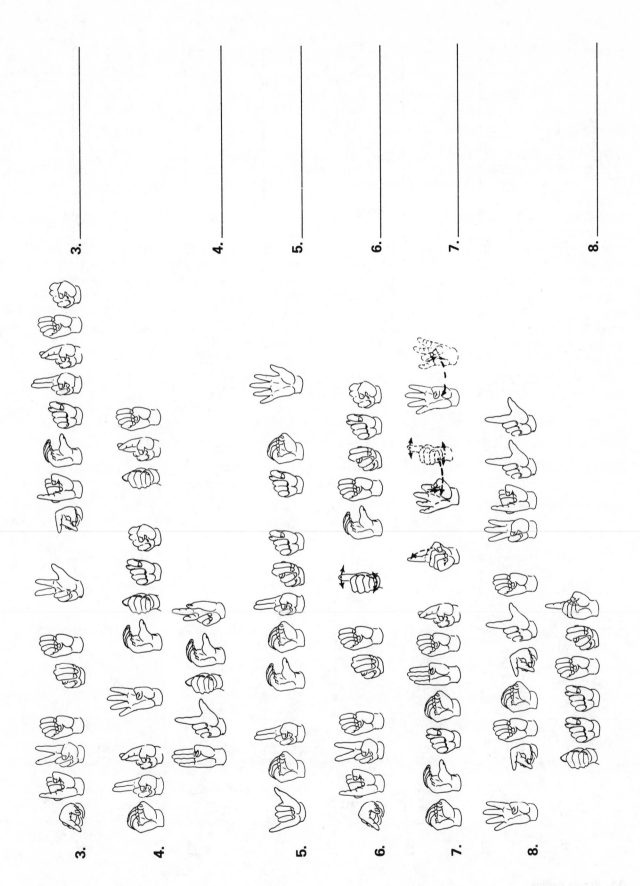

3. _____

4. _____

5. _____

6. _____

7. _____

8. _____

3.

4.

5.

6.

7.

8.

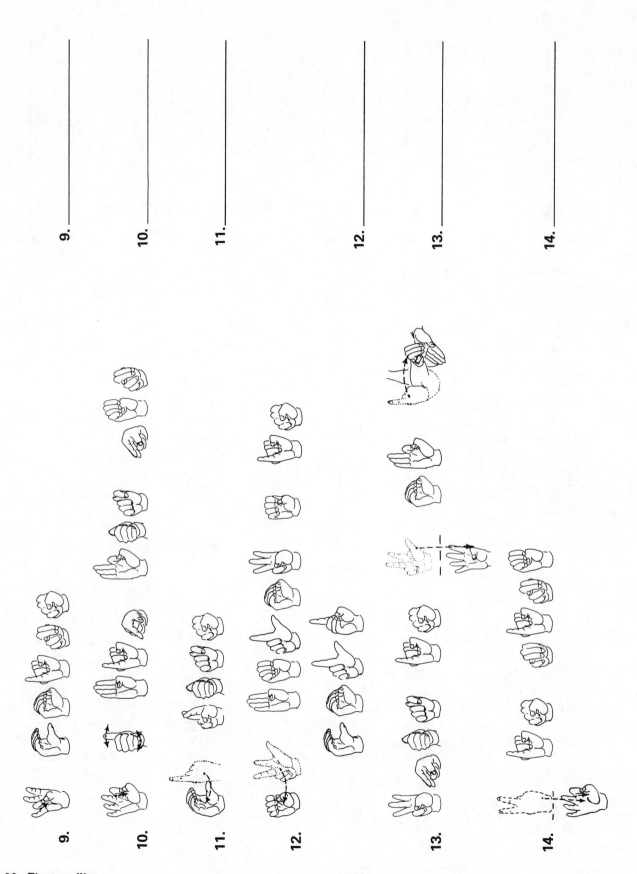

9.

10.

11.

12.

13.

14.

9.

10.

11.

12.

13.

14.

15.

16.

17.

18.

19.

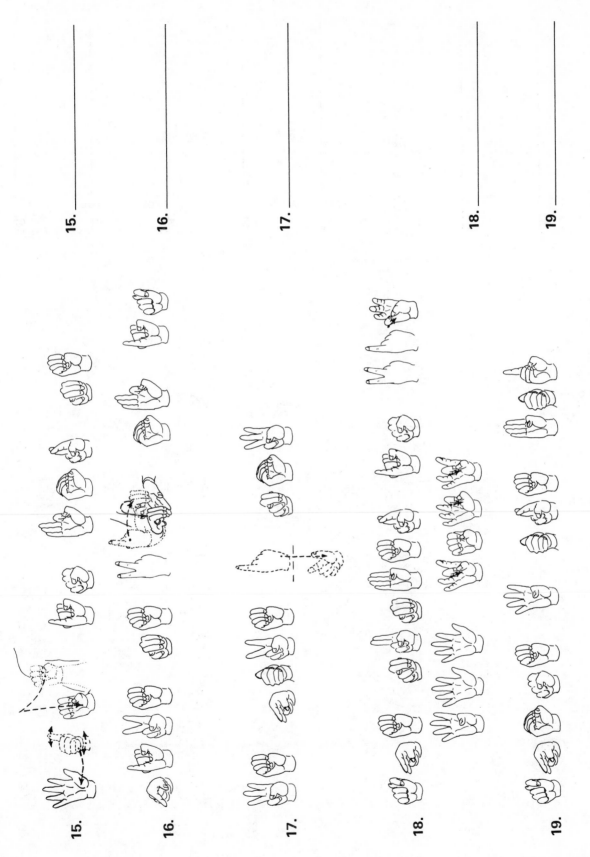

15.

16.

17.

18.

19.

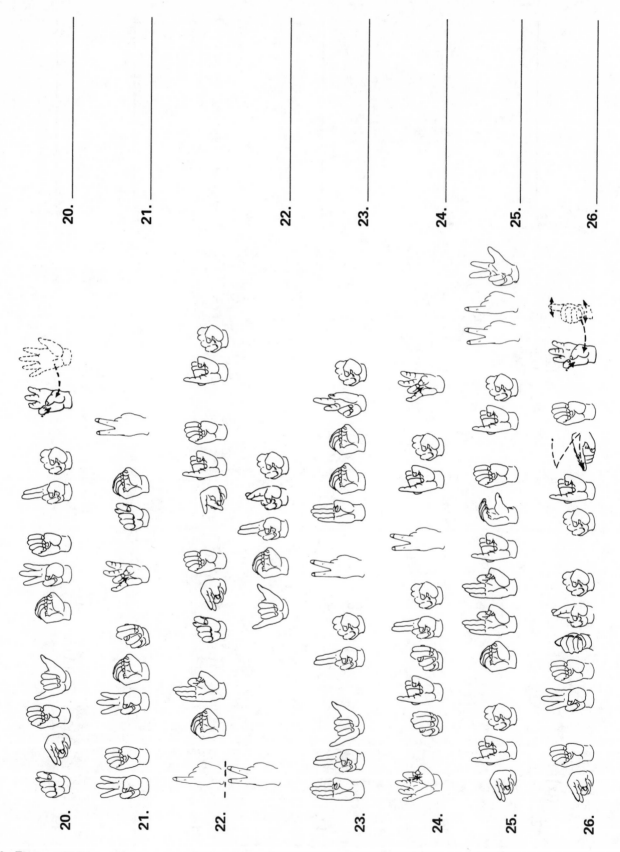

20. _____

21. _____

22. _____

23. _____

24. _____

25. _____

26. _____

20.

21.

22.

23.

24.

25.

26.

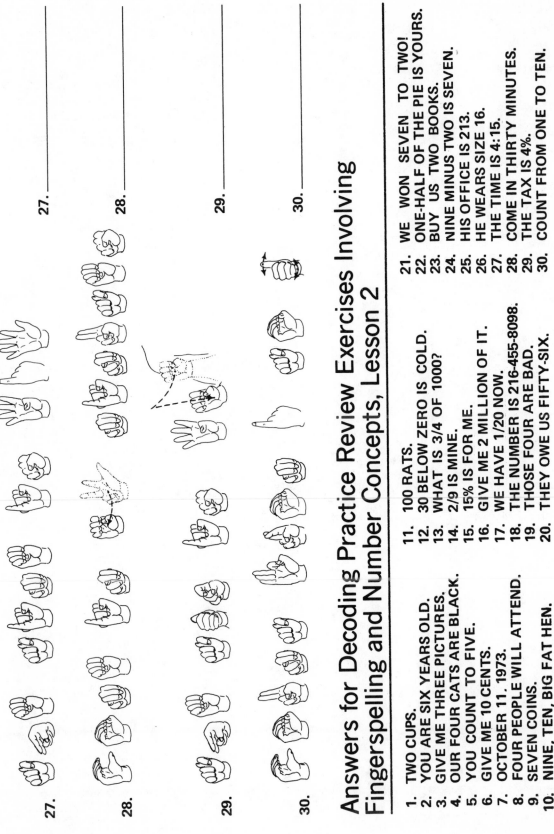

27. _____

28. _____

29. _____

30. _____

Answers for Decoding Practice Review Exercises Involving Fingerspelling and Number Concepts, Lesson 2

1. TWO CUPS.
2. YOU ARE SIX YEARS OLD.
3. GIVE ME THREE PICTURES.
4. OUR FOUR CATS ARE BLACK.
5. YOU COUNT TO FIVE.
6. GIVE ME 10 CENTS.
7. OCTOBER 11. 1973.
8. FOUR PEOPLE WILL ATTEND.
9. SEVEN COINS.
10. NINE, TEN, BIG FAT HEN.
11. 100 RATS.
12. 30 BELOW ZERO IS COLD.
13. WHAT IS 3/4 OF 1000?
14. 2/9 IS MINE.
15. 15% IS FOR ME.
16. GIVE ME 2 MILLION OF IT.
17. WE HAVE 1/20 NOW.
18. THE NUMBER IS 216-455-8098.
19. THOSE FOUR ARE BAD.
20. THEY OWE US FIFTY-SIX.
21. WE WON SEVEN TO TWO!
22. ONE-HALF OF THE PIE IS YOURS.
23. BUY US TWO BOOKS.
24. NINE MINUS TWO IS SEVEN.
25. HIS OFFICE IS 213.
26. HE WEARS SIZE 16.
27. THE TIME IS 4:15.
28. COME IN THIRTY MINUTES.
29. THE TAX IS 4%.
30. COUNT FROM ONE TO TEN.

CHAPTER 2

COMMUNICATING WITH SIGNS

The lessons contained in this chapter present to the student the basic "building blocks" (vocabulary) needed to communicate with signs. To enhance the student's mastery in the acquisition of this aspect of Manual Communication, each lesson presents:

1. An illustration of how a given sign "typically" is made. It should be remembered, however, that any system of signs, including those used in America, is a cultural phenomenon reflecting basically man's invention to satisfy his need to communicate. Thus, it is highly probable that a referent object may be referred to by more than one sign depending on the state or region where it is used. That is to say, signs are not *absolute*. Variants of a given sign often are found in different regions of the country akin to regional dialects in speech. When applicable, your instructor may wish to familiarize you with some of the alternate signs used for the same referent. Accordingly, try to learn the alternate signs as this will enhance your ability to communicate with deaf persons from diverse regional backgrounds.

2. A verbal description of each of the illustrated signs accompanied with helpful verbal cues aimed at further reinforcing the learning process.

3. Presentation of practice material involving both an encoding and a decoding process which the student may utilize to stabilize his/her newly acquired skill of communicating with signs and fingerspelling.

You can facilitate the acquisition of this skill by keeping the following hints in mind as you progress through the lessons presented:

1. Practice with someone as frequently as possible.
2. Play a game. For example, Password. Make cards with signs already learned. One member of one team can fingerspell the word, then the other members must offer the sign for the fingerspelled word. Roles can be reversed.
3. Use the sign(s) in sentences of your own.
4. Select a highly descriptive picture and describe it to another person using signing, fingerspelling and by moving your lips, but without using your voice.
5. Make up a short story and relate it using fingerspelling along with the signs you have learned.

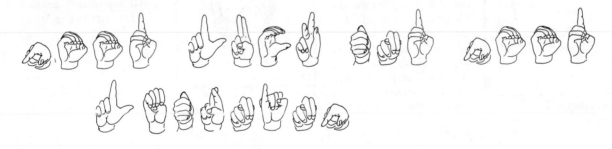

lesson three

Signs presented in this lesson are:

I	IT	ARE	SEE
YOU (singular)	WE	THE	AND
YOU (plural)	THEY	A	BOY
HE	AM	AN	CAR
SHE	IS	HELP, ASSIST	DRIVE

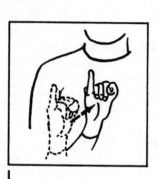

I

The right hand assumes the configuration of the fingerspelled letter *I* and is held in front of the body so that the palmar side of the *I* hand is facing to the left; next, the *I* hand is moved toward the body of the signer and comes to rest on the chest.

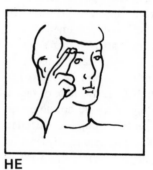

HE

The right hand, in the configuration of the letter *H*, is moved toward the signer's forehead. The palmar side of the extended fingers of the *H* hand touches the right side of the forehead.

YOU (singular)

The right hand, with only the index finger extended (all other fingers are clasped to the palm with the thumb resting on the knuckles), is held in front and slightly to the right side of the body, pointing to the viewer; next, the pointing hand is moved slightly forward (away from the signer's body).

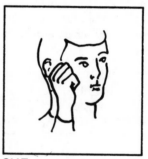

SHE

The right hand, in the configuration of the letter *S*, is moved toward the cheek so that the back side of the thumb makes contact with the signer's cheek.

YOU (plural)

The right hand, with only the index finger extended (all other fingers are clasped to the palm with the thumb resting on the knuckles), is held in front of the body and pointing to the viewer; next, the pointing hand is moved to the right to show inclusion of more than one person.

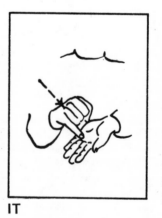

IT

The left hand, with the thumb and fingers extended and joined, is held in front of the body with the fingertips pointing to the reviewer and the palmar side facing up. The right hand assumes the configuration of the letter *I* and then is moved downward so that the tip of the finger touches the left palm.

36

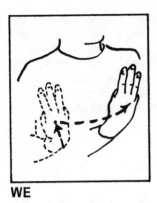

The right hand, in the configuration of the letter *W*, is moved toward the signer with the fingertips of the *W* hand touching the right side of the chest; next, the *W* hand crosses over and touches the left side of the signer's chest. NOTE: If the right hand is involved, move left to right.

WE

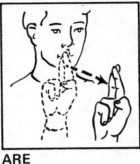

The right hand assumes the configuration of the letter *R* with its back side placed near or over the lips of the signer; then, the *R* hand is pulled straight forward.

ARE

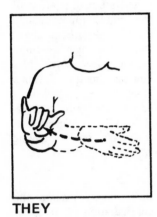

The right hand, with the thumb and fingers extended and joined, is held in front of the body with the palmar side facing the signer; next, the hand is moved to the right side of the body while twisting in a counter-clockwise direction to form the letter *Y*. The sign ends with the palmar side of the *Y* hand facing the viewer.

THEY

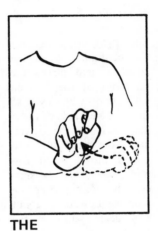

The right hand assumes the configuration of the letter *T* and is held in front and slightly to the right side of the body so that the knuckles of the *T* hand are facing the viewer; next, the *T* hand makes a slight movement to the right while simultaneously flexing upward at the wrist. The sign ends with the back side of the *T* hand facing the signer.

THE

The right hand assumes the configuration of the letter *A*, which is placed near or over the lips so that the back side of the thumb is near or makes contact with the lips; then, the *A* hand is pulled straight forward.

AM

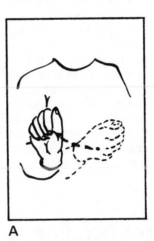

The right hand assumes the configuration of the letter *A* and is held in front and slightly to the right side of the body so that the back side of the *A* hand is facing the viewer; then, the *A* hand makes a slight movement sideways (to the right) while simultaneously flexing upward at the wrist. The sign ends with the back side of the *A* hand facing the signer.

A

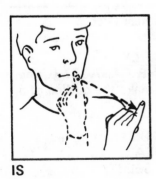

The right hand assumes the configuration of the letter *I*, which is placed near or over the lips so that the palmar side of the *I* hand is facing to the left; then, the *I* hand is pulled forward, away from the signer.

IS

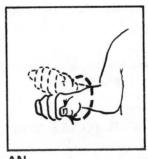

The right hand assumes an *A* configuration and is held in front and to the right side of the body with the back side facing down; next, the *A* hand tilts inward (counter-clockwise) so that now the back side is facing upward.

AN

Lesson Three 37

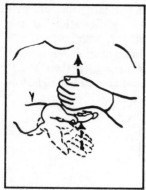

HELP, ASSIST

The left hand assumes the configuration of the letter *A* and is held in front of the signer's body with the fingers pointing to the viewer and the palm facing up. The right hand, with the fingers extended and joined, moves from below so that its palmar side touches the bottom portion of the *A* hand and lifts it up.

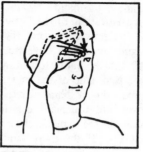

BOY

The right hand, with the fingers and thumb extended and touching, is placed near the signer's forehead; then, the hand tilts downward as if to suggest putting on a hat.

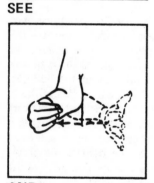

SEE

The right hand assumes the configuration of the letter *V* and places the fingertips of the *V* hand near or over the eyes so that the back side of the *V* hand is facing the viewer; next, the wrist tilts and moves the *V* hand forward—away from the signer. The *V* fingertips are pointing upward at about a 45-degree angle as the sign comes to an end.

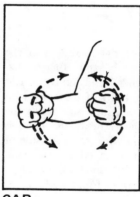

CAR

Both hands assume the configuration of the letter *S* and are held in front of the body, approximately six to eight inches apart; then, the hands simultaneously are moved in a circular direction, first in a clockwise and then in a counter-clockwise direction as if to suggest that they are on a steering wheel.

AND

The right hand, with the thumb and fingers extended and apart, is held in front of the body with the palmar side facing to the left; next, the hand is pulled toward the right side of the body while the fingers join and curve to touch the thumb as it bends.

DRIVE

Both hands assume the configuration of the letter *D* and are held in front of the body, approximately six to eight inches apart; then, the hands simultaneously are moved in a circular direction, first in a clockwise and then in a counter-clockwise direction as if to suggest that they are on a steering wheel.

A) Exercises in Encoding

Encode the following material using signs and fingerspelling. Use fingerspelling for all underlined words.

1. I SEE YOU (singular).
2. HE AND I ARE <u>HERE</u>.
3. SHE <u>WILL</u> DRIVE THE CAR.
4. THEY <u>CAN</u> HELP YOU (plural).
5. I AM A <u>BOY</u>.
6. WE ARE <u>IN</u> AN <u>ACCIDENT</u>.
7. I <u>WILL</u> DRIVE <u>MY</u> CAR <u>TO</u> SEE YOU (singular).
8. WE <u>SHALL</u> HELP <u>THIS</u> BOY.
9. THEY <u>WANT IT</u>.
10. YOU <u>AND I</u> ARE <u>EARLY</u>.
11. IS THE CAR <u>IN</u> THE <u>GARAGE</u>? (Using your right index finger, make the outline of a question mark.)
12. I SEE AN <u>APPLE</u>.
13. THEY <u>WILL</u> <u>ASSIST</u> <u>US</u>.
14. <u>WHY</u> IS HE <u>IN</u> THE CAR?
15. THE BOY <u>DID</u> <u>NOT</u> SEE IT.

B) Exercises in Decoding

Decode the following illustrated exercises:

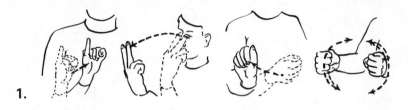

1. 1. _____

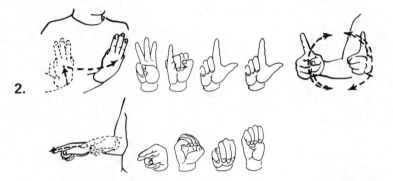

2. 2. _____

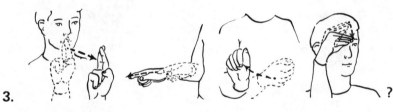

3. ? 3. _____

4. 4. _____

5. 5. _____

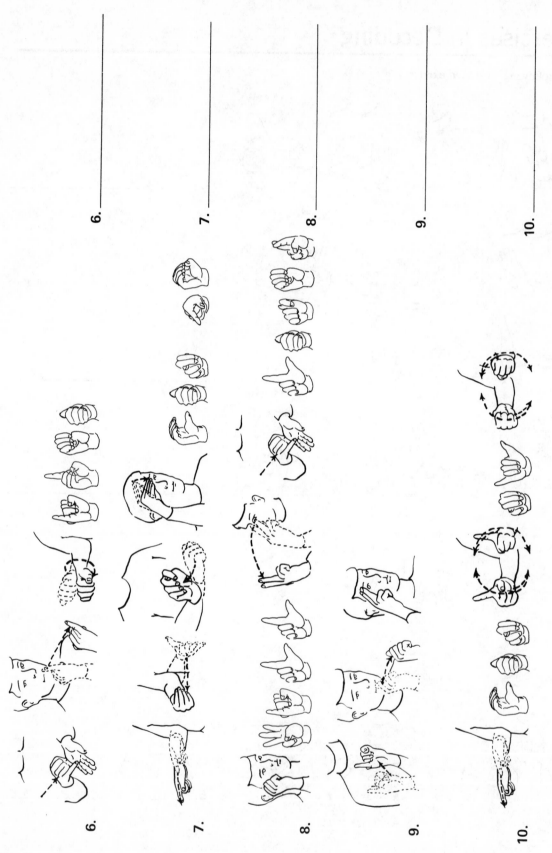

6.

7.

8.

9.

10.

6.

7.

8.

9.

10.

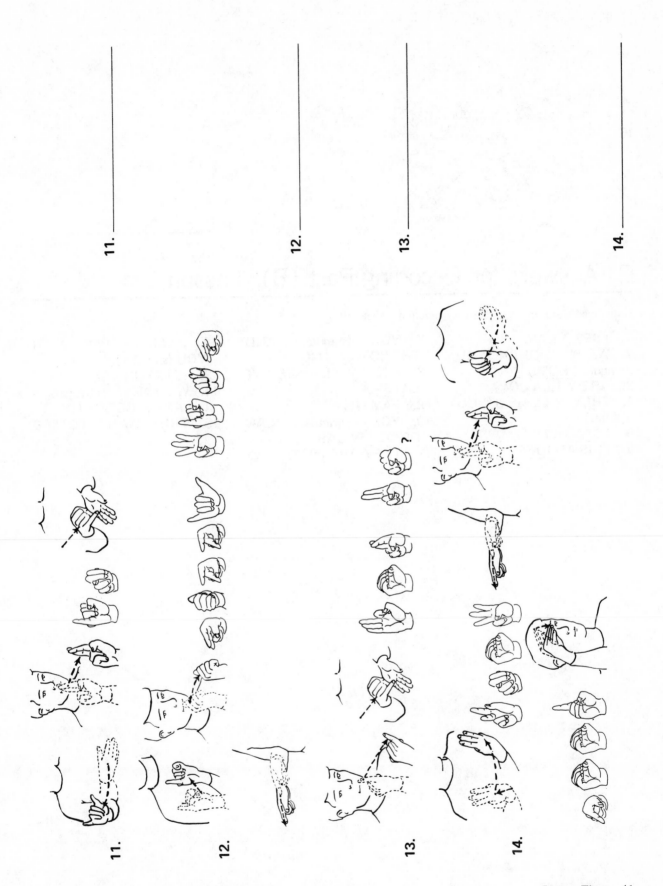

11.

12.

13.

14.

15.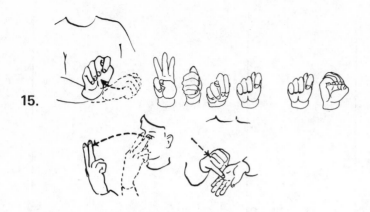

15. _____

C) Answers for Decoding Part (B), Lesson 3

Underlined words indicate that they should have been fingerspelled.

1. I SEE A CAR.
2. WE <u>WILL</u> DRIVE YOU (singular) <u>HOME</u>.
3. ARE YOU A BOY?
4. THEY <u>WILL</u> HELP YOU (plural).
5. I <u>CAN</u> HELP IT.
6. IT IS AN <u>IDEA</u>.

7. YOU (singular) AND THE BOY <u>CAN GO</u>.
8. SHE <u>WILL</u> SEE IT <u>LATER</u>.
9. I AM HE.
10. YOU (singular) <u>CAN</u> DRIVE <u>MY</u> CAR.
11. THEY ARE <u>IN</u> IT.

12. I AM <u>HAPPY</u> <u>WITH</u> YOU (singular).
13. IS IT <u>FOR US</u>?
14. WE <u>KNOW</u> YOU (singular) ARE A <u>GOOD</u> BOY.
15. THEY <u>WANT</u> <u>TO</u> SEE IT.

lesson four

Signs presented in this lesson are:

BLACK (color)	OUR	WHO	WILL
FAST, QUICK, SUDDEN	OURSELF, OURSELVES	WHOM	TELL
ME	THEM	WHOSE	STOP
MY, MINE	HIM	BE	THIS
US	HER	SHALL	WHAT

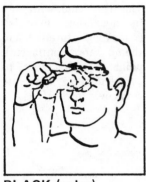

BLACK (color)

The right hand, with only the index finger extended (remaining fingers and thumb are contracted), is moved toward and placed on the signer's forehead. The index fingertip is pointing to the left with the back side facing up; then, the hand is drawn across the forehead from left to right.

NOTE: Be careful *not* to bend the index finger as your hand is moved across the forehead since doing so would produce the sign for "because."

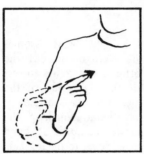

ME

The right hand, with only the index finger extended (remaining fingers and thumb are contracted) is moved toward and points to or touches the signer's chest. The back of the hand is toward the viewer.

MY, MINE

The right hand, with the fingers extended and joined, is held about six to eight inches in front of the body with the back side facing the viewer; then, the right hand is moved toward the signer with the palm coming to rest on the chest.

FAST, QUICK, SUDDEN

The right thumbnail touches the extreme tip of the right index finger which is crooked (all other fingers are contracted and clasped to the palm); then, the right thumb is flicked up as the hand is moved downward.

US

The right hand assumes the configuration of the letter *U*, which is then placed near the right shoulder so that the back side of the *U* hand is facing the viewer; next, the *U* hand crosses over to touch the left side of the signer's chest.

NOTE: Reverse directions if you sign left-handed.

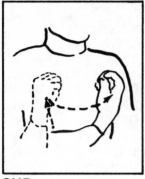

OUR

The right hand assumes the configuration of the letter *O* and comes to rest on the right side of the chest with the back side of the thumb touching the chest; then, the *O* hand crosses over to the left side of the chest as the wrist twists so that the bottom portion of the *O* hand is now touching the chest.

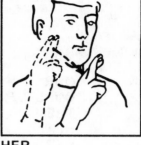

HER

This sign is made by combining *H* on the right cheek plus *R*. The right *H* hand touches the right cheek so that the back side of the *H* hand is facing the viewer; next, the *H* hand is moved forward as it quickly assumes the configuration of the letter *R*.

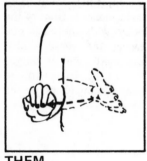

OURSELF, OURSELVES

The right hand assumes the configuration of the letter *A* and comes to rest on the right side of the chest with the back side of the thumb touching the chest; then, the *A* hand crosses over to the left side of the chest as the wrist twists so that the bottom portion of the *A* hand is now touching the chest.

WHO

The right hand, with only its index finger extended (remaining fingers and thumb are contracted), points to, and is moved to complete a clockwise circle over the lips.

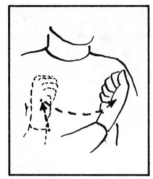

THEM

The right hand, with fingers extended and joined, is held in front of the body, with the palmar side facing left; then, the hand is moved sideways (to the right) while twisting to make the letter *M*.

WHOM

This sign is made by combining "who" plus *M*. Make the sign as you would for "who"; then, the right hand is moved forward and down, making the letter *M*, which is held in front of the body with the knuckles of the *M* hand facing the viewer.

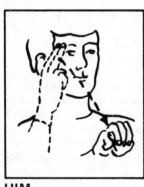

HIM

This sign is made by combining "he" plus "m." The right hand assumes the configuration of the letter *H* which is placed on the right side of the forehead with the back side of the *H* hand facing the viewer; next, the *H* hand is moved forward and slightly downward as it quickly fingerspells the letter *M*.

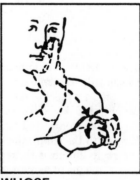

WHOSE

The right hand assumes the configuration of the letter *L*; the thumb of the *L* hand is placed on the chin with the index finger of the *L* hand pointing vertically. The *L* hand is held with the back side facing the viewer; then, the index finger of the *L* hand is bent in and out several times. Lastly, the *L* hand is pulled away from the chin as the hand makes the letter *S* and twists quickly in a clockwise direction.

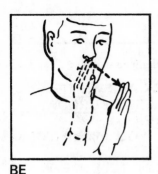

BE

The right hand makes the letter *B*, which is placed near or over the lips so that the palmar side of the *B* hand is facing to the left; next, the *B* hand is pulled straight forward.

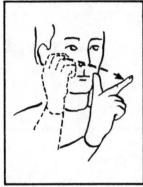

SHALL

The right hand, in the configuration of the letter *S*, is placed on the right cheek so that the edge of the *S* hand is facing the viewer; then, the *S* hand is moved straight forward as the configuration is changed to the fingerspelled letter *L*. The sign ends with the back side of the *L* hand facing to the right.

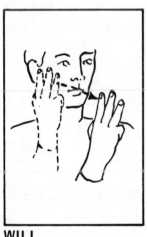

WILL

The right hand, in the configuration of the letter *W*, is placed on the right cheek with the back side of the *W* hand facing to the right; next, the *W* hand is pulled straight forward. NOTE: In this, as in the previous sign ("shall"), the forward motion is suggestive of "time ahead" or "time in the future."

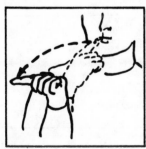

TELL

The right hand, with only the index finger extended (remaining fingers and thumb are contracted), points to, or touches the lips of the signer; then, the hand bends forward (away from the body) and comes to rest with the back side of the hand facing down.

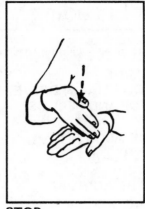

STOP

The left hand, with all the fingers extended and joined, is held in front of the body with the palmar side facing up. The right hand, with the fingers extended and joined (back of hand is facing the viewer), is held about three to four inches above the left hand. Then, the right hand descends; with its edge coming to rest on the left palm.

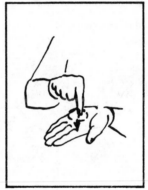

THIS

The left hand, with the thumb and fingers extended and joined, is held in front of the body with the fingers pointing to the viewer and the palm facing up. With the right index finger (remaining fingers and thumb are contracted), start making a circle in a clockwise direction. As you approach the completion of the circle, *press* the index finger *down* onto the *center* of your left palm.

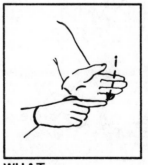

WHAT

The left hand, with the fingers extended and joined, is held in front of the body with the palm facing to the right. The right index fingertip (remaining fingers and thumb are contracted) grazes the fingers of the left hand as the right hand is moved downward.

A) Exercises in Encoding

Encode the following material using signs and fingerspelling. Use fingerspelling for all underlined words.

1. THE BLACK CAR IS MINE.
2. <u>HOW</u> FAST WILL YOU (singular) DRIVE?
3. WILL YOU (plural) STOP AND TELL US?
4. WHAT IS IT?
5. WE SHALL BE QUICK <u>ABOUT</u> IT.
6. TELL THEM WHAT SHE <u>DID</u>.
7. I <u>CAN</u> SEE HER <u>LATER.</u>
8. WHOSE CAR WILL THEY DRIVE?
9. WHAT IS HER <u>NAME</u>?
10. WE SHALL HELP OURSELVES.
11. WHAT <u>DID</u> YOU (singular) TELL HIM <u>ABOUT</u> ME?
12. OUR CAR IS BLACK AND <u>WHITE</u>.
13. WILL THEY SEE HER <u>TOMORROW</u>?
14. IS THIS BOY <u>DEAF</u>?
15. <u>FOR</u> WHOM <u>ARE</u> YOU (plural) <u>LOOK-ING</u>?
16. <u>CAN</u> YOU (singular) TELL ME WHAT THIS IS?
17. WHAT SHALL WE <u>TEACH</u> OUR BOY?
18. I <u>NEED</u> <u>TO</u> SEE THEM <u>TODAY</u>.
19. WHO IS HE?
20. WHAT WILL YOU (singular) TELL THEM <u>WHEN</u> THEY <u>COME</u>?

B) Exercises in Decoding

Decode the following illustrated exercises:

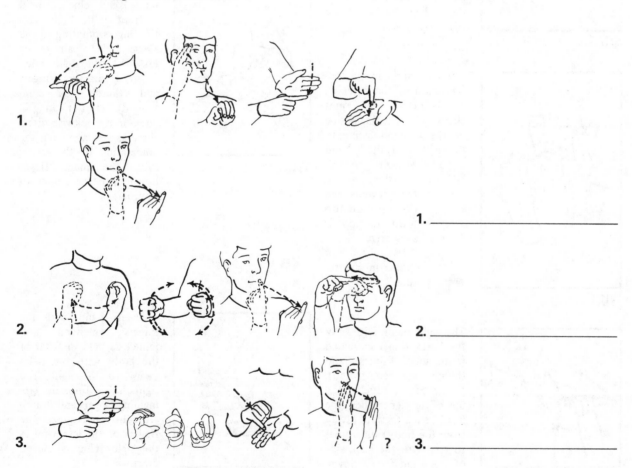

1. _____

2. _____

3. _____

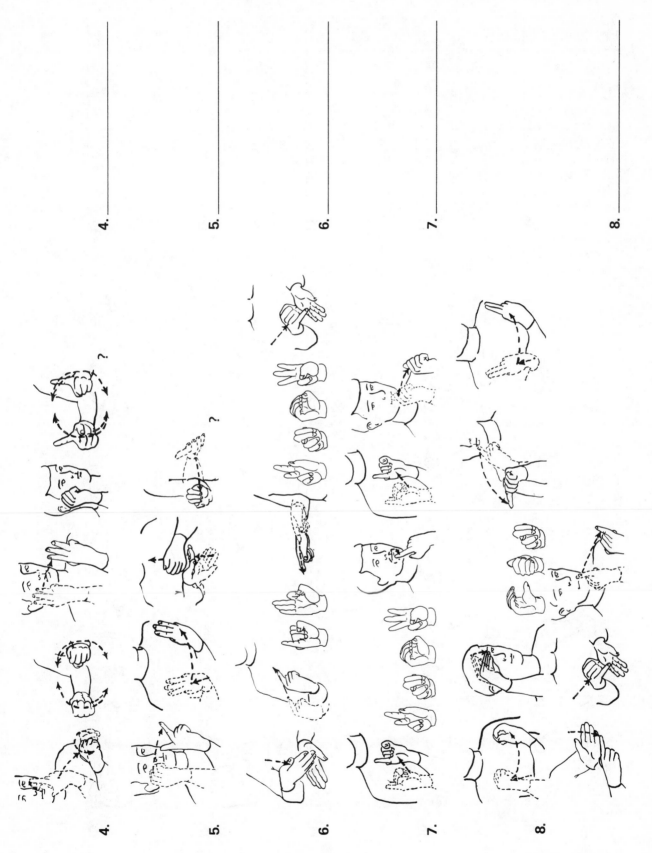

4.

5.

6.

7.

8.

4.

5.

6.

7.

8.

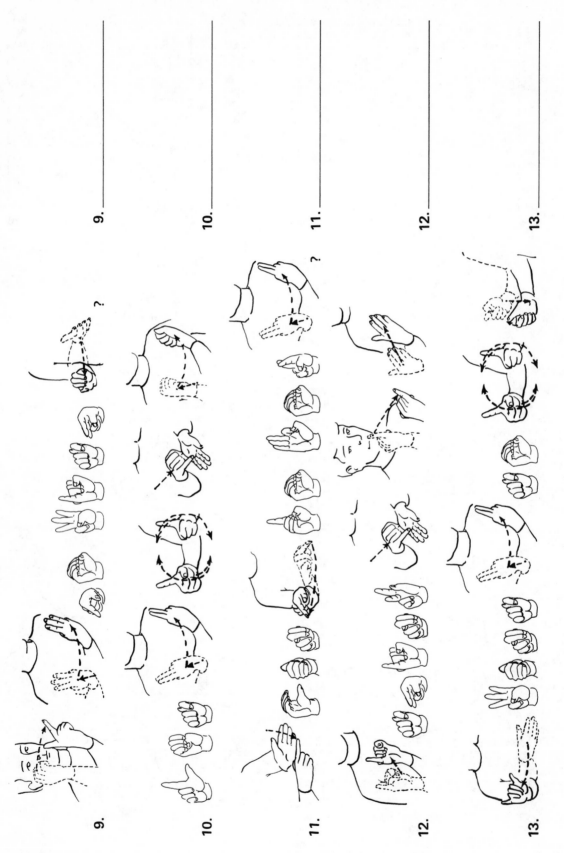

9.

10.

11.

12.

13.

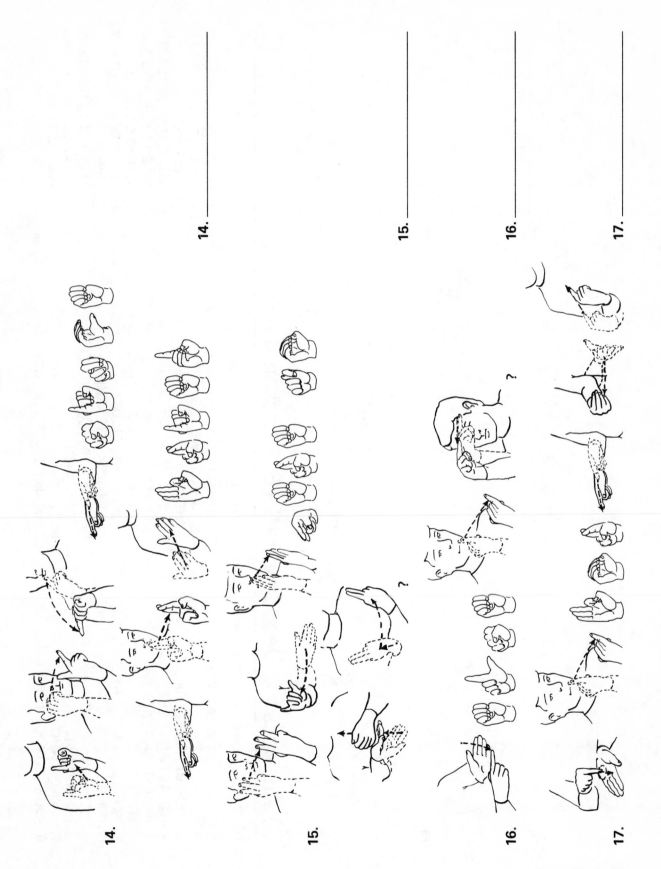

14.

15.

16.

17.

14.

15.

16.

17.

18.

19.

20.

C) Answers for Decoding Part (B), Lesson 4

Underlined words indicate that they should have been fingerspelled.

1. TELL HIM WHAT THIS IS.
2. OUR CAR IS BLACK.
3. WHAT CAN IT BE?
4. WHOSE CAR WILL SHE DRIVE?
5. SHALL WE HELP THEM?
6. STOP ME IF YOU (singular) KNOW IT.
7. I KNOW WHO I AM.
8. OUR BOY CAN TELL

US WHAT IT IS.
9. SHALL WE GO WITH THEM?
10. LET US DRIVE IT OURSELVES.
11. WHAT CAN YOU (plural) DO FOR US?
12. I THINK IT IS MINE.
13. THEY WANT US TO DRIVE FAST.
14. I SHALL TELL YOU (singular) SINCE YOU ARE

MY FRIEND.
15. WILL THEY BE HERE TO HELP US?
16. WHAT ELSE IS BLACK?
17. THIS IS FOR YOU (singular) AND ME.
18. SEE ME ABOUT IT LATER.
19. I LEFT IT IN HER CAR.
20. TELL ME WHAT YOU (singular) SEE.

lesson five

Signs presented in this lesson are:

WITH	AT	COLLEGE	YOURSELVES
WITHOUT	WHY	NOT	YOURSELF
GIRL	IN, INSIDE	DON'T	HIMSELF
NAME (noun)*	SCHOOL*	YOUR (singular)	HERSELF
OR	UNIVERSITY	MYSELF	ITSELF

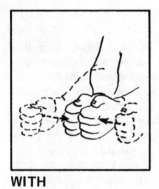

WITH

Both hands, in the configurations of the letter *A*, are held approximately four to six inches apart in front of the body; next, the *A* hands are brought together so that they touch at the knuckles.

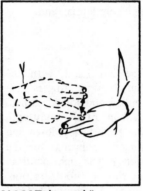

NAME (noun)*

The left hand assumes the configuration of the letter *H* and is held in front of the body with the back side facing the viewers. The right hand also assumes the configuration of the letter *H*, descends and strikes the left *H* hand edgewise (contact is made at the second joint) with *several* quick up and down movements.

NOTE: This sign carries an asterisk (*) which indicates that the motion should be repeated several times.

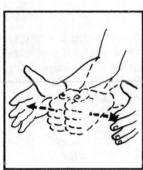

WITHOUT

This sign is made similarly to "with" except that once the *A* hands are together, quickly pull them apart and extend all ten fingers.

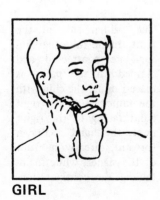

GIRL

The palmar side of the right thumb (remaining fingers are contracted and clasped to the palm) touches the signer's right cheek; then, the thumb slides down the cheek in the direction of the chin.

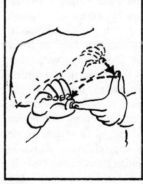

OR

The left hand assumes the configuration of the letter *L* and is held in front of the body with the back side of the *L* hand facing the viewer. (The thumb is pointing upward, while the index finger is pointing to the right.) The right hand, in the configuration of the letter *O*, first touches the thumb (contact is made between the back side of the right thumb and the palmar side of the left thumb); then, the right *O* hand is moved forward and the joined *O* fingertips touch the tip of the index finger of the left *L* hand.

51

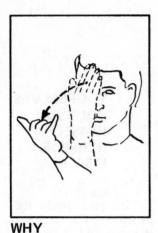

WHY

The right hand, with its fingers and thumb extended and joined, touches the forehead (contact is made between the forehead and the palmar side of the joined fingertips); then quickly the right hand is pulled away from the forehead and forms the letter Y. The back side of the Y hand should be facing the viewer as the sign comes to an end.

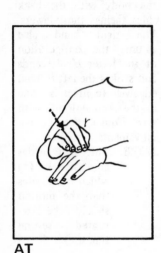

AT

The left hand, with the thumb and fingers extended and joined, is held in front of the body with the palm facing down and fingers pointing to the viewer. The right hand, in a similar configuration, moves horizontally from the right side of the body, sliding over the left hand to make contact with it. (Contact is made between the right fingertips and the back side of the left hand.)

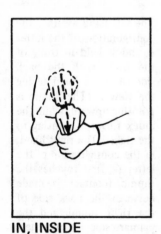

IN, INSIDE

The right hand, with the fingers extended, joined and with the thumb touching them, is held in front of the body with the joined fingertips pointing downward; next, the right hand is moved in a downward direction and places the joined fingertips inside of the left hand which is held in front of the body in the configuration of the letter O.

NOTE: The sign for "out, outside" is made by reversing the motion used to execute "in, inside."

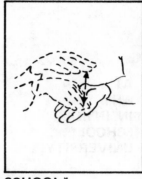

SCHOOL*

The left hand, with the fingers and thumb extended and joined, is held in front of the body with the palm facing up. The right hand, in a similar configuration, but with the palmar side facing down and the fingertips pointing to the left, descends, and claps the left hand *several* times.

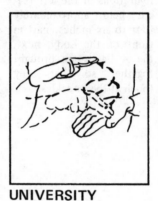

UNIVERSITY

The left hand, with the thumb and fingers extended and joined, is held in front of the body with the palm facing up. The right hand assumes the configuration of the letter U; the palmar side of the U hand touches the left palm and then, the U hand is raised upward in a spiraling motion.

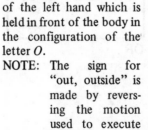

COLLEGE

Bring your hands together as you would if you were making the sign for ("school"); then, raise your right hand in a spiraling motion.

NOTE: This sign intends to suggest "higher school."

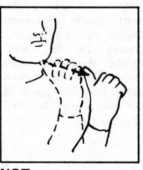

NOT

The palmar side of the right thumb (all other fingers are contracted and clasped to the palm) is placed under the chin with the knuckles of the right hand facing to the right; next, the hand is drawn forward, directly in front of the signer, while maintaining the configuration.

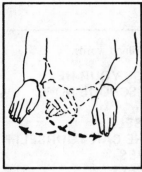

DON'T

Both hands have the thumbs and fingers extended and joined, and are placed one on top of the other (palms are facing down) in front of the body so that a right angle is formed; then, twist the wrists so that the hands separate clockwise and counter-clockwise, respectively.

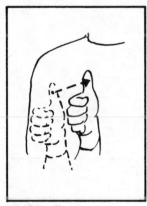

YOUR (singular)

The right hand, with the thumb and fingers extended and joined, is held in front and slightly to the right side of the body with the fingertips pointing upward and the palm facing the viewer; next, the hand is moved away from the signer's body, while preserving the configuration.

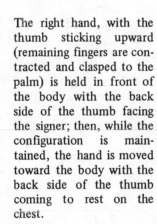

MYSELF

The right hand, with the thumb sticking upward (remaining fingers are contracted and clasped to the palm) is held in front of the body with the back side of the thumb facing the signer; then, while the configuration is maintained, the hand is moved toward the body with the back side of the thumb coming to rest on the chest.

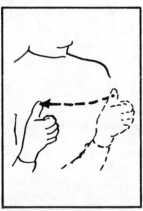

YOURSELVES

The right hand, with the thumb sticking upward (remaining fingers are contracted and clasped to the palm) is held in front and slightly to the left side of the body; next, the right hand, while maintaining the configuration, is moved across to the right side of the body.

NOTE: This sign intends to show inclusion of more than one person.

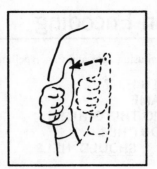

YOURSELF

The right hand, with the thumb sticking upward (all other fingers are contracted and clasped to the palm) is held in front of the body with the palmar side of the thumb facing the viewer; next, the right hand is moved forward, while maintaining the configuration.

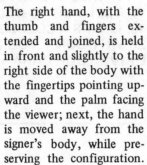

HIMSELF

This sign is made by combining the signs for "he" and "self" or "yourself." Make the sign for "he"; then, move your right hand forward while making the sign for "yourself."

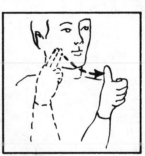

HERSELF

The right hand, in the configuration of the letter *H*, touches the right cheek (contact is made between the cheek and the palmar side of the *H* hand); then, the *H* hand is moved forward as the shape is changed to make the sign for "yourself."

ITSELF

This sign is made by combining the signs for "it" and "self" or "yourself." Make the sign for "it"; then, the right hand makes a slight movement to the right as the configuration for the sign "yourself" is made.

A) Exercises in Encoding

Encode the following material using signs and fingerspelling. Use fingerspelling for all underlined words.

1. WHY ARE YOU WITH HIM?
2. TELL ME YOUR NAME.
3. <u>DO</u> YOU <u>KNOW</u> WHO THIS GIRL IS?
4. I SHALL <u>GO</u> WITHOUT HIM.
5. YOU (singular) OR I <u>SHOULD</u> HELP THEM.
6. SHE WILL <u>COME</u> <u>TO</u> SEE YOU (singular) AT NOON.
7. HE <u>PUT</u> IT IN OUR CAR.
8. WHAT IS THE NAME <u>OF</u> YOUR SCHOOL?
9. THEY WILL BE AT THE UNIVERSITY <u>LATER</u>.
10. OUR COLLEGE <u>NEEDS</u> YOUR HELP.
11. THIS BOY IS NOT IN SCHOOL <u>NOW</u>.
12. WE DON'T <u>WANT</u> IT.
13. I <u>ALWAYS</u> HELP MYSELF.
14. WILL YOU DRIVE THE CAR YOURSELF?
15. TELL US YOURSELVES.
16. <u>LET</u> HIM <u>DO</u> IT HIMSELF.
17. IT WILL STOP <u>BY</u> ITSELF.
18. TELL HER <u>TO</u> HELP HERSELF.
19. IS THIS A COLLEGE OR A UNIVERSITY?
20. WHY DON'T YOU (singular) <u>WANT</u> ME <u>TO</u> DRIVE YOUR CAR?

B) Exercises in Decoding

Decode the following illustrated exercises:

1. _____

2. _____

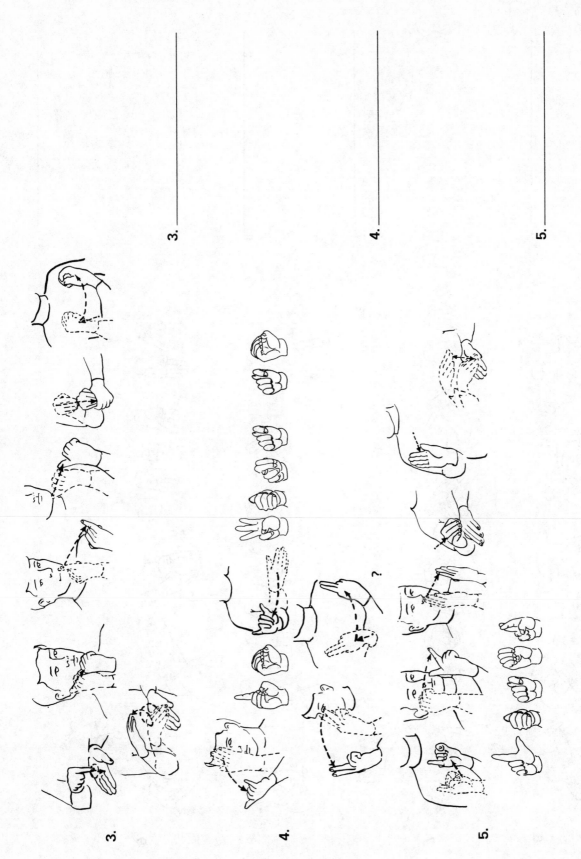

3.

4.

5.

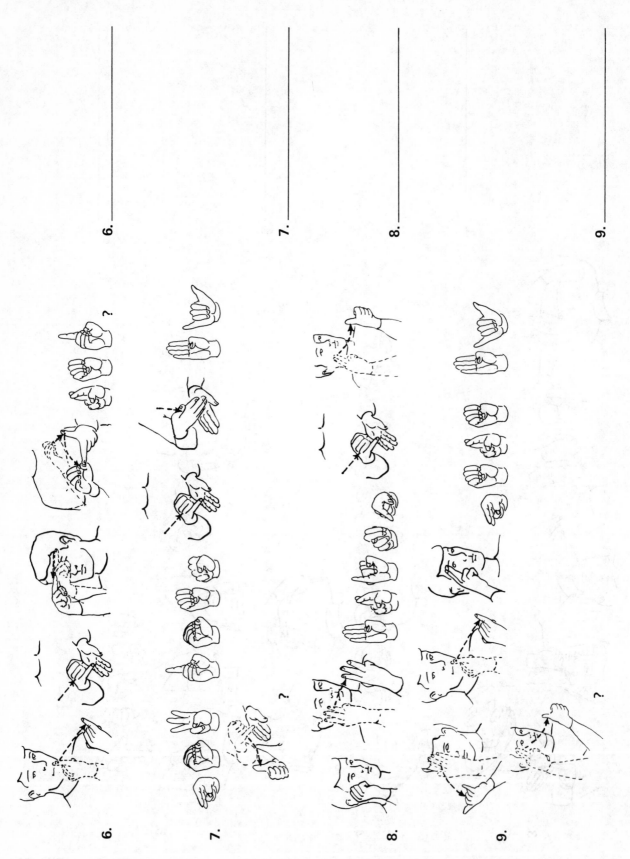

6.

7.

8.

9.

6.

7.

8.

9.

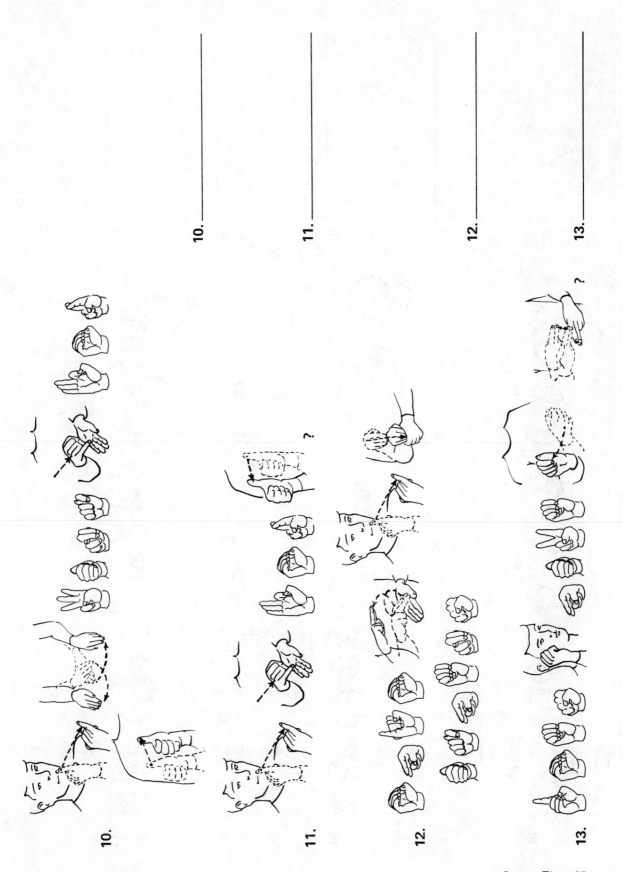

10. _____

11. _____

12. _____

13. _____

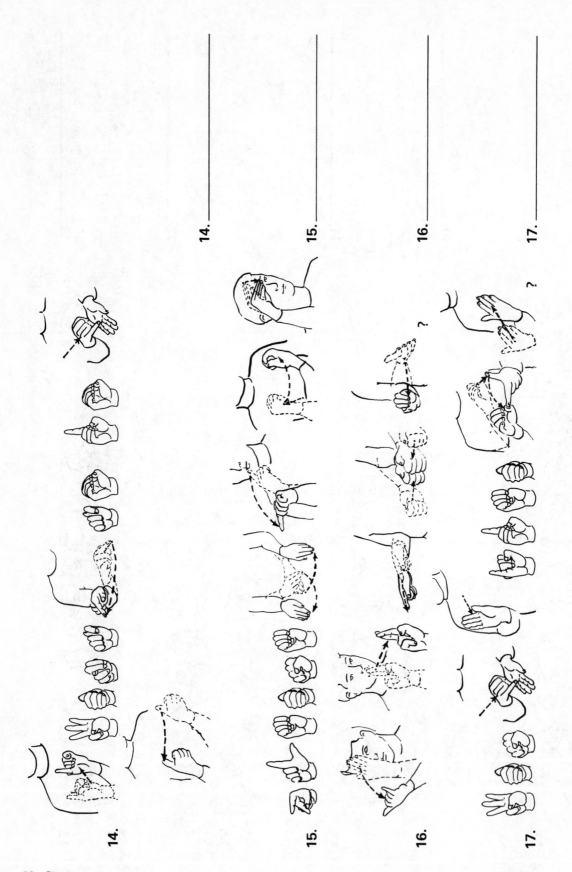

14.

15.

16.

17.

14.

15.

16.

17.

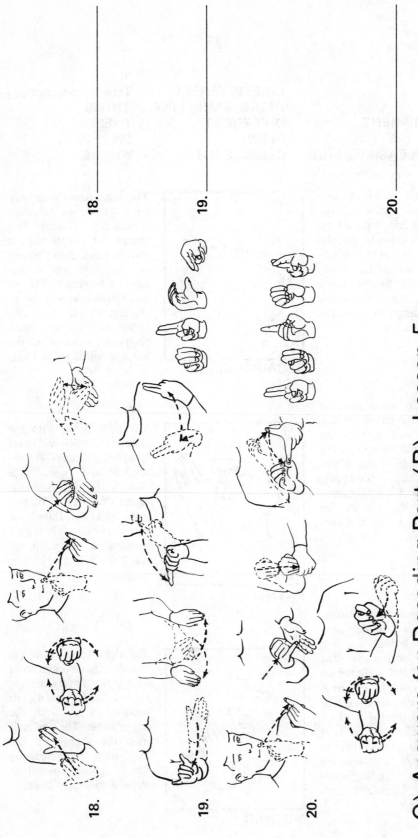

18.

19.

20.

C) Answers for Decoding Part (B), Lesson 5

Underlined words indicate that they should have been fingerspelled.

1. IS THIS YOUR BLACK CAR?
2. WHO WILL DRIVE WITH YOU (singular)?
3. THIS GIRL IS NOT IN OUR COLLEGE.
4. WHY DO THEY WANT TO SEE US?
5. I SHALL BE AT YOUR SCHOOL LATER.

6. IS IT BLACK OR RED?
7. HOW DOES IT STOP BY ITSELF?
8. SHE WILL BRING IT HERSELF.
9. WHY IS HE HERE BY HIMSELF?
10. I DON'T WANT IT FOR MYSELF.
11. IS IT FOR YOURSELF?
12. OHIO UNIVERSITY IS IN ATHENS.
13. DOES SHE HAVE A NAME?

14. I WANT YOU TO DO IT YOUR-SELVES.
15. PLEASE DON'T TELL OUR BOY.
16. WHY ARE YOU (singular) WITH THEM?
17. WAS IT YOUR IDEA OR MINE?
18. MY CAR IS AT SCHOOL.
19. THEY DON'T TELL US MUCH.
20. IS IT IN OR UNDER THE CAR?

Lesson Five 59

lesson six

Signs presented in this lesson are:

WAS	MOTHER	LIKE, INTEREST	THAT (conjunction)
WERE	PARENT	ALIKE, SAME, LIKE	THOSE
HIS	FOSTER PARENT	DIFFERENT	THESE
BECAUSE, SINCE	ORPHAN	OPEN	ON
FATHER	ENJOY, PLEASURE, LIKE	CLOSE, SHUT	WHERE

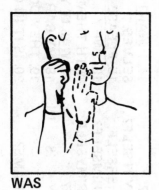

WAS

The right hand assumes the configuration of the letter *W* and is placed on the right cheek so that the palmar side of the *W* fingertips touches the cheek; then, the *W* hand is moved towards the ear as the hand changes to an *S* configuration.

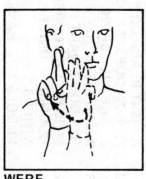

WERE

The right hand assumes the configuration of the letter *W* and is placed on the right cheek so that the palmar side of the *W* fingertips touches the cheek; then, the *W* hand is moved towards the ear as the hand changes to an *R* configuration.

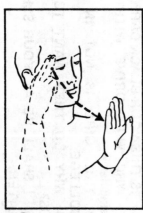

HIS

This sign is made by combining two other signs ("He," lesson 3, and "Your," lesson 5). The right *H* hand is placed on the right side of the forehead (with the back side facing to the right); then, the hand turns and is moved forward so that the palmar side is now facing the viewer with the fingers extended, joined and pointing upward.

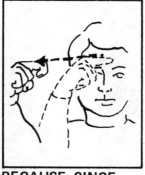

BECAUSE, SINCE

The right hand, with only the index finger extended (remaining fingers and thumb are contracted), is moved toward and placed on the right side of the signer's forehead. The index fingertip is pointing to the left with the back side facing up; then, the index finger is crooked as the hand is pulled to the right.

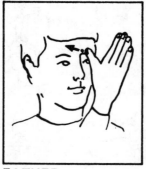

FATHER

The right hand, with the thumb extended and apart (remaining fingers are extended and joined), is brought in to touch the signer's forehead. The sign ends with the thumb on the forehead while the remaining fingers point upward at about a 45-degree angle.

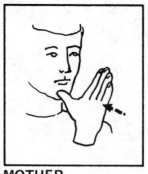

MOTHER

The right hand, with the thumb extended and apart (remaining fingers are extended and joined), is brought in to touch the signer's chin. The sign ends with the thumb on the chin while the remaining fingers point upward at about a 45-degree angle.

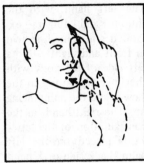

PARENT

The right hand, in the configuration of the letter *P*, is moved toward and with the tip of the middle finger touches the signer's chin. The back side of the hand is facing the viewer; then, with the configuration preserved, the hand is raised and touches the forehead.

FOSTER PARENT

The right hand, in the configuration of the letter *F*, is moved toward and with the tips of the "F" fingers touches the signer's chin. The back side of the *F* fingers is facing to the left; then, with the configuration preserved, the hand is raised and touches the forehead.

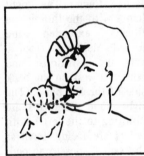

ORPHAN

The right hand, in the configuration of the letter *O*, touches the chin and is held so that its back side is facing to the right; next, the *O* hand is raised and touches the middle of the forehead.

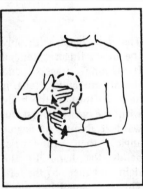

ENJOY, LIKE, PLEASURE

Both hands, with the thumbs extended and pointing upward (remaining fingers are extended and joined), are placed with one above the other against the body so that the thumbs are pointing upward and the fingers are pointing in opposite directions (left and right); next, the hands simultaneously rub the body as circles are completed in a clockwise and counter-clockwise direction, respectively.

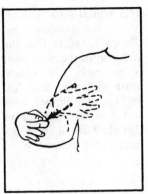

LIKE, INTEREST

The right hand, with the thumb and fingers extended and apart, touches the chest with the thumb and fingertips; next, the hand is moved forward as the thumb bends inward to touch the middle fingertip, which is flexed inward to about a 45-degree angle. The back side of the hand is facing the viewer as the sign comes to an end.

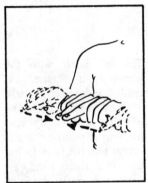

ALIKE, SAME, LIKE

Both hands, with only the index fingers extended (remaining fingers and thumb are contracted), are held in close proximity with each other in front of the body so that the index fingers are pointing to the viewer and the wrists are facing down; next, with the configuration maintained, both hands are moved toward each other and touch the sides of the index fingers together.

DIFFERENT

This sign is made by reversing the previous sign ("same"). Start the sign by placing both index fingers side-by-side (and touching) in front of the body (both fingers point to the viewer with the palmar sides facing down); then, pull the index fingers apart in opposite directions.

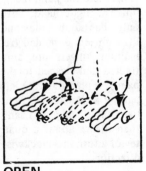

OPEN

This sign begins with both hands placed side-by-side in front of the body while the sides of the index fingers touch and the palms are facing down; the hands are then turned over onto their back sides as the hands are pulled apart.

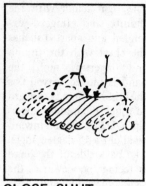

CLOSE, SHUT

This sign is made similarly to the previous one ("open"), except that the *direction* of the movement is *reversed*. The hands, apart with the palms facing up, are flipped over and brought together so that the sides of the index fingers are touching.

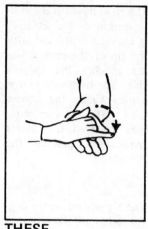

THESE

The left hand, with the thumb and fingers extended and joined, is held in front and slightly to the left side of the body with the fingers pointing to the viewer and the palm facing up. The right hand, in the configuration of the letter Y, is placed on the left palm (back side of Y hand is facing up) and then makes about a quarter of a turn in a clockwise direction.

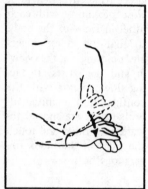

THAT (conjunction)

The left hand, with the thumb and fingers extended and joined, is held in front and slightly to the left side of the body with the fingers pointing to the viewer and the palm facing up. The right hand assumes the configuration of the letter Y, descends and comes to rest on the left palm with the back side of the Y hand facing up.

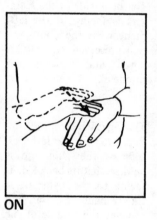

ON

The left hand, with the thumb and fingers extended and joined, is held in front and slightly to the left side of the body with the fingers pointing to the viewer while the palm faces down. The right hand, with the thumb and fingers extended and joined, descends from a vertical position and comes to rest on the back side of the left hand. (The right hand fingertips are pointing to the left.) Both wrists are facing down as the sign comes to an end.

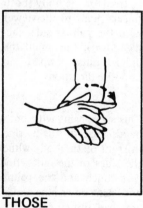

THOSE

The left hand, with the thumb and fingers extended and joined, is held in front and slightly to the left side of the body with the fingers pointing to the viewer and the palm facing up. The right hand, with only the thumb, index and little fingers extended (remaining fingers are contracted and clasped to the palm), is placed on the left palm (back side of right hand is facing up) and then makes about a quarter of a turn in a clockwise direction.

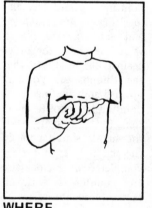

WHERE

The right hand, with only the index finger extended (remaining fingers and thumb are contracted), is held in front of the body with the wrist flexed upward at about a 45-degree angle; then, the wrist bends the hand to the right and then, to the left. This is a small but quick movement of about two or three inches in each direction.

A) Exercises in Encoding

Encode the following material using signs and fingerspelling. Use fingerspelling for all underlined words.

1. WHERE IS YOUR FATHER <u>NOW</u>?
2. IT WAS ON OUR <u>TABLE</u>.
3. THESE <u>THINGS</u> ARE <u>FOR</u> OUR MOTHER AND FATHER.
4. I AM NOT THE PARENT <u>OF</u> THIS BOY.
5. WILL IT CLOSE <u>BY</u> ITSELF?
6. DON'T OPEN IT IN THE CAR.
7. WHERE <u>DOES</u> YOUR FOSTER PARENT LIVE?
8. WE <u>KNOW</u> THAT YOU ARE AN ORPHAN.
9. IT IS DIFFERENT <u>BUT</u> I LIKE IT.
10. <u>DID</u> YOU ENJOY YOUR <u>VACATION</u>?
11. <u>BOTH OF</u> THEM ARE THE SAME.
12. WE DON'T LIKE IT BECAUSE IT IS DIFFERENT.
13. SINCE YOU ARE <u>HERE</u>, I SHALL HELP YOU.
14. IT WAS HIS <u>IDEA TO</u> DRIVE.
15. <u>DO</u> YOU <u>HAVE</u> AN INTEREST IN OUR SCHOOL?
16. WHY ARE THESE THE SAME?
17. DID YOUR MOTHER OPEN OUR <u>GIFT YET</u>?
18. MY FATHER <u>WORKS FOR</u> THE UNIVERSITY.
19. I SEE THAT YOU <u>FOUND</u> YOUR CAR.
20. TELL YOUR MOTHER THAT WE ARE NOT <u>HERE</u>.

B) Exercises in Decoding

Decode the following illustrated exercises:

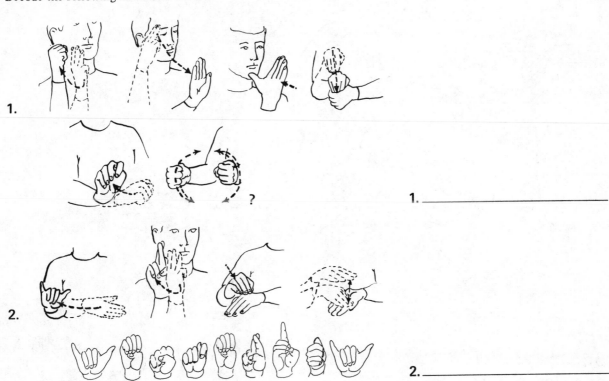

1. _____

2. _____

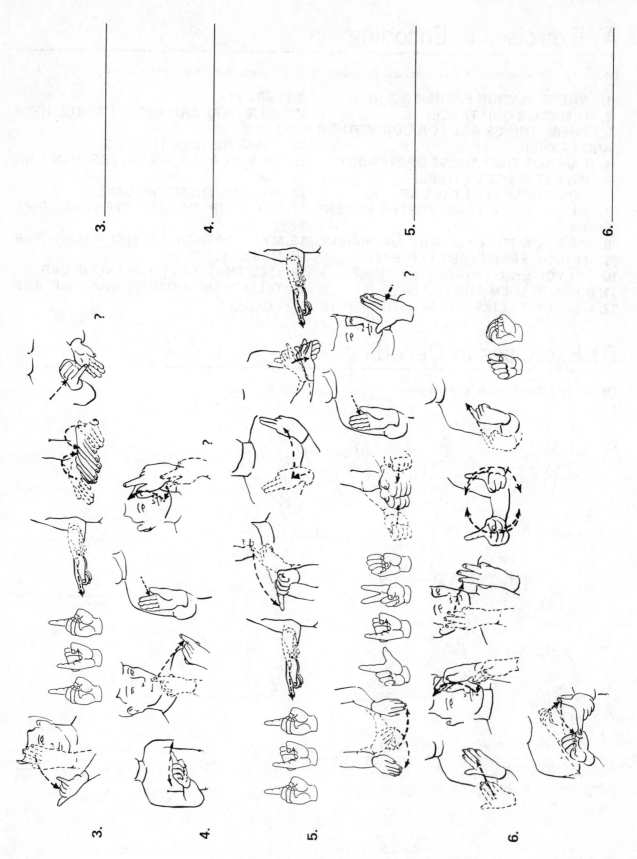

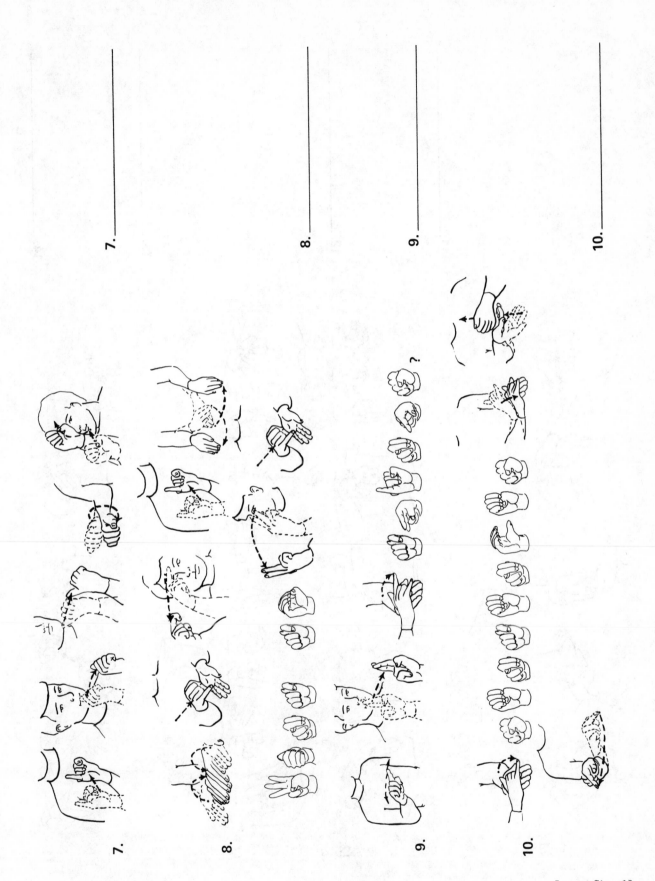

7.

8.

9.

10.

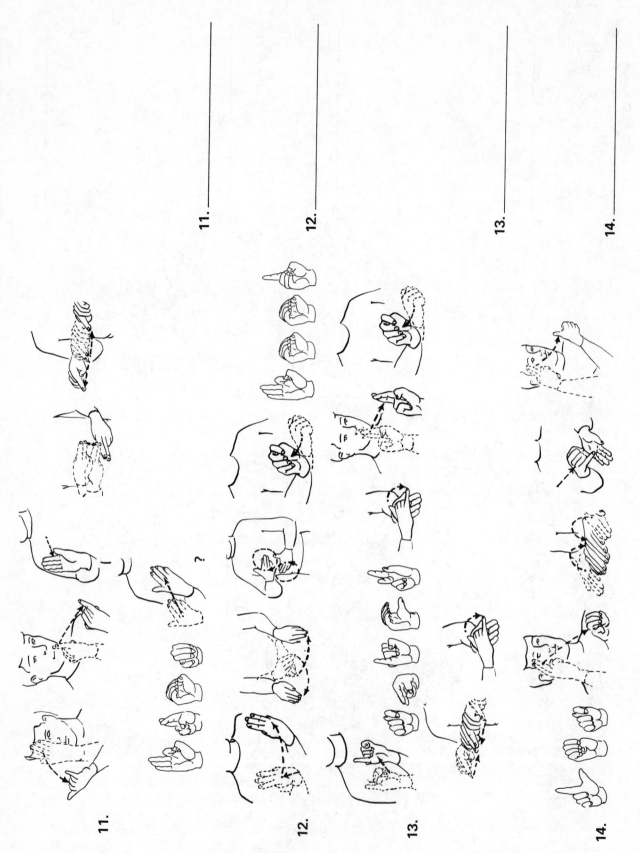

11.

12.

13.

14.

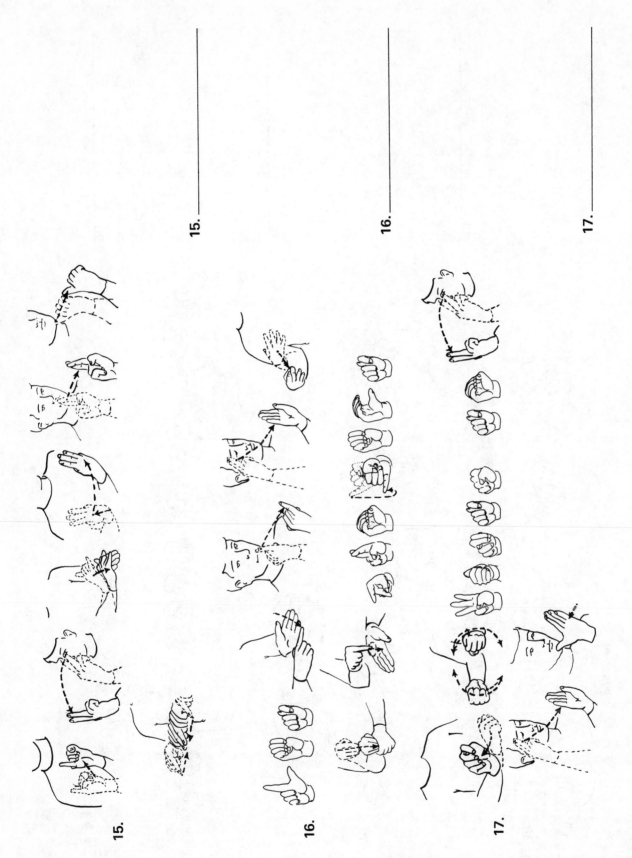

15.

16.

17.

15.

16.

17.

Lesson Six   67

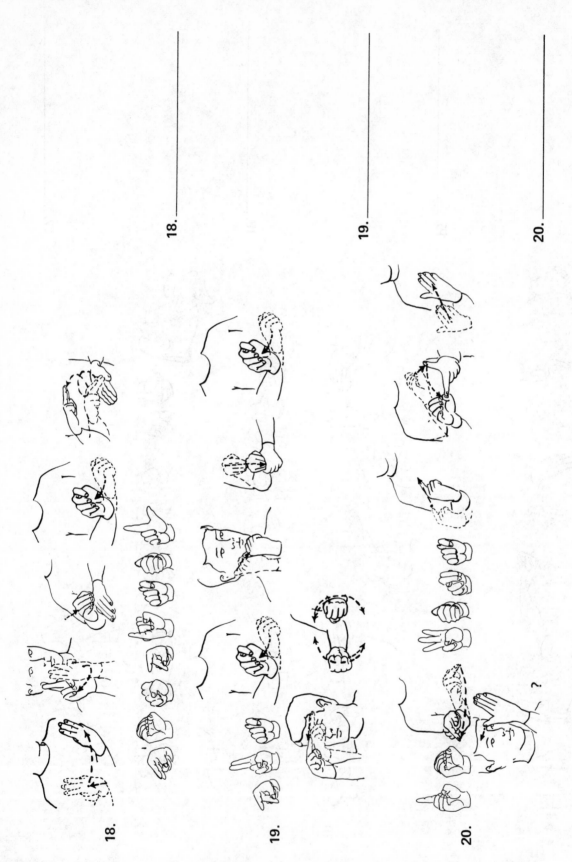

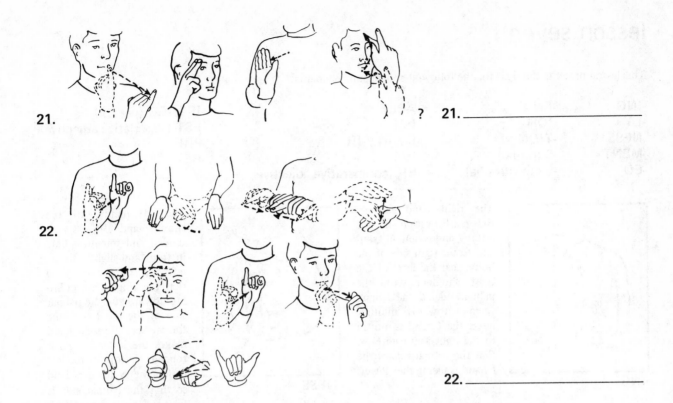

21. .... **?**   21. _____

22. 22. _____

C) Answers for Decoding Part (B), Lesson 6

Underlined words indicate that they should have been fingerspelled.

1. WAS HIS MOTHER IN THE CAR?
2. THEY WERE AT SCHOOL <u>YESTERDAY</u>.
3. WHY <u>DID</u> YOU (singular) CLOSE IT?
4. WHERE IS YOUR PARENT.
5. <u>DID</u> YOU (singular) TELL US THAT YOU DON'T <u>LIVE</u> WITH YOUR MOTHER?
6. MY FOSTER PARENT WILL DRIVE ME <u>TO</u> COLLEGE.
7. I AM NOT AN ORPHAN.
8. CLOSE IT BECAUSE I DON'T <u>WANT</u> <u>TO</u> SEE IT.
9. WHERE ARE THOSE <u>THINGS</u>?
10. THESE <u>SENTENCES</u> WILL HELP YOU (plural).
11. WHY IS YOUR NAME DIFFERENT <u>FROM</u> MINE?
12. WE DON'T LIKE THE <u>FOOD</u>.
13. I <u>THINK</u> THESE ARE THE SAME <u>AS</u> THOSE.
14. <u>LET</u> HIM CLOSE IT HIMSELF.
15. I SEE THAT WE ARE NOT ALIKE.
16. WHAT IS HIS INTEREST IN THIS <u>PROJECT</u>?
17. THE BOY <u>WANTS</u> <u>TO</u> SEE HIS MOTHER.
18. WE ARE AT THE UNIVERSITY <u>HOSPITAL</u>.
19. <u>PUT</u> THE GIRL INSIDE THE BLACK CAR.
20. <u>DO</u> YOU (plural) <u>WANT</u> ME OR MY FATHER?
21. IS HE YOUR PARENT?
22. I DON'T LIKE SCHOOL BECAUSE I AM <u>LAZY</u>.

lesson seven

This lesson presents the signs for the following morphemic elements:[1]

-ING	-EN	-ABLE	-IST, -ER (person)
-LY	-ION	-ISH	-EST (superlative adjective)
-NESS	-TION	-IM, -IL, -IR	-PRE
-MENT	-S (plural)	-IVE	-RE
-ED	-S (apostrophe)	-ER (comparative adjective)	-Y

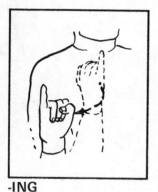

-ING

The right hand assumes the configuration of the letter *I* and is held in front and to the right side of the body near the level of the right shoulder with the palmar side of the *I* hand facing toward midline; next, the *I* hand is moved to the right as it rotates so that the palmar side of the *I* hand is facing the viewer.

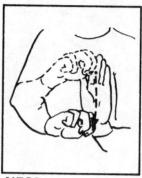

-NESS

The left hand, with the thumb and fingers extended and joined, is held in front and slightly to the left side of the body so that the fingers are pointing upward and the palmar side of the hand is facing the viewer; the right hand makes the letter *N*, which touches the tips of the left hand (the *N* hand is held so that the palmar side is facing down); next, the *N* hand brushes past the palmar side of the left fingers as it is moved downward toward the wrist.

-LY

The right hand, with only the thumb, index and little fingers extended (remaining fingers are contracted and clasped to the palm), is held in front and to the right side of the body near the level of the right shoulder with the palmar side of the fingers facing the viewer; next, with the configuration preserved, the right hand makes a quick wiggling motion downward. The sign ends with the palmar side of the hand still facing the viewer.

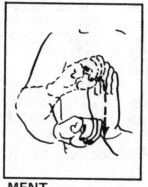

-MENT

This sign is made similarly to the previous one ("-ness"), except that the right hand assumes the configuration of the letter *M*.

---

[1] Morphemic elements are considered to be the most basic elements of the English language, of which one class adds meaning by forming new words. For example, in the sentence "The girls walked home," the -s after girl is the "plural" morpheme; the -ed after walk is the "past tense" morpheme. It is assumed that since the student is already familiar with the rules of grammar governing the English language, he/she can use, as well as understand, the morphemes presented here in encoding and decoding sentences.

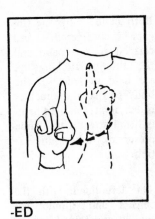

-ED

The right hand assumes the configuration of the letter *D* and is held in front and to the right side of the body near the level of the right shoulder with the palmar side of the *D* hand facing toward midline; next, the *D* hand is moved to the right as it rotates so that the palmar side of the *D* hand is facing the viewer.

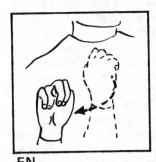

-EN

The right hand assumes the configuration of the letter *N* and is held in front of the body with the palmar side of the *N* hand facing midline; next, the *N* hand is moved to the right as it rotates so that the palmar side of the *N* hand is facing the viewer.

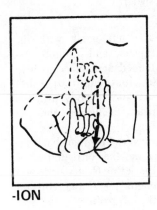

-ION

The left hand, with the thumb and fingers extended and joined, is held in front of the body with the fingers pointing upward and the palmar side of the hand facing the viewer. The right hand assumes the configuration of the letter *I*; then, the back side of the thumb of the *I* hand grazes past the palmar side of the left fingers in a downward direction.

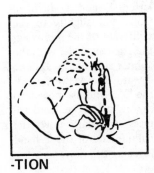

-TION

This sign is made similarly to the previous one ("-ion"), except that the configuration of the right hand is that of the letter *O*. The top portion of the right hand grazes past the palmar side of the left fingers in the direction of the palm.

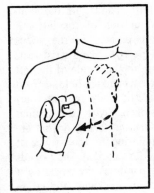

-S (plural)

The right hand assumes the configuration of the letter *S* and is held in front and slightly to the right side of the body near the level of the shoulder with the back side of the *S* hand facing to the right; next, the *S* hand is moved to the right as the hand rotates so that the palmar side of the *S* hand is facing the viewer.

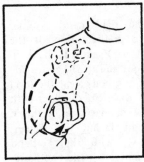

-S (apostrophe)

Both hands assume the configuration of the letter *A* and are held in a parallel position (three to four inches apart) in front of the body with the wrists facing the viewer; then, with the configuration maintained, both *A* hands tilt forward so that the wrists are facing down.

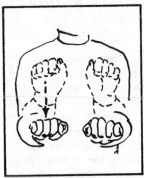

-ABLE

The right hand assumes the configuration of the letter *S* and is held in front and to the right side of the body near the level of the right shoulder with the back side of the *S* hand facing the signer; next, the *S* hand rotates clockwise and drops slightly so that the back side of the *S* hand is facing down.

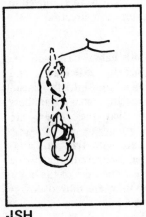

-ISH

The right hand assumes the configuration of the letter *I* and is held in front and to the right side of the body near the level of the right shoulder with the *I* hand pointing upward and the palmar side facing midline; then, with the configuration maintained, the *I* hand makes a wiggling motion as the hand descends in a downward direction.

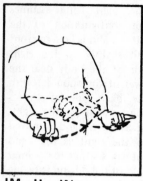

-IM, -IL, -IN

Both hands, in the configuration of the letter *I*, are crossed at the wrists (the right hand wrist rests on the back side of the left wrist) and are held in front of the body so that the *I* fingers (with the palmar surfaces facing down) are pointing to the viewer at an angle; next, the *I* hands separate as the wrists twist them clockwise and counter-clockwise, respectively.

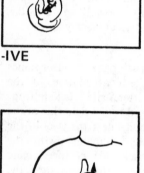

-IVE

The right hand assumes the configuration of the letter *V* and is held in front and to the right side of the body near the level of the right shoulder with the palmar side of the *V* hand facing the viewer; next, with the *V* hand maintaining the configuration, a wiggling motion is made as the hand is moved downward.

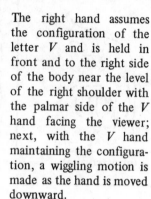

-ER (comparative adjective)

The right hand, with only the thumb sticking upward (remaining fingers are contracted and clasped to the palm), is held in front and slightly to the right side of the body with the palmar side of the thumb facing midline; next, with the configuration preserved, the right hand is moved in an upward direction.

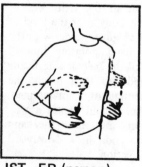

-IST, -ER (person)

Both hands, each with its fingers extended and joined, are initially placed near the signer's shoulders so that the fingers are pointing to the viewer; next, with the configuration preserved, the hands graze the sides of the body as they are moved downward.

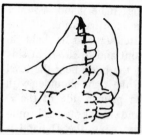

-EST (superlative) adjective

Both hands, with the fingers contracted and clasped to the palm and the thumbs sticking up, are held in front of the body so that the knuckles touch; next, the right hand is lifted straight up, while preserving the configuration.

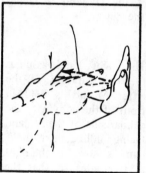

PRE-

The left hand, with the fingers and thumb extended and joined, is held in front and slightly to the left side of the body with the fingers pointing upward and the palmar side facing the viewer. The right hand assumes the configuration of the letter *P* with the middle fingertip of the *P* hand touching the back side of the left hand; then, the right *P* hand is pulled straight toward the signer.

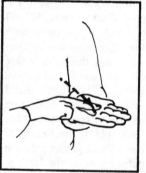

RE-

The left hand, with the fingers and thumb extended and joined, is held in front and to the left side of the body with the palm facing up and the fingers pointing to the viewer. The right hand assumes the configuration of the letter *R*, descends and plants the *R* fingertips on the left palm.

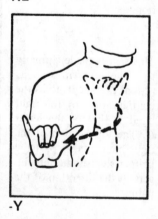

-Y

The right hand assumes the configuration of the letter *Y* and is held in front and slightly to the right side of the body near the right shoulder with the palmar side of the *Y* hand toward the viewer; next, the *Y* hand is moved to the right as the hand rotates so that now the palmar side of the *Y* hand is facing the viewer.

A) Exercises in Encoding

Encode the following material using signs and fingerspelling. Use fingerspelling for all underlined words.

1. WE ARE DRIVING OUR CAR <u>TO</u> THE UNIVERSITY. (For "driving," first make the sign for "drive," followed by "-ing.")
2. IT WILL NOT <u>HAPPEN</u> SUDDENLY.
3. HIS QUICKNESS <u>SURPRISED</u> US. (For "quickness," sign "quick" plus "-ness.")
4. SHE CLOSED <u>EARLY</u> <u>TODAY</u>.
5. <u>HAVE</u> YOU DRIVEN OUR CARS <u>YET</u>? (For "driven," sign "drive" plus "-en.")
6. IS THIS YOUR FATHER'S <u>BOOK</u>?
7. WHAT ARE THE NAMES <u>OF</u> YOUR PRE-SCHOOL <u>CHILDREN</u>?
8. WILL HE RE-OPEN THE <u>CASE</u>?
9. THIS <u>TEAM</u> WILL BE UNSTOPPABLE. (For "unstoppable," fingerspell "un," followed by the signs for "stop" plus "-able.")
10. HE IS THE QUICKEST BOY IN THE <u>LEAGUE</u>.
11. SHE IS FASTER <u>THAN</u> I.
12. WHY ARE YOU (singular) STOPPING <u>HERE</u>?
13. I <u>THINK</u> IT IS QUICKER THIS <u>WAY</u>.
14. WE SEE IT <u>AS</u> BLACKISH. (For "blackish," sign "black" plus "-ish.")
15. THE BOY'S NAME IS <u>JOHN</u>.
16. WHY WAS IT PLEASURABLE?

B) Exercises in Decoding

Decode the following illustrated exercises:

1.

? 1._____

2.

? 2._____

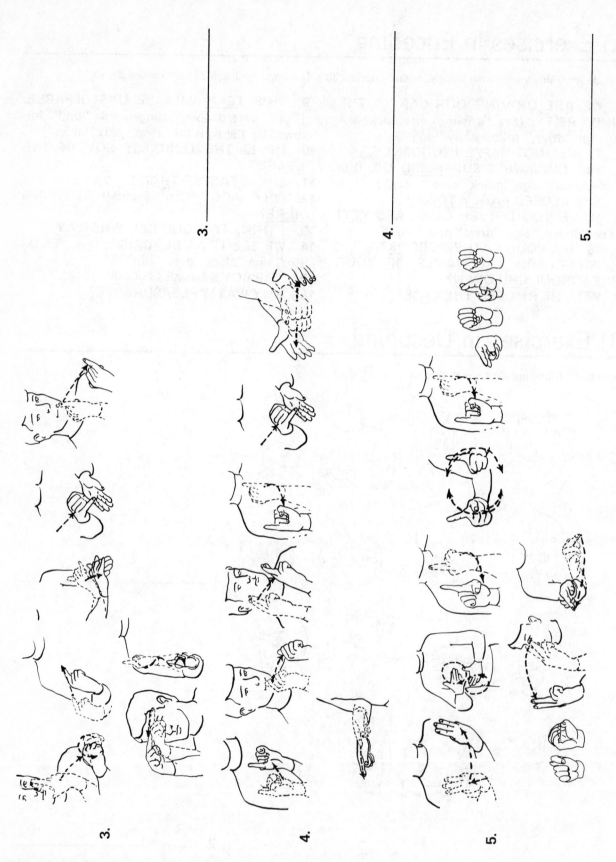

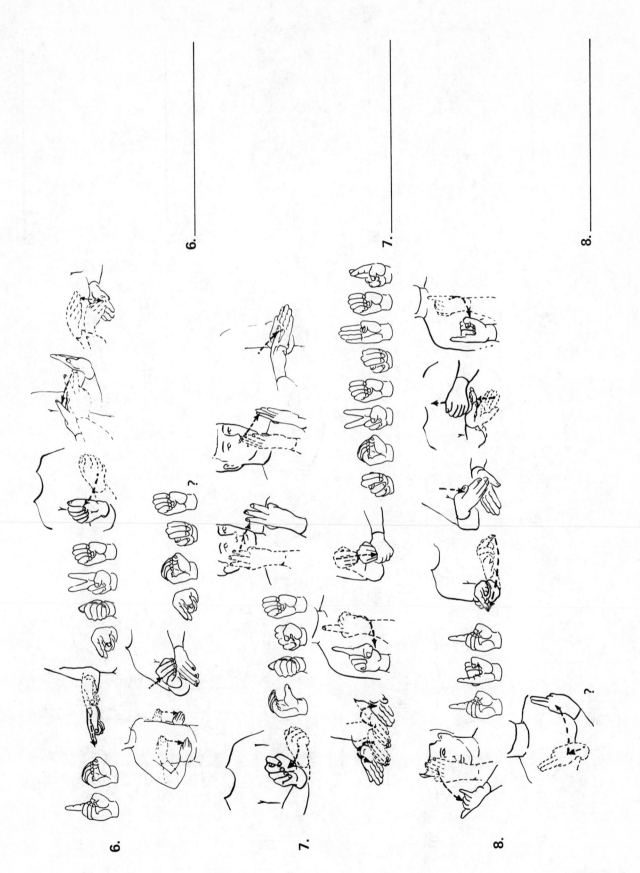

6.

7.

8.

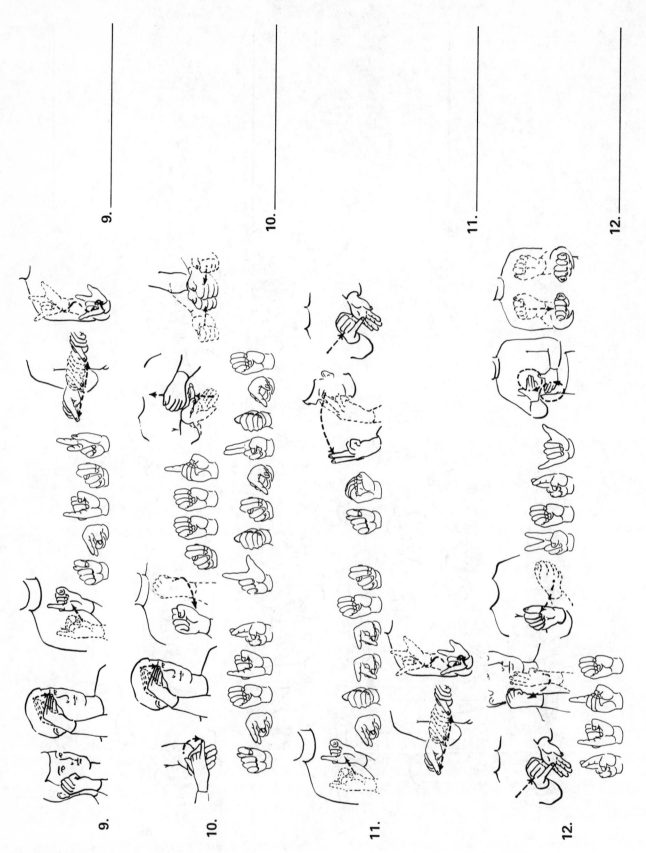

9.

10.

11.

12.

9.

10.

11.

12.

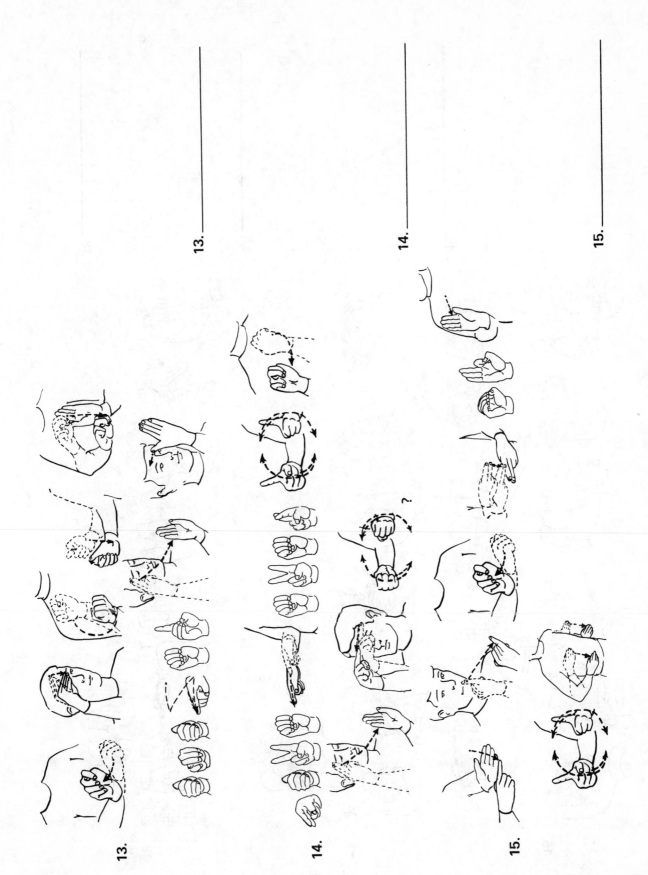

13.

14.

15.

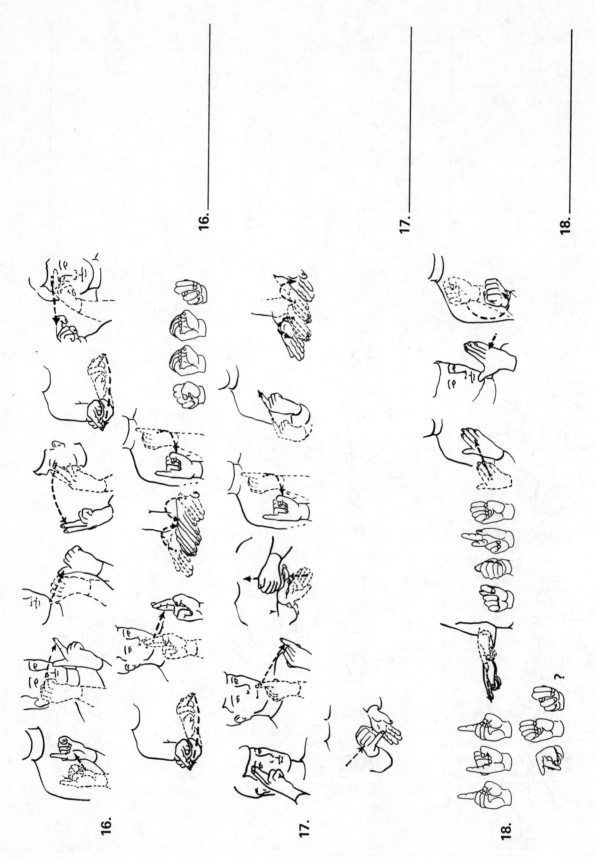

16.

17.

18.

16.

17.

18.

C) Answers for Decoding Part (B), Lesson 7

Underlined words indicate that they should have been fingerspelled.

1. WHY ARE THEY STOPPING THE CARS?
2. WHOSE CAR WILL HE BE DRIVING <u>TO</u> SCHOOL?
3. TELL ME THAT IT IS BLACKISH.
4. I AM OPENING IT WITHOUT YOU (singular).
5. WE ENJOYED DRIVING <u>HERE</u> <u>TO</u> SEE YOU (plural).
6. <u>DO</u> YOU <u>HAVE</u> A PRESCHOOLER AT <u>HOME</u>?
7. THE <u>CASE</u> WILL BE REOPENED IN <u>NOVEMBER</u>.
8. WHY <u>DID</u> YOU (plural) STOP HELPING US?
9. SHE AND I <u>THINK</u> DIFFERENTLY.
10. THESE BOYS <u>NEED</u> HELP WITH <u>THEIR</u> <u>LANGUAGE</u>.
11. I <u>HAPPEN</u> <u>TO</u> SEE IT DIFFERENTLY.
12. IT WAS A <u>VERY</u> PLEASURABLE <u>RIDE</u>.
13. THE BOY'S QUICKNESS <u>AMAZED</u> HIS FATHER.
14. <u>HAVE</u> YOU (singular) <u>EVER</u> DRIVEN HIS BLACK CAR?
15. WHAT IS THE NAME <u>OF</u> YOUR DRIVER?
16. I SHALL NOT SEE YOU (plural) SINCE YOU ARE CLOSING <u>SOON</u>.
17. HE IS HELPING ME OPEN IT.
18. <u>DID</u> YOU <u>TAKE</u> MY MOTHER'S <u>PEN</u>?

lesson eight

Signs presented in this lesson are:

EITHER	HAS (auxiliary)	TOGETHER	WALK
NEITHER	NEVER	TABLE	WHEN
HAVE (possessive)	FOR	READ	THING
HAVE (auxiliary)	HOW	BRING	WANT
HAS (possessive)	PAST, AGO, LAST	CARRY	BOOK

EITHER

The left hand assumes the configuration of the letter *L* and is held in front and slightly to the left side of the body with the thumb sticking upward and the back side of the *L* hand facing the viewer. The right hand, in the configuration of the letter *E*, is placed on the left thumb so that the fingernails of the *E* hand touch the palmar surface of the thumb; next, the *E* hand separates, touches the tip of the left index finger and returns to its original starting position.

NEITHER

The left hand assumes the configuration of the letter *L* and is held in front and slightly to the left side of the body with the thumb sticking upward and the back side of the *L* hand facing the viewer. The right hand, in the configuration of the letter *N*, is brought over to touch the thumb (contact is made between the tips of the *N* hand and the palmar side of the left thumb); next, the *N* hand separates and is moved past the tip of the left index finger as it quickly changes into the configuration of the fingerspelled letter *R* as the hand is flexed slightly upward.

HAVE (possessive)

Both hands, with the thumbs extended and sticking upward, while the fingers are joined and cupped, are held in front of the body about six to eight inches apart so that the back sides of the hands are facing the viewer; next, bend the hands toward the body so that the joined fingertips touch the chest.

HAVE (auxiliary verb)

The left hand assumes the configuration of the letter *H* and is held in front and slightly to the left side of the body with the fingers pointing to the viewer and the back side of the hand facing to the left. The right hand, also in the configuration of the letter *H*, is placed across the left hand so that the back side of the right hand is facing the viewer; next, the right *H* hand grazes the left *H* hand as it is moved toward the tip of the left *H* hand, and then changes to a *V* configuration as it drops downward sharply. The sign ends with the palmar side of the *V* hand facing the viewer.

NOTE: This motion intends to suggest the completion of action.

HAS (possessive)

The right hand, in the configuration of the letter *S*, is held approximately six to eight inches in front and slightly to the right side of the body with the back side of the hand facing the viewer; next, the *S* hand comes straight toward the body and rests on the right side of the chest.

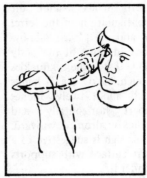

FOR

The sign begins by touching the right index finger (all other fingers and thumb are contracted) on the right side of the forehead and then quickly pulling the hand away, while twisting the wrist so that the index finger points forward and the back of the hand faces the signer.

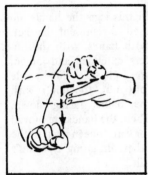

HAS (auxiliary verb)

The left hand assumes the configuration of the letter *H* and is held in front and slightly to the left side of the body so that the *H* fingers are pointing to the viewer with the back side facing to the left. The right hand, in the configuration of the letter *S*, touches the left *H* hand (contact is made between the back side of the thumb of the *S* hand and the third joint of the index finger of the left *H* hand); next, the *S* hand grazes past the fingertip of the left *H* hand and then quickly is dropped downward.

NOTE: This motion intends to suggest the completion of action.

HOW

Both hands are held side-by-side in front of the body so that the thumbs are extended upward, fingers half flexed and the backs of the hands are touching each other; next both hands are quickly flipped forward so that the thumbs are pointing to the viewer as the sign ends.

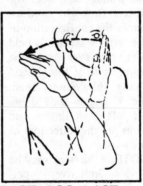

PAST, AGO, LAST

The right hand, with fingers and thumb extended and joined, is held in front and slightly to the right side of the body near the level of the right shoulder with the palmar side facing the signer and the fingers pointing upward; next, the right hand moves toward and is flipped over the right shoulder.

NOTE: This sign intends to suggest that something took place prior to now.

NEVER

The right hand, with the fingers and thumb extended and joined, is held in front and slightly to the right side of the body near the level of the right shoulder with the palmar side of the hand facing to the left and the fingertips pointing upward; next, with the configuration preserved, the hand makes a wiggling line as it descends.

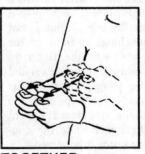

TOGETHER

Both hands assume the configuration of the letter *T* and are placed side-by-side in front of the body so that the knuckles touch; then, with the configuration preserved, both hands are moved forward, away from the signer's body.

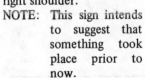

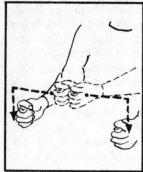

TABLE

Both hands assume the configuration of the letter *T* and are placed side-by-side in front of the body so that the knuckles touch; next, the *T* hands pull about twelve inches apart horizontally and quickly drop downward. This sign is suggestive of a flat surface with supports under it.

NOTE: The sign for "desk" is made similarly to "table," except that both hands assume the configuration of the letter *D*.

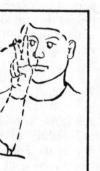

READ

The left hand, with the fingers joined and extended vertically, is held in front of the body so that the palmar side faces the signer. The right hand assumes the configuration of the letter *V*, which is held near the eyes with the palmar side of the *V* hand facing the viewer; then, the *V* fingers slide down the left hand fingers and palm in the direction of the wrist.

NOTE: This sign may be imitative, perhaps, of the eyes scanning a page for information.

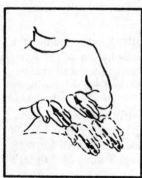

BRING

Both hands, with the fingers and thumbs extended and joined, are placed side-by-side (but not touching) in front of the body with the fingertips pointing to the viewer and the palmar sides of the hands facing up; next, the hands are moved toward the signer while the configuration is preserved.

CARRY

Both hands, with the fingers and thumbs extended and joined, are placed side-by-side (but not touching) in front of the body with the fingertips pointing to the viewer and the palmar sides facing up; next, with the configuration preserved, the hands simultaneously are moved to the right.

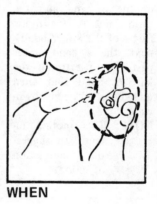

WALK

In this sign the hands are used to represent the feet. Both hands, with the fingers extended and joined, are placed side-by-side (but not touching) with the palms facing down. Then, the hands are moved forward, one in front of the other, imitating a person's gait.

WHEN

The left hand, with only the index finger extended (remaining fingers and thumb are contracted), is held vertically in front and slightly to the left side of the body with the palmar side of the left index finger facing to the right. The right hand, with only the index finger extended, touches the left index finger, separates to complete a clockwise circle along a horizontal plane and ends in the same spot again.

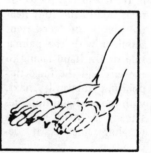

THING

The right hand, with the fingers and thumb extended and joined, is held in front of the body with the fingers pointing to the viewer and the palmar side facing up; next, the hand makes several arc motions as it is moved to the right side of the body.

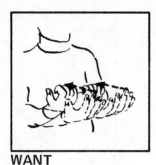

WANT

Both hands are held side-by-side in front of the body and with the back sides facing down. The configuration of the hands is a slight cupping of the palms with the fingers spread apart in a clawlike manner; next, with the configuration preserved, both hands are moved toward the body, while the fingers and thumbs are curled inward.

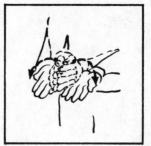

BOOK

This sign is made by pantomiming opening a book. Begin by bringing the hands (thumbs and fingers extended, joined and pointing to the viewer) together so that the palms join; then, open the hands so that the palms are facing up.

A) Exercises in Encoding

Encode the following material using signs and fingerspelling. Use fingerspelling for all underlined words.

1. IS THE <u>GIFT</u> FOR US?
2. HOW <u>DO</u> YOU <u>KNOW</u> MY NAME?
3. I SAW HIM AT SCHOOL <u>YESTERDAY</u>. (The word "saw," which is the imperfect tense of "see," is signed as "see" plus "past." Other irregular verbs are formed similarly.)
4. HE IS TELLING US THAT WE <u>SHOULD GO</u> TOGETHER.
5. IS THE BLACK BOOK ON THE TABLE?
6. WHY ARE YOU READING HIS BOOK?
7. <u>DO</u> YOU WANT ME <u>TO</u> BRING IT WITH ME?
8. <u>PLEASE</u> HELP HIM CARRY IT <u>TO</u> THE CAR.
9. WHEN ARE THEY <u>FINISHING</u> THIS THING?
10. WHY ARE YOU TELLING ME THAT I SHALL NEVER SEE IT?
11. WE HAVE THE BOOKS WITH US.
12. HAVE YOU <u>EVER</u> DRIVEN HER CAR?
13. I <u>THINK</u> HE IS CARRYING IT WITH HIM.
14. WE WALKED QUICKLY BECAUSE WE WERE <u>LATE</u>.
15. NEITHER <u>OF</u> THESE THINGS IS FOR YOU.
16. <u>PLEASE</u> READ EITHER THE BLACK OR <u>RED</u> BOOK.
17. SHE HAS IT ON HER DESK. ("Desk" is signed similarly to "table," except that both hands assume the configuration of the letter D.)
18. HAS HE BEEN READING IT?
19. WE HAD NEVER SEEN IT <u>UNTIL</u> <u>NOW</u>.
20. THEY TOLD YOU <u>SEVERAL</u> <u>MONTHS</u> AGO.
21. <u>DID</u> YOU BRING YOUR <u>SPEECH</u> BOOK WITH YOU?
22. TELL US WHEN YOU <u>DECIDE</u> <u>TO</u> BRING IT.
23. WE SHALL READ IT TOGETHER <u>NOW</u>.
24. IS IT ON OR <u>UNDER</u> THE TABLE?
25. WHY DON'T YOU WANT <u>TO</u> CARRY IT FOR ME?

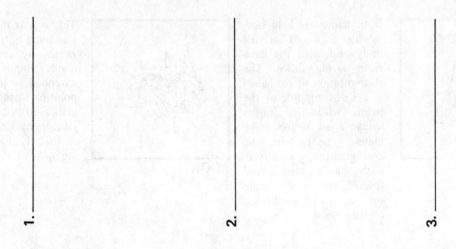

1.

2.

3.

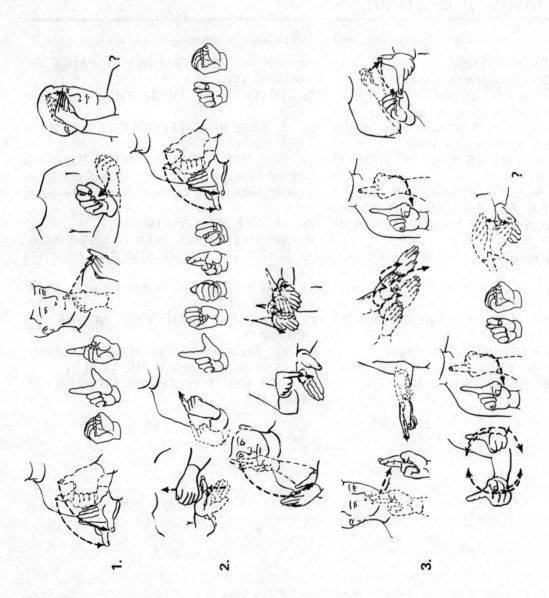

1.

2.

3.

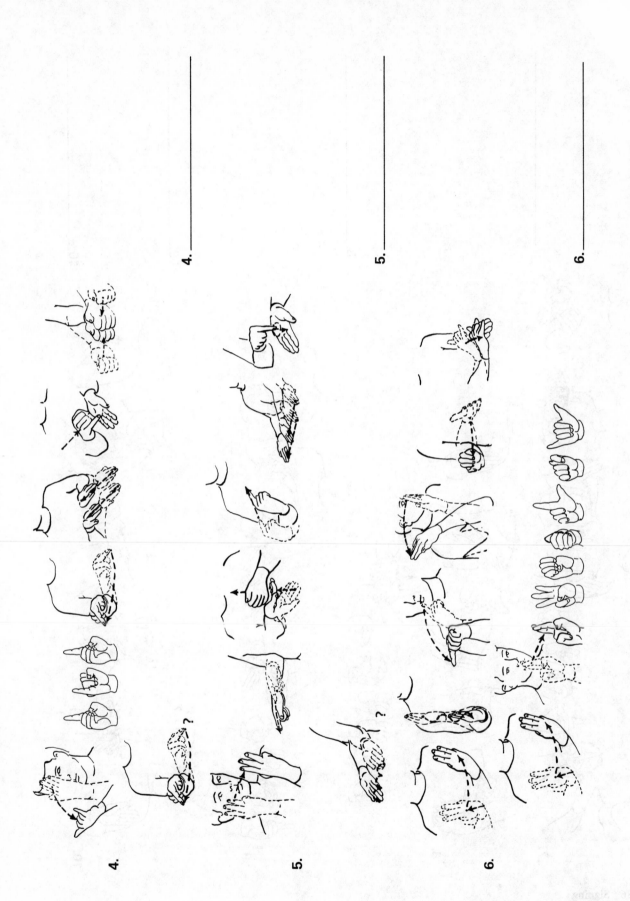

4.

5.

6.

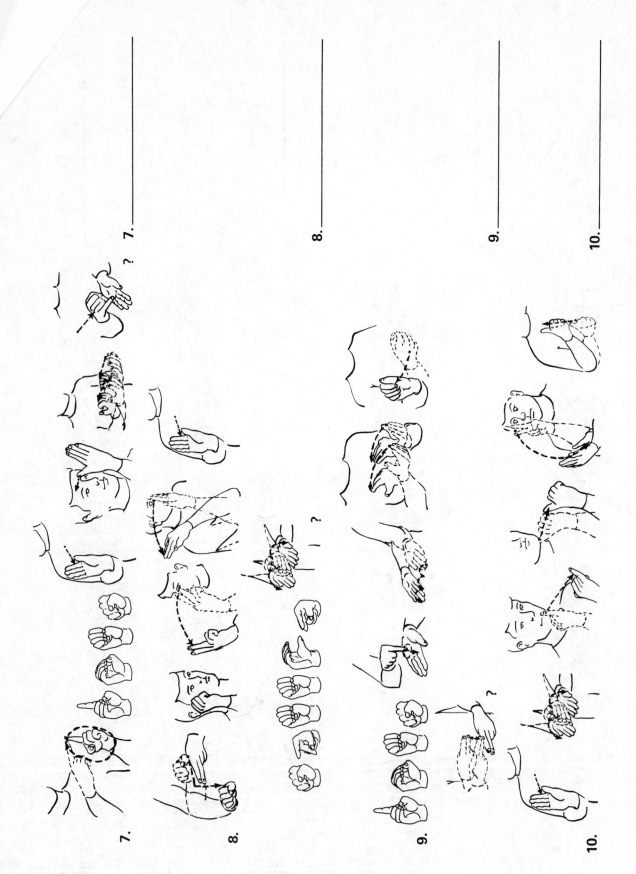

7.

8.

9.

10.

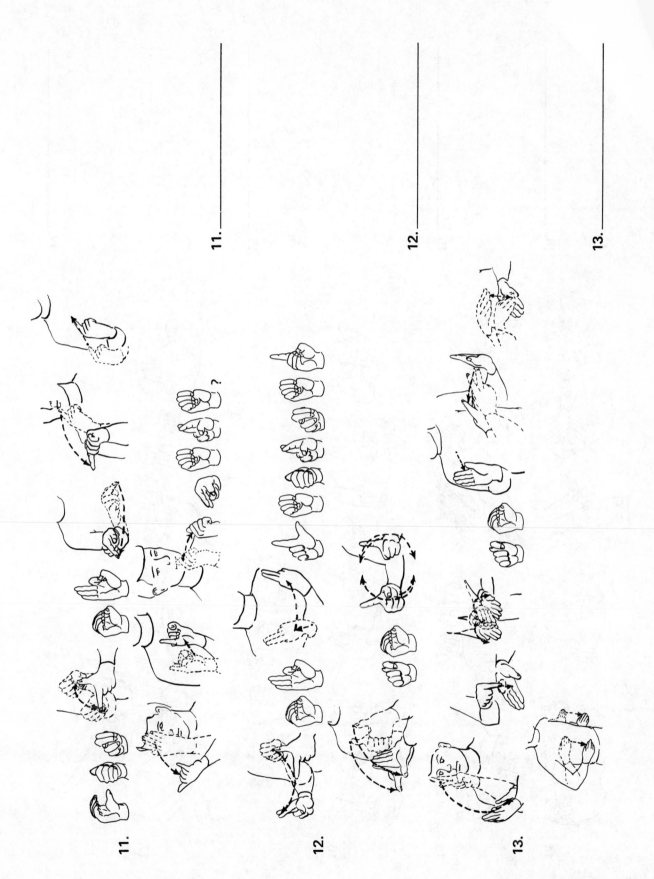

11.

12.

13.

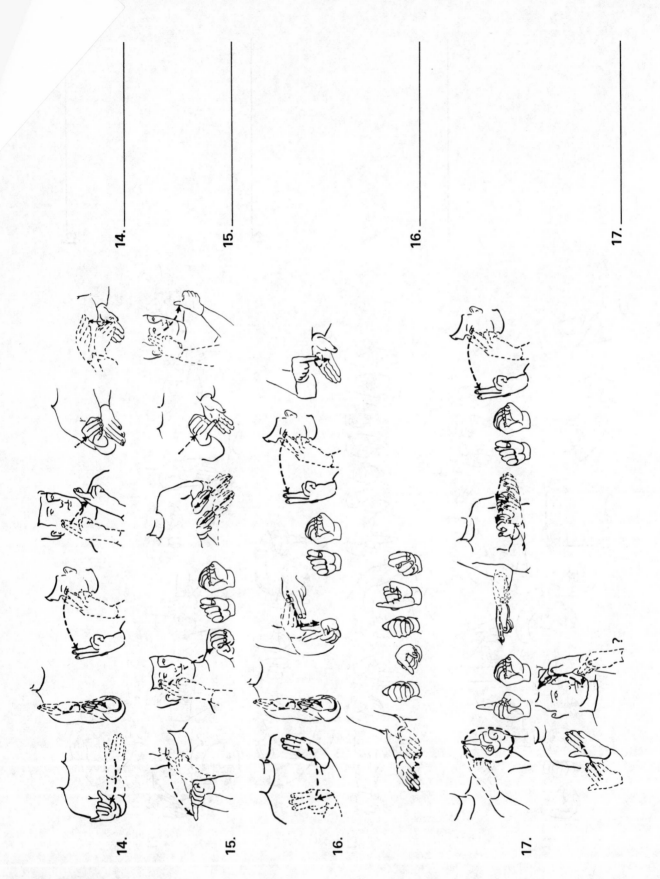

14.

15.

16.

17.

14.

15.

16.

17.

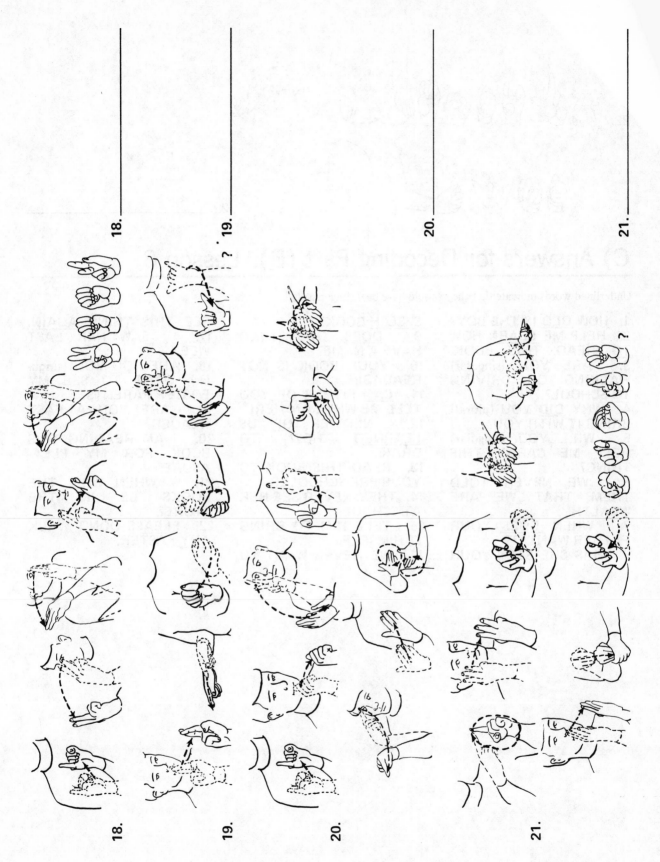

18.

19.

20.

21.

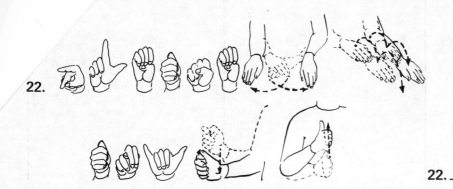

22. _____

C) Answers for Decoding Part (B), Lesson 8

Underlined words indicate that they should have been fingerspelled.

1. HOW <u>OLD</u> IS THE BOY?
2. HELP ME <u>LEARN</u> HOW <u>TO</u> READ THIS BOOK.
3. ARE YOU (singular) WALKING OR DRIVING TO SCHOOL?
4. WHY <u>DID</u> YOU (plural) BRING IT WITH YOU?
5. WILL YOU (singular) HELP ME CARRY THIS THING?
6. WE NEVER TOLD THEM THAT WE ARE <u>WEALTHY</u>.
7. WHEN <u>DOES</u> YOUR FATHER WANT IT?
8. HAS SHE SEEN YOUR <u>SPEECH</u> BOOK?
9. <u>DOES</u> THIS THING HAVE A NAME?
10. YOUR BOOK IS NOT READABLE.
11. <u>CAN</u> EITHER <u>OF</u> YOU TELL ME WHY I AM HERE?
12. NEITHER <u>OF</u> US <u>LEARNED</u> HOW <u>TO</u> DRIVE.
13. READ THIS BOOK <u>TO</u> YOUR PRE-SCHOOLER.
14. THEY NEVER SEE HER AT SCHOOL.
15. TELL HIM <u>TO</u> BRING IT HIMSELF.
16. WE NEVER WANT TO SEE THIS THING <u>AGAIN</u>.
17. I SAW HER LAST <u>WEEK</u>.
18. WHEN <u>DO</u> YOU (singular) WANT <u>TO</u> SEE MY FOSTER PARENTS?
19. ARE YOU A FAST READER?
20. I AM READING THIS BOOK FOR MY PLEA-ASURE.
21. WHEN WILL THE BOOKS BE IN THE <u>STORE</u>?
22. <u>PLEASE</u> DON'T WALK <u>ANY</u> FASTER.

lesson nine

MASS ACLD INC.
1296 WORCESTER ROAD
FRAMINGHAM CTR MASS 01701

Signs presented in this lesson are:

GO	YES*	CHILDREN	CAN'T
COME	NO	ALL, WHOLE	(ALL) RIGHT
OLD, AGE	NONE, NO (quantitative)	BOTH	THERE (expletive)
NOW	WRITE	COULD	CORRECT, RIGHT
ALWAYS	CHILD*	WOULD	EXACT

GO

With only the index fingers of both hands extended (the back sides of the hands face the viewer), place the fingers close together at midline pointing at each other; next, move the hands away from your body as the fingers construct alternate circles in a clockwise direction.

NOW

Both hands, with the fingers extended and joined (the thumbs also are extended but not joined), are held side-by-side (but not touching) in front of the signer's body with the fingertips of each hand pointing in a vertical direction; then, with the configuration preserved, the hands simultaneously are moved in a downward direction.

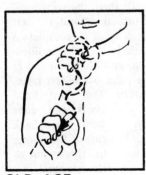

COME

With only the index fingers of both hands extended (the back sides of the hands face the viewer), place the index fingers close together pointing at each other; next, move the hands toward your body as the index fingers construct alternate circles in a counter-clockwise direction.

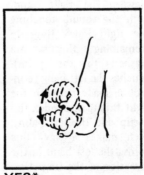

ALWAYS

The right hand, with only the index finger extended and pointing to the viewer, is held in front and slightly to the right side of the body near the level of the right shoulder; next, with the configuration preserved, the right hand is moved to formulate a circle in a clockwise direction along a vertical plane.

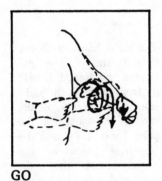

OLD, AGE

The right hand assumes the configuration of the letter S. The top portion of the S hand is placed near or over the chin; then, the S hand performs a wavering in and out motion as it is pulled in a downward direction.

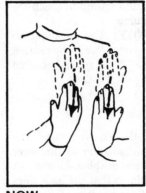

YES*

The right hand forms the letter S, which is held in front and to the right side of the body so that the back side faces up; then, the S hand nods up and down *several* times.

91

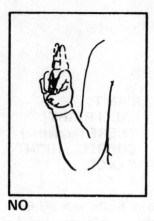

NO

The right hand, with the thumb extended and the index and middle fingers joined and also extended (remaining fingers are clasped to the palm), is held in front and to the right side of the body near the level of the right shoulder so that the palmar surface of the *U* fingers faces the viewer; next, the *U* fingers are flexed inward to touch the thumb.

NOTE: For an emphatic "no," the motion may be repeated twice.

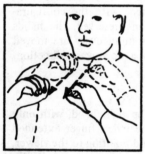

**NONE,
NO (quantitative)**

Both hands assume the configuration of the letter *O* and are placed under the chin so that the back sides of the hands are facing up; next, with the configuration preserved, both *O* hands are moved forward simultaneously.

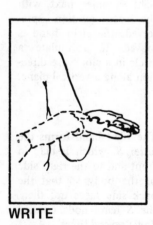

WRITE

The left hand, with the fingers extended and joined, is held in front and slightly to the left side of the body with the palm facing up and the joined fingertips pointing to the viewer. The right hand, with the thumb touching the right index fingertip (remaining fingers are clasped to the palm), touches the left palm (contact is made between the right thumb and index fingertip and the left palm); then makes a wavy line across the left hand in the direction of the fingertips.

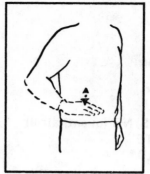

CHILD*

The right hand, with the thumb and fingers extended and joined, is held to the right side of the body at the level of the waist line with the palm facing down and the fingertips pointing to the viewer; then, the hand makes several small bouncing up and down movements.

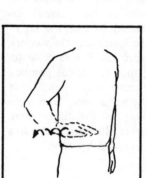

CHILDREN

The right hand, with the thumb and fingers extended and joined, is held in front and to the right side of the body at the level of the waist line; the palm faces down and the fingertips point to the viewer; next, the right hand makes several bouncing movements as it is moved to the right.

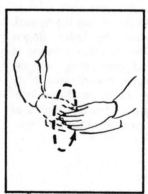

ALL, WHOLE

The left hand, with the thumb and fingers extended and joined, is held in front of the body at waist height with the palm facing the signer. The right hand, with the thumb and fingers extended and joined, is planted into the palm of the left hand (the back side of the right hand fingers touches the palmar side of the left hand fingers); then, the right hand is moved around the left hand so as to complete a circle in a clockwise direction, and comes to end in the palm of the left hand.

NOTE: The right hand starts and ends with the back side of the fingers in the palm of the left hand.

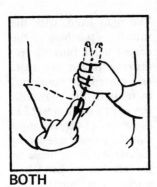

BOTH

The left hand is clasped around the *V* configuration of the right hand (both hands have their back sides facing the viewer); next, the right hand passes downward through the left hand, as the right hand changes its configuration to the letter *U*

CAN'T

The left hand, with only the index finger extended (remaining fingers and thumb are contracted), is held in front of the body with the index finger pointing to the right and the palmar side facing down. The index finger of the right hand (in a similar configuration) is positioned about four to five inches above the left index finger with the right index finger pointing to the viewer; next, the right hand is moved downward with the index finger striking the tip of the left index finger while continuing the path of motion for four to six inches past the struck finger.

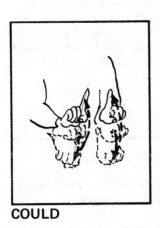

COULD

Both hands assume the configuration of the letter *S* and are held side-by-side (about four to six inches apart) in front of the body with the back sides of the hands facing the signer; then, both hands tilt forward so that now the back sides are facing up; as they are bent back to the original position, the letter *D* is fingerspelled. The sign ends with the palmar sides of the *D* hands facing the viewer.

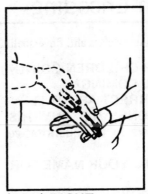

(ALL) RIGHT

The left hand, with the thumb extended (but not joined) and the fingers extended and joined, is held in front of the body with the palm facing up and the fingertips pointing to the right. The right hand, with the thumb and fingers extended and joined, is moved so that the bottom edge of the right hand touches the left palm, and then is moved forward at a right angle across the left hand.

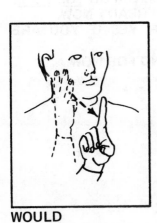

WOULD

The right hand assumes the configuration of the letter *W*, which is placed on the right cheek with the back side of the right *W* hand facing to the right; next, the *W* hand is moved forward, while simultaneously changing its configuration to that of the letter *D*. The sign ends with the palmar side of the *D* hand facing the viewer.

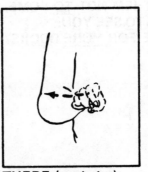

THERE (expletive)

The right hand assumes the configuration of the letter *R* and is held in front of the body with the *R* fingers pointing to the viewer; next, the *R* hand is moved to the right side of the body.

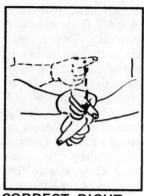

The left hand, with only the index finger extended (remaining fingers and thumb are contracted), is held in front of the body with the back side facing to the right and the index finger pointing to the viewer at about a 45-degree angle. The right hand, in a similar configuration, is moved downward and comes to rest on the top portion of the left hand so that the index fingertip also is pointing to the viewer at about a 45-degree angle to the left with the back side facing to the right.

CORRECT, RIGHT

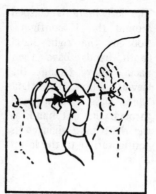

The right hand, with the thumb touching the curved index fingertip (remaining fingers are apart and curved) is positioned in front of the body with the wrist flexed upward at about a 45-degree angle and the palmar side facing the viewer at an angle to the left. The left hand, in a similar configuration, is held in front of (closer to the viewer) and approximately two to three inches from the right hand so that the palmar sides of the hands are facing each other; then, the hands are moved toward each other and touch their joined thumbs and index fingertips.

EXACT

A) Exercises in Encoding

Encode the following material using signs and fingerspelling. Use fingerspelling for all underlined words.

1. WHERE ARE YOUR CHILDREN GOING?
2. ARE BOTH OF YOU COMING?
3. YES, YOU ARE CORRECT ABOUT IT.
4. WE HAVE NO MONEY TO BUY HIS CAR. ("No" is used here in the quantitative sense).
5. WOULD YOU WRITE YOUR NAME FOR US?
6. HOW OLD IS THIS BOY?
7. DO WE KNOW HER AGE?
8. DOES SHE WANT US TO COME NOW OR LATER?
9. HOW CAN WE HELP THIS CHILD?
10. WE CAN'T TELL THEM NOT TO COME.
11. ALL OF US WANT TO SEE YOU.
12. COULD WE WRITE FOR MORE BOOKS?
13. IT IS IMPOSSIBLE TO TELL YOU NOW.
14. YOUR ANSWERS ARE CORRECT.
15. IT MUST BE EXACT.
16. IS EVERYTHING ALL RIGHT WITH YOU?
17. TELL US EXACTLY THE WAY YOU SAW IT.
18. I DON'T WANT TO TELL YOU THAT IT IS RIGHT. ("Right" is signed as "correct.")
19. CAN THEY READ AND WRITE?
20. WHEN IS SHE COMING FOR THERAPY?
21. NONE OF THEM IS READY NOW.
22. DON'T TELL HER YES IF YOU ARE NOT SURE.
23. OUR ANSWER IS NO FOR NOW.

B) Exercises in Decoding

Decode the following illustrated exercises:

1. _____

2. _____

3. _____

4.

5.

6.

7.

8.

9.

10.

11.

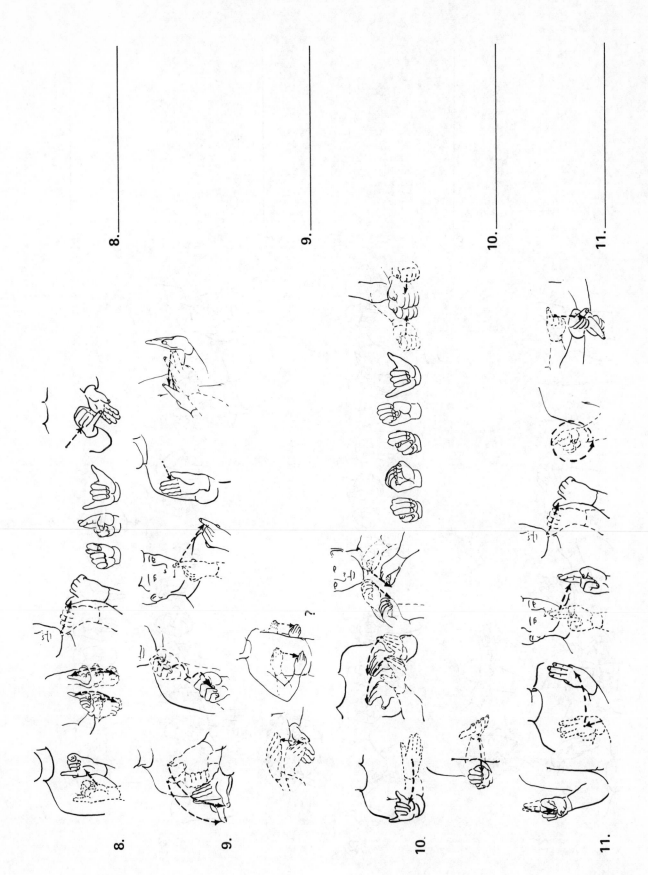

8.

9.

10.

11.

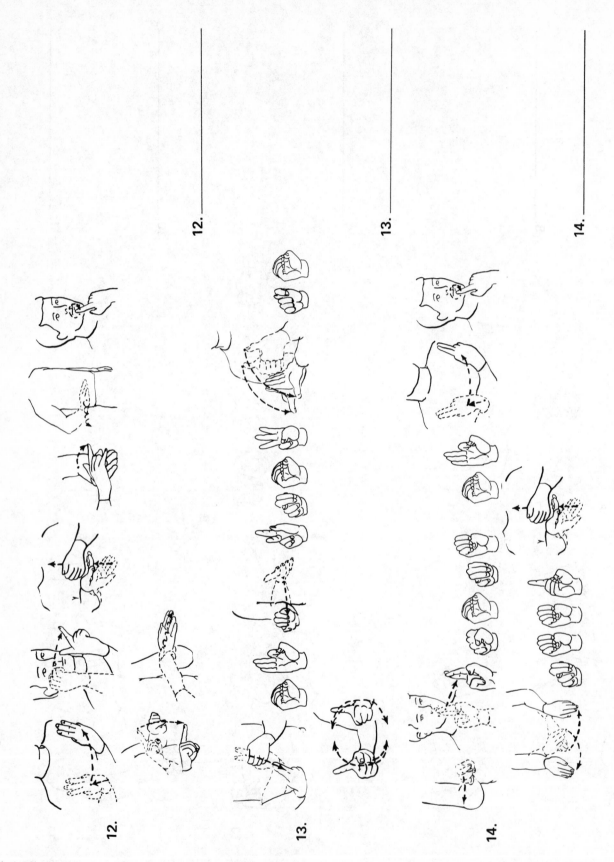

12.

13.

14.

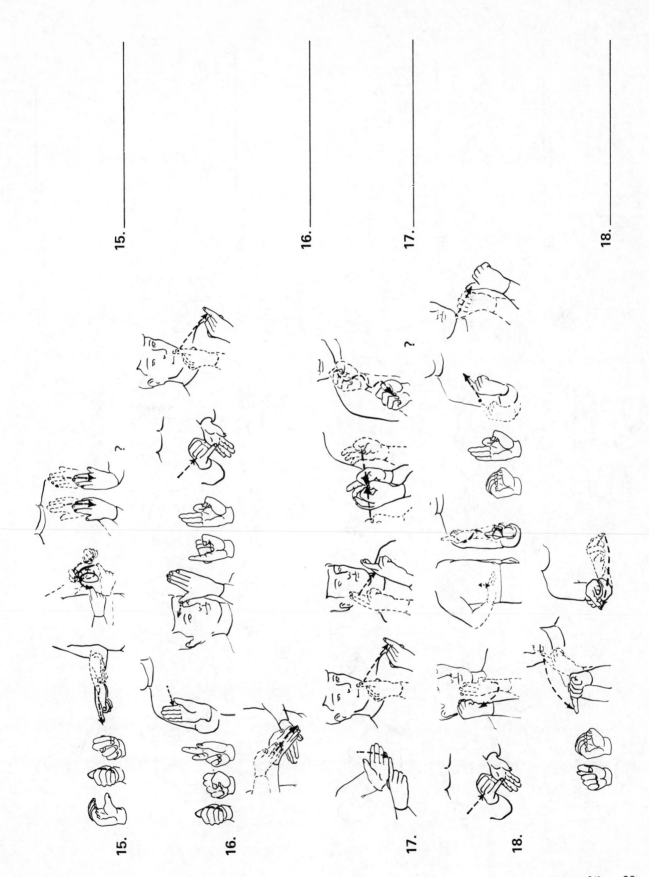

15.

16.

17.

18.

15.

16.

17.

18.

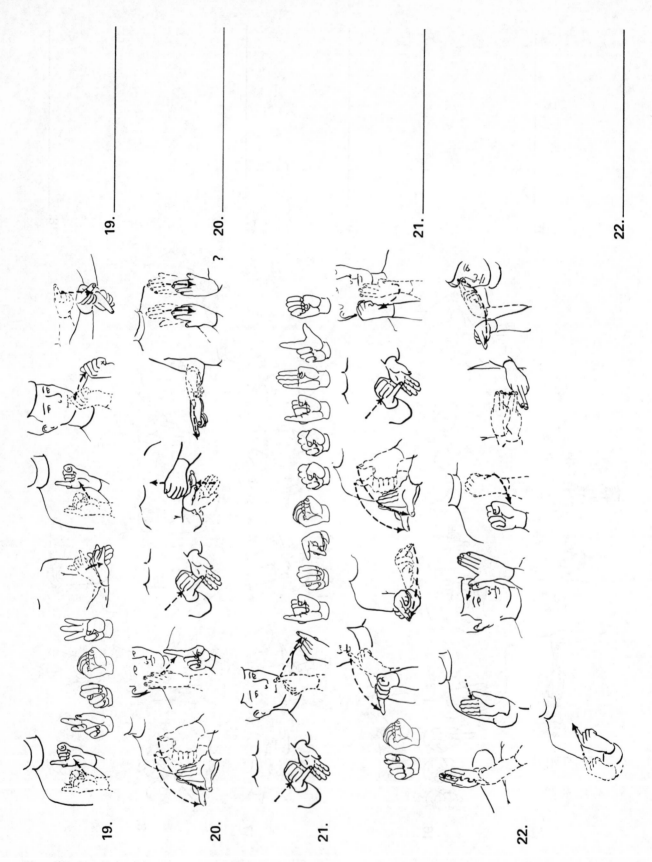

19.

20.

21.

22.

19.

20.

21.

22.

C) Answers for Decoding Part (B), Lesson 9

Underlined words indicate that they should have been fingerspelled.

1. HOW EXACT <u>DO</u> YOU (singular) WANT <u>ME</u> <u>TO</u> BE?

2. NO, IT IS NOT COR-RECT.

3. IS THE CHILD COMING WITH HIS MOTHER?

4. WHY <u>DO</u> YOU (plural) ALWAYS <u>SAY</u> NO?

5. NONE <u>OF</u> THEM WANTS IT FOR NOW.

6. WRITE YOUR NAME FOR ME.

7. WOULD YOU (singular) LIKE <u>TO</u> GO WITH US?

8. I COULD NOT <u>TRY</u> IT.

9. HOW OLD IS YOUR PRE-SCHOOLER?

10. THEY HAVE NO <u>MON-EY</u> WITH THEM.

11. NO, WE ARE NOT AL-WAYS RIGHT.

12. WE SHALL HELP THOSE CHILDREN WHO CAN'T WRITE.

13. BOTH <u>OF</u> THEM <u>KNOW</u> HOW <u>TO</u> DRIVE.

14. THERE ARE <u>SOME</u> <u>OF</u> US WHO DON'T <u>NEED</u> HELP.

15. <u>CAN</u> YOU COME NOW?

16. <u>ASK</u> YOUR FATHER <u>IF</u> IT IS ALL RIGHT.

17. WHAT IS HER EXACT AGE?

18. IT WAS CHILDISH <u>OF</u> ME NOT <u>TO</u> TELL YOU (plural).

19. I <u>KNOW</u> THAT I AM RIGHT.

20. HOW WOULD IT HELP YOU (singular) NOW?

21. IT IS <u>IMPOSSIBLE</u> <u>TO</u> TELL YOU (plural) HOW IT WAS.

22. WRITE YOUR FA-THER'S NAME FOR ME.

lesson ten

Signs presented in this lesson are:

NOTHING
TRUE, SURE
BUT
REAL
WRONG, MISTAKE, ERROR
SIGN (SIGN LANGUAGE)
FINGERSPELL, SPELL

LIPREAD, SPEECHREAD
ORAL (method or school)
TEACH
PERHAPS, PROBABLE, MAYBE
LIVE, ADDRESS
FIRST
LAST, FINAL

LARGE
BIG
SMALL*
LITTLE*
EASE*
ALMOST

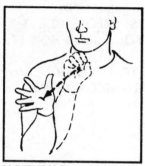

NOTHING

The right hand assumes the configuration of the letter *O* and is placed under the chin so that the palmar side of the *O* hand is facing left; then, the *O* hand is moved forward as the fingers fan out. (The hand has the fingers pointing broadly to the viewer and the palm facing left as the sign comes to an end.)

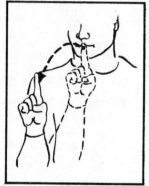

TRUE, SURE

With the right index finger in a vertical position (all other fingers and the thumb are contracted), place the index fingertip near or over the lips so that the palmar side of the hand is facing left. Next, make an upward arc as you move your finger forward away from the lips. Be sure that both plane and hand configuration are maintained.

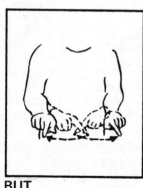

BUT

Both hands, with only their index fingers extended and crossed (remaining fingers and thumbs are contracted), are held in front of the body with their back sides facing up; then, the hands are pulled apart right and left respectively, while retaining their original configuration.

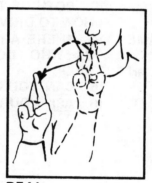

REAL

This sign is made similarly to the previous one ("true," "sure"), except that an *R* configuration is used. The right hand makes the letter *R*, which is placed near or over the lips with the palmar side of the *R* hand facing to the left; then, with the configuration maintained, the *R* hand makes an upward arc as it is moved forward, away from the lips.

WRONG, MISTAKE, ERROR

The right hand first assumes the configuration of the letter *Y* and is held about six inches in front of the signer's chin with the back of the hand facing the viewer; then, the *Y* hand is moved toward the signer and is planted on the chin.

NOTE: Facial expression often will suggest whether the signer is implying a "small mistake" or a "great moral wrongdoing."

102

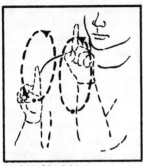

SIGN (SIGN LANGUAGE)

With only the index fingers of both hands extended vertically (remaining fingers and thumbs are contracted) and held about six inches apart in front of the body; with their palmar sides facing the viewer, move the hands *alternately* in a counter-clockwise direction while several circles are completed.

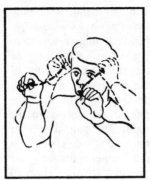

TEACH

Both hands, each in the configuration of the fingerspelled letter *O*, are placed on the side of each temple so that their palmar sides face inward. Next, the hands, while maintaining their *O* configuration, move forward (away from the body) and simultaneously land in a parallel manner as they twist so that their palmar sides are now facing the viewer.

NOTE: The sign for "educate" is made similarly to "teach," except that *E* hands are used. Both signs intend to suggest that something is being transferred from one mind to another.

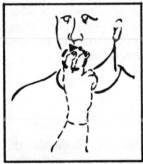

FINGERSPELL, SPELL

With the fingers of the right hand extended, spread apart and held in front of the body with the palmar side facing down, wiggle the fingers up and down several times (without bending the hand itself) as the hand is moved to the right side of the body.

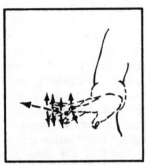

LIPREAD, SPEECHREAD

The right hand assumes the configuration of the letter *V*; the *V* fingers are hooked and point to the signer's lips. Then, the *V* hand is moved to perform a circular motion in a clockwise direction over the lips, while maintaining the configuration.

PERHAPS, PROBABLE, MAYBE

Both hands, with their fingers and thumbs extended and joined, are held about three to four inches apart in front of the body with the fingers pointing to the viewer and the palms facing up. Then, the hands, while preserving their configuration, alternately are moved up and down.

ORAL (method or school)

The right hand, in the configuration of the letter *O*, is placed near or over the lips so that the palmar side of the *O* hand is facing to the left. Then, the *O* hand is moved to perform a circular motion in a clockwise direction over the lips.

LIVE, ADDRESS

Both hands, with their thumbs extended and remaining fingers contracted and clasped to the palm, are placed about three to four inches apart on the body with the thumbs pointing upward and the back sides of the hands facing the viewer; then, the hands graze the body as they simultaneously are moved upward in a parallel manner.

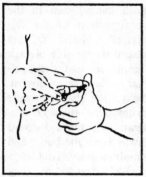

FIRST

The left hand, with only the thumb extended (remaining fingers are contracted and clasped to the palm), is held in front of the body with the thumb sticking upward and the palmar side facing to the right. The palmar side of the right index fingertip (all other fingers and thumb remain clasped) strikes the palmar side of the left thumb.

BIG

This sign is made similarly to the previous one ("large"), except that B hands are used. Both hands make the letter B and are held side-by-side (but not touching) in front of the body with the fingers pointing to the viewer and their palmar sides facing each other; then, the B hands are moved laterally in opposite directions, while maintaining their configuration.

LAST, FINAL

The left hand, with only the little finger extended (remaining fingers and thumb are contracted), is held in front of the body with the little finger pointing to the right and the back side of the hand facing the viewer. The right hand assumes a similar configuration and is held about six inches above the left I hand with the little finger pointing to the viewer and the palmar side facing to the left; then, the right I hand is moved downward and brushes past the tip of the left little finger.

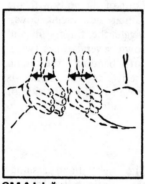

SMALL*

Both hands, with their fingers extended and joined and their thumbs extended but sticking upward, are placed approximately eight inches apart in front of the body so that their fingers are pointing to the viewer and their palms are facing each other; next, the hands are moved toward each other, but stop short of touching. This motion is repeated several times.

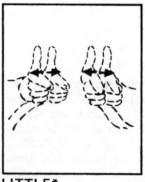

LITTLE*

This sign is made the opposite way of "large." Both hands first make the letter L and are held about eight inches apart in front of the body with their thumbs sticking upward, index fingers pointing to the viewer and palmar sides facing each other. Next, the hands are moved toward each other, but stop short of touching. This motion is repeated several times.

LARGE

Both hands, in the configuration of the letter L, are positioned side-by-side (but not touching) in front of the body so that their palmar sides face each other and their index fingers are pointing to the viewer; then, the L hands are moved laterally in opposite directions, while maintaining their configuration.

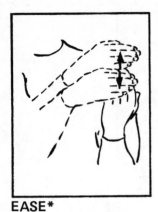

EASE*

The left hand, with the thumb and fingers extended and joined, is held in front and slightly to the left side of the body with the fingers pointing upward and the back side facing the viewer. The right hand, in a similar configuration, first places the palmar side of the fingers on the back side of the left fingers (the right hand fingers are positioned so that they point to the left); then, the right hand makes several quick strokes in an upward direction.

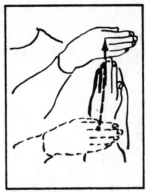

ALMOST

The left hand, with the thumb and fingers extended and joined, is held in front and slightly to the left side of the body with the fingers pointing upward and the back side facing the viewer. The right hand, in a similar configuration, first places the palmar side of the fingers on the back side of the left wrist (the fingers point to the left); then, the right hand grazes the back side of the left hand as it is moved upward past the left fingertips.

A) Exercises in Encoding

Encode the following material using signs and fingerspelling. Use fingerspelling for all underlined words.

1. WE WANT <u>TO</u> <u>LEARN</u> HOW <u>TO</u> LIP-READ.
2. WHAT IS THE SIGN FOR THIS <u>WORD</u>?
3. <u>DO</u> THEY <u>KNOW</u> HOW <u>TO</u> FINGER-SPELL?
4. WHAT IS HIS FIRST NAME?
5. ARE YOU DRIVING A LARGE CAR?
6. PERHAPS THERE IS NOTHING <u>TO</u> TELL YOU.
7. IS IT TRUE THAT YOU ARE TEACHING HIM SIGNS?
8. WE ARE <u>SORRY</u> BUT WE CAN'T HELP YOU.
9. TEACH THIS BOY <u>MORE</u> ORAL <u>SKILLS</u>.
10. WHAT IS THE NAME <u>OF</u> YOUR TEACH-ER? (For "teacher" sign "teach" plus "er"—person.)
11. WE ARE DRIVING IT FOR THE LAST <u>TIME</u>.
12. HOW SHALL WE EDUCATE THIS BOY? (For "educate" sign it as you would "teach," but with *E* hands.)
13. IT IS WRONG FOR US NOT <u>TO</u> TELL THEM.
14. HE ALMOST <u>FORGOT</u> <u>TO</u> BRING IT.
15. IS YOUR CAR SMALL?
16. NO, IT IS NOT <u>VERY</u> BIG.
17. YES, SHE <u>CAN</u> READ IT WITH EASE.
18. WHOSE ERROR WAS IT?
19. FIRST, TELL ME WHERE YOU LIVE.
20. DON'T <u>MAKE</u> IT <u>SO</u> EASY FOR THEM. (For "easy" sign "ease" plus "-y".)
21. I <u>KNOW</u> BUT IS IT REAL?
22. WHY ARE YOU <u>GIVING</u> US <u>SO</u> LITTLE?

B) Exercises in Decoding

Decode the following illustrated exercises:

1.   ? 1._____

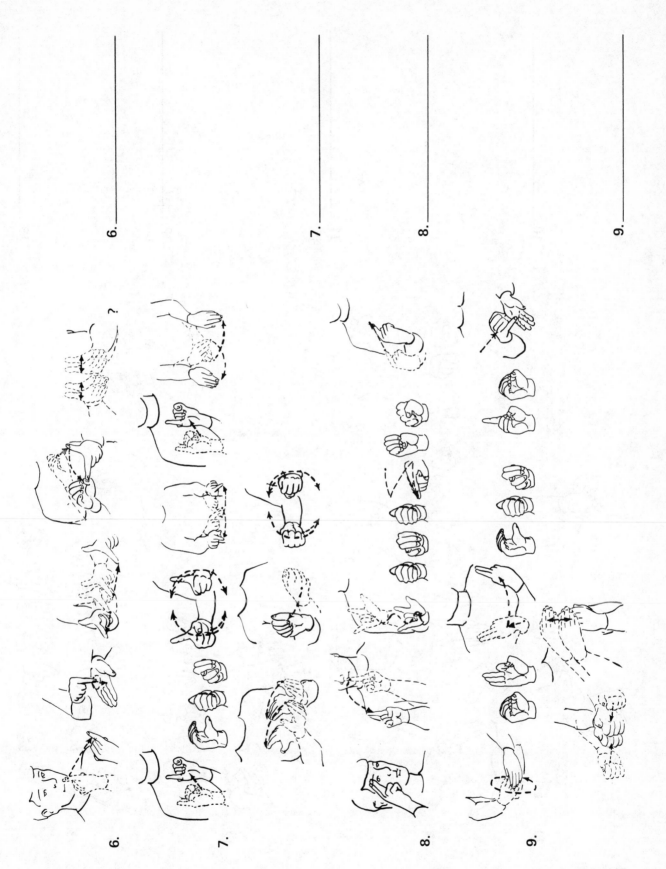

6.

7.

8.

9.

6.

7.

8.

9.

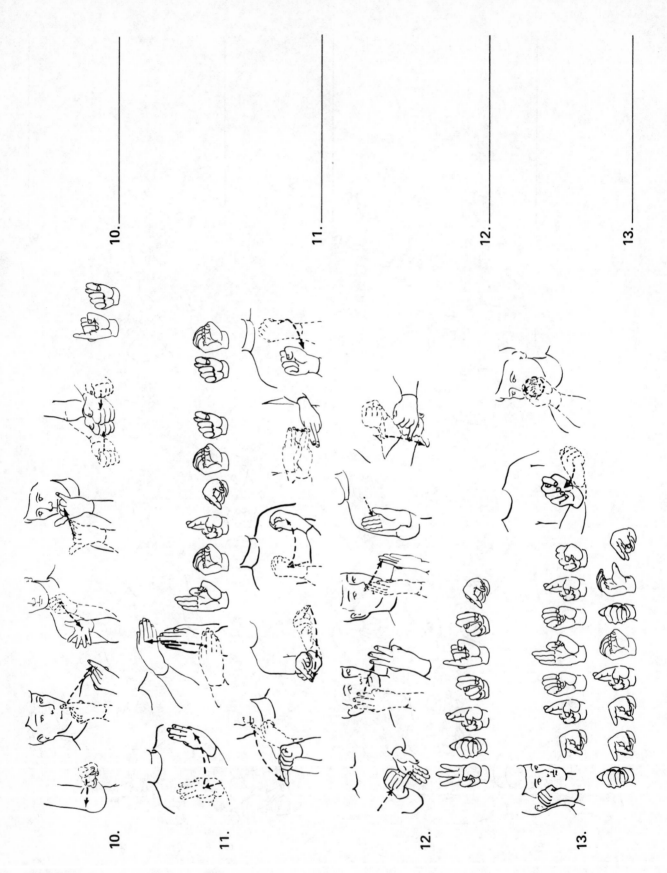

10.

11.

12.

13.

10.

11.

12.

13.

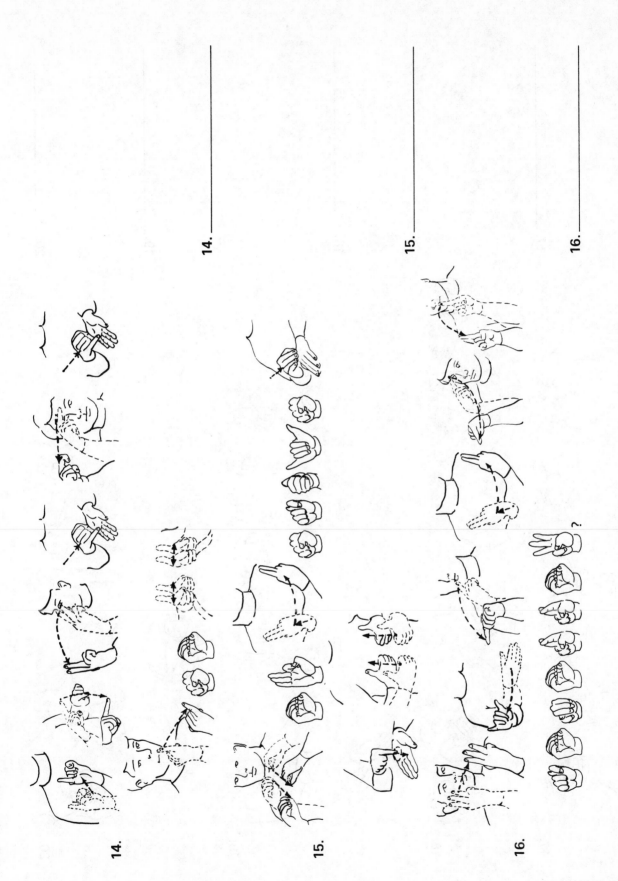

14.

15.

16.

14.

15.

16.

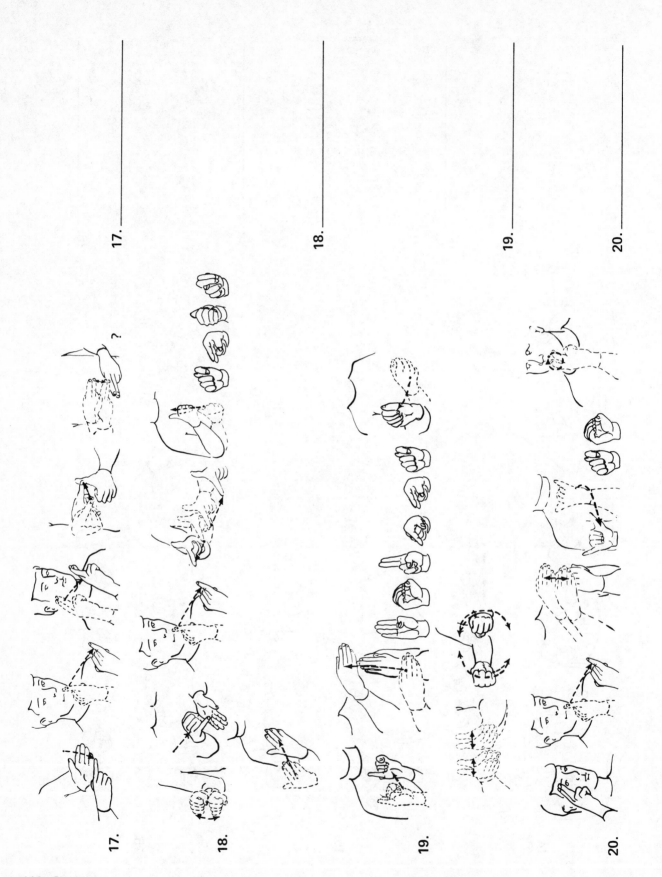

17.

18.

19.

20.

21. _____

22. _____

23. _____

21.

22.

23.

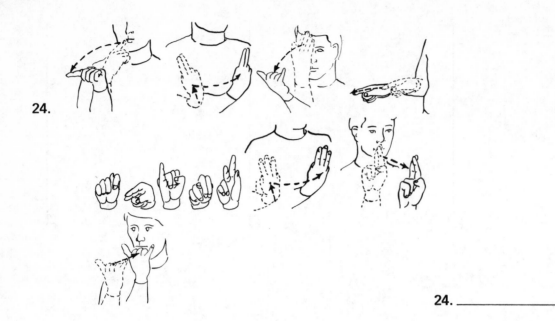

24. _____

C) Answers for Decoding Part (B), Lesson 10

Underlined words indicate that they should have been fingerspelled.

1. HOW BIG IS IT?
2. ARE YOU (singular) SURE THAT THEY LIVE <u>HERE</u>?
3. THEY ARE TEACHING US HOW <u>TO</u> SIGN AND FINGERSPELL.
4. I CAN'T LIPREAD YOU (singular) <u>TOO WELL</u>.
5. IT WILL BE MY LAST MISTAKE.
6. IS THIS LARGE OR SMALL?
7. I <u>CAN</u> DRIVE, BUT I DON'T HAVE A CAR.
8. HE TRULY <u>AMAZES</u> ME.
9. ALL <u>OF</u> US <u>CAN</u> <u>DO</u> IT WITH EASE.

10. THERE IS NOTHING WRONG WITH IT.
11. WE ALMOST <u>FORGOT</u> <u>TO</u> TELL YOU (plural) OUR NAMES.
12. IT WILL BE YOUR FINAL <u>WARNING</u>.
13. SHE <u>PREFERS</u> THE ORAL <u>APPROACH</u>.
14. I CAN'T SEE IT BECAUSE IT IS <u>SO</u> LITTLE.
15. NONE <u>OF</u> US <u>STAYS</u> AT THIS ADDRESS.
16. WILL THEY TELL US FOR SURE <u>TOMORROW</u>?
17. WHAT IS HER FIRST NAME?

18. YES, IT IS LARGER <u>THAN</u> MINE.
19. I ALMOST <u>BOUGHT</u> A SMALL CAR.
20. HE IS EASY <u>TO</u> LIPREAD.
21. THEY TELL ME THAT YOU ARE AN ORALIST.
22. FIRST, I WANT <u>TO</u> TELL YOU (plural) THAT IT IS REAL.
23. WOULD YOU (singular) TEACH OUR BOY HOW <u>TO</u> SIGN?
24. TELL US WHY YOU (singular) <u>THINK</u> WE ARE WRONG.

lesson eleven

Signs presented in this lesson are:

MORE*	UNTIL	SOME	ONLY
MANY*	ABOVE	PART	ACROSS, OVER
MUCH	BELOW	NEW	BY
TO, TOWARD	ANY	AGAIN, REPEAT*	HERE*
FROM	SLOW	OFTEN	TOO

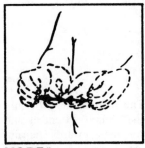

MORE*

With the fingertips of both hands facing each other (fingers are curved, touching the thumbs, and the backs of the hands are facing sideways), move the hands back and forth (sideways) so that the fingertips touch and separate several times.

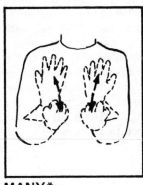

MANY*

Both hands first assume the configuration of the letter *S* and are placed side-by-side (but not touching) in front of the body so that the backs of the fingers are facing the viewer; then, the hands fan out as they are moved slightly upward. The sign ends with the thumbs and fingers of both hands extended, apart and with the back sides of the hands facing the viewer.

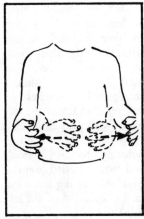

MUCH

Both hands, with their thumbs and fingers apart and slightly bent, are positioned side-by-side (but not touching), in front of the body so that their fingertips point to each other and the back sides of the hands are facing the viewer; then, with the configuration maintained, the hands are moved in opposite directions (sideways) along a horizontal plane.

TO, TOWARD

The left hand, with only the index finger extended (remaining fingers and thumb are contracted), is held in front and to the left side of the body with the index finger pointing upward and the palmar side of the hand facing to the right. The right hand, with only the index finger extended (remaining fingers and thumb are contracted), is flexed to midline; then the hand is moved toward and touches the left fingertip.

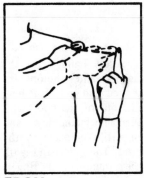

FROM

The left hand, with only the index finger extended (remaining fingers and thumb are contracted), is held in front and to the left side of the body with the index finger pointing upward and the palmar side facing the signer. The right hand, with only the index finger extended and crooked (remaining fingers and thumb are fully contracted), touches the left fingertip. (Contact is made between the palmar side of the left index finger and the back side of the right index finger; the right wrist is not flexed.) Then, the right hand is pulled away in the direction of the signer.

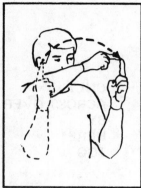

UNTIL

The left hand, with only the index finger extended (remaining fingers and thumb are contracted), is held in front and to the left side of the body near the level of the shoulder with the index finger pointing upward and the palmar side facing midline. The right hand, with only the index finger extended (remaining fingers and thumb are contracted), is held in front and to the right side of the body near the level of the right shoulder so that the index finger is pointing upward and the palmar side is facing to the left; next, the right hand makes an upward arc as the hand is crossed over to touch the left fingertip.

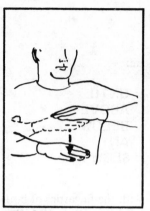

BELOW

The left hand, with the fingers and thumb extended and joined, is held in front of the body with the palm facing down and the fingertips pointing to the right. The right hand, in a similar configuration, touches the left hand (the back side of the right fingers touches the palmar side of the left fingers) and then is pulled straight down.

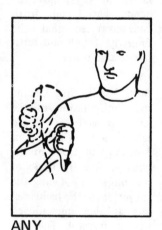

ANY

The right hand, with only the thumb extended and sticking upward (remaining fingers are contracted and clasped to the palm), is held in front and to the right side of the body with the palmar side of the thumb facing the viewer; next, the right hand makes a counter-clockwise movement toward midline. The sign ends with the thumb pointing downward.

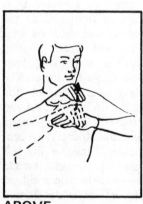

ABOVE

The left hand, with the fingers and thumb extended and joined, is held in front of the body with the palm facing down and fingertips pointing to the right. The right hand, with the thumb and fingers extended, joined and slightly cupped, comes to rest on the back side of the left hand (the palm is facing down and the fingertips are pointing to the viewer); then, with the configuration preserved, the right hand is raised vertically five to six inches.

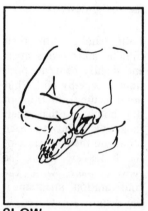

SLOW

The left hand, with the thumb and fingers extended and joined, is held in front of the body with the palm facing down and with the fingertips pointing to the viewer. The right hand, in a similar configuration, comes to rest on the back of the left hand (with the palm facing down and the fingertips pointing to the viewer) and then is pulled over the back side of the left hand in the direction of the left forearm.

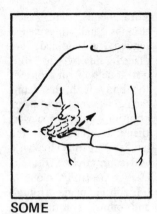

SOME

The left hand, with the thumb and fingers extended and joined, is held in front of the body with the palm facing up and the fingertips pointing to the right. The right hand is shaped similarly, but is held vertically so that the palm faces the left side. The right hand touches the left palm with its edge so that a right angle is created (fingertips point to the viewer and the palmar side faces midline); then, the right hand, with the configuration preserved, is pulled straight toward the signer.

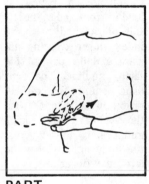

PART

The left hand, with the thumb and fingers extended and joined, is held in front of the body with the palm facing up and the fingertips pointing to the right. The right hand, in the configuration of the letter *P*, first touches the left palm (the tip of the middle finger touches the palm) and then grazes it as the right hand is moved across the palm in the direction of the signer.

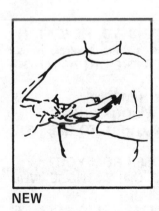

NEW

The left hand, with the thumb and fingers extended and joined, is held in front of the body with the palm facing up and the fingertips pointing to the right. The right hand, with the thumb and fingers extended, joined and slightly cupped, touches the left palm with its back side (the fingertips are pointing to the left), and then slides across the left palm in the direction of the wrist as the right hand is curved upward.

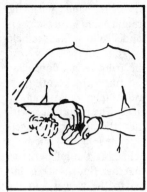

AGAIN, REPEAT*

The left hand, with the thumb and fingers extended and joined, is held in front of the body with the palm facing up and the fingertips pointing to the viewer. The right hand, with the thumb and fingers joined, slightly curved and pointing upward, is raised slightly; then, turns in a counter clockwise direction and places the right fingertips in the palm of the left hand.

NOTE: The sign for "repeat" is made by signing "again" several times.

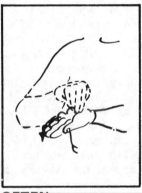

OFTEN

The left hand, with the thumb and fingers extended and joined, is held in front of the body with the palm facing up and the fingertips pointing to the viewer. The right hand, with the thumb and fingers extended, joined and slightly cupped, touches the left palm with its fingertips (the back side of the right hand is facing the viewer) and then makes several bouncing type movements as the right hand is moved toward the left fingertips.

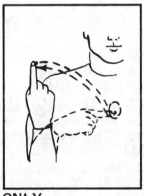

ONLY

The right hand, with only the index finger extended (remaining fingers and thumb are contracted), is held in front and to the right side of the body near the level of the shoulder with the index finger pointing upward and the back side facing the viewer. Then, with the configuration preserved, the right hand is moved downward, makes a small circle, and is raised again to its original position.

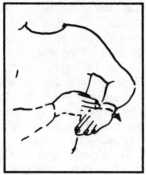

ACROSS, OVER

The left hand, with the thumb and fingers extended and joined, is held in front of the body with the palm facing down and the fingertips pointing toward the viewer at an angle. The right hand, with the thumb and fingers extended and joined, is held near the left wrist so that the fingers are pointing to the viewer and the palmar side is facing to the left; then, the lower edge of the right hand slides over the top (back side) of the left hand.

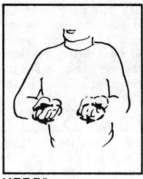

HERE*

Both hands, with their thumbs and fingers extended and joined, are placed side-by-side (but not touching) in front of the body with the palms facing up and the fingers pointing to the viewer; then, simultaneously, the hands perform clockwise and counter-clockwise circles respectively along a horizontal plane (round-and-round). This motion is repeated several times.

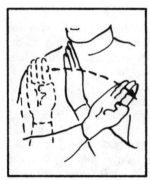

BY

The left hand, with the thumb and fingers extended and joined, is held in front of the body with the fingertips pointing upward and the palmar side facing to the right. The right hand makes the letter *B* (palm of *B* hand faces the viewer) and is moved across (to the left of) the body, past the left hand in the direction of the left forearm.

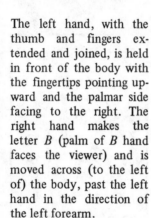

TOO

The left hand, with only the index finger extended (remaining fingers and thumb are contracted), is held in front and to the left side of the body with the index finger pointing upward and the palmar side facing midline. The right hand assumes the configuration of the letter *O* (with the palmar side facing midline), is moved across the body and touches the left index fingertip.

A) Exercises in Encoding

Encode the following material using signs and fingerspelling. Use fingerspelling for all underlined words.

1. <u>DO</u> YOU HAVE ANY MORE BOOKS WITH YOU?
2. HOW MANY <u>OF</u> THEM <u>DO</u> THEY WANT?
3. I <u>THINK</u> IT IS TOO MUCH.
4. WE CAN DRIVE TO SCHOOL <u>LATER</u>.
5. THE <u>GIFT</u> IS FROM YOUR MOTHER.
6. <u>PLEASE</u> DRIVE UNTIL I TELL YOU <u>TO</u> STOP. ("To stop" is an infinitive; "To" is fingerspelled. The sign for "To" is used when direction is being implied.)
7. WHO LIVES ABOVE YOU?
8. SOME <u>OF</u> US ARE TOO SLOW.
9. <u>CAN</u> YOU SEE THIS PART?
10. HOW MUCH <u>DID</u> YOU <u>PAY</u> FOR YOUR NEW CAR?
11. TELL ME AGAIN BECAUSE I SHALL FORGET IT.
12. <u>DO</u> THEY WANT US <u>TO</u> REPEAT IT? ("Repeat" is signed as "again" several times.)
13. HOW OFTEN <u>DOES</u> SHE DRIVE TO THE UNIVERSITY?
14. IS HE COMING BY HIMSELF?
15. <u>LEAVE</u> YOUR NEW BOOKS HERE.
16. SHE WILL <u>WALK</u> OVER <u>TO</u> SEE YOU AT <u>NOON</u>.
17. WHO LIVES ACROSS FROM YOU?
18. WE SHALL HELP ONLY THOSE WHO ARE HERE.
19. I <u>CAN</u> ONLY <u>DO</u> <u>SO</u> MUCH BY MYSELF.
20. MY FATHER IS A SLOW DRIVER.
21. HOW <u>FAR</u> IS IT FROM YOUR COLLEGE?
22. I CAN'T TELL YOU UNTIL I SEE IT.

B) Exercises in Decoding

Decode the following illustrated exercises:

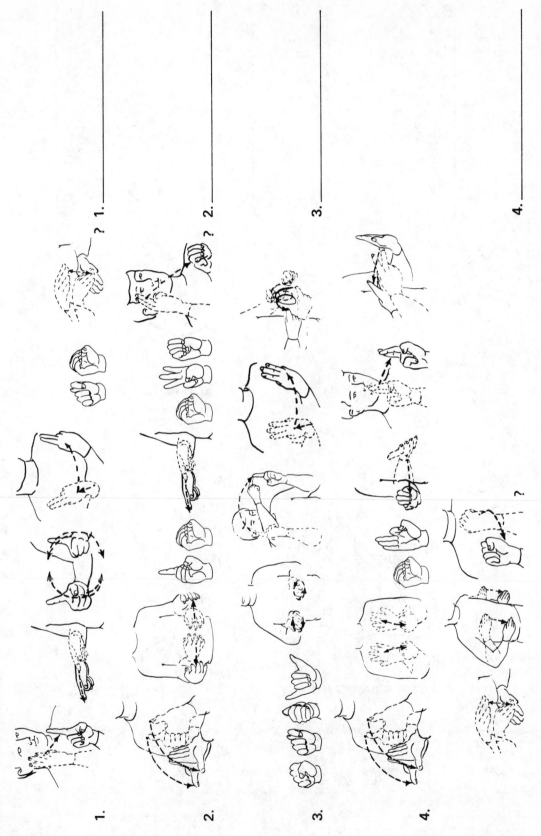

1. _____

2. _____

3. _____

4. _____

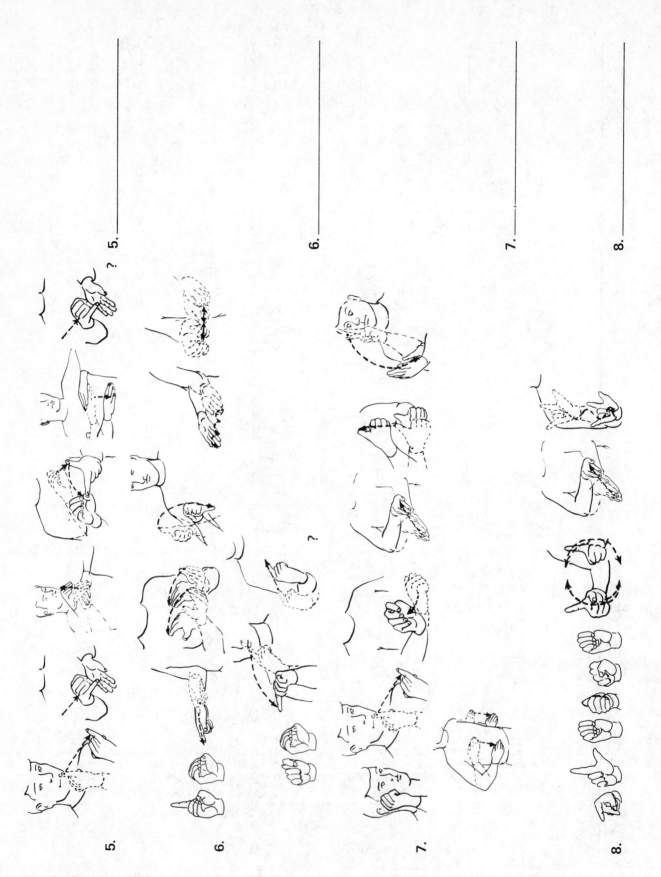

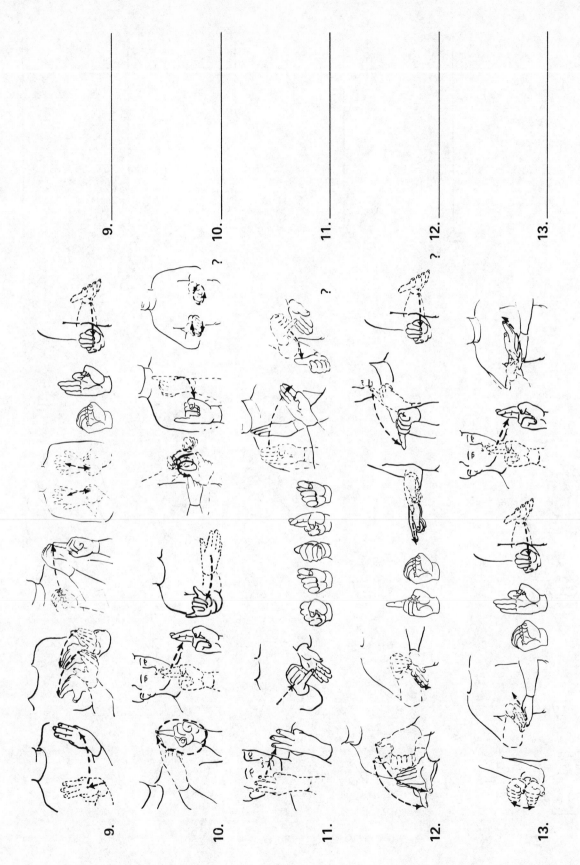

9.

10. ?

11. ?

12. ?

13.

9.

10.

11.

12.

13.

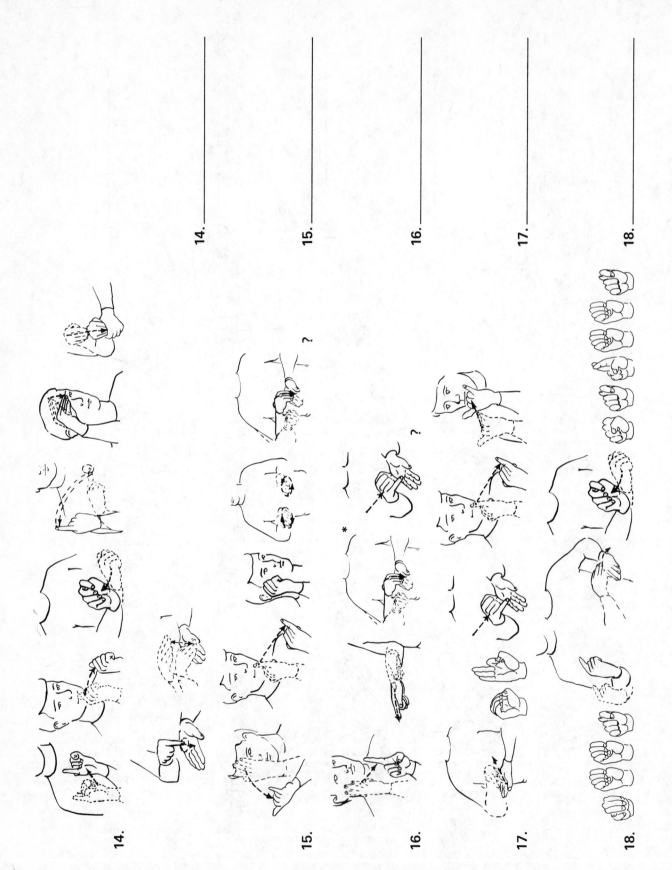

14.

15.

16.

17.

18.

14.

15.

16.

17.

18.

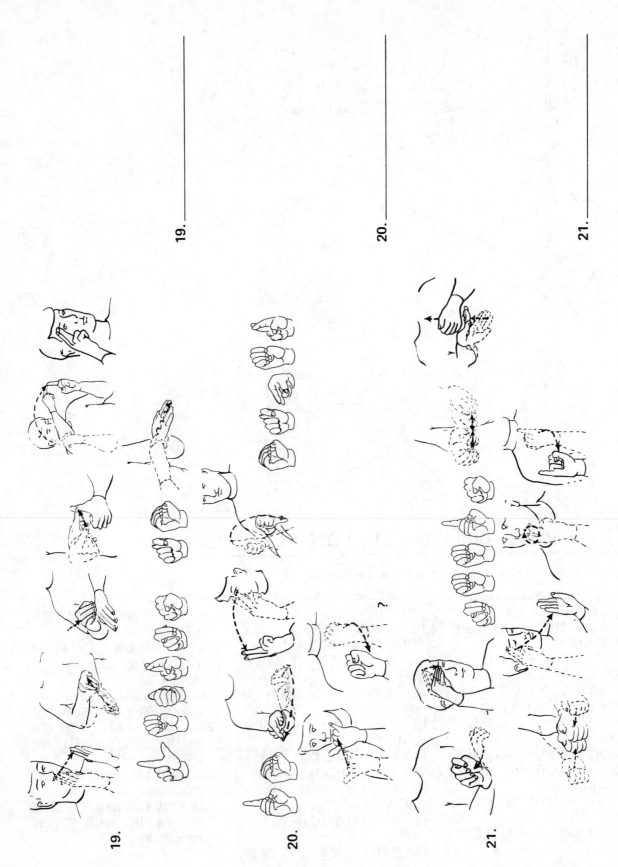

19.

20.

21.

19.

20.

21.

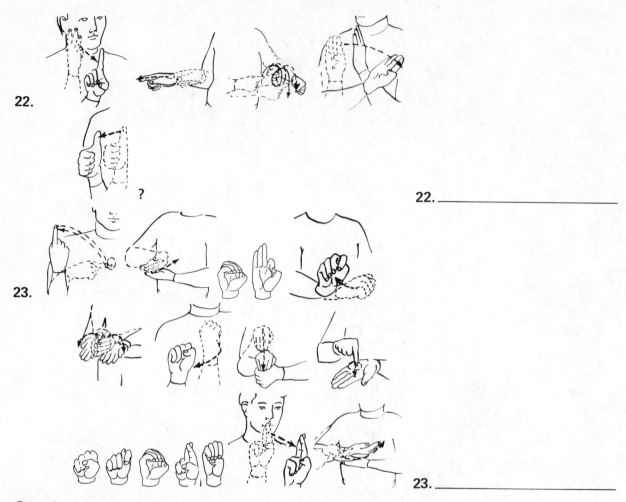

22. _____

23. _____

C) Answers for Decoding Part (B), Lesson 11

Underlined words indicate that they should have been fingerspelled.

1. WOULD YOU DRIVE US TO SCHOOL?
2. HOW MUCH <u>DO</u> YOU <u>OWE</u> HIM?
3. <u>STAY</u> HERE UNTIL WE COME.
4. HOW MANY <u>OF</u> THEM ARE PRE-SCHOOLERS?
5. IS IT ABOVE OR BELOW IT?
6. <u>DO</u> YOU (singular) HAVE ANYTHING MORE <u>TO</u> TELL ME?
7. SHE IS THE SLOWEST READER.
8. <u>PLEASE</u> DRIVE SLOWLY.

9. WE HAVE TOO MANY <u>OF</u> THEM.
10. WHEN ARE THEY COMING HERE?
11. WILL IT <u>START</u> BY ITSELF?
12. HOW OFTEN <u>DO</u> YOU TELL THEM?
13. YES, SOME <u>OF</u> THEM ARE NEW.
14. I AM THE ONLY BOY IN THIS SCHOOL.
15. WHY IS SHE HERE AGAIN?
16. WOULD YOU REPEAT* IT?
17. PART <u>OF</u> IT IS

WRONG.
18. <u>MEET</u> ME ACROSS THE <u>STREET</u>.
19. BE SLOW AT FIRST UNTIL HE <u>LEARNS</u> <u>TO</u> WRITE.
20. <u>DO</u> YOU (plural) SEE ANY <u>OTHER</u> MISTAKES?
21. THE BOY <u>NEEDS</u> MORE HELP WITH HIS LIPREADING.
22. WOULD YOU GO BY YOURSELF?
23. ONLY SOME <u>OF</u> THE BOOKS IN THIS <u>STORE</u> ARE NEW.

lesson twelve

Signs presented in this lesson are:

ENTER, INTO	ELSE	PLEASE	EVERY, EACH*
BOTHER*	HAPPEN, OCCUR	VERY	USE
BETWEEN	THANK	COMPLAIN*	WEAR
EVER	LOVE	BEFORE	INDIVIDUAL
OTHER, ANOTHER	JUST	AFTER	PERSON

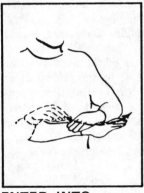

ENTER, INTO

The left hand, with the thumb and fingers extended and joined, is held in front of the body with the palm facing down and the fingers pointing to the right. The right hand, with the thumb and fingers extended and joined, is held in front of the body with the palm facing down and the fingers pointing to the viewer at an angle to the left; then, without changing the configuration, the right hand is moved under the left hand, continuing three to four inches beyond the left hand as the right hand is curved slightly upward.

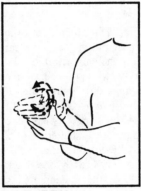

BETWEEN

The left hand, with the fingers extended and joined, is held in front of the body at mid-chest height (in line with the right side of the body) with the thumb sticking upward, the fingers pointing to the right and the palmar side of the hand facing the signer. The right hand, in the configuration of the letter *B*, touches the left hand near the base of the thumb. (Contact is made between the bottom portion of the *B* hand and the "fleshy" part of the left hand near the base of the thumb. The *B* hand has its fingertips pointing to the viewer at an angle and its palmar side facing to the left.) Then, the *B* hand quickly completes a small arc movement in a clockwise direction and then another arc in a counter-clockwise direction.

BOTHER*

The left hand, with the fingers extended and joined, is held at mid-chest level in front of the right side of the body with the thumb extended vertically, the fingers pointing to the right and the palmar side toward the signer. The right hand, with the thumb extended and the remaining fingers also extended, joined and pointing to the viewer at an angle, descends and strikes the base of the left thumb with its bottom edge. This motion is repeated several times.

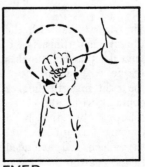

EVER

The right hand, in the configuration of the letter *E*, is held in front and to the right side of the body near the level of the right shoulder, with the wrist flexed upward at about a 45-degree angle; then, the *E* hand is moved to complete a circle in a clockwise direction.

123

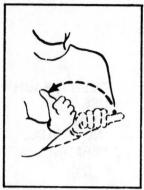

OTHER, ANOTHER

The right hand, with the fingers contracted and clasped to the palm, is held in front of the body with the thumb extended and pointing to the left and the back of the hand facing up; then, with the configuration maintained, the forearm rotates the right hand about 135 degrees in a clockwise direction.

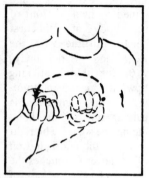

ELSE

The right hand, in the configuration of the letter E, is held in front of the body with the back side facing up; then, the E hand is moved to the right as the wrist twists the hand 180 degrees in a clockwise direction. The sign ends with the back side of the E hand facing down.

HAPPEN, OCCUR

Both hands, each with its index finger extended (remaining fingers are contracted), are placed side-by-side (but not touching) in front of the body with the index fingers pointing to the viewer and the back sides facing down; next, with the configuration preserved, the hands are rolled over inward so that now their back sides are facing up while their index fingers continue to point to the viewer.

THANK

The right hand, with the thumb and fingers extended and joined, touches the lips (the palmar side of the right fingertips makes contact with the lips), followed by the hand flipping forward so that the joined and extended fingers point to the viewer.

LOVE

Make this sign first by crossing your wrists (the hands assume a fist configuration with their back sides facing the viewer); then, move the crossed wrists in the direction of the chest so that the fist hands are touching the chest.

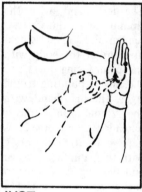

JUST

The left hand, with the thumb and fingers extended and joined, is held in front and to the left side of the body near the level of the left shoulder with the fingertips pointing upward and the palmar side of the left hand facing to the right. The right hand adopts the configuration of the letter I; then, the extended fingertip of the I hand makes the letter J over the palm of the left hand.

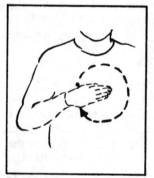

PLEASE

The palm of the right hand, with the thumb and fingers extended and joined, is placed on the chest with the fingertips pointing to the left; then, the hand is moved to make a large circular motion on the chest.

VERY

First, both hands are in the configuration of the letter V and are moved to the center of the body so that the palmar sides of the index and second fingers touch; then, the V hands are pulled apart in opposite directions along a horizontal plane.

COMPLAIN*

The right hand, with the thumb and fingers apart and curved, is positioned in front of the body at chest level with the back side of the hand facing the viewer; then, with the configuration preserved, the hand is moved in to touch the chest. This motion is repeated several times.

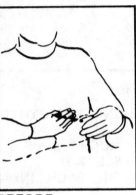

BEFORE

The left hand, with the thumb and fingers extended and joined, is held in front and slightly to the left side of the body with the palm facing the signer and the fingertips pointing to the right. The right hand, with the thumb and fingers extended and joined, is planted in the palm of the left hand with the fingertips pointing to the left and the palmar side facing the signer; then, with the left hand remaining stationary, move the right hand (the palm facing you) *toward* the body.

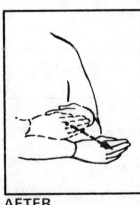

AFTER

The left hand, with the thumb and fingers extended and joined, is held in front and slightly to the left side of the body with the palm facing the signer and the fingertips pointing to the right. The right hand, in a similar configuration, touches the back side of the left fingertips so that its back side is facing the viewer with the fingertips pointing to the left; then, with the left hand remaining stationary, move the right hand (the palm facing you) *away* from the body.

EVERY, EACH*

The left hand, in the configuration of the letter *A*, is held in front of the body with the back side facing to the left. The right hand has its thumb extended and pointing upward (remaining fingers are contracted and clasped to the palm); then, the palmar side of the right thumb first touches the side of the left thumb and then slides downward over the back side of the contracted fingers. This downward motion continues for about two to three inches past the left hand.

NOTE: The sign for "each" is made by simply repeating the motion for "every" several times.

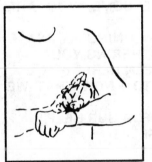

USE

The left forearm, with the hand in an *S* configuration, is laid across the body with the back side of the *S* hand facing up. The right hand makes the letter *U*; the wrist of the *U* hand touches the top side of the left hand wrist; then, the *U* hand completes several small circular movements.

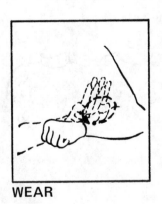

WEAR

This sign is made similarly to the previous one ("use"), except that the right hand first makes the configuration for the letter *W* and then completes several small circular movements.

Both hands, each in the configuration of the letter *I*, are held on each side of the body near the level of the shoulders with the *I* fingers pointing to the viewer and the palmar sides facing midline; then, with the configuration maintained, the wrists of the *I* hands graze the sides of the body as the hands are moved downward.

INDIVIDUAL

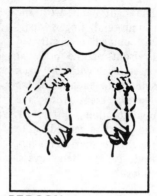

This sign is made similarly to the previous one ("individual"), except the hands assume the configuration of the letter *P*. The *P* hands are positioned on each side of the body near the level of the shoulders with the back sides facing up and the sides of the wrists touching the body; then, the wrists of the *P* hands graze the sides of the body as the hands are moved downward.

PERSON

A) Exercises in Encoding

Encode the following material using signs and fingerspelling. Use fingerspelling for all underlined words.

1. WHEN WILL THIS PERSON BE COMING?
2. I CAN'T <u>DECIDE</u> WHAT <u>TO</u> WEAR.
3. PLEASE <u>DON'T</u> USE IT AGAIN.
4. WHAT ELSE <u>DO</u> YOU WANT EACH <u>OF</u> US <u>TO DO</u>. ("Each" is signed similarly to "every," but is repeated several times.)
5. EVERY <u>TIME</u> WE COME, YOU ARE <u>GONE</u>.
6. WHY IS SHE COMPLAINING AGAIN?
7. WHAT ELSE IS BOTHERING YOU?
8. <u>DID</u> IT EVER HAPPEN HERE?
9. WE WANT YOU <u>TO KNOW</u> THAT WE LOVE YOU.
10. THEY THANK US FOR OUR HELP.
11. I JUST WANT <u>TO</u> SEE IT.
12. WILL YOU BE DRIVING THE OTHER CAR?
13. THANK THEM VERY MUCH FOR US.
14. DON'T GO BEFORE I SEE YOU.
15. WE <u>MUST</u> <u>PLAN</u> FOR EACH INDIVIDUAL.
16. PUT IT BETWEEN THE BOOKS.
17. I DON'T WANT TO BOTHER YOU AGAIN.
18. WE ARE NOW ENTERING THE <u>TUNNEL</u>.
19. BRING IT TO ME AFTER YOU SEE IT.
20. SOME <u>OF</u> US ARE <u>LUCKY</u>.
21. WHAT <u>IS</u> THIS PERSON'S NAME?
22. WHAT IS HAPPENING AT YOUR SCHOOL?

B) Exercises in Decoding

Decode the following illustrated exercises:

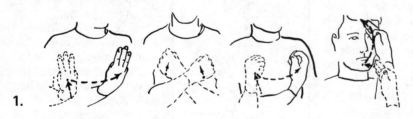

1.   1. _____

2.

3. ?

4.

5.

2.

3.

4.

5.

?

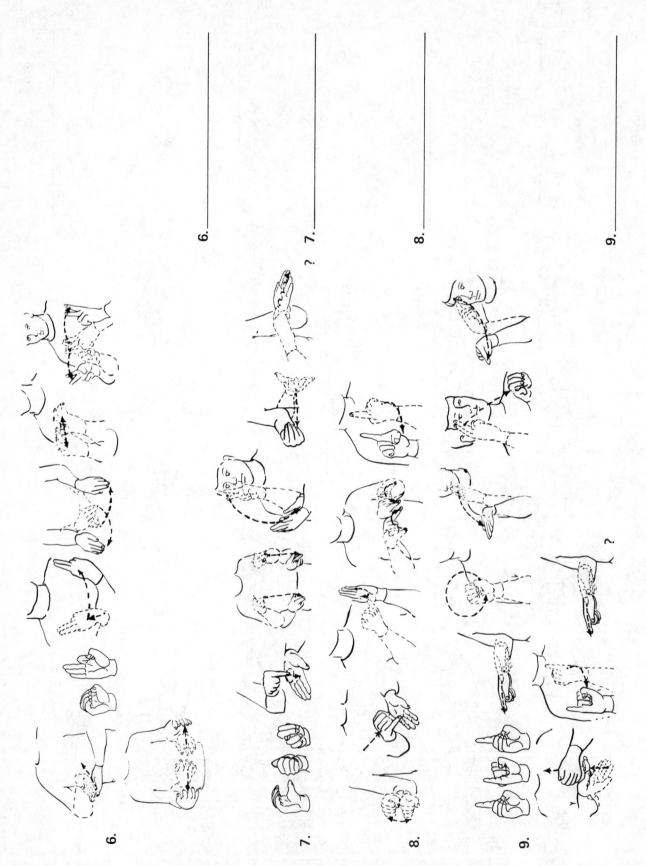

6.

7.

8.

9.

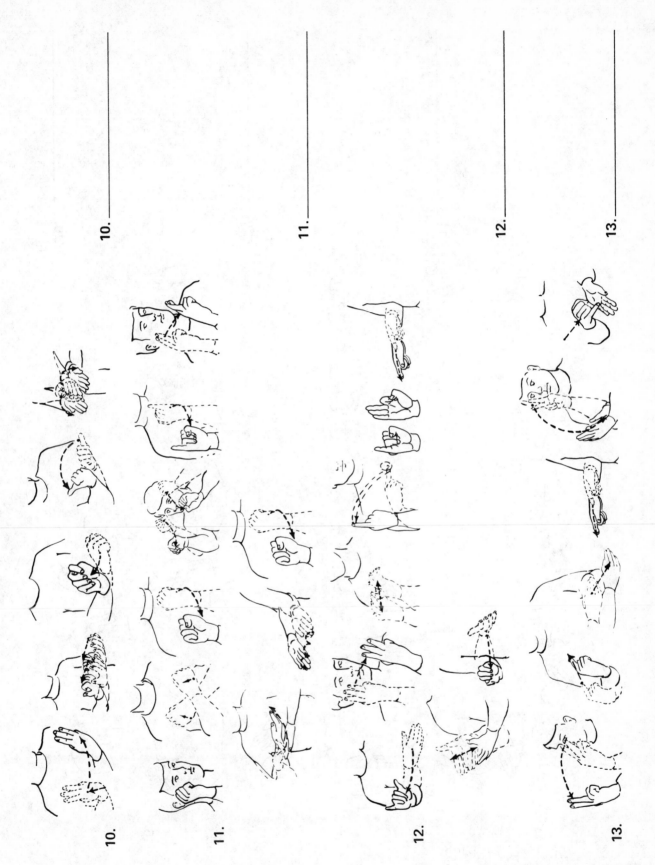

10.

11.

12.

13.

10.

11.

12.

13.

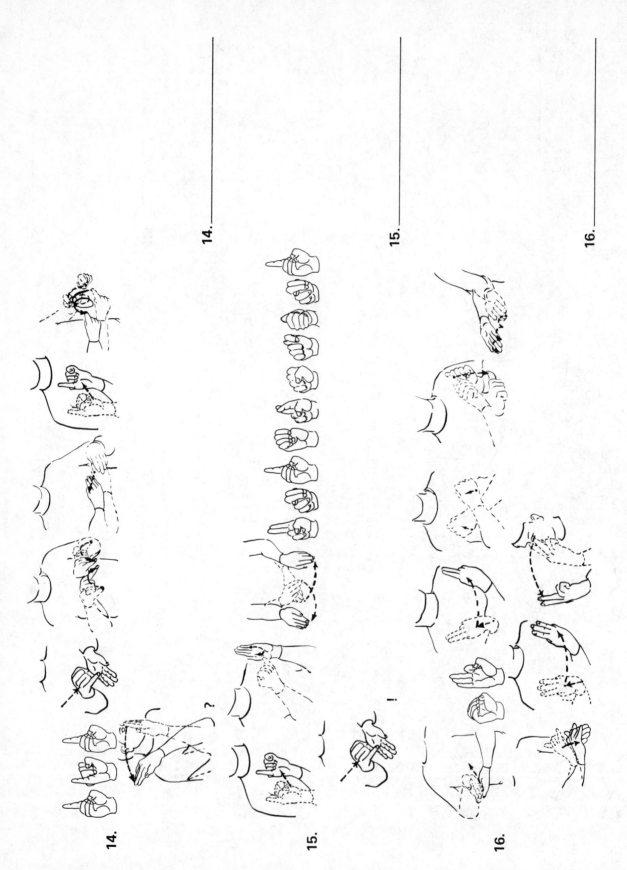

14.

15.

16.

14.

?

15.

!

16.

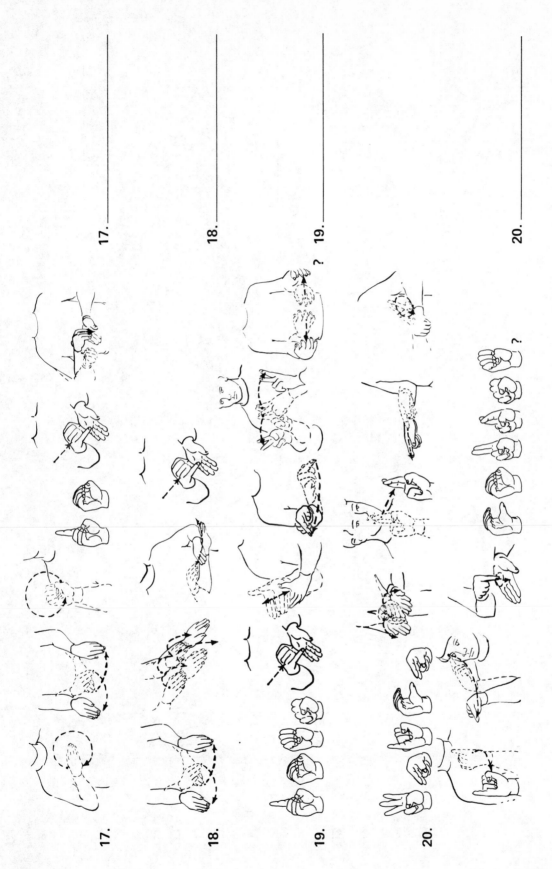

17.

18.

19. ?

20.

?

17.

18.

19.

20.

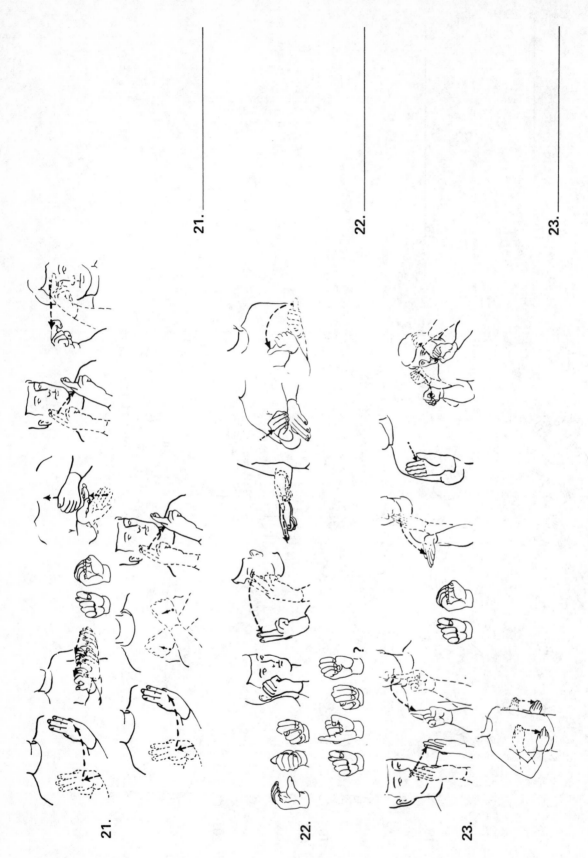

21.

22.

23.

21.

22.

23.

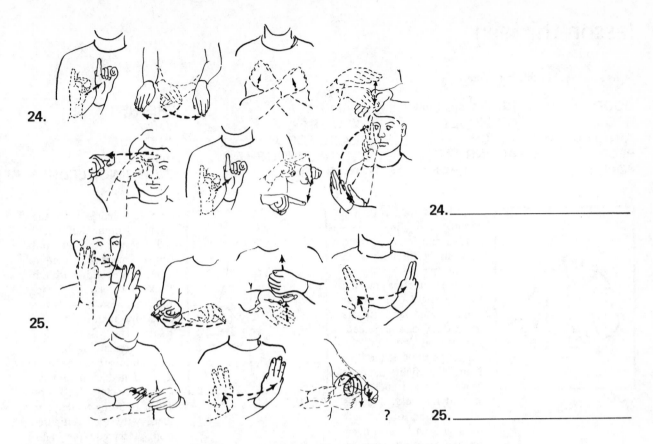

24. _____

25. _____

C) Answers for Decoding Part (B), Lesson 12

Underlined words indicate that they should have been fingerspelled.

1. WE LOVE OUR FOSTER PARENTS.
2. IT WAS AN INDIVIDUAL <u>EFFORT</u>.
3. <u>WHAT</u> <u>IS</u> THE BOY WEARING?
4. PLEASE TELL ME WHEN YOU (plural) WANT <u>TO</u> USE IT.
5. WHO ELSE IS COMING WITH YOU (singular)?
6. SOME <u>OF</u> US DON'T COMPLAIN VERY MUCH.
7. <u>CAN</u> THIS PERSON READ AND WRITE?
8. YES, IT JUST HAPPENED.
9. <u>DID</u> YOU EVER THANK HIM FOR HELPING YOU (singular)?
10. WE WANT THE OTHER BOOK.
11. SHE LOVES TEACHING HER NEW THINGS.
12. THEY WILL COMPLAIN ONLY <u>IF</u> YOU (singular) BOTHER THEM.
13. SEE ME AFTER YOU READ IT.
14. DID IT HAPPEN BE<u>FORE</u> I CAME?
15. I JUST DON'T <u>UNDERSTAND</u> IT!
16. SOME <u>OF</u> US LOVE EVERYTHING THAT WE SEE.
17. PLEASE DON'T EVER <u>DO</u> IT AGAIN.
18. DON'T WALK INTO IT.
19. <u>DOES</u> IT BOTHER YOU (plural) VERY MUCH?
20. <u>WHICH</u> BOOK ARE YOU (singular) USING FOR THIS <u>COURSE</u>?
21. WE WANT <u>TO</u> HELP HER BECAUSE <u>WE</u> LOVE HER.
22. <u>CAN</u> SHE SEE YOU (singular) AT ANOTHER <u>TIME</u>?
23. BE SURE <u>TO</u> THANK YOUR TEACHER.
24. I DON'T LOVE SCHOOL BECAUSE I CAN'T READ.
25. WILL YOU (plural) HELP US BEFORE WE GO?

lesson thirteen

Signs presented in this lesson are:

GOOD	KIND (adjective)	PAPER*	WHETHER
BAD	DIFFICULT	WATER*	NOR
ABOUT	WHICH*	EAT*, FOOD*	NEXT
PEOPLE	AMONG	THINK, THOUGHT	FINE
POLITE*	NICE, CLEAN*	RATHER	KNOW, KNOWLEDGE*

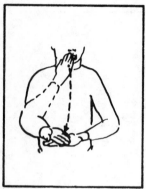

GOOD

The left hand, with the thumb and fingers extended and joined, is held in front of the body with the palmar side facing up and the fingertips pointing to the right. The right hand thumb and fingers are extended and joined; the palmar side of the fingertips touches the lips; then, the right hand is moved forward and down so that its back side lands on the palm of the left hand and with the fingertips pointing to the viewer.

ABOUT

The left hand, with the thumb bending and touching the contracted and joined fingertips, is held in front of the body with the back of the knuckles facing the viewer and the fingertips pointing to the right. The right index finger (remaining fingers and thumb are contracted) is positioned about an inch above the left fingertips and is pointing to the left; then, with the configuration preserved, the right hand is moved to complete a clockwise circle around the fingers of the stationary left hand.

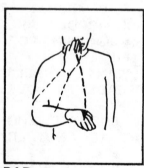

BAD

As with the previous sign ("good"), the palmar side of the right hand fingertips touches the lips, followed by the hand reversing its position (the right palm now faces the ground) as the hand is moved forward and in a downward direction.

NOTE: This sign may be suggestive, perhaps, of the notion that something is not worthy of propagation, and thus it is thrown to the ground.

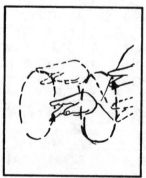

PEOPLE

Both hands assume the configuration of the letter *P* and are held approximately six to eight inches apart in front of the body near the level of the chest with their back sides facing up; then, the *P* hands alternately complete a forward, clockwise circle in front of the signer's body near the level of the chest.

134

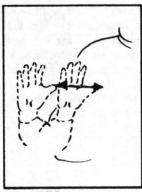

POLITE*

The right hand, with the thumb and fingers extended and apart, is moved in the direction of the signer with the extended thumb touching the breastbone (remaining fingers are pointing upward and the palm of the right hand is facing to the left); then, quickly, the hand is pulled away. Repeat several such back and forth movements; however, be sure that the sign ends with the thumb resting on the chest.

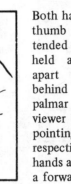

KIND (adjective)

Both hands, each with the thumb and fingers extended and joined, are held about two inches apart (one *has* to be behind the other) with the palmar sides facing the viewer and the fingertips pointing left and right respectively; then, the hands alternately complete a forward, clockwise circle around each other in front of the signer's body.

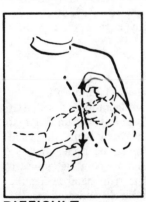

DIFFICULT

Both hands, each in the configuration of the letter *V*, but with the *V* fingers crooked (remaining fingers and thumb are contracted), are positioned in front of the body with their back sides facing the viewer and the right hand held approximately three to four inches higher than the left hand; then, with the configuration maintained, the hands simultaneously are moved in opposite (upward and downward) directions while rubbing the back sides of their crooked *V* fingers as the hands pass each other.

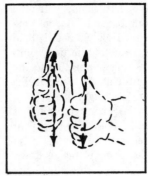

WHICH*

Both hands, with the thumbs extended and remaining fingers contracted and clasped to the palm, are placed side-by-side (but not touching) in front of the body with the thumbs sticking upward and the back sides of the hands facing sideways; then, alternately, the hands are moved up and down several times, while preserving their configuration.

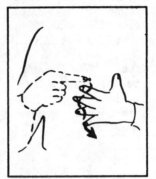

AMONG

The left hand, with the thumb and fingers extended and apart, is held in front of the body with the fingers pointing to the right and the palmar side facing the signer. The right index fingertip (remaining fingers and thumb are contracted) weaves an in-and-out path through the fingers as it is moved from the index to the little finger of the left hand.

NICE, CLEAN*

The left hand, with the thumb and fingers extended and joined, is held in front of the body with the palm facing up and the fingertips pointing to the right. The right hand, with the thumb and fingers extended and joined, touches the left palm (the palm is facing down and the fingertips are pointing to the viewer) and then slides across the palm in the direction of the left fingertips.

NOTE: For "clean," the hand performs a double motion. That is, the hand slides back and forth several times as if to suggest that something is being rubbed out.

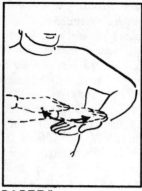

PAPER*

The left hand, with the thumb and fingers extended and joined, is held in front of the body with the fingers pointing to the right and the palm facing up. The right hand, in a similar configuration, is held about three to four inches above the left hand (the palm is facing down and the fingertips are pointing to the left); then, the right hand descends so that its palm touches the left palm as the right hand continues its movement toward the wrist. This motion is repeated several times.

NOTE: This sign may be imitative, perhaps, of sheets of paper passing through a printing press.

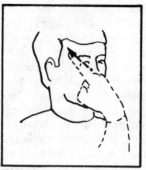

THINK, THOUGHT

The right hand, with only the index finger extended (remaining fingers and thumb are contracted), is moved toward and touches the right side of the forehead with the extended index fingertip.

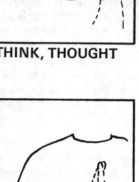

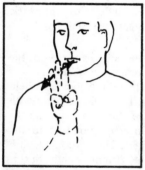

WATER*

The right hand, in the configuration of the letter *W*, is held near the lips with the *W* fingers pointing upward and the palmar side of the hand facing to the left; then, the *W* hand is moved to and from the lips several times.

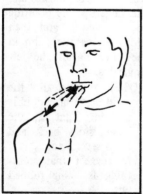

EAT*, FOOD*

The right thumb bends to touch the fingers, which are together and half flexed at the base (the hand is held approximately four to six inches in front of the signer's mouth with the joined thumb and fingertips pointing at the signer); then, the hand is moved to-and-from the mouth several times.

RATHER

The left hand assumes the configuration of the letter *L* and is held in front of the body so that the palm is facing the signer and the thumb is pointing upward. The right hand makes the letter *R*, which first touches the left thumb (contact is made between the palmar side of the left thumb and the back side of the right thumb) and then is moved laterally to touch the left fingertip (the back side of the right thumb touches the tip of the left index finger). The *R* fingers are pointing upward at about a 45-degree angle as the sign ends.

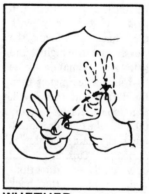

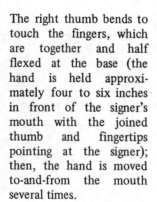

WHETHER

The left hand assumes the configuration of the letter *L* and is held in front of the body with the palm facing the signer and the thumb pointing upward. The right hand makes the letter *W* and touches the left thumb (the back side of the right thumb touches the palmar side of the left thumb); then, the *W* hand is moved toward and touches the tip of the left index finger with the back side of the right thumb.

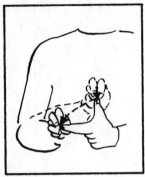

NOR

The left hand, in the configuration of the letter L, is held in front of the body with the index finger of the L hand pointing to the right and the thumb sticking upward. The right hand makes the letter N, the tips of the index and middle fingers of the N hand touch the palmar side of the left thumb, separate, and are moved forward to touch the left index fingertip.

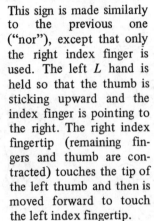

NEXT

This sign is made similarly to the previous one ("nor"), except that only the right index finger is used. The left L hand is held so that the thumb is sticking upward and the index finger is pointing to the right. The right index fingertip (remaining fingers and thumb are contracted) touches the tip of the left thumb and then is moved forward to touch the left index fingertip.

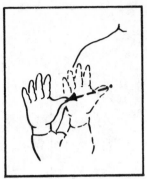

FINE

The right hand, with the thumb and fingers extended and apart, is moved in the direction of the signer with the extended thumb touching the breastbone (remaining fingers are pointing upward and the palm of the hand is facing left); then, the right hand is moved away (forward) from the signer's chest just *once*. The right hand fingertips are pointing upward at about a 45-degree angle as the sign ends.

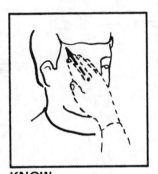

KNOW, KNOWLEDGE*

The right hand, with the thumb and fingers extended and joined, is moved toward the signer and the palmar side of the fingertips touches the right side of the forehead.

NOTE: The sign for "knowledge" is made by repeating the motion for "know" several times.

A) Exercises in Encoding

Encode the following material using signs and fingerspelling. Use fingerspelling for all underlined words.

1. THESE PEOPLE ARE VERY POLITE.
2. IS IT ABOUT OUR PAPER?
3. IT IS VERY DIFFICULT FOR HIM <u>TO</u> <u>LEARN</u> HOW <u>TO</u> READ.
4. I KNEW <u>THAT</u> YOU ARE AMONG THEM.
5. WE ARE <u>HAPPY</u> THAT YOU ARE FINE AGAIN.
6. WHICH <u>OF</u> THOSE <u>DO</u> YOU WANT US <u>TO</u> BRING?
7. THEY WOULD RATHER NOT COME <u>TODAY</u>.
8. HAVE YOU EATEN <u>YET</u>?
9. PLEASE BRING HIM A <u>GLASS</u> <u>OF</u> WATER.
10. IT WAS VERY NICE <u>OF</u> YOU <u>TO</u> <u>DO</u> IT.
11. I <u>ADMIT</u> I WAS BAD NOT <u>TO</u> THINK ABOUT IT.
12. GOOD PEOPLE ARE DIFFICULT <u>TO</u> <u>FIND</u>.
13. THANK YOU FOR BEING <u>SO</u> KIND.
14. NEITHER YOU NOR I <u>CAN</u> HAVE IT.
15. THINK ABOUT IT BEFORE NEXT <u>WEEK</u>.
16. WHO WILL HELP YOU CLEAN* IT? ("Clean" is signed similarly to "nice," but is repeated several times.)
17. WOULD YOU RATHER DRIVE TO THE UNIVERSITY?
18. IS IT WRONG FOR HER <u>TO</u> KNOW IT?
19. WE <u>RESPECT</u> HIS KNOWLEDGE* VERY MUCH.
20. <u>DO</u> YOU KNOW THIS <u>TO</u> BE TRUE?
21. THE FOOD IS VERY <u>EXPENSIVE</u> HERE.
22. SHE IS THE KINDEST PERSON I KNOW.
23. THERE IS A <u>THIEF</u> AMONG US.
24. I WANT YOU <u>TO</u> BE MORE POLITE NEXT <u>TIME</u>.

B) Exercises in Decoding

Decode the following illustrated exercises:

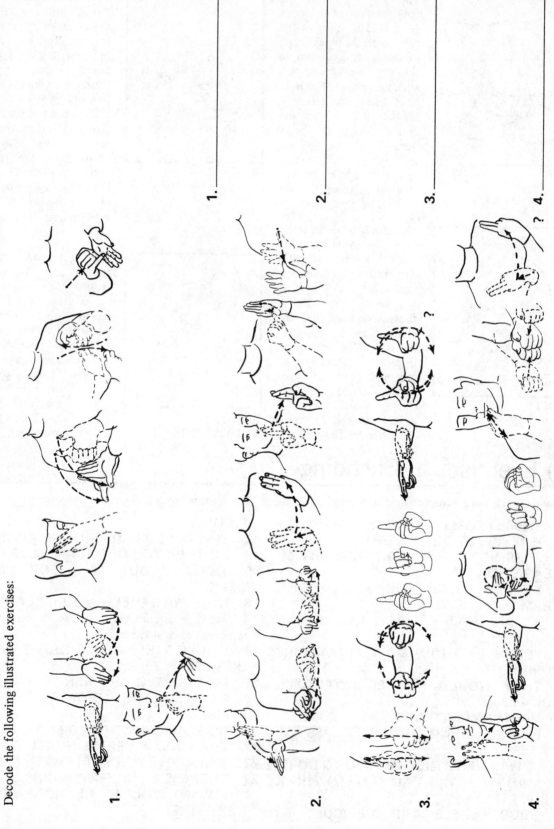

1.

2.

3.

4.

1.

2.

3.

4.

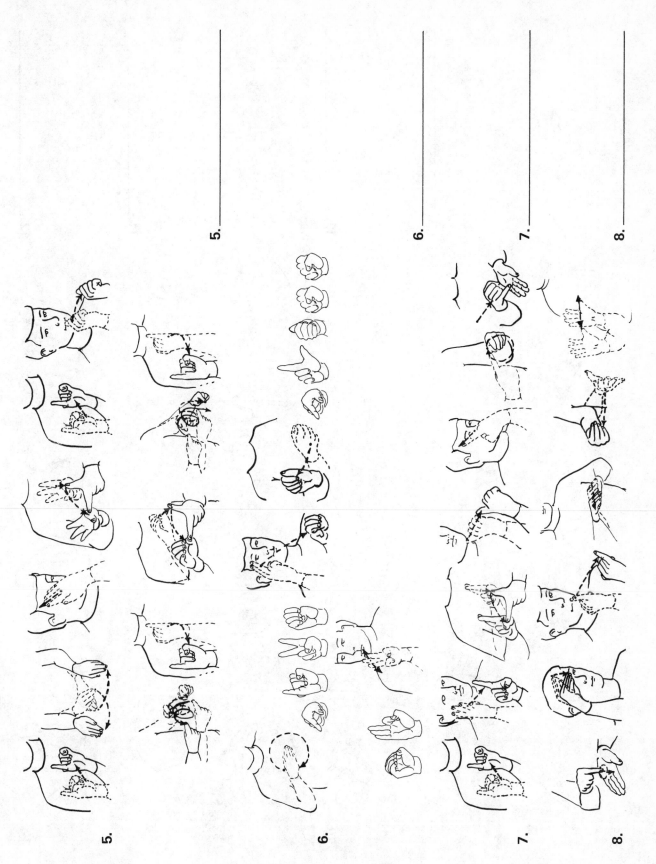

5.

6.

7.

8.

5.

6.

7.

8.

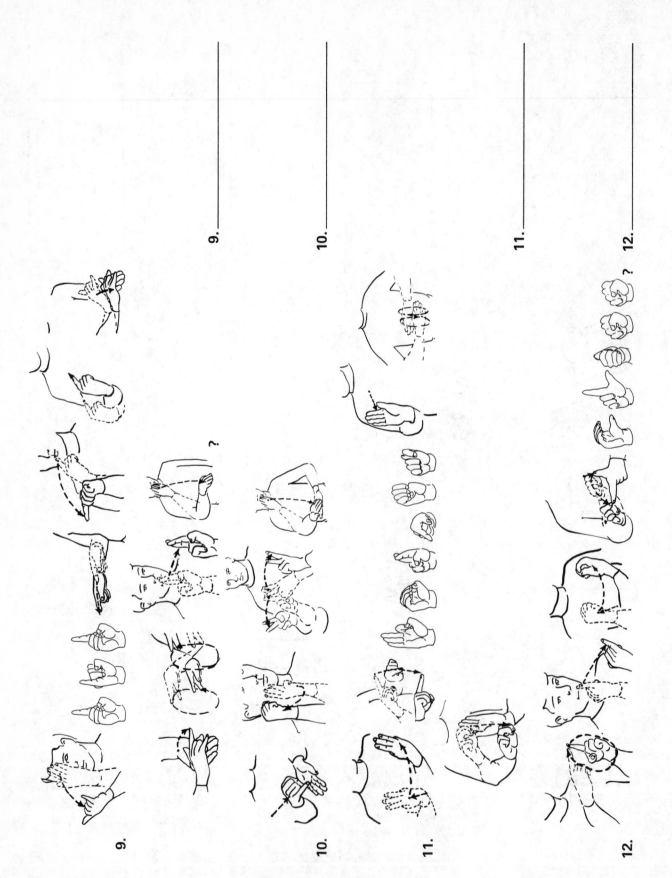

9.

10.

11.

12.

9.

10.

11.

12.

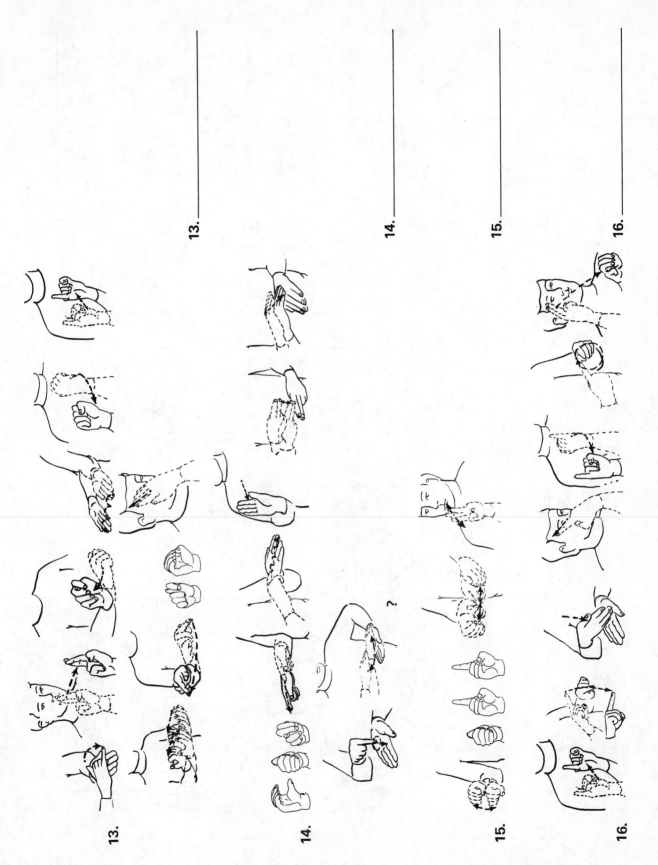

13.

14.

15.

16.

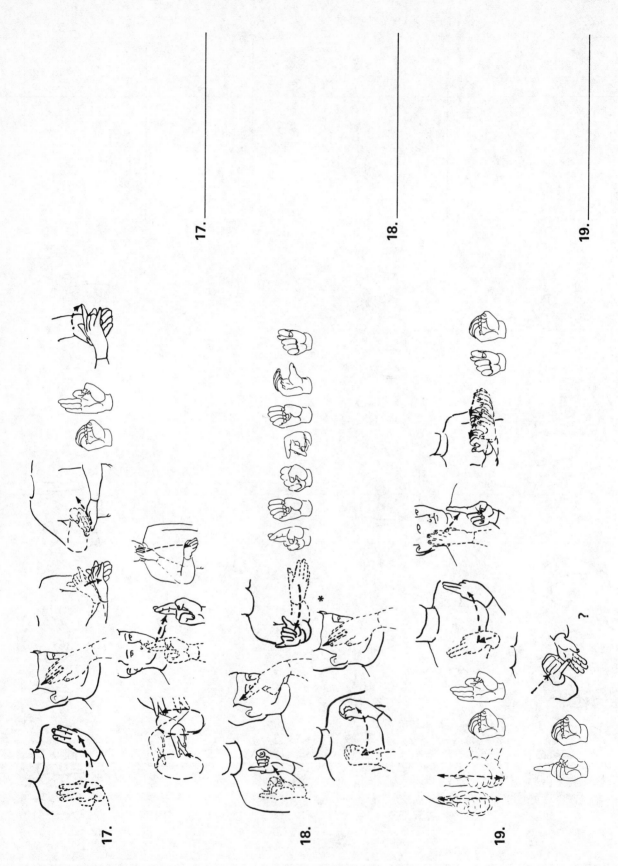

17.

18.

19.

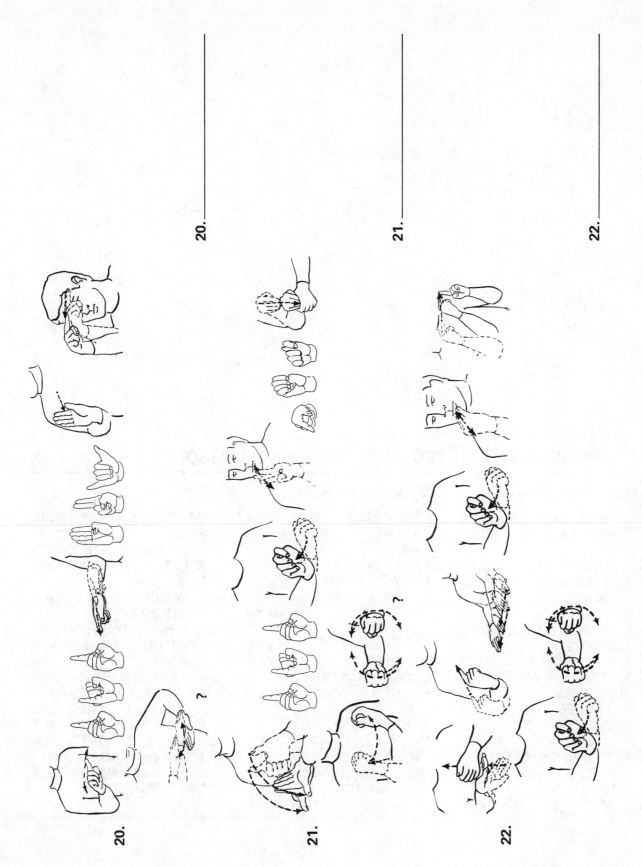

20.

21.

22.

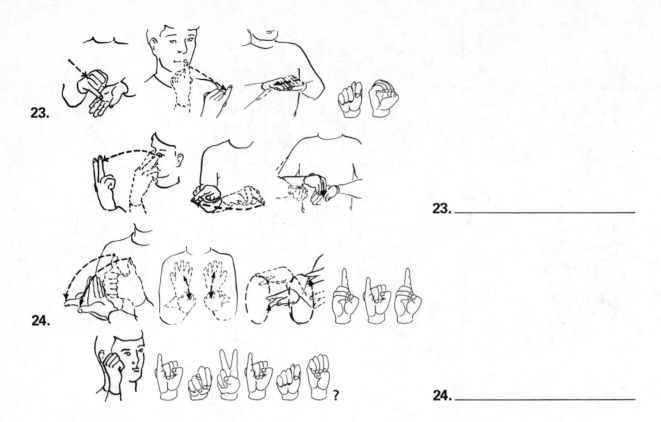

23. _____

24. _____

C) Answers for Decoding Part (B), Lesson 13

Underlined words indicate that they should have been fingerspelled.

1. YOU (singular) DON'T KNOW HOW DIFFICULT IT IS.
2. THANK YOU (plural), BUT WE ARE JUST FINE.
3. WHICH CAR <u>DID</u> YOU DRIVE?
4. WOULD YOU LIKE <u>TO</u> EAT WITH US?
5. I DON'T KNOW WHETHER I AM COMING OR GOING.
6. PLEASE <u>GIVE</u> HIM A <u>GLASS</u> OF WATER.
7. I WOULD RATHER NOT THINK ABOUT IT.
8. THIS BOY IS NICE AND POLITE.
9. WHY <u>DID</u> YOU (singular) TELL ME THAT THOSE PEOPLE ARE BAD?
10. IT WAS VERY GOOD.
11. WE CAN'T <u>FORGET</u> YOUR KINDNESS.
12. WHEN IS OUR NEXT <u>CLASS?</u>
13. THESE ARE THE THINGS I WANT YOU (plural) <u>TO</u> KNOW.
14. <u>CAN</u> YOU (singular) WRITE YOUR NAME ON THIS PAPER?
15. YES, <u>ADD</u> MORE WATER.
16. I CAN'T STOP THINKING ABOUT HIM.
17. WE KNOW THAT SOME OF THOSE PEOPLE ARE BAD.
18. I THINK THEY <u>RE-SPECT</u> OUR KNOWL-EDGE.
19. WHICH <u>OF</u> US WOULD WANT <u>TO DO</u> IT?
20. WHERE <u>DID</u> YOU (singular) <u>BUY</u> YOUR BLACK PAPER?
21. HOW <u>DID</u> THE WATER <u>GET</u> INSIDE OUR CAR?
22. HELP ME CARRY THE FOOD TO THE CAR.
23. IT IS NICE <u>TO</u> SEE YOU (plural) AGAIN.
24. HOW MANY PEOPLE <u>DID</u> SHE <u>INVITE?</u>

lesson fourteen

Signs presented in this lesson are:

CAN, ABLE	**HARD-OF-HEARING**	**WORD***	**ALONG**
MAY	**HEARING AID**	**VOCABULARY***	**FUTURE**
POSSIBLE	**DEAF**	**AROUND**	**FRIEND**
HEAR	**TELEPHONE, CALL**	**SMART, CLEVER**	**HAPPY***
HEARING IMPAIRED	**LEARN**	**UNDERSTAND**	**IDEA**

CAN, ABLE

Both hands assume the configuration of the letter *A* and are held in a parallel position in front of the body with the back sides facing the signer; the *A* hands are then bent forward once. The sign ends with the back side of the *A* hands facing up.

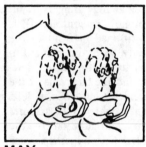

MAY

Both hands make the letter *M* and are held in a parallel position in front of the body with the back sides of the *M* hands facing the signer; then, the *M* hands simultaneously are bent forward once.

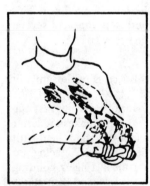

POSSIBLE

Both hands, in the configuration of the letter *P*, are moved toward and touch the chest with the tips of their middle fingers (the *P* hands are held in a parallel position on the chest with the back sides facing the viewer); then, the *P* hands simultaneously are pulled away (forward) from the chest, rotated in a clockwise and counter-clockwise direction respectively, fingerspell the letter *A* and execute the sign for "can" or "able."

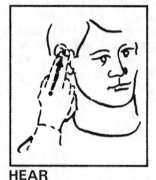

HEAR

The right hand, in the configuration of the letter *H*, points to the right ear. The back of the *H* hand faces the viewer.

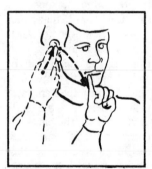

HEARING-IMPAIRED

This sign is made by combining "hear" plus the fingerspelled letter *I*. First, make the sign for "hear"; then, the *H* hand is moved forward as it changes its configuration to the letter *I* which is held approximately four inches in front of the chin with its palmar side facing the viewer.

HARD-OF-HEARING

The right hand makes the letter *H*, which is held in front and slightly to the right side of the body with its palmar side facing left; then, without altering its configuration, the *H* hand makes an upward movement toward the right side of the body.

HEARING AID

This sign is made by combining the signs for "hear" plus "help." First, make the sign for "hear," followed by the sign for "help" (lesson 3). The sign for "help" is made in the following manner: The left hand, with the fingers clasped to the palm and the thumb sticking upward, is held in front of the body with the back side of the hand facing the viewer. The right hand, with the fingers extended, joined and pointing to the left, is moved up from below, its palmar surface makes contact with the bottom portion of the left hand, and lifts it upward.

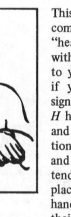

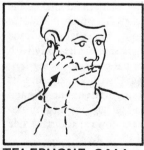

DEAF

This sign is made by combining the signs for "hear" plus "close." First, with your *H* hand, point to your ear as you would if you were making the sign for "hear"; then, the *H* hand is moved forward and in a downward direction as the right thumb and fingers become extended and joined and are placed next to the left hand so that the sides of their index fingers are touching, pointing to the viewer and with the palms facing down.

NOTE: This sign means literally "hearing-closed."

TELEPHONE, CALL

The right hand forms the letter *Y* and then the *Y* hand is brought near the face so that the thumb is pointing to the ear and the little finger is near the mouth.

NOTE: This sign imitates the way this instrument is used.

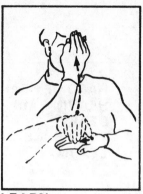

LEARN

The left hand, with the fingers extended and joined, is held in front of the body with the fingers pointing to the right and the palm facing up. The extended fingers and thumb of the right hand first touch the left palm and then come together so that the thumb touches the fingertips as the right hand is moved toward the signer and touches the forehead with its joined thumb and fingertips.

NOTE: This sign may be imitative, perhaps, of gathering information from a printed page.

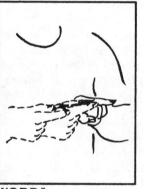

WORD*

The left hand, with only the index finger extended (remaining fingers and thumb are contracted), is positioned in front of the body with the index fingertip pointing at the viewer and the back side of the hand facing to the left. The right hand assumes the configuration of the letter *G*, and marks a space of about an inch by touching the side part of the left index finger. This motion is repeated several times.

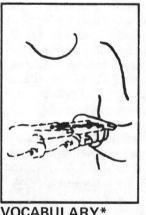

VOCABULARY*

This sign is made similarly to the previous one ("word"), except that the right hand makes the letter *V* (the *V* hand is held with the back side facing up and the *V* fingers pointing to the left) and then marks a space of about an inch by touching the side part of the left index finger which is pointing to the viewer. This motion is repeated several times.

AROUND

The left hand, with the thumb extended and touching the joined fingertips, is held in front of the body with the joined fingertips pointing upward and the back of the fingers facing the viewer. The right index finger (remaining fingers and thumb are contracted) is held about two inches above the left fingertips and points to them; then, the right hand is moved to complete a clockwise circle in a horizontal plane around the left fingers.

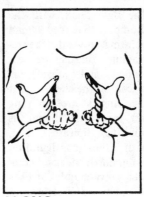

ALONG

Both hands, each in the configuration of the letter *A*, are held side-by-side (but not touching) in front of the body so that the back sides are facing up; then, the *A* hands are moved forward as the wrists flip them clockwise and counter-clockwise respectively, while the hands form the letter *L* (the back sides of the *L* hands face the viewer with the index fingers of the *L* hands cocked at about a 45-degree angle).

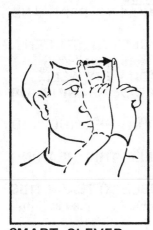

SMART, CLEVER

The right hand, with only the index finger extended (remaining fingers and thumb are contracted), is moved toward and placed on the middle of the forehead. (The index fingertip is pointing upward and the back side of the hand is facing to the right.) Then, with the configuration preserved, the right hand is moved approximately three to four inches forward.

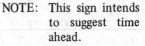

FUTURE

The right hand, in the configuration of the letter *F*, is placed on the signer's right cheek (the side of the thumb touches the cheek) so that the palmar side of the *F* hand is facing left with the joined fingers pointing upward; then, the *F* hand is moved straight forward (away from the body) without altering its configuration.

NOTE: This sign intends to suggest time ahead.

UNDERSTAND

The right hand, with the index finger in a curved position (remaining fingers and thumb are contracted), is moved toward and with the index fingertip touches the forehead; then, the hand tilts forward causing the curved index finger to separate from the forehead as it straightens. The back of the hand faces the viewer as the sign comes to an end.

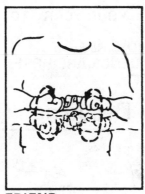

FRIEND

Both hands assume the configuration of the letter *X* and are held, one above the other, in front of the body so that the *X* hands face each other (the left *X* hand has its back side facing down, while the right *X* hand has its back facing up); then, the right *X* hand is moved downward so that the crooked index finger hooks the crooked index finger on the left hand. This motion is then reversed. (That is, the hands separate, reverse their spatial positions, and then re-hook their crooked index fingers.)

The right hand, with the thumb extended and pointing upward (the remaining fingers are extended and joined), is placed on the chest so that the fingers are pointing left and its thumb is pointing upward; then, with the configuration maintained, the hand completes several quick strokes in an upward direction.

HAPPY*

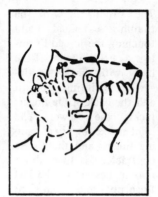

The right hand, in the configuration of the letter *I*, is moved toward and touches the right side of the forehead. The little finger is pointing upward and the back side of the hand is facing the viewer; then, with the configuration preserved, the *I* hand is curved slightly upward and outward.

IDEA

A) Exercises in Encoding

Encode the following material using signs and fingerspelling. Use fingerspelling for all underlined words.

1. WE ARE VERY HAPPY WITH YOU.
2. WOULD YOU <u>DRAW</u> A <u>LINE</u> AROUND THIS WORD?
3. THEY DON'T HAVE A LARGE VOCABULARY.
4. SHE IS A SMART GIRL.
5. COULD YOU UNDERSTAND ME VERY <u>WELL</u>?
6. <u>DO</u> THEY WANT <u>TO</u> COME ALONG WITH US?
7. I DON'T KNOW WHAT WILL HAPPEN IN THE FUTURE.
8. CAN YOU TELL US MORE ABOUT IT?
9. WE ARE NOT ABLE <u>TO</u> HELP YOU NOW.
10. MAY WE DRIVE YOUR CAR TO SCHOOL?
11. YES, I THINK IT IS POSSIBLE.
12. SOME <u>OF</u> YOUR FRIENDS ARE HERE.
13. WHOSE IDEA WAS IT?
14. MAY SHE USE YOUR TELEPHONE?
15. CALL US <u>IF</u> YOU <u>NEED</u> HELP.
16. I AM LEARNING HOW <u>TO</u> READ AND WRITE.
17. HE IS A VERY CLEVER STUDENT. ("Student" is signed as "learn" plus "-er.")
18. WE CAN'T HEAR YOU VERY <u>WELL</u>.
19. IS THE BOY HARD-OF-HEARING OR DEAF?
20. PLEASE USE YOUR HEARING AID MORE.
21. HOW CAN WE HELP THIS HEARING IMPAIRED PERSON?
22. IT IS NOT IMPOSSIBLE <u>TO</u> TEACH THIS DEAF GIRL. ("Impossible" is signed as "-im" plus "possible.")
23. I CAN HEAR YOU WHEN I USE MY HEARING AID.
24. PLEASE SIGN FOR US BECAUSE WE ARE DEAF.

B) Exercises in Decoding

Decode the following illustrated exercises:

1.

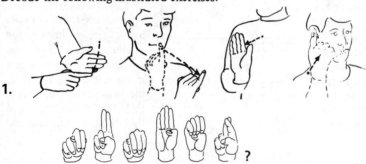

1._____

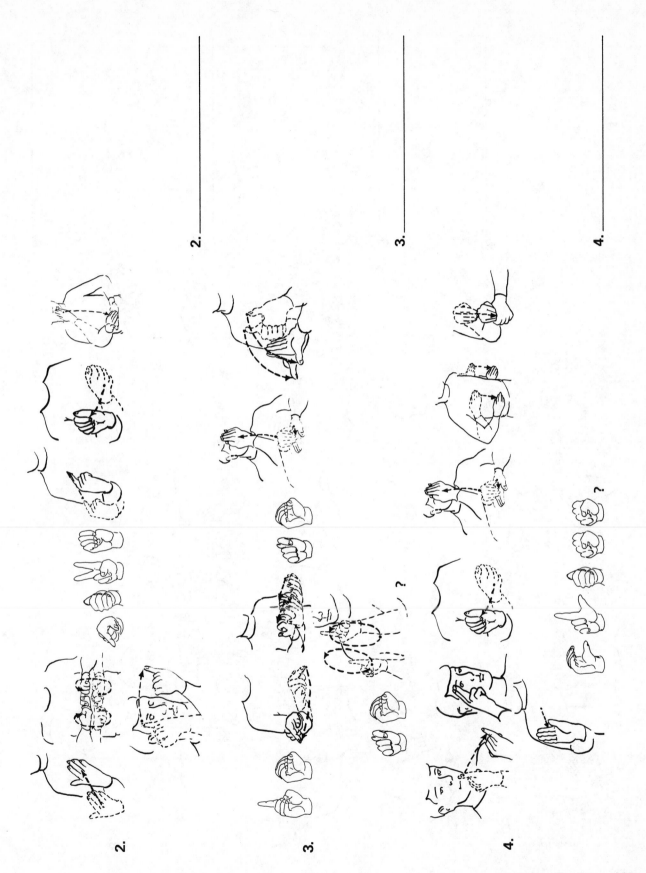

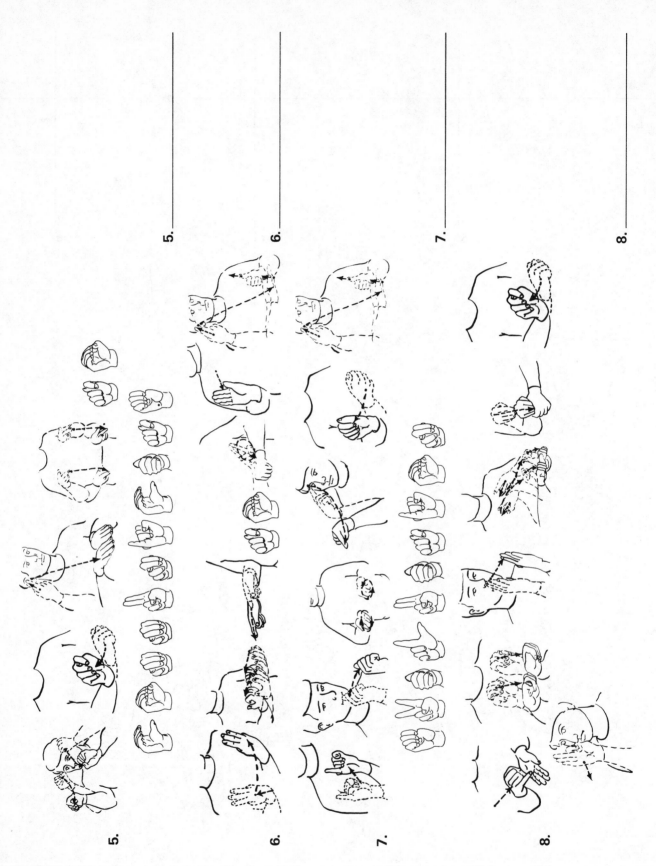

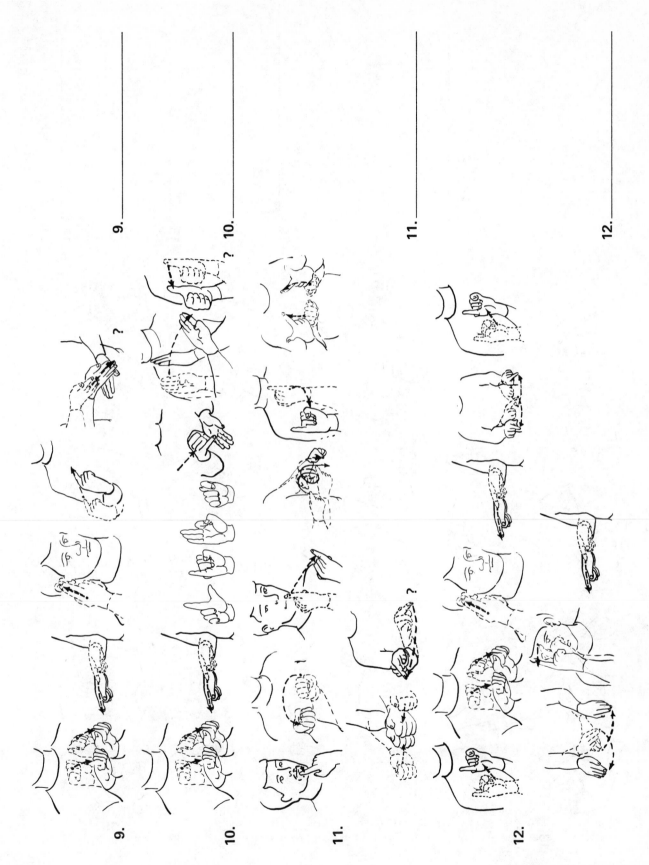

9.

10.

11.

12.

9.

10.

11.

12.

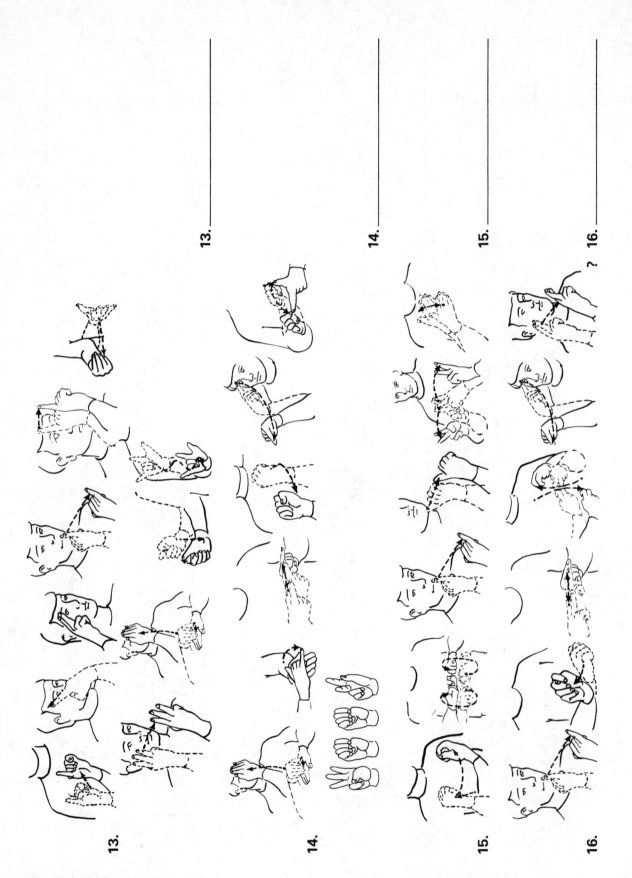

13.

14.

15.

16.

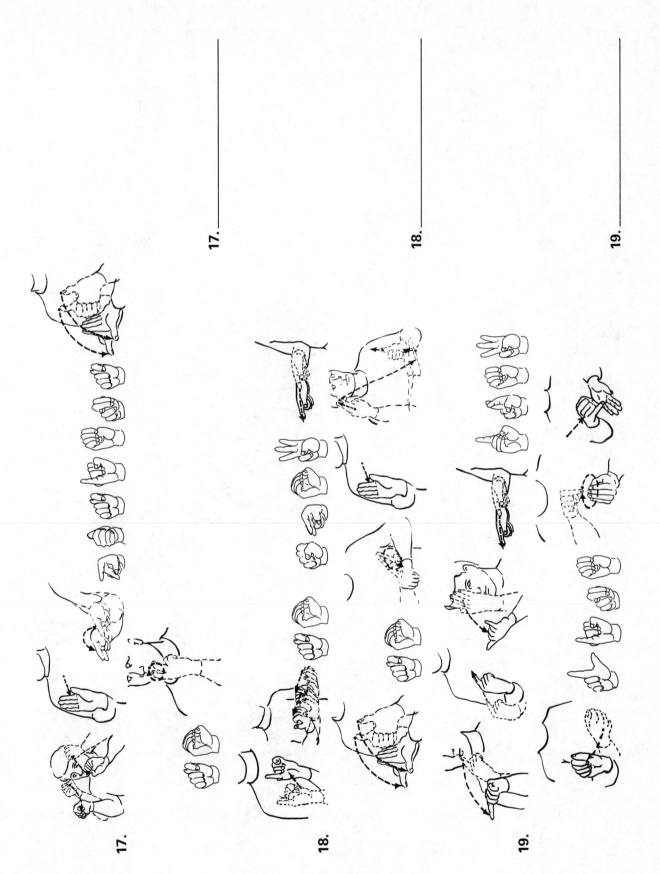

17.

18.

19.

17.

18.

19.

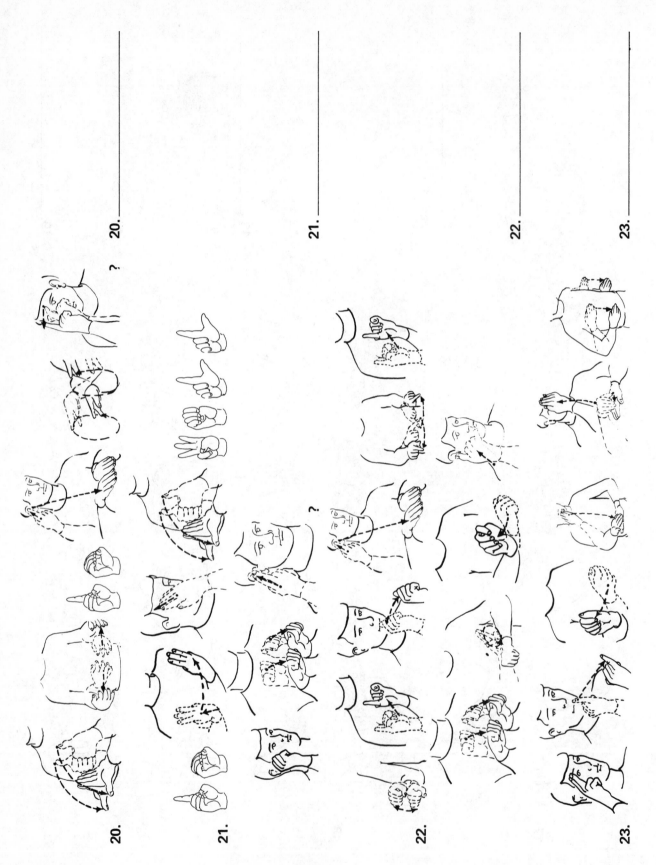

20.

21.

22.

23.

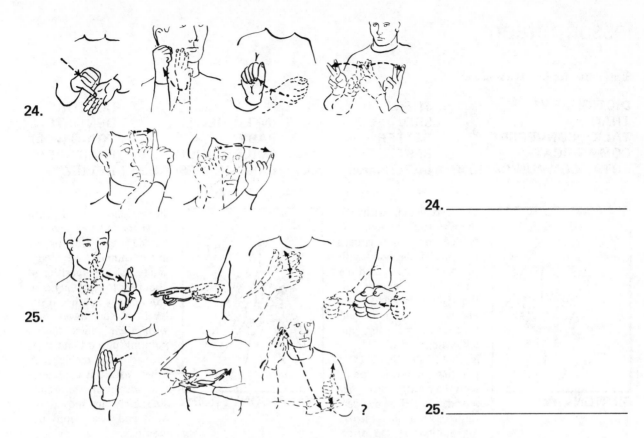

24. _____

25. _____

C) Answers for Decoding Part (B), Lesson 14

Underlined words indicate that they should have been fingerspelled.

1. WHAT IS YOUR TELE-PHONE <u>NUMBER</u>?
2. MY FRIEND <u>GAVE</u> ME A GOOD IDEA.
3. <u>DO</u> YOU (plural) WANT <u>TO</u> LEARN HOW <u>TO</u> SIGN?
4. IS HE A STUDENT IN YOUR <u>CLASS</u>?
5. TEACH THE DEAF PERSON <u>TO COMMUNI-CATE</u>.
6. WE WANT YOU (singular) <u>TO</u> USE YOUR HEAR-ING <u>AID</u>.
7. I AM HERE FOR A HEARING AID <u>EVALUA-TION</u>.
8. IT MAY BE POSSIBLE IN THE FUTURE.
9. CAN YOU HEAR ME ALL RIGHT?
10. CAN YOU <u>LIFT</u> IT BY YOURSELF?
11. WHO ELSE IS GOING ALONG WITH YOU (plu-ral)?
12. I CAN HEAR YOU (sin-gular), BUT I DON'T UN-DERSTAND YOU.
13. I THINK HE IS SMART AND WILL LEARN QUICKLY.
14. LEARN THESE WORDS FOR NEXT <u>WEEK</u>.
15. OUR FRIEND IS NOT VERY HAPPY.
16. IS THE VOCABULARY DIFFICULT FOR HER?
17. TEACH YOUR HARD-OF-HEARING <u>PATIENT</u> HOW <u>TO</u> LIPREAD.
18. I WANT <u>TO SHOW</u> YOU (singular) HOW <u>TO</u> USE YOUR HEARING AID.
19. TELL ME WHY YOU (singular) <u>DREW</u> A <u>LINE</u> AROUND IT.
20. HOW MUCH <u>DO</u> DEAF PEOPLE UNDERSTAND?
21. <u>DO</u> WE KNOW HOW <u>WELL</u> SHE CAN HEAR?
22. YES, I AM DEAF BUT I CAN USE THE TELE-PHONE.
23. HE IS A GOOD STU-DENT.
24. IT WAS A VERY CLEV-ER IDEA.
25. ARE YOU (singular) HAPPY WITH YOUR NEW HEARING AID?

lesson fifteen

Signs presented in this lesson are:

DICTIONARY*	THEN	IF*	DOCTOR*
THAN	SICK	INTERVIEW*	DENTIST*
TALK*, CONVERSE*	BETTER	BABY*	TRAIN (verb)*
COMMUNICATE*	BEST	SMILE, LAUGH*	PRACTICE*
TOTAL COMMUNICATION*	LATER (after awhile)	EXPLAIN, DESCRIBE	REVIEW*

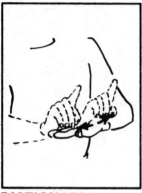

DICTIONARY*

The left hand, with the thumb and fingers extended and joined, is held in front of the body with the palm facing up and the joined fingers pointing to the right. The right hand makes the letter *D* and touches the left palm (the index finger of the *D* hand is held so that it is pointing upward); next, with the configuration preserved, the *D* hand performs several quick stroking motions in the direction of the left wrist.

TALK*, CONVERSE*

Both hands, each with only its index finger extended (remaining fingers and thumb are contracted), are positioned about six to eight inches in front of one another at the level of the lower face with their index fingers pointing upward and their palmar sides facing each other. With this configuration preserved, the hands alternately are moved toward and away from the mouth.

COMMUNICATE*

This sign is made similarly to the previous one ("talk," "converse"), except that *C* hands are used to execute the alternate movements toward and away from the mouth. This motion is repeated several times.

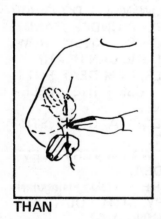

THAN

The left hand, with the thumb and fingers extended and joined, is held in front of the body with the palm facing down and the fingers pointing to the right. The right hand, with the fingers in a similar configuration and pointing to the viewer, descends and brushes past the left fingertips. The sign comes to an end with the right hand fingertips pointing toward the viewer.

TOTAL COMMUNICATION*

This sign is made similarly to the previous one ("communicate"), except that the configuration of the right hand is the letter *T*. The right *T* hand and the left *C* hand are moved to perform alternate movements toward and away from the mouth. This motion is repeated several times.

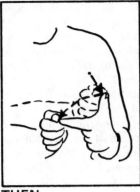

THEN

The left hand, in the configuration of the letter *L*, is held in front of, and slightly to the left side of, the body with the thumb pointing upward and the palmar side of the *L* hand facing the signer. The right hand makes the letter *T* and is moved to touch the left thumb (contact is made between the side of the right thumb and the palmar side of the left thumb); then, the *T* hand is moved forward and touches the tip of the left index finger.

SICK

Both hands, each with its middle finger flexed inward to about a 45-degree angle (remaining fingers and thumb are extended and apart), are held in front of the body (left hand at stomach level and right hand about twelve inches higher) with their back sides facing the viewer; next, simultaneously the hands are brought toward the body so that the tip of the right middle finger touches the forehead, while the tip of the left middle finger touches the abdomen.

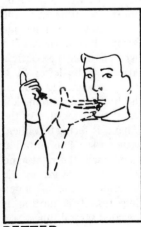

BETTER

The right hand, with the thumb extended vertically (remaining fingers are both extended and joined), is placed near or on the lips so that the joined fingertips are pointing to the left and the back of the hand faces the viewer; next, the hand is moved to the right and in an upward direction as the fingers bend to touch the palm. Note that the thumb is sticking up as the sign ends.

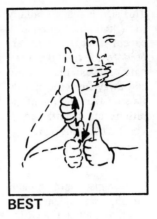

BEST

The left hand, with the thumb sticking up (remaining fingers are contracted and clasped to the palm) is placed in front of the body so that the palmar side of the thumb is facing the viewer. The right hand, with the thumb extended vertically and remaining fingers extended and joined, is placed near or on the lips so that the back of the hand faces the viewer; next, the fingers clasp shut as the right hand is moved downward and placed next to the left hand so that their clasped fingers touch while their thumbs point vertically. The sign finishes with the right hand moving in an upward direction.

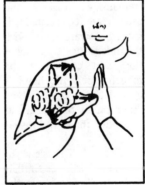

LATER
(after awhile)

The left hand, with the thumb and fingers extended and joined, is held in front of the body with the fingers pointing upward and the palmar side facing to the right. The right hand makes the letter *L* and is moved toward the left hand so that the thumb makes contact with the left palm; without separating, the *L* hand is then tilted forward.

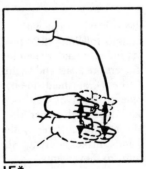

IF*

Both hands, in the configuration of the letter *F*, are held side-by-side (but not touching) in front of the body with their palmar sides facing each other; then, with both distance and configuration maintained, the *F* hands alternately are moved up and down several times.

INTERVIEW*

This sign is made similarly to ("talk," "converse"), except that *I* hands are used to execute the alternate movements toward and away from the mouth. Be sure that the *I* configurations are maintained as you execute this sign.

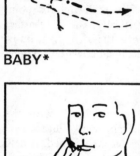

BABY*

Pantomime holding and rocking an infant. The hand, as well as the whole right forearm, is laid on top of the left one; then, alternately swing the arms sideways several times.

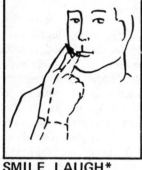

SMILE, LAUGH*

The right hand, with only the index finger extended (remaining fingers and thumb are contracted), is moved toward and with the index fingertip touches the right corner of the mouth; then the hand is moved to the right (in the direction of the cheek) as the index fingertip brushes the skin.

NOTE: The sign for "laugh" is made similarly to "smile," but the motion is repeated several times.

EXPLAIN, DESCRIBE

Both hands, each with its thumb touching the tip of its index finger (remaining fingers are apart and slightly bent), are held side-by-side in front of the body and face each other (but do not touch); next, the hands make alternate to-and-fro movements.

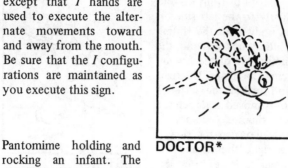

DOCTOR*

The left hand assumes an *A* configuration and is held in front and to the left side of the body so that the back side is facing down. The right hand assumes the configuration of the letter *M*; then, the *M* fingertips touch the inside of the wrist of the left hand. This motion is repeated several times.

NOTE: The sign for a non-medical doctor, Ph.D., for example, is made similarly, except that the letter *D* is used instead of *M*. Similarly, an *N* hand and a *P* hand configuration would signify "Nurse" and "Psychiatrist," respectively.

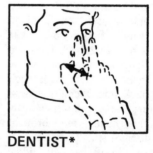

DENTIST*

The right hand assumes the configuration of the letter *D* and is moved toward and touches the corner of the mouth several times (the back of the *D* hand faces the viewer).

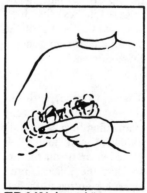

TRAIN (verb)*

The left hand, with only the index finger extended (remaining fingers and thumb are contracted inward), is held in front of the body with the index finger pointing to the viewer and the palmar side facing to the right. The right hand, in the configuration of the letter *T*, is moved toward and touches the top portion of the left hand (the back side of the *T* hand is facing up); then, with the configuration maintained, the right hand is moved forward in the direction of the left index fingertip. This motion is repeated several times.

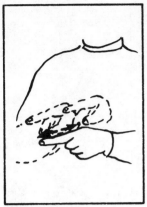

PRACTICE*

This sign is made similarly to the previous one ("train"), except that the letter *P* is used instead of *T*. The tip of the middle finger of the right *P* hand touches the left index finger at the third joint (the right *P* hand is held so that the back side is facing up and the index finger is pointing at the viewer); then, the *P* hand slides along the left index finger in the direction of the fingertip. This motion is repeated several times.

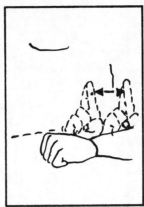

REVIEW*

The left forearm, with the hand in the configuration of the letter *S*, is laid across the body with the back of the *S* hand facing up. The right hand makes the letter *R*; then, the wrist of the right hand touches the side of the wrist of the left hand and completes several back-and-forth type brushing movements on the left forearm.

A) Exercises in Encoding

Encode the following material using signs and fingerspelling. Use fingerspelling for all underlined words.

1. IS THE WORD IN THE DICTIONARY?
2. I THINK THAT THE STUDENTS KNOW MORE THAN THE TEACHER.
3. WE SHALL TALK WITH YOU LATER.
4. WILL YOU TEACH US HOW <u>TO</u> COMMUNICATE?
5. <u>DOES</u> HE WANT ME <u>TO</u> USE "TOTAL COMMUNICATION"?
6. SHE CAN'T COME <u>TODAY</u> BECAUSE SHE IS SICK.
7. CAN YOU UNDERSTAND ME ANY BETTER NOW?
8. WHO IS THE BEST STUDENT IN YOUR <u>CLASS</u>?
9. WE SHALL HELP HER IF WE CAN.
10. SHE WAS SLOWER THEN.
11. WHEN IS HE COMING HERE FOR AN INTERVIEW?
12. WAS YOUR BABY <u>BORN</u> DEAF?
13. <u>DO</u> YOU KNOW HOW <u>TO</u> SMILE?
14. WHY ARE THEY LAUGHING AT US?
15. WHO IS YOUR <u>FAMILY</u> DOCTOR?
16. MY PSYCHIATRIST CAN'T UNDERSTAND WHY I <u>DID</u> IT. ("Psychiatrist" is signed similarly to "doctor," but with a *P* hand.)
17. WHEN WILL HE SEE THE DENTIST?
18. PLEASE EXPLAIN IT AGAIN.
19. I AM TRAINING <u>TO</u> BE A NURSE. ("Nurse" is signed similarly to "doctor," but with an *N* hand.)
20. HOW OFTEN <u>DO</u> YOU PRACTICE AT <u>HOME</u>?
21. NOW WE WANT <u>TO</u> STOP AND REVIEW.
22. WHY DON'T YOU WANT <u>TO</u> PRACTICE MORE?
23. <u>DID</u> YOU TALK WITH MY DOCTOR?
24. <u>DESCRIBE</u> FOR US WHAT YOU SEE.

B) Exercises in Decoding

Decode the following illustrated exercises:

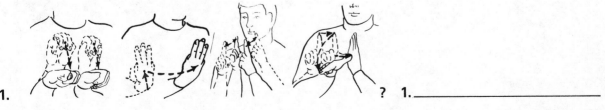

1. _____? 1._____

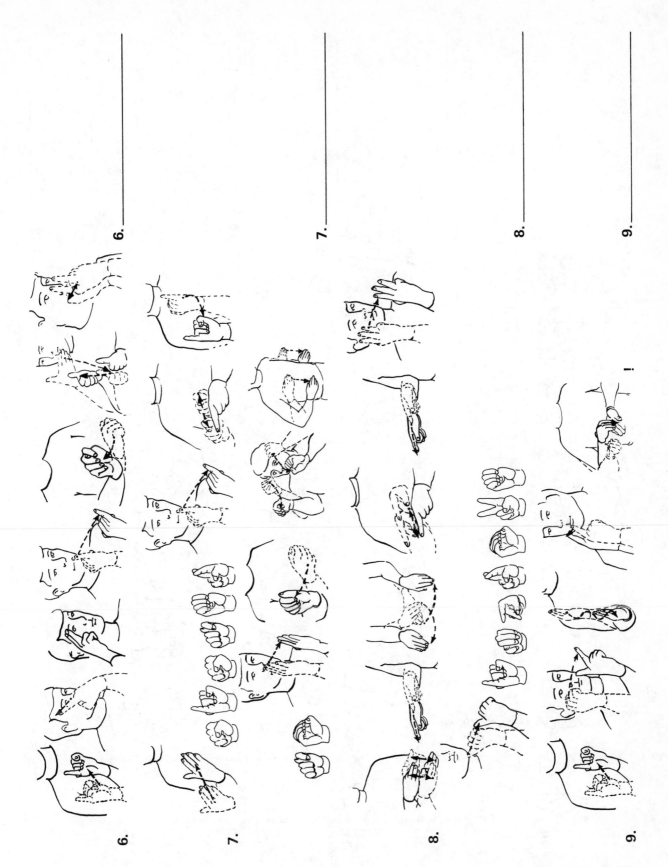

6.

7.

8.

9.

6.

7.

8.

9.

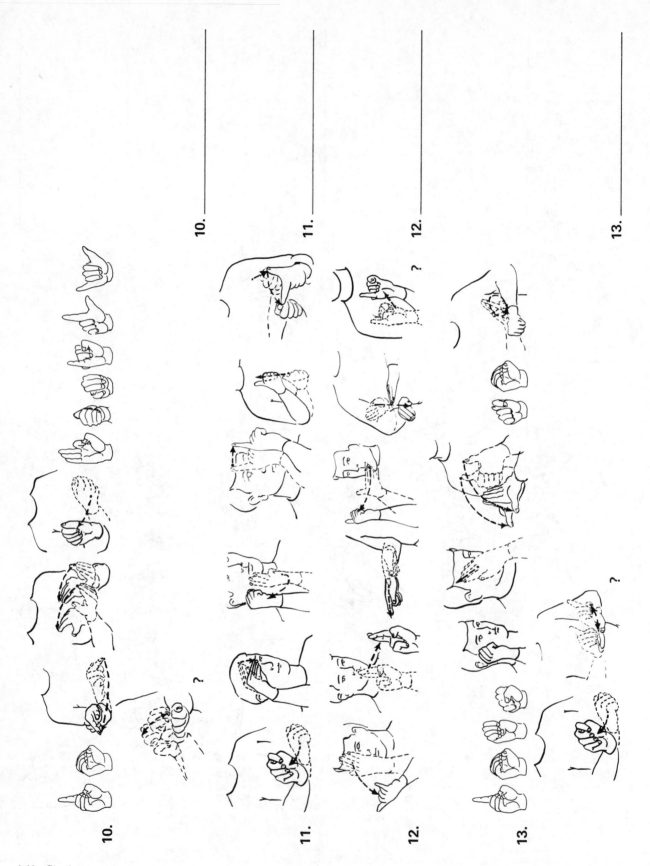

10.

11.

12.

13.

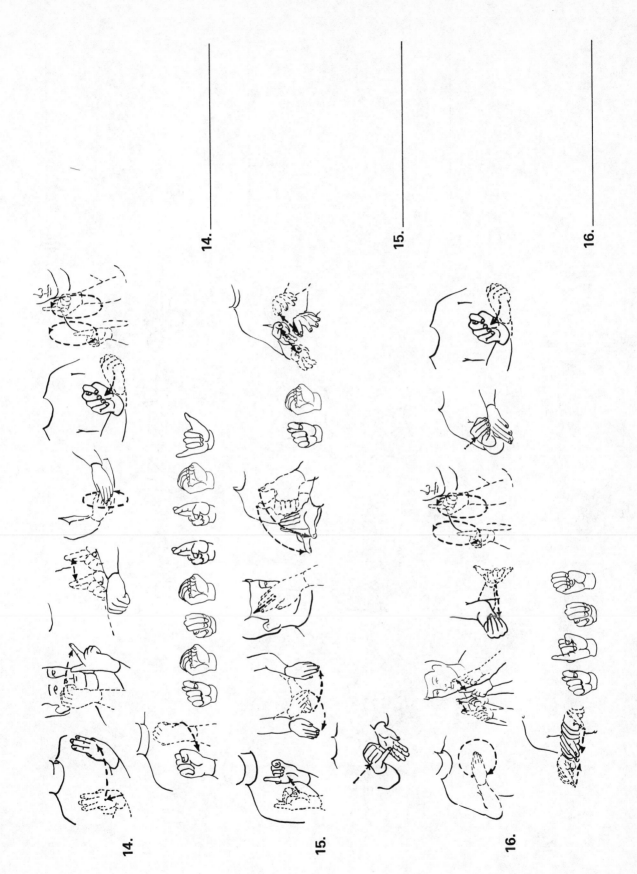

14.

15.

16.

14.

15.

16.

17.

18.

19.

17.

18.

19.

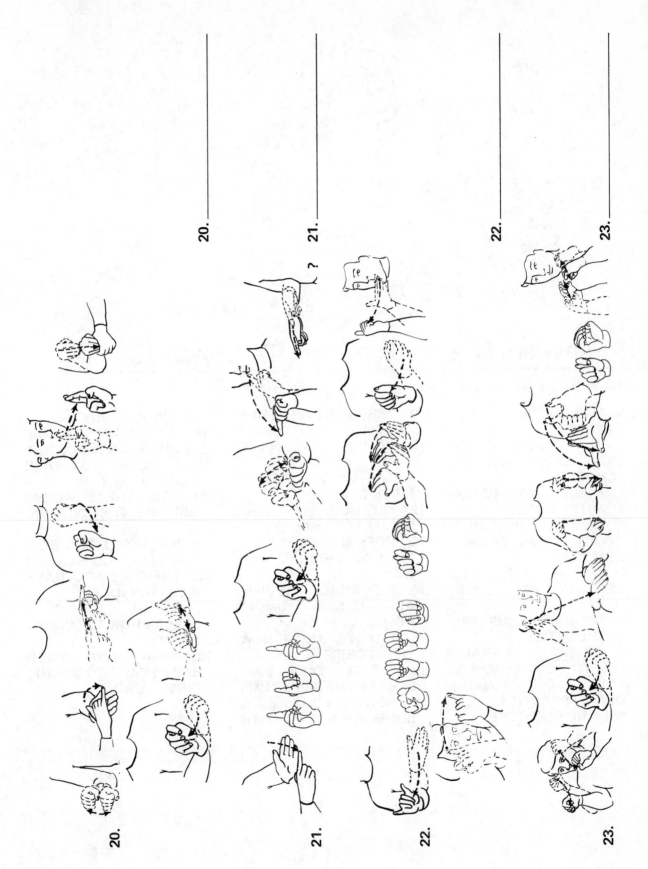

20.

21.

22.

23.

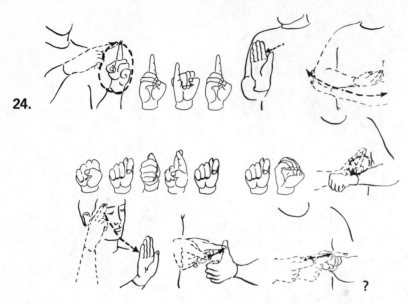

24.

24. _____

C) Answers for Decoding Part (B), Lesson 15

Underlined words indicate that they should have been fingerspelled.

1. MAY WE TALK LATER?
2. IF YOU (singular) ARE SICK, DON'T GO TO SCHOOL.
3. I SHALL <u>TRY TO</u> EXPLAIN IT BETTER.
4. HOW <u>DO</u> THEY <u>FEEL</u> ABOUT TOTAL COMMUNICATION?
5. THE MOTHER TELLS US THAT THE BABY IS DEAF.
6. I THINK HE IS THE BEST DENTIST.
7. MY <u>SISTER</u> IS TRAINING <u>TO</u> BE A TEACHER.
8. IF YOU (singular) DON'T PRACTICE, YOU WILL NOT <u>IMPROVE</u>.

9. I SHALL NEVER SMILE AGAIN!
10. <u>DO</u> YOU (plural) HAVE A <u>FAMILY</u> DOCTOR?
11. THE BOY WAS SMARTER THEN.
12. WHY ARE YOU (singular) BETTER THAN I?
13. <u>DOES</u> SHE KNOW HOW <u>TO</u> USE THE DICTIONARY?
14. WE SHALL REVIEW ALL THE SIGNS <u>TOMORROW</u>.
15. I DON'T KNOW HOW <u>TO</u> DESCRIBE IT.
16. PLEASE TALK AND SIGN AT THE SAME <u>TIME</u>.
17. HOW <u>DO</u> YOU (singular) COMMUNICATE WITH

YOUR DEAF BOY?
18. IF HE IS SICK, HE <u>SHOULD</u> SEE A DOCTOR.
19. I <u>PLAN TO</u> TALK ABOUT IT LATER.
20. YES, THESE WORDS ARE IN THE DICTIONARY.
21. WHAT <u>DID</u> THE DOCTOR TELL <u>YOU</u> (singular)?
22. THEY <u>SEEM TO</u> HAVE A BETTER IDEA.
23. TEACH THE DEAF PERSON HOW <u>TO</u> COMMUNICATE.
24. WHEN <u>DID</u> YOUR BABY <u>START TO</u> USE HIS FIRST <u>WORD</u>?

lesson sixteen

Signs presented in this lesson are:

SON	ASK	DAUGHTER	SUNDAY
MUST	QUESTION	TEAR, CRY*	MONDAY
NEED*	DAILY*	COLOR	VOICE
HAVE TO	BROTHER	WHITE	GLASS*
SHOULD	DRILL*	FIGHT*	SISTER

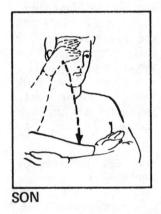

SON

This sign is made by combining the signs for "boy" and "baby." However, the side-to-side movement which belongs to the sign for "baby" is omitted.

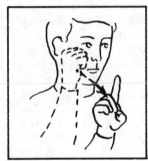

HAVE TO

This sign is made in two steps: First, the right hand, held in front of the body at chest height, assumes the configuration of the letter *X* and then, with the tip of the bent index finger pointing downward, the hand is moved straight down; next, the right hand returns to its original starting position and fingerspells the word "to."

MUST

The right hand, in the configuration of the letter *M*, is held in front and slightly to the right side of the body at shoulder height; then, the *M* hand is moved straight down.

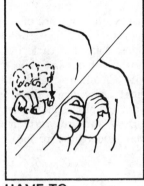

SHOULD

The right hand, in the configuration of the letter *S*, touches the right cheek and is held so that its back side faces to the right; then, the *S* hand is moved forward as it changes its configuration to the fingerspelled letter *D*, with the palmar side of the *D* hand facing the viewer.

NEED*

This sign is made similarly to the previous one ("must"), except that an *N* configuration is used. The right *N* hand initiates several small up-and-down motions, while maintaining the elevated position.

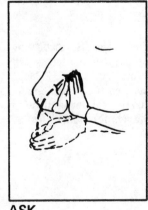

ASK

Begin this sign by bringing your hands (fingers and thumbs extended and joined) together so that the palms touch and the fingertips are pointing to the viewer; then, the joined hands are tilted backwards (toward the signer) with the hands maintaining their configuration and pointing vertically as the sign comes to an end.

167

QUESTION

The right hand, with only the index finger extended (remaining fingers and thumb are contracted), is held in front and to the right side of the body at the level of the shoulder with the hand cocked at about a 45-degree angle upward so that the palmar side of the index finger is facing the viewer; then, the hand is moved downward as the index finger makes the outline of a question mark (i.e., completes half of a circle by moving forward in a clockwise direction, makes a slight movement downward and pushes the finger slightly forward as if it were adding the period).

DRILL*

The left hand, in the configuration of the letter *B*, is held in front of the body with the palmar side toward the signer and the fingertips pointing to the right. The right hand makes the letter *D* and then the tips of the thumb and middle finger of the right *D* hand touch the top portion of the left hand near the base of the thumb (the *D* hand is held with the palmar side of the index finger facing the viewer); then, the hand is moved back and forth laterally several times, grazing the left hand as it does so.

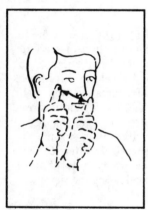

DAILY*

The right hand, with the thumb extended and remaining fingers contracted and clasped to the palm, is held on the right cheek with the side of the thumb touching it (the back side of the hand is facing to the right); then, the hand makes a quick movement forward without altering its configuration. This motion is repeated several times.

DAUGHTER

This sign is made by combining the signs for "girl" and "baby"; however, the side-to-side movement which belongs to the sign for "baby" is omitted. Make the sign for "girl," immediately following it with the sign for "baby."

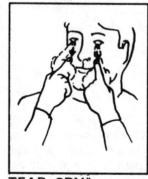

TEAR, CRY*

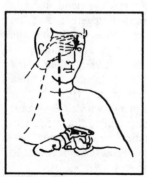

BROTHER

This sign is made by combining the signs for "boy" and "same." Make the sign for "boy," immediately following it with the sign for "same."

Both hands, each with only its index finger extended (remaining fingers and thumb are contracted), are moved toward the face with the index fingertips placed near the lower border of the eyes and with the back sides of the hands facing the viewer; then, with the configuration preserved, both hands are moved downward in the direction of the cheeks. This sign intends to suggest tears rolling down the cheeks. NOTE: For "cry," the motion is repeated several times.

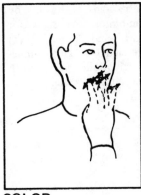

COLOR

The right hand, with the thumb curled in and touching the palm (remaining fingers are extended and apart), is held in front of the mouth so that the palmar sides of the fingers are facing the signer and with the fingertips pointing upward; then, with the hand remaining stationary, the fingers perform small front-to-back wiggling movements.

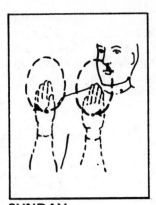

SUNDAY

Both hands, with their thumbs and fingers extended and joined, are held side-by-side (but not touching) in front of the body so that their fingertips are pointing upward and their palmar sides are facing the viewer; then, simultaneously, the hands are moved in a circular direction (clockwise for the right hand, counterclockwise for the left hand), while maintaining their configuration.

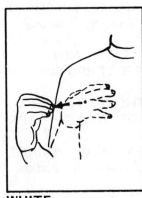

WHITE

The right hand, with the thumb and fingers extended and apart, touches the chest with its fingertips (the back side of the hand faces the viewer), followed by a movement away from the chest as the thumb flexes inward and touches the extended, but joined fingertips. The sign ends with the joined fingertips pointing at the signer with the back side of the hand toward the viewer.

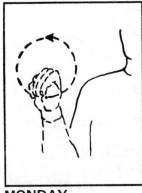

MONDAY

The right hand assumes the configuration of the letter *M* and is held in front and to the right side of the body at the level of the shoulder; then, the *M* hand is moved to make several circular movements in a clockwise direction.

NOTE: The remaining days of the week are similarly formed once the hand first assumes the configuration of the letters *T* for "Tuesday," *W* for "Wednesday," *H* for "Thursday," *F* for "Friday" or *S* for "Saturday."

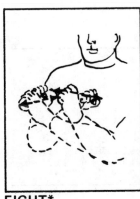

FIGHT*

Both hands make the letter *S* and are held in a parallel manner (about six to eight inches apart) in front of the body with the back sides of their *S* configurations facing left and right, respectively; then, the *S* hands are moved toward each other and cross at the sides of their wrists. The sign ends with the back sides of the *S* hands still facing sideways. This motion is repeated several times.

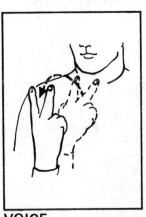

VOICE

The right hand, in the configuration of the letter *V*, is positioned on the throat with the first and second fingers straddling the thyroid (voice box) area; then, a small arc is formed as the *V* hand is moved up and away from the upper region of the throat (the back of the right *V* hand faces the viewer as the sign is completed).

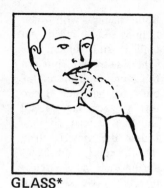

With the tip of your right index finger, which is bent (remaining fingers and thumb are contracted), tap your upper front teeth *several* times.

GLASS*

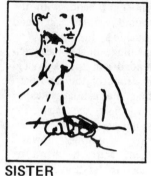

This sign is made by combining the signs for "girl" and "same." Make the sign for "girl," immediately following it with the sign for "same."

SISTER

A) Exercises in Encoding

Encode the following material using signs and fingerspelling. Use fingerspelling for all underlined words.

1. WE HELP OUR SON DAILY.
2. WHEN ARE YOUR BROTHER AND SISTER COMING TO SEE YOU?
3. WHY MUST WE DRILL MORE NOW?
4. TELL ME WHY YOU NEED TO KNOW IT?
5. SHOULD I USE MY VOICE WHEN I SIGN?
6. WE HAVE TO GO WITH THEM.
7. MAY I ASK YOU ABOUT IT?
8. PLEASE BRING US A GLASS OF WATER.
9. STOP FIGHTING US SO MUCH.
10. WHAT COLOR IS YOUR NEW CAR?
11. DO WE WANT TO GO ON SUNDAY OR MONDAY?
12. THERE IS NOTHING WRONG WITH YOUR VOICE.
13. MAY WE SEE YOU ON TUESDAY? ("Tuesday" is signed similarly to "Monday," but with a *T* hand.)
14. WHY ARE THE BOYS FIGHTING?
15. IS YOUR DAUGHTER LEARNING TOTAL COMMUNICATION?
16. SHOW ME WHERE THE WHITE CAR IS.
17. I DON'T WANT TO SEE YOU IN TEARS AGAIN.
18. DO YOU KNOW WHY HE IS CRYING? ("Cry" is signed as "tear," but is repeated several times.)
19. I HAVE TO QUESTION IT.
20. WE DRILL ON THESE WORDS DAILY.
21. WHY DO THEY NEED OUR HELP?
22. ASK ME IF YOU DON'T UNDERSTAND.
23. WHEN DOES YOUR SON SEE THE DOCTOR?

B) Exercises in Decoding

Decode the following illustrated exercises:

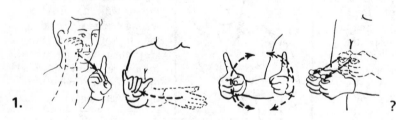

1.   ? 1._____

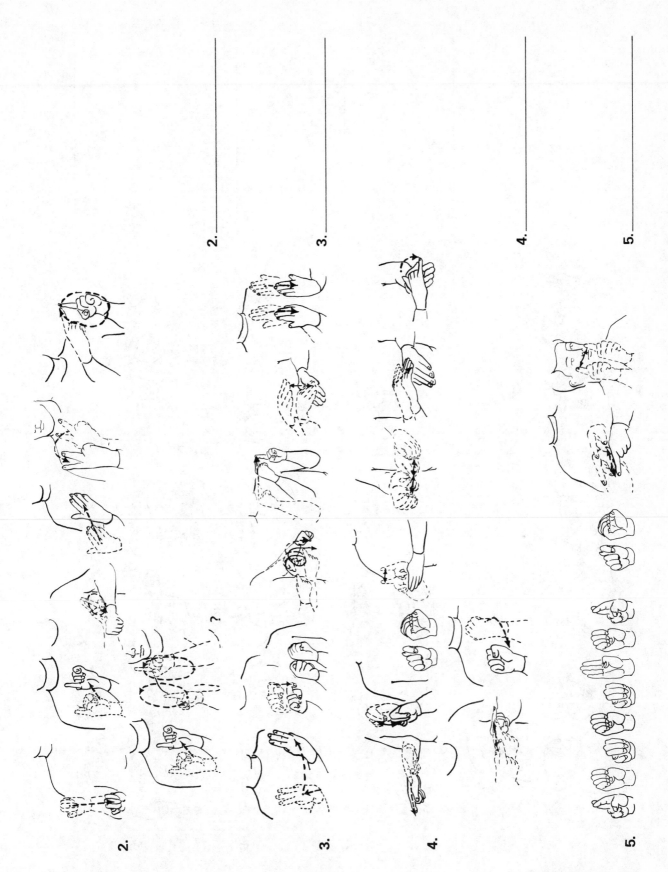

6.

7.

8.

9.

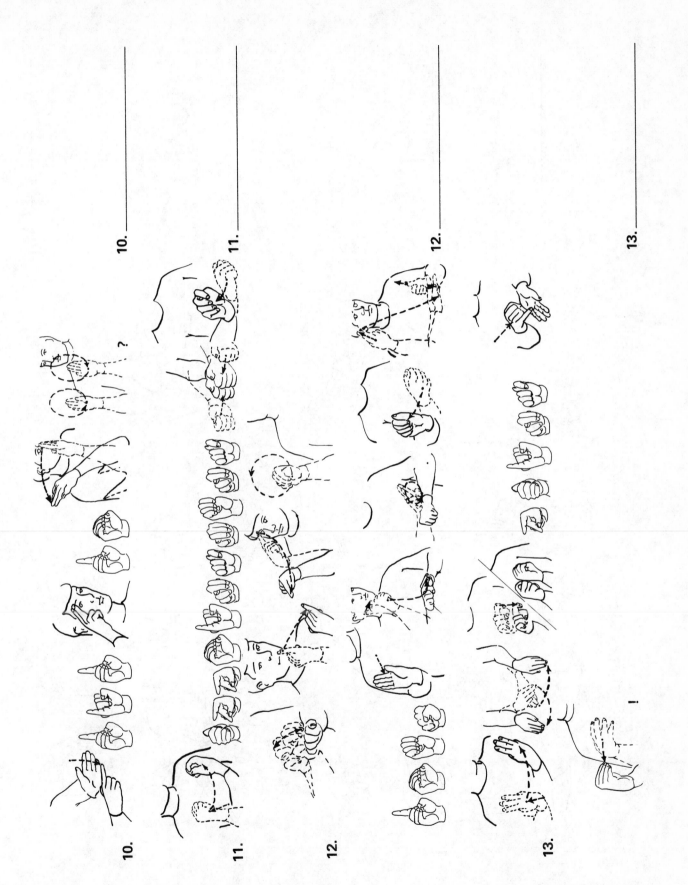

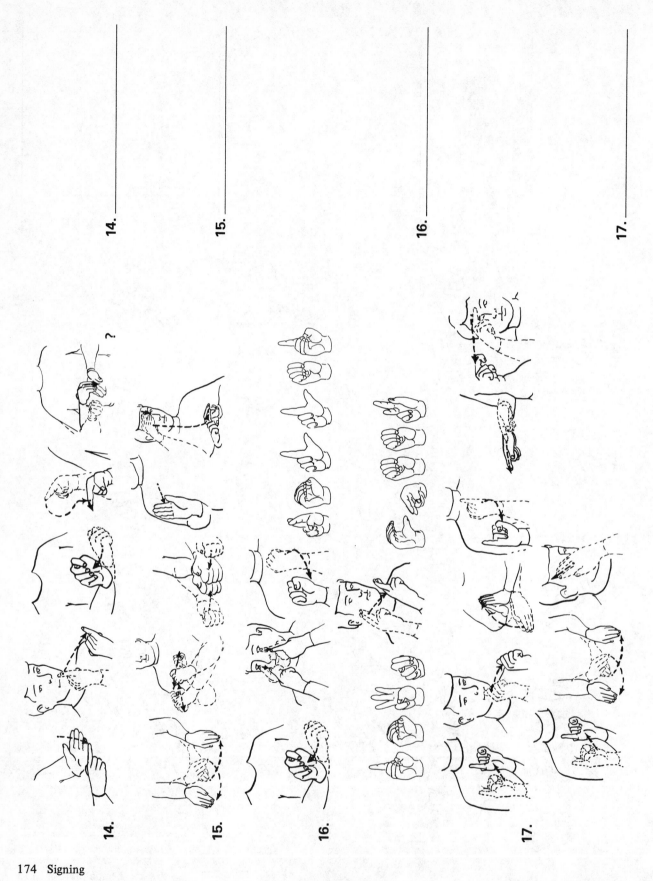

14.

15.

16.

17.

14.

15.

16.

17.

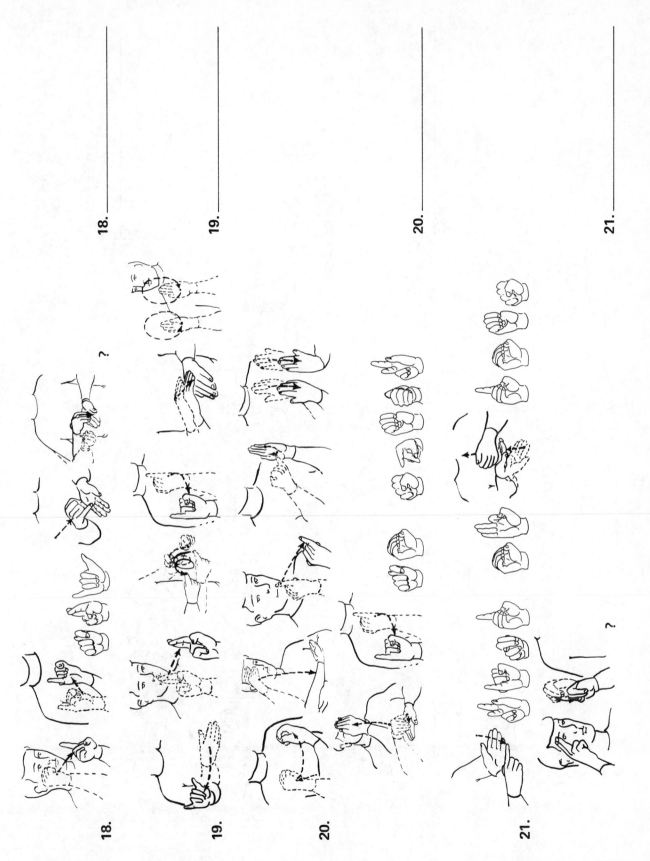

18.

19.

20.

21.

18.

19.

20.

21.

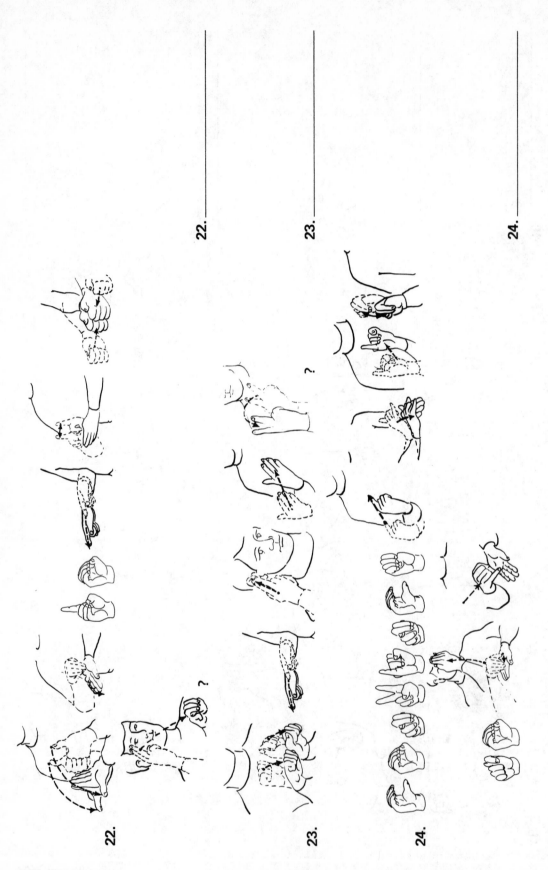

22.

23.

24.

C) Answers for Decoding Part (B), Lesson 16

Underlined words indicate that they should have been fingerspelled.

1. SHOULD THEY DRIVE TOGETHER?

2. MUST I USE MY VOICE WHEN I SIGN?

3. WE HAVE <u>TO</u> GO TO SCHOOL NOW.

4. YOU (singular) NEED <u>TO</u> DRILL MORE ON THESE WORDS.

5. <u>REMEMBER</u> <u>TO</u> PRACTICE DAILY.

6. DON'T ASK US BECAUSE WE DON'T KNOW.

7. IS YOUR BROTHER IN COLLEGE?

8. WHAT IS YOUR DAUGHTER'S NAME?

9. <u>DO</u> YOU (singular) WANT A GLASS <u>OF</u> <u>MILK?</u>

10. WHAT <u>DID</u> HE <u>DO</u> LAST SUNDAY?

11. OUR <u>APPOINTMENT</u> WITH THE DOCTOR IS FOR MONDAY.

12. <u>DOES</u> YOUR SISTER USE A HEARING AID?

13. WE DON'T HAVE <u>TO</u> <u>PAINT</u> IT WHITE!

14. WHAT IS THE QUESTION AGAIN?

15. DON'T FIGHT WITH YOUR BROTHER.

16. THE TEARS <u>ROLLED</u> <u>DOWN</u> HER <u>CHEEK.</u>

17. I AM ASKING YOU BECAUSE I DON'T KNOW.

18. SHOULD I <u>TRY</u> IT AGAIN?

19. THEY ARE COMING ON SUNDAY.

20. OUR SON IS JUST NOW LEARNING <u>TO</u> <u>SPEAK.</u>

21. WHAT <u>KIND</u> <u>OF</u> HELP <u>DOES</u> HE NEED?

22. HOW OFTEN <u>DO</u> YOU (singular) DRILL WITH HIM?

23. CAN YOU (singular) HEAR MY VOICE?

24. <u>CONVINCE</u> ME THAT I NEED <u>TO</u> LEARN IT.

lesson seventeen

Signs presented in this lesson are:

TOMORROW	LIFE	YESTERDAY	ORANGE (color)*
CUP	MONTH	TOILET*	CAT*
BROWN	WEEK	MONEY*	GRAY*
MIRROR	YEAR	EXPENSIVE	UNDER
PARDON*, EXCUSE*	ANIMAL*	DOG*	WASTE*

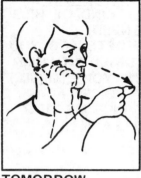

TOMORROW

The right hand, with the thumb extended (remaining fingers are contracted and clasped to the palm), first touches the right cheek with the palmar side of the thumb (the back side of the hand is facing to the right); then, the hand tilts out as it is moved forward. The thumb points to the viewer as the sign comes to an end.

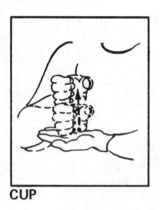

CUP

The left hand, with the thumb and fingers extended and joined, is held in front of the body with the palm facing up and the fingers pointing to the right. The right hand, in the configuration of the letter C, touches the left hand (the palmar side of the C hand faces left) and then is lifted two to three inches in an upward direction. This sign intends to suggest the shape of a cup.

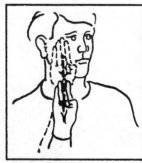

BROWN

The right hand assumes the configuration of the letter B, and is moved toward and, with the top portion of the hand, touches the right cheek. The hand is held with the palmar side facing the viewer; then, the B hand is moved slightly downward while grazing the cheek.

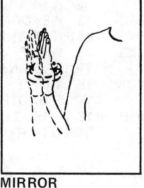

MIRROR

The right hand, with the thumb and fingers extended and joined, is held in front and to the right side of the body at the level of the shoulder with the fingers pointing upward and the palmar side facing the signer; then, with the configuration preserved, the hand is turned in a counter-clockwise direction so that the palmar side is now facing the viewer, and is returned to its original position.

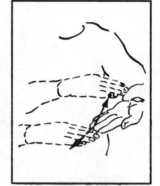

PARDON,* EXCUSE*

The left hand, with the thumb and fingers extended and joined, is held in front and slightly to the left side of the body with the fingers pointing to the right and the palmar side facing up. The right hand, in a similar configuration but with the palm facing down and fingertips pointing to the viewer, is moved downward and touches the left hand near the edge of the fingertips; then, the right hand fingertips brush past the left fingertips. This motion is repeated several times.

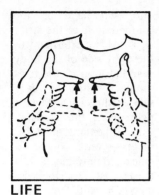

LIFE

Both hands assume the configuration of the letter *L* and are positioned in a parallel manner on the body so that their thumbs are sticking upward and their index fingers are pointing at each other; with their configuration preserved, the *L* hands simultaneously are moved upward while grazing the body.

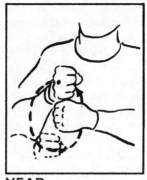

YEAR

Both hands assume the configuration of the letter *S* and are held with the right hand on top of the left (their back sides are facing sideways); then, the right *S* hand completes a forward moving circle around the stationary left hand and comes to rest on top of the left hand (the original starting point).

NOTE: This sign may be imitative of the earth's revolution around the sun.

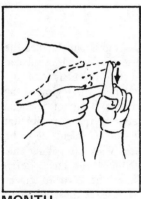

MONTH

The left hand, with only the index finger extended (remaining fingers and thumb are contracted), is held in front and to the left side of the body with the index finger pointing upward and the palmar side facing the viewer. The back side of the right index finger (remaining fingers and thumb are contracted) touches the left index fingernail and then, the right index finger slides down the back side of the left index finger while grazing it.

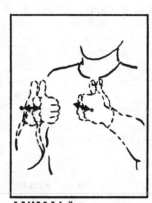

ANIMAL*

Both hands, each with its thumb extended and pointing upward (remaining fingers are curved and joined), are placed side-by-side (but not touching) with their fingertips touching the chest (the thumbs are pointing upward) and the back sides of the fingers are facing each other; then, the hands, without separating from the chest, are bent toward each other and then are returned to their original position. This motion is repeated several times.

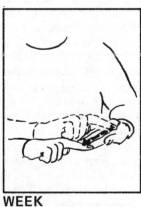

WEEK

The left hand, with the thumb and fingers extended and joined, is held in front and slightly to the left side of the body with the palm facing up and fingers pointing to the right. The right hand, with only the index finger extended (remaining fingers and thumb are contracted), is placed on the left palm so that the index finger is pointing to the viewer (the back side of the right index finger is facing up); then, the right hand slides toward the left fingertips, grazing the left hand as it slides.

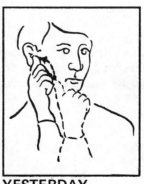

YESTERDAY

The right hand, with only the thumb extended (remaining fingers are contracted and clasped to the palm), touches the right cheek with the palmar side of the thumb (the back side of the hand is facing to the left); then, the thumb moves back in the direction of the ear as the hand tilts backward.

Lesson Seventeen 179

TOILET*

The right hand, in the configuration of the letter *T*, is held in front and to the right side of the body near the level of the shoulder with the back side of the *T* hand facing to the right; then, the *T* hand, without bending its wrist, makes several short but quick back and forth movements along a horizontal plane.

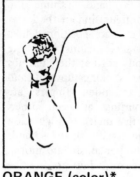

ORANGE (color)*

The right hand, in the configuration of the letter *O*, is held in front and to the right side of the body near the level of the right shoulder with the back side of the *O* hand facing right; then the *O* hand, without bending the wrist, makes several short but quick arc movements as it twists, first, in a clockwise direction and then in a counter-clockwise direction.

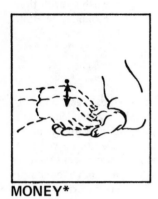

MONEY*

The left hand, with the thumb and fingers joined and extended, is held in front and slightly to the left side of the body with the palm facing up and the fingers pointing to the right. The right hand, with the thumb touching its extended and joined fingertips, descends so that the back sides of the fingers touch the left palm. This motion is repeated several times.

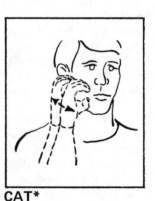

CAT*

The right hand makes the letter *C*, which is placed on the right side of the face near the region of the mouth. (Contact is made between the top portion of the *C* hand and the face, with the palmar side of the hand facing left.) Then, the *C* hand grazes the face as it is pulled to the right, in the direction of the cheek. This motion is repeated several times.

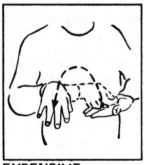

EXPENSIVE

First, the hands assume the configuration and execute the sign for "money"; next, the right hand, with the wrist performing a twisting movement to the right, rises in an arc and then descends with the fingers and thumb fanning out and the palmar side of the hand facing down.

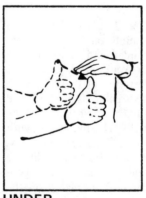

UNDER

The left hand, with the thumb and fingers extended and joined, is held in front and to the left side of the body with the palm facing down and the fingers pointing to the right. The right hand, with only the thumb extended (remaining fingers are contracted and clasped to the palm), first is held about three to four inches away from the chest with the thumb pointing upward and the palmar side facing the viewer; then, the right hand, without altering its configuration, is moved forward and stops directly under the left palm.

DOG*

With your right hand, pat your right thigh a few times and then snap your fingers as if you were calling a dog.

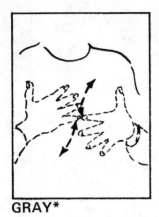

Both hands, with the thumbs and fingers extended and apart, are placed in front of the body so that the tip of the right small finger is touching the tip of the left index finger (both hands have their back sides facing the viewer); then, alternately, the hands are moved up and down several times as their fingertips brush past each other.

GRAY*

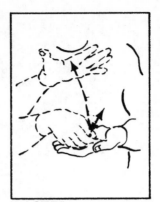

The hands first assume the configuration of and execute the sign for "money"; then, the right hand is moved in an upward direction as the fingers fan apart. The back side of the right hand faces down as the sign comes to an end.

WASTE*

A) Exercises in Encoding

Encode the following material using signs and fingerspelling. Use fingerspelling for all underlined words.

1. I SHALL <u>GIVE</u> YOU THE MONEY TOMORROW.
2. WHERE IS MY BROWN CUP?
3. PRACTICE THESE WORDS WITH THE USE <u>OF</u> A MIRROR.
4. PARDON ME FOR ASKING YOU AGAIN.
5. HAVE YOU SEEN OUR BROWN CAT?
6. I MUST <u>START</u> IT BY NEXT MONTH.
7. PLEASE COME AND <u>STAY</u> FOR A WEEK.
8. HOW MANY WEEKS ARE THERE IN A YEAR?
9. <u>DO</u> YOU KNOW THE <u>NAME OF</u> THIS ANIMAL?
10. HOW BIG IS HER DOG?
11. WHAT IS HE <u>DOING</u> UNDER MY CAR?
12. DON'T WASTE ANY MORE <u>OF</u> OUR MONEY.
13. HOW EXPENSIVE WAS YOUR NEW CAR?
14. <u>DID</u> YOU GO TO SCHOOL YESTERDAY?
15. IS THE BOY TOILET-TRAINED?
16. MAY WE <u>PAINT</u> IT ORANGE AND GRAY?
17. USE A MIRROR WHEN YOU PRACTICE THESE WORDS.
18. WHAT COLOR IS YOUR CAT?
19. SOME THINGS ARE VERY <u>IMPORTANT</u> IN LIFE.
20. EXCUSE US FOR BOTHERING YOU AGAIN.
21. WAS SHE VERY DIFFICULT <u>TO</u> TOILET-TRAIN?
22. <u>DOES</u> YOUR DOG HAVE A NAME?
23. WE DON'T WANT <u>TO</u> WASTE ANY MORE <u>OF</u> HIS <u>TIME</u>.

B) Exercises in Decoding

Decode the following illustrated exercises:

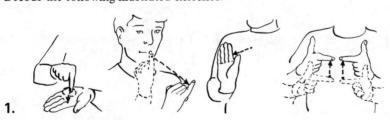

1. _____

1. _____

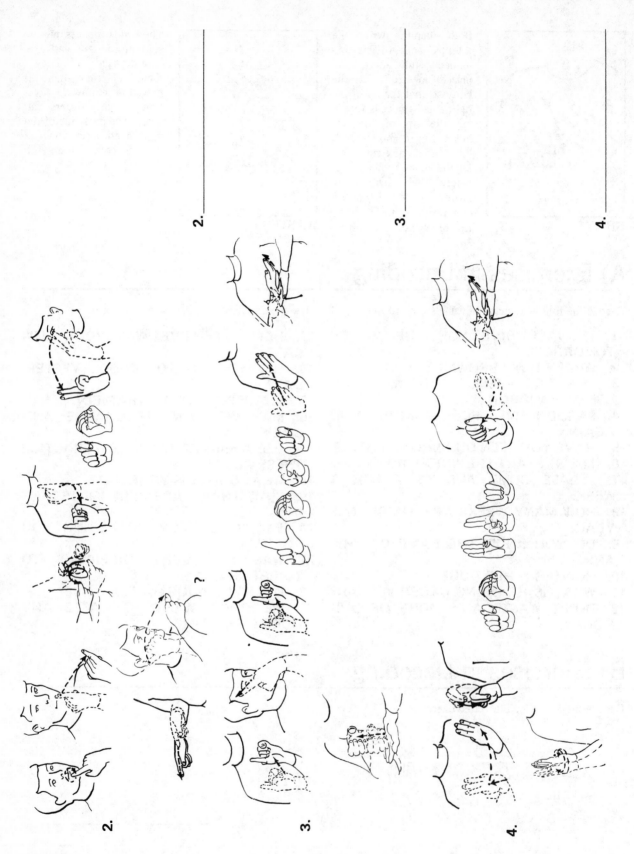

2.

3.

4.

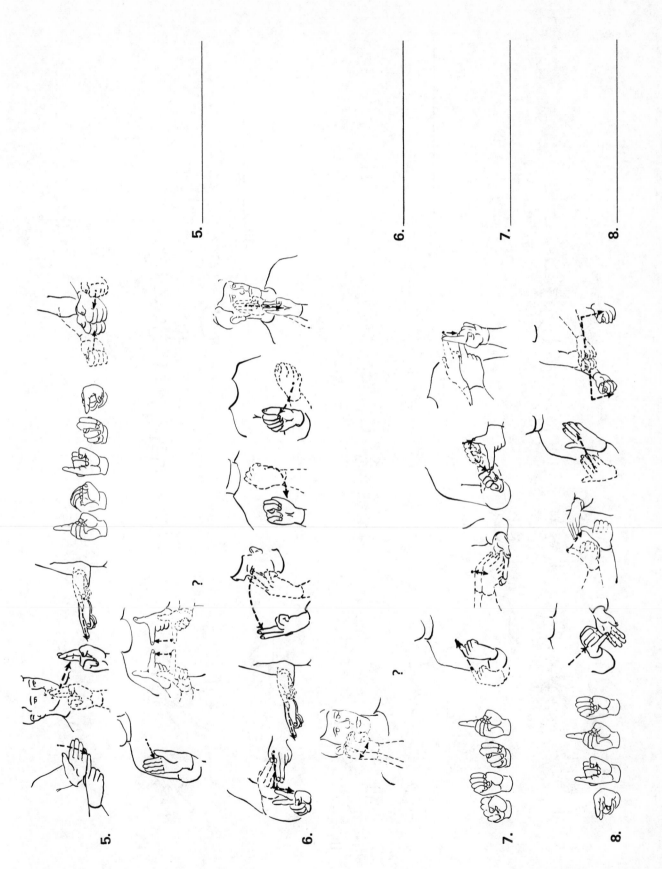

5.

6.

7.

8.

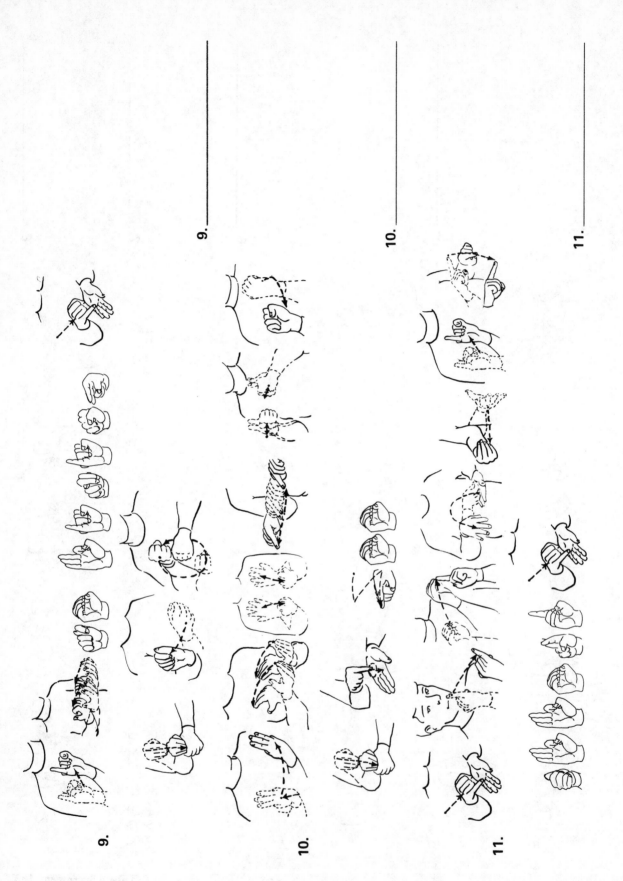

9.

10.

11.

9.

10.

11.

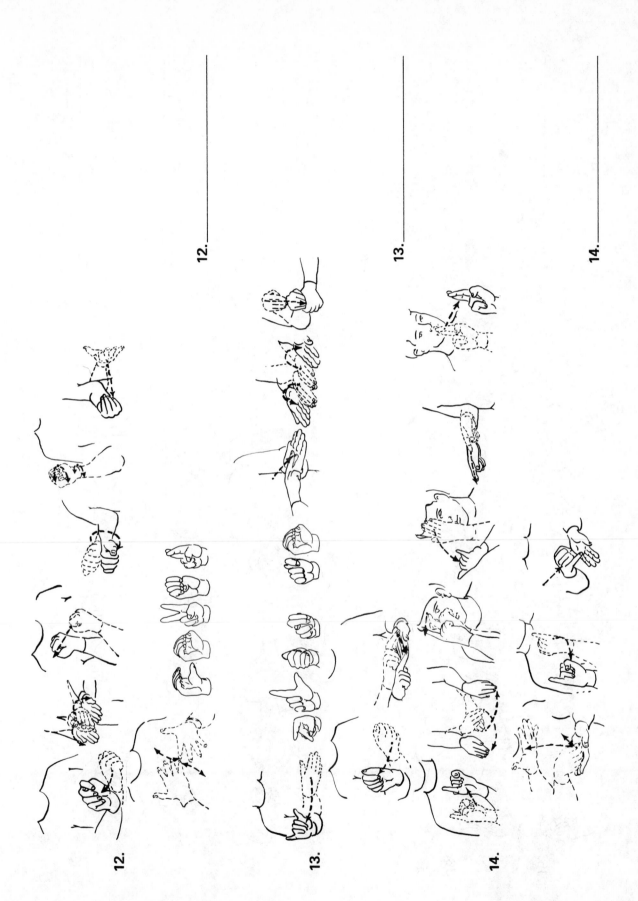

12.

13.

14.

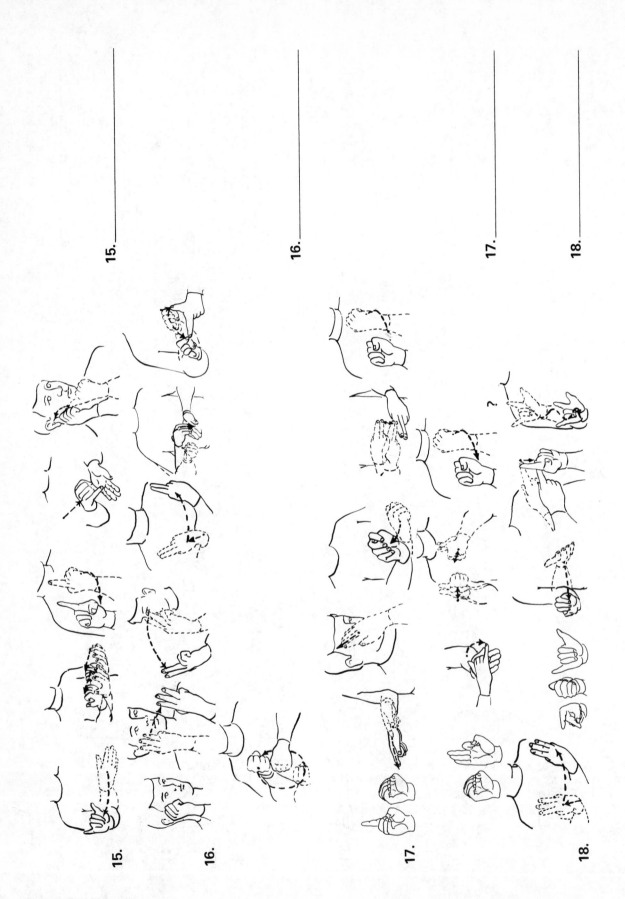

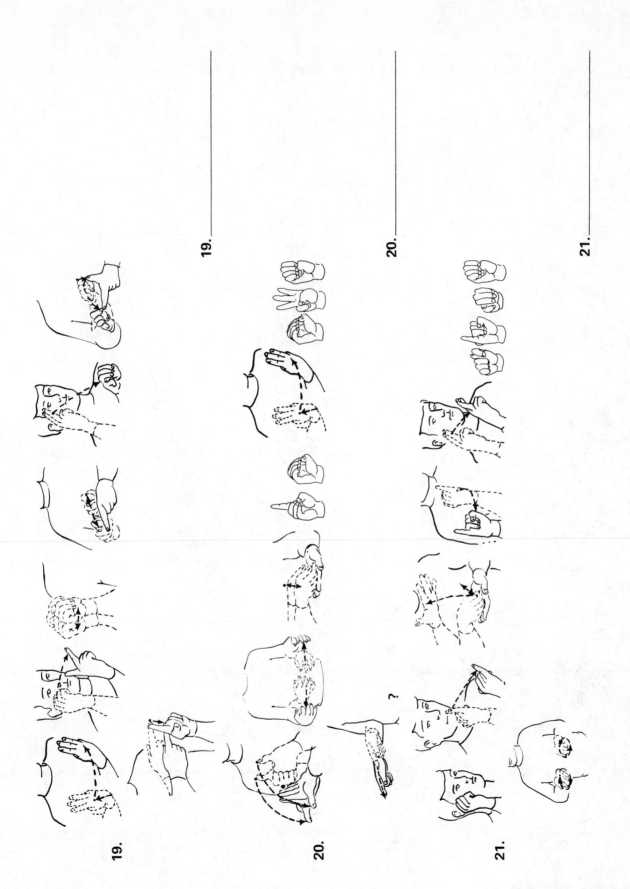

19.

20.

21.

19.

20.

21.

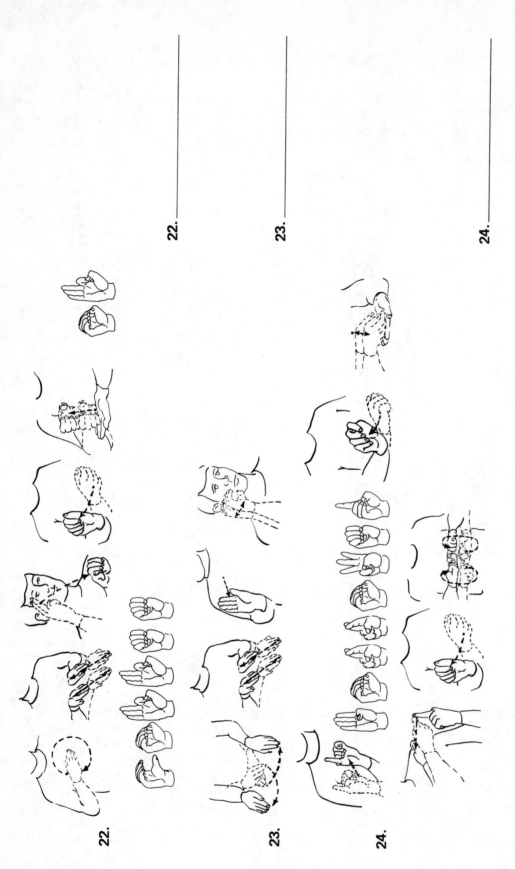

22.

23.

24.

C) Answers for Decoding Part (B), Lesson 17

Underlined words indicate that they should have been fingerspelled.

1. THIS IS YOUR LIFE.
2. WHO IS COMING <u>TO</u> SEE YOU TOMORROW?
3. I THINK I <u>LOST</u> MY NEW CUP.
4. WE NEED <u>TO BUY</u> A NEW MIRROR.
5. WHAT ARE YOU <u>DO-ING</u> WITH YOUR LIFE?
6. HAVE YOU SEEN A BROWN CAT?
7. <u>SEND</u> ME MONEY NEXT MONTH.
8. <u>HIDE</u> IT UNDER MY TABLE.
9. I WANT <u>TO FINISH</u> IT IN A YEAR.

10. WE HAVE MANY DIF-FERENT ANIMALS IN THIS <u>ZOO.</u>
11. IT IS TOO EXPENSIVE AND I CAN'T <u>AFFORD</u> IT.
12. THE BOOK HAS AN ORANGE AND GRAY <u>COVER.</u>
13. THEY <u>PLAN TO</u> RE-OPEN IN A WEEK.
14. I DON'T UNDERSTAND WHY YOU ARE WASTING IT.
15. THEY WANTED IT YESTERDAY.
16. SHE WILL SEE US AGAIN NEXT YEAR.

17. <u>DO</u> YOU KNOW THE NAMES <u>OF</u> THESE ANI-MALS?
18. WE <u>PAY</u> THEM MONTHLY
19. WE SHALL TOILET TRAIN HIM NEXT MONTH.
20. HOW MUCH MONEY <u>DO</u> WE <u>OWE</u> YOU?
21. SHE IS WASTING HER <u>TIME</u> HERE.
22. PLEASE BRING HIM A CUP <u>OF COFFEE.</u>
23. DON'T BRING YOUR CAT.
24. I <u>BORROWED</u> THE MONEY FROM A FRIEND.

lesson eighteen

Signs presented in this lesson are:

ANSWER	SEEM, APPEAR	PURPLE*	UNCLE*
RESPOND	BUY, PURCHASE	FAT	AUNT*
REASON*	TREE*	BLAME	LONG (time)
VISIT	FOREST*	INTERPRET, TRANSLATE	UP
TIRED	SHOE*	FAMILY	DOWN

ANSWER

With only the index fingers extended (remaining fingers and thumbs are contracted) and held vertically, begin the sign by placing the palmar side of the right index finger over the lips. The left hand forms an identical configuration, but is held about six to eight inches in front of, and parallel to, the right hand (the backs of both hands face the viewer); then, both hands are moved forward while turning so that the sign ends with the palmar sides of both index fingers facing the viewer.

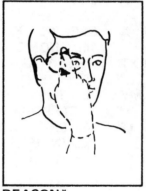

REASON*

The right hand, in the configuration of the letter *R*, is moved toward the signer and positions the *R* fingertips on the right side of the forehead with the back side of the *R* hand facing the viewer. Then, without bending the wrist, the *R* hand makes several small circular movements in a counter-clockwise direction.

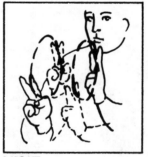

VISIT

Both hands make the letter *V* and are held in a parallel manner in front of the body near the level of the face with the palmar sides of the *V* hands facing each other. Then, the *V* hands are moved alternately to complete a forward circular motion.

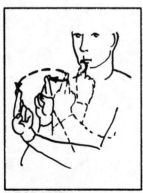

RESPOND

This sign is made similarly to the previous one ("answer"), except that *R* formations are used. The right *R* hand is held over the lips while the left *R* hand is held about six to eight inches in front of the right hand. The backs of both hands, in line, face the viewer; then, both hands are moved forward while turning so that the sign ends with the palmar sides of the *R* hands facing the viewer.

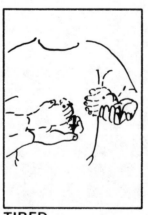

TIRED

Both hands, with their fingers joined and slightly bent, touch the lower portion of the chest with their fingertips. (The hands are placed side-by-side with the back sides of the fingers facing each other.) Then, without separating from the body, the hands are rolled forward so that their fingertips are pointing upward as the sign comes to an end.

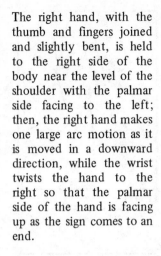

The right hand, with the thumb and fingers joined and slightly bent, is held to the right side of the body near the level of the shoulder with the palmar side facing to the left; then, the right hand makes one large arc motion as it is moved in a downward direction, while the wrist twists the hand to the right so that the palmar side of the hand is facing up as the sign comes to an end.

SEEM, APPEAR

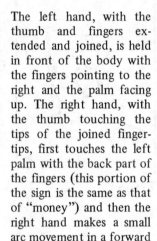

The left hand, with the thumb and fingers extended and joined, is held in front of the body with the fingers pointing to the right and the palm facing up. The right hand, with the thumb touching the tips of the joined fingertips, first touches the left palm with the back part of the fingers (this portion of the sign is the same as that of "money") and then the right hand makes a small arc movement in a forward direction.

BUY, PURCHASE

The left forearm is laid across the signer's body with the fingers of the left hand joined and extended and with the palm facing down. The elbow of the raised right hand rests on the back side of the left hand, with the right hand in the configuration of the letter *T*. Next, with an agitating motion, the wrist turns the hand first in a clockwise direction and then in a counter-clockwise direction. This agitating motion, suggestive of the leaves of a tree, is repeated several times.

TREE*

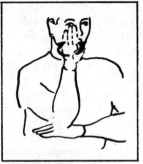

This sign is made similarly to the previous one ("tree"), except that the configuration of the right hand is the fingerspelled letter *F*. Again, the agitating motion of the *F* hand, suggestive of the rustling of the leaves, is repeated several times.

FOREST*

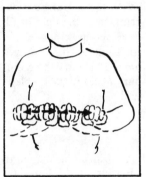

Both hands assume the configuration of the letter *S* and touch as they are placed side-by-side in front of the body with their wrist sides facing down. Then, the *S* hands separate sideways (right and left, respectively) and return again to their former position. This motion is repeated several times.

SHOE*

The right hand, in the configuration of the letter *P*, is held in front and to the right side of the body near the level of the right shoulder; next, the *P* hand performs an agitating motion first to the right and then, to the left along a horizontal plane. This motion is repeated several times.

PURPLE*

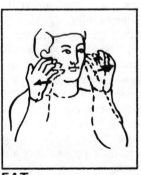
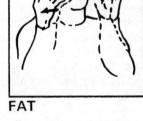

Both hands, with their fingers apart and curved, are placed near each cheek so that their palmar sides face the cheeks. Then, the hands are pulled sideways, suggesting "puffed cheeks."

FAT

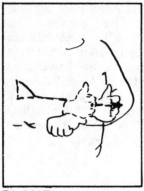

BLAME

The left hand, in an *S* configuration, is held in front of the body with the wrist facing down. The right hand, with the thumb extended and sticking upward (remaining fingers are contracted and clasped to the palm), first is placed on the back side of the left hand so that the thumb is sticking upward and the palmar side is facing the viewer. Next, with the configuration maintained, the right hand grazes the back side of the left hand as it is moved forward about three to four inches past the left hand.

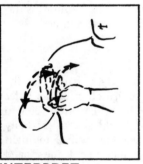

INTERPRET, TRANSLATE

Both hands, in the configuration of the letter *F*, are placed in front of the body so that only their joined thumbs and index fingertips touch (their palmar sides face each other). Next, the *F* hands are rocked alternately up and down in an interchanging action.

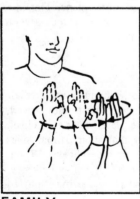

FAMILY

Both hands, in the configuration of the letter *F*, are placed in front of the body so that their joined thumbs and index fingertips are touching (the palmar sides of the *F* hands are facing the viewer). Next, the *F* hands separate, are moved forward to complete semicircles along a horizontal plane and come together again so that now their little fingers are touching and their palmar sides are facing the signer.

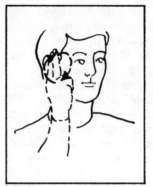

UNCLE*

The right hand, in the configuration of the letter *U*, is placed near the right temple so that the *U* fingers are pointing upward and with their palmar sides toward the face. Then, the *U* hand completes several small, circular movements in a clockwise direction.

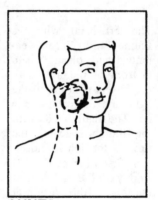

AUNT*

The right hand, in the configuration of the letter *A*, is held near the right cheek with the back side of the *A* hand facing to the right. Next, the *A* hand completes several small, circular movements in a clockwise direction over the cheek.

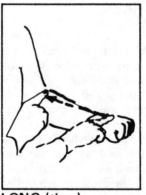

LONG (time)

The left forearm is bent at the elbow and extended in front of the body with the hand in a fist position with the wrist facing down. The right hand, with only the index finger extended (remaining fingers and thumb are contracted), touches the back side of the left hand with its index fingertip; then, the right index finger grazes the left hand and forearm as the hand is moved toward the left elbow.

NOTE: This sign refers to "long time"; it does not pertain to "long" in the sense of linear measurement.

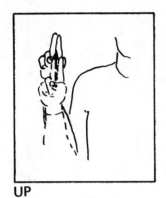

The right hand, in the configuration of the letter *U*, is placed to the right side of the body near the level of the right shoulder with the palmar side facing the viewer. Next, the *U* hand is moved straight up.

UP

The right hand, with the thumb and fingers extended and joined, is held to the right side of the body near the level of the right shoulder with the hand positioned so that the fingers are pointing downward, at an oblique angle. Then, the forearm and hand move downward at an oblique angle.

DOWN

A) Exercises in Encoding

Encode the following material using signs and fingerspelling. Use fingerspelling for all underlined words.

1. I DON'T NEED A REASON <u>TO</u> BUY IT.
2. HOW OFTEN <u>DO</u> YOU VISIT YOUR FAMILY?
3. MY UNCLE IS A VERY KIND PERSON.
4. WHY ARE YOU BLAMING YOUR AUNT FOR IT?
5. CAN YOU INTERPRET WHAT HE IS SAYING?
6. I WAS FAT THEN.
7. WAS YOUR PURPLE <u>TIE</u> EXPENSIVE?
8. I CAN'T <u>FIND</u> MY <u>LEFT</u> SHOE.
9. WHAT <u>IS</u> THE <u>NAME</u> <u>OF</u> THIS FOREST?
10. HOW MANY TREES <u>DO</u> YOU SEE IN THIS <u>PICTURE</u>?
11. WE ARE NOT SURE, BUT IT APPEARS <u>TO</u> BE <u>SO</u>.
12. FOR SOME REASON, I SEEM <u>TO</u> BE TIRED.
13. HOW <u>DID</u> THEY RESPOND TO YOUR QUESTION?
14. WHY CAN'T SHE ANSWER ME NOW?
15. HE IS ALWAYS BLAMING US FOR SOMETHING. ("Something" is signed as "some" plus "thing.")
16. I AM GOING UP TO MY <u>ROOM</u>.
17. HOW LONG MUST WE <u>WAIT</u> FOR HIS ANSWER? (Note: the sign for "long" is used in the sense of "long time"; not linear measurement.)
18. I SHALL NOT BE WEARING THOSE PURPLE SHOES.
19. THE BOY IS <u>WALKING</u> DOWN THE <u>STAIRS</u>.
20. TELL ME WHAT THE BOY IS <u>DOING</u>.
21. WHEN ARE YOUR AUNT AND UNCLE COMING <u>TO</u> VISIT US?
22. DON'T BLAME ME FOR YOUR MISTAKE.
23. I HAVE NOT SEEN YOUR FAMILY FOR A LONG <u>TIME</u>.

B) Exercises in Decoding

Decode the following illustrated exercises:

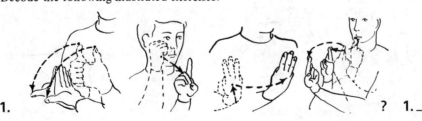

1. ? 1._____

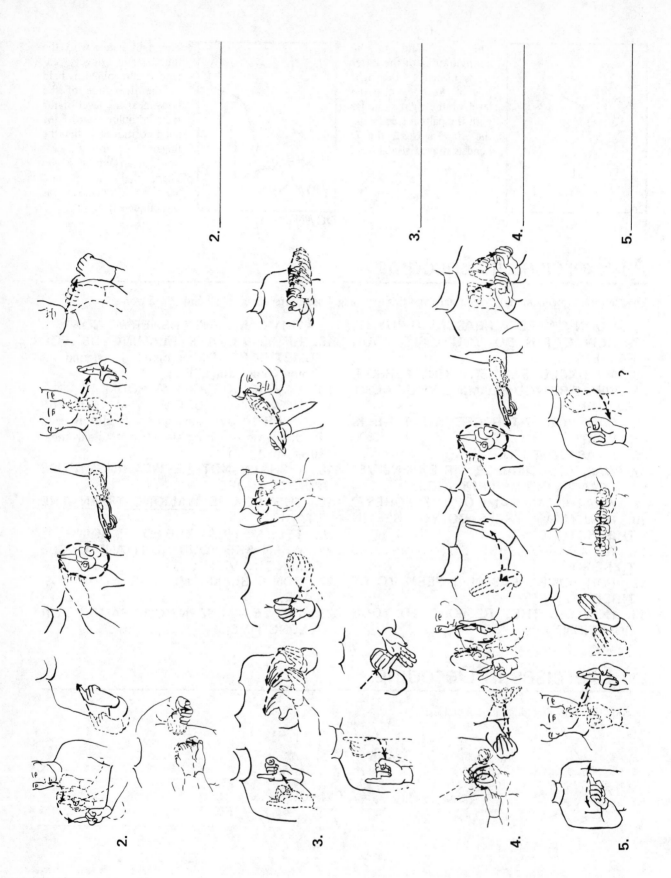

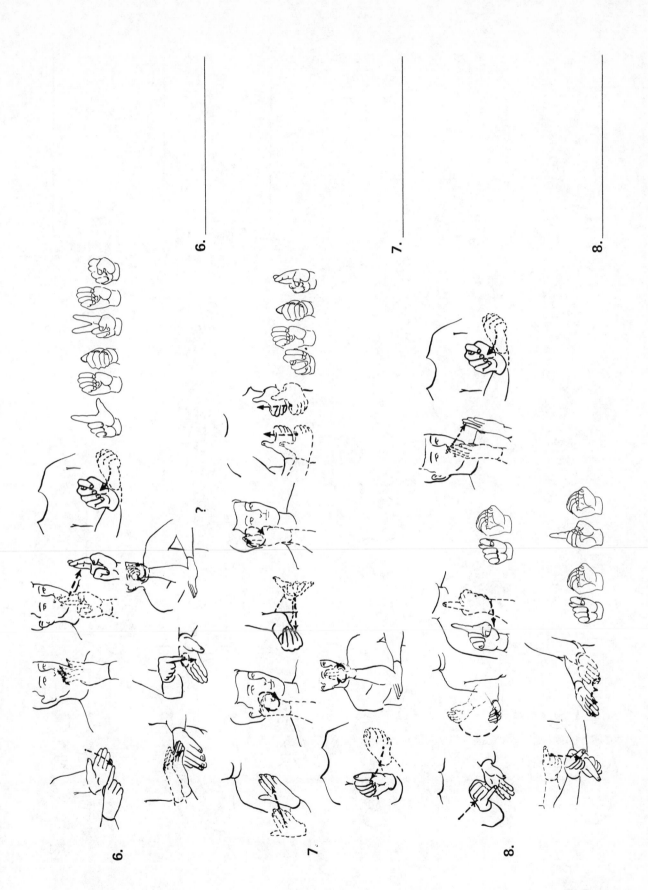

6.

7.

8.

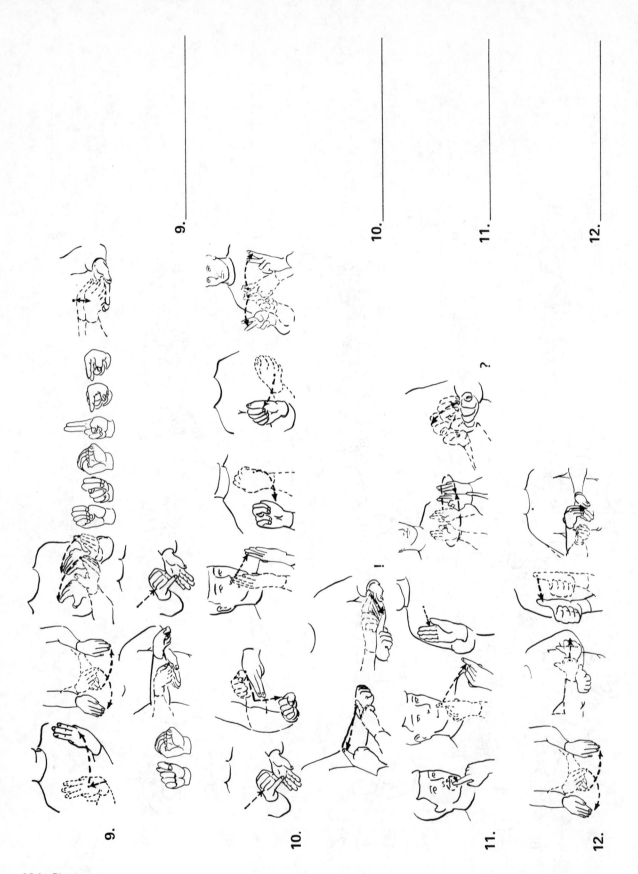

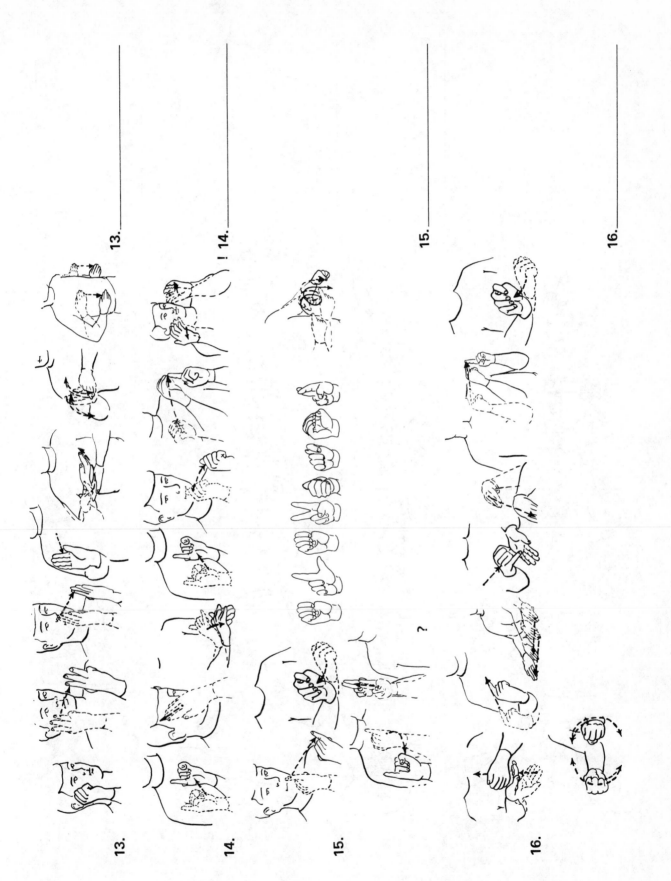

13.

14.

15.

16.

13.

! 14.

15.

16.

17.

18.

19.

20.

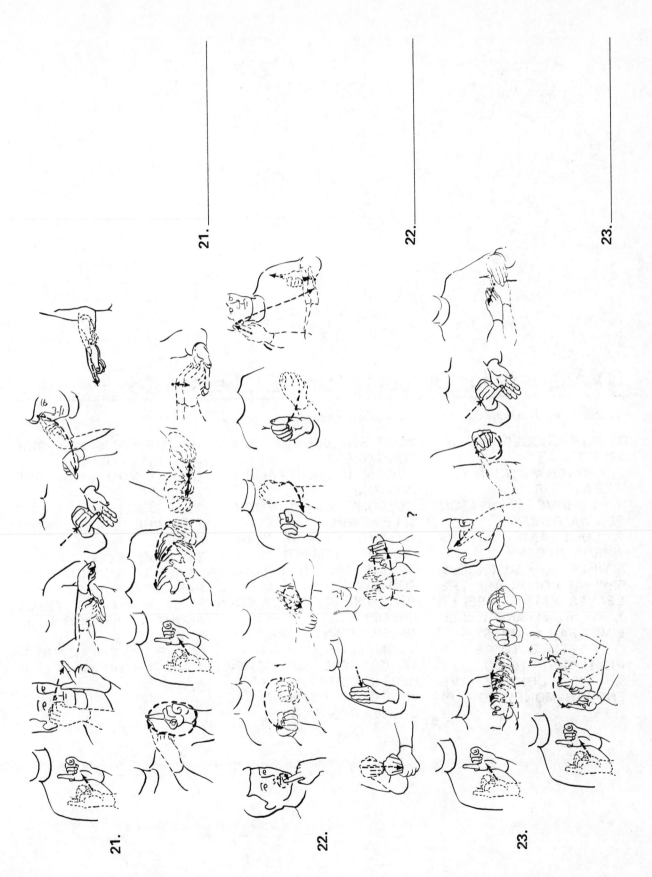

21.

22.

23.

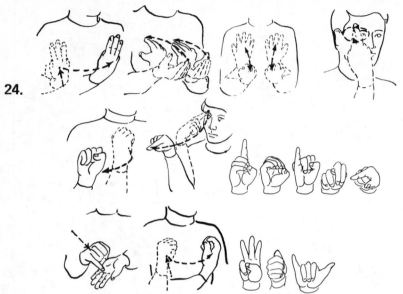

24.

24._____

C) Answers for Decoding Part (B), Lesson 18

Underlined words indicate that they should have been fingerspelled.

1. HOW SHOULD WE RE-SPOND?
2. ANSWER ME WHEN YOU ARE NOT TIRED.
3. I HAVE A REASON FOR WANTING IT
4. COME AND VISIT US WHEN YOU CAN.
5. WHERE ARE MY SHOES?
6. WHAT COLOR ARE THE LEAVES ON THIS TREE?
7. MY AUNT AND UNCLE LIVE NEAR A FOREST.
8. IT SEEMED TO BE THE RIGHT THING TO DO.
9. WE DON'T HAVE ENOUGH MONEY TO BUY IT.

10. IT HAS BEEN A VERY LONG WEEK!
11. WHO IS YOUR FAMILY DOCTOR?
12. DON'T BLAME YOUR-SELF AGAIN.
13. SHE WILL BE YOUR NEW INTERPRETER.
14. I KNOW THAT I AM TOO FAT!
15. IS THE ELEVATOR GO-ING UP?
16. HELP ME CARRY IT DOWN TO THE CAR.
17. IS THERE ANY DEAF-NESS IN YOUR FAMILY?
18. I CAN'T RESPOND BE-CAUSE I DON'T KNOW.

19. PURPLE IS NOT OUR FAVORITE COLOR.
20. DO YOU EVER GET TIRED?
21. I SHALL BUY IT FOR YOU WHEN I HAVE MORE MONEY.
22. WHO ELSE USES A HEARING AID IN YOUR FAMILY?
23. I WANT TO THINK ABOUT IT BEFORE I RE-SPOND.
24. WE HAVE MANY REA-SONS FOR DOING IT OUR WAY.

lesson nineteen

Signs presented in this lesson are:

INCLUDE, INVOLVE	BLUE*	COFFEE*	LANGUAGE
GREEN*	WINDOW	TEA*	GRAMMAR
MISUNDERSTAND	HOME	DEVELOP	COUSIN*
AGREE	NIECE*	HARD	RED*
DRINK	NEPHEW*	SENTENCE	MAKE*

INCLUDE, INVOLVE

The left hand, in the configuration of the letter *O*, is held in front of the body with the back side of the hand facing to the left. The right hand, with the thumb and fingers extended and apart, is positioned in front and slightly to the right side of the body at shoulder level with the palmar side of the hand facing the viewer; then, the right hand makes a wide semi-circular sweep to the right, ending with the thumb flexed inward to touch the extended and joined fingertips. The hand is then moved downward and the joined fingertips are placed inside the left *O* hand. The last motion in this sign is the same movement used to execute the sign for "in" or "inside."

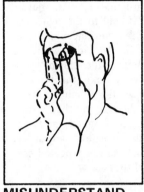

MISUNDERSTAND

The right hand, in the configuration of the letter *V*, is moved toward the forehead so that contact is made between the forehead and the tip of the index finger. The palmar side of the *V* fingers is facing left. Next, the *V* hand is rotated horizontally and in a counterclockwise direction so that now the middle finger of the *V* hand is touching the forehead and the palmar side of the hand is facing right.

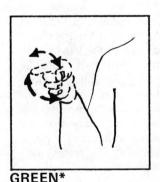

GREEN*

The right hand, in the configuration of the letter *G*, is held to the right side of the body near the level of the right shoulder; then, the forearm turns the *G* hand so that it makes several quick motions, first in a clockwise direction and then, in a counterclockwise direction.

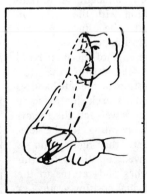

AGREE

This sign is made by combining two other signs: "think" (lesson 13) and "same" (lesson 6). The right index fingertip touches the forehead and then the right hand is moved forward and downward and places the side of its index finger next to the left index finger so that both fingers are side-by-side and touching with their palmar sides facing down. The sign intends to suggest the idea that the signer "is of the same mind."

DRINK

The right hand, in the configuration of the letter *C*, is held near the lips so that the back of the thumb is near the lips and with the palmar side of the *C* hand facing left. Next, the *C* hand is tilted toward the signer, suggesting that a liquid is being imbibed.

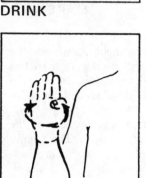

BLUE*

The right hand, in the configuration of the letter *B*, is held to the right side of the body near the level of the shoulder with the palmar side facing the viewer. Next, the forearm causes the *B* hand to twist to the left and then return to its original position. This twisting motion is quick and is repeated several times.

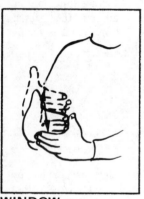

WINDOW

The left hand, with the thumb extended and pointing upward (remaining fingers are extended and joined), is placed in front of the body with the back side of the hand facing the viewer and the fingertips pointing to the right. The right hand forms an identical configuration with the exception that the fingertips are pointing to the left; then the edge of the right hand is placed on the top portion of the left hand so that its back side is facing the viewer and the fingers are pointing to the left; next, the right hand is moved up three to four inches and returns to the original position again.

NOTE: This sign may be imitative, perhaps, of upper and lower window sashes.

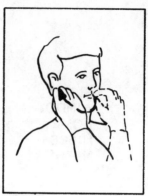

HOME

The right hand, with the thumb flexed inward to touch the joined and curved fingertips, first is placed about an inch in front of the mouth with the joined thumb and fingertips pointing to the mouth. Next, with the configuration maintained, the hand is moved to the right, in the direction of the ear.

NOTE: This sign may intend to suggest, perhaps, a place to eat and sleep.

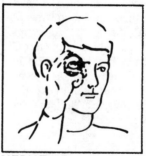

NIECE*

The right hand, in the configuration of the letter *N*, is placed near the right cheek so that the *N* fingertips are pointing at the cheek; next, the right *N* hand is moved to complete several small circles over the cheek.

NEPHEW*

The right hand, in the configuration of the letter *N*, is placed near the right temple so that the *N* fingertips are pointing at the temple; then, the *N* hand is moved to complete several small circles over the temple.

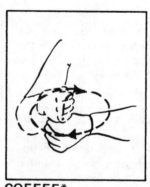

COFFEE*

With both hands in the configuration of the letter *S*, the right hand is placed on top of the left hand so that their back sides are facing in opposite directions (sideways). The right hand then completes several large clockwise circles along a horizontal plane, imitative of grinding coffee beans.

MASS AULD INC.
1296 WORCESTER ROAD
FRAMINGHAM CTR MASS 01701

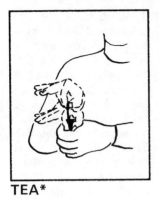

TEA*

The left hand assumes the configuration of the letter *O* and is held in front of the body while the right hand first makes the letter *F*, inserts part of the *F* hand (its thumb and index finger) into the left *O* hand and completes several clockwise motions.
NOTE: This sign is imitative of a tea bag being swirled about in a cup.

SENTENCE

Both hands, each with its thumb and index finger curved and touching (remaining fingers are apart and slightly curved), are positioned in front of the body so that the hands are in contact at the tips of their joined index fingers and thumbs and with their palmar sides facing each other. Next, the hands flutter as they are pulled apart to the right and left, respectively.

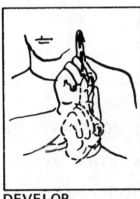

DEVELOP

The left hand, with the thumb and fingers extended and joined, is held in front and slightly to the left side of the body with the fingers pointing upward and the palmar side facing the viewer. The right hand makes the letter *D*, which is laid against the left palm so that the right index finger is pointing upward and the back side is facing right; then, the right *D* hand slides upward past the left fingertips.

LANGUAGE

This sign is made similarly to the previous one ("sentence"), except that the hands are in the formation of the letter *L*, touch their thumbs (the palmar sides of the *L* hands are facing the viewer), and then flutter as the hands are pulled apart to the right and left, respectively.

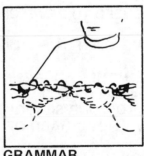

GRAMMAR

This sign is made similarly to the previous ones ("sentence" and "language"), except that the hands are in the formation of the letter *G*, touch their thumbs and fingertips, and then flutter as the *G* hands are pulled apart to the right and left, respectively.

HARD

The left hand, in the configuration of the letter *V*, but with the *V* fingers crooked (remaining fingers and thumb are contracted), is held in front of the body so that the crooked *V* fingertips are pointing to the signer. The right hand forms an identical configuration and is held about three to four inches above the left hand; then, with the configuration maintained, the right hand is moved straight down and strikes the top portion of the left *V* hand.

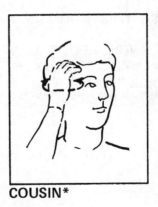

COUSIN*

The right hand, in the configuration of the letter *C*, is held near the signer's temple so that the palmar side is facing the head; then, the forearm twists the *C* hand by moving it slightly to the right and then to the left along a horizontal plane. This motion is repeated several times.

Lesson Nineteen 203

The right hand, with only the index finger extended (remaining fingers and thumb are contracted), is positioned in front of the mouth with the fingertip pointing to the mouth and the back side of the hand facing the viewer. Next, with the hand remaining stationary, the index fingertip brushes the lips as it moves downward. The motion is repeated several times.

RED*

Both hands, in the configuration of the letter *S*, are positioned one on top of the other so that their back sides are facing in opposite directions (sideways). Next, both hands twist. The left hand twists to the right and the right hand twists to the left. This motion is repeated several times.

NOTE: The sign for "fix" is done similarly, except that the hands are in the configuration of the letter *F*.

MAKE*

A) Exercises in Encoding

Encode the following material using signs and fingerspelling. Use fingerspelling for all underlined words.

1. I DON'T WANT <u>TO</u> MISUNDERSTAND YOU AGAIN.
2. WHAT <u>DOES</u> THIS <u>COURSE</u> INCLUDE?
3. <u>DO</u> YOU WANT ME <u>TO</u> MAKE TEA OR COFFEE?
4. I AGREE THAT WE NEED <u>TO</u> DEVELOP A BETTER <u>PROGRAM</u>.
5. CAN YOU HELP ME OPEN THE WINDOW?
6. WHAT IS YOUR HOME ADDRESS? ("Address" is signed similarly to "live.")
7. OUR NIECE GOES TO YOUR SCHOOL.
8. MY NEPHEW IS NOT HARD-OF-HEARING.
9. <u>DOES</u> YOUR FAMILY HAVE BLUE <u>CROSS</u> <u>INSURANCE</u>?
10. WOULD YOU <u>USE</u> THIS WORD IN A SENTENCE?
11. WHAT <u>DO</u> YOU KNOW ABOUT LANGUAGE DEVELOPMENT? ("Development" is signed as "develop" plus "ment.")
12. I THINK YOU NEED MORE HELP WITH YOUR GRAMMAR.
13. THE DOCTOR THINKS THAT MY BABY COUSIN IS DEAF.
14. WE AGREE THAT YOU SHOULD <u>PAINT</u> IT RED.
15. THIS <u>BREAD</u> IS TOO HARD <u>TO</u> EAT.
16. HOW <u>DOES</u> A DEAF PERSON LEARN LANGUAGE?
17. WE SHALL HELP YOU MAKE A BETTER SENTENCE.
18. <u>ASK</u> YOUR MOTHER <u>TO</u> HELP YOU PRACTICE THESE SENTENCES AT HOME.
19. I AM MAKING SOMETHING FOR MY NIECE.
20. WHO <u>BROKE</u> YOUR CAR WINDOW?
21. IT IS A GOOD IDEA, BUT IT NEEDS <u>TO</u> BE DEVELOPED MORE.
22. ARE YOU DRINKING TEA OR COFFEE?
23. <u>TRY</u> NOT <u>TO</u> MISUNDERSTAND WHAT I AM TELLING YOU.

B) Exercises in Decoding

Decode the following illustrated exercises:

1. _____

2. _____

3. _____

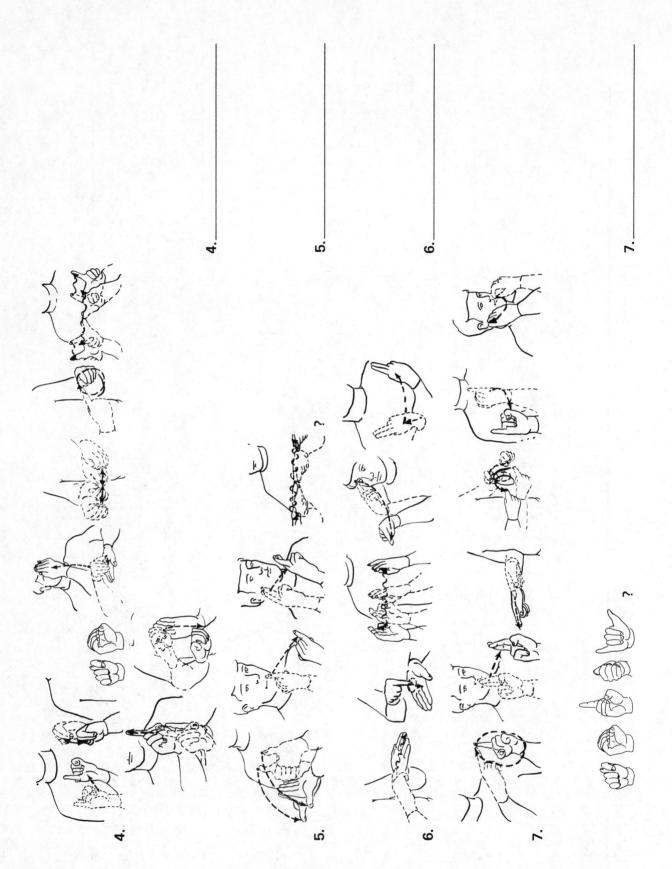

4.

5.

6.

7.

4.

5.

6.

7.

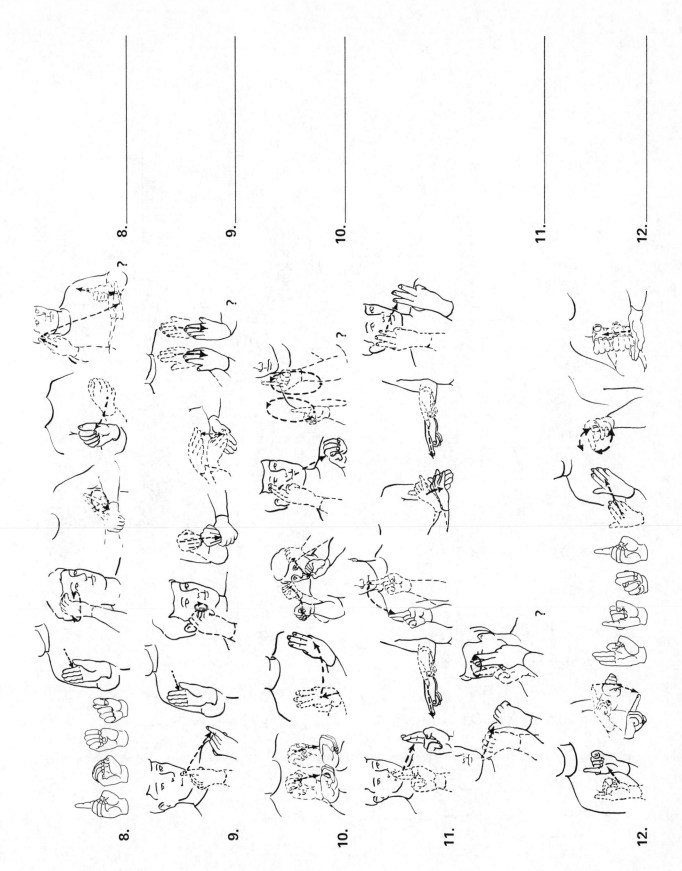

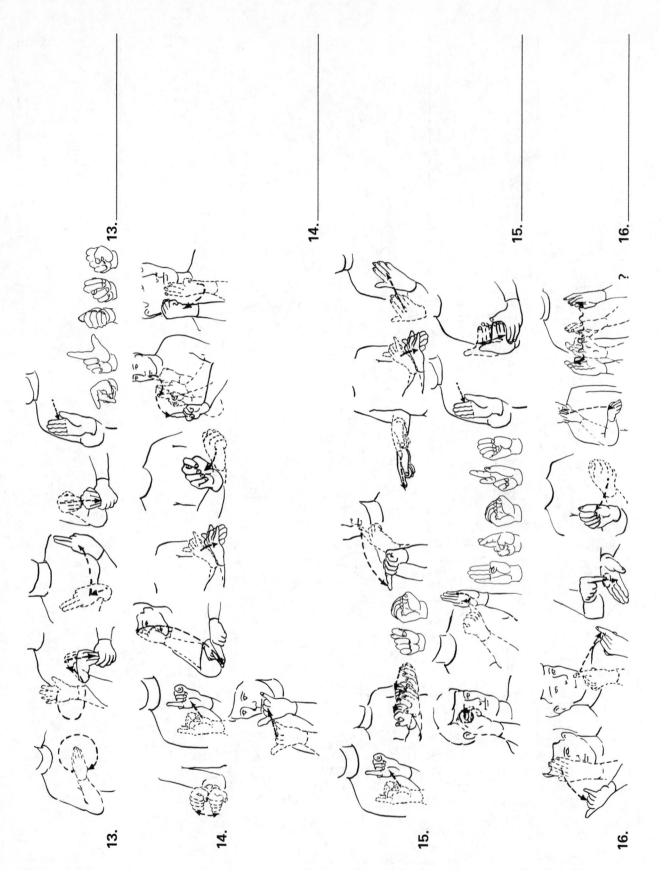

13.

14.

15.

16.

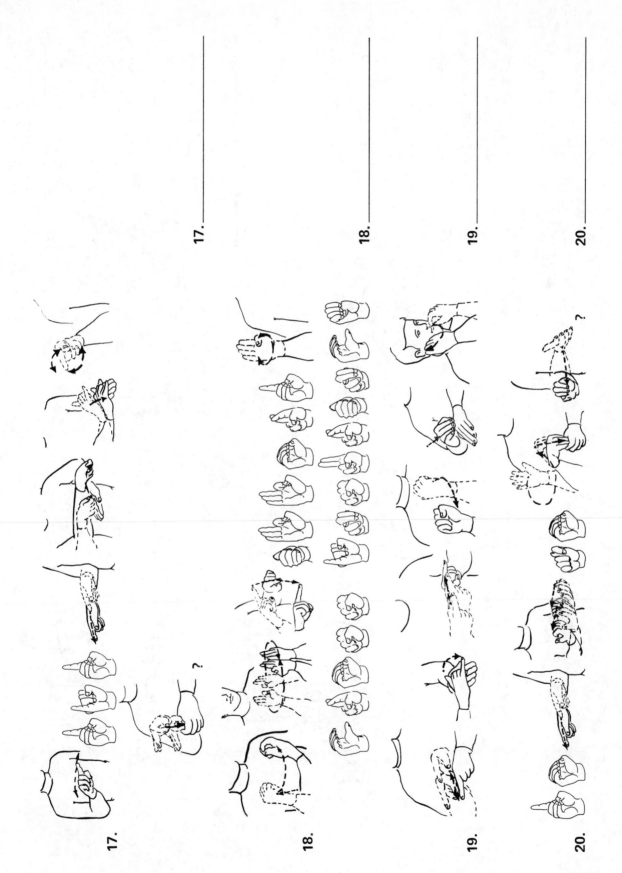

17.

18.

19.

20.

17.

18.

19.

20.

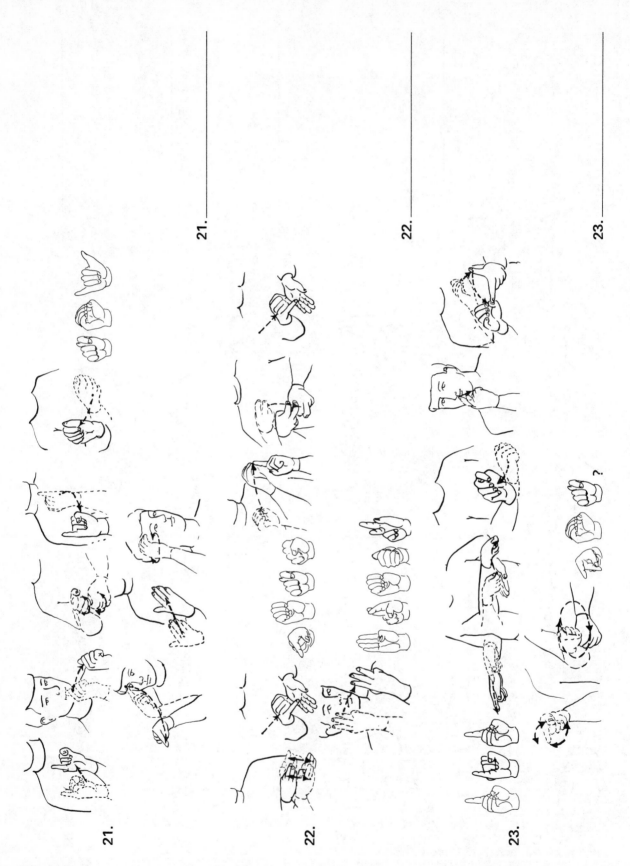

21.

22.

23.

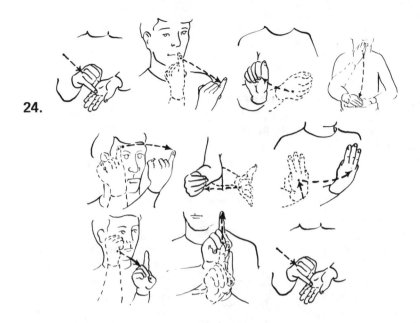

24.

24. _____

C) Answers for Decoding Part (B), Lesson 19

Underlined words indicate that they should have been fingerspelled.

1. IS THIS A DIFFICULT SENTENCE FOR YOU?
2. DO YOU WANT <u>SUGAR</u> IN YOUR TEA?
3. PLEASE BRING HER A CUP <u>OF</u> COFFEE.
4. I NEED <u>TO</u> LEARN MORE <u>ABOUT</u> LANGUAGE DEVELOPMENT.
5. HOW IS HER GRAMMAR?
6. WRITE THIS SENTENCE FOR US.
7. WHEN ARE YOU COMING HOME <u>TODAY</u>?
8. <u>DOES</u> YOUR COUSIN USE A HEARING AID?
9. IS YOUR NIECE IN SCHOOL NOW?

10. MAY WE TEACH HIM SIGN LANGUAGE?
11. ARE YOU SURE THAT YOU WILL NOT MISUNDERSTAND?
12. I CAN'T <u>FIND</u> MY GREEN CUP.
13. PLEASE INCLUDE US IN YOUR <u>PLANS</u>.
14. YES, I AGREE THAT THE ANSWER WAS WRONG.
15. I WANT <u>TO</u> TELL YOU THAT MY NEPHEW JUST <u>BROKE</u> YOUR WINDOW.
16. WHY IS THIS A BAD SENTENCE?
17. WHERE <u>DID</u> YOU BUY THAT GREEN TEA?

18. OUR FAMILY CAN'T <u>AFFORD</u> BLUE <u>CROSS</u> <u>INSURANCE</u>.
19. PRACTICE THESE WORDS AT HOME.
20. <u>DO</u> YOU WANT <u>TO</u> INVOLVE THEM?
21. I AM MAKING A <u>TOY</u> FOR MY COUSIN.
22. IF IT <u>GETS</u> TOO HARD, IT WILL <u>BREAK</u>.
23. <u>DID</u> YOU BUY THE RED OR GREEN COFFEE <u>POT</u>?
24. IT IS A GOOD IDEA AND WE SHOULD DEVELOP IT.

lesson twenty

Signs presented in this lesson are:

PROBLEM	**PEPPER***	**CAREFUL***	**WISH**
BREATHE*	**SIT**	**ATTEMPT**	**DESIRE**
HURRY	**CHAIR**	**EFFORT**	**PENCIL**
SOMEONE	**COMPARE***	**TRY**	**EVALUATE***
SALT*	**DOUBT***	**OPINION**	**LISTEN**

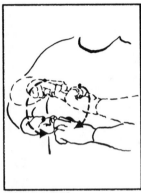

PROBLEM

Both hands, each in the configuration of the letter *V*, but with the *V* fingers crooked (remaining fingers and thumb are contracted), are positioned in front of the body at mid-chest level with their knuckles touching. (The right hand is held with its back side facing up, while the left hand has its back side facing down.) Next, with the configuration preserved, the hands reverse this position of their back sides 180 degrees (but are still touching their knuckles) as both hands are moved downward.

HURRY

Both hands assume the configuration of the letter *H* and are placed in a parallel manner in front of the body with their palmar sides facing each other. Next, with the configuration maintained, the *H* hands make a jagged line as they are moved forward.

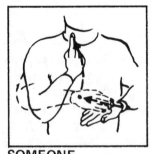

SOMEONE

This sign is made by combining the signs "some" (lesson 11) and "one." The sign for "one" is made by holding your index finger straight up (remaining fingers and thumb are contracted) and with the palmar side of the finger facing the signer.

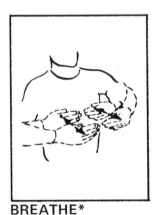

BREATHE*

Both hands, with their thumbs and fingers extended and joined, are held side-by-side approximately one to two inches in front of the signer's chest so that their fingertips point to each other and their palmar sides are facing the signer. Then, the hands are moved simultaneously two to three inches away from the signer's chest and return to their original position. This motion is repeated several times, suggesting the inhalation and exhalation phases of breathing.

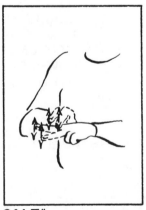

SALT*

Both hands, in the configuration of the letter *V*, are positioned one over the other with the palmar sides of the *V* fingers facing down. The left *V* fingertips are pointing to the right, while the right *V* fingertips are pointing to the viewer; then, with the hands remaining stationary, the *V* fingers of both hands are wiggled up and down several times.

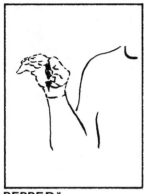

PEPPER*

The right hand, with the index finger and thumb forming a loop while the remaining fingers are apart and slightly bent, is held to the right side of the body near the level of the shoulder with the back side facing up and the wrist half flexed. Next, the right hand makes several quick up and down (vertical) movements.

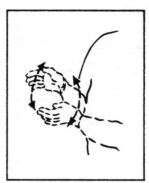

COMPARE*

Both hands, each with its thumb and fingers joined and slightly cupped, are held apart and at an angle (the right hand is higher than the left hand) in front of the body with their palmar sides facing each other. Next, a small arc is formed as the hands alternately are moved up and down several times.

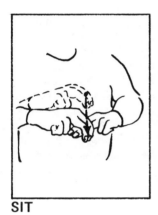

SIT

The left hand assumes the configuration of the letter H and is held in front of the body with the palmar side facing down and the H fingertips pointing to the viewer at an angle. The right hand, also in an H configuration, but with the H fingers bent so that the knuckles are toward the viewer, is moved down and hooks over the extended fingers of the left H hand. The sign ends with the back sides of both H hands facing up.

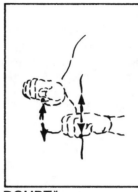

DOUBT*

Both hands assume the configuration of the letter A and are held in front of the body approximately four to six inches apart, and with the right hand held three to four inches higher than the left one. Both A hands have their wrists facing down. Next, the A hands alternately perform several up and down movements.

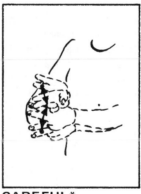

CAREFUL*

The left hand, in the configuration of the letter V, is placed in front of the body so that the V fingertips are pointing to the viewer at an angle with the palmar side of the V fingers facing right. The right hand, in a similar configuration, but with the palmar side of the V fingers facing left, is held about two inches above the left hand. Next, both hands move toward each other (the left hand is moved upward, while the right hand is moved in a downward direction) so that the top part of the left hand makes contact with the bottom portion of the right hand near the wrist area. The hands then separate and repeat the motion.

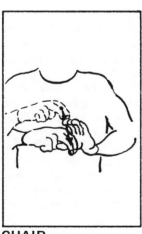

CHAIR

The left hand, in the configuration of the letter C, is held in front of the body with the palmar side of the thumb facing up while the palmar surface of the C hand is facing to the right. The right hand, in the configuration of the letter H, but with the H fingers bent so that the knuckles are toward the viewer, is moved down and hooks over the extended left thumb.

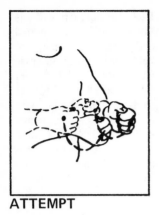

ATTEMPT

Both hands, in the configuration of the letter *A*, are placed side-by-side near the signer's chest so that the knuckles face each other. Next, both *A* hands execute an arc motion as they dip down while moving forward and come up again. Note that the *A* hands maintain both the configuration and the parallelism throughout.

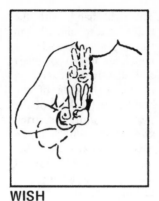

WISH

The right hand, in the configuration of the letter *W*, is held against the signer's chest with the *W* fingertips pointing up, while their palmar sides are facing to the left. Next, the right *W* hand grazes the body as it is moved straight down.

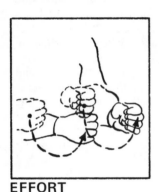

EFFORT

This sign is made similarly to the previous one ("attempt"), except that the initial configuration of both hands is the letter *E* instead of the letter *A*.

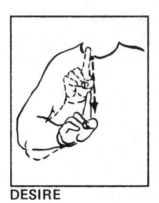

DESIRE

This sign is made similarly to the previous one ("wish"), except that the letter *D* is used instead of *W*. The right *D* hand is held against the chest with the index finger pointing upward and the palmar side facing to the left. Next, the right *D* hand is moved in a downward direction.

TRY

This sign is made similarly to the two previous signs ("attempt" and "effort"), except that the initial configuration of both hands is the letter *T* instead of the letters *A* ("attempt") and *E* ("effort").

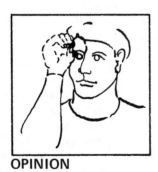

OPINION

The right hand, in the configuration of the letter *O*, is placed near the right side of the forehead so that the back side is facing to the right. Next, the *O* hand is moved to complete a small circle in a counterclockwise direction over the right forehead.

PENCIL

The left hand, with the thumb and fingers extended and joined, is held in front of the body with the palm facing up and the fingers pointing to the right. The joined thumb and index finger (remaining fingers are contracted and clasped to the palm) of the right hand first touch the lips and then the left palm; lastly, the right hand makes a wavy line across the left palm in the direction of the fingertips. This latter motion is the same movement used to execute the sign for "write."

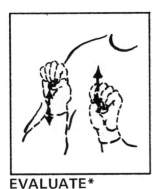

Both hands, each in the configuration of the letter *E*, are held apart at an angle (one higher than the other) in front of the body with their back sides facing the signer. Next, the *E* hands alternately are moved up and down several times.

EVALUATE*

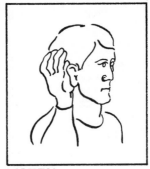

The right hand is cupped and placed behind the right ear so that the palmar side of the cupped hand is facing the viewer. NOTE: This sign may be imitative, perhaps, of anticipating sound.

LISTEN

A) Exercises in Encoding

Encode the following material using signs and fingerspelling. Use fingerspelling for all underlined words.

1. FIRST, TEACH THE BOY HOW <u>TO</u> BREATHE CORRECTLY.
2. <u>DO</u> YOU WANT <u>TO</u> TELL ME YOUR PROBLEM?
3. PLEASE HURRY BECAUSE WE ARE <u>LATE</u>.
4. SOMEONE SHOULD EVALUATE HIS HEARING AID.
5. I <u>PUT</u> TOO MUCH SALT AND PEPPER IN THE FOOD.
6. HOW SHOULD WE COMPARE THEM?
7. I DOUBT <u>IF</u> HER PROBLEM IS REAL.
8. THE BOY IS <u>STANDING</u> ON THE RED CHAIR.
9. PLEASE DRIVE CAREFULLY.
10. I SHALL ATTEMPT <u>TO</u> <u>FINISH</u> IT BY NEXT MONTH.
11. <u>LET</u> US TRY <u>TO</u> EVALUATE HIM AGAIN.
12. LISTEN CAREFULLY AND TELL ME WHAT I <u>SAID</u>.
13. I DON'T THINK YOU ARE LISTENING.
14. I WISH <u>TO</u> KNOW WHY I AM DEAF.
15. <u>DID</u> YOU BRING YOUR PENCIL <u>TO-DAY</u>?
16. IT IS OUR OPINION THAT YOU NEED <u>TO</u> BUY A HEARING AID.
17. WHY IS SHE <u>AFRAID</u> <u>TO</u> ATTEMPT IT?
18. <u>DO</u> THEY HAVE ANY <u>GREAT</u> DESIRES IN LIFE?
19. WE NEED YOUR HELP <u>TO</u> <u>SOLVE</u> THIS PROBLEM.
20. YOU ARE NOT COMPARING THEM VERY CAREFULLY.
21. NOW, WE WANT <u>TO</u> EVALUATE YOUR <u>SPEECH</u>.
22. IT IS MY DOCTOR'S OPINION THAT I AM A SLOW LEARNER. ("Learner" is signed as "learn" plus "er.")
23. WHAT COLOR IS YOUR PENCIL?
24. TRY NOT <u>TO</u> BREATHE TOO SLOWLY.

B) Exercises in Decoding

Decode the following illustrated exercises:

1.

1. _____

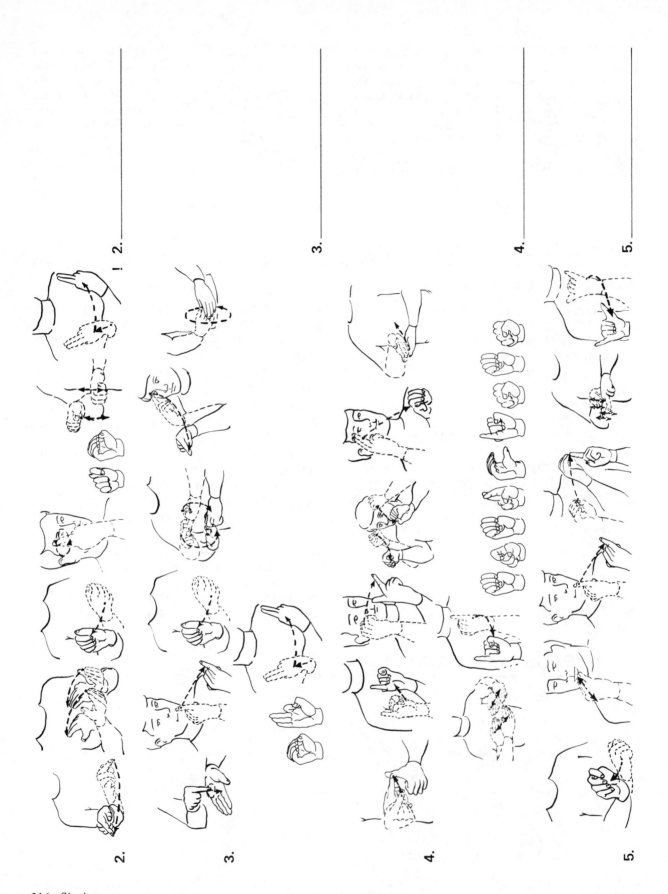

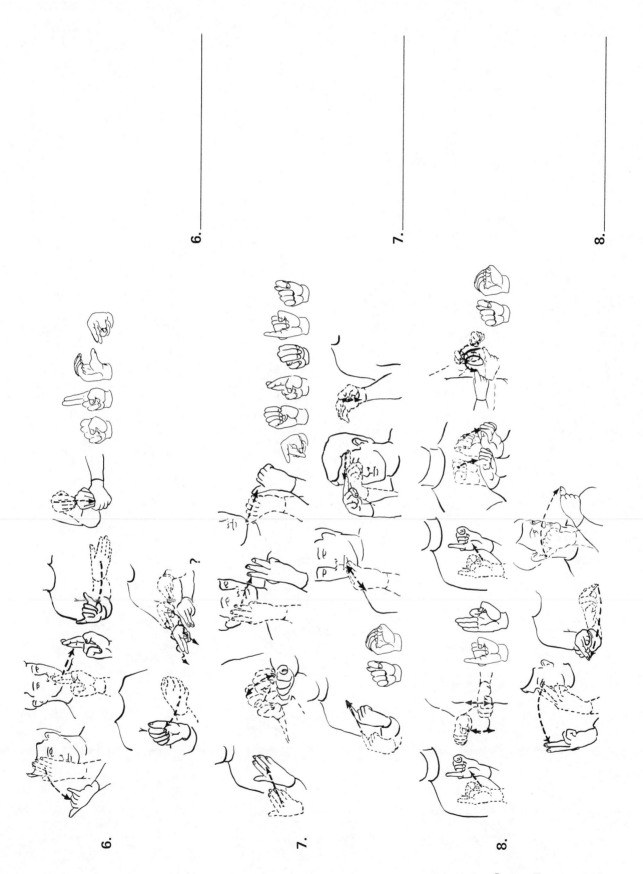

6.

7.

8.

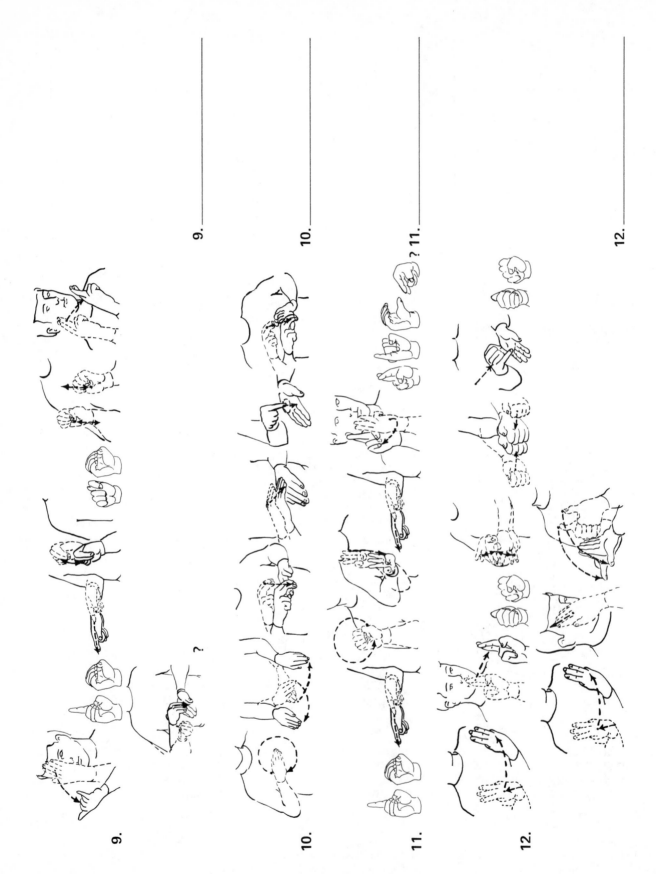

13.

14.

15.

16.

13.

14.

15.

16.

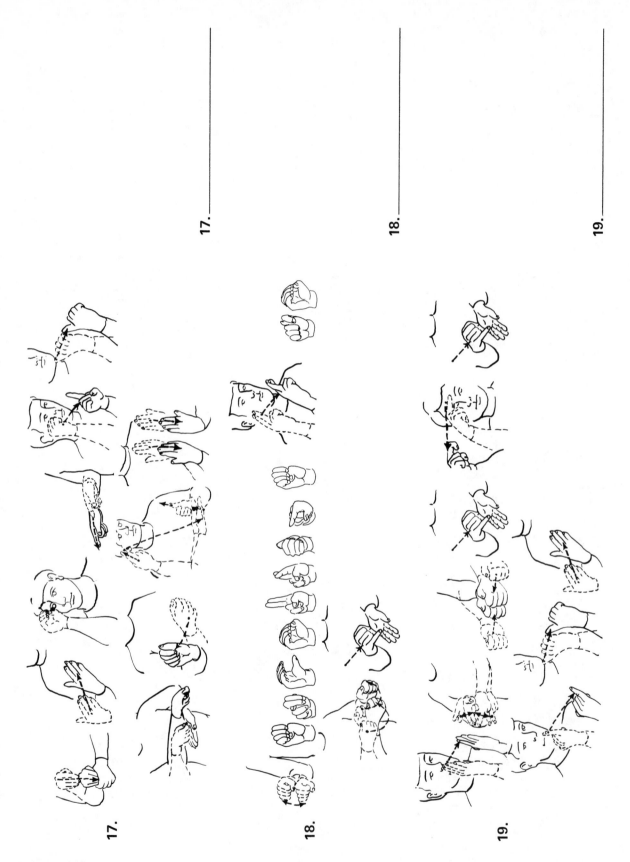

17.

18.

19.

20.

21.

22.

20.

21.

22.

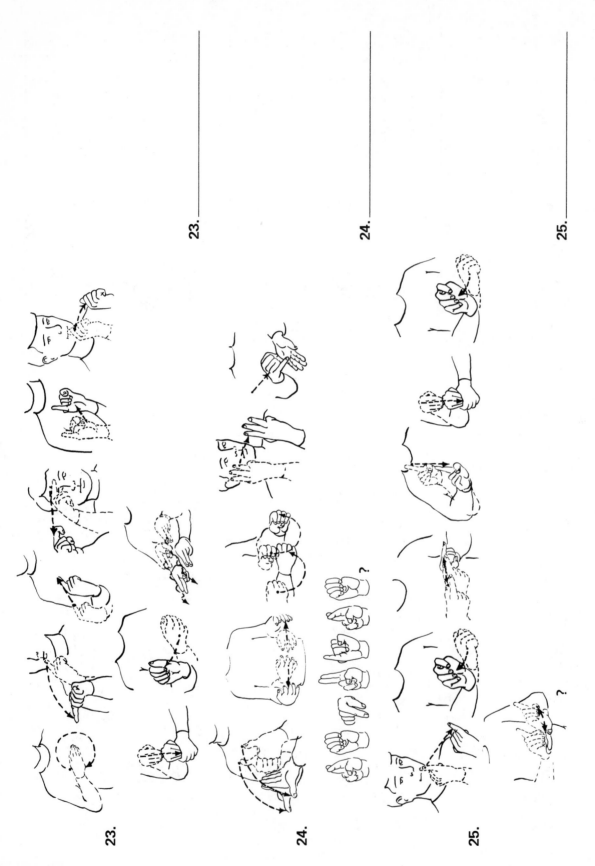

23.

24.

25.

C) Answers for Decoding Part (B), Lesson 20

Underlined words indicate that they should have been fingerspelled.

1. PLEASE LISTEN FOR YOUR <u>SOUND</u>.
2. YOU (plural) HAVE A REASON <u>TO</u> DOUBT US!
3. THIS IS A PROBLEM FOR ALL <u>OF</u> US.
4. FIRST, I SHALL TEACH HIM SOME BEATHING <u>EXERCISES</u>.
5. THE FOOD IS TOO SALTY.
6. WHY ARE THEY IN <u>SUCH</u> A HURRY?
7. MY DOCTOR WILL NOT <u>PERMIT</u> ME <u>TO</u> EAT BLACK PEPPER.
8. I DOUBT <u>IF</u> I CAN COME <u>TO</u> SEE YOU (plural) TOMORROW.
9. WHY <u>DO</u> YOU (singular) NEED <u>TO</u> EVALUATE HER AGAIN?
10. PLEASE DON'T SIT ON THIS CHAIR.
11. <u>DO</u> YOU (singular) EVER WISH YOU WERE <u>RICH</u>?
12. WE ARE <u>AS</u> CAREFUL WITH IT <u>AS</u> WE KNOW HOW.
13. SOMEONE SHOULD TELL HIS FATHER.
14. I CAN'T ATTEMPT IT BY MYSELF.
15. TRY <u>TO</u> LEARN THESE WORDS BY TOMORROW MORNING.
16. MAY I PLEASE USE YOUR PENCIL <u>TO</u> WRITE IT?
17. IN MY OPINION YOU (singular) SHOULD NOT BUY A HEARING AID NOW.
18. YES, <u>ENCOURAGE</u> HER <u>TO</u> ATTEMPT IT.
19. BE CAREFUL WITH IT BECAUSE IT IS NOT MINE.
20. WHAT ARE THEY TRYING <u>TO</u> COMPARE?
21. I EVALUATED HIS <u>SPEECH</u> YESTERDAY.
22. HE IS MAKING A CHAIR FOR HIS FATHER.
23. PLEASE TELL ME BECAUSE I AM IN A HURRY.
24. HOW MUCH EFFORT WILL IT <u>REQUIRE</u>?
25. IS THE WORD DESIRE IN THE DICTIONARY?

lesson twenty-one

Signs presented in this lesson are:

STORY*	BODY	COPY, IMITATE	THIRST
HUNGER	BASIC	NOTICE	JOIN
COMFORT	ATTENTION, CONCENTRATE	RECOGNIZE	SEVERAL
ENCOURAGE*	NORTH	COOPERATE	MORNING
BLIND	SUPERVISE, TAKE CARE OF	SUSPECT* (verb)	REMEMBER

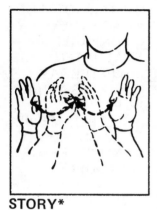

STORY*

Both hands, each with its thumb and index finger curved and touching (remaining fingers are apart and slightly curved), are positioned in front of the body so that the hands are in contact at the tips of their joined index fingers and thumbs and with their palmar sides facing each other. Then, the hands are twisted so that their palmar sides now face the viewer as the hands are pulled apart sideways and then return to their former position. This motion is repeated several times.

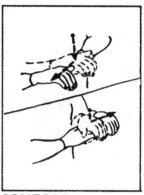

COMFORT

The left hand, with the thumb and fingers extended and joined, is held in front of the body with the fingers pointing to the right and the palm facing down. The right hand, with the thumb extended and apart (remaining fingers are joined and slightly curved), descends and clasps the top of the left hand. Then, the right hand slides over and past the left fingertips. Next, the hands reverse their spatial position and repeat the motion. That is, the right hand now is held in front of the body with the palm facing down and the fingers pointing to the left; the left hand descends and clasps the top of the right hand and then slides over and past the right fingertips.

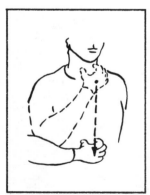

HUNGER

This sign starts at the level of the neck with the palmar side of the thumb and fingers of the right *C* hand touching the throat; then, the *C* hand is moved downward, while grazing the body.
NOTE: Facial expression can alter the connotative meaning of this sign from a mild feeling of hunger to extreme and painful starvation.

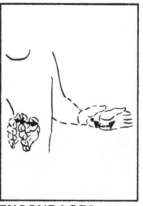

ENCOURAGE*

Both hands, each with its thumb and fingers joined and slightly curved, initially are placed on each side of the body at waist level with their palmar sides facing the viewer. Next, both hands simultaneously make several small, pushing type motions as they are moved forward, return to their original position and repeat the motion.

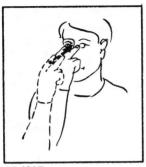

BLIND

The right hand, in the configuration of the letter *V*, first is held approximately six inches in front of the eyes with the *V* fingertips pointing at them. Then, with the configuration maintained, the *V* hand is moved towards the eyes, suggesting that sight is now blocked.

ATTENTION, CONCENTRATE

Both hands, each with its thumb and fingers extended and joined, are placed near each side of the face so that their fingertips are pointing up and their palmar sides are facing each other; next, the hands, while preserving their configuration, simultaneously are moved forward.

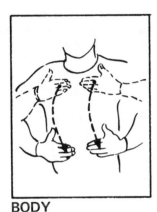

BODY

Both hands, each with its thumb extended and pointing upward (remaining fingers are extended and joined), are placed side-by-side on the signer's chest so that their fingertips are pointing at each other and with their thumbs sticking up. Next, the hands separate from the body and simultaneously move downward, and retouch the body near the waist line.

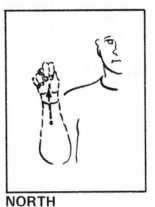

NORTH

The right hand, in the configuration of the letter *N*, is held in front and to the right side of the body near the level of shoulder with the back side of the *N* hand toward the signer. Next, the *N* hand moves straight up.

NOTE: The remaining directional movements are performed similarly. For "south" the *S* hand moves down. For "east," the *E* hand moves to the signer's right and for "west," the *W* hand moves to the signer's left. That is, the signer executes the diagram:

```
        N
   W ---+--- E
        S
```

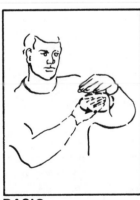

BASIC

The left hand, with the thumb and fingers extended and joined, is held in front and slightly to the left side of the body near the level of the left shoulder with the fingers pointing to the right and the palm facing down. The right hand, with the thumb and fingers extended and joined, first is held directly beneath the left hand (palm is facing down and fingers are pointing to the left). Then, the right hand completes a circle in a counterclockwise direction along a horizontal plane beneath the left hand.

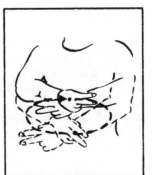

SUPERVISE, TAKE CARE OF

Both hands, each in the configuration of the letter *V*, are crossed so that the sides of their wrists touch as the *V* hands point approximately 45 degrees in opposite directions along a horizontal plane. Next, without separating the hands, complete a large horizontal circle in front of the body.

COPY, IMITATE

The left hand, with the thumb and fingers extended and joined, is held in front of the body with the palm facing up and the fingers pointing to the viewer; the fingers of the right hand first are spread (palmar side toward the viewer) and then become contracted (the thumb touches the extended fingertips) as the hand moves down and with its joined thumb and fingertips touches the palm of the left hand.

NOTICE

The left hand, with the thumb and fingers extended and joined, is held in front and to the left side of the body with the fingers pointing up and the palmar side facing to the right. The right index finger (remaining fingers and thumb are contracted) first points to the eye and then the tip of the right index finger touches the left palm.

RECOGNIZE

This sign is made similarly to the previous one ("notice"), except that the right hand, in the configuration of the letter *R*, points to the eye and then the *R* hand moves down so that the *R* fingertips touch the palm of the left hand.

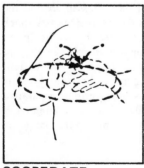

COOPERATE

This sign is produced by first making the sign for "join" and then moving the interlocked hands counter-clockwise to form a large horizontal circle in front of the body.

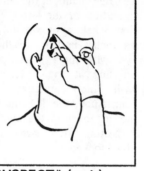

SUSPECT* (verb)

The right index fingertip (remaining fingers and thumb are contracted) first touches the right side of the forehead and then quickly is flexed. This "scratching" motion is repeated several times.

NOTE: Facial expression can be used to convey the degree of suspicion.

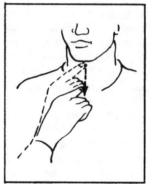

THIRST

The right index finger (remaining fingers and thumb are contracted) first touches the upper region of the throat and then grazes it as the right hand is moved several inches in a downward direction.

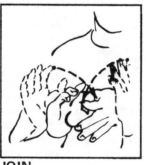

JOIN

Both hands, each with its thumb and fingers apart and slightly curved, are positioned in front of the body with their palmar sides facing each other. Next, the hands are moved toward each other as their thumbs and index fingers form an interlocking circle with each other.

SEVERAL

First, the right *A* hand is held in front of the body with the back side facing down. Next, as the hand is moved from left to right, the thumb passes across the fingertips as they straighten and extend one by one.

REMEMBER

The left hand, in the configuration of the letter *A*, is held in front and slightly to the left side of the body with the back side facing to the left; the right hand, with only the thumb extended (remaining fingers are contracted to the palm), first touches the right side of the forehead and then is dropped down so that the palmar side of the right thumb touches the thumbnail of the left *A* hand.

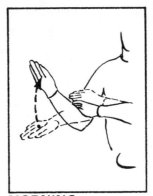

MORNING

The left hand, with the thumb and fingers extended and joined, is placed on the inside of the right arm which is held outstretched in front of the body with the fingers of the hand extended and joined and the palm facing up. Then, the right forearm bends up at the elbow.

NOTE: The sign may be suggestive, perhaps, of the sun rising.

A) Exercises in Encoding

Encode the following material using signs and fingerspelling. Use fingerspelling for all underlined words.

1. WILL YOU TELL US THE STORY AGAIN?
2. NO, WE ARE NOT VERY HUNGRY NOW. ("Hungry" is signed as "hunger" plus "y.")
3. MY COUSIN IS BOTH DEAF AND BLIND.
4. ENCOURAGE YOUR PATIENT TO LEARN LIPREADING.
5. WE ARE ENJOYING ALL THE COMFORTS OF HOME. ("Enjoying" is signed as "enjoy" plus "ing.")
6. HE NEEDS TO BUY A BODY HEARING AID.
7. CAN YOU REMEMBER THE BASIC IDEA?
8. PLEASE PAY ATTENTION WHEN I EXPLAIN IT.
9. I KNOW I NEED TO LEARN HOW TO CONCENTRATE.
10. OUR HOME IS NORTH OF HERE.
11. WHO WILL SUPERVISE US TOMORROW?
12. COPY THIS SENTENCE FOR US.
13. DID YOU NOTICE THAT HE WAS NOT WEARING HIS HEARING AID?
14. I ALMOST DID NOT RECOGNIZE HIM.
15. WE SUSPECT THAT HER STORY IS NOT TRUE.
16. PLEASE COME AND TELL ME WHY TOMORROW MORNING.
17. I AM VERY THIRSTY. ("Thirsty" is signed as "thirst" plus "y.")
18. MAY I PLEASE JOIN YOU LATER?
19. PLEASE ENCOURAGE THEM TO COOPERATE.
20. SEVERAL OF MY FRIENDS DID NOTICE IT.
21. DO YOU WANT TO TAKE CARE OF IT? ("Take care of" is signed similarly to "supervise.")
22. WHO IS YOUR SUPERVISOR IN THE CLINIC?
23. I DON'T FEEL VERY COMFORTABLE THIS MORNING. ("Comfortable" is signed as "comfort" plus "able." "This morning" is signed as "now" plus "morning.")
24. WHAT CAUSED HIS BLINDNESS? ("Blindness" is signed as "blind" plus "ness.")
25. DID YOU (singular) NOTICE THAT HE CAN'T COMMUNICATE?

B) Exercises in Decoding

Decode the following illustrated exercises:

1.

2.

3.

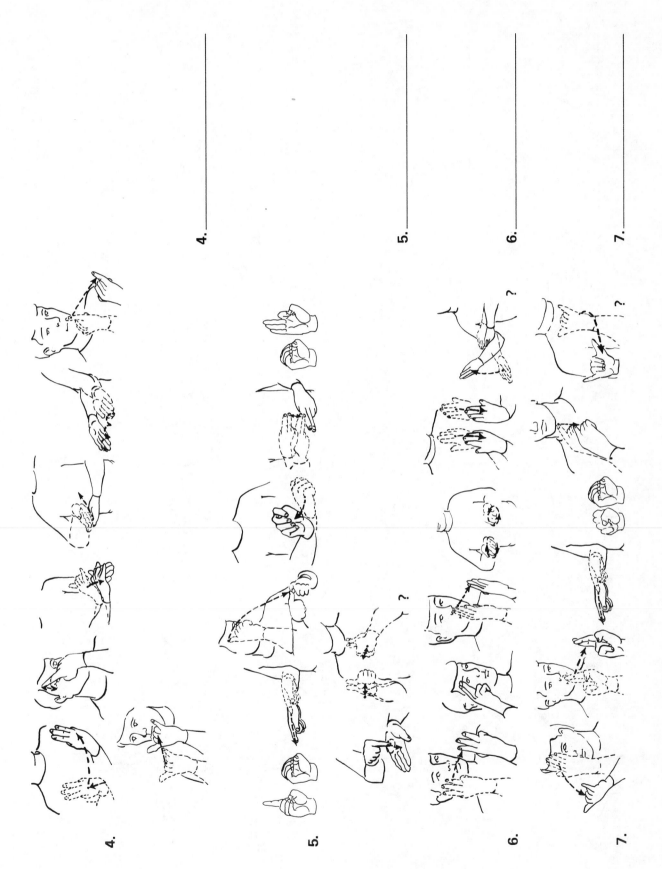

4.

5.

6.

7.

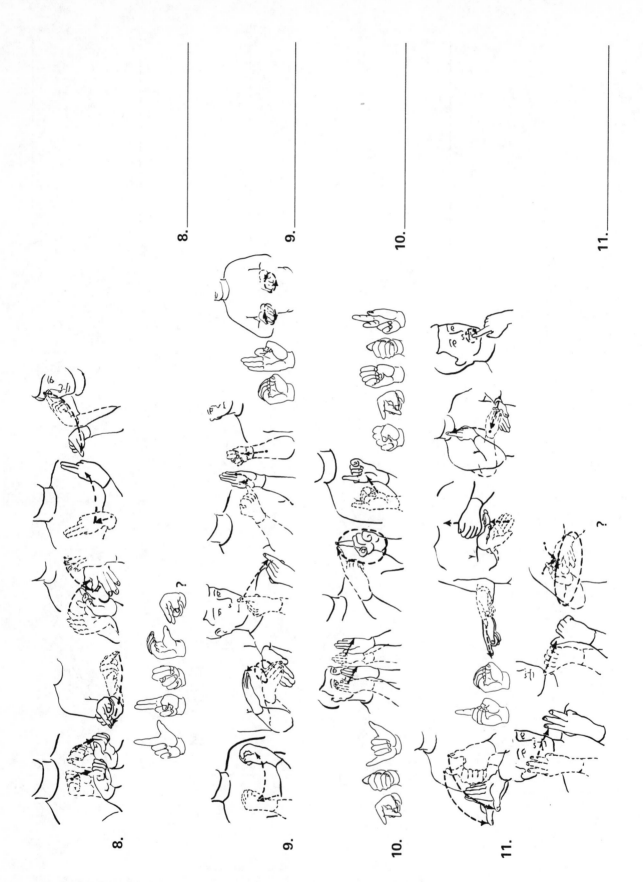

8.

9.

10.

11.

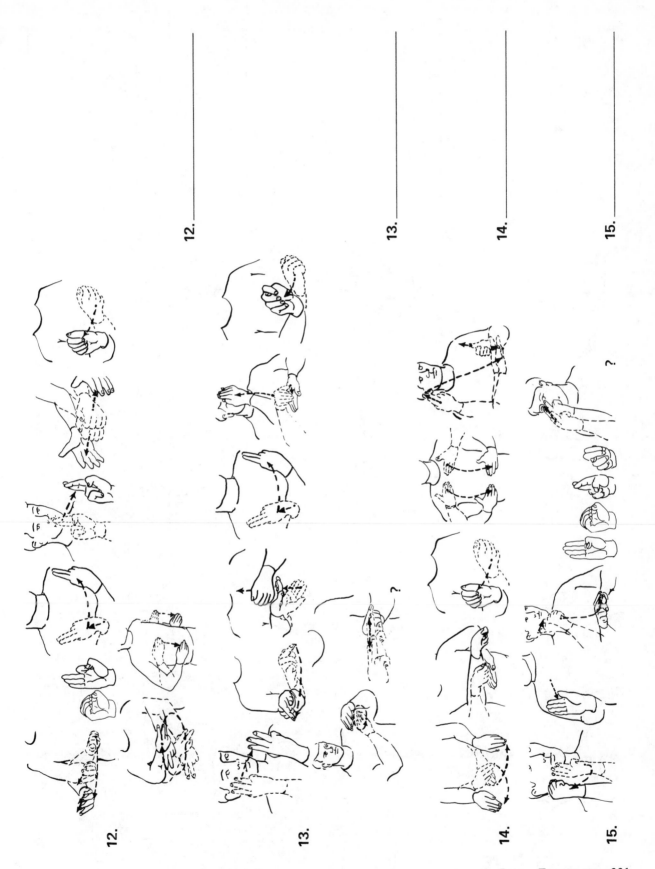

12. _____

13. _____

14. _____

15. _____

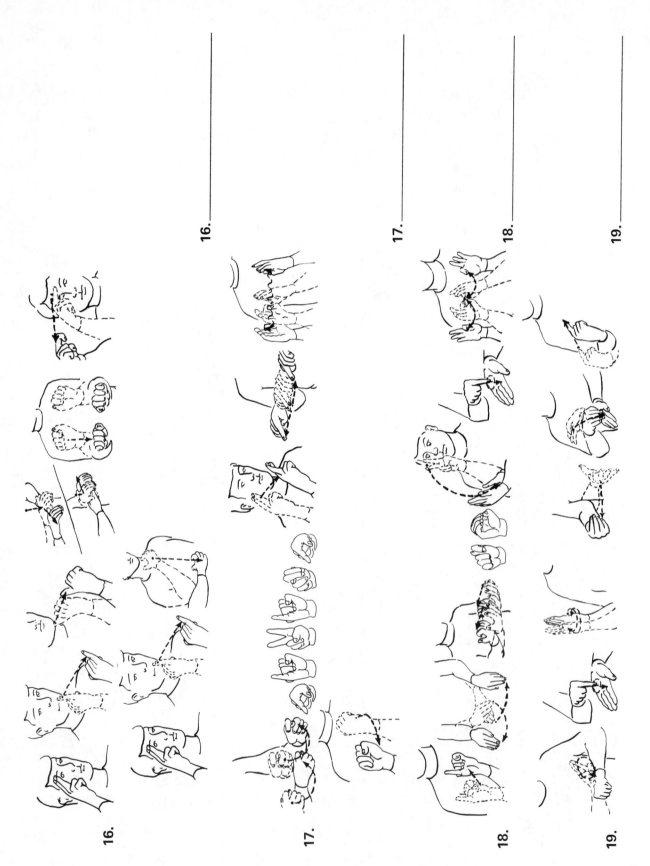

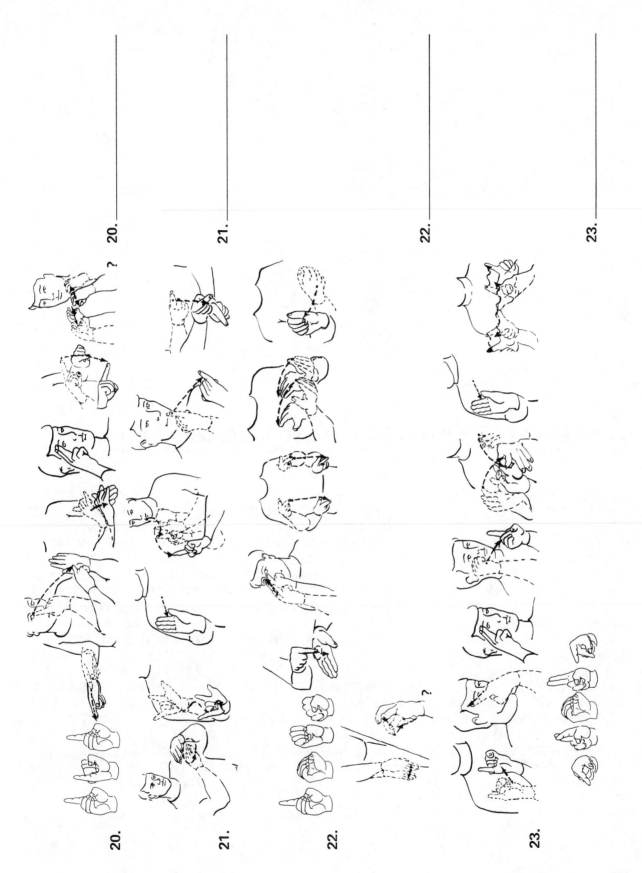

20.

21.

22.

23.

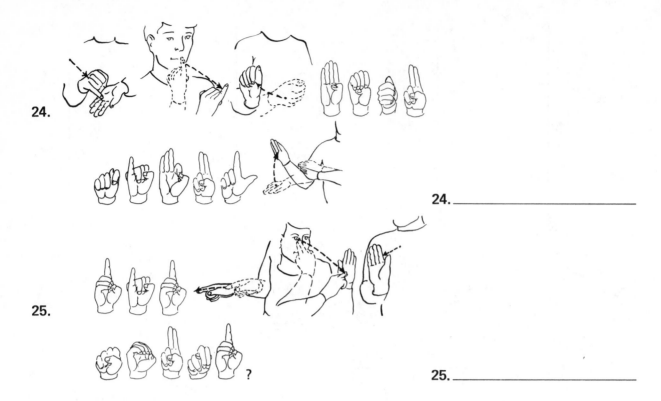

24. _____

25. _____

C) Answers for Decoding Part (B), Lesson 21

Underlined words indicate that they should have been fingerspelled.

1. <u>DO</u> YOU (singular) WANT ME <u>TO</u> COPY IT NOW?
2. <u>DID</u> YOU (singular) NOTICE ANY PROBLEMS?
3. HE WAS NOT ABLE <u>TO</u> RECOGNIZE ANY <u>OF</u> THEM.
4. WE SUSPECT THAT SOMETHING IS WRONG.
5. <u>DO</u> YOU (singular) REMEMBER THE NAME <u>OF</u> THIS ANIMAL?
6. WILL HE BE HERE THIS MORNING?
7. WHY ARE YOU (singular) <u>SO</u> THIRSTY?
8. CAN YOU (plural) JOIN US FOR <u>LUNCH</u>?
9. OUR COLLEGE IS JUST NORTH <u>OF</u> HERE.
10. <u>PAY</u> ATTENTION WHEN I <u>SPEAK</u>.
11. HOW <u>DO</u> YOU (singular) HELP SOMEONE WHO WILL NOT COOPERATE?
12. SEVERAL <u>OF</u> US ARE WITHOUT A SUPERVISOR.
13. WILL YOU (plural) HELP US LEARN THE BASIC VOCABULARY?
14. DON'T BUY A BODY HEARING AID.
15. WAS YOUR SISTER <u>BORN</u> BLIND?
16. HE IS NOT COMFORTABLE BECAUSE HE IS HUNGRY.
17. TRY <u>GIVING</u> HER DIFFERENT SENTENCES.
18. I DON'T WANT <u>TO</u> READ THIS STORY.
19. USE THIS MIRROR AND IMITATE ME.
20. <u>DID</u> YOU (singular) NOTICE THAT HE CAN'T COMMUNICATE?
21. BASICALLY, YOUR ANSWER IS CORRECT.
22. <u>DOES</u> THIS BLIND PERSON HAVE A DOG?
23. I THINK HE SHOULD JOIN YOUR LANGUAGE <u>GROUP</u>.
24. IT IS A <u>BEAUTIFUL</u> MORNING.
25. <u>DID</u> YOU (singular) RECOGNIZE YOUR <u>SOUND</u>?

lesson twenty-two

Signs presented in this lesson are:

COOK* (verb)	EQUAL,* EVEN*	ENGLISH	DAY
NOON	DOOR	TOUCH, CONTACT	THROUGH
AFTERNOON	MEASURE*	EMPHASIZE	INTRODUCE
NIGHT	HOUSE	HOUR	POP (soda)
OVERNIGHT	BUILD	MINUTE	MACHINE*

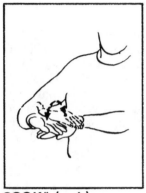

COOK* (verb)

The left hand, with the thumb and fingers extended and joined, is held in front of the body with the fingers pointing to the right and the palm facing up. The right hand with the thumb and fingers extended and joined, descends and touches the left hand so that their palms touch and with the fingers of the right hand pointing to the left. Then, the right hand is flipped over on its back. This motion is repeated several times; it may be suggestive, perhaps, of cooking a piece of meat.

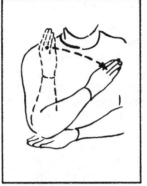

AFTERNOON

As with the previous sign ("noon"), the left hand (palm facing down) is placed under the elbow of the right arm (which is held first in a vertical position) in front and to the right side of the body (fingers are both extended and joined, pointing upward and with the palm facing to the left). Next, the right arm swings to the left (counter-clockwise) about 135 degrees. Again, this sign may be suggestive, perhaps, of the course of the sun.

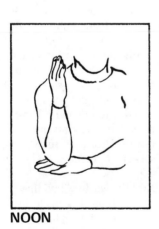

NOON

The left hand, with the thumb and fingers extended and joined (the palm is facing down), is placed under the elbow of the right arm (which is held in a vertical position) in front and to the right side of the body with the palm of the hand facing to the left (fingers and thumb are extended, joined and are pointing upward). This sign may be suggestive, perhaps, of the position of the sun: straight up and down.

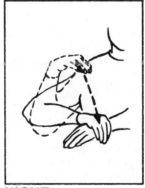

NIGHT

The left hand, with the thumb and fingers extended and joined, is held in front of the body with the palm facing down and the fingers pointing to the viewer at an angle. The right hand, with the thumb and fingers joined and slightly curved, is moved downward so that the palm comes to rest on the back side of the left wrist. (The right hand fingertips, with their back sides facing the viewer at an angle, are pointing down as the sign comes to an end.) This sign may be suggestive, perhaps, of the sun setting.

235

OVERNIGHT

The left forearm is positioned horizontally across the signer's body with the hand touching the inner side of the right arm, which is extended downward with the thumb and fingers extended and joined. From this position, the right forearm swings up in the direction of the left elbow where contact is made against the palm of the right hand.

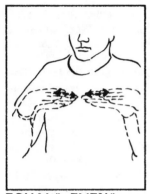

EQUAL*, EVEN*

Both hands, each with its thumb and fingers joined, extended and with the fingers flexed at the base, are held side-by-side in front of the body with the palmar sides of their fingers facing down and their fingertips pointing at each other. Next, with the configuration maintained, the hands are moved toward each other so that their fingertips touch, separate about three or four inches to the right and left, respectively and then retouch.

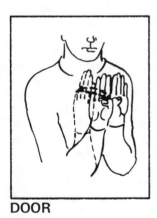

DOOR

This sign is executed in two steps. *Step one*: Both hands assume the configuration of the letter *B* and are held in front of the body with the sides of their index fingers touching and their palmar sides facing the viewer. *Step two*: The wrist rotates (horizontally) the right hand first in a clockwise, then counterclockwise, direction.
NOTE: This sign may be imitative, perhaps, of the opening and closing of a double leaved door.

MEASURE*

Both hands assume the configuration of the letter *Y* and are held side-by-side in front of the body so that their wrists are facing down. Next, the *Y* hands are moved toward each other so that their thumbs touch, separate about three or four inches to the right and left, respectively and then retouch.

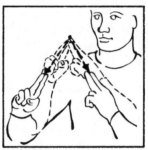

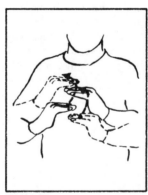

HOUSE

Both hands, each in the configuration of the letter *H*, are held in front of the body at chest level so that their *H* fingertips are touching each other at an oblique angle; next, both *H* hands separate and are moved downward at oblique angles.

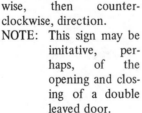

BUILD

Both hands, each with its thumb and fingers joined, extended and with the fingers flexed at the base, are positioned one above the other in front of the body with the palmar sides of the fingers facing down. (The right hand fingertips are pointing to the left, while the fingertips of the left hand are pointing to the right.) Next, with the configuration maintained, the left hand is raised so that now it is positioned above the right hand, followed by the right hand repeating the same movement. This sign may be suggestive, perhaps, of laying bricks.
NOTE: Sign for "building" (noun) is made by combining the signs for ("build") plus ("house").

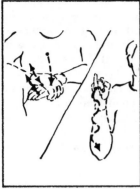

ENGLISH

This sign is made first by executing the sign for England, followed by the sign for "ish." *Step one*: The left hand, with the thumb and fingers extended and joined, is held in front of the body with the palm facing down and the fingers pointing to the viewer. The right hand (in a similar configuration) is moved down and clasps the outer edge of the left hand and together move back and forth several times at an oblique angle. *Step two*: Following this movement, the right hand makes the sign for "ish" as described in lesson 7.

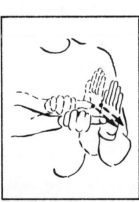

TOUCH, CONTACT

The left hand, in the configuration of the letter *S*, is held in front of the body with the wrist facing down. The right hand, with the middle finger flexed to about a 45-degree angle (remaining fingers and thumb are extended and apart), is moved down and with its middle fingertip touches the back side of the left *S* hand.

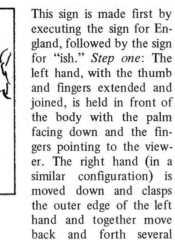

EMPHASIZE

The left hand, with the thumb and fingers extended and joined, is held in front and to the left side of the body so that the fingers are pointing upward and with the palmar side facing the right. The right thumb is extended, sticking out and pointing to the left (remaining fingers are contracted to the palm) and first touches the left palm, and then *both* hands are moved in a forward direction, while holding their contact.

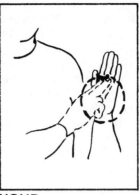

HOUR

The left hand, with the thumb and fingers extended and joined, is held in front and to the left side of the body with the fingers pointing upward and the palmar side of the hand facing to the right. The right hand, in the configuration of the letter *U*, is moved to touch the left hand fingers near their base with the palmar side of the *U* fingers; then, the *U* hand is moved forward to complete a circle in a clockwise direction over the left palm and returns to the original position.

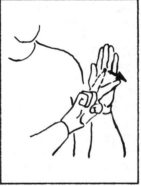

MINUTE

As with the previous sign ("hour"), the left hand with the thumb and fingers extended and joined, is held in front and to the left side of the body with the fingers pointing upward and the palm facing to the right. The right index finger (remaining fingers and thumb are contracted) first touches the left hand fingers near their base with its side (the back side of the right hand is facing the signer) and then the index finger is flicked forward *once*.

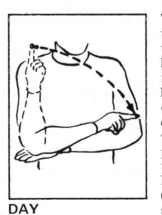

DAY

The right hand configuration for this sign is the letter *D*, with the *D* hand held so that its back side is facing to the right. The left hand (palm is facing down) is placed under the elbow of the right forearm which is held in a vertical position in front, and to the right side of the body. Next, the right forearm (hand in *D* configuration) swings to the left (counterclockwise) and comes to rest on the elbow of the left hand.

THROUGH

The left hand, with the thumb and fingers joined, extended and with the fingers flexed upward at about a 45-degree angle, is held in front of the body with the back side of the hand facing down. The right hand, with the thumb and fingers extended and joined, first is positioned in front of the body (closer to the signer) with the fingers pointing to the viewer and the palmar side facing to the left. Next, with the configuration maintained, the right hand is moved forward while the bottom edge of the hand slips through between the second and third fingers of the left hand.

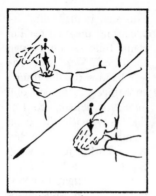

POP (SODA)

This sign is executed in two steps. *Step one*: The left hand, in the configuration of the letter *O*, is held in front of the body with the back side facing left. The right hand, with the thumb and index finger touching (remaining fingers are extended and apart) is moved down and places the joined thumb and index finger inside the left *O* hand. *Step two*: The right hand first is pulled our of the left *O* hand, straightens its fingers, and then descends and comes to rest on top of the left *O* hand. This sign intends to suggest, perhaps, a capped bottle.

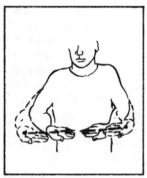

INTRODUCE

Both hands, each with its thumb and fingers extended and joined, are held on each side of the body with their palms facing up and their fingers pointing to each other. Next, the hands are moved toward each other (but do not touch) as if to suggest that two people are coming closer together.

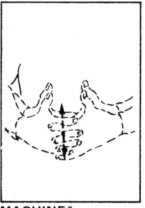

MACHINE*

Both hands have their thumbs extended and pointing upward and their remaining fingers interlocked with each other. The hands are placed in front of the body so that their palmar sides are facing the signer. Next, the interlocked hands quickly are rocked back and forth several times, suggesting the vibrations produced by a machine.

A) Exercises in Encoding

Encode the following material using signs and fingerspelling. Use fingerspelling for all underlined words.

1. I COOKED THE <u>MEAT</u> WITHOUT SALT.
2. ARE YOUR FRIENDS COMING AT NOON?
3. SHE IS AT THE <u>OFFICE</u> THIS AFTERNOON. ("This afternoon" is signed as "now" plus "afternoon.")
4. WE CAN EVALUATE HER TOMORROW NIGHT.
5. YOUR MOTHER CAN <u>STAY</u> WITH US OVERNIGHT.
6. PLEASE OPEN THE DOOR BECAUSE IT IS <u>HOT</u> IN HERE.
7. I WANT <u>TO</u> KNOW <u>IF</u> THEY ARE EQUAL.
8. WE DON'T KNOW HOW <u>TO</u> MEASURE HIS <u>LOSS</u>.
9. <u>DO</u> YOU LIVE IN THIS HOUSE TOO?
10. CAN SHE HELP US BUILD IT?
11. WHAT IS THE NAME <u>OF</u> YOUR NEW BUILDING? ("Building" is signed as "build" plus "house.")
12. HOW <u>WELL</u> <u>DOES</u> HE USE THE ENGLISH LANGUAGE? ("English" is signed as "England" plus "ish.")
13. DON'T TOUCH IT BECAUSE IT IS <u>HOT</u>.
14. I WANT YOU <u>TO</u> EMPHASIZE THE BASIC IDEAS.
15. WE SHALL BE DRIVING THROUGH YOUR <u>TOWN</u> IN THE MORNING.
16. MAY I SEE YOU FOR A MINUTE?
17. I WANT <u>TO</u> BUY SOME POP BEFORE WE GO.
18. WHAT <u>DOES</u> THIS MACHINE <u>DO</u>?
19. YES, I SHALL INTRODUCE YOU TO OUR FAMILY DOCTOR.
20. <u>DO</u> YOU KNOW WHAT DAY THIS IS?
21. TODAY I WANT <u>TO</u> EMPHASIZE SOME IDEAS ABOUT LANGUAGE. ("Today" is signed as "now" plus "day.")
22. WE ARE <u>MOVING</u> TO OUR NEW HOUSE NEXT WEEK.
23. <u>DOES</u> HE HAVE A <u>CLASS</u> THIS HOUR?
24. <u>DO</u> YOU WANT ME <u>TO</u> CLOSE YOUR DOOR?

B) Exercises in Decoding

Decode the following illustrated exercises:

1.

?

1._____

2.

?

2._____

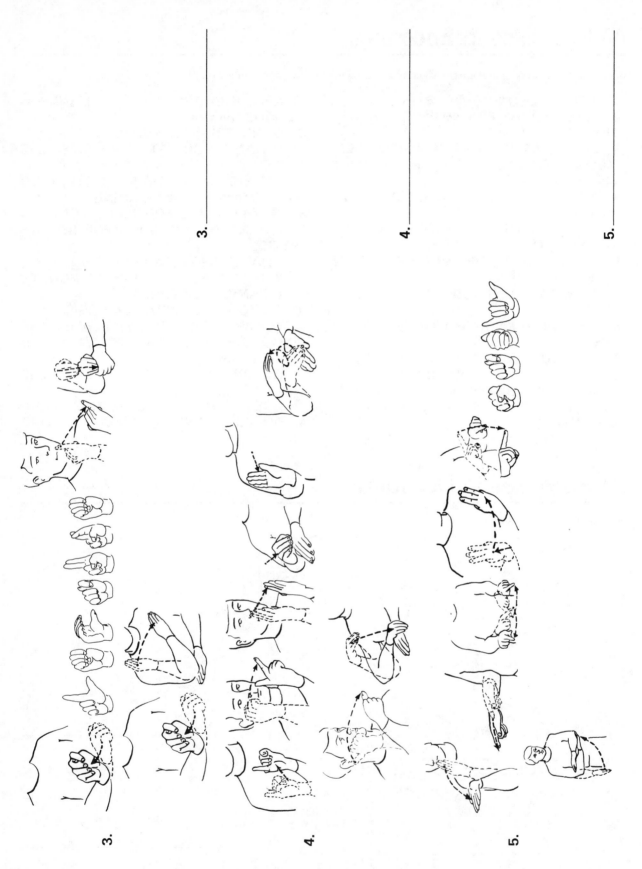

3.

4.

5.

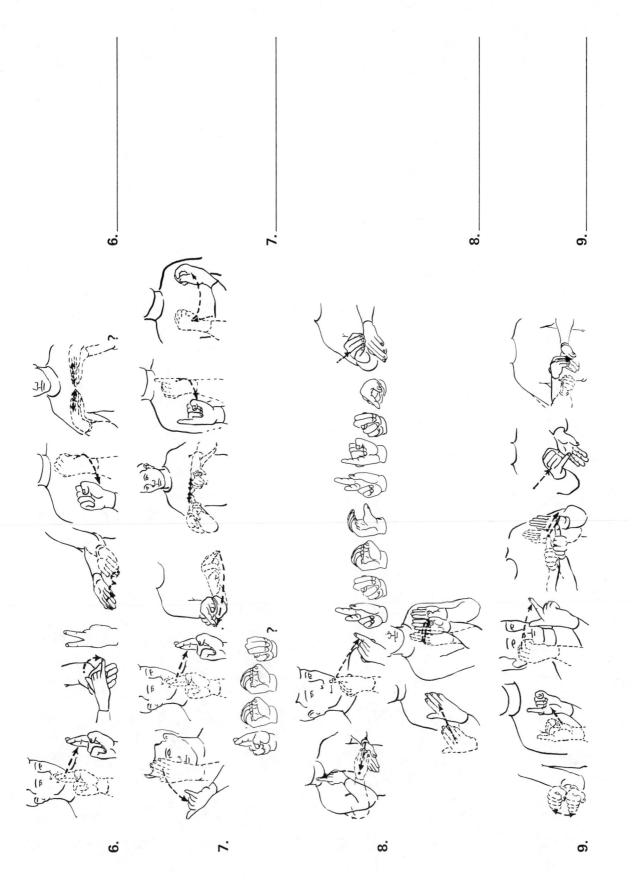

6.

7.

8.

9.

6.

7.

8.

9.

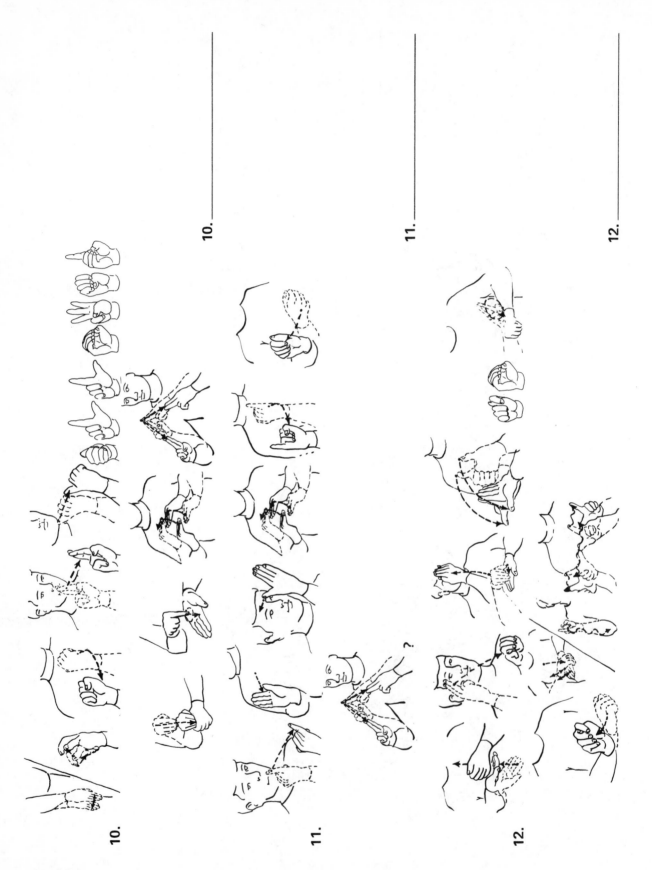

10.

11.

12.

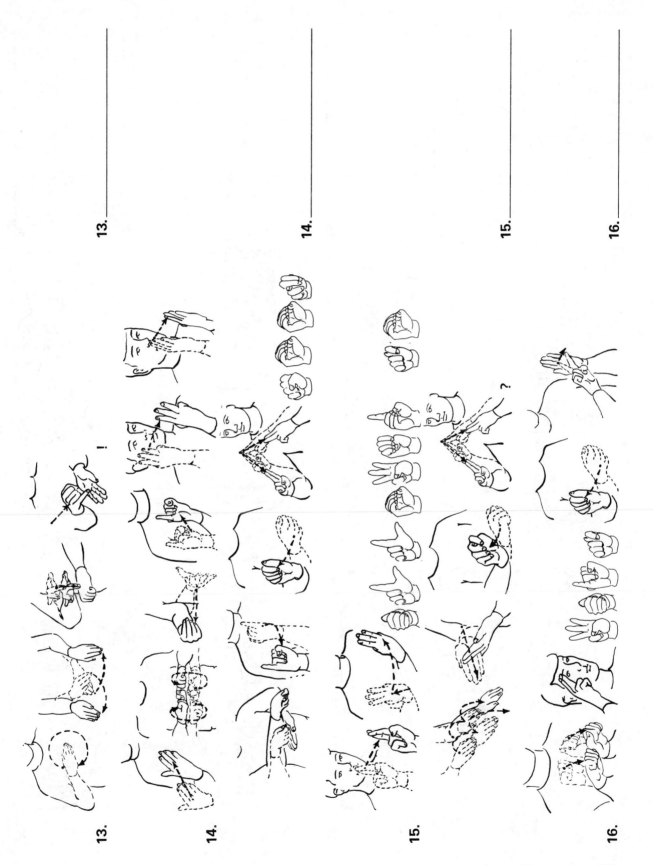

13.

14.

15.

16.

17.

18.

19.

20.

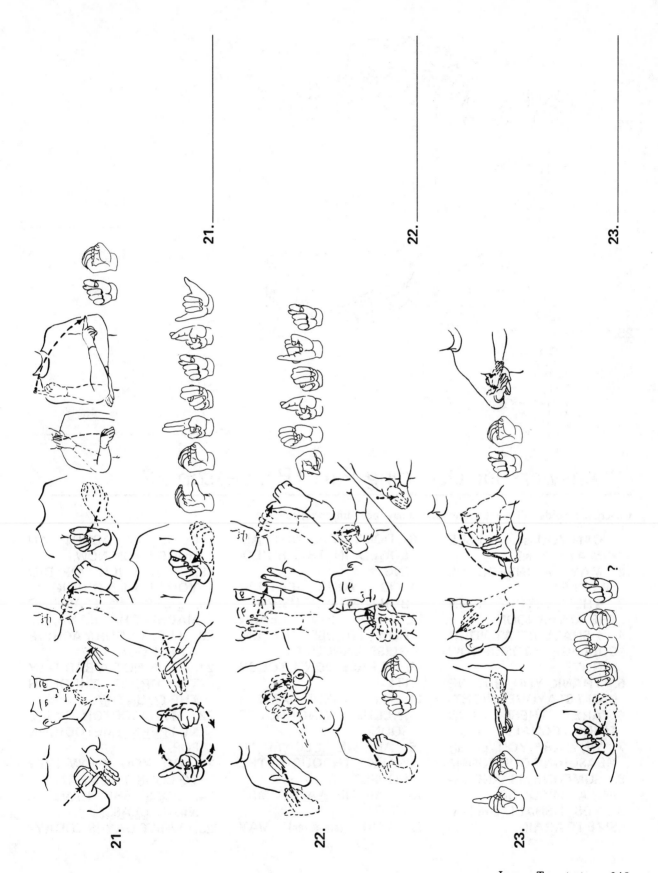

21.

22.

23.

21.

22.

23.

24._____

25._____

C) Answers for Decoding Part (B), Lesson 22

Underlined words indicate that they should have been fingerspelled.

1. CAN YOU (singular) SEE HIM AT NOON?
2. MAY I INTRODUCE MYSELF?
3. THE LECTURE IS IN THE AFTERNOON.
4. I SHALL BE AT YOUR COLLEGE TOMORROW NIGHT.
5. THANK YOU, BUT WE CAN'T STAY OVERNIGHT.
6. ARE THESE TWO THINGS EQUAL?
7. WHY ARE YOU (plural) MEASURING OUR ROOM?
8. SOMEONE IS KNOCKING AT MY DOOR.
9. YES, I SHALL EMPHASIZE IT AGAIN.
10. DOGS ARE NOT ALLOWED IN THIS BUILDING.
11. IS YOUR FATHER BUILDING A HOUSE?
12. HELP HIM LEARN HOW TO USE THE ENGLISH LANGUAGE.
13. PLEASE DON'T TOUCH IT!
14. MY FRIEND AND I WILL BE BUYING A HOUSE SOON.
15. ARE WE ALLOWED TO WALK THROUGH THE HOUSE?
16. CAN HE WAIT A MINUTE?
17. YOU (singular) MAY COME IN ABOUT AN HOUR FROM NOW.
18. HOW MUCH POP DID YOU (singular) DRINK?
19. DOES THIS TEACHING MACHINE HAVE A NAME?
20. I LEFT YOUR MACHINE AT SCHOOL.
21. IT IS NOT A BAD DAY TO DRIVE THROUGH THE COUNTRY.
22. MY DOCTOR WILL NOT PERMIT ME TO DRINK POP.
23. DO YOU KNOW HOW TO COOK THE MEAT?
24. DOES SHE HAVE A NIGHT CLASS?
25. WHAT DAY IS TODAY?

lesson twenty-three

Signs presented in this lesson are:

FEAR	**TIME (abstract)**	**RUN**	**MEMORIZE**
FRIGHT	**PLEASANT***	**BECOME, GET**	**CANCEL**
SCARE	**YELLOW***	**LOSE**	**GET, OBTAIN**
AFRAID	**ALONE**	**POOR***	**RECEIVE**
TIME, O'CLOCK	**EXPERIENCE***	**OCCUPATION***	**NECESSARY**

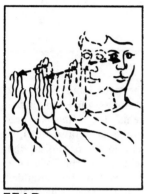

FEAR

Both hands, each with its thumb and fingers extended and joined, first are placed side-by-side and are held to the right side of the body near the level of the face so that their fingers are pointing upward and with their palms facing the viewer. Then, both hands simultaneously are pushed in a forward direction while the signer's head turns to the left as if to suggest, perhaps, that one is shielding himself from something and, furthermore, refuses to face it.

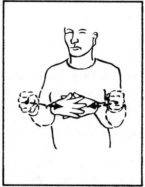

SCARE

This sign is made similarly to the previous one ("fright"), except that, initially, the hands are in an *S* configuration (their back sides face to the right and left, respectively). Then, the *S* hands are moved quickly toward the midline of the body as their thumbs and fingers become extended and apart, and stop when one hand is directly in front of the other. Both hands have their palmar sides facing the signer as the sign comes to an end.

FRIGHT

Both hands, each with its thumb and fingers extended and apart, first are held on both sides of the body (approximately three to four inches from the chest area) so that their fingers are pointing to each other and with their palmar sides facing the signer. Then, the hands are moved quickly toward the midline of the body and stop when one hand is directly in front of the other.

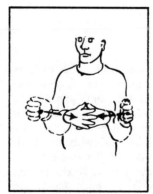

AFRAID

This sign is made similarly to the previous one ("scare"), except that, initially, the hands are in an *A* configuration (their back sides face to the right and left, respectively). Then, the *A* hands are moved quickly toward the midline of the body as their thumbs and fingers become extended and apart, and stop when one hand is directly in front of the other. Both hands have their palmar sides facing the signer as the sign comes to an end.

247

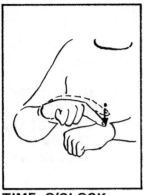

TIME, O'CLOCK

The left hand, in the configuration of the letter *S*, is held across the front of the body with its wrist facing down. The right index finger (remaining fingers are contracted) touches the back side of the left *S* hand near the back of the wrist region.

NOTE: This sign is imitative of pointing to one's watch.

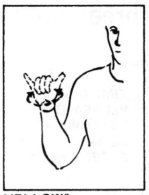

YELLOW*

The right hand first makes the letter *Y* and is held in front and to the right side of the body near the level of the shoulder with its back side facing the signer. Next, without changing position, the hand is turned at the wrist several times, first in a clockwise and then counter-clockwise direction. The arm maintains its position.

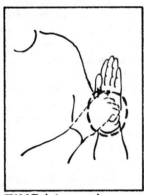

TIME (abstract)

The left hand, with the fingers extended and joined, is held in front and to the left side of the body with the palm facing the viewer at an angle and with the fingers of the left hand pointing upward. The right hand first makes the letter *T*, touches the left palm (its back side is facing to the right) and then completes a circle in a clockwise direction over the left palm.

NOTE: This sign conveys "time" in the abstract or indefinite sense.

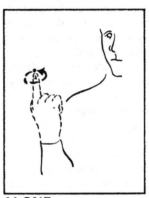

ALONE

The right hand, with only its index finger extended (remaining fingers and thumb are contracted), is held in front and to the right side of the body near the level of the shoulder with its back side facing the viewer and with the right index finger pointing upward. Next, without altering the configuration, the hand is moved to complete a small circle in a counter-clockwise direction.

PLEASANT*

Both hands, each with its thumb and fingers extended and joined, are held near each cheek with their fingers pointing upward and with the back sides of the hands facing the viewer. Next, the fingers of both hands are flexed at their base and then returned to their original positions. This motion is repeated several times.

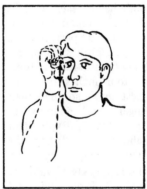

EXPERIENCE*

The right hand, in the configuration of the letter *E*, is held near the signer's right temple with the back side facing to the right. Then, the *E* hand is moved slightly downward. This motion is repeated several times.

NOTE: The sign may intend to suggest, perhaps, the white hair usually associated with elderly people with experience.

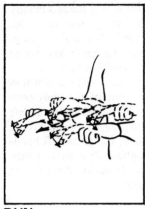

RUN

Both hands first assume the configuration of the letter *L* and are placed in front of the body so that their thumbs touch and their index fingers are pointing to the viewer (both wrists are facing down). Next, their index fingertips are flexed and extended several times as the *L* hands, with their thumbs still touching, are moved forward.

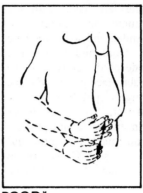

POOR*

The left forearm is held vertically in front and to the left side of the body, while the right hand, with the thumb and fingers extended and slightly apart, first touches the left elbow and then is moved downward as the right thumb bends in and touches the extended fingertips. This motion is repeated several times.

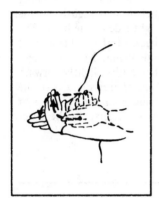

BECOME, GET

Both hands, each with its thumb and fingers extended and joined, are positioned in front of the body so that their palms touch. (The fingers of the left hand are pointing to the viewer while those of the right hand are pointing upward.) Next, the hands reverse positions as they rub each other (the right hand tilts in a clockwise direction - forward, while the left hand tilts in a counter-clockwise direction - vertically) as the hands are moved forward --away from the signer.

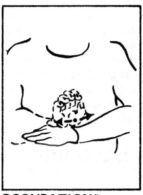

OCCUPATION*

The left forearm is stretched across the front of the body with the thumb and fingers of the left hand joined, extended, and with the palm facing down. The right hand makes the letter *O*. The wrist of the right *O* hand first touches the side of the left wrist and is held so that the palmar side of the *O* hand is facing the viewer. Then, the right *O* hand grazes the left forearm as it makes several quick movements first to the left and then to the right - toward the left wrist.

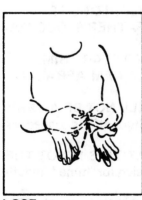

LOSE

Both hands (with the fingertips touching their thumbs) are positioned in front of the signer's body and are touching (the back sides of the fingers of both hands face down). Quickly, open the hands (the fingers and thumbs become extended and joined) in a downward direction so that the hands are in a parallel position with their fingertips pointing obliquely downward as the sign comes to an end.

MEMORIZE

The right hand, with the thumb and fingers joined and slightly bent, first touches the forehead. The hand is held so that its back side is facing the viewer. Next, the right hand is moved forward and in a downward direction as the hand assumes an *S* configuration. The sign ends with the back side of the right *S* hand facing down.

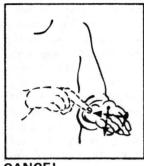

CANCEL

The left hand, with the thumb and fingers extended and joined, is held in front and to the left side of the body with the palm facing up and the fingers pointing to the viewer. The right index finger (remaining fingers and thumb are contracted) draws an "X" pattern on the palm of the left hand.

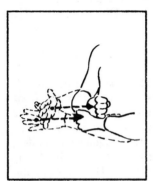

GET, OBTAIN

Both hands, each with its fingers and thumb extended and apart, are held in a crossed position, one above the other, in front of the body so that their palms are facing left and right and with their fingers pointing to the viewer at an angle. Then, the hands contract into fists as they are brought toward the signer.

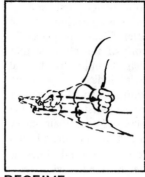

RECEIVE

This sign is made similarly to the previous one ("get," "obtain"), except that the hands assume an *R* configuration and are held in a crossed position in front of the body with their back sides facing left and right, respectively. Then, the crossed *R* hands contract into fists as they are brought toward the signer.

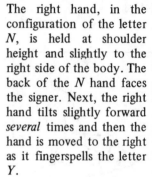

NECESSARY*

The right hand, in the configuration of the letter *N*, is held at shoulder height and slightly to the right side of the body. The back of the *N* hand faces the signer. Next, the right hand tilts slightly forward *several* times and then the hand is moved to the right as it fingerspells the letter *Y*.

A) Exercises in Encoding

Encode the following material using signs and fingerspelling. Use fingerspelling for all underlined words.

1. WHAT TIME CAN YOU SEE ME TOMOR-ROW?
2. YES, WE SHALL COME AT THREE O'CLOCK THIS AFTERNOON. ("This afternoon" is signed as "now" plus "afternoon.")
3. HOW MANY YELLOW CHAIRS <u>DOES</u> HE WANT?
4. DON'T <u>FEEL</u> THAT YOU ARE ALONE.
5. <u>DO</u> YOU HAVE ANY EXPERIENCE TEACHING THE DEAF?
6. IT IS NECESSARY THAT YOU TRY <u>TO</u> MEMORIZE IT.
7. WHY IS THE BOY RUNNING?
8. WHEN I GET IT, I SHALL <u>SHOW</u> IT TO YOU.
9. I <u>STRUGGLED</u> <u>TO</u> OBTAIN IT.
10. WE RECEIVED THE MONEY YESTER-DAY.
11. ARE YOU GETTING TIRED? ("Getting" is signed as "become" plus "ing.")
12. IF WE ARE NOT MORE CAREFUL, WE COULD LOSE IT.
13. IS IT TRUE THAT YOUR FAMILY IS POOR?
14. I DON'T WANT <u>TO</u> CANCEL THE LANGUAGE EVALUATION.
15. HOW <u>DID</u> YOU LOSE OUR PAPERS?
16. IT IS NECESSARY FOR ME <u>TO</u> CANCEL MY <u>TRIP</u> TODAY. ("Today" is signed as "now" plus "day.")
17. FOR NOW, TRY MEMORIZING IT.
18. WHAT IS YOUR FATHER'S OCCUPA-TION?
19. BE CAREFUL NOT <u>TO</u> SCARE HIM.
20. I DON'T KNOW WHY I AM AFRAID <u>OF</u> YOU.
21. I FEAR THAT I SHALL NOT BE A VERY GOOD STUDENT. ("Student" is signed as "learn" plus "er.")
22. WE ARE SURE THAT THIS IS NOT THE TIME FOR IT. (Use the sign for "time" (indefinite) here.)
23. HOW MUCH EXPERIENCE IS NECES-SARY FOR THIS OCCUPATION?
24. I DON'T THINK HIS FAMILY IS POOR.
25. IT IS PLEASANT TODAY.

B) Exercises in Decoding

Decode the following illustrated exercises:

1. _____

2. _____

3. _____

4. _____

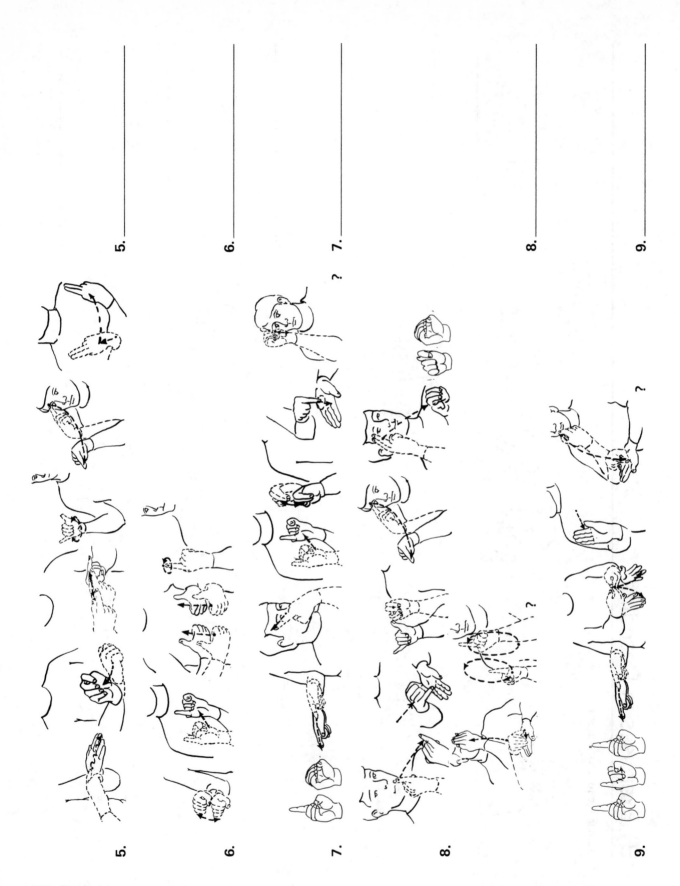

5.

6.

7.

8.

9.

5.

6.

7.

8.

9.

10.

11.

12.

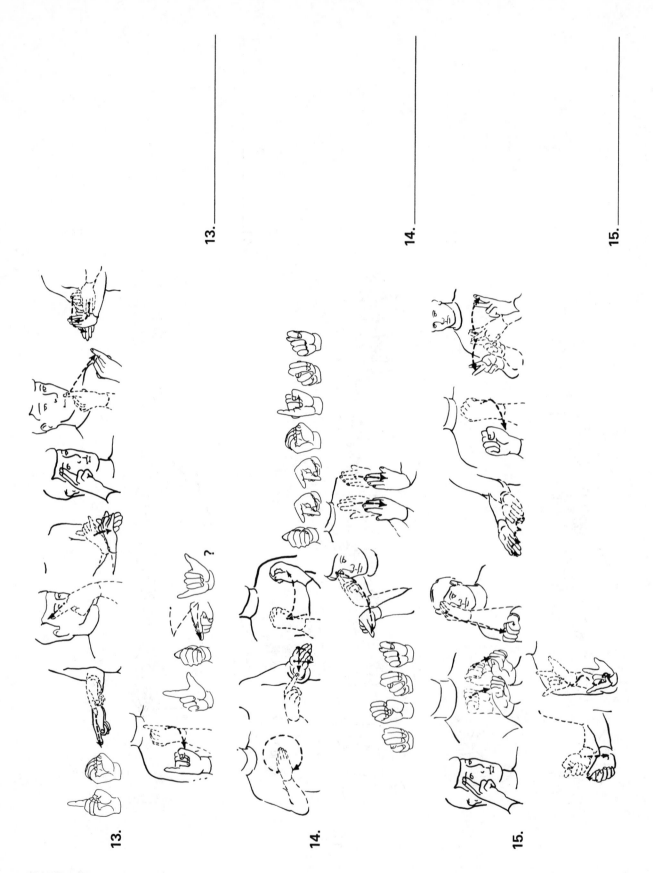

13.

14.

15.

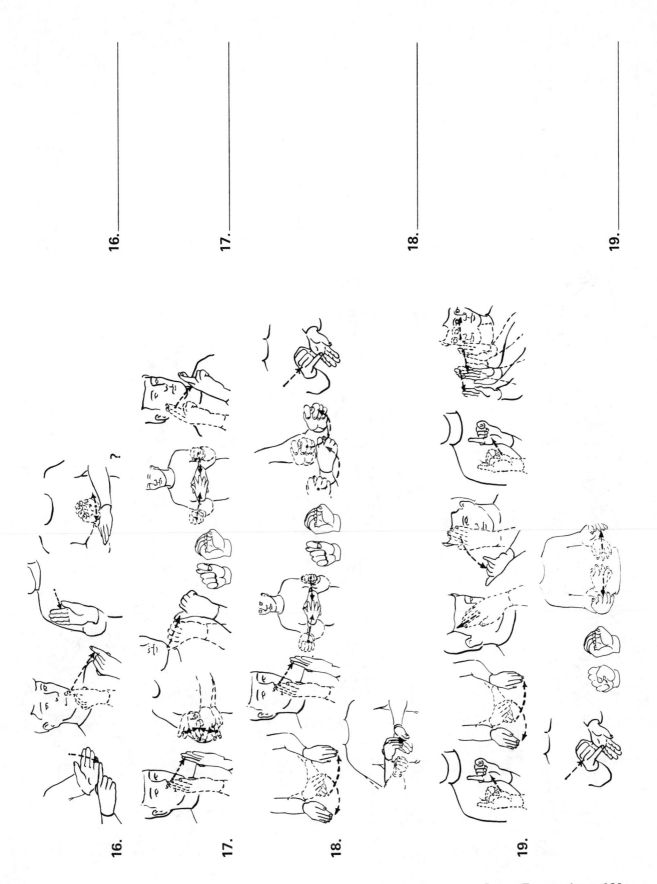

16.

17.

18.

19.

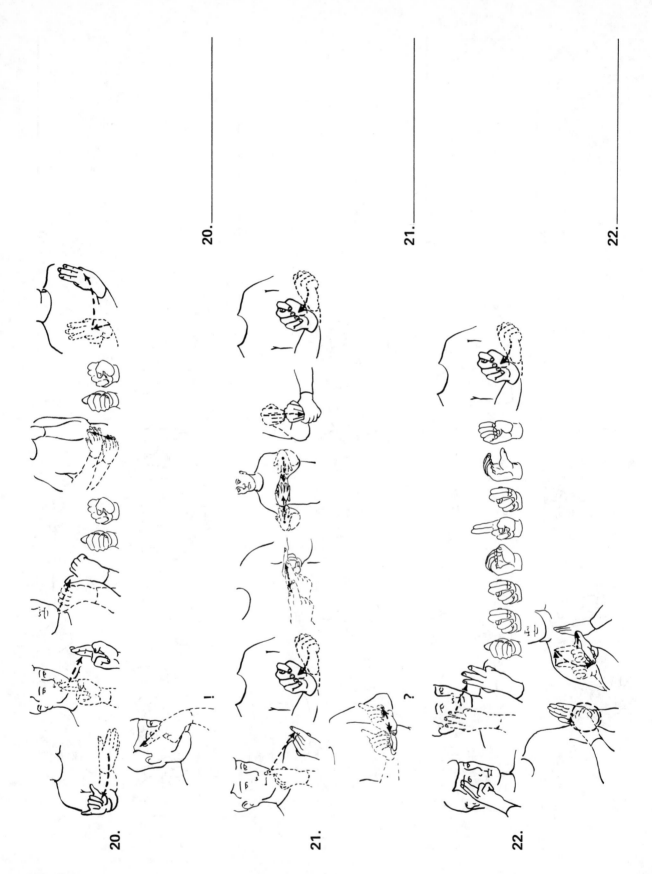

20.

21.

22.

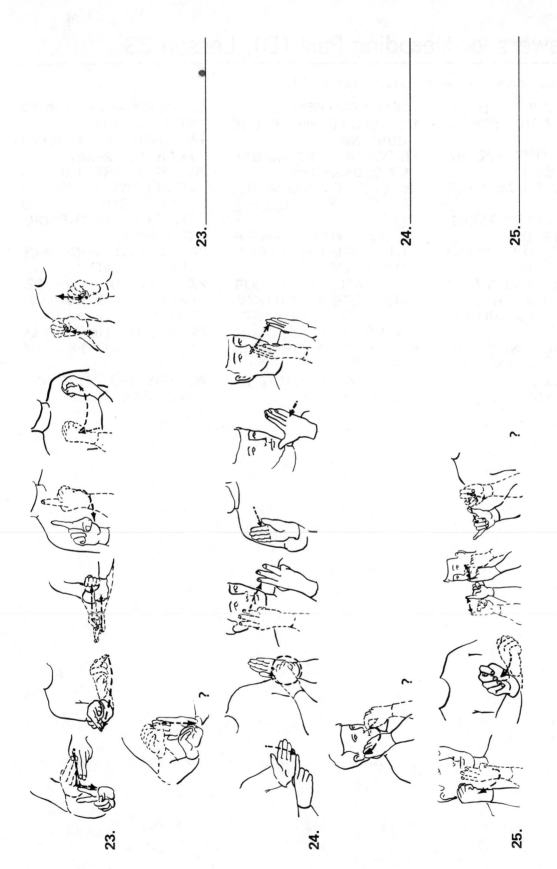

23.

24.

25.

23.

24.

25.

C) Answers for Decoding Part (B), Lesson 23

Underlined words indicate that they should have been fingerspelled.

1. MEMORIZE THESE WORDS FOR TOMORROW.
2. WHAT TIME ARE WE GOING TODAY?
3. IT WAS A LONG TIME AGO.
4. IT WAS VERY PLEASANT YESTERDAY.
5. WRITE THE WORD "YELLOW" FOR US.
6. YES, I LIVE ALONE.
7. <u>DO</u> YOU (singular) THINK I NEED THIS EXPERIENCE?
8. IS IT NECESSARY FOR HIM <u>TO</u> LEARN SIGN LANGUAGE?
9. <u>DID</u> YOU (singular) LOSE YOUR PENCIL?
10. TELL ME WHY SHE IS RUNNING?
11. MAY I COME AND GET MY BOOKS NOW?
12. <u>DID</u> YOU (plural) RECEIVE OUR <u>LETTER</u> <u>YET</u>?
13. <u>DO</u> YOU (singular) THINK THAT HE IS GETTING <u>LAZY</u>?
14. PLEASE CANCEL OUR <u>APPOINTMENT</u> FOR NOW.
15. HE CAN MEMORIZE THINGS VERY QUICKLY.
16. WHAT IS YOUR OCCUPATION?
17. BE CAREFUL NOT <u>TO</u> SCARE HER.
18. DON'T BE AFRAID <u>TO</u> TRY IT AGAIN.
19. I DON'T KNOW WHY I FEAR IT <u>SO</u> MUCH.
20. THEY ARE NOT <u>AS</u> POOR <u>AS</u> WE THINK!
21. IS THE WORD "FRIGHT" IN THE DICTIONARY?
22. HE WILL <u>ANNOUNCE</u> THE TIME LATER.
23. HAVE YOU (plural) RECEIVED OUR EVALUATION?
24. WHAT TIME WILL YOUR MOTHER BE HOME?
25. WAS THE INTERVIEW NECESSARY?

lesson twenty-four

Signs presented in this lesson are:

HOPE,* EXPECT*
IGNORANT, STUPID
MAJOR (line of work)
POSTPONE
PAIN*

HEADACHE
GOAL
OBJECTIVE
ARGUE,* QUARREL*
WAIT*

DEBT,* OWE*
BEGIN, START
HONEST
STUDY*
PRISON

DISCUSS,* DEBATE*
GUESS
BELIEVE
ADULT
SHOWER*

HOPE,* EXPECT*

The left hand, with the thumb and fingers extended and joined, is held in front and to the left side of the body at shoulder level (the fingers are pointing upward and the palmar side faces the signer). The right hand, with only the index finger extended (remaining fingers and thumb are contracted and the back of the hand towards the viewer), touches the right side of the forehead and then is pulled away with the right hand adopting the configuration of the left hand (that is, the thumb and fingers become fully extended, are joined and are pointing upward with the palmar sides of both hands facing each other). Lastly, the fingers of both hands simultaneously flex at the base. This latter motion is repeated several times.

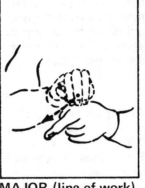

MAJOR (line of work)

The left hand, with only the index finger extended (remaining fingers and thumb are contracted), is held in front of the body with the back side facing to the left and the index finger pointing to the viewer; the right hand, in the configuration of the letter *M*, touches the left index finger near the base of the finger, and then the *M* hand slides forward in the direction of the signer, while grazing the left index finger.

NOTE: The signs for "profession" and "field" (specialty) are made similarly with the exception that *P* and *F* hand configurations, respectively, are used instead of *M*.

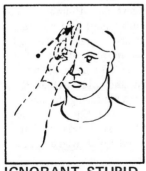

IGNORANT, STUPID

The right hand, in the configuration of the letter *V*, with the palm facing the viewer, is moved toward and touches the center of the forehead with the back side of the right hand (the *V* fingers are pointing upward as the sign comes to an end).

POSTPONE

Both hands, in the configuration of the letter *F*, are placed side-by-side (but not touching) in front of the body so that the palms are facing each other and with the fingers pointing to the viewer; next, without altering the configuration, the hands are moved forward simultaneously to complete an upward arc (clockwise direction).

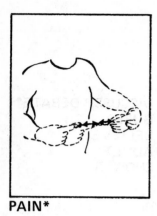

PAIN*

Both hands, each with only its index finger extended (remaining fingers and thumb are contracted), are placed about three to four inches apart in front of the body so that their index fingers are pointing toward each other (back sides of the hands face the viewer); next, the hands are moved toward each other, touch their fingertips, separate right and left, respectively and return to the original position. This motion is repeated several times.

HEADACHE*

This sign is performed by executing the sign for "pain" on the forehead. The motion is repeated several times.

NOTE: This applies to other words which make reference to pain, i.e., for "toothache" the sign would be executed in the region of the tooth where the discomfort and/or pain is being experienced.

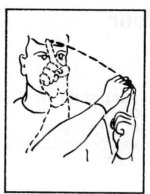

OBJECTIVE

The left hand, with only the index finger extended (remaining fingers and thumb are contracted), is held in front and to the left side of the body at the level of the shoulder with the index finger pointing upward and the back side facing the viewer. The back side of the right index finger (remaining fingers and thumb are con- of the forehead and then is moved forward as the hand configuration changes to an *O*; the *O* hand then touches the index fingertip of the left hand (the back side of the right *O* hand faces up as the sign is completed).

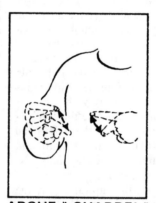

ARGUE,* QUARREL*

Both hands, each with only its index finger extended (remaining fingers and thumb are contracted), are placed about three to four inches apart in front of the body so that their index fingers are pointing at each other (the back sides of the hands face the viewer); next, the wrists simultaneously turn the hands inward so that the index fingers are now pointing in a downward direction, and then return to the former hand position. This motion is repeated several times.

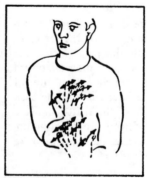

WAIT*

Both hands, each with its fingers and thumb apart, slightly bent and pointing upward, are positioned one in front of the other to the left side of the body and are held so that the palms are facing the signer. Next, the fingers of the stationary hands perform several quick wiggling motions.

GOAL

The left hand, with only the index finger extended, is held in front and to the left side of the body at the level of the shoulder with the index finger pointing upward (remaining fingers and thumb are contracted) and the back side of the hand toward the viewer; the back side of the right index finger (remaining fingers and thumb are contracted) touches the center of the forehead and then is moved forward to touch the fingertip of the left hand.

DEBT,* OWE*

The left hand, with the thumb and fingers extended and joined, is held in front and slightly to the left side of the body with the palm facing up and the fingers pointing to the viewer; the index *fingertip* of the right hand (remaining fingers and thumb are contracted) descends to touch the left palm, is raised up and retouches the palm. This motion is repeated several times.

NOTE: Do not confuse this sign with that for ("discuss") where the *edge* of the index finger strikes the left palm.

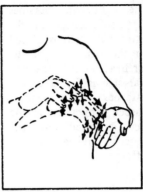

STUDY*

The left hand, with the thumb and fingers extended and joined, is held in front and slightly to the left side of the body with the palm facing up and the fingers pointing to the right; the right hand, with the thumb and fingers extended and apart, is held in front of the body so that the fingers point to the left palm at an angle; then, the hand, with the fingers executing a wiggling motion, is moved toward the left palm (but does not touch it) and then returns to the original position. This motion is repeated several times.

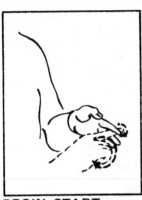

BEGIN, START

The left hand, with the fingers and thumb extended and joined, is held in front and to the left side of the body with the palm facing to the right and the fingers pointing to the viewer; the right index finger (remaining fingers and thumb are contracted) is placed between the first and second fingers of the left hand and then the right hand is rotated clockwise.

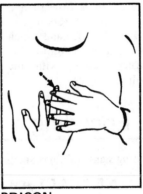

PRISON

The left hand, with the thumb and fingers extended and apart, is placed in front of the signer with the palm facing toward the body and the fingers pointing to the right. The right hand, also with the thumb and fingers extended, apart and pointing upward, is moved toward the left hand so that the back sides of the right fingers (which are pointing upward) touch the palmar sides of the left fingers, suggesting the bars associated with this institution.

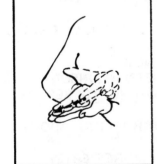

HONEST

The left hand with the thumb and fingers extended and joined, is held in front and slightly to the left side of the body with the palm facing up and the fingers pointing to the viewer; the right hand assumes the configuration of the letter *H*, touches the left palm (the side of the middle finger of the right *H* hand makes contact with the left palm); then, the *H* hand slides across the left palm in the direction of the viewer.

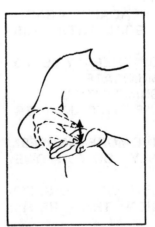

DISCUSS,* DEBATE*

The left hand, with the thumb and fingers extended and joined, is held in front of the body with the palm facing upward and the fingers pointing to the viewer. The right hand, with only the index finger extended (thumb and remaining fingers are contracted) descends so that the *side* of the right index finger strikes the left palm several times as if "making a point."

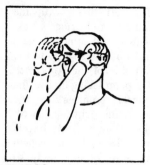

GUESS

The right hand assumes the configuration of the letter *C*, which is placed on the right side of the forehead so that the palmar side is facing to the left; next, the *C* hand is clasped into a fist as the hand is moved across the signer's forehead to the left.

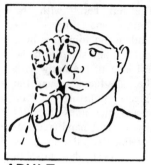

ADULT

The right hand, in the configuration of the letter *A*, is moved in and touches the right side of the forehead with the back side of the thumb; then, the *A* hand descends and touches the right side of the signer's chin (the back side of the *A* hand is facing to the right as the sign ends).

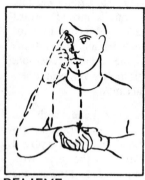

BELIEVE

The right index finger (remaining fingers and thumb are contracted) first touches the forehead; next all of the fingers of the right hand simultaneously extend as the hand is moved in a forward and downward direction and clasps the left hand which is extended in front of the signer's body, with the palm facing up.

SHOWER*

The right hand, with the thumb flexed to touch the extended but joined fingertips, is positioned three to four inches above the right side of the head; then, the hand extends and moves downward - toward the head - as the thumb and fingers spread apart. This motion is repeated several times.

A) Exercises in Encoding

Encode the following material using signs and fingerspelling. Use fingerspelling for all underlined words.

1. WHY <u>DID</u> YOU TELL ME THAT I AM STUPID?
2. I HOPE SHE COMES TODAY. ("Today" is signed as "now" plus "day.")
3. THE DOCTOR <u>FEELS</u> THAT THE PAIN WILL STOP BY ITSELF.
4. <u>DO</u> YOU HAVE A HEADACHE AGAIN?
5. WHAT IS YOUR GOAL WITH THIS <u>PATIENT</u>?
6. AN OBJECTIVE <u>OF</u> <u>THERAPY</u> IS <u>TO</u> TEACH HIM <u>TO</u> COMMUNICATE.
7. PLEASE STOP ARGUING WITH US.
8. MAY WE DISCUSS THIS <u>MATTER</u> AGAIN?
9. CAN YOU WAIT FIVE MORE MINUTES?
10. HOW MUCH MONEY <u>DO</u> YOU OWE THEM?
11. WHY CAN'T WE POSTPONE BUYING IT?
12. IT IS MY OPINION THAT HE IS HONEST.
13. GUESS HOW OLD I AM.
14. TRY STUDYING MORE.
15. WHY DON'T YOU BELIEVE HIS ANSWER?
16. WHEN <u>DOES</u> THE EVALUATION BEGIN?
17. THE <u>EXAMINATION</u> WILL START IN TEN MINUTES.
18. HOW <u>DO</u> WE HELP THE ADULT DEAF PERSON?
19. HE IS SHOWERING NOW.
20. HAVE YOU EVER BEEN IN PRISON?
21. GUESS WHO IS COMING <u>TO</u> SEE US TODAY.
22. WHY ARE WE QUARRELING ABOUT IT?
23. <u>DO</u> YOU HAVE ANY MORE DEBTS?
24. WE BELIEVE THAT YOU CAN LEARN HOW <u>TO</u> READ AND WRITE.
25. WHAT IS YOUR PROFESSION? ("Profession" is signed similarly to "major," but with a *P* hand.)

B) Exercises in Decoding

Decode the following illustrated exercises:

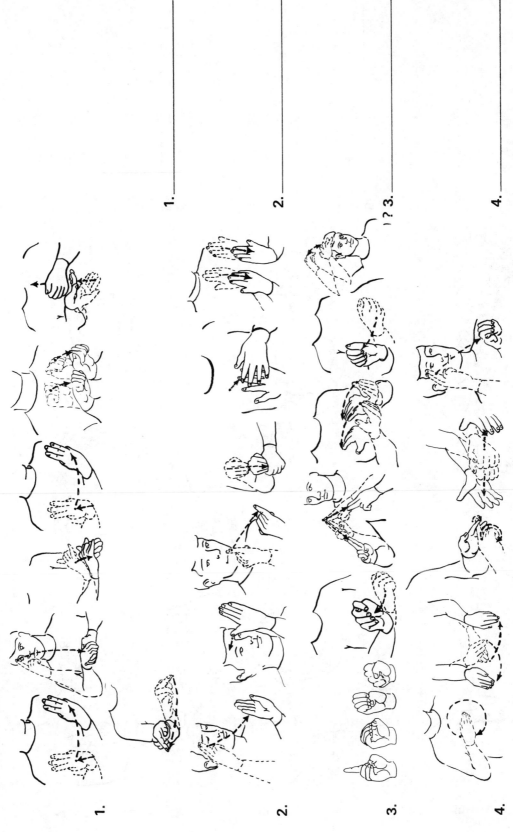

1.

2.

3.

4.

1.

2.

? 3.

4.

5.

6.

7.

8.

9.

10.

? 11.

11.

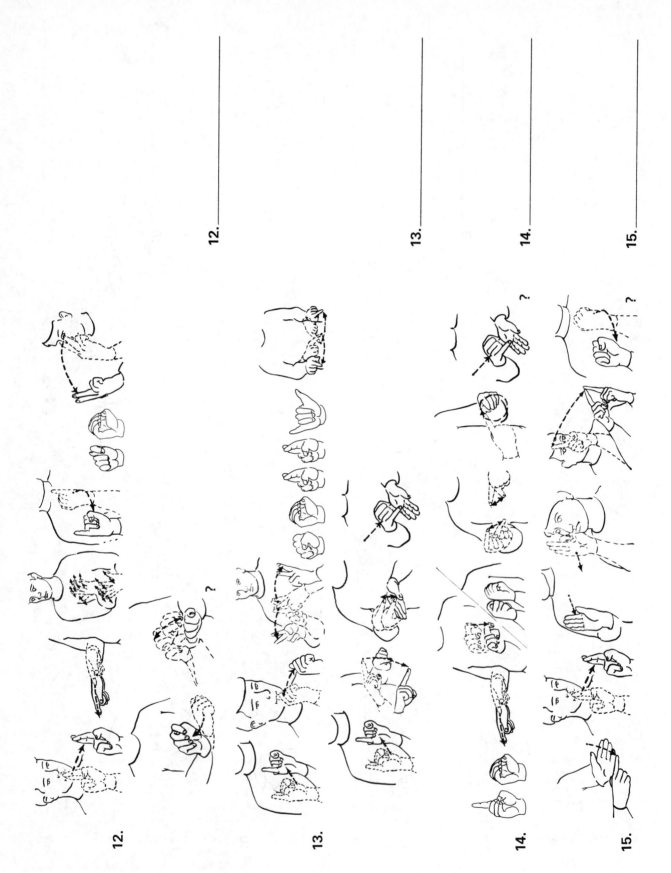

12.

13.

14.

15.

16.

17.

18.

16.

17.

18.

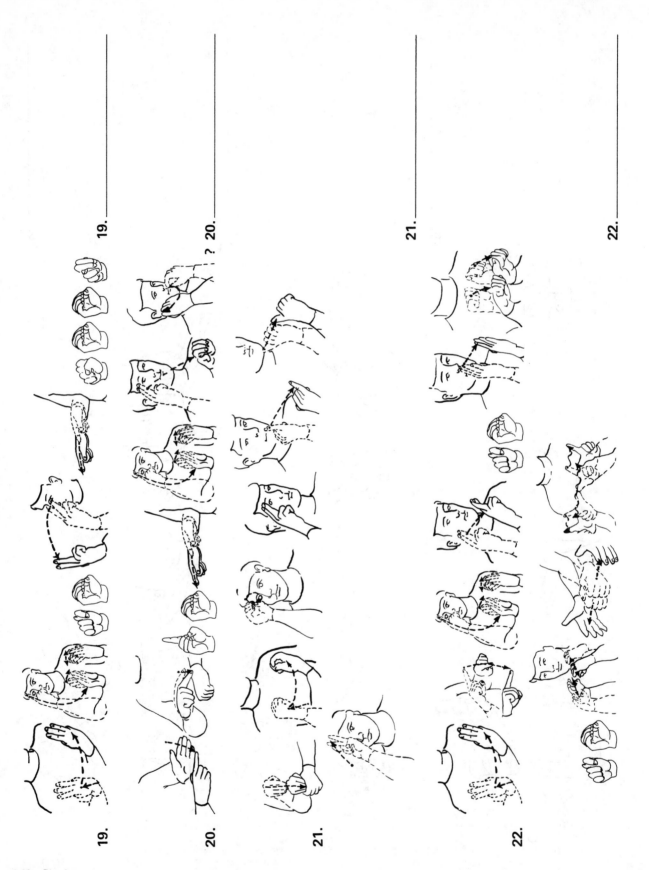

19.

20.

21.

22.

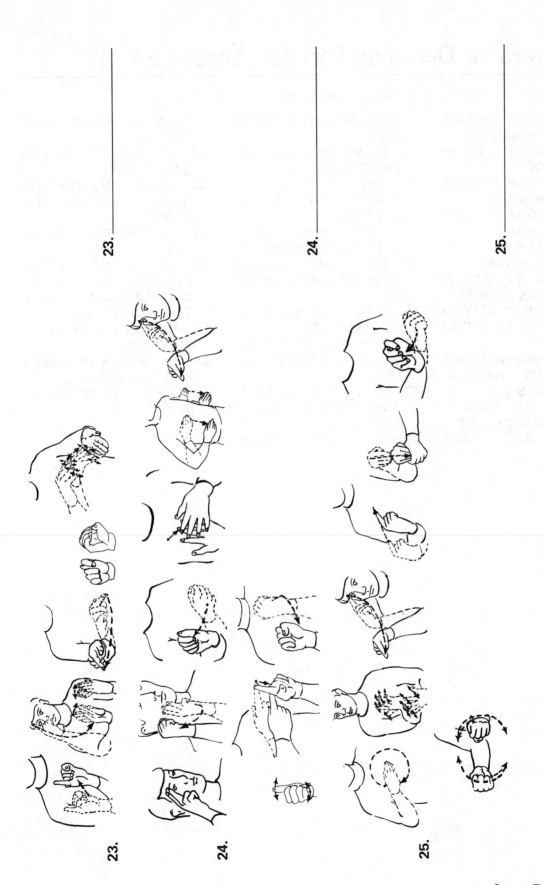

23.

24.

25.

C) Answers for Decoding Part (B), Lesson 24

Underlined words indicate that they should have been fingerspelled.

1. WE BELIEVE THAT WE CAN HELP YOU (plural).
2. HIS FATHER IS IN PRISON NOW.
3. <u>DOES</u> THE HOUSE HAVE A SHOWER?
4. PLEASE DON'T START WITHOUT HIM.
5. OUR MAJOR IS IN DEAF EDUCATION.
6. IS YOUR <u>PATIENT</u> A CHILD OR AN ADULT?
7. I BELIEVE THAT YOU (plural) OWE US MORE MONEY.
8. IF YOU (singular) DON'T KNOW THE ANSWER, PLEASE GUESS.
9. HE IS AN HONEST HEARING AID <u>DEALER</u>.
10. WHAT ARE YOUR REASONS FOR POSTPON-ING IT?
11. <u>DO</u> WE OWE YOU ANY-THING ELSE?
12. ARE YOU (singular) WAITING <u>TO</u> SEE THE DOCTOR?
13. I AM VERY <u>SORRY</u>, BUT I CAN'T DISCUSS IT.
14. <u>DO</u> YOU (singular) HAVE <u>TO</u> ARGUE ABOUT IT?
15. WHAT ARE YOUR FU-TURE GOALS?
16. WHY <u>DID</u> YOU (singu-lar) <u>CHOOSE</u> THIS OBJEC-TIVE?
17. HOW OFTEN <u>DOES</u> HE HAVE THESE HEAD-ACHES?
18. CAN YOU (singular) TELL ME WHERE YOUR PAIN IS?
19. WE HOPE <u>TO</u> SEE YOU (plural) <u>SOON</u>.
20. WHAT TIME <u>DO</u> YOU (singular) EXPECT HIM HOME?
21. IN OUR OPINION, HE IS NOT STUPID.
22. WE CAN'T EXPECT HER <u>TO</u> BE ABLE <u>TO</u> COMMUNICATE WITH-OUT LANGUAGE.
23. I EXPECT YOU (plural) <u>TO</u> STUDY.
24. HE WAS A PRISONER FOR TEN MONTHS.
25. PLEASE WAIT FOR ME IN THE CAR.

lesson twenty-five

Signs presented in this lesson are:

PROGRESS (noun)   SELL, STORE* (noun)   REVERSE   EXAMPLE
PAY   JEALOUS   LECTURE,* SPEECH*   LAW
SHORT (TIME)*   STUBBORN   SHOW (verb)   LEAVE, DEPART
LIMIT   RULE   DEMONSTRATE   INVESTIGATE,* EXAMINE*
AGAINST   CHANGE   ILLUSTRATE   PRINCIPLE

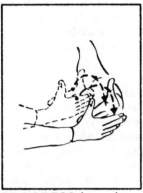

PROGRESS (noun)

Both hands, each with its thumb extended and apart (remaining fingers are extended and joined), are placed one in front of the other with the right hand nearer the viewer. (Both hands have their palmar sides towards the signer and their fingertips pointing in opposite direction, left and right respectively.) Next, the left hand completes an upward arc motion in a forward direction so that now it is in front of the right hand. Then the right hand makes a similar motion so that when the sign comes to an end, the right hand is directly in front of the left one (closest to the viewer) while the original configuration is preserved.

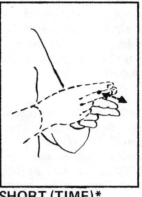

SHORT (TIME)*

Both hands first assume the configuration of the letter *H*. The left *H* hand is placed in front and slightly to the left side of the body pointing to the viewer with the back side of the left *H* hand facing to the left. The right *H* hand is placed over the left *H* hand and points to the left (its back side is toward the viewer). The lower edge of the right second finger touches the second knuckle of the left index finger; then the right *H* hand grazes the left index finger as it is moved back and forth (toward the wrist and away from it). This motion is repeated several times.

NOTE: "Short" here refers to time and is not applicable to linear measurement.

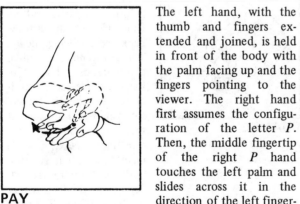

PAY

The left hand, with the thumb and fingers extended and joined, is held in front of the body with the palm facing up and the fingers pointing to the viewer. The right hand first assumes the configuration of the letter *P*. Then, the middle fingertip of the right *P* hand touches the left palm and slides across it in the direction of the left fingertips with the right wrist curving slightly upward.

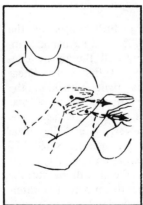

LIMIT

Both hands, each with its thumb and fingers joined and flexed at the base, are placed with the right hand above the left in front of the body so that their palms are facing down and their fingers are pointing in opposite directions (left and right, respectively). Next, with the configuration maintained, the hands simultaneously are moved forward.

271

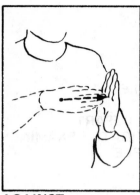

AGAINST

The left hand, with the thumb and fingers extended and joined, is held in front and to the left side of the body with the fingers pointing upward and the palm facing to the right. The right hand, with the thumb and fingers extended and joined, is moved horizontally toward the left hand so that contact is made between the right fingertips and the left palm (back side of the right hand is facing the viewer as the sign comes to an end).

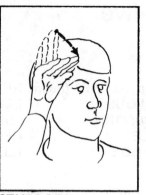

STUBBORN

The right hand, with the thumb extended and apart (remaining fingers are extended and joined), first moves toward and touches the right side of the forehead with the thumb (palm of hand is facing the viewer and with the right fingertips pointing upward). Next, with the right thumb maintaining contact with the side of the forehead, the fingers are bent forcefully in a forward direction.

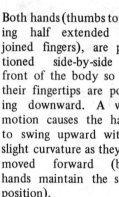

SELL, STORE* (noun)

Both hands (thumbs touching half extended and joined fingers), are positioned side-by-side in front of the body so that their fingertips are pointing downward. A wrist motion causes the hands to swing upward with a slight curvature as they are moved forward (both hands maintain the same position).
NOTE: The sign for "store" (noun) is made by signing "sell" several times. That is, "store" is done with a repeated motion.

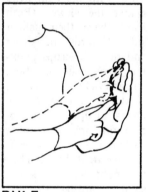

RULE

The left hand, with the thumb and fingers extended and joined, is held in front and to the left side of the body with the fingers pointing upward and the palm facing to the right. The right hand makes the letter *R* and touches the left hand near the fingertips. Next, the *R* hand separates, is moved down, and retouches the left palm.

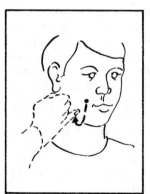

JEALOUS

The little finger of the right hand (remaining fingers and thumb are contracted) first is placed near the right corner of the mouth and is held so that its back side is facing the viewer. Next, the little finger makes a small "J" formation near the corner of the mouth by turning the forearm in a counter-clockwise direction.

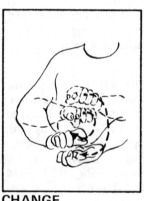

CHANGE

The right hand, with the thumb and index finger curved to touch each other (remaining fingers are contracted and clasped to the palm), is positioned in front of the body with the back side facing down. The left hand, in a similar configuration, but with the back side facing up, is placed on the right hand so that the knuckles of their contracted fingers are touching. Next, while maintaining their contact, both hands are turned 180 degrees to the left so that the back of the right hand is now facing up as the sign comes to an end.

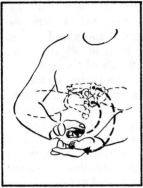

REVERSE

This sign is made similarly to the previous one ("change"), except that the hands assume an *R* configuration. The right *R* hand, with the *R* fingertips pointing toward the viewer, is placed in front of the body with the back side facing down. The left *R* hand, in a similar configuration but with the back facing up, is placed on the right hand so that the back sides of their contracted thumbs and fingers are touching. Next, while maintaining their contact, both hands are turned 180 degrees to the left so that the back of the right hand is now facing up as the sign comes to an end.

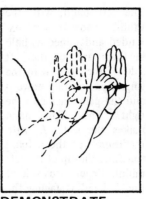

DEMONSTRATE

This sign is made similarly to the previous one ("show"), except that the right hand first adopts a *D* configuration. The *D* hand is moved from a horizontal position and touches the left palm. (The joined thumb and fingertips of the *D* hand touch the left palm, while the index finger of the *D* hand, with its back side toward the signer, is pointing upward.) Then, without separating, the hands are moved forward.

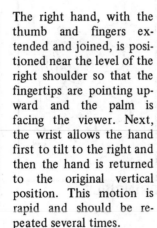

LECTURE,* SPEECH*

The right hand, with the thumb and fingers extended and joined, is positioned near the level of the right shoulder so that the fingertips are pointing upward and the palm is facing the viewer. Next, the wrist allows the hand first to tilt to the right and then the hand is returned to the original vertical position. This motion is rapid and should be repeated several times.

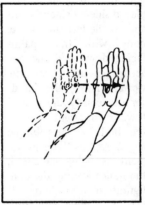

ILLUSTRATE

This sign is made similarly to the previous one ("demonstrate"), except that the right hand first adopts an *I* configuration. The *I* hand is moved from a horizontal position and, with the top portion of the *I* hand, touches the left palm. (The *I* hand is held with the back side toward the signer.) Then, without separating, the hands are moved forward.

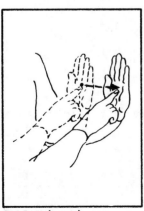

SHOW (verb)

The left hand, with the thumb and fingers extended and joined, is held in front and to the left side of the body with the fingers pointing upward and the palm facing to the right. The right index finger (thumb and remaining fingers are contracted) touches the palm of the left hand and holds that contact as both hands are moved forward.

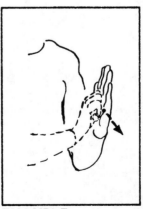

EXAMPLE

This sign is made similarly to the previous one ("illustrate"), except that the right hand first adopts an *E* configuration. The *E* hand is moved from a horizontal position and, with the top part of the *E* hand, touches the left palm. (The *E* hand is held with the back side toward the signer.) Then, without separating, both hands are moved forward.

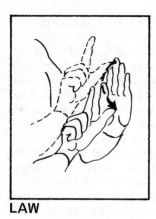

LAW

The left hand, with the thumb and fingers extended and joined, is held in front and to the left side of the body with the fingertips pointing upward and the palm facing to the right. The right hand makes the letter *L*, with the thumb of the *L* hand touching the tip of the left middle finger (back side of the *L* hand is facing the signer). Next, the *L* hand separates, is moved down, and retouches the left palm.

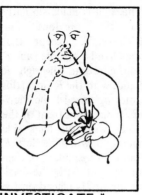

INVESTIGATE,*
EXAMINE*

The left hand, with the thumb and fingers extended and joined, is held in front and slightly to the left side of the body with the palm facing up and the fingertips pointing to the viewer. The right index fingertip (thumb and remaining fingers are contracted) first touches the nose and then is moved downward to touch the left palm, grazing the left hand with the index finger as it moves forward toward the left fingertips. Then, the right index finger quickly returns to the left palm and repeats the grazing motion.

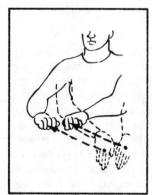

LEAVE, DEPART

Both hands, each with its thumb and fingers extended and joined, are placed side-by-side in front and to the left side of the body with their palms facing down and the fingertips pointing at the viewer. Next, the hands simultaneously are moved toward the right side of the body at an oblique angle. As this latter movement is being executed, the hands assume the configuration of the letter *A*. (The sign ends with both *A* hands side-by-side and with their wrists facing down.)

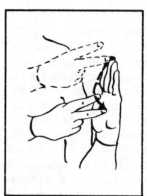

PRINCIPLE

The left hand, with the thumb and fingers extended and joined, is held in front and to the left side of the body so that the fingers are pointing upward and the palm faces to the right. The right hand first makes the letter *P*, with the middle fingertip of the *P* hand touching the tip of the left middle finger. Then, the *P* hand separates, is moved downward and retouches the palm of the left hand.

A) Exercises in Encoding

Encode the following material using signs and fingerspelling. Use fingerspelling for all underlined words.

1. PLEASE PAY US THE MONEY THAT YOU OWE US.
2. SHE IS AGAINST THE IDEA YOU <u>PROPOSED</u> YESTERDAY.
3. <u>LET</u> ME KNOW IF YOU <u>DECIDE</u> <u>TO</u> SELL IT.
4. IS YOUR SISTER A JEALOUS PERSON?
5. WE CAN <u>STAY</u> ONLY FOR A SHORT TIME.
6. FIRST, YOU NEED <u>TO</u> LEARN THE RULES <u>OF</u> OUR LANGUAGE.
7. WHY <u>IS</u> HE BEING <u>SO</u> STUBBORN?
8. <u>DO</u> YOU WANT <u>TO</u> CHANGE YOUR ANSWER?
9. WHY <u>DID</u> SHE REVERSE THE WORDS IN THIS <u>SENTENCE</u>?
10. IT IS AGAINST THE RULE <u>TO</u> RE-VERSE THESE.
11. SOME <u>OF</u> US DON'T <u>WORK</u> TO OUR LIMIT.
12. WHO CAN EXPLAIN THE LAW FOR US?
13. IS HE A GOOD LAWYER? ("Lawyer" is signed as "law" plus "er"-person.)
14. <u>DO</u> YOU KNOW WHEN HE IS LEAVING FOR THE <u>CONVENTION</u>?
15. HIS <u>LECTURE</u> WAS ABOUT TOTAL COMMUNICATION.
16. SHOW US THAT YOU KNOW HOW <u>TO</u> USE THE RULE.
17. ASK HIM <u>TO</u> DEMONSTRATE IT AGAIN.
18. THIS IS A GOOD EXAMPLE <u>OF</u> THE BASIC IDEA.
19. I CAN'T BE SURE THAT THEY WILL NOT INVESTIGATE US.
20. WE DON'T THINK THAT WE CAN <u>SUPPORT</u> THIS PRINCIPLE.
21. THIS IS ANOTHER <u>WAY</u> <u>OF</u> ILLUS-TRATING THE SAME IDEA.
22. SHE IS BEGINNING <u>TO</u> SHOW SOME PROGRESS.
23. TODAY, I WANT <u>TO</u> DEMONSTRATE HOW A HEARING AID <u>WORKS</u>.
24. IS THERE A RULE AGAINST IT?
25. WILL YOU DRIVE ME TO THE STORE? ("Store" is signed similarly to "sell," but is repeated several times.)

B) Exercises in Decoding

Decode the following illustrated exercises:

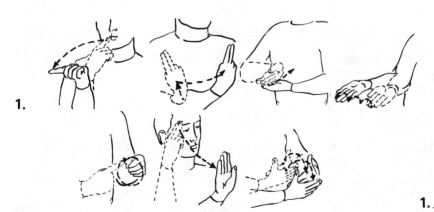

1.

1. _____

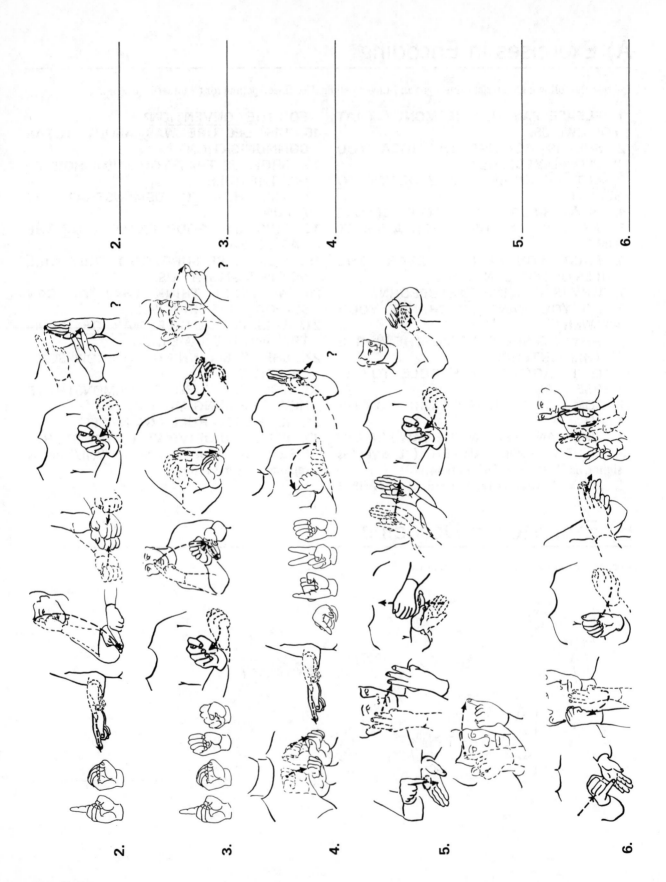

2.

3.

4.

5.

6.

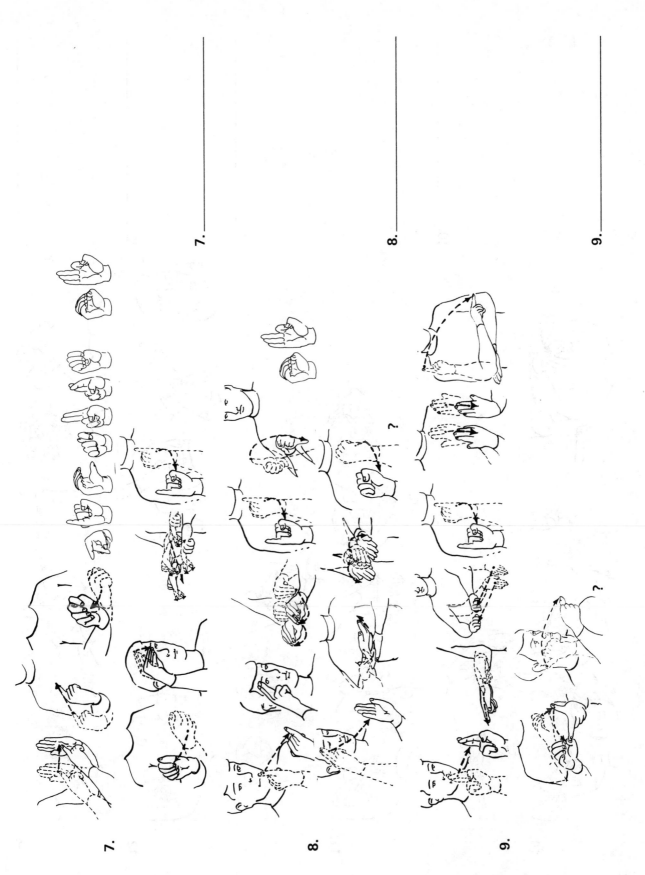

7.

8.

9.

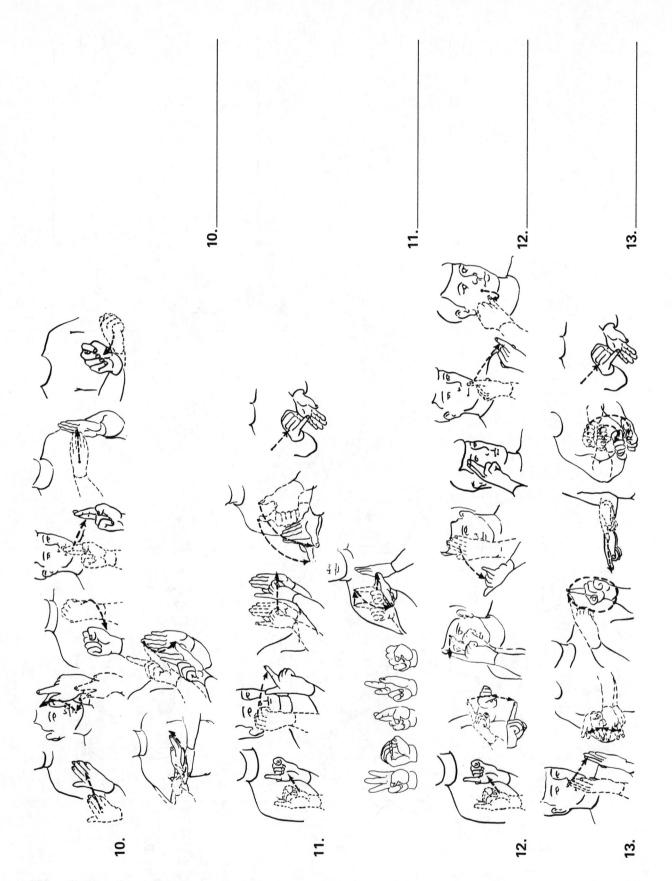

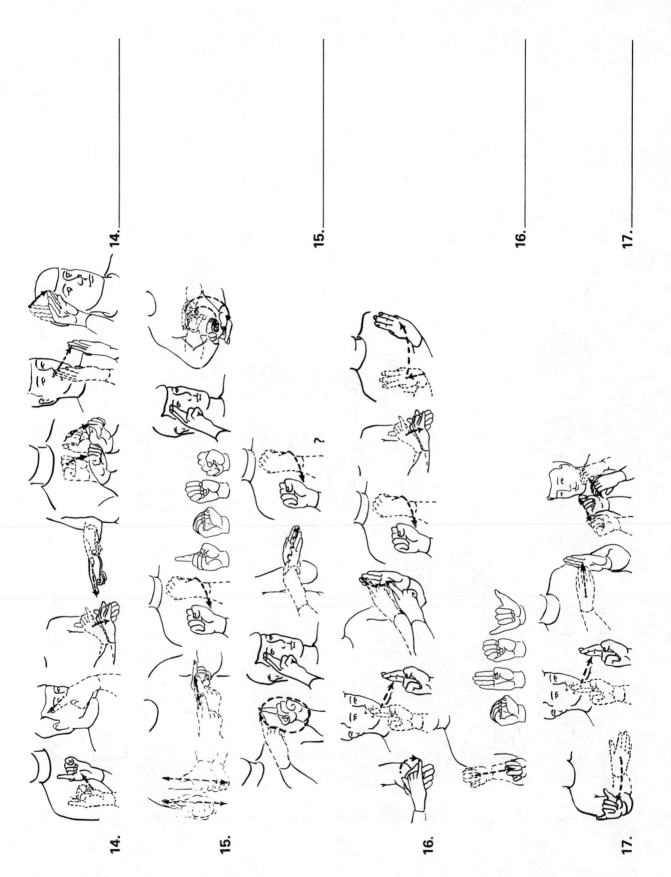

14.

15.

16.

17.

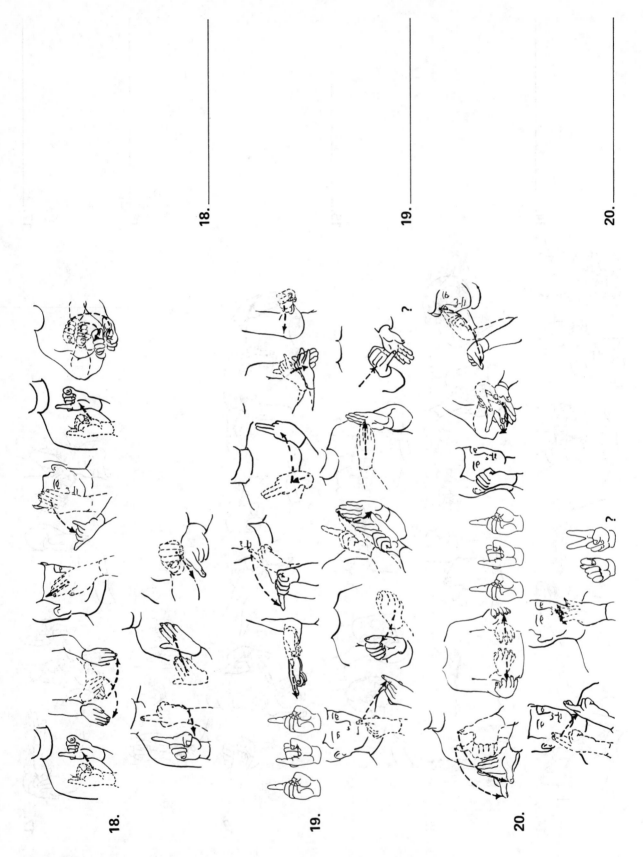

18.

19.

20.

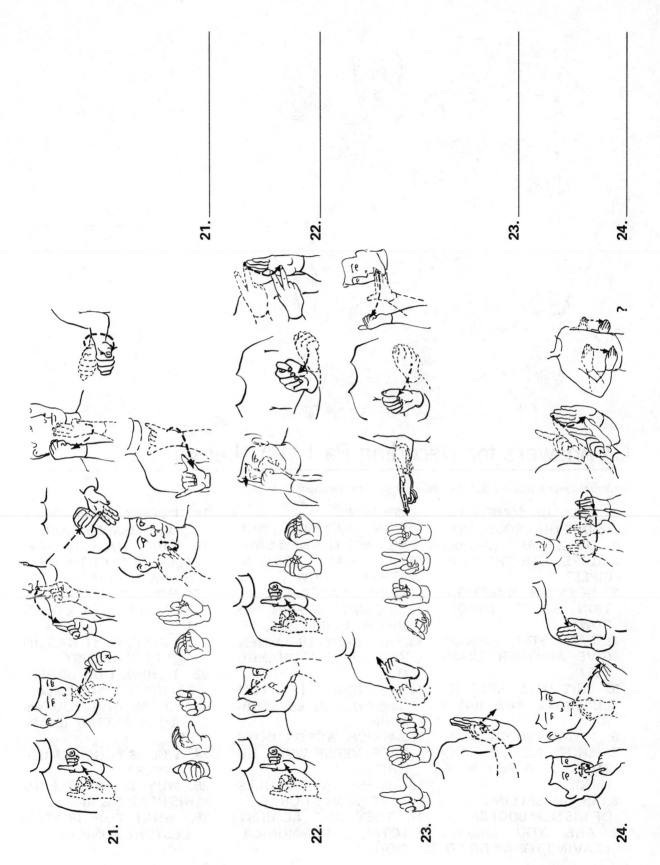

21.

22.

23.

24.

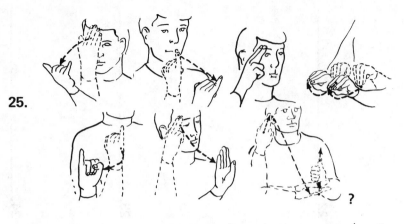

25. _____

26. _____

C) Answers for Decoding Part (B), Lesson 25

Underlined words indicate that they should have been fingerspelled.

1. TELL US SOMETHING ABOUT HIS PROGRESS.
2. <u>DO</u> YOU (singular) AGREE WITH THE PRINCIPLE?
3. <u>DOES</u> THE INVESTIGATION START TOMORROW?
4. CAN YOU (singular) <u>GIVE</u> ANOTHER EXAMPLE?
5. THIS WILL HELP ILLUSTRATE THE BASIC IDEA.
6. IT WAS A SHORT VISIT.
7. SHOW ME THE <u>PICTURE OF</u> A BOY RUNNING.
8. IS HE SELLING ANY <u>OF</u> HIS NEW BOOKS?
9. ARE YOU (singular) LEAVING TODAY OR TOMORROW?
10. MY PARENTS ARE AGAINST THE NEW LAW.
11. I SHALL DEMONSTRATE HOW IT <u>WORKS</u> LATER.
12. I CAN'T UNDERSTAND WHY HE IS JEALOUS.
13. BE CAREFUL WHEN YOU (singular) CHANGE IT.
14. I THINK THAT YOU (singular) CAN BE STUBBORN.
15. WHICH WORDS <u>DOES</u> HE REVERSE WHEN HE WRITES?
16. THESE ARE RULES THAT WE MUST <u>OBEY</u>.
17. THEY ARE AGAINST TOTAL COMMUNICATION.
18. I DON'T KNOW WHY I CHANGED MY MAJOR.
19. <u>DID</u> YOU (singular) TELL US THAT THERE IS A LAW AGAINST IT?
20. HOW MUCH <u>DID</u> SHE PAY FOR HER COLOR <u>T.V.</u>?
21. I AM SURE IT WAS AN <u>ACT OF</u> JEALOUSY.
22. I THINK I <u>DO</u> UNDERSTAND THE PRINCIPLE.
23. <u>LET</u> ME <u>GIVE</u> YOU (singular) A BETTER EXAMPLE.
24. WHO IS YOUR FAMILY LAWYER?
25. WHY IS HE SELLING HIS HEARING AID?
26. WHAT TIME IS YOUR LECTURE TONIGHT?

lesson twenty-six

Signs presented in this lesson are:

SAY*	REFUSE, OBJECT	COLD*	YOUNG*
WONDERFUL	FOLD	NUMBER	BATH*
FALSE	LEAVE (transitive verb)	WINTER*	CRITICIZE, CORRECT
RESPONSIBLE	HANDKERCHIEF, * COLD*	FREEZE	HONOR
FAULT	OPERATE, SURGERY	ASSOCIATE, MINGLE	RESPECT

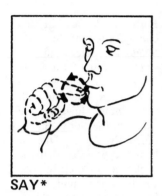

SAY*

With the right index finger (remaining fingers and thumb are contracted) extended and pointing to the left in front of the lips, complete a circle by moving the index finger in a forward and clockwise direction. This motion is repeated several times.

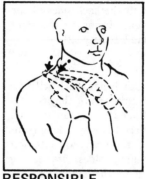

RESPONSIBLE

Both hands make the letter *R* and then both are placed on the signer's right shoulder with the tips of the *R* fingers touching the shoulder.

NOTE: This sign may intend to suggest, perhaps, that a burden is weighing down the shoulder.

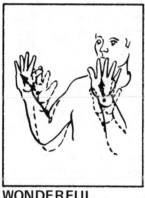

WONDERFUL

Both hands, each with its thumb and fingers extended and apart, are positioned near each side of the body at shoulder level with the fingertips pointing upward and their palmar sides facing the viewer. Next, with the configuration maintained, the hands are pushed slightly forward and in an upward direction.

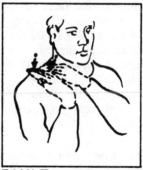

FAULT

Both hands, each with its fingers and thumb extended and joined, are placed on the signer's right shoulder with the palmar sides of the fingers of both hands touching the shoulder.

FALSE

The right hand, with only the index finger extended (thumb and remaining fingers are contracted), is held near the right cheek so that the index finger is pointing upward and with its back side facing to the right. Then, the hand tilts (bending at the wrist) to the left, in front of the face.

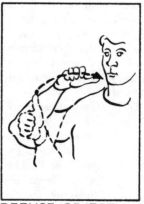

REFUSE, OBJECT

The right hand, with only the thumb extended and apart (remaining fingers are contracted and clasped to the palm), first is held in front and to the right side of the body with the thumb sticking upward and the back side of the hand facing to the right. Next, the hand is jerked up and back so the thumb points over the signer's shoulder.

283

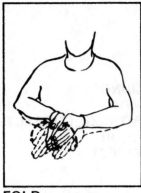

FOLD

Both hands, with their thumbs and fingers extended and joined, are held in front of the body so that their edges are touching and the fingertips are pointing toward the viewer. The palms are facing up. Next, without separating, the hands tilt inward so that their palmar surfaces are now touching. The sign ends with the back sides of the hands facing to the right and left, respectively.

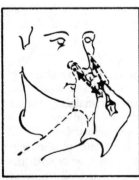

**LEAVE
(transitive verb)**

Both hands, each with its thumb and fingers extended and apart, are placed side-by-side in front of the body so that their palmar sides are facing each other and their fingertips are pointing somewhat in an upward direction. (The hands are tilted at about a 45 degree upward angle.) Next, the hands simultaneously are tilted downward so that now their fingertips are pointing to the ground as the sign comes to an end.

**HANDKERCHIEF,*
COLD***

The right hand assumes the configuration of the letter *G*, which first faces and then is moved in to touch both sides of the nostrils. Next, the *G* hand is moved slightly downward as the right thumb and index finger touch. This motion is repeated several times.
NOTE: Context will determine whether the signer is referring to "handkerchief" or "cold" in the sense of "infection."

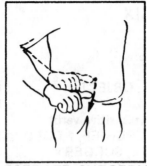

OPERATE, SURGERY

The right hand, with only the thumb extended (remaining fingers are contracted and clasped to the palm), first touches the region of the abdomen with its thumbnail and then the right thumb grazes the abdomen as the hand is moved downward.

COLD*

Both hands are in the configuration of the letter *S* and are placed side-by-side in front of the body so that their wrists are facing each other and with the elbows hugging the sides of the body. Simultaneously, bring the *S* hands together so that the back sides of their thumbs touch. Then, pull the *S* hands apart, right and left, and return them to their former position. The motion is quick and is repeated several times.

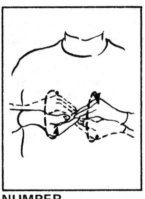

NUMBER

The left hand, with the thumb bending inward to touch the palmar sides of the extended and joined fingers, first is held in front of the body with the back sides of the left fingers facing down and the fingertips pointing to the right. The right hand, in a similar configuration (except that the back sides of the fingers face up and the fingertips point to the left), is brought to midline so that the hands touch their tips. Next, the wrists rotate the hands clockwise and counter-clockwise so that now the backs of the right fingers are facing down while the backs of the left fingers are facing up.

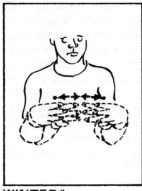

WINTER*

This sign is made similarly to the previous one ("cold"), except that the hands assume a *W* configuration and are placed side-by-side in front of the body with the *W* fingertips pointing at each other (the backs of the *W* hands face the viewer) and the elbows hugging the sides of the body. Simultaneously, bring the *W* hands together so that their fingertips touch, and then pull them apart (right and left). The motion is quick and is repeated several times.

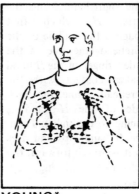

YOUNG*

Both hands, each with its thumb extended and apart (remaining fingers are extended and joined), are placed side-by-side on the signer's chest so that only their fingertips are touching the body (their thumbs are pointing upward and the back sides of both hands are facing the viewer). Next, the hands simultaneously brush upward and outward on the chest and then return to their former position to repeat the motion.

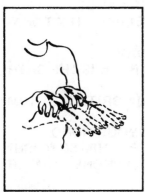

FREEZE

Both hands, each with its thumb curled inward and remaining fingers extended and apart, are placed side-by-side in front of the body so that the sides of their index fingers are touching (the palms are facing down and the fingertips are pointing to the viewer). Next, the hands simultaneously are moved toward the signer as their fingers assume a claw-like configuration, suggesting the effect of freezing.

BATH*

Both hands, each in the configuration of the letter *A*, are positioned side-by-side on the chest so that they are parallel with each other (the back sides of the *A* hands face the viewer). Simultaneously, the *A* hands graze the chest as they are moved up and down as if to suggest that the body is being washed.

ASSOCIATE, MINGLE

The left hand, with only the thumb extended and held vertically (remaining fingers are contracted to the palm), is held in front of the body with the back side to the viewer. The right hand, with only the thumb extended (remaining fingers are contracted to the palm), then is tilted downward and held directly above the left thumb. Then, the right thumb performs a clockwise circular motion around the stationary left thumb.

CRITICIZE, CORRECT

The left hand, with the thumb and fingers extended and joined, is held in front and to the left side of the body, with the fingers pointing to the viewer and the palm facing up. The right index fingertip (thumb and remaining fingers are contracted) first touches the lips and then the right hand is moved forward and downward with the index finger drawing an "X" pattern on the left palm.

The right hand forms the letter *H*, which first touches the middle of the forehead (the side of the index finger of the *H* hand makes contact with the forehead, while the back side of the *H* hand is facing to the right). Then, the *H* hand dips and rises as it is moved forward, the fingertips pointing upward.

HONOR

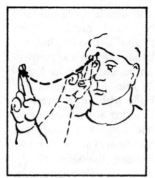

The right hand, in the configuration of the letter *R* (the side of the extended *R* fingers makes contact with the middle of the forehead), is held so that its back side is facing to the right. Then, the *R* hand dips and rises as it is moved forward, the extended fingers pointing upward.

RESPECT

A) Exercises in Encoding

Encode the following material using signs and fingerspelling. Use fingerspelling for all underlined words.

1. MAY WE FOLD THE PAPER?
2. PLEASE LEAVE THE BOOKS ON MY DESK.
3. MY DOCTOR REFUSES <u>TO</u> OPERATE ON ME UNTIL NEXT YEAR.
4. <u>DO</u> YOU WANT SOME <u>MEDICINE</u> FOR YOUR COLD?
5. WHY IS YOUR <u>ROOM</u> SO COLD?
6. WE GO TO <u>FLORIDA</u> EVERY WINTER.
7. I THINK SHE WANTS <u>TO</u> FREEZE THE <u>VEGETABLES</u>.
8. WE REFUSE <u>TO</u> ASSOCIATE WITH THEM.
9. SAY THESE WORDS FOR ME.
10. WE THINK THAT YOU ARE WONDERFUL.
11. I MUST SAY THAT IT IS FALSE.
12. HE IS NOT RESPONSIBLE FOR WHAT HAPPENED.
13. I GUESS IT WAS OUR FAULT.
14. WE REFUSE <u>TO</u> BELIEVE THAT WINTER IS HERE.
15. I <u>FEEL</u> YOUNG TODAY.
16. EXCUSE ME, BUT WHERE IS THE BATH <u>ROOM</u>?
17. WHY MUST YOU CRITICIZE HIM AGAIN?
18. THIS WAS <u>DONE</u> IN YOUR HONOR.
19. WHY <u>DO</u> YOU RESPECT HIM <u>SO</u> MUCH?
20. WHAT IS YOUR TELEPHONE NUMBER AT THE <u>OFFICE</u>?
21. OUR BABY <u>DID</u> NOT SAY ANY WORDS UNTIL HE WAS FOUR.
22. SHE WAS TOO YOUNG FOR SURGERY.
23. WHOSE FAULT WAS IT THAT I WAS <u>BORN</u> DEAF?
24. <u>DO</u> YOU HAVE A HANDKERCHIEF WITH YOU?

B) Exercises in Decoding

Decode the following illustrated exercises:

1.

1. _____

2.

3.

4.

2.

3.

4.

5.

6.

7.

8.

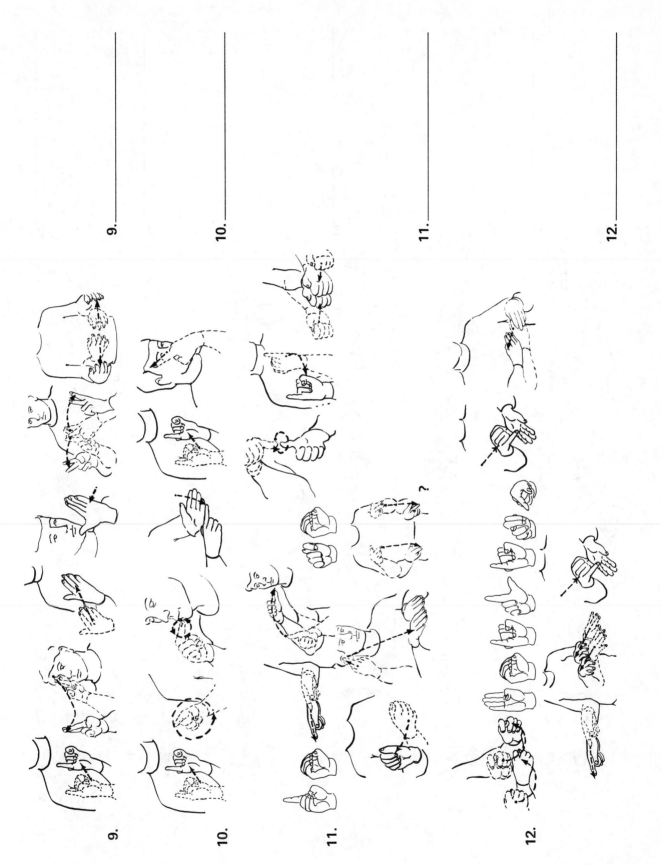

9.

10.

11.

12.

9.

10.

11.

12.

13.

14.

15.

16.

13.

14.

15.

16.

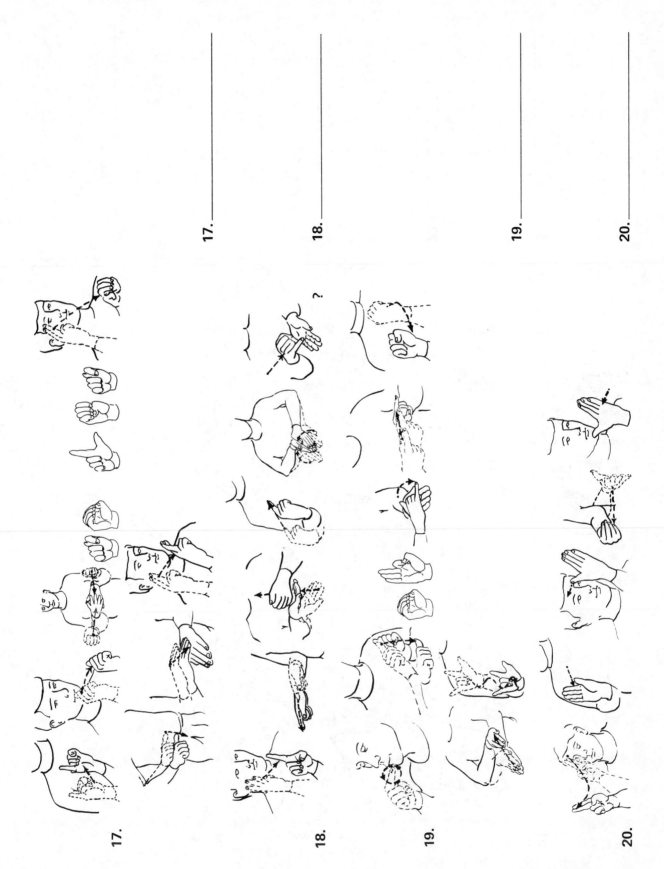

17.

18.

19.

20.

17.

18.

19.

20.

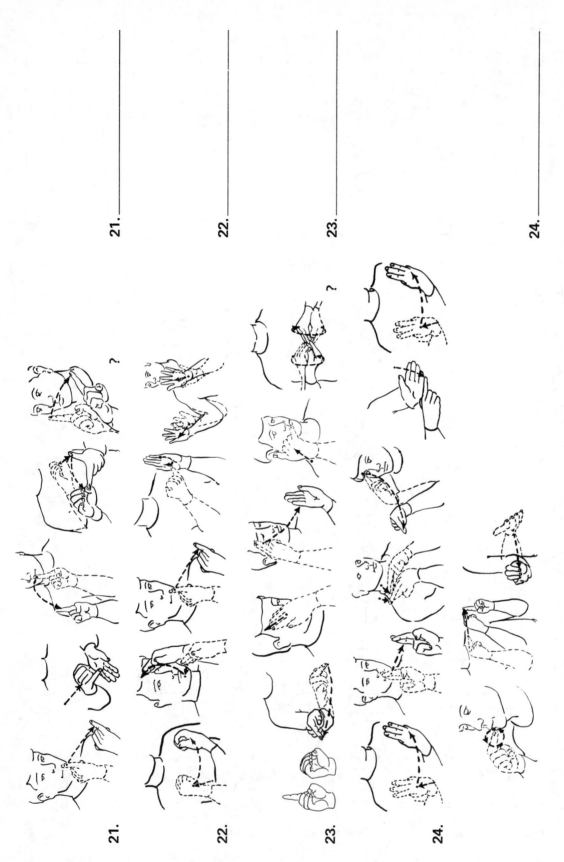

21.

22.

23.

24.

25.

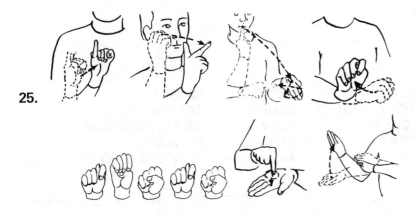

25._____

C) Answers for Decoding Part (B), Lesson 26

Underlined words indicate that they should have been fingerspelled.

1. IT IS A FALSE <u>ALARM</u>.
2. WE DON'T WANT <u>TO</u> BE RESPONSIBILE FOR IT.
3. I REFUSE <u>TO</u> BELIEVE THAT IT WAS MY FAULT.
4. <u>DO</u> YOU (singular) THINK HE IS TOO YOUNG FOR A HEARING AID?
5. IS SHE <u>TAKING</u> A BATH NOW?
6. WHY ARE THEY CRITICIZING US?
7. WHAT IS HER TELEPHONE NUMBER?
8. HE THINKS THAT YOU ARE A WONDERFUL PERSON.
9. I RESPECT MY MOTHER VERY MUCH.
10. I ALWAYS SAY WHAT I THINK.
11. <u>DO</u> YOU (singular) OBJECT <u>TO</u> ASSOCIATING WITH A DEAF PERSON?
12. TRY <u>BOILING</u> IT BEFORE YOU FREEZE IT.
13. I ALWAYS GET SICK IN THE WINTER.
14. I CANCELLED <u>CLASS</u> TODAY BECAUSE THE <u>ROOM</u> WAS COLD.
15. <u>DO</u> YOU HAVE A HANDKERCHIEF WITH YOU?
16. LEAVE THE DICTIONARY ON MY TABLE.
17. I AM AFRAID <u>TO LET</u> HIM OPERATE ON HER.
18. WOULD YOU (singular) HELP ME FOLD IT?
19. SAY EACH <u>OF</u> THESE WORDS SLOWLY.
20. "HONOR YOUR FATHER AND MOTHER."
21. IS IT TRUE OR FALSE?
22. OUR FOSTER PARENT IS JUST WONDERFUL.
23. <u>DO</u> YOU (plural) KNOW HIS TELEPHONE NUMBER?
24. WE ARE RESPONSIBLE FOR WHAT WE SAY TO THEM.
25. I SHALL CORRECT THE <u>TESTS</u> THIS MORNING.

lesson twenty-seven

Signs presented in this lesson are:

PRAISE,* CONGRATULATE* DECIDE   LESSON   WORK*
WASH*   SORRY, SORROW COURSE   SCREAM, YELL
CHEAP   SECRET   PLAY (verb)* STILL, CONTINUE
SIZE   BREAK   READY   SOUND*
SUBSTITUTE   AWFUL   AMBITION MOVIE (MOTION PICTURE)*

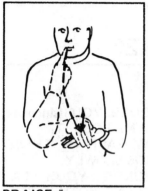

PRAISE,*
CONGRATULATE*

The left hand, with the thumb and fingers extended and joined, is held in front and slightly to the left side of the body with the fingers pointing to the viewer and the palmar side facing up. The right index fingertip (thumb and remaining fingers are contracted) first touches the lips and then is pulled away so that the entire hand (thumb and fingers extended and joined), together with the left hand imitate the motion for "applause") by clasping, separating, and re-clasping each other.

NOTE: The sign may be suggestive, perhaps, of the idea that the lips are expressing applause.

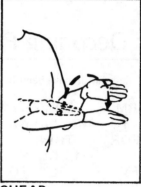

CHEAP

The left hand, with the thumb and fingers extended and joined, is held in front and to the left side of the body with the fingers pointing at the viewer and with the palm facing to the right. The right hand, with the thumb and fingers extended and joined, is held in front of the body with the palm facing up and the fingers pointing to the viewer. Then, the right hand makes a counter-clockwise movement (to the left) as the side of the right index finger brushes downward past the palm of the left hand, ending an inch or two below the left hand, palmar side down.

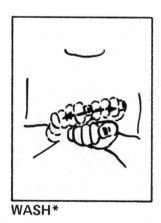

WASH*

Both hands, in the configuration of the letter *A*, are held in front of the body so that their knuckles are touching and with the back side of the left hand facing down, while the back of the right hand is facing up. Next, the right hand grazes the left hand knuckles as the former is moved back and forth several times.

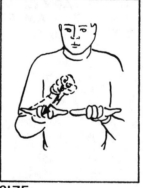

SIZE

The left hand, in the configuration of the letter *Y*, is held in front of the body with the wrist facing down. The right hand first makes the letter *S* and is held in front and to the right side of the body at chest level; then, as the right *S* hand is moved downward, it changes to a *Y* configuration which is placed next to the left *Y* hand so that the thumbs of both *Y* hands are touching and their little fingers are pointing to the viewer.

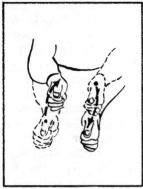

SUBSTITUTE

The left hand, in the configuration of the letter *A*, is held in front of the body with the wrist facing to the right. The right hand, in a similar configuration, but with the wrist facing to the left, is placed in front of (closer to the viewer) the left *A* hand. Next, the *A* hands simultaneously exchange spatial positions. That is, the right hand makes a small upward arc motion as it is moved toward the signer, while the left *A* hand makes a small downward motion as it is moved away from the signer.

NOTE: The sign for "exchange" is done similarly to "substitute," except that both hands first assume an *E* configuration with their wrists facing to the left and right, respectively. Next, the *E* hands simultaneously swap spatial positions.

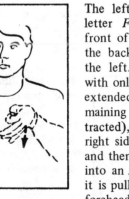

DECIDE

The left hand makes the letter *F* and is held in front of the body so that the back side is facing to the left. The right hand, with only the index finger extended (thumb and remaining fingers are contracted), first touches the right side of the forehead and then the hand changes into an *F* configuration as it is pulled away from the forehead, and is brought downward and placed next to the left *F* hand. Then, both *F* hands are moved downward about three to four inches.

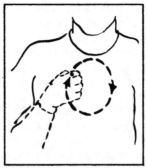

SORRY, SORROW

The right hand, in the configuration of the letter *S* and with the back side toward the viewer, is moved to complete several circular motions in a clockwise direction on the chest.

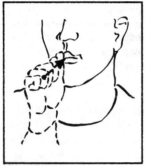

SECRET

The right hand, in the configuration of the letter *A*, is moved in the direction of the lips, with the back side of the thumb resting firmly over the lips as if to suggest that the lips are now sealed.

BREAK

Both hands, each in the configuration of the letter *S*, are held in front of the body so that they are touching (both *S* hands have their wrists facing down). Next, the *S* hands separate as they are quickly turned over on their back sides.

NOTE: This sign is imitative of something being snapped.

AWFUL

Both hands, each in the configuration of the letter *A*, are held on each side of the temples so that their back sides are facing sideways. Next, the *A* hands simultaneously are moved slightly downward and forward as their thumbs and fingers fan out and their palms turn toward the viewer.

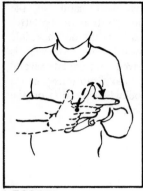

LESSON

The left hand, with the thumb and fingers extended and joined, is held in front and slightly to the left side of the body with the fingers pointing to the viewer and the palm facing up. The right hand, in the configuration of the letter *L*, first is placed on the left fingertips so that the thumb points upward and the index finger points to the left (back of the hand is facing the viewer). Next, the *L* hand is lifted up, moved toward and set down again on the left palm.

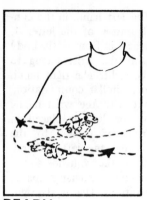

READY

Both hands, each in the configuration of the letter *R*, are held in a crossed position (the wrist of the right hand touches the back of the left wrist) in front of the body. (Both *R* hands have their fingertips pointing to the viewer at an angle and with the back sides of the hands facing up.) Next, with the *R* configuration maintained, both hands bend their wrists to the right and left as the hands are pulled apart.

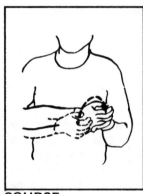

COURSE

This sign is done similarly to the previous one ("lesson"), except that the right hand assumes the configuration of the letter *C*. The *C* hand, with the palmar side facing to the left, first touches the left hand near the fingertips. Then, the *C* hand is lifted up, moved toward the left palm and comes to rest on it. The sign ends with the back of the *C* fingers facing the viewer.

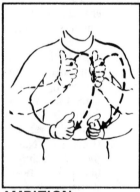

AMBITION

With only their thumbs extended (remaining fingers are clasped to the palms), both hands are placed side-by-side on the chest so that the back sides of the thumbs make contact with the body. Then, the hands simultaneously are moved forward and downward in an arched manner and re-touch the body at the level of the abdomen. The thumbs are pointing at a 45-degree upward angle as the sign comes to an end.

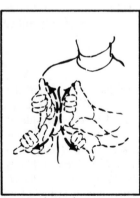

PLAY (verb)*

Both hands, each in the configuration of the letter *Y*, are held about six inches from each other in front of the body so that their palmar sides face each other. Next, the *Y* hands simultaneously are moved downward while rotating slightly inward (left hand rotated clockwise, the right one in a counter-clockwise direction). Then, the hands are returned to their original position and repeat the motion.

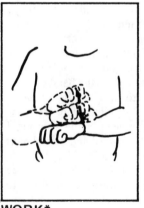

WORK*

The left hand, in the configuration of the letter *S*, is held in front of the body with the wrist facing down. The right hand, also in an *S* configuration, is held above the left hand with the wrist facing down. Next, the right *S* hand is moved up and down several times and touches the back of the left wrist on its downward movements.

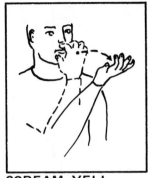

The right hand, in a claw-like configuration (thumb and fingers are apart and curved), first is held over the mouth so that its back side is facing the viewer. Next, the right claw-like hand is moved slightly upward and then curved in a forward direction so that the sign ends with the palm of the claw-like hand facing up.

SCREAM, YELL

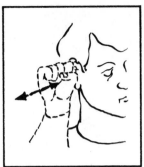

The right hand, in the configuration of the letter *S*, is moved laterally to and from the ear (the wrist faces the viewer) several times, suggesting the pathway of the imaginary sound waves.

SOUND*

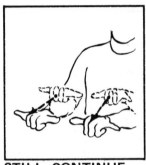

Both hands first assume the configuration of the letter *Y* and are placed side-by-side (but not touching) in front of the body with their wrists facing down. Next, with the configuration and distance between them maintained, both *Y* hands are moved in a forward direction.

STILL, CONTINUE

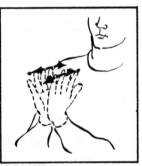

With their thumbs and fingers fanned apart and extended vertically, both hands are positioned in front of the body and with their palmar sides touching. Next, the hands rub each other as they perform alternating back and forth movements. Keep the fingers apart, and touch only the palms together.

MOVIE (MOTION PICTURE)*

A) Exercises in Encoding

Encode the following material using signs and fingerspelling. Use fingerspelling for all underlined words.

1. WHEN WILL YOU BE READY <u>TO</u> GO?
2. WHY <u>DID</u> HE BREAK MY PENCIL?
3. I AM SORRY, BUT YOU MAY NOT SEE THIS MOVIE.
4. IT IS MY AMBITION <u>TO</u> BECOME A TEACHER <u>OF</u> THE DEAF.
5. HE REFUSES <u>TO</u> TELL US HIS SECRET.
6. CAN YOU HEAR THIS SOUND?
7. WHAT <u>DID</u> YOU DECIDE <u>TO</u> <u>DO</u> ABOUT IT?
8. ARE YOU STILL <u>PLANNING</u> <u>TO</u> EVALUATE HER TOMORROW MORNING?
9. IT WAS JUST AWFUL!
10. <u>DO</u> YOU WANT <u>TO</u> PLAY A <u>GAME</u>?
11. THIS COURSE WILL TEACH YOU HOW <u>TO</u> SIGN AND FINGERSPELL.
12. <u>DOES</u> YOUR BROTHER WORK FOR THE UNIVERSITY?
13. HE WEARS A SIZE TEN AND ONE-HALF.
14. WHY IS THE CHILD SCREAMING?
15. MY TEACHER PRAISED ME FOR MY GOOD WORK.
16. DON'T <u>FORGET</u> <u>TO</u> CONGRATULATE THEM.
17. I <u>PLAN</u> <u>TO</u> WASH ON TUESDAY.
18. WE REFUSE <u>TO</u> BUY THEM A CHEAP <u>GIFT</u>.
19. WHEN <u>DO</u> WE START THE NEXT LESSON?
20. I CAN'T DECIDE HOW <u>TO</u> ANSWER YOU.
21. WE WERE SORRY <u>TO</u> HEAR ABOUT YOUR <u>ACCIDENT</u>.
22. ARE YOU READY <u>TO</u> LISTEN NOW?
23. IS HE STILL WEARING HIS NEW HEARING AID?
24. SHOW ME THE <u>PICTURE</u> <u>OF</u> A BOY PLAYING WITH A <u>BALL</u>.
25. WHY <u>DO</u> YOU WANT <u>TO</u> EXCHANGE IT? ("Exchange" is signed similarly to "substitute," but with *E* hands.)

B) Exercises in Decoding

Decode the following illustrated exercises:

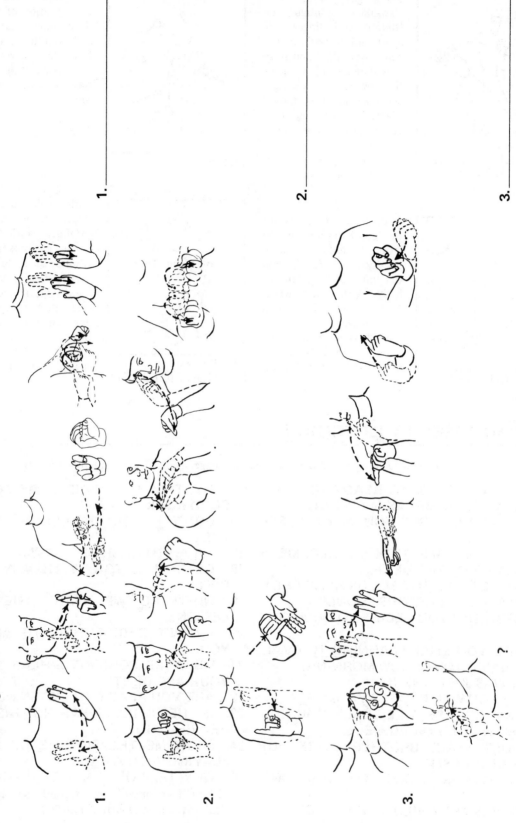

1.

2.

3.

1. _____

2. _____

3. _____

4.

5.

6.

7.

8.

9.

10.

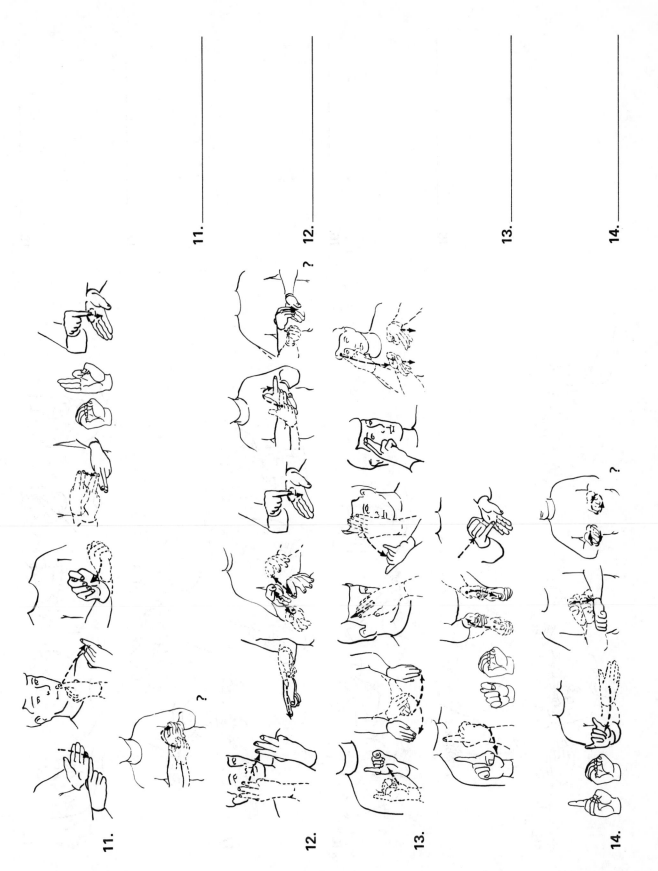

11.

12.

13.

14.

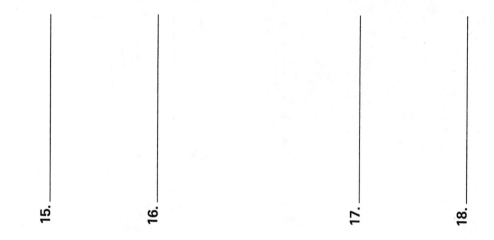

15.

16.

17.

18.

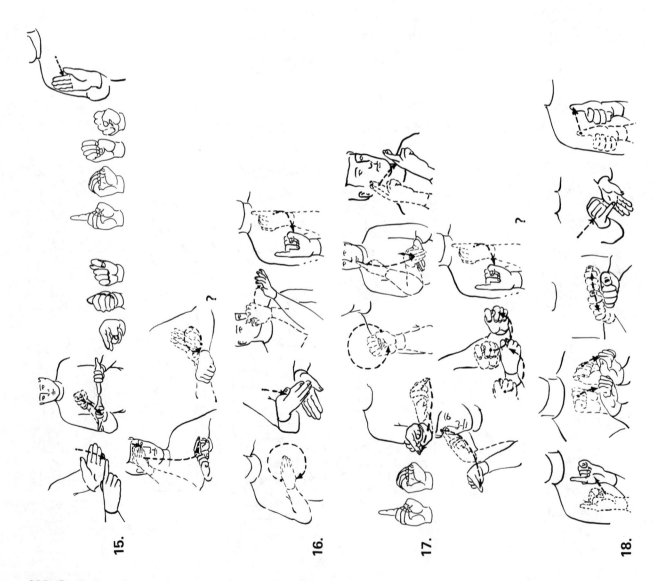

15.

16.

17.

18.

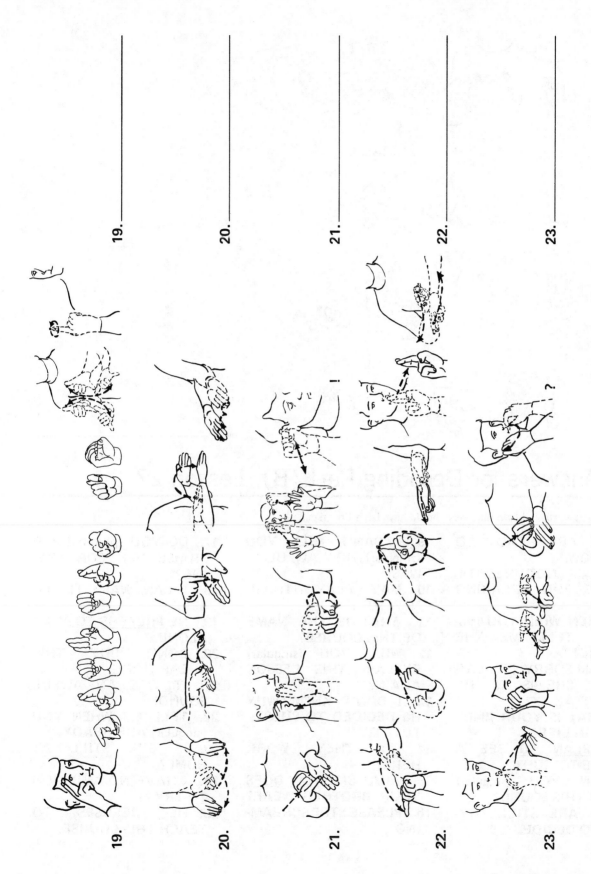

19.

20.

21.

22.

23.

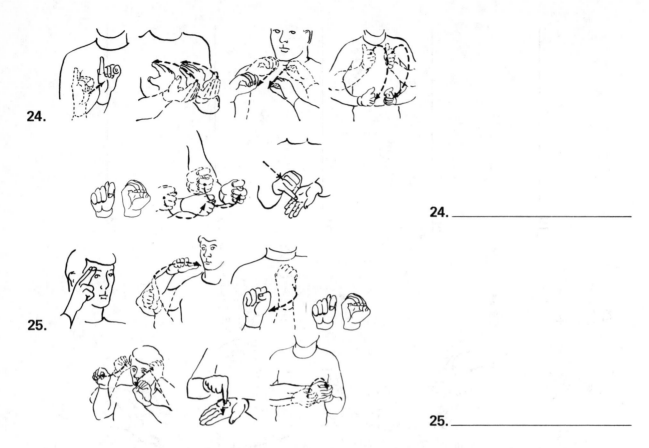

24. _____

25. _____

C) Answers for Decoding Part (B), Lesson 27

Underlined words indicate that they should have been fingerspelled.

1. WE ARE READY <u>TO</u> GO NOW.
2. I AM NOT RESPONSIBLE FOR BREAKING IT.
3. WHEN WILL YOU (singular) TELL ME THE SECRET?
4. I AM SORRY <u>TO</u> HEAR THAT SHE IS <u>IN</u> THE <u>HOSPITAL</u>.
5. WHAT IS YOUR AMBITION IN LIFE?
6. I <u>PLAN TO</u> SEE A MOVIE TONIGHT.
7. CAN YOU (singular) HEAR THIS SOUND?
8. WE ARE STILL TRYING <u>TO</u> DECIDE.
9. I CAN'T TELL YOU (singular) HOW AWFUL IT WAS!
10. MAY I PLAY WITH MY NEW <u>TOY</u>?
11. WHAT IS THE NAME <u>OF</u> THIS COURSE?
12. WILL YOU (singular) EXPLAIN THIS LESSON AGAIN?
13. I DON'T KNOW WHY HE DECIDED <u>TO</u> SUBSTITUTE IT.
14. <u>DO</u> THEY WORK HERE?
15. WHAT SIZE <u>HAT</u> <u>DOES</u> YOUR BROTHER WEAR?
16. PLEASE STOP SCREAMING.
17. <u>DO</u> YOU (plural) EVER PRAISE HER FOR TRYING?
18. I CAN WASH IT MYSELF.
19. HE <u>PREFERS</u> <u>TO</u> PLAY ALONE.
20. DON'T BUY THIS CHEAP THING.
21. IT WAS AN AWFUL SOUND!
22. TELL ME WHEN YOU (singular) ARE READY.
23. IS SHE STILL AT HOME?
24. I HAVE NO AMBITION <u>TO</u> TRY IT.
25. HE REFUSES <u>TO</u> TEACH THIS COURSE.

lesson twenty-eight

Signs presented in this lesson are:

JUDGE* (verb)	MEET (a person)	SUFFER*	LAZE (verb)
MILK*	MEETING*	VARIOUS	WARN*
DEPEND	PATIENT (adjective)	SILLY,* RIDICULOUS*	LOW
PAGE	VOLUNTEER,* CANDIDATE*	QUIT, RESIGN	SING*
PROUD	FOLLOW	HATE	INSTITUTION

JUDGE* (verb)

The left hand makes the letter *F* and is held in front of the body so that the fingers are pointing to the viewer and the palm of the hand is facing to the right. The right hand, with only the index finger extended (remaining fingers and thumb are contracted), first touches the forehead and then it changes into an *F* configuration as the hand is pulled away from the forehead, brought downward and placed next to the left *F* hand (the palmar sides of the *F* hands face the midline). Lastly, the *F* hands are moved to execute alternating up and down movements.

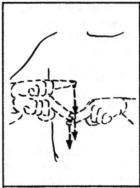

DEPEND

The left hand, with only the index finger extended (remaining fingers and thumb are contracted), is held in front of the body so that the index finger is pointing to the viewer and the wrist is facing down. The right hand, with only the index finger extended (remaining fingers and thumb are contracted), is moved downward so that the palmar side of the right fingertip makes contact with the back side of the index fingertip of the left hand. (The tip of the right index finger is pointing to the left.) Next, both hands, with their index fingers touching, are moved in a downward direction.

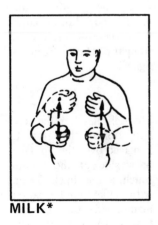

MILK*

Initially, the left hand assumes the configuration of the letter *C* (with the palmar side facing to the right), while the right hand forms the letter *S*, which is held with the wrist facing to the left. (The hands are held about three inches apart and at approximately a 45-degree angle to each other in front of the body.) Next, the left *C* and the right *S* hands reverse their configurations as they are moved alternately up and down several times.

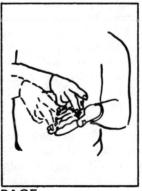

PAGE

The left hand, with the fingers and thumb extended and joined, is held in front and slightly to the left side of the body with the palm facing up and the fingers pointing to the viewer. The right hand, in the configuration of the letter *P*, first touches the left hand near the fingertips with the tip of the middle finger of the right *P* hand; then, the right hand, which is held with the back to the viewer, lifts up, moves toward the left palm and retouches it.

305

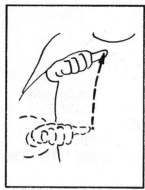

PROUD

The right hand, with only the thumb extended and apart (remaining fingers are contracted to the palm), first touches the lower portion of the signer's chest. (Contact is made between the thumbnail and the chest, with the hand held so that the back side is facing up.) Next, the right thumb grazes the body as the hand is moved upward (in the direction of the neck), stopping near the collar bone.

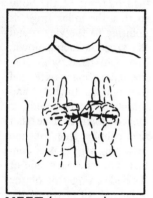

MEET (a person)

Both hands, each with only the index finger extended (remaining fingers and thumb are contracted), are held about six to eight inches apart in front of the body so that their index fingers are pointing upward and with the palmar sides facing each other. Next, the hands simultaneously are brought together to the center of the body so that the backs of the thumbs touch.

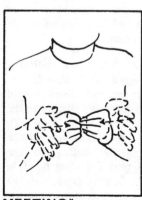

MEETING*

Both hands, each with the fingers and thumb extended and apart, are positioned approximately six inches from each other in front of the body so that the fingers are pointing to the viewer and their palmar sides are facing each other. Next, both hands are moved toward the midline as their thumbs flex to touch their extended and joined fingertips. The sign ends with both hands touching their joined thumbs and fingertips and with the backs of the fingers facing the viewer. This motion is repeated several times.

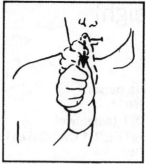

PATIENT (adjective)

The right hand, in the configuration of the letter *A*, is placed over the lips (the back side of the thumb touches the lips). Then, with the configuration maintained, the *A* hand is moved in a downward direction and stops when it reaches the chin.

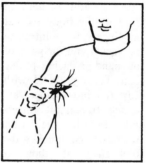

VOLUNTEER,*
CANDIDATE*

The right thumb and index finger (remaining fingers are contracted) pinch the clothing on the right side of the chest and tug it out repeatedly.

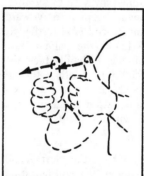

FOLLOW

Both hands, with only their thumbs extended and pointing vertically (remaining fingers are contracted), first are positioned one in front of the other so that the back sides of the thumbs are facing the signer. Next, with the configuration maintained, both hands simultaneously are moved straight out (away from the signer).

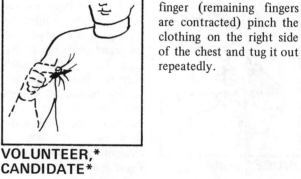

SUFFER*

The right hand, in the configuration of the letter *A*, is placed over the lips (the back side of the thumb touches the lips). Then, with the configuration maintained, the *A* hand first is rolled to the left and then to the right side. This motion is repeated several times.

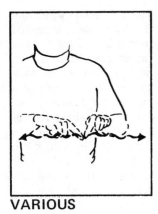

VARIOUS

Both hands, each with only the index finger extended (remaining fingers and thumb are contracted), are positioned at an angle in front of the body so that the sides of their index fingertips are touching while pointing downward at about a 45-degree angle (both hands have their wrists facing down). Next, the index fingers of both hands make small wiggling motions as the hands are moved in opposite directions (to the right and left, respectively).

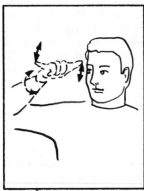

SILLY,*
RIDICULOUS*

The right hand first forms the letter Y which is held in front and on the level of the forehead with the wrist facing down and with the little finger of the Y hand pointing to the viewer. Next, with the upper arm held in place, the right forearm provides a quick rocking motion for the Y hand (the wrist does not move), which first tilts slightly downward and then returns to the original position. This motion is repeated several times.

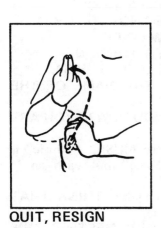

QUIT, RESIGN

The right hand, in the configuration of the letter H, is placed in front of the body with the H fingers pointing downward and the back of the hand facing the viewer. The left hand wraps its fingers around the right H fingers. Next, the right H hand is pulled out of the left hand, and upward, as it moves to the right, so that the sign ends with the H fingers pointing upward and the back side toward the signer.

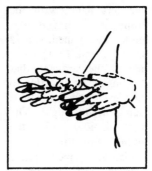

HATE

Both hands, each with the middle fingertip under its thumb (remaining fingers are semi-curved and apart), are placed side-by-side in front of the body so that their palmar sides are facing each other; next, the hands snap open as they are moved forward.

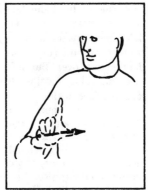

LAZE (verb)

The right hand first assumes the configuration of the letter L and then is brought toward the body so that the thumb of the L hand strikes the chest. The sign ends with the index finger of the L hand pointing upward.

NOTE: The sign for "lazy" is made by combining "laze" plus "y."

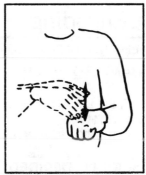

WARN*

The left hand, in the configuration of the letter S, is held in front and slightly to the left side of the body with the wrist facing down. The right hand, with the fingers and thumb extended and joined, slaps the back side of the left S hand several times with the palmar side of its fingertips.

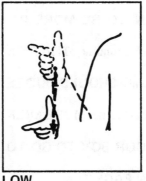

LOW

The right hand, in the configuration of the letter L, is held in front and to the right side of the body at the level of the shoulder with the thumb pointing upward and the back side of the L hand facing to the right. Next, without bending the wrist, the L hand is moved in a downward direction.

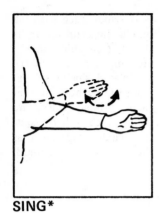

SING*

The left hand, with the thumb and fingers extended and joined, is held in front and to the left side of the body so that the fingers are pointing to the viewer and the palm is facing to the right. The right hand, with the thumb and fingers extended and joined, is held over the left forearm so that the fingers are pointing to the left and with the back side of the hand facing the viewer. Then the right hand makes a semicircular motion (dips and then rises) over the left forearm. This motion is repeated several times.

NOTE: The signs for "poetry," "song," and "music" are made similarly once the right hand assumes the appropriate letter configuration "p" for "poetry," "s" for "song," and "m" for "music."

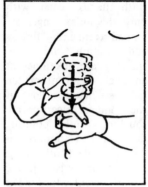

INSTITUTION

The left hand, with only the little finger extended (remaining fingers and thumb are contracted), is held in front of the body with the little finger pointing to the viewer at an angle (the palmar side of the little finger is facing to the right). The right hand, with only the little finger extended (remaining fingers and thumb are contracted), is held three to four inches above the left *I* hand with the little finger pointing to viewer at an angle. (The palmar side of the little finger is facing to the left.) Then, the right *I* hand is moved downward and strikes the top portion of the left *I* hand.

NOTE: Often, this sign is used to connote a residential school for the deaf.

A) Exercises in Encoding

Encode the following material using signs and fingerspelling. Use fingerspelling for all underlined words.

1. <u>DOES</u> SOMEONE WANT <u>TO</u> VOLUNTEER FOR IT?
2. I DON'T THINK IT IS A SILLY ANSWER.
3. PLEASE SING ALONG WITH ME.
4. I CAN'T FOLLOW YOU TO SCHOOL TODAY.
5. FOR VARIOUS REASONS, WE DECIDED NOT <u>TO</u> GO.
6. WE DON'T WANT <u>TO</u> SEE HIM SUFFER ANYMORE.
7. YOU MUST LEARN <u>TO</u> BE MORE PATIENT WITH ME.
8. <u>DID</u> WE TELL YOU (singular) THAT WE ARE PROUD <u>OF</u> YOU?
9. I THINK YOU (plural) SHOULD JUDGE FOR YOURSELVES.
10. WOULD YOU (singular) LIKE MORE MILK IN YOUR COFFEE?
11. WE DON'T WANT OUR BOY <u>TO</u> GO TO AN INSTITUTION.
12. THE ANSWER IS ON PAGE TEN.
13. I CAN'T SAY THAT I HATE IT.
14. <u>DOES</u> HE GET LAZY IN THE WINTER? ("Get" is signed as "become." "Lazy" is signed as "laze" plus "-y.")
15. WHY <u>DID</u> YOU QUIT SCHOOL?
16. WE WARNED THEM NOT <u>TO</u> TRY IT.
17. <u>DO</u> I HAVE A LOW VOICE?
18. I AM NOT READY <u>TO</u> RESIGN.
19. YES, WE CAN DEPEND ON THEM.
20. <u>DO</u> YOU KNOW THE NAME <u>OF</u> THE CANDIDATE?
21. I CAN FOLLOW YOU NOW IF YOU ARE READY.
22. I DON'T LIKE THE MUSIC. ("Music" is signed similarly to "sing" but with an <u>M</u> hand.)
23. WHY <u>DO</u> YOU (singular) THINK THAT YOU ARE SUFFERING?
24. WHAT TIME IS OUR MEETING THIS AFTERNOON? ("This afternoon" is signed as "now" plus "afternoon.")

B) Exercises in Decoding

Decode the following illustrated exercises:

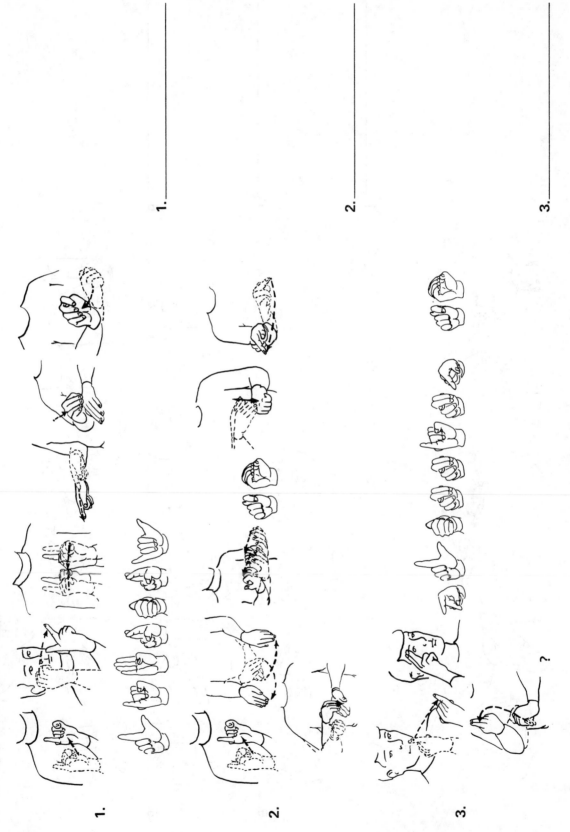

1. _____

2. _____

3. _____

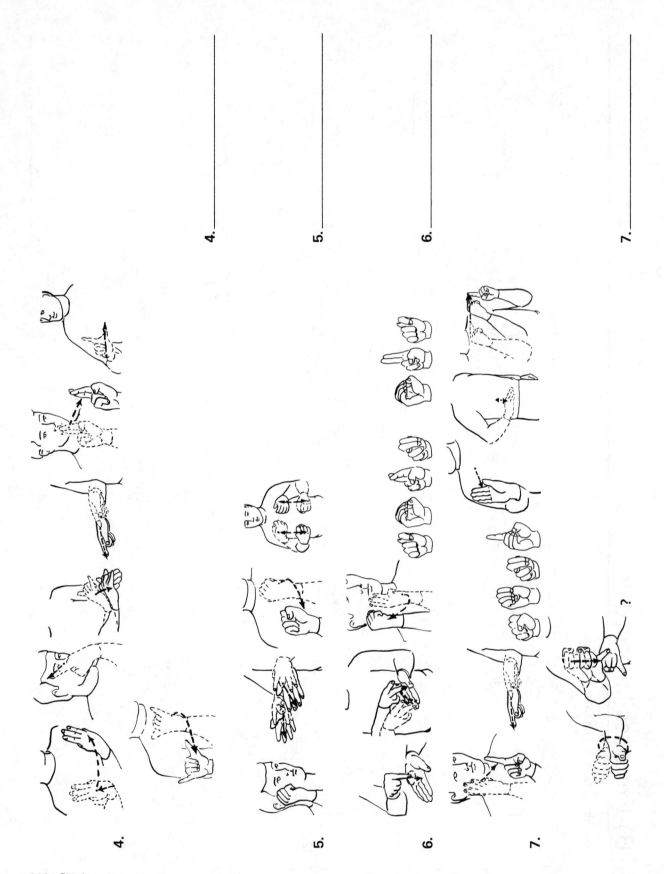

4.

5.

6.

7.

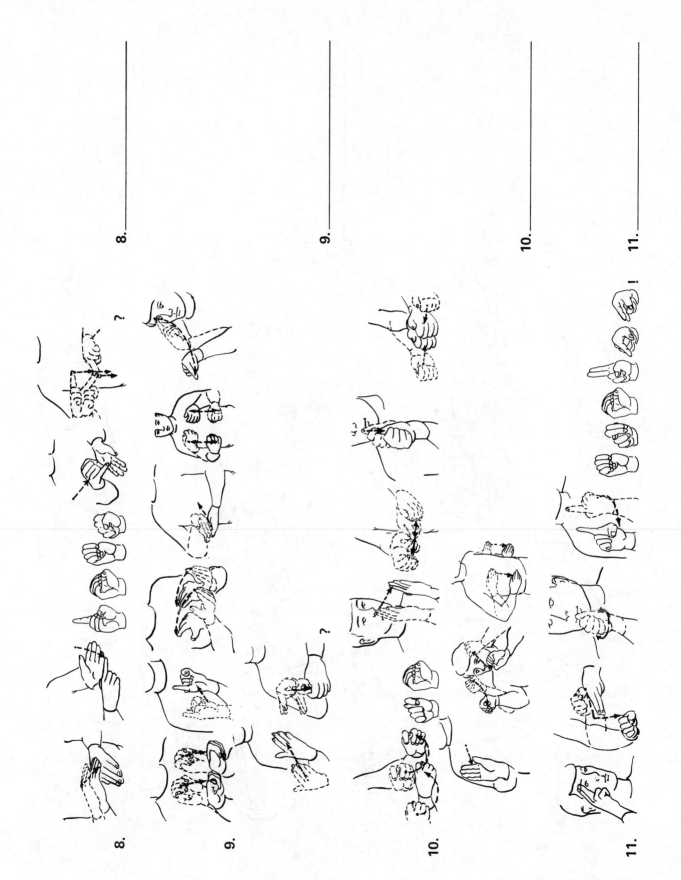

8.

9.

10.

11.

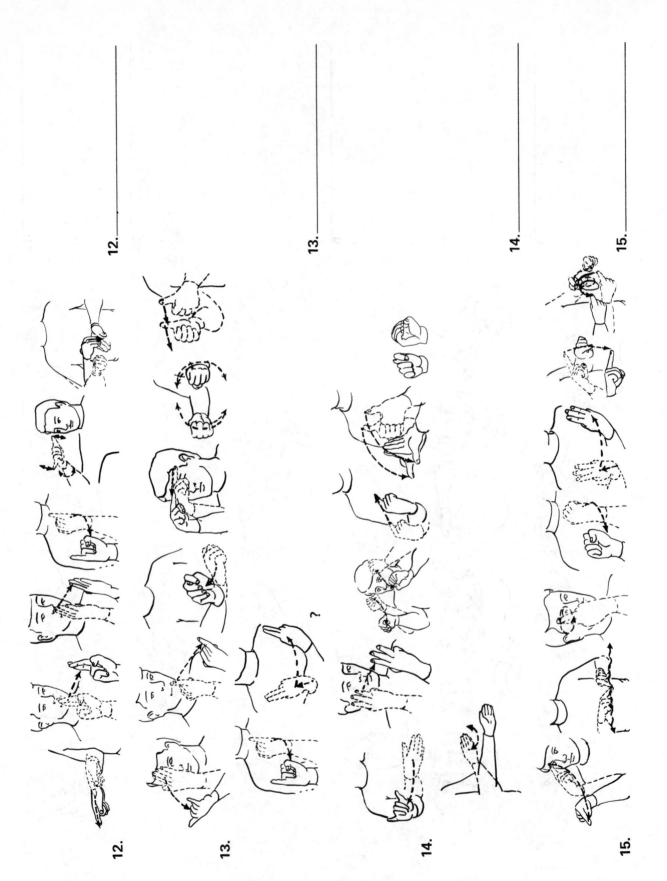

12.

13.

14.

15.

12.

13.

14.

15.

MASS ACLD INC.
1296 WORCESTER ROAD
FRAMINGHAM CTR MASS 01701

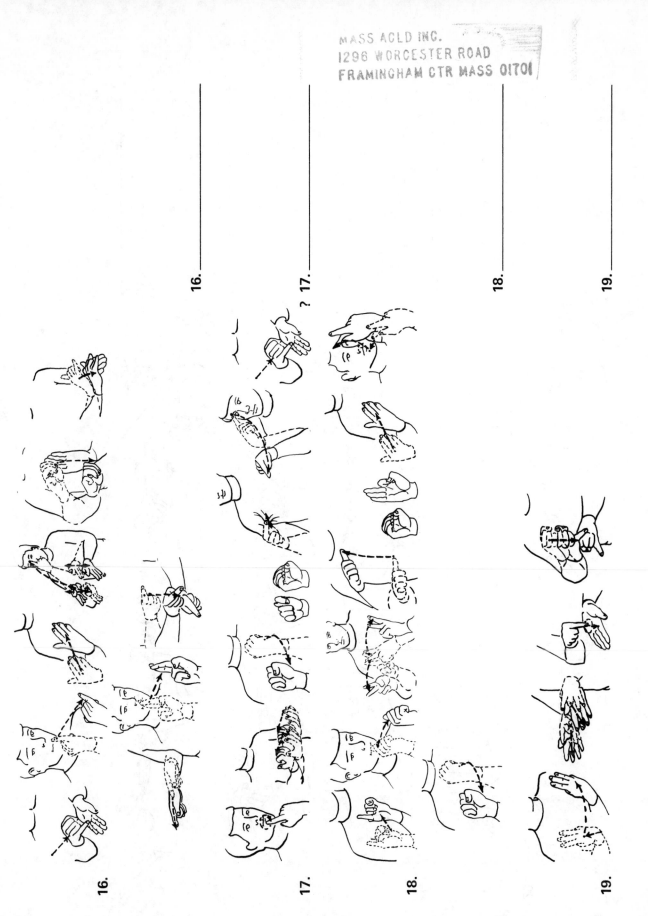

16.

17.

18.

19.

16.

? 17.

18.

19.

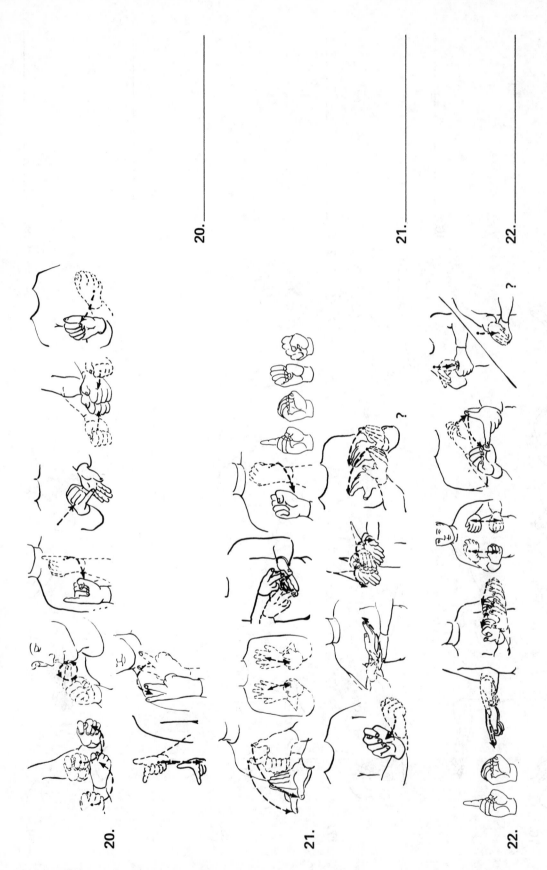

20.

21.

22.

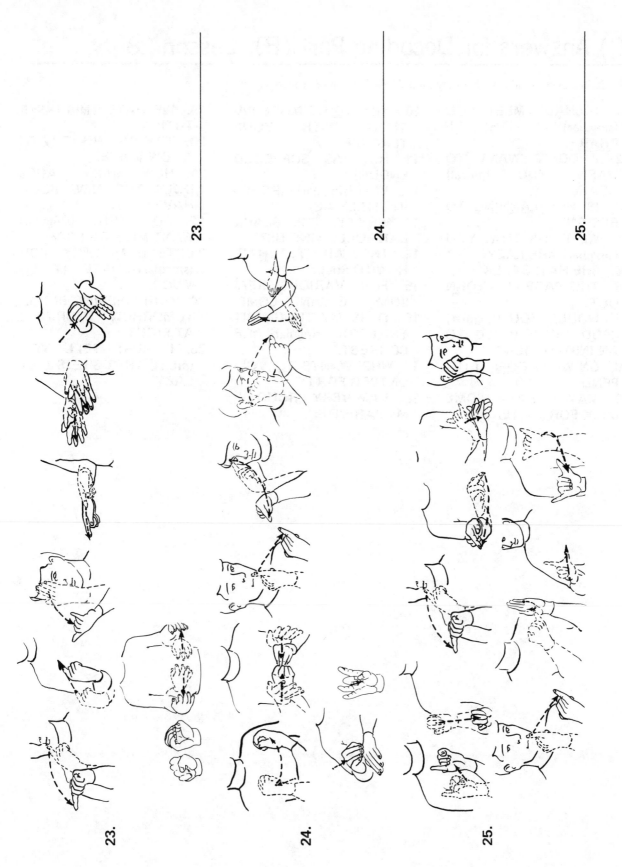

23.

24.

25.

C) Answers for Decoding Part (B), Lesson 28

Underlined words indicate that they should have been fingerspelled.

1. I SHALL MEET YOU (singular) AT THE LI-BRARY.
2. I DON'T WANT TO WARN YOU (plural) AGAIN.
3. IS HE PLANNING TO RESIGN?
4. WE THINK THAT YOU (singular) ARE LAZY.
5. SHE HATES MILK.
6. THIS PAGE WAS TORN OUT.
7. WOULD YOU (singular) SEND YOUR CHILD TO AN INSTITUTION?
8. ON WHAT DOES IT DE-PEND?
9. MAY I HAVE SOME MILK FOR MY TEA?
10. TRY TO BE MORE PA-TIENT WITH YOUR TEACHER.
11. HE HAS SUFFERED ENOUGH!
12. YOU (singular) ARE BE-ING SILLY AGAIN.
13. WHY IS THE BLACK CAR FOLLOWING US?
14. THEY WILL TEACH ME HOW TO SING.
15. FOR VARIOUS REA-SONS, WE CAN'T COME.
16. IT IS MY JUDGMENT THAT YOU (singular) ARE CORRECT.
17. WHO WANTS TO VOL-UNTEER FOR IT?
18. I AM VERY PROUD OF MY PARENTS.
19. WE HATE THIS INSTI-TUTION.
20. TRY SAYING IT WITH A LOW VOICE.
21. HOW MANY PAGES DOES THE NEW BOOK HAVE?
22. DO YOU (singular) WANT MILK OR POP?
23. TELL ME WHY YOU (singular) HATE IT SO MUCH.
24. OUR MEETING IS FOR TOMORROW MORNING AT EIGHT.
25. I MUST TELL YOU (plural) THAT SHE IS JUST LAZY.

lesson twenty-nine

Signs presented in this lesson are:

IMPORTANT	ARRIVE	PROMISE	EMOTION*
FIRE (noun)	STAND	BROTHER-IN-LAW	THRILL
NOTIFY, INFORM	TASTE*	DURING, WHILE	ACCEPT
FORCE, COMPEL	PROVE, PROOF	MEDICINE	OBEY
FIND	DUTY*	SURRENDER, GIVE UP	INTEND

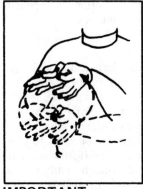

IMPORTANT

Both hands, each with the tip of the thumb and index finger touching to form circles (remaining fingers are apart and slightly curved), are held side-by-side in front of the body so that the joined thumbs and index fingers touch (back sides of the hands are facing sideways). Next, the hands (without altering the configuration) separate, make semi-circles (clockwise for the left hand and counter-clockwise for the right one) in an upward direction and come together again, meeting at the tips of the thumbs and forefingers. The palmar surfaces continue to face each other as the sign comes to an end.

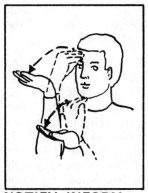

NOTIFY, INFORM

First, the right hand (with the thumb touching the extended and joined fingers) touches the right side of the forehead (the back side of the hand faces the viewer). Then, the left hand, in a similar configuration, is held six to eight inches away from the body at the level of the face with the joined thumb and fingertips pointing toward the signer. Then, both hands are tilted forward as they open so that the palms of both hands are facing up and with the thumbs and fingers extended, joined and pointing to the viewer.

NOTE: This sign may be imitative, perhaps, of the dissemination of information.

FIRE (noun)

Both hands, with their thumbs and fingers apart and slightly curved, are held side-by-side in front of the body at the level of the waist so that their palmar surfaces are facing up. Next, the hands simultaneously are moved upward as the fingers perform a series of wiggling motions suggestive, perhaps, of flickering flames.

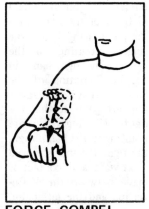

FORCE, COMPEL

The right hand, in the configuration of the letter *C*, is held in front and slightly to the right side of the body near the level of the chest with the palmar side of the *C* hand facing the viewer. Next, the right forearm moves downward, while the wrist tilts the hand forward. The sign ends with the palmar side of the *C* hand facing down.

317

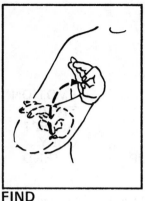

FIND

The right hand, with the thumb and index fingertip touching (remaining fingers are apart and slightly curved), is held in front of the body at the level of the abdomen with the palmar side facing down. Next, with the configuration maintained, the hand is flexed upward to about a 45-degree angle as the hand is moved toward the signer. The sign ends with the palmar surface of the hand facing the viewer.

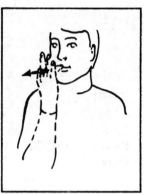

TASTE*

The right hand, with the middle finger flexed to about a 45-degree angle (remaining fingers and thumb are extended and apart), is held in front of the signer's face with the middle fingertip pointing to the lips. Next, with the configuration maintained, the hand is moved toward the signer with the middle fingertip touching the lips. This motion is repeated several times.

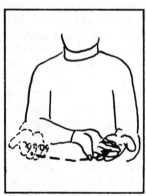

ARRIVE

The left hand, with the thumb extended and apart, while the fingers are joined and slightly curved, is held in front and to the left side of the body with the back side facing down and the fingers toward the viewer. The right hand, in a similar configuration, is held in front and to the right side of the body; then, with the configuration preserved, the right hand is moved to the left and with its back side touches the palm of the left hand.

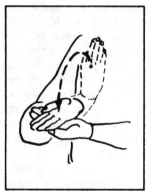

PROVE, PROOF

The left hand, with the thumb and fingers extended and joined, is held in front of the body with the palm facing up and the fingers pointing to the right. The right hand, with the thumb and fingers joined and the palm bent slightly, is held at chest level about five to six inches from the body with the fingers pointing upward and the palmar side toward the signer. Next, the right hand performs an upward arc motion as it is moved in a forward and downward direction so that its back side touches the left palm.

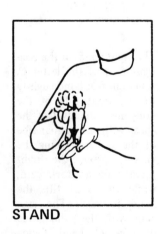

STAND

The left hand, with the thumb and fingers extended and joined, is held in front of the body with the palm facing up and the fingers pointing to the viewer. The right hand, in the configuration of the letter *V*, first is held above the left palm so that the right *V* fingertips are pointing to the palm; then, the right *V* hand is moved downward and contact is made between the *V* fingertips and the left palm.

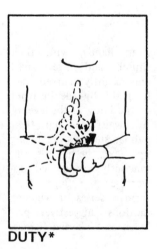

DUTY*

The left hand, in the configuration of the letter *S*, is held in front of the body with the wrist facing down. The right hand makes the letter *D* and is held above the left hand; then, the *D* hand (with the index finger pointing upward and its palmar side toward the viewer) is moved downward and touches the back side of the left hand. This motion is repeated several times.

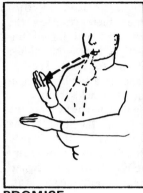

PROMISE

The left forearm is placed horizontally across the front of the body with the thumb and fingers of the left hand extended, joined and the palmar side facing down. The right index finger (remaining fingers and thumb are contracted) first touches the lips and then is pulled away as the entire forearm is moved forward and makes contact with the wrist of the left hand. The sign ends with the right forearm tilted at about a 45-degree angle with the palm of the right hand (its fingers joined and extended) facing the viewer.

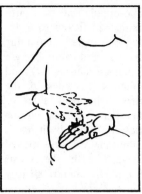

MEDICINE

The left hand, with the thumb and fingers extended and joined, is held in front of the body with the palm facing up and the fingers pointing to the viewer. The right hand, with only the middle finger flexed to about a 45-degree angle (remaining fingers and thumb are extended and apart), touches the left palm with its middle fingertip and then the hand is moved to perform a circular motion on the left palm.

NOTE: The sign may be imitative, perhaps, of the way medicine used to be prepared. Also, the sign for "drug" is done similarly to "medicine," except that the configuration of the right hand is that of the letter *D*.

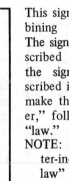

BROTHER-IN-LAW

This sign is made by combining two other signs: The sign for "brother" described in lesson 16 and the sign for "law" described in lesson 25. First, make the sign for "Brother," followed by that for "law."

NOTE: Other signs ("sister-in-law," "father-in-law" and "mother-in-law") are made by combining "sister," "father," or "mother" with "law."

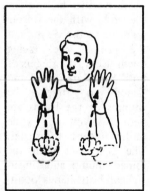

SURRENDER, GIVE UP

Both hands assume the configuration of the letter *S* and are placed side-by-side in front of the body at waist level so that their back sides are facing up; then, the hands are lifted vertically and moved toward the signer as their thumbs and fingers fan out. The sign ends with the palmar sides of the hands facing the viewer.

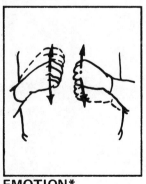

EMOTION*

Both hands, each in the configuration of the letter *E*, are placed approximately four inches apart from each other on the body so that their back sides are facing the viewer. Next, the *E* hands alternately are moved up and down, while grazing the body. This sign is repeated several times.

DURING, WHILE

Both hands, each with only the index finger extended (remaining fingers and thumb are contracted), are held in close proximity (two to three inches) to each other in front of the body with their index fingers pointing to the viewer. (Both hands have their wrists facing down.) Next, both hands are moved simultaneously in a forward direction.

THRILL

The middle fingers of both hands are flexed to a 45-degree angle (remaining fingers and thumbs are extended and apart) and touch both sides of the chest (the back sides of the hands are facing the viewer). Next, both hands simultaneously are moved upward with the wrists tilting the hands slightly (in a clockwise direction for the right hand and in a counter-clockwise direction for the left one) so that the sign ends with the back sides of both hands facing the viewer and the fingers pointing upward.

OBEY

The right hand fingertips (the thumb touches the extended and joined fingertips) touch the middle of the forehead. The left hand, in a similar configuration, is held about six to eight inches away from the body at the level of the face with the joined thumb and fingertips pointing to the signer. Next, both hands are moved forward and in a downward direction as they open so that the palms of both hands are facing each other and with the thumbs and fingers extended, joined and pointing at an angle downward.

ACCEPT

Both hands, each with the thumb and fingers extended and apart, are placed in close proximity to each other in front of the body with the fingers pointing to the viewer and the palmar sides facing down. Next, the fingers of both hands are joined and flexed to touch the thumbs as the hands are bent downward while pulled towards the signer. The sign ends with the joined thumb and fingertips of both hands pointing downward.

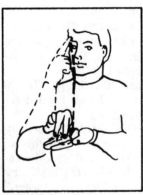

INTEND

The left hand, with the thumb and fingers extended and joined, is held in front of the body with the palm facing up and the fingers pointing to the viewer. The right index finger (remaining fingers and thumb are contracted) first is placed on the right side of the forehead. Then, the right hand is pulled away as the letter *V* is formed. The fingertips of the *V* hand are then placed on the palm of the left hand and rotated clockwise.

A) Exercises in Encoding

Encode the following material using signs and fingerspelling. Use fingerspelling for all underlined words.

1. WHERE <u>DID</u> YOU FIND IT?
2. I INTEND <u>TO DO</u> IT THIS MORNING. ("This morning" is signed as "now" plus "morning.")
3. YOUR EVALUATION IS NOT ACCEPT-ABLE. ("Acceptable" is signed as "accept" plus "able.")
4. WE SHOULD OBEY ALL THE LAWS.
5. WE ARE THRILLED <u>TO</u> BE HERE. ("Thrilled" is signed as "thrill" plus "ed.")
6. WAIT FOR US WHILE WE TRY <u>TO</u> CLOSE IT.
7. I CAN'T HELP YOU DURING THE <u>EXAMINATION</u>.
8. PLEASE DON'T FORCE HIM <u>TO PAY</u> ATTENTION.
9. I AM COMPELLED <u>TO</u> GO.
10. WHO INFORMED YOU THAT HE RE-SIGNED?
11. <u>DID</u> YOU NOTIFY HIS PARENTS?
12. PLEASE STAND UP FOR A MINUTE.
13. WHO STARTED THE FIRE IN THIS BUILDING? ("Building" is signed as "build" plus "house.")
14. IT IS IMPORTANT AND YOU SHOULD REMEMBER IT.
15. WHO IS YOUR BROTHER-IN-LAW?
16. I PROMISE YOU THAT I SHALL BE HERE WHEN YOU COME.
17. CAN YOU PROVE THAT IT WAS NOT YOUR FAULT?
18. WE NEED <u>TO</u> GET MORE PROOF.
19. <u>DOES</u> YOUR FOOD TASTE ALL RIGHT?
20. <u>DID</u> YOUR DOCTOR <u>GIVE</u> YOU ANY MEDICINE?
21. WHAT KIND <u>OF</u> A DRUG IS IT? ("Drug" is signed similarly to "medicine," but with a <u>D</u> hand.)
22. IT IS YOUR DUTY <u>TO</u> INFORM US.
23. I DON'T KNOW WHEN SHE IS ARRIV-ING.
24. TRY SHOWING US MORE RESPECT FOR OUR EMOTION.
25. DON'T GIVE UP NOW! ("Give up" is signed similarly to "surrender.")

B) Exercises in Decoding

Decode the following illustrated exercises:

1. _____

2. _____

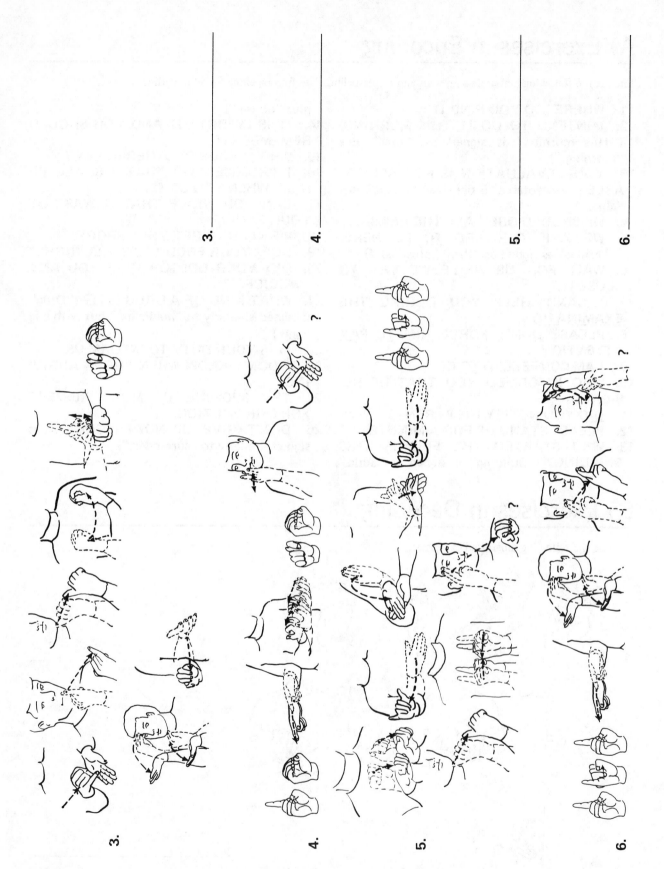

3.

4.

5.

6.

7.

8.

9.

10.

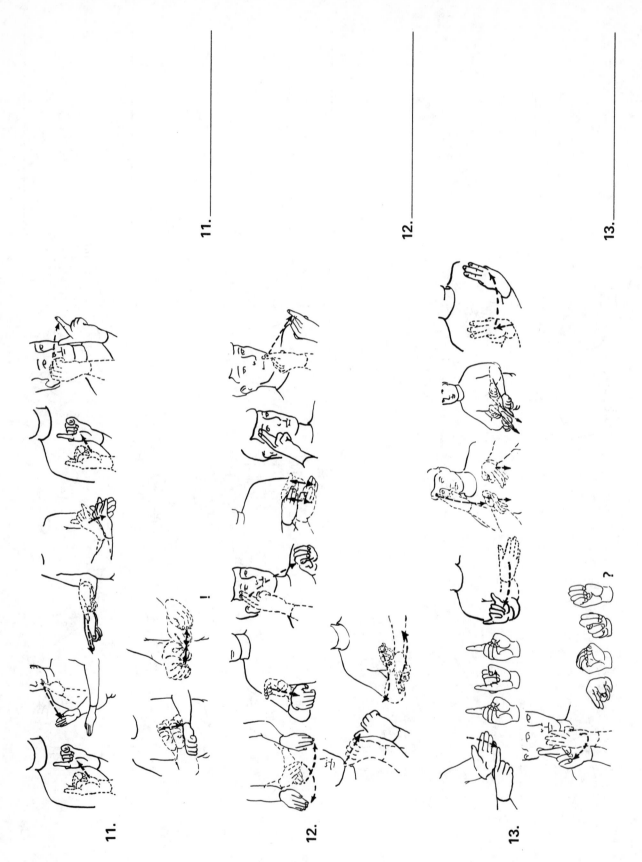

11.

12.

13.

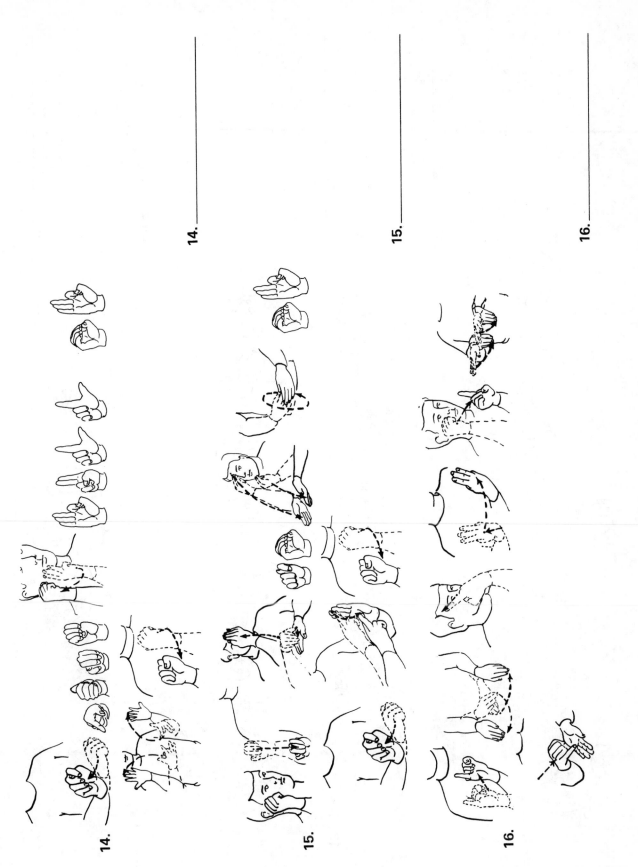

14.

15.

16.

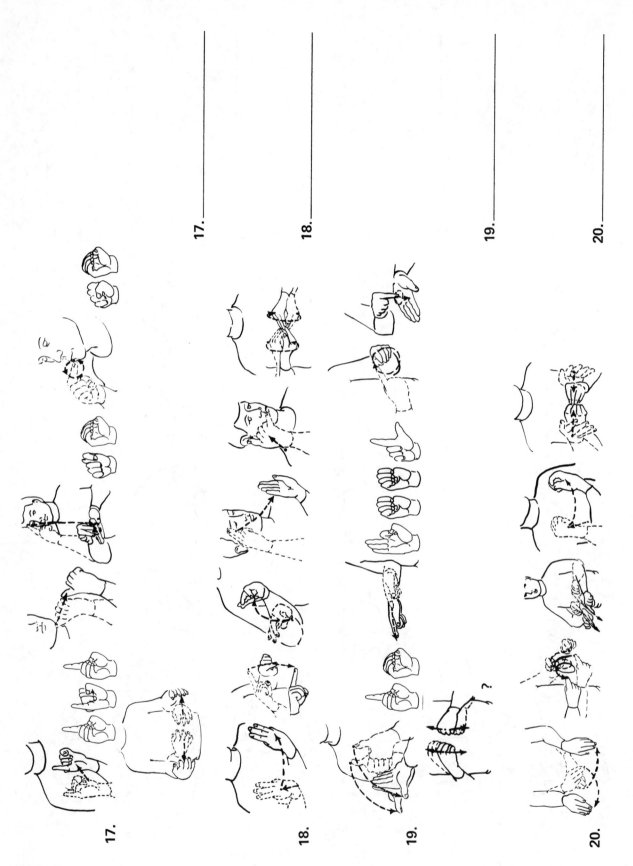

17.

18.

19.

20.

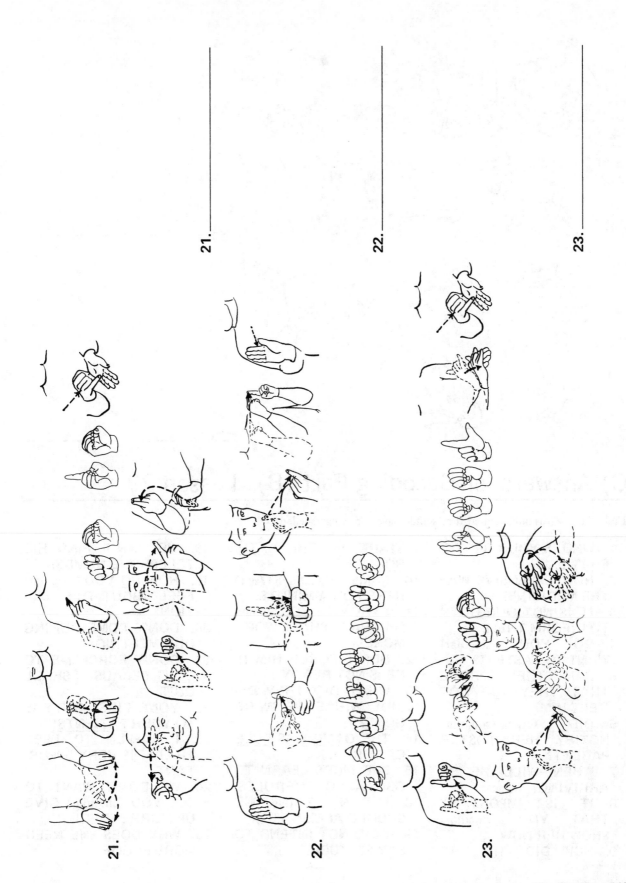

21.

22.

23.

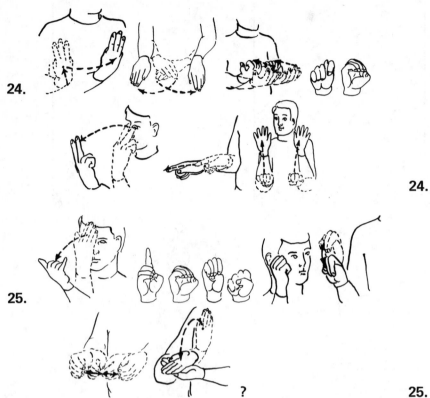

24. _____

25. _____

C) Answers for Decoding Part (B), Lesson 29

Underlined words indicate that they should have been fingerspelled.

1. WHO IS YOUR BROTH-ER-IN-LAW?
2. HOW EXPENSIVE WAS THE MEDICINE?
3. IT IS NOT OUR DUTY TO INFORM THEM.
4. DO YOU (singular) WANT TO TASTE IT?
5. CAN THEY PROVE THAT THEY DID NOT MEET HIM?
6. DID YOU (singular) NOTIFY HER FOSTER PARENT?
7. WHEN WILL HE BE ARRIVING?
8. IT IS IMPORTANT THAT YOU (singular) SHOW HER NOW.
9. HOW DID THE FIRE START IN THE BATH-ROOM?
10. COME AND STAND HERE FOR A MINUTE.
11. I PROMISE YOU (singular) THAT I SHALL WORK MORE!
12. DON'T FORCE HIM IF HE IS NOT READY.
13. WHAT DID THEY DE-CIDE WHILE WE WERE GONE?
14. THE GAME WAS FULL OF THRILLS.
15. SHE MUST LEARN TO OBEY ALL OF THE RULES.
16. I DON'T THINK WE SHOULD ACCEPT IT.
17. I DID NOT INTEND TO SAY SO MUCH.
18. WE CAN'T FIND HIS TELEPHONE NUMBER.
19. HOW DO YOU (singular) FEEL ABOUT THIS EMO-TION?
20. DON'T COME DURING OUR MEETING.
21. DON'T FORCE ME TO DO IT BECAUSE I SHALL QUIT.
22. YOUR FIRST DUTY IS TO YOUR PATIENTS!
23. I HAPPEN TO FEEL THAT IT IS VERY IMPOR-TANT.
24. WE DON'T WANT TO SEE YOU (singular) GIVE UP (SURRENDER).
25. WHY DOES SHE NEED MORE PROOF?

lesson thirty

Signs presented in this lesson are:

PROFIT
EARN, COLLECT
GIVE, DONATE
HAND
IMPROVE

FORGET
COUNSEL*, ADVISE*
FIRE (to terminate some
  other person's employment)
FEEL
SMELL*

LEAD, GUIDE
ADMIT, CONFESS
BEHIND (preposition)
PICTURE
PRINT*

THIN
MAN
PUT, PLACE
WOMAN
WISE*

PROFIT

The right hand, with the thumb and index finger curved and touching (remaining fingers are extended and apart), is held on the right side of the body so that it touches the body near the lower level of the chest (the joined thumb and index finger are pointing downward). Next, the hand grazes the body as it makes a small movement in a downward direction.

NOTE: This sign may be imitative, perhaps, of sticking a coin into the vest pocket.

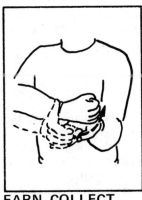

EARN, COLLECT

The left hand, with the thumb and fingers extended and joined, is held in front and slightly to the left side of the body with the palm facing up and the fingers pointing to the viewer. The right hand, with the thumb extended and pointing vertically (the remaining fingers are joined and slightly curved), comes to rest on the left hand fingers (the back side of the right hand is facing the viewer). Next, the right hand is quickly pulled back over the left palm in the direction of the signer as it closes to a fist position.

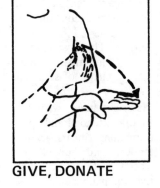

GIVE, DONATE

The right hand, with the thumb touching the extended and joined fingertips, is placed in front of the body so that the fingertips are pointing upward. Then, the hand is flipped forward and flattens out (the thumb is extended and apart, while the remaining fingers are extended and joined) with the fingertips pointing to the viewer. The palmar side of the hand is facing up as the sign ends.

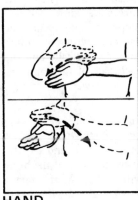

HAND

This sign is executed in two steps. *Step one:* The left hand, with the thumb and fingers extended and joined, is placed in front and slightly to the left side of the body with the fingers pointing to the viewer and the palm facing right. The right hand, with the thumb and fingers extended and joined, touches the left hand near the wrist with its edge (the right hand is held with the fingers pointing to the left and the back side facing the viewer). Then, the right hand is pulled toward the signer at an oblique angle. *Step two:* The hands reverse their spatial relationship and execute the movements described above.

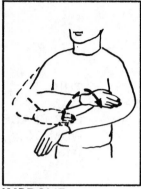

IMPROVE

The left forearm is held in front and to the left side of the body with the thumb and fingers of the hand extended, joined and pointing downward at an oblique angle. The right hand, with its fingers and thumb extended and joined, first touches the back side of the left wrist with its edge (the right hand is held with its back side toward the viewer and the fingers pointing to the left), and again, on the upper arm.

NOTE: This sign may be imitative, perhaps, of steps up.

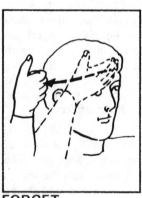

FORGET

The right hand, with the thumb extended and apart (remaining fingers are extended and joined), is placed on the forehead so that the palmar side of the fingers touches the skin; then, the hand is quickly pulled to the right as the fingers are contracted and clasped to the palm. The sign ends with the thumb pointing vertically and the back side of the hand facing the viewer.

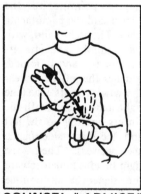

COUNSEL,* ADVISE*

The left hand, in the configuration of the letter *S,* is held in front and slightly to the left side of the body with the wrist facing down. The right hand, with the thumb touching the joined fingertips, is positioned on the back side of the left *S* hand with the joined fingertips touching the hand. Then, the fingers of the right hand fan out as the hand is moved outward (away from the signer). This motion is repeated several times.

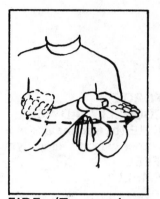

FIRE (To terminate some other person's employment)

The left hand, with the thumb bending inward to touch the joined fingertips, is held in front and slightly to the left side of the body so that the fingertips are pointing upward. The right hand, with its thumb and fingers extended and joined, is held in front of the body with the palm facing up and the fingertips pointing toward the viewer. Next, with the configuration maintained, the right hand is moved to the left as its knuckles brush past the left fingertips.

NOTE: This sign may be imitative, perhaps, of someone being severed or removed from his/her position.

FEEL

The thumb and fingers of the right hand are extended and apart, except for the middle finger which is flexed to a 45-degree angle. Then, the tip of the middle finger grazes over the region of the heart as the right hand is moved upward.

SMELL*

The right hand, with the thumb and fingers joined (and the fingers bending slightly at the palm), is held in front of the chin so that the palmar side is facing the signer and the fingers are pointing to the left. Next, with the configuration preserved, the right hand tilts slightly forward as it is lifted upward past the nose. This motion is repeated several times.

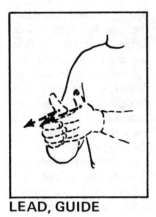

LEAD, GUIDE

Both hands, each with the thumb extended and pointing vertically (remaining fingers are extended and joined), are held in front of the body with their palmar sides touching (the palmar sides of the left fingers are touching the right palm, while the right hand fingers bend to close over the fingertips and fingers of the left hand). Then, holding this position, both hands are moved forward.

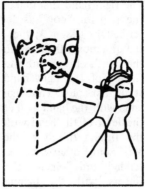

PICTURE

The left hand, with the thumb and fingers extended and joined, is held in front and slightly to the left side of the body with the palm facing to the right and the fingers pointing upward. The right hand assumes the configuration of the letter *C*, which first is placed over the right cheekbone (the back side of the *C* hand is facing to the right); then the hand is pulled away and placed on the palm of the left hand so that the back side of the *C* hand is facing the signer as the sign comes to an end.

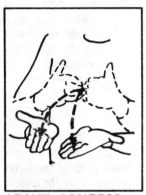

ADMIT, CONFESS

Both hands, each with the thumb extended and apart (remaining fingers are extended and joined), are positioned side-by-side so that the fingertips are touching the chest (the thumbs of both hands are pointing upward and the back sides of the fingers are facing each other). Then, the hands are flipped forward so that now the palmar sides are facing up.

NOTE: This sign may be imitative, perhaps, of getting something off your chest.

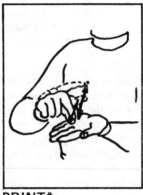

PRINT*

The left hand, with the thumb and fingers extended and joined, is held in front of the body with the palm facing up and the fingers pointing to the viewer. The right hand, in the configuration of the letter *G*, is held over the left palm so that the wrist of the *G* hand is facing down. Then, the thumb and index finger touch as the *G* hand is moved downward and touches the left palm. This motion is repeated several times.

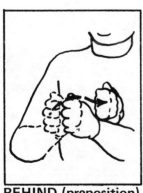

BEHIND (preposition)

Both hands, each in the configuration of the letter *A*, are placed side-by-side in front of the body so that the knuckles touch. Next, the right *A* hand is moved upward and curves over the top of the left hand, moving backward as it goes to stop above and near the left wrist.

THIN

The right hand, with the thumb and index finger extended and separated (remaining fingers are contracted), touches both sides of the face near the level of the cheek bone (the back side of the hand is facing the viewer). Next, the thumb and index finger graze the cheeks as the hand is moved downward past the chin. This sign may be imitative, perhaps, of cheeks drawn in.

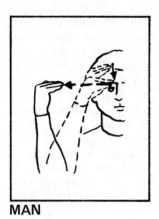

MAN

The right hand first makes the sign for "boy" as described in lesson 3; then, the arm moves the hand to the right as the thumb and fingers of the right hand straighten out. The sign ends with the hand held at the level of the head with the fingers flexed at the base but otherwise extended and joined. The fingers, with the palmar sides facing down, are pointing to the left.

NOTE: The sign for "men" is made similarly to "man," except that the right hand makes one additional movement to the right, thus suggesting one more man.

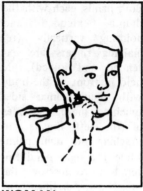

WOMAN

The right hand first makes the sign for "girl" as described in lesson 3; then, the arm moves the hand to the right as the thumb and fingers of the right hand straighten out. The sign ends with the hand held at the level of the cheek with the fingers flexed at the base but otherwise extended and joined. The fingers, with the palmar sides facing down, are pointing to the left.

NOTE: The sign for "women" is made similarly to "woman," except that the right hand makes one additional movement to the right, thus suggesting one more woman.

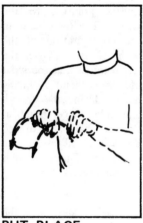

PUT, PLACE

Both hands, each with the thumb flexed inward to touch the extended and joined fingers, are positioned side-by-side (but are not touching) in front of the body with the joined fingertips of both hands pointing downward. Next, with the configuration preserved, the hands simultaneously are moved to complete an upward arc motion while moving forward.

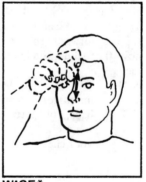

WISE*

The right hand, in the configuration of the letter X, is placed on the middle of the forehead so that the crooked index finger of the right X hand is pointing downward; Next, the X hand is moved to execute several quick up and down movements.

A) Exercises in Encoding

Encode the following material using signs and fingerspelling. Use fingerspelling for all underlined words.

1. <u>DO</u> YOU THINK THAT SHE IS IMPROVING?
2. DON'T FORGET <u>TO</u> BRING ME MY NEW BOOK TOMORROW.
3. IF YOU WILL NOT WORK, I SHALL FIRE YOU.
4. I DON'T KNOW WHY, BUT I FEEL LAZY TODAY. ("Lazy" is signed as "laze" plus "y.")
5. <u>DO</u> YOU SMELL ANYTHING BURNING?
6. I ADVISED THEM NOT <u>TO</u> ATTEMPT IT. ("Attempt" is signed similarly to "try," but with A hands.)
7. HOW MUCH MONEY <u>DID</u> YOU GIVE THEM?
8. ARE YOU DONATING YOUR HEARING AID?
9. PUT THE BLACK CAR BEHIND THE RED <u>BALL</u>.
10. I CAN'T ADMIT THAT IT WAS MY FAULT.
11. WHAT ELSE <u>DO</u> YOU SEE IN THIS PICTURE?
12. WHO WILL PRINT OUR NEW BOOK?
13. MY FATHER IS A PRINTER. ("Printer" is signed as "print" plus "er.")
14. HOW MUCH PROFIT <u>DO</u> YOU HOPE <u>TO</u> MAKE?
15. WHY IS SHE <u>SO</u> THIN?
16. I THINK <u>IT</u> WAS A WISE DECISION. ("Decision" is signed as "decide" plus "ion.")
17. HOW <u>DID</u> HE <u>HURT</u> HIS HAND?
18. HE <u>IS</u> AN IMPORTANT MAN IN OUR SCHOOL.
19. A WOMAN ANSWERED THE TELEPHONE.
20. I SHALL LEAD YOU TO OUR NEW BUILDING. ("Building" is signed as "build" plus "house.")
21. WE NEED SOMEONE <u>TO</u> GUIDE US.
22. SHOW HIM SOME PICTURES AND ASK HIM <u>TO</u> DESCRIBE THEM.
23. I PUT THE PAPERS ON YOUR DESK.
24. HOW MUCH MONEY <u>DO</u> YOU EARN EACH MONTH? ("Each" is signed similarly to "every," but is repeated several times.)
25. PLEASE BRING ME MY NEWSPAPER. ("Newspaper" is signed as "print" plus "paper".)

B) Exercises in Decoding

Decode the following illustrated exercises:

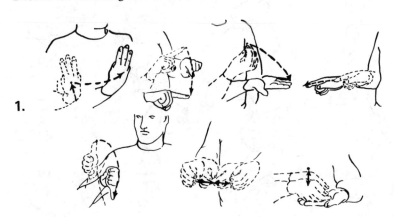

1.

1._____

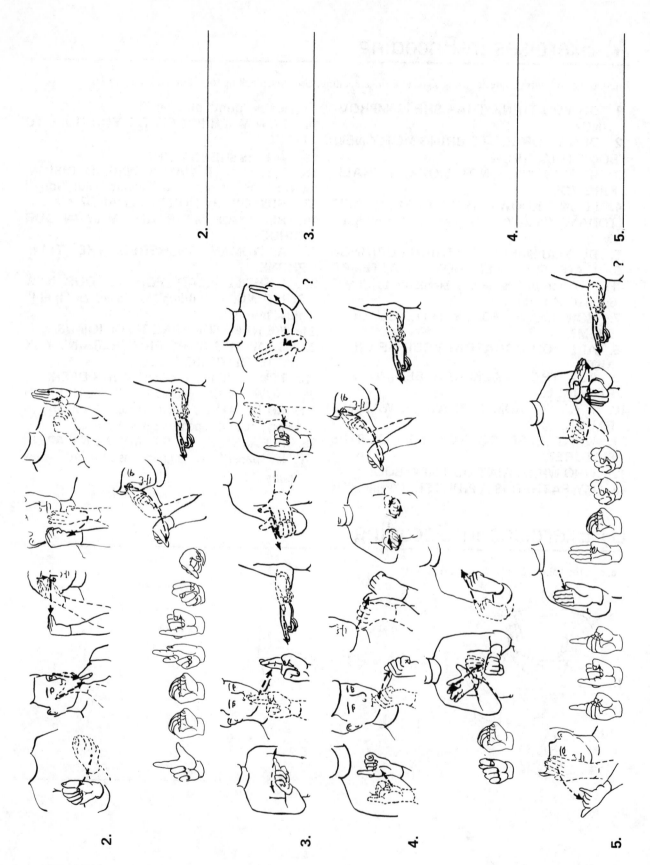

6.

7.

8.

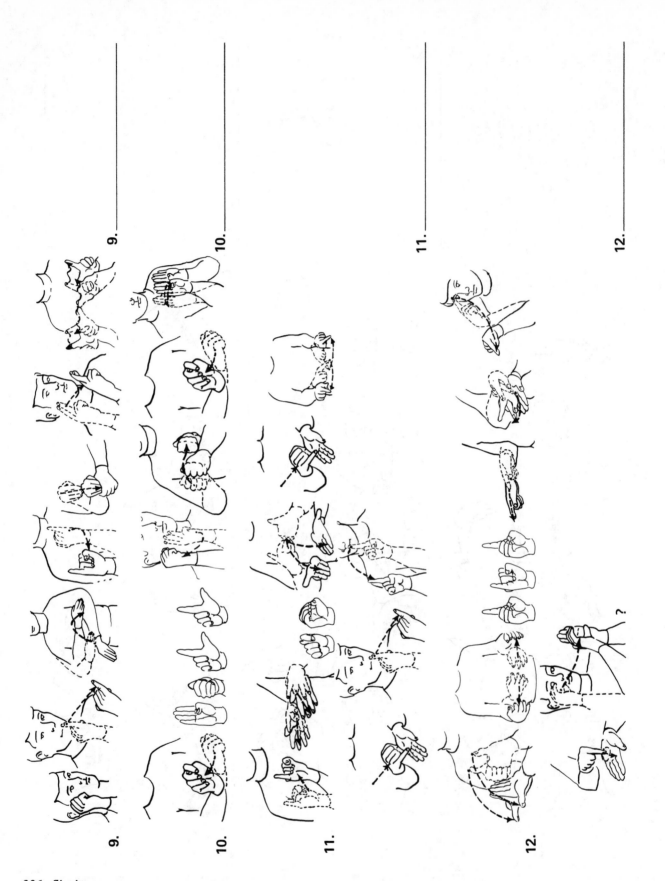

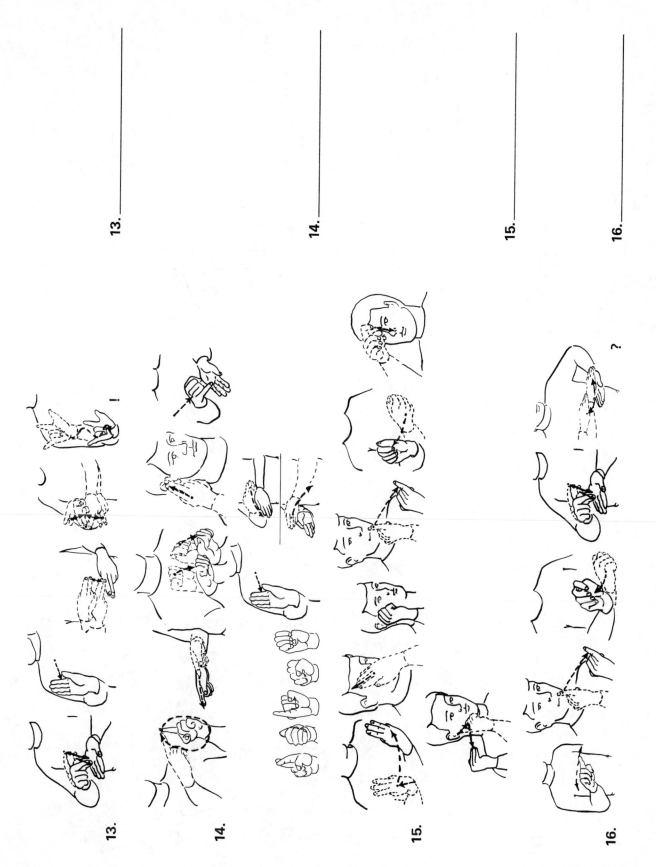

13.

14.

15.

16.

13.

14.

15.

16.

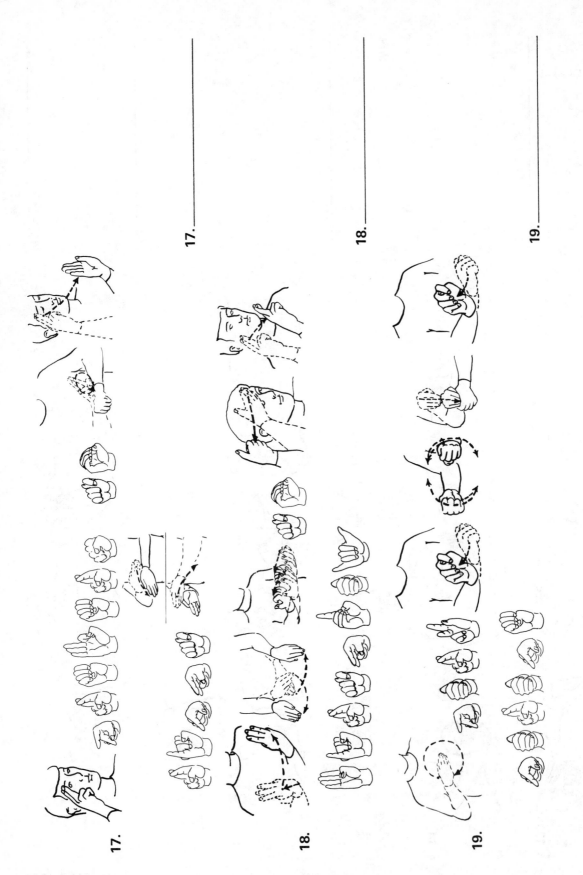

17.

18.

19.

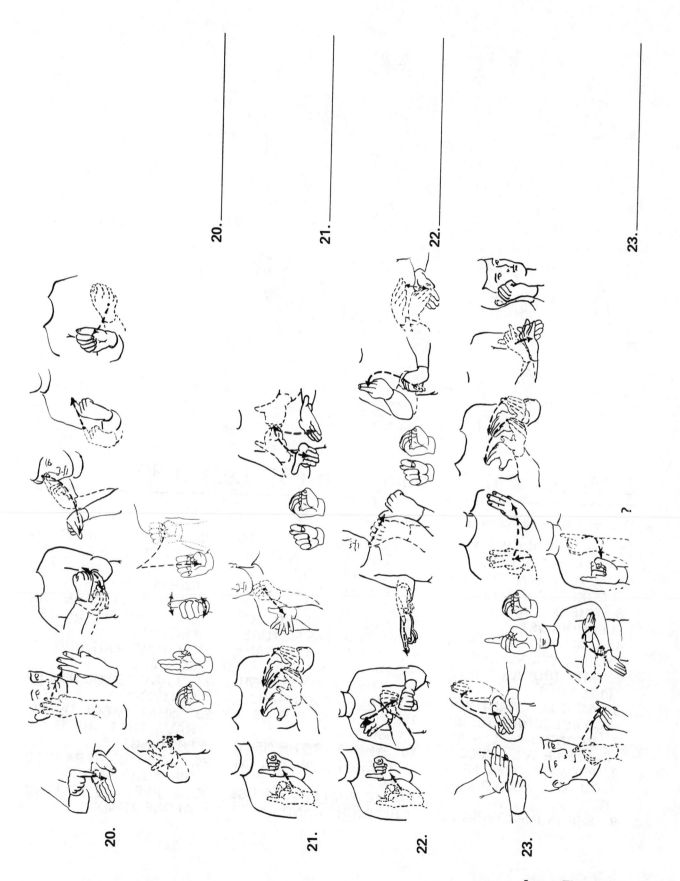

20.

21.

22.

23.

20.

21.

22.

23.

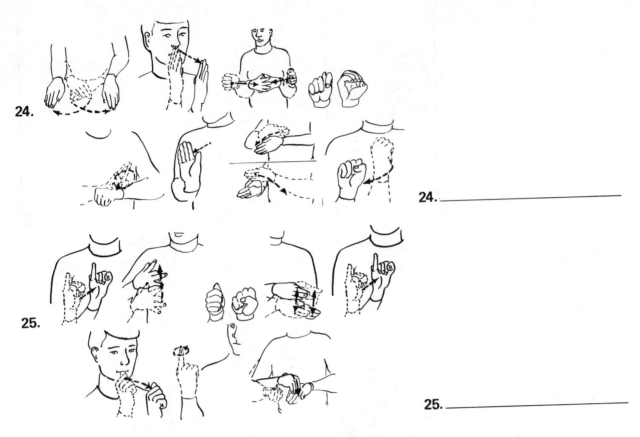

24. _____

25. _____

C) Answers for Decoding Part (B), Lesson 30

Underlined words indicate that they should have been fingerspelled.

1. WE CAN'T GIVE YOU ANY MORE MONEY.
2. A THIN MAN WAS JUST <u>LOOKING</u> FOR YOU.
3. WHERE ARE YOU LEADING US?
4. I AM NOT HERE FOR YOU <u>TO</u> COUNSEL ME.
5. WHY <u>DID</u> YOUR <u>BOSS</u> FIRE YOU?
6. WE DON'T WANT YOU <u>TO</u> FEEL SORRY FOR US.
7. I CAN'T SMELL IT BE-CAUSE I HAVE A COLD.
8. PROMISE ME THAT YOU WILL NOT FORGET IT.
9. SHE IS IMPROVING IN HER LANGUAGE.
10. THE <u>BALL</u> WAS BE-HIND THE DOOR.
11. I HATE <u>TO</u> ADMIT IT, BUT IT IS TRUE.
12. HOW MUCH <u>DID</u> YOU PAY FOR THIS PICTURE?
13. PRINT YOUR NAME CAREFULLY!
14. WHEN YOU CAN HEAR IT, <u>RAISE</u> YOUR HAND.
15. WE KNOW SHE IS A WISE WOMAN.
16. WHERE IS THE NEWS-PAPER? ("print" plus "pa-per")
17. HE <u>PREFERS</u> <u>TO</u> USE HIS <u>RIGHT</u> HAND.
18. WE DON'T WANT <u>TO</u> FORGET HER <u>BIRTHDAY</u>.
19. PLEASE <u>PARK</u> THE CAR IN THE <u>GARAGE</u>.
20. THIS WILL EARN FOR ME A PROFIT <u>OF</u> TEN PER CENT.
21. I HAVE NOTHING <u>TO</u> CONFESS.
22. I ADVISE YOU NOT <u>TO</u> QUIT SCHOOL.
23. WHAT PROOF <u>DO</u> WE HAVE THAT SHE IS IM-PROVING?
24. DON'T BE AFRAID <u>TO</u> USE YOUR HANDS.
25. I FEEL <u>AS</u> IF I AM ALONE AGAIN.

340 Signing

lesson thirty-one

Signs presented in this lesson are:

WAY
METHOD
ROAD, PATH
ODD, STRANGE, PECULIAR
REST

WIN, VICTORY
LADY
GENTLEMAN
SEARCH,* SEEK*
SKILL

MANAGE, CONTROL
CREAM
PLACE (noun)
AREA
GROW, SPRING*

LOAF (verb)
SLIM, SLENDER
REGISTER, SIGN
  (your name)
BREAD
PROGRAM (noun)

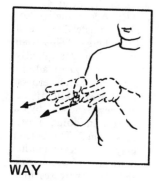

WAY

Both hands, in the configuration of the letter *W*, are placed side-by-side in front of the body with the *W* fingers pointing to the viewer and the palmar sides facing each other. Next, the *W* hands simultaneously are moved forward while staying parallel.

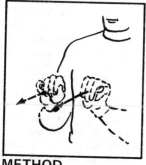

METHOD

Both hands, in the configuration of the letter *M*, are placed side-by-side in front of the body so that the knuckles are facing up and the back sides are toward the signer. Next, the *M* hands simultaneously are moved forward while maintaining a parallel position.

ROAD, PATH

Both hands, with the thumbs and fingers extended and joined, are placed about six inches apart in front of the body with the palmar surfaces facing each other and the fingertips pointing to the viewer at an angle to the right. Then, while the hands remain parallel, both hands bend right and left as they are moved forward, imitative of the bends and turns of a path or road.

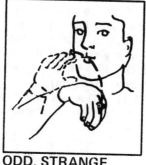

ODD, STRANGE, PECULIAR

The right hand first assumes the configuration of the letter *C* and is held near the right cheek with the back side of the *C* hand facing to the right. Then, the *C* hand is moved across (to the left) the lower portion of the face with the wrist bending acutely as the *C* hand is tilted downward.

REST

Both hands first make the letter *R* and are crossed at the wrists. The crossed *R* hands are held in front of the body at chest level with the back sides facing the viewer. Next, the crossed *R* hands are moved toward the signer and come to rest on the chest so that the *R* fingertips are touching the body.

WIN, VICTORY

The left hand assumes the configuration of the letter *S* and is held in front of the body with the back side of the *S* hand facing to the left. The right hand, with the thumb and fingers extended and apart, is held over the left hand so that its back side is facing to the right. Then, the right hand quickly is moved toward the signer as it clenches into a fist position.

LADY

First, the palmar side of the right thumb (remaining fingers are contracted) grazes the right cheek as the hand is moved toward the chin. This is the sign for "girl" described in lesson 5. Then, the right hand leaves the chin, performing a large forward arc motion as the fingers and thumb fan out and come to rest at the chest (the thumb touches the chest and the fingers are pointing upward at about a 45-degree angle, with the back side of the hand facing to the right).

NOTE: This sign intends to suggest a "polite girl."

GENTLEMAN

First, the right hand makes the sign for "boy" described in lesson 3. Next, the thumb and fingers fan out as the hand performs a large forward arc motion in front of the body and is returned to the body with the thumb resting on the breast bone. The hand is held so that the back side is facing to the right and the fingers are pointing at about a 45-degree upward angle.

NOTE: This sign intends to suggest a "polite boy."

SEARCH,* SEEK*

The right hand assumes the configuration of the letter *C* and is held near the right side of the chin with the back side of the hand facing to the right. Then, the *C* hand is moved to complete several circular motions over the entire face.

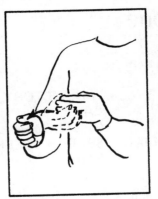

SKILL

The left hand, with the thumb and fingers extended and joined, is held in front of the body with the fingers pointing to the viewer and the back side facing to the left. The right hand grasps the lower edge of the left hand and then is snapped outwardly. The sign ends with the right hand in the configuration of the letter *A*.

NOTE: According to Stokoe, Casterline, and Croneberg[1] "This is an expression (frequently exclamatory) of admiration to the cleverness, adroitness, skill or expertness shown by a person in doing a certain thing. The person may be a clever mathematician in which case the sign expresses high admiration of his skill in manipulating figures. He may be a lady-killer; the sign then expresses admiration of his romantic prowess. Or he may have won ten thousand dollars on the horses the first time he ever went to a race track; in this case the sign shows the signer's admiration and amazement at the accidental but nevertheless astounding feat of gambling done by the person. The person may be a professional parachute jumper giving an exhibition, and the sign will then indicate the signer's admiration of his nerve and skill.

---

[1] Stokoe, W., Casterline, D., Croneberg, C., *A Dictionary of American Sign Language on Linguistic Principles*, Gallaudet College Press, 1965, Page 155.

MANAGE, CONTROL

Both hands assume the configuration of the letter *A* and are positioned in front of the body so that the left *A* hand is slightly ahead (closer to the viewer) of the right *A* hand. The wrist of the right *A* hand is facing to the left, while that of the left *A* hand is facing up. Next, the *A* hands execute alternate movements forward and back, in the direction of the viewer.

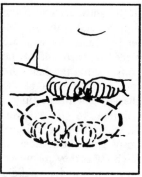

AREA

Both hands assume the configuration of the letter *A* and are held in front of the body so that the backs of the thumbs are touching. Then, the *A* hands separate and make halves of a *horizontal* circle in the direction of the signer and touch again to close the circle.

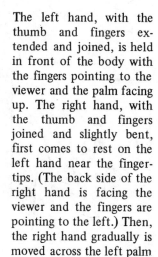

CREAM

The left hand, with the thumb and fingers extended and joined, is held in front of the body with the fingers pointing to the viewer and the palm facing up. The right hand, with the thumb and fingers joined and slightly bent, first comes to rest on the left hand near the fingertips. (The back side of the right hand is facing the viewer and the fingers are pointing to the left.) Then, the right hand gradually is moved across the left palm in the direction of the wrist.

NOTE: This sign may be imitative, perhaps, of skimming the cream once it has risen to the top.

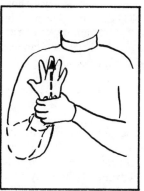

GROW, SPRING*

The right hand, with the thumb bending inward to touch the extended and joined fingers, is held in front of the body with the fingers pointing upward. The left hand, in the configuration of the letter *C,* is moved toward the right hand and, with its palmar side, touches the back sides of the right hand fingers and thumb. Next, with the left hand remaining stationary, the right hand is moved upward and stops when its thumb and fingers are fully extended and apart. (The back side of the hand faces the viewer.)

NOTE: The sign for "Spring" is made by repeating this motion several times.

PLACE (noun)

Both hands assume the configuration of the letter *P,* with the tips of the second fingers touching. The *P* hands are held in front of the body with the back sides facing right and left, respectively. Then, the *P* hands separate and make halves of a *horizontal* circle in the direction of the signer and touch again to close the circle.

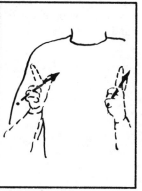

LOAF (verb)

Both hands assume the configuration of the letter *L* and are held in front of the body with the back sides of the *L* hands facing to the right and left, respectively. Next, the *L* hands simultaneously are brought toward the body so that the thumbs strike the chest near each shoulder. The sign ends with the index finger of both *L* hands pointing upward at a 45-degree angle.

SLIM, SLENDER

Both hands, each with the thumb and fingers extended and joined, are placed on each side of the body so that the palms are touching the sides of the chest and with the fingers pointing to the viewer. Next, the hands simultaneously graze both sides of the body as they are moved downward, and then flare slightly outward when the hands reach the waistline. NOTE: This sign may be imitative, perhaps, of a tapered body.

BREAD

The left hand, with the thumb and fingers extended and joined, is held in front of the body at chest level with the fingers pointing to the right and the back side facing the viewer. The right hand, with the thumb and fingers joined and flexed at the base, touches the back side of the left hand with its fingertips. Then, the right hand fingertips graze the back of the left hand while moving up and down, possibly imitative of slicing a long loaf of bread.

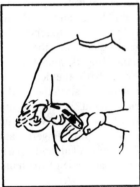

REGISTER, SIGN (your name)

The left hand, with the thumb and fingers extended and joined, is held in front of the body with the palm facing up and the fingers pointing to the viewer. The right hand assumes the configuration of the letter *H* and is held in front and to the right side of the body so that the index and middle fingers are pointing to the viewer (the back sides of the fingers are facing to the right). Then, the wrist turns the right *H* hand to the left so that the palmar sides of the *H* fingers touch the palm of the left hand.

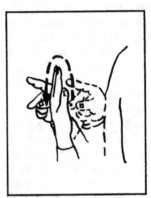

PROGRAM (noun)

The left hand, with the thumb and fingers extended and joined, is held in front of the body with the fingers pointing upward and the palm facing the signer. The right hand, in the configuration of the letter *P*, first touches the left palm (contact is made between the tip of the middle finger and the palm). Then, the *P* hand makes an arc motion as it is moved toward and over the left fingertips and touches the back side of the left hand near the knuckles. (The back side of the right thumb makes contact with the back side of the left hand.)

A) Exercises in Encoding

Encode the following material using signs and fingerspelling. Use fingerspelling for all underlined words.

1. MAY WE <u>DO</u> IT OUR WAY?
2. THIS IS A NEW METHOD <u>OF</u> TEACHING LANGUAGE DEVELOPMENT. ("Development" is signed as "develop" plus "ment.")
3. WHAT IS THE NAME <u>OF</u> THIS ROAD?
4. THE GENTLEMAN IS FROM <u>FLORIDA</u>.
5. HE IS SLOW IN LEARNING THE <u>SKILL</u>.
6. <u>DO</u> YOU WANT MORE CREAM IN YOUR TEA?
7. WHO WILL WIN THE <u>GAME</u> TOMORROW?
8. <u>DO</u> YOU THINK I AM SLIM?
9. DON'T FORGET <u>TO</u> BUY SOME BREAD.
10. I THINK YOU SHOULD REST FOR A MINUTE.
11. DON'T <u>LET</u> HIM <u>CATCH</u> YOU LOAFING AGAIN.
12. I WANT <u>TO</u> SEE THIS PLACE FOR MYSELF.
13. PLEASE WAIT FOR US IN THIS AREA.
14. HOW CAN IT GROW WITHOUT WATER?
15. SPRING IS ALMOST HERE! ("Spring" is signed as "grow," which is repeated several times.)
16. I SEARCHED FOR IT THIS MORNING, BUT I WAS NOT ABLE <u>TO</u> FIND IT.
17. WHEN <u>DID</u> YOU REGISTER?
18. PLEASE SIGN HERE, IF YOU AGREE WITH IT. ("Sign" in this sentence refers to "sign your name.")
19. WHO HELPED YOU <u>PLAN</u> THIS PROGRAM?
20. WHAT METHOD ARE YOU USING WITH YOUR <u>PATIENT</u>?
21. THE PARENTS ARE IN THE WAITING AREA.
22. WHEN ARE YOU <u>MOVING</u> TO YOUR NEW PLACE?
23. IT WAS A VICTORY FOR US.
24. I FEEL ODD GOING ALONE.

B) Exercises in Decoding

Decode the following illustrated exercises:

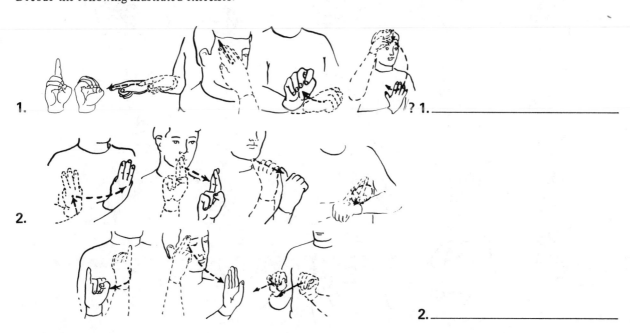

1. _____

2. _____

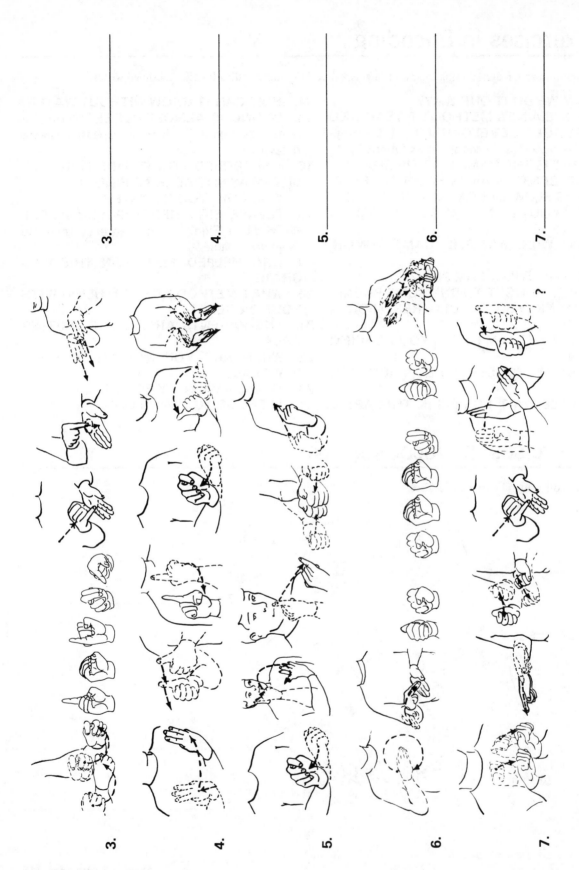

3.

4.

5.

6.

7.

8.

9.

10.

11.

8.

9.

10.

11.

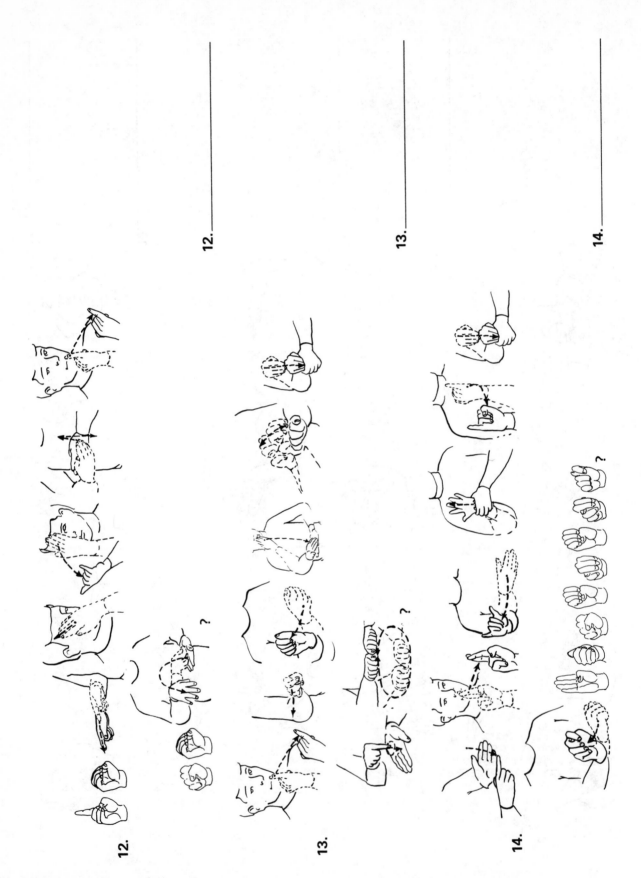

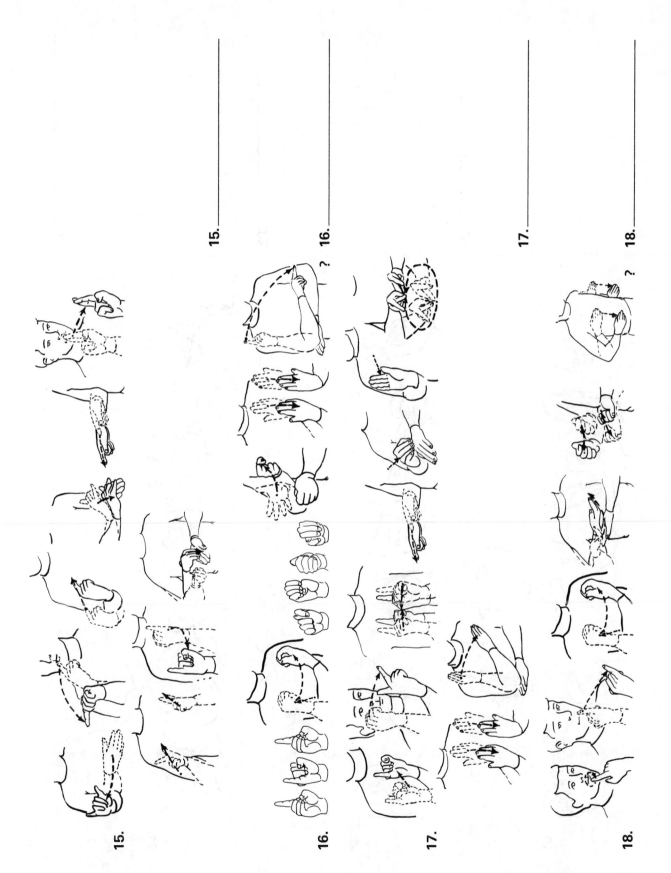

15.

16.
?

17.

18.
?

15.

16.

17.

18.

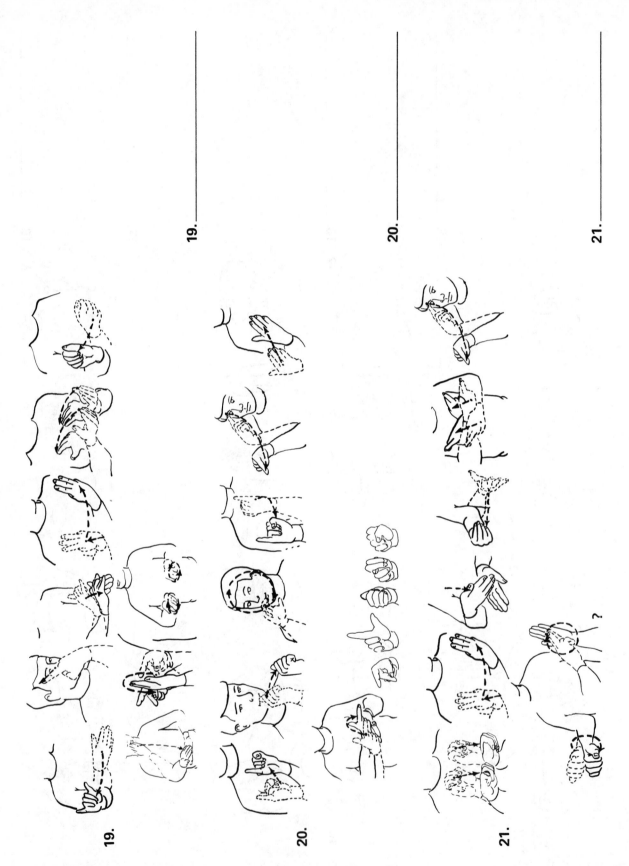

19.

20.

21.

22.

23.

24.

25. _____

C) Answers for Decoding Part (B), Lesson 31

Underlined words indicate that they should have been fingerspelled.

1. <u>DO</u> YOU KNOW THE GENTLEMAN?
2. WE ARE NOT USING HIS METHOD.
3. TRY <u>DOING</u> IT THIS WAY.
4. WE FOLLOWED THE OTHER ROAD.
5. THE LADY IS WITH ME.
6. PLEASE REGISTER <u>AS SOON AS</u> POSSIBLE.
7. CAN YOU MANAGE IT BY YOURSELF?
8. HE NEEDS TO LEARN THESE SKILLS.
9. WHO WILL PRINT OUR PROGRAM?
10. DON'T SIGN ANYTHING BEFORE YOU READ IT.
11. SHE IS VERY <u>TALL</u> AND SLIM.
12. <u>DO</u> YOU KNOW WHY BREAD IS <u>SO</u> EXPENSIVE?
13. IS THERE A GOOD DOCTOR IN THIS AREA?
14. WHAT ARE THEY GROWING IN THE <u>BASEMENT</u>?
15. THEY TELL ME THAT YOU ARE LOAFING AGAIN.
16. <u>DID</u> OUR <u>TEAM</u> WIN TODAY? ("Today" is formed by signing "now" and then "day.")
17. I SHALL MEET YOU AT YOUR PLACE THIS AFTERNOON.
18. WHO IS OUR NEW MANAGER?
19. THEY THINK THAT WE HAVE A GOOD PROGRAM HERE.
20. I AM SEARCHING FOR MY LESSON <u>PLANS</u>.
21. MAY WE STOP AND REST FOR AN HOUR?
22. I DON'T WANT ANY CREAM IN MY COFFEE.
23. THERE ARE OTHER METHODS THAT WE CAN USE.
24. I CAN'T REMEMBER THE NAME <u>OF</u> THIS PLACE.
25. THE GENTLEMAN IS FROM MY HOME <u>TOWN</u>.

lesson thirty-two

Signs presented in this lesson are:

CHEESE*	DOLLAR	HORSE*	CHEW
FUN	WEAK*	COOKIE*	BUTTER*
ESTABLISH	CENTER	SPOON	BIRTH
SINCE (time)	HIGH	KNIFE*	ICE CREAM
SEPARATE	HOT	FORK*	BORN

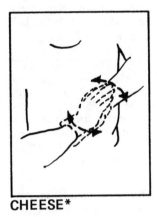

CHEESE*

The left hand, with the thumb and fingers extended and joined, is held in front of the body with the palm facing up and the fingers pointing to the right. The right hand forms a similar configuration, but with the palm facing down and the fingertips pointing to the left. Then, with the palmar sides of both hands still touching each other, execute small twisting motions backward-and-forward to the viewer. While doing this, rub the palmar surfaces of both hands together.

NOTE: This probably is an attempt to illustrate early cheese making where the cheese was placed in a cloth and simultaneously pressed and twisted to force out liquid and congeal the cheese curds.

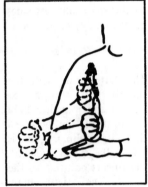

ESTABLISH

The left hand, with the thumb and fingers extended and joined, is placed in front of the body with the palm facing down and the fingers facing to the right. The right hand, in the configuration of the letter *A*, is held in front and slightly to the right side of the body. Next, the *A* hand swings to the left and in an upward direction, extending the thumb vertically in the process. (The right hand is now directly over the left hand with the thumb pointing upward and its palmar side toward the viewer.) With this configuration held, the right hand is moved downward and comes to rest on the back of the left hand.

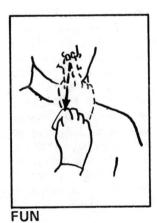

FUN

The right hand assumes the configuration of the letter *H.* The palmar sides of the *H* fingertips first touch the nose and then, without bending the wrist, the hand is dropped downward as the *H* fingers are bent over the thumb.

NOTE: The sign for "funny" is made by combining the sign for "fun" plus "Y," which is fingerspelled.

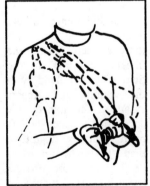

SINCE (time)

Both hands, with only their index fingers extended (remaining fingers and thumbs are contracted), place the palmar sides of their index fingers on the right shoulder. Then, both hands are flipped forward. The sign ends with both hands positioned side-by-side in front of the body with their back sides facing down, index fingers pointing at the viewer.

353

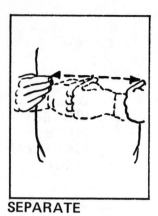

SEPARATE

Both hands, each with the thumb and fingers extended and joined (fingers are flexed at the base), are held side-by-side in front of the body so that the back sides of the fingers are facing each other. (The fingertips of both hands are pointing to the signer.) Next, without altering their configuration, the hands are pulled sideways, to the right and left sides of the body, respectively.

CENTER

The left hand, with the thumb and fingers extended and joined, is placed in front of the body with the palm facing up and the fingers pointing to the right. The right hand, with its thumb and fingers joined and slightly curved, first completes a large circle along a horizontal plane above the left palm before the hand descends to touch the left palm with its fingertips.

NOTE: The sign for "middle" is made similarly, except that the right hand makes the letter *M*, then completes a circular motion before descending so that its *M* fingertips touch the left palm.

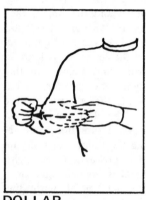

DOLLAR

The left hand, with the thumb and fingers extended and joined, is held in front of the body so that its palmar side is facing the signer and with the fingers pointing to the right. The right hand forms a similar configuration so that the fingers and palm cover the back of the left hand, and the right thumb presses against the palm of the left hand. Then, the right hand is pulled to the right as the thumb bends inward to touch the extended and joined fingers.

HIGH

The right hand, in the configuration of the letter *H*, is held in front and to the right side of the body at the level of the waistline so that the *H* fingers are pointing to the viewer, and the back side of the hand is facing to the right. Next, with the configuration preserved and with no wrist movement, the *H* hand is lifted straight upward, stopping near the level of the shoulder.

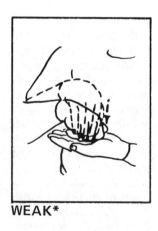

WEAK*

The left hand, with the thumb and fingers extended and joined, is held in front of the body with the palm facing up and the fingers pointing to the right. The right hand, with the thumb and fingers extended and joined in a curve, first touches the left palm with its fingertips; then, the right fingertips bend and collapse into the left palm several times as if to suggest, perhaps, that their muscles are flaccid.

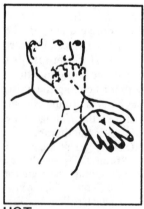

HOT

The right hand, with the thumb and fingers apart and crooked, is held in front of the mouth so that the back side of the hand is facing the viewer. Next, the hand is pulled away from the mouth as the wrist turns the hand so that the palmar side now is facing down and with the fingers fully extended, apart and pointing downward at an angle.

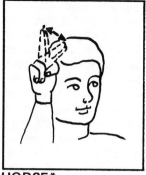

HORSE*

The right hand, in the configuration of the letter *H*, is placed on the right temple so that the *H* fingers are pointing upward, and with their palmar sides facing the viewer. Next, the *H* fingers bend forward and then return to the original position. This motion is repeated several times.

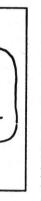

The left hand, with the thumb and fingers extended and joined, is held in front and slightly to the left side of the body with the palm facing up and the fingers pointing to the viewer. The right hand, with the thumb and fingers separated and extended in a curve, first is held over the left palm so that the right thumb and fingertips are pointing to it. Then, the right hand is moved downward so that the thumb and fingertips touch the left palm, and then the right hand is raised to its original position. The motion is then repeated.

NOTE: The sign intends to suggest how cookies are cut out.

COOKIE*

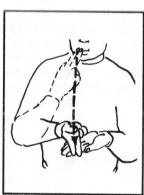

SPOON

The left hand, with the thumb and fingers extended and joined, is held in front of the body with the palm facing up and the fingers pointing to the viewer. The right hand, in the configuration of the letter *H*, first places the palmar sides of the *H* fingertips over the lips and then the *H* hand is moved forward, in a downward direction, and places the back sides of the *H* fingers on the left palm.

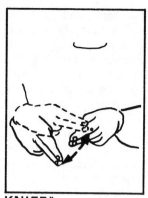

KNIFE*

The left hand, in the configuration of the letter *H*, is held in front of the body with the *H* fingers pointing to the viewer at an angle and the back side of the *H* hand is facing to the left. The right hand, also in the configuration of the letter *H*, first touches the left *H* hand (contact is made at the first joint between the middle finger of the right *H* hand and the index finger of the left *H* hand). Next, the right *H* hand, which is held with its back side toward the viewer, slides forward past the left *H* fingertips. This motion, intending to suggest that something is being sliced, is repeated several times.

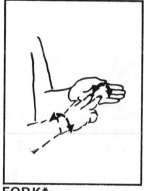

FORK*

The left hand, with the thumb and fingers extended and joined, is held in front and to the left side of the body with the fingers pointing to the viewer and the back side facing to the left. The right hand, in the configuration of the letter *V*, touches the left palm with its *V* fingertips and then is moved to complete a semicircle in a clockwise direction. This motion is repeated several times.

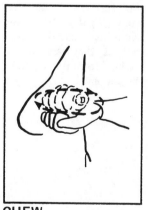

CHEW

Both hands, each in the configuration of the letter *A*, are placed in front of the body so that their knuckles are touching and with the back side of the left *A* hand facing down, while the back of the right *A* hand is facing up. Next, the right *A* hand completes several circular movements in a clockwise direction while rubbing the stationary left *A* hand.

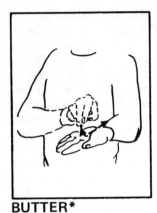

BUTTER*

The left hand, with its thumb and fingers extended and joined, is held in front and slightly to the left side of the body with the palm facing up and its fingers pointing to the viewer. The right hand, in the configuration of the letter *H*, is held with the palmar surfaces of the *H* fingers directly over the left palm. Next, the *H* fingers move down to touch the left palm and then the hand is pulled toward the signer as the *H* fingers brush past the palm. This motion is repeated several times.

NOTE: This sign may be imitative, perhaps, of the way butter is scooped up with a knife.

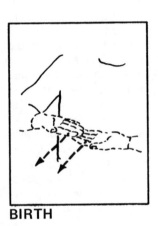

BIRTH

The left hand, with the thumb and fingers extended and joined, is placed in front of the body at the level of the abdomen with the palm facing up and the fingers pointing to the right. The right hand adopts a similar configuration, except that the fingers are pointing to the left. The fingers of the right hand are placed so that their backs overlap the fingers of the left hand, slightly. Next, the hands maintain their contact as they are moved forward from the region of the abdomen.

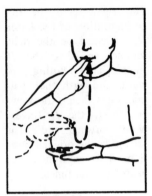

ICE CREAM

The left hand, with the thumb and fingers extended and joined, is held in front of the body with the palm facing up and the fingers pointing to the right. The right hand makes the letter *H*, which is held over the left hand so that the back side of the *H* hand is facing the viewer and the *H* fingers are pointing to the left. Next, the right *H* hand is dipped down to the palm and then raised to the mouth.

NOTE: An "ice cream cone" is signed by licking an imaginary cone.

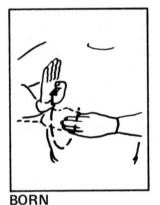

BORN

The left hand, with the thumb and fingers extended and joined, is held in front of the body at the level of the abdomen with the back side of the hand facing the viewer and the fingers pointing to the right. The right hand, with the thumb and fingers extended and joined, has its back side placed against the palmar side of the left hand so that the fingers are pointing to the left. Next, the right hand is moved downward and forward beyond the left hand as it assumes the configuration of the letter *B* with the hand flexed upward. The sign ends with the palm of the right *B* hand facing the viewer and the fingertips pointing upward.

A) Exercises in Encoding

Encode the following material using signs and fingerspelling. Use fingerspelling for all underlined words.

1. WHAT <u>KIND</u> <u>OF</u> CHEESE <u>DO</u> YOU WANT US <u>TO</u> BUY?
2. WOULD YOU <u>LOAN</u> US TEN DOLLARS?
3. WHEN WAS YOUR PROGRAM ESTAB-LISHED?
4. MY PARENTS WILL BUY ME A HORSE FOR MY BIRTHDAY. ("Birthday" is signed as "birth" plus "day.")
5. THIS <u>PATIENT</u> HAS A VERY HIGH VOICE.
6. PLEASE DON'T TOUCH IT BECAUSE IT IS HOT.
7. SINCE I AM HERE, <u>LET</u> ME HELP YOU.
8. <u>DID</u> YOU WANT ME <u>TO</u> SEPARATE THEM?
9. I WILL GIVE YOU A COOKIE BECAUSE YOU ARE A GOOD BOY.
10. ARE YOU BRINGING ICE CREAM FOR <u>DESSERT</u>?
11. WOULD YOU LIKE MORE BUTTER ON YOUR BREAD?
12. THIS SPOON IS <u>DIRTY</u>.
13. BE CAREFUL BECAUSE THIS KNIFE IS VERY <u>SHARP</u>.
14. HOW MANY FORKS <u>DO</u> WE NEED FOR OUR <u>PARTY</u>?
15. IF YOU DON'T EAT, YOU WILL GET WEAK. ("Get" is signed as "become.")
16. WHEN IS YOUR BIRTHDAY?
17. I WAS NOT BORN DEAF.
18. WE ENJOY WORKING BECAUSE IT IS FUN.
19. HOW MUCH <u>DID</u> YOUR BABY <u>WEIGH</u> AT BIRTH?
20. IS IT IN THE MIDDLE OR AT THE <u>END</u>? ("Middle" is signed similarly to "center," but with an *M* hand.)
21. CHEW YOUR FOOD <u>WELL</u> BEFORE YOU <u>SWALLOW</u> IT.
22. SHE WAS BORN DEAF AND BLIND.
23. SINCE I AM NOT GOING, I CAN <u>DO</u> IT TOMORROW.
24. WOULD YOU HELP US SEPARATE THESE <u>TOYS</u>?
25. WHY DID YOU THINK IT WAS FUNNY? ("Funny" is signed as "fun" plus "Y.")

B) Exercises in Decoding

Decode the following illustrated exercises:

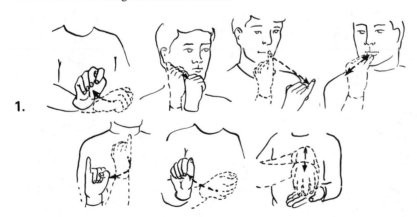

1.

1._____

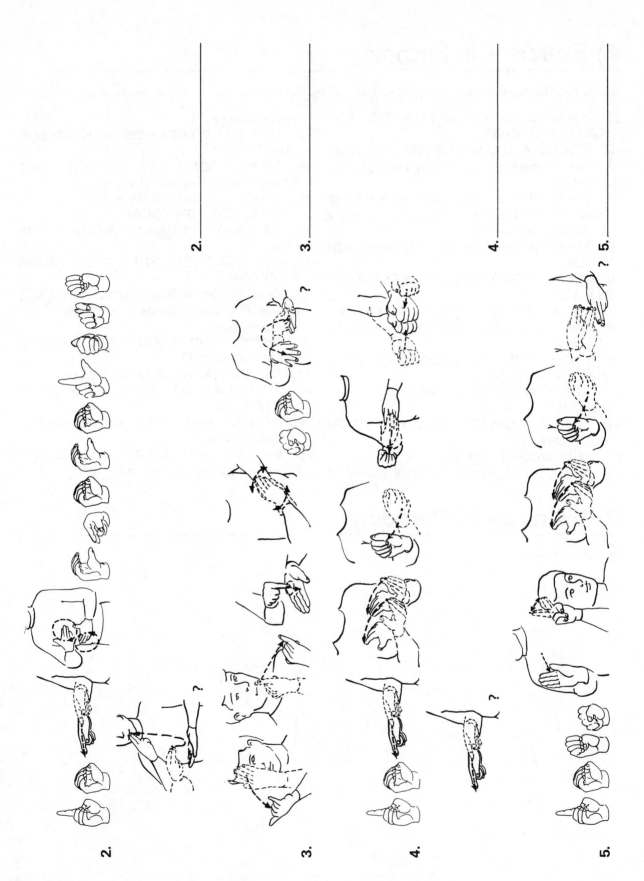

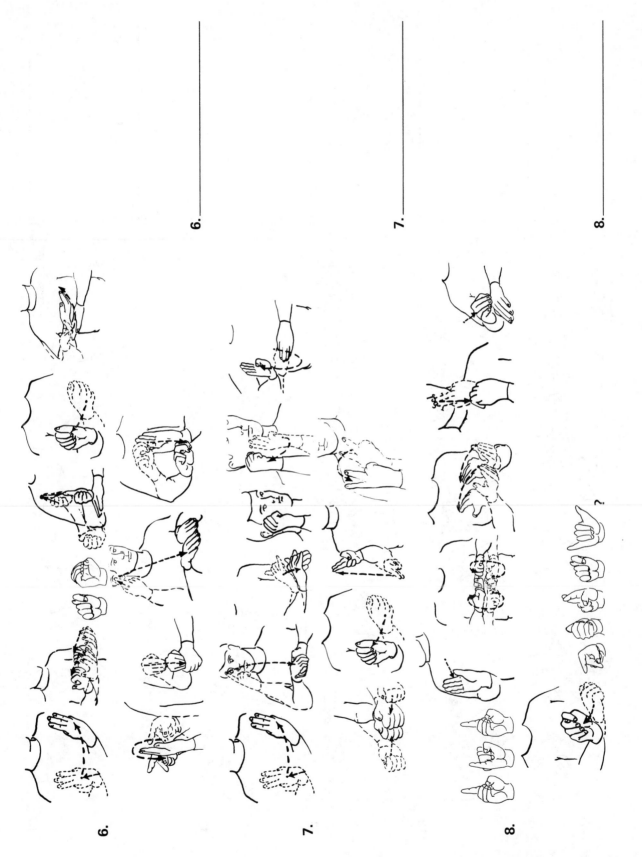

6.

7.

8.

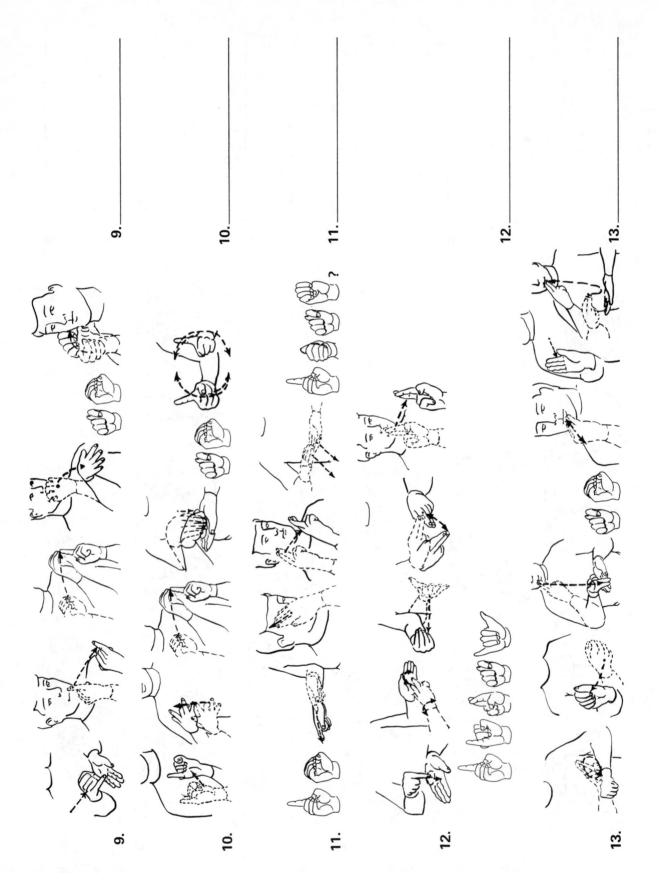

9.

10.

11.

12.

13.

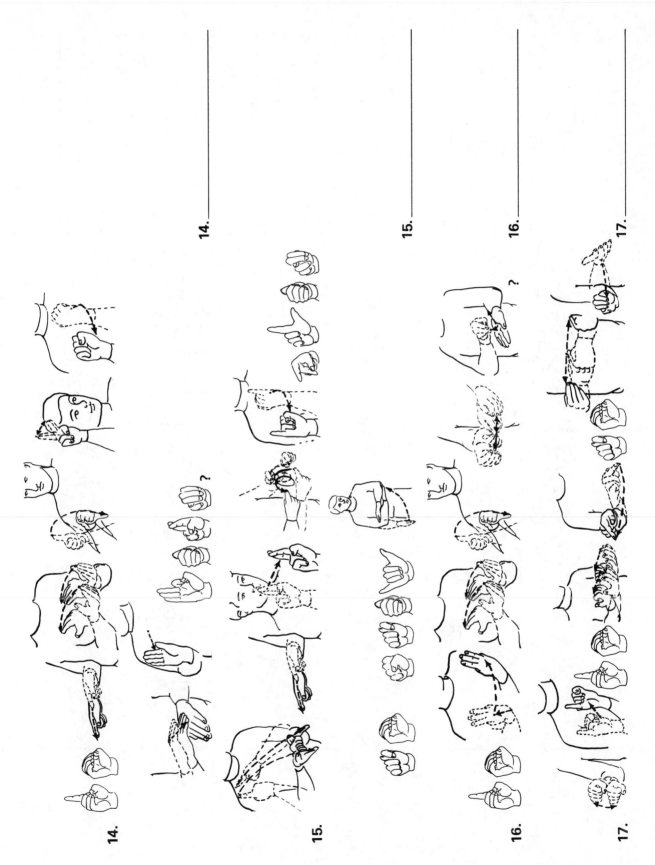

14.

15.

16.

17.

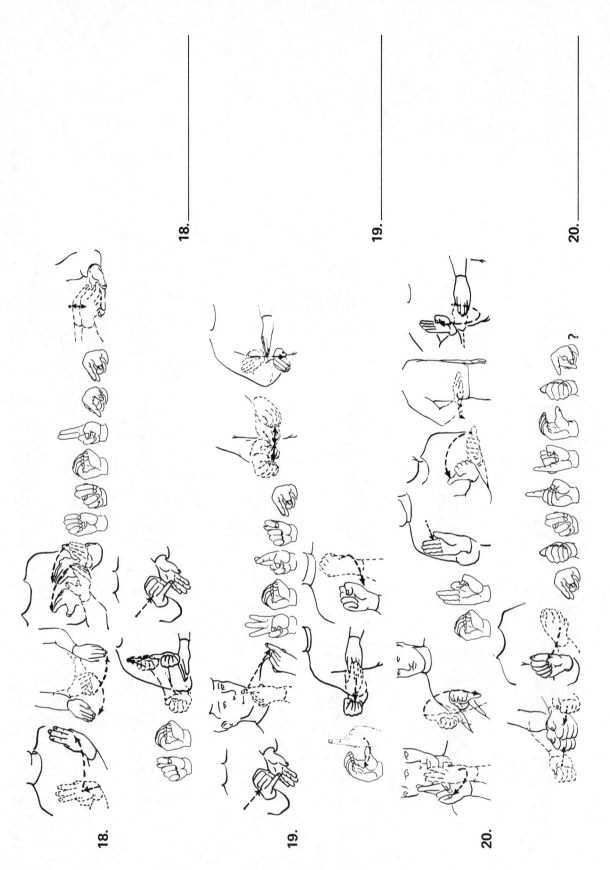

18.

19.

20.

18.

19.

20.

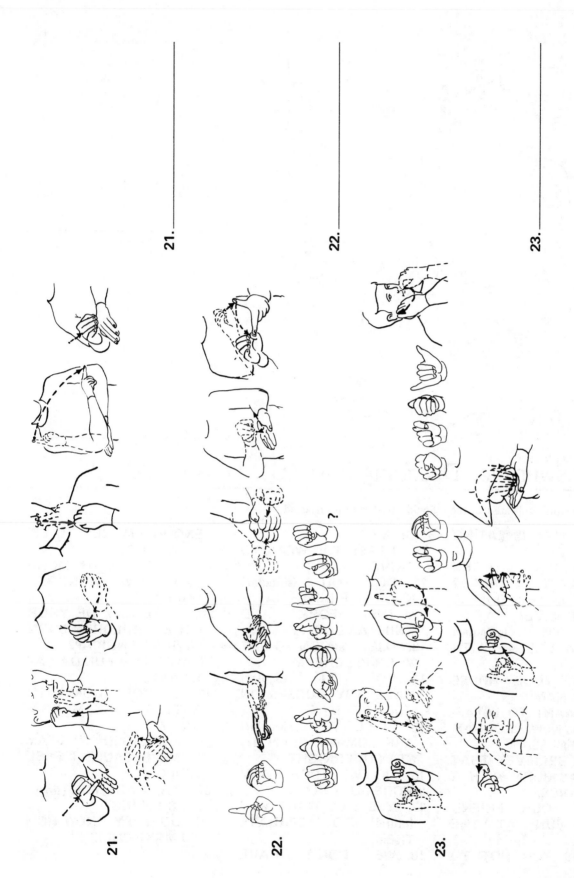

21.

22.

23.

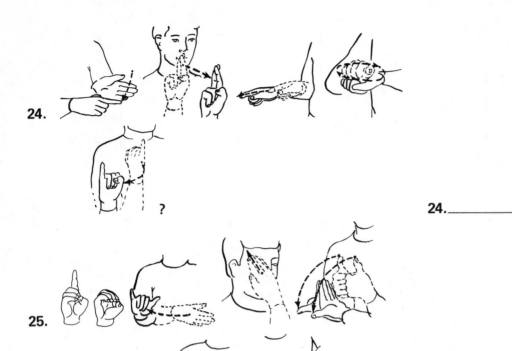

24. _____

25. _____

C) Answers for Decoding Part (B), Lesson 32

Underlined words indicate that they should have been fingerspelled.

1. THE GIRL IS EATING A COOKIE.
2. DO YOU (singular) LIKE CHOCOLATE ICE CREAM?
3. WHY IS THIS CHEESE SO EXPENSIVE?
4. DO YOU (singular) HAVE A DOLLAR WITH YOU?
5. DOES YOUR HORSE HAVE A NAME?
6. WE WANT TO ESTABLISH A NEW PROGRAM IN DEAFNESS.
7. WE BELIEVE THAT SHE WAS BORN WITH A HIGH VOICE.
8. DID YOUR FRIEND HAVE FUN AT THE PARTY?
9. IT IS TOO HOT TO DRINK.
10. I FEEL TOO WEAK TO DRIVE.
11. DO YOU (singular) KNOW HER BIRTH DATE?
12. THIS FORK AND KNIFE ARE DIRTY.
13. USE A SPOON TO EAT YOUR ICE CREAM.
14. DO YOU (singular) HAVE ANY HORSES ON YOUR FARM?
15. SINCE YOU (singular) ARE COMING, PLAN TO STAY OVERNIGHT.
16. DO WE HAVE ANY MORE BUTTER?
17. YES, I DO WANT YOU (plural) TO SEPARATE THEM.
18. WE DON'T HAVE ENOUGH MONEY TO ESTABLISH IT.
19. IT IS WORTH MORE THAN ONE HUNDRED DOLLARS.
20. WERE ANY OF YOUR OTHER CHILDREN BORN WITH A HANDICAP?
21. IT WAS A FUN DAY AT SCHOOL.
22. DO YOU COOK WITH BUTTER OR MARGARINE?
23. I DECIDED TO STAY HOME BECAUSE I FEEL WEAK.
24. WHAT ARE YOU (singular) CHEWING?
25. DO THEY KNOW HOW TO MAKE CHEESE?

lesson thirty-three

Signs presented in this lesson are:

VOTE*	CHECK (√)	EXAGGERATE	ROOM
BEHAVE*	NERVOUS	CLIMB	NOISE
ENTHUSIASM*	APPLE*	SUPPORT	STEAL
FALL (verb)	CHOCOLATE*	BEAT, DEFEAT	SWALLOW
AUTUMN*	WORTH	BOX	WATCH (verb)

VOTE*

The left hand, in the configuration of the letter O, is held in front of the body with the wrist facing to the right. The right hand, with only the thumb and index finger curved and touching (remaining fingers are extended and apart), first is held above the left O hand so that the joined thumb and index finger of the right hand are pointing downward. Next, the right hand is moved downward and places the thumb and index finger inside the left O hand, and then is returned to the original position. This motion is repeated several times. The sign intends to suggest, perhaps, putting ballots in ballot box.

ENTHUSIASM*

Both hands, each with the thumb and fingers extended and joined, are held in front of the body so that their palms are touching, fingertips pointing to the viewer and with their backs facing to the right and left, respectively. Next, both hands rub their palmar surfaces together as they alternately are moved back and forth. This motion is repeated several times.

NOTE: The speed with which this sign is executed may indicate the degree of enthusiasm.

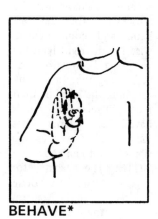

BEHAVE*

The right hand, in the configuration of the letter B, is placed on the breastbone so that the B fingers are pointing upward, and with the back side of the B hand facing to the right. Next, the B hand brushes slightly upward before moving forward to execute a small circular motion which is completed when the B hand is returned to its original position. This motion is repeated several times.

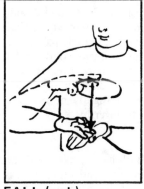

FALL (verb)

The left hand, with the thumb and fingers extended and joined, is held in front of the body with the palm facing up and the fingers pointing to the viewer. The right hand, in the configuration of the letter V, first is held over the left palm so that the V fingers are pointing to the left side and with the palmar sides of the fingers facing down. Next, the V hand is moved to complete a circle in a clockwise direction before descending and turning over so that the back sides of the V fingers make contact with the palmar side of the left hand.

365

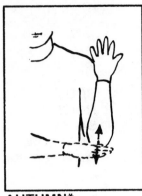

AUTUMN*

The left forearm is held vertically in front and to the left side of the body with the thumb and fingers extended, apart and the back side of the hand facing the viewer. The right hand, with the fingers and thumb extended and joined, is held near the elbow with the fingers pointing to the left and the palm of the hand facing down. Next, the side of the index finger of the right hand brushes the elbow several times as the hand is moved up and down (past the elbow).

NOTE: This sign may be suggestive, perhaps, of falling leaves.

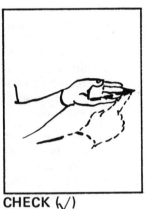

CHECK (√)

The left hand, with the thumb and fingers extended and joined, is held in front and slightly to the left side of the body with the palm facing to the right and the fingers pointing to the viewer. The right index fingertip (remaining fingers and thumb are contracted) first touches the left palm, and then traces the outline of a check mark over it. The sign ends with the index finger slightly beyond the left fingertips.

NERVOUS

Both hands, each with the thumb and fingers extended and apart, are held side-by-side in front of the body with their palmar sides facing down and their fingers pointing to the viewer. Next, both hands execute a trembling motion.

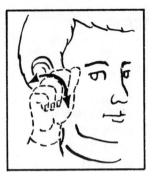

APPLE*

The right hand, in the configuration of the letter *A*, is held on the right cheek so that the tip of the thumb touches it. The back side of the hand is facing to the right. Next, the *A* hand is rocked back and forth several times at the wrist.

CHOCOLATE*

The left hand, in the configuration of the letter *S*, is held in front of the body with the wrist facing down. The right hand forms the letter *C*, which is placed on the back side of the left *S* hand so that only the back side of the thumb of the *C* hand is touching the left hand. (The back side of the *C* hand is facing up.) Next, the *C* hand is moved to complete several circles in a clockwise direction.

WORTH

Both hands, each in the configuration of the letter *W*, are held in front of the body so that the sides of their index fingers are touching (the palmar sides of *W* hands are facing the viewer). Next, the *W* hands separate, make semi-circles (clockwise for the left hand and counter-clockwise for the right hand) in an upward direction and come together again by touching the sides of their index fingers. Both hands have their palmar sides facing the viewer as the sign comes to an end.

NOTE: The sign for "value" is done similarly, except the hands assume the configuration of the letter *V*.

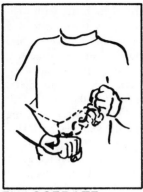

EXAGGERATE

The left hand, in the configuration of the letter *S*, is placed in front and slightly to the left side of the body with the back side facing left. The right hand, also in an *S* configuration, first touches the edge of the left hand, and then the right hand is moved away from the left hand. As the right hand is moved forward and downward at an oblique angle, it bends repeatedly at the wrist.

NOTE: The sign for "advertise*" is made similarly to "exaggerate," except that the right hand is moved away in a *straight line,* instead of performing a waving motion. Then, the hand is returned to the original position and repeats the motion.

CLIMB

Both hands, in the configuration of the letter *C*, are placed side-by-side in front of the body so that their palmar sides are facing the viewer. Next, both hands clench into fists as they perform alternate movements in an upward direction, imitative of the way one would grasp the rungs of an imaginary ladder.

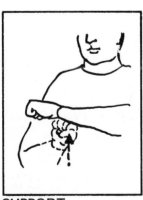

SUPPORT

The left forearm is placed in front of and across the body with the hand in a fist position and facing down. The right hand, in the configuration of the letter *S*, first is held below the left forearm near the wrist. Next, the right *S* hand is moved up so that contact is made between the right knuckles and the left wrist.

BEAT, DEFEAT

The left forearm is placed in front of, and across the body, with the hand in a fist position and facing down. The right hand, in the configuration of the letter *S*, is held above the back side of the left wrist so that the back side of the *S* hand is facing the signer. Next, the right forearm moves slightly forward as the hand is flipped downward so that the wrist touches the back side of the left wrist.

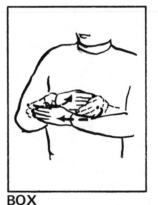

BOX

In this sign, the hands attempt to illustrate the four sides of a square box. First, both hands, in the configuration of the letter *B*, are positioned in a parallel manner in front of the body so that the hands are within six to eight inches of each other, with the fingers pointing to the viewer and their palmar surfaces facing each other. Next, the *B* hands (with their parallel structure maintained) are moved so as to complete the other two sides of the square. The hands are now one in front of the other with their fingers pointing to the right and left, respectively, and with their back sides facing the viewer.

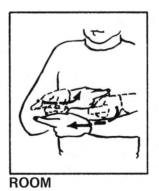

ROOM

In this sign, as with the previous one, the hands attempt to illustrate the four sides or walls of a room. The sign is done similarly to the previous one "box," except that both hands assume the configuration of the letter *R*.

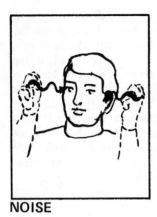

NOISE

Both hands, each in the configuration of the letter *N*, are held approximately six inches opposite the right and left ears so that the wrists of the *N* hands are facing to the left and right, respectively. Next, the *N* hands simultaneously are moved toward the ears. As the hands are moved toward the ears, they bend repeatedly at the wrist to produce waving (up and down) motions.

NOTE: An accompanying facial expression further may indicate the degree of discomfort associated with the source of noise.

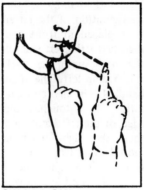

SWALLOW

The right hand, with only the index finger extended (remaining fingers and thumb are contracted), first is positioned approximately six to eight inches in front of the mouth with the index finger pointing upward and the back side facing to the right. Next, with the configuration maintained, the hand is brought toward the mouth so that the index finger first touches the lips, and then grazes the chin and the area under the chin as the index finger moves downward before coming to stop on the throat.

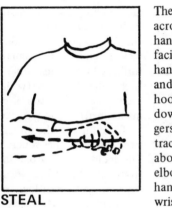

STEAL

The left forearm is bent across the body with the hand in a fist position and facing down. The right hand, with only the index and second fingers apart, hooked and pointing downward (remaining fingers and thumb are contracted), first is placed above and near the left elbow. Then, the right hand is moved toward the wrist as it grazes the left forearm.

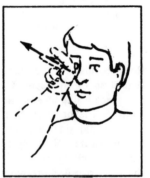

WATCH (verb)

The right hand, in the configuration of the letter *V*, is held near the right cheek bone and under the area of the eye. The *V* fingertips of the flexed hand are pointing to the viewer with the palmar side of the fingers facing down. Next, the *V* hand is moved straight forward.

NOTE: This sign may be suggestive, perhaps, of vision being directed to something or someone.

A) Exercises in Encoding

Encode the following material using signs and fingerspelling. Use fingerspelling for all underlined words.

1. HOW MANY APPLES <u>DID</u> HE EAT YESTERDAY?
2. WE LOVE CHOCOLATE ICE CREAM.
3. THEY FEEL THAT THEY CAN BEAT US.
4. I THINK SHE IS EXAGGERATING AGAIN.
5. WE DON'T WANT YOU <u>TO</u> ADVERTISE IT. ("Advertise"* is signed similarly to "exaggerate," but without the waving motion. Also, the movement is repeated several times.)
6. <u>DID</u> YOU VOTE FOR OUR CANDI-DATE?
7. PLEASE TRY <u>TO</u> BEHAVE YOURSELF.
8. I DON'T THINK IT IS WORTH DISCUSS-ING AGAIN.
9. IT IS A THING <u>OF</u> MUCH VALUE. ("Value" is signed similarly to "worth," but with V hands.)
10. I WANT <u>TO</u> CLIMB IT WITHOUT YOUR HELP.
11. PLEASE BE CAREFUL NOT <u>TO</u> FALL.
12. SHE WILL START SCHOOL NEXT AUTUMN.
13. WHY <u>DID</u> YOU PUT A CHECK ON MY PAPER?
14. THIS INTERVIEW IS BEGINNING <u>TO</u> MAKE ME NERVOUS.
15. MY CAR IS MAKING A FUNNY NOISE. ("Funny," in this context, would be signed as "odd" or "strange.")
16. PUT THE <u>BALL</u> IN THE BOX.
17. <u>DID</u> YOU FIND SOMETHING IN YOUR <u>MAIL</u> BOX YESTERDAY?
18. THE DOCTOR IS IN THE NEXT ROOM.
19. I WANT YOU <u>TO</u> KNOW THAT YOUR ENTHUSIASM IS <u>CONTAGIOUS</u>!
20. WILL YOU SUPPORT OUR NEW IDEA?
21. PLEASE BE CAREFUL NOT <u>TO</u> SWAL-LOW IT.
22. WATCH HOW I MAKE IT.
23. <u>DID</u> HE STEAL THE APPLES?
24. I WANT YOU <u>TO</u> WATCH HOW I <u>DO</u> IT.

B) Exercises in Decoding

Decode the following illustrated exercises:

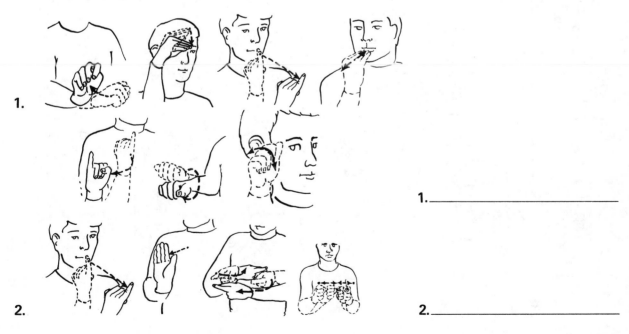

1.

1._____

2._____

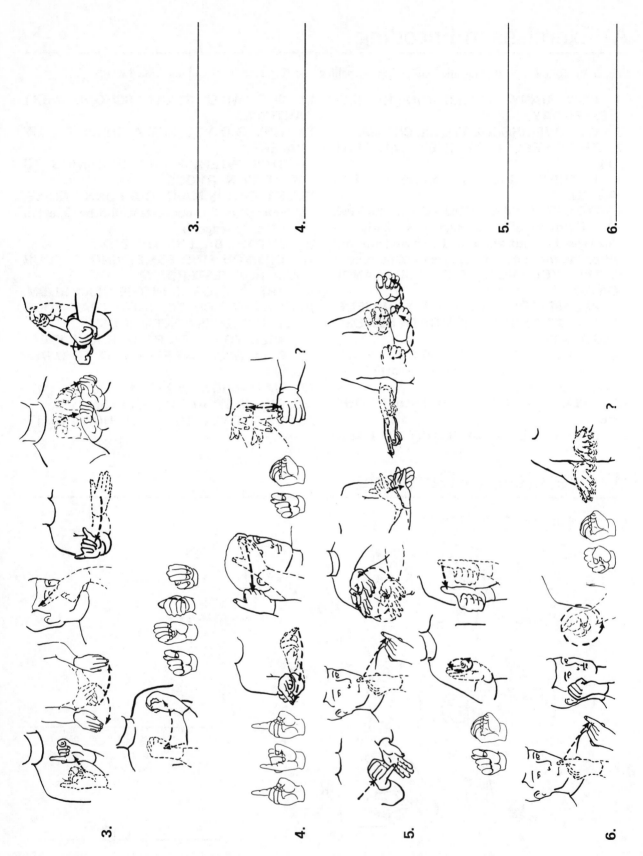

3.

4.

5.

6.

3.

4.

5.

6.

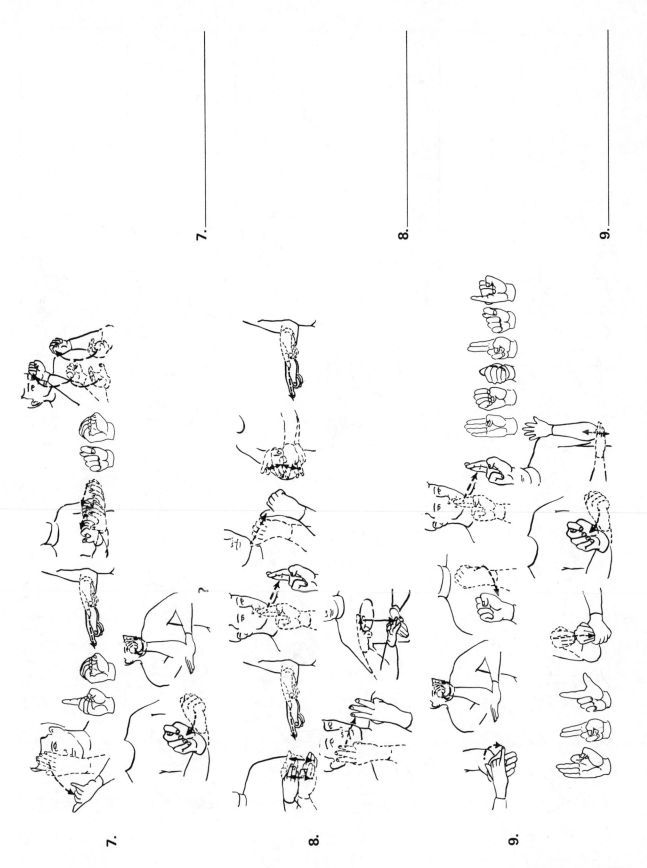

7.

8.

9.

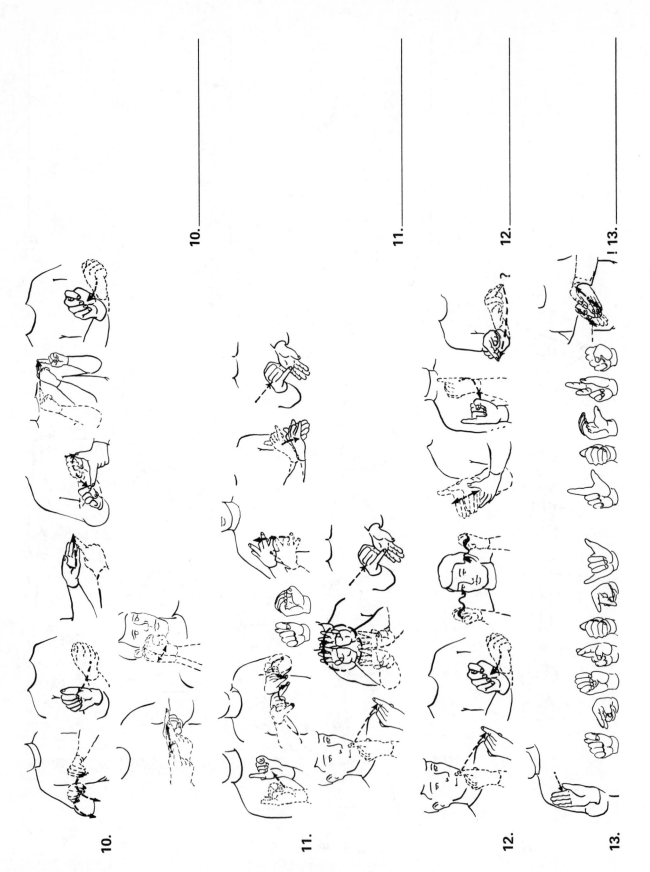

10.

11.

12.

13.

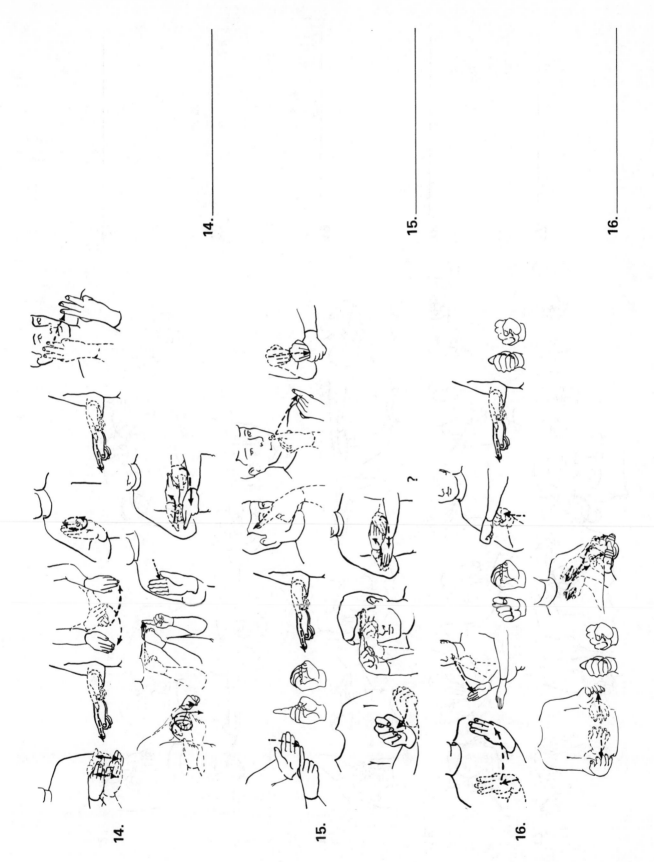

14.

15.

16.

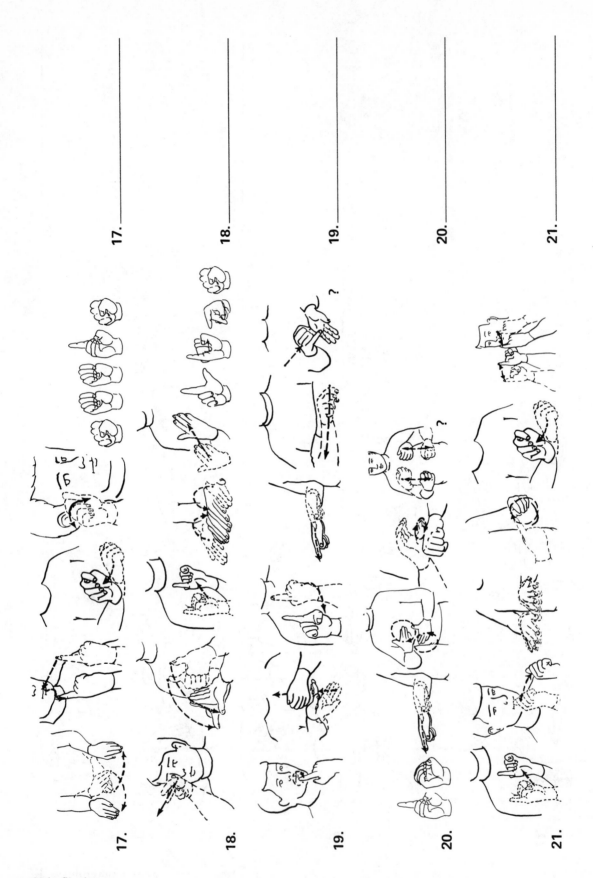

17.
18.
19.
20.
21.

17.
18.
19.
20.
21.

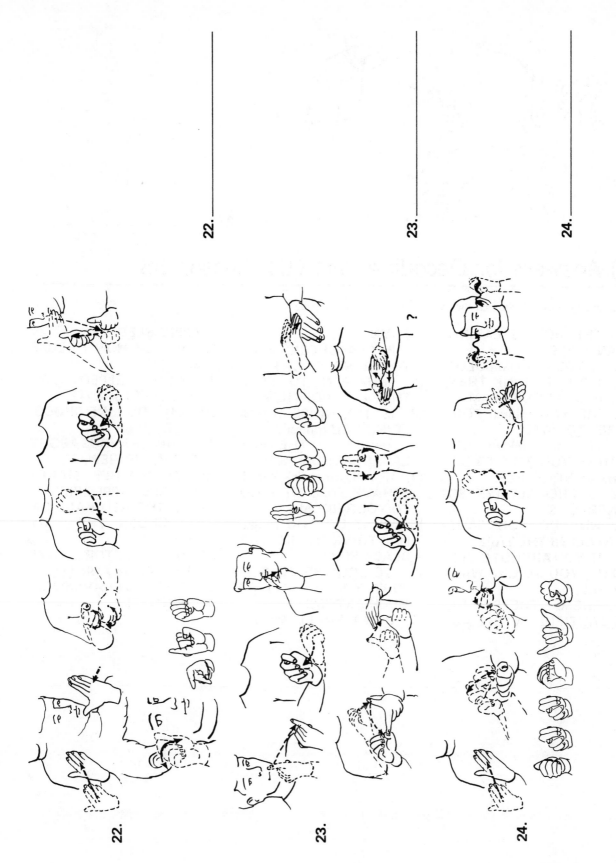

22.

23.

24.

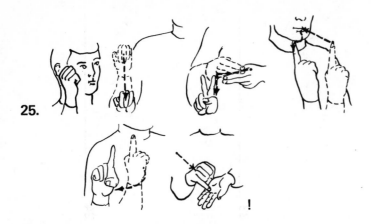

25. _____

C) Answers for Decoding Part (B), Lesson 33

Underlined words indicate that they should have been fingerspelled.

1. THE BOY IS EATING AN APPLE.
2. IS YOUR ROOM COLD?
3. I DON'T THINK THEY CAN BEAT OUR <u>TEAM</u>.
4. <u>DID</u> YOU (plural) FORGET <u>TO</u> VOTE?
5. IT IS IMPORTANT THAT YOU TRY TO BEHAVE YOURSELF.
6. IS SHE ALWAYS <u>SO</u> NERVOUS?
7. WHY <u>DO</u> YOU WANT <u>TO</u> CLIMB THE TREE?
8. IF YOU ARE NOT CAREFUL, YOU (singular) WILL FALL.
9. THESE TREES ARE <u>BEAUTIFUL</u> IN THE AU-
TUMN.
10. PUT A CHECK NEXT TO THE WORD "CAT."
11. I HAPPEN <u>TO</u> FEEL THAT IT IS WORTH IT.
12. IS THE NOISE BOTHERING YOU (plural)?
13. YOUR <u>THERAPY</u> <u>LACKS</u> ENTHUSIASM!
14. IF YOU (singular) DON'T BEHAVE, YOU WILL GO TO YOUR ROOM.
15. WHAT <u>DO</u> YOU (singular) THINK IS IN THE BLACK BOX?
16. WE PROMISE TO SUPPORT YOU (singular) <u>AS</u> MUCH <u>AS</u> POSSIBLE.
17. DON'T SWALLOW THE
APPLE <u>SEEDS</u>.
18. WATCH HOW I CLOSE MY <u>LIPS</u>.
19. WHO HELPED YOU (singular) STEAL IT?
20. <u>DO</u> YOU LIKE CHOCOLATE MILK?
21. I AM NERVOUS ABOUT THE INTERVIEW.
22. MY MOTHER MAKES THE BEST APPLE <u>PIE</u>.
23. IS THE RED <u>BALL</u> ON OR UNDER THE BLUE BOX?
24. MY DOCTOR SAYS THAT NOISE <u>ANNOYS</u>.
25. SHE MUST HAVE SWALLOWED IT!

lesson thirty-four

Signs presented in this lesson are:

SCIENCE	PUNISH, PENALIZE	POLICE	WORLD
CARELESS*	FAMOUS	DARK	DUMB
FARM (noun)	HEART	BALL*	THROAT
COUNTRY	BOAT	SELFISH	COAT (noun)
MONKEY*	TOOTHBRUSH*	AMERICA	HABIT

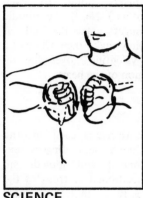

SCIENCE

Both hands, each with the thumb fully extended and apart (remaining fingers are contracted and clasped to the palm), are positioned about three to four inches apart in front of the body, and with their thumbs pointing downward. Then, the hands alternately are moved to complete clockwise and counter-clockwise circles along a vertical plane. That is, the left hand is moved in a clockwise direction, while the right hand is moved to complete a circle in a counter-clockwise direction.

NOTE: This sign may intend to suggest, perhaps, the way chemicals would be poured into a beaker.

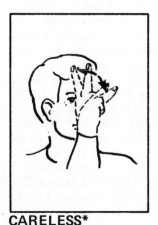

CARELESS*

The right hand, in the configuration of the letter *V*, is placed on the forehead so that the side of the index finger of the *V* hand is touching the forehead. The *V* fingers are pointing vertically and with the palmar sides facing to the left. Then, the wrist tilts the *V* hand in an arc to the left, across the forehead. This motion is repeated several times.

FARM (noun)

The right hand, with the thumb and fingers fully extended and apart, is held in front and slightly to the left side of the face with the thumb placed under the chin (the fingers are pointing upward at an angle and the back side of the hand is facing to the right). Next, with the configuration preserved, the thumb scrapes the undersurface of the chin as the hand is moved from left to right.

COUNTRY

The left forearm is bent across the body with its hand in a fist configuration, touching the right side of the chest. The back side of the hand is facing the viewer. The right hand, in the configuration of the letter *Y*, first is placed near the left elbow so that the back side of the *Y* hand is facing the viewer. Then, the *Y* hand is moved to complete a circle in a clockwise direction over the left elbow.

NOTE: This sign refers to country in the sense of a "rural area" as well as to a "foreign land."

MONKEY*

Both hands, each with the thumb and fingers joined and cupped, are placed side-by-side on the body at the level of the abdomen so that only the fingertips are touching the body (both hands have the back sides of their fingers facing downward). Next, the hands simultaneously perform a quick scratching type of motion as both brush upward and then return to repeat the motion.

NOTE: This sign is imitative of one characteristic behavior associated with this animal.

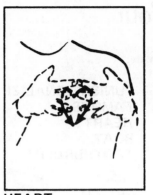

HEART

Both hands have their middle fingers flexed to a 45-degree angle (remaining fingers and thumbs are extended). The hands are placed side-by-side over the region of the heart so that the palmar sides of their middle fingers touch the body. (The back sides of the hands are facing the viewer, and the remaining fingers point to each other.) Next, the middle fingers graze the body as they make the outline of a "valentine" over the region of the heart.

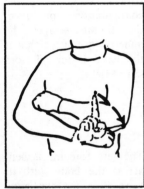

PUNISH, PENALIZE

The left forearm is bent across the body with the hand in a fist configuration and facing down. The right hand, with only the index finger extended (remaining fingers and thumb are contracted), first is held near the left elbow with the index finger pointing upward and the back side of the hand facing to the right. Then, the right index finger strikes the left elbow as the right hand is tilted to the left side.

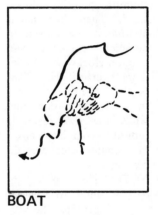

BOAT

Both hands, each with the thumb and fingers extended and joined, are positioned in front of the body so that their lower edges are touching. Both hands have their fingers pointing to the viewer and are tilted sideways to about a 45-degree angle. Then, the joined hands make a wavy motion as they are moved forward while holding the initial contact position.

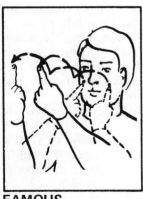

FAMOUS

With both index fingers extended (remaining fingers and thumbs are contracted), touch both cheeks simultaneously. (The back sides of the hands are facing the viewer.) Next, with the hand configuration preserved, make two continuous forward arcs in an upward direction, toward the viewer.

TOOTHBRUSH*

The index finger of the right hand is extended (remaining fingers and thumb are contracted) and is placed at the right corner of the mouth so that the index finger is pointing to the left (the back of the hand is facing up). Next, with the teeth visible, the hand is moved back and forth in front of the teeth, imitative of how a toothbrush is used. This motion is repeated several times.

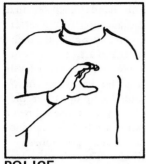

POLICE

The right hand makes the letter *C* and then places the *C* hand on the left side of the chest so that the back side of the *C* hand is facing to the right.

NOTE: This sign is suggestive of the location where a policeman's badge would be worn.

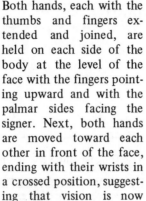

DARK

Both hands, each with the thumbs and fingers extended and joined, are held on each side of the body at the level of the face with the fingers pointing upward and with the palmar sides facing the signer. Next, both hands are moved toward each other in front of the face, ending with their wrists in a crossed position, suggesting that vision is now blocked.

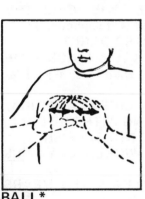

BALL*

Both hands, each in the configuration of the letter *C*, are placed side-by-side about an inch apart in front of the body with the back sides of the *C* hands facing sideways. Next, the *C* hands are moved toward each other so that their thumbs and fingertips are touching. This motion is repeated several times.

SELFISH

Both hands assume the configuration of the letter *V* and are placed side-by-side in front of the body so that their *V* fingertips are pointing to the viewer and with their palmar sides facing down. Next, the *V* hands simultaneously are pulled toward the body as their extended *V* fingers bend in a claw-like formation.

AMERICA

Both hands, with their thumbs separately extended and their remaining fingers locked together, are moved to form a horizontal circle in a clockwise direction in front of the body, while maintaining their locked position.

NOTE: This sign may be suggestive, perhaps, of a fence associated with rural America.

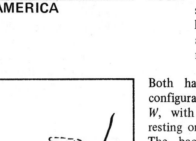

WORLD

Both hands assume the configuration of the letter *W*, with the right hand resting on top of the left. The back sides of the hands are facing sideways while their fingers point to the viewer at a slight angle. Next, the right *W* hand is moved forward and completes a circle around the left hand, and then is returned to the original position.

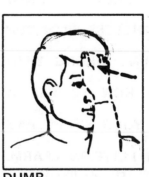

DUMB

The right hand, in the configuration of the letter *A*, is held in front of the body at forehead level with the back of the *A* hand toward the viewer. Then, the *A* hand is moved toward the middle of the forehead so that contact is made at the second joints of the fingers.

THROAT

The right hand first makes the letter *G* and then with the thumb and index finger lightly pinches both sides of the throat.

Both hands, each in the configuration of the letter *C*, are placed on each shoulder so that their back sides are facing to the right and left. Next, the *C* hands simultaneously are moved to complete an arc motion in a forward and downward direction as both hands change to a letter *A* formation.

NOTE: The hands in this sign are pantomiming the way a coat is thrown over the shoulders.

COAT (noun)

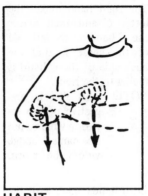

Both hands, each in the configuration of the letter *S*, are crossed at their wrists and are held in front of the body at chest level with the backs of the *S* hands facing up. Then, the *S* hands are moved downward, while maintaining their crossed position.

NOTE: The sign for "custom" is made similarly, except that the hands assume the configuration of the letter *C*.

HABIT

A) Exercises in Encoding

Encode the following material using signs and fingerspelling. Use fingerspelling for all underlined words.

1. <u>DO</u> YOU KNOW WHY I AM PUNISHING <u>YOU</u>?
2. OUR SCIENCE TEACHER IS ILL TODAY.
3. HE IS A VERY FAMOUS SCIENTIST. ("Scientist" is signed as "science" plus "-ist.")
4. SHE MAY BE DEAF, BUT SHE IS NOT DUMB.
5. DON'T BE <u>SO</u> CARELESS WITH OUR MONEY.
6. THERE IS NOTHING WRONG WITH YOUR THROAT.
7. <u>DO</u> YOU KNOW HOW <u>TO</u> USE A TOOTHBRUSH?
8. HOW MUCH <u>DID</u> YOUR SISTER PAY FOR HER NEW COAT?
9. MY BROTHER AND I LIVE ON A FARM.
10. WE LIVE ALONE IN THE COUNTRY.
11. WERE YOU AND YOUR BROTHER BORN IN ANOTHER COUNTRY?
12. THE SCIENTIST IS TEACHING THIS MONKEY HOW <u>TO</u> SIGN. (The word "sign" here refers to "sign language.")
13. MY DAUGHTER SUFFERED A HEART <u>ATTACK</u> YESTERDAY.
14. HOW BIG IS YOUR NEW BOAT?
15. IF YOU DON'T GO, I WILL CALL THE POLICE. ("Call" is signed as "telephone.")
16. WHY IS THIS ROOM <u>SO</u> DARK?
17. IT IS HARD FOR US <u>TO</u> CHANGE SOME OF OUR HABITS. ("Hard" is signed as "difficult.")
18. <u>DOES</u> HER FAMILY LIVE IN AMERICA?
19. THE CAT IS PLAYING WITH THE BALL.
20. SOME PEOPLE ARE NOT SELFISH.
21. I WATCHED THE WORLD <u>OLYMPICS</u> ON <u>TELEVISION</u>.
22. WE CAME TO AMERICA TEN YEARS AGO.
23. TRY <u>TO</u> UNDERSTAND OUR CUSTOMS. ("Custom" is signed similarly to "habit," but with *C* hands.)
24. IT WAS A DUMB MISTAKE AND YOU KNOW IT.

B) Exercises in Decoding

Decode the following illustrated exercises:

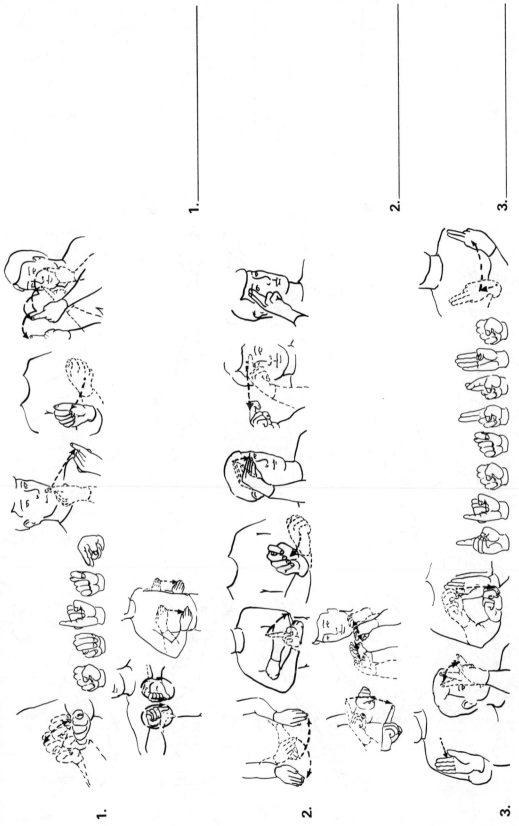

1. _____

2. _____

3. _____

1.

2.

3.

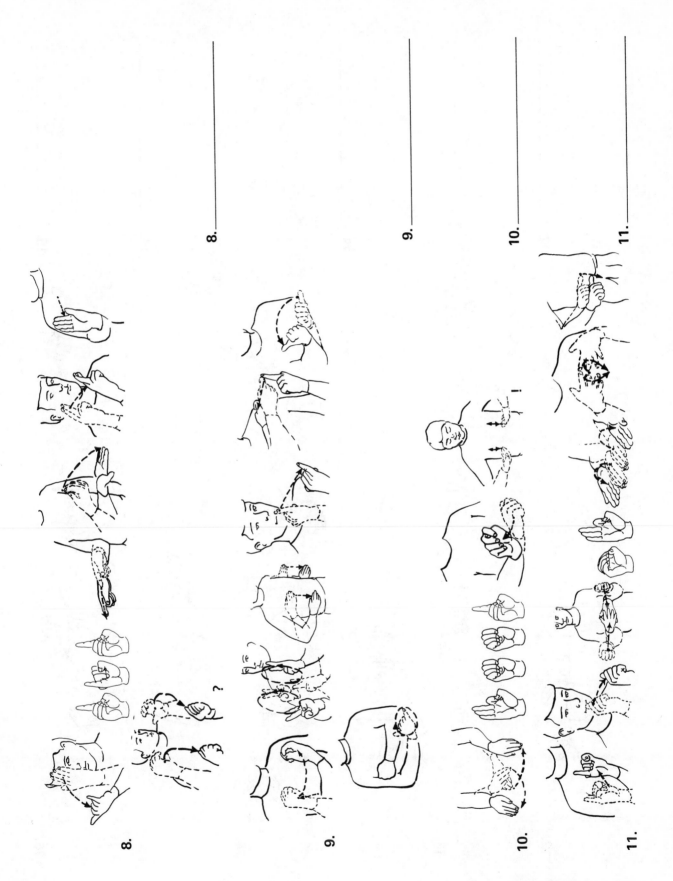

8.

9.

10.

11.

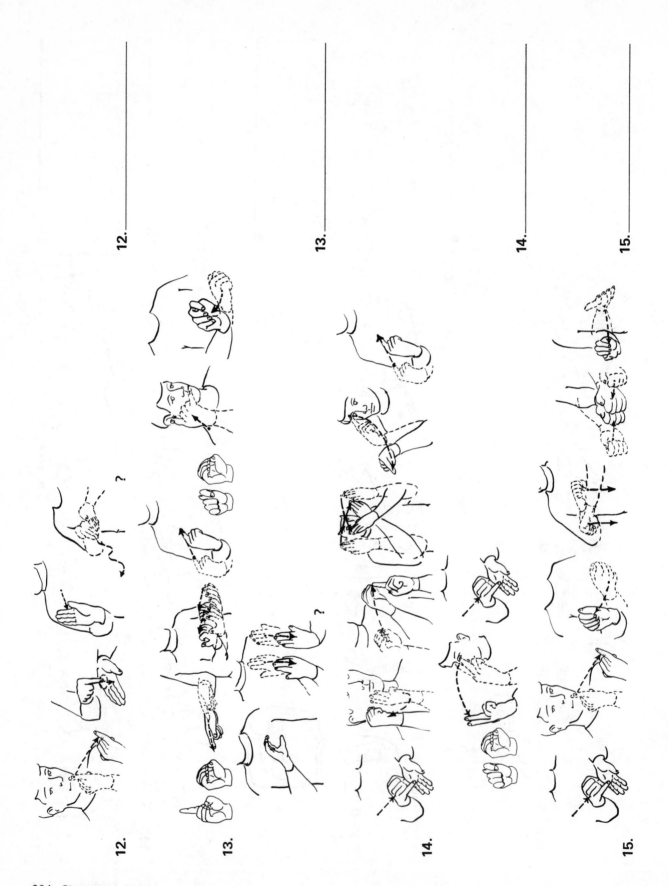

12.

13.

14.

15.

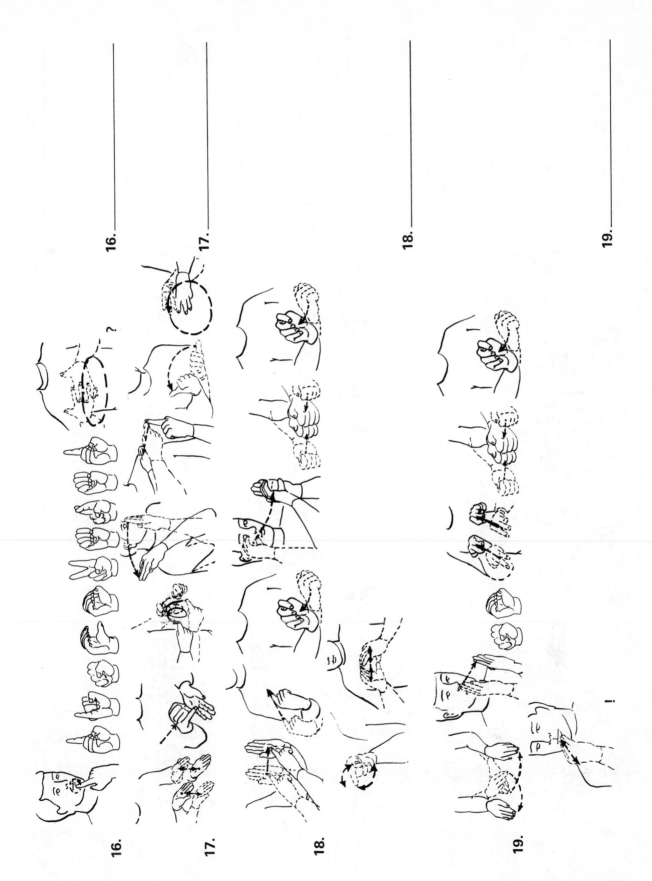

16.

17.

18.

19.

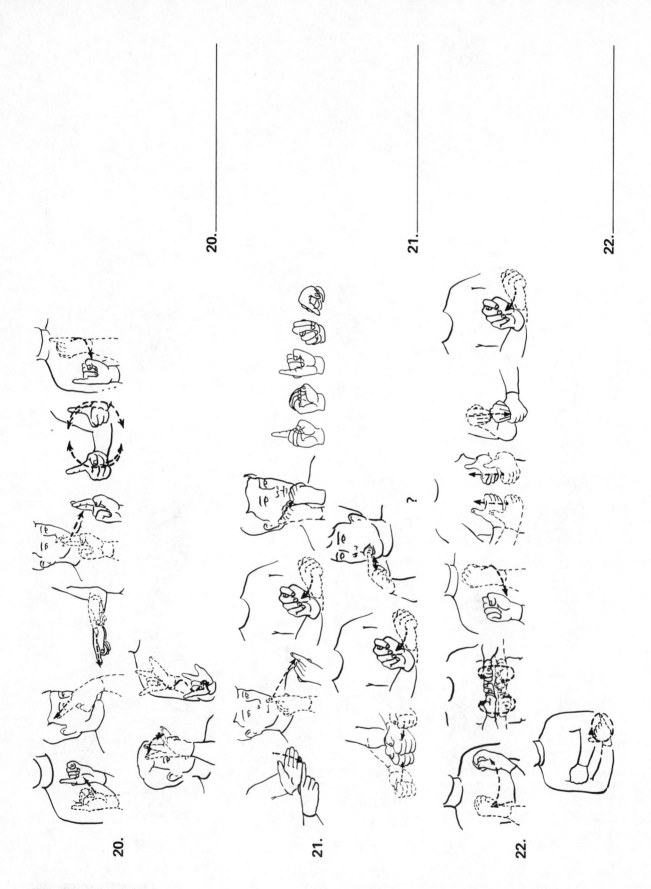

20.

21.

22.

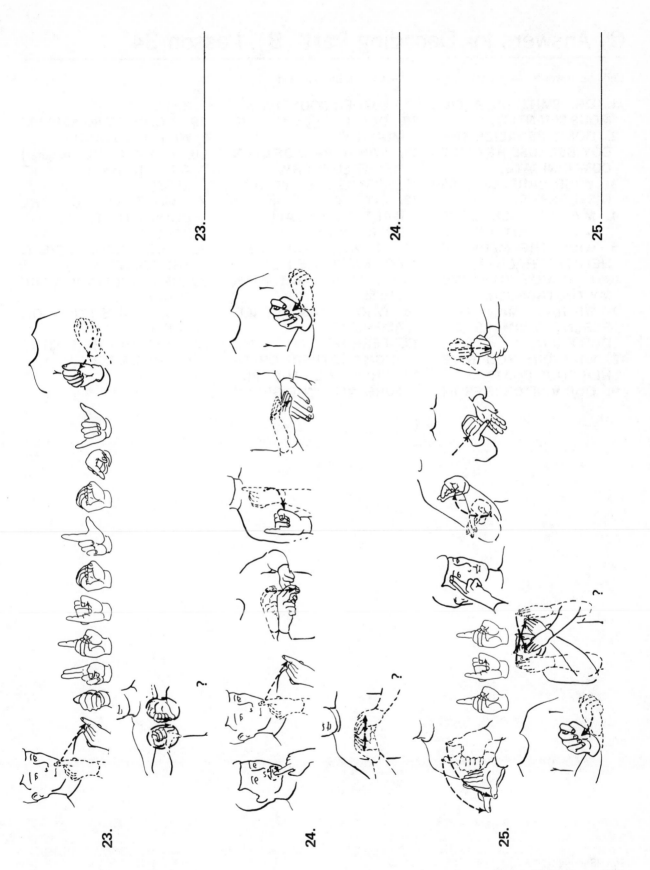

23.

24.

25.

C) Answers for Decoding Part (B), Lesson 34

Underlined words indicate that they should have been fingerspelled.

1. DR. <u>SMITH</u> IS A FAMOUS SCIENTIST.
2. DON'T PENALIZE THE BOY BECAUSE HE CAN'T COMMUNICATE.
3. YOUR CARELESSNESS <u>DISTURBS</u> US.
4. MY TEACHER SAYS THAT I AM NOT DUMB.
5. WILL THE MEDICINE HELP MY THROAT?
6. I FORGOT <u>TO</u> BRING MY TOOTHBRUSH.
7. WE HAVE MANY DIFFERENT ANIMALS ON OUR FARM.
8. WHY <u>DID</u> YOU GIVE HER YOUR COAT?
9. OUR VISITOR IS FROM ANOTHER COUNTRY.
10. DON'T <u>FEED</u> THE MONKEY!
11. I AM AFRAID <u>OF</u> OPEN HEART SURGERY.
12. IS THIS YOUR BOAT?
13. <u>DO</u> YOU (singular) WANT ME <u>TO</u> CALL THE POLICE NOW?
14. IT WAS TOO DARK FOR ME TO SEE IT.
15. IT IS A HABIT WITH THEM.
16. WHO <u>DISCOVERED</u> AMERICA?
17. PERHAPS IT CAME FROM ANOTHER WORLD.
18. SHOW ME THE PICTURE WITH THE GREEN BALL.
19. DON'T BE <u>SO</u> SELFISH WITH THE FOOD!
20. I THINK YOU (singular) ARE DRIVING CARELESSLY.
21. WHAT IS THE GIRL <u>DOING</u> WITH THE TOOTHBRUSH?
22. OUR FRIENDS LIVE IN THE COUNTRY.
23. IS <u>AUDIOLOGY</u> A SCIENCE?
24. WHO IS SITTING ON THE BALL?
25. HOW <u>DID</u> HE FIND IT IN THE DARK?

lesson thirty-five

Signs presented in this lesson are:

SUMMER	SO	AWAKE	YET
BORROW	LATE	SURPRISE	WORKSHOP
LOAN	FLOWER	AIRPLANE, FLY	SHAVE*
TRAIN* (noun), RAILROAD*	MEAN (verb)	STUCK	PAINT*
TALL	MAGAZINE, PAMPHLET	PITY*	DISAPPOINT

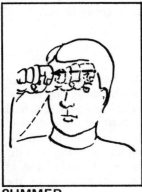

SUMMER

The right hand assumes the configuration of the letter *X*, which first touches the left side of the forehead and is held so that the tip of the flexed index finger is pointing downward. Next, the flexed index finger scrapes the forehead as the hand is moved from left to right. This sign may be imitative, perhaps, of wiping perspiration from the forehead.

NOTE: This sign often is confused with the signs for "because," lesson 6 and "black" (color), lesson 4. For "because," the index finger is flexed as the hand is drawn to the right; while in the sign for "black," the index finger does *not* flex as the hand is moved to the right.

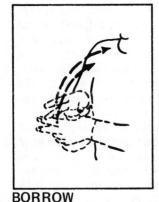

BORROW

Both hands, each in the configuration of the letter *V*, are positioned one on top of the other in front of the body with their back sides facing left and right, and the *V* fingertips pointing to the viewer at a slight angle. Next, both *V* hands are arched up and back in the direction of the body, while maintaining their original contact. The *V* fingertips are pointing upward as the sign comes to an end.

LOAN

This sign is made in reverse of the order used in the previous sign ("borrow"). Both hands, in the configuration of the letter *V*, are crossed near their wrists and are positioned in front of the body at chest level with the *V* fingertips pointing upward, and with the backs of the *V* fingers facing to the right and left, respectively. Next, with the contact maintained, the *V* hands are arched forward and down so that their *V* fingertips are now pointing to the viewer at an angle.

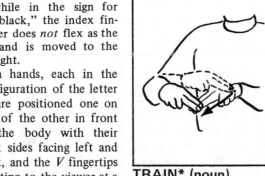

TRAIN* (noun), RAILROAD*

The left hand, in the configuration of the letter *H*, is held in front of the body with the wrist facing down and the *H* fingertips pointing to the viewer. The right hand, also in an *H* configuration, first touches the back sides of the left fingers. The right *H* hand is held with the wrist facing down and the fingertips pointing to the left. Then, without separating, the right *H* hand rubs the left fingers while moving front-to-back (toward the left fingertips and then in the direction of the knuckles). This motion is repeated several times.

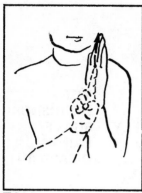

TALL

The left hand, with the thumb and fingers extended, joined, and pointing upward, is held in front of the body with the palm facing to the right. The right index finger (remaining fingers and thumb are contracted) first is placed parallel to the left palm so that it is pointing upward and with the back side of the right hand facing the signer. Then, the right hand slides up the left palm in the direction of the fingertips.

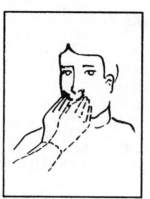

FLOWER

The right hand, with the thumb bending inward to touch the extended but joined fingertips (the back of the hand is toward the viewer), first touches the upper lip (under the left nostril) with its joined thumb and fingertips and then moves right and touches the upper lip under the right nostril. This sign is imitative of smelling an imaginary flower.

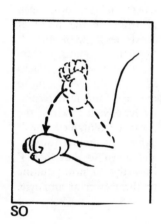

SO

The right hand, in the configuration of the letter *S*, is held in front and to the right side of the body at the level of the shoulder with the wrist of the *S* hand facing the viewer. Next, the right forearm moves slightly forward as the wrist tilts the *S* hand downward so that now the wrist of the *S* hand is facing down.

NOTE: This sign is not to be confused with the sign for "yes" (lesson 9) which is made with the *S* hand bending at the wrist *repeatedly*.

MEAN (verb)

The left hand, with the thumb and fingers extended and joined, is held in front of the body with the palm facing up and the fingers pointing to the viewer. The right hand, in the configuration of the letter *M*, first touches the left palm with the tips of its first three fingers. (The back sides of the *M* fingers are facing to the left.) Next, the wrist flexes the *M* hand to the right, with the fingertips grazing the left palm and fingers.

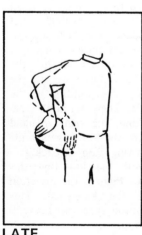

LATE

The right hand, with the thumb and fingers extended and joined, is placed in front and to the right side of the body at the level of the waistline with the fingertips pointing downward and the back side of the hand facing the viewer. Next, the hand sweeps past the hip (while moving toward the rear) as the wrist bends the hand in an upward direction.

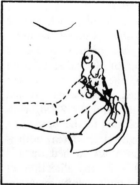

MAGAZINE, PAMPHLET

The left hand, with the thumb and fingers extended and joined, is held in front of the body with the palm facing to the right and the fingers pointing to the viewer. The thumb and remaining fingers of the right hand first encircle the palmar and back sides of the left hand respectively, then slide forward past and beyond the left fingertips as the right thumb bends inward to touch the palmar surfaces of the fingertips.

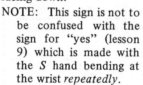

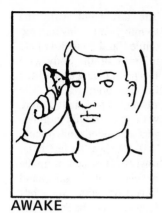

SURPRISE

AWAKE

The right hand, with only the thumb and index finger extended and touching (remaining fingers are contracted), is placed near the corner of the right eye (the back of the thumb touches the face) so that the joined thumb and index fingertip are pointing to it. Next, the right index finger is flicked upward, suggesting the opening of the eyes.

Both hands, each with the thumb touching the extended index finger (remaining fingers are contracted and clasped to the palm), are positioned near the corner of each eye with the back sides of the hands facing to the right and left, respectively. Next, both hands are moved in an upward direction, while changing their configuration to a letter *L* and with the back sides of the *L* hands facing right and left. The index fingers of the *L* hands are pointing upward at about a 45-degree angle as the sign comes to an end.

AIRPLANE, FLY

The right hand, with the thumb, index and little finger extended and apart (remaining fingers are contracted and clasped to the palm), is held in front and slightly to the right side of the body with the palm facing down and the fingers pointing to the viewer. Next, the hand is moved forward and curved slightly upward, while holding the original configuration.

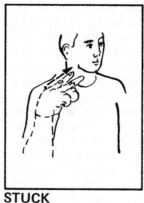

STUCK

The right hand, in the configuration of the letter *V*, is held approximately four to five inches in front and to the right side of the body with the *V* fingertips pointing to the side of the signer's neck and the palmar side facing down. Then, the *V* hand is moved toward the body and the fingertips touch the side of the neck.

NOTE: This sign intends to convey the idea that one is "stuck" in the sense of being "frustrated" or "helpless."

PITY*

The right hand, with the middle finger flexed to a 45-degree angle (the thumb and remaining fingers are extended and apart), touches the region of the signer's heart with the tip of its middle finger. Next, the hand is turned out as it is moved forward, while preserving the original configuration. (The hand now is positioned in front of the body, with the palm facing down and the fingers pointing to the viewer.) Then, the hand performs several stroking type motions by completing small circular movement.

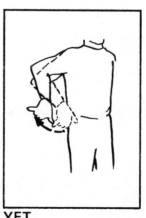

YET

This sign is made similarly to ("late") which appeared on the previous page, except that the right hand assumes the configuration of the letter *Y* and is held by the side of the body at waist level with its back side facing the viewer. Next, the *Y* hand sweeps past the hip while moving toward the rear as the wrist bends the hand in an upward direction.

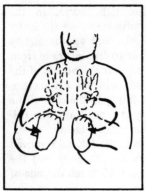

WORKSHOP

Both hands, each in the configuration of the letter *W*, are placed side-by-side in front of the body with the *W* fingertips pointing upward and their palmar sides facing the viewer. Next, the *W* hands simultaneously complete semicircles along a horizontal plane (in a clockwise direction for the right hand and counter-clockwise for the left one) as both hands are moved forward, while changing their configuration to a letter *S*. Both *S* hands are positioned side-by-side in front of the body and with their backs facing the viewer as the sign comes to an end.

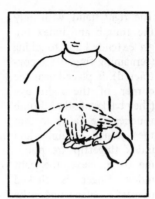

PAINT*

The left hand, with the thumb and fingers extended and joined, is held in front of the body with the palm facing up and the fingers pointing to the viewer. The right hand, with the thumb and fingers extended and joined, first touches the left hand fingers. (Contact is made between the right hand fingertips and the left fingers. The back of the right hand is toward the viewer.) Then, the right hand is moved in the direction of the left wrist with the fingers grazing the left palm and then flexing to a 45-degree angle. This motion is repeated several times.

SHAVE*

The right hand assumes the configuration of the letter *Y* and positions the thumb of the *Y* hand near the signer's right cheek bone. (The little finger is pointing upward at an angle and the wrist of the *Y* hand is facing left.) Next, the *Y* hand is moved in the direction of the chin with the thumb grazing the cheek. This motion is repeated several times.

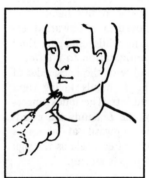

DISAPPOINT

The right hand, with only the index finger extended (remaining fingers and thumb are contracted), is held about three to four inches in front of the chin with the index finger pointing to the chin. Next, the hand is brought toward the signer as the index fingertip touches the chin *once*.

A) Exercises in Encoding

Encode the following material using signs and fingerspelling. Use fingerspelling for all underlined words.

1. MAY I BORROW YOUR PENCIL FOR A MINUTE?
2. <u>DID</u> YOU LOAN THEM ANY MONEY?
3. <u>DO</u> YOU WANT <u>TO</u> <u>RIDE</u> THE TRAIN WITH ME?
4. HOW TALL IS YOUR SISTER-IN-LAW?
5. SHE IS SO NERVOUS ABOUT HER INTERVIEW.
6. I THINK I CAN POSTPONE IT UNTIL SUMMER.
7. SHE IS ALWAYS LATE FOR <u>THERAPY</u>.
8. WHO IS NOT HERE YET?
9. TRY NOT <u>TO</u> DISAPPOINT YOUR FRIEND AGAIN.
10. THE FLOWERS ARE FOR YOUR <u>GRANDMOTHER</u>.
11. WHAT <u>DOES</u> THIS WORD MEAN?
12. I PUT THE MAGAZINE ON YOUR DESK.
13. I AM NOT AWAKE YET.
14. WE HAVE A SURPRISE FOR YOU TODAY.
15. HAVE YOU EVER BEEN IN AN AIRPLANE?
16. ARE YOU FLYING OR DRIVING?
17. DON'T PITY US BECAUSE WE ARE BLIND.
18. I GOT STUCK WHEN I COULD NOT ANSWER HIM. ("Stuck" is used here in the sense of being "frustrated.")
19. THE WORKSHOP WAS <u>HELD</u> AT <u>OHIO</u> UNIVERSITY.
20. WHAT COLOR WILL YOU PAINT IT?
21. MAY I WATCH YOU SHAVE?
22. WE WERE DISAPPOINTED WITH YOUR WORKSHOP.
23. IS THE RAILROAD <u>STATION</u> OPEN?
24. HER ANSWER <u>DID</u> NOT SURPRISE ME.

B) Exercises in Decoding

Decode the following illustrated exercises:

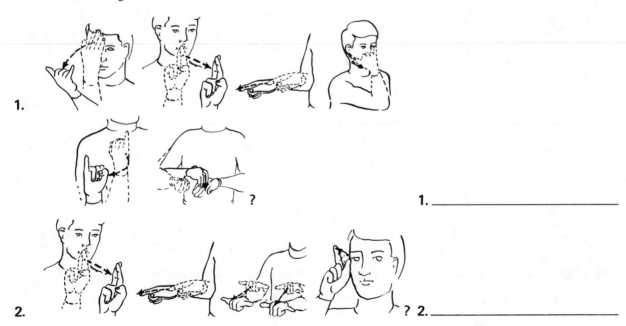

1. _____

2. _____

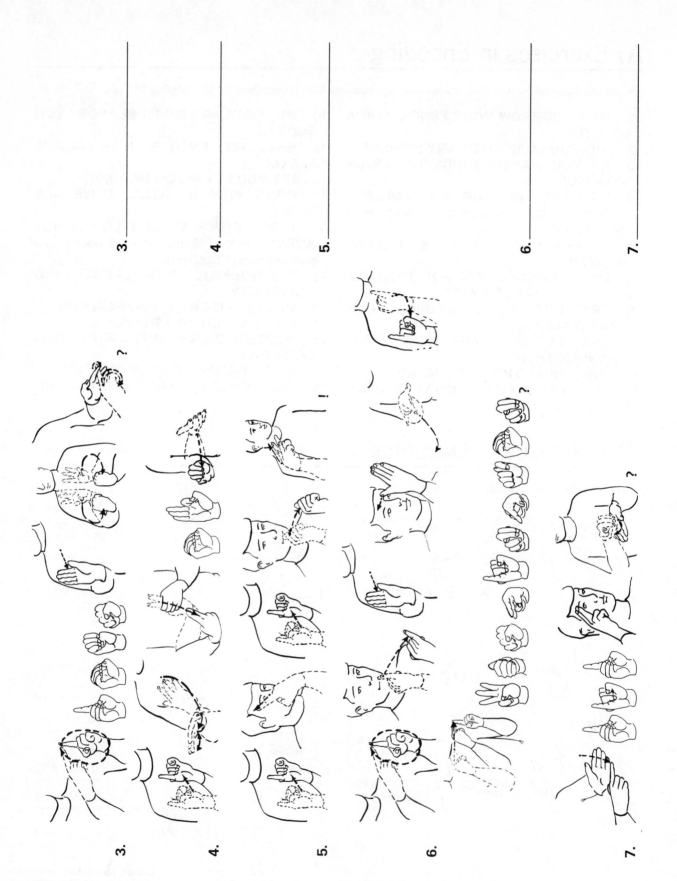

3.

4.

5.

6.

7.

8.

9.

10.

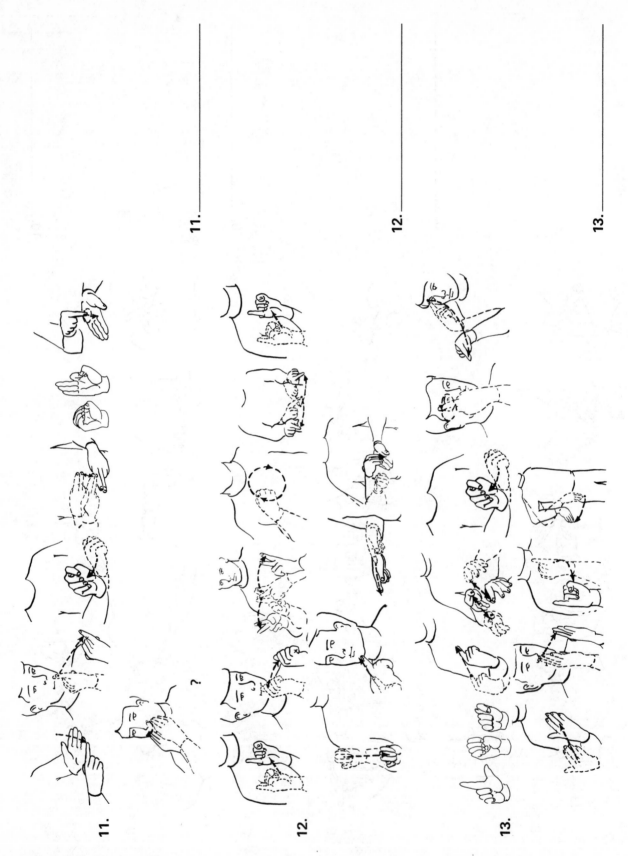

11.

12.

13.

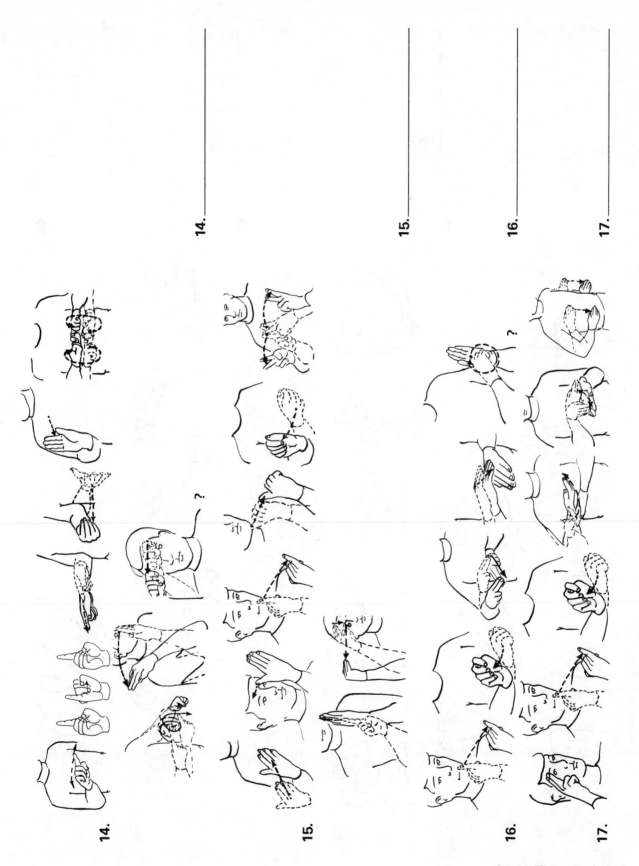

14.

15.

16.

17.

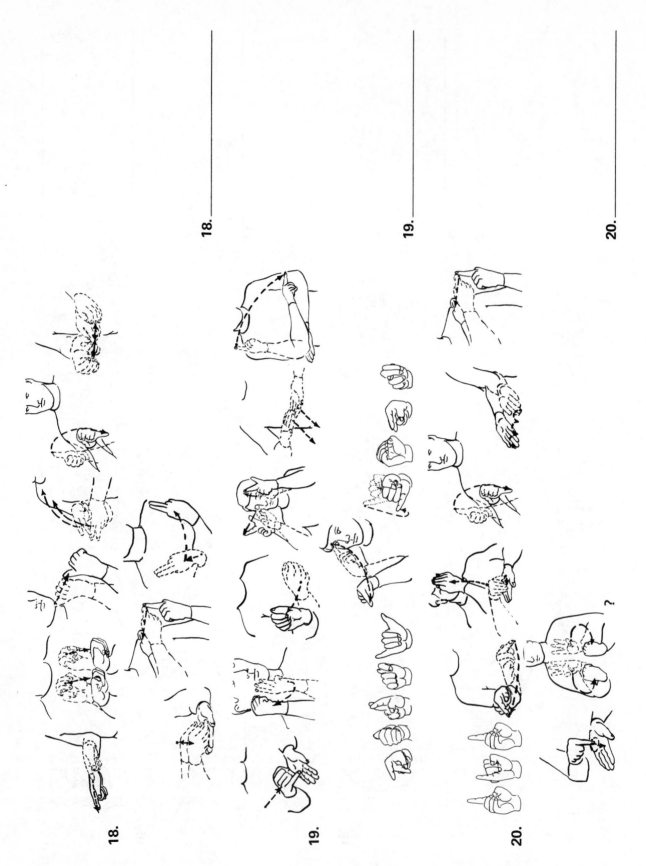

18.

19.

20.

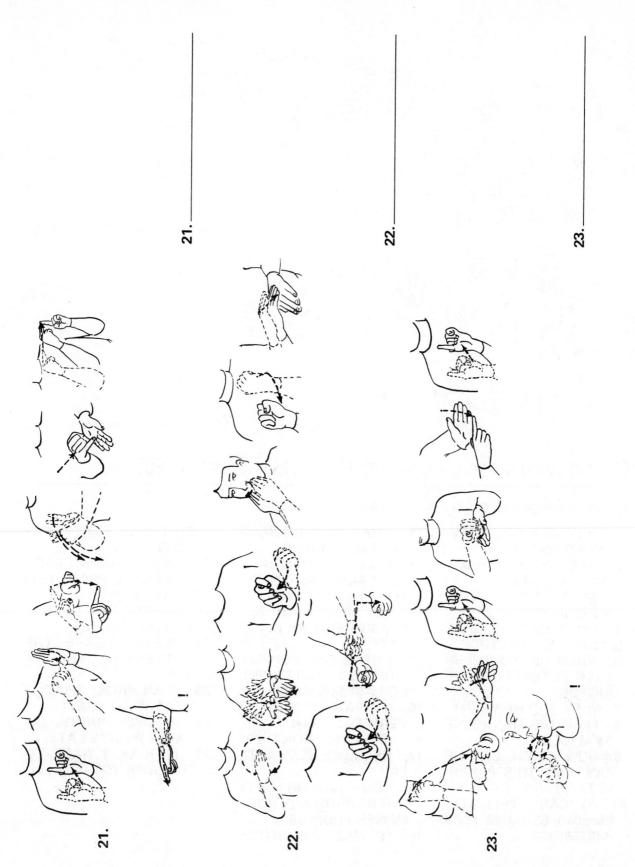

21.

22.

23.

21.

22.

23.

24. _____

25. _____

C) Answers for Decoding Part (B), Lesson 35

Underlined words indicate that they should have been fingerspelled.

1. WHY ARE YOU SHAV-ING AGAIN?
2. ARE YOU (singular) STILL AWAKE?
3. WHEN <u>DOES</u> YOUR WORKSHOP START?
4. I PITY BOTH <u>OF</u> <u>THEM</u>.
5. I THINK I AM STUCK!
6. WHEN IS YOUR FA-THER FLYING TO <u>WASH-INGTON</u>?
7. WHAT <u>DID</u> HE MEAN?
8. I PAINTED THIS HOUSE BY MYSELF.
9. HOW MUCH <u>DID</u> HE PAY FOR THIS PAMPH-LET?
10. WE CAN'T TELL YOU (singular) BECAUSE IT IS A SURPRISE.

11. WHAT IS THE NAME <u>OF</u> THIS FLOWER?
12. I AM VERY SORRY, BUT I MUST DISAPPOINT YOU (singular) AGAIN.
13. <u>LET</u> ME EXPLAIN THE REASON FOR MY BEING LATE.
14. WHERE <u>DID</u> YOU (sin-gular) AND YOUR FRIEND GO LAST SUMMER?
15. MY FATHER IS NOT A VERY TALL MAN.
16. ISTHETRAINONTIME?
17. HE IS THE NEW PAINT-ER.
18. YOU (singular) MAY NOT BORROW ANY MORE MONEY FROM US.
19. IT WAS A SURPRISE

BIRTHDAY <u>PARTY</u> FOR <u>JOHN</u>.
20. <u>DID</u> YOU (plural) LEARN ANYTHING FROM THIS WORKSHOP?
21. I JUST CAN'T LOAN IT TO YOU (singular)!
22. PLEASE LEAVE THE FLOWERS ON THE TA-BLE.
23. REMEMBER THAT I MEAN WHAT I SAY!
24. PLEASE HURRY BE-CAUSE WE ARE LATE.
25. I THINK I WANT <u>TO</u> SURPRISE YOU (singular).

lesson thirty-six

Signs presented in this lesson are:

BLOOD	OBVIOUS	EGG	SELECT
DIVORCE	PAIR	NEAR	FAR
SLEEP*	JELLY*	WIND* (noun)	HIDE, CONCEAL
KEY*	RELIGION	LOCK	PEN (writing instrument)
KILL	INTELLIGENT, BRILLIANT	SECRETARY	EXCEPT

BLOOD

The left hand, with the thumb and fingers extended and joined, is held in front of the body with the palmar side toward the signer and the fingers pointing to the right. The right hand, with the thumb and fingers fully extended and apart, first touches the mouth with the palmar side of its index finger (the hand is held with the back side toward the viewer and the fingers pointing to the left). Then, the fingers of the right hand perform a fluttering motion as the hand is moved downward with the fingers brushing past the back side of the left hand.

NOTE: This sign intends to suggest the flowing movement of blood.

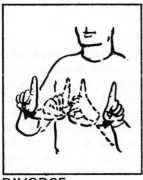

DIVORCE

Both hands first assume the configuration of the letter *D* and are positioned in front of the body so that their palmar surfaces face each other as the *D* hands touch. Next, the *D* hands are pulled apart sideways as they twist so that their palmar surfaces are now facing the viewer.

NOTE: This sign is suggestive of the growing distance between two parties.

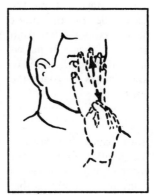

SLEEP*

The right hand, with the thumb and fingers extended and apart, is placed over the face with the fingers pointing upward and the back of the hand facing the viewer. Then, the hand is moved downward as the thumb bends inward and touches the fingers which are joined and flexed at the base. The sign ends with the hand at chin level and with its back toward the viewer. This motion is repeated several times.

NOTE: A facial expression (drooping of the eyes) may be used to supplement the sign.

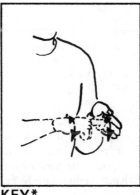

KEY*

The left hand, with the thumb and fingers extended and joined, is positioned in front and to the left side of the body with the fingers pointing to the viewer and the palmar side of the hand facing to the right. The right hand first makes the letter *X* and touches the palm of the left hand (contact is between the left palm and right second joint). Then, the *X* hand is moved to perform *several* small clockwise and counterclockwise movements at or against the left palm.

401

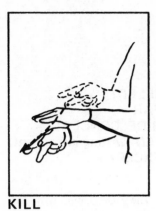

KILL

The left forearm is positioned at a 45-degree angle across the body with the thumb and fingers extended, joined and with the palm facing down. The right hand, in the configuration of the letter *K*, first is held in front and to the right side of the body so that the index finger of the *K* hand is pointing to the left fingers. Then, the back side of the index finger grazes the left palm as the *K* hand is passed under it, stopping three to four inches beyond the left hand.

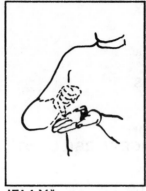

JELLY*

The left hand, with the thumb and fingers extended and joined, is held in front of the body with the palm facing up and the fingers pointing to the viewer. The right hand, with only its little finger extended (the thumb and remaining fingers are contracted), touches the left palm with the tip of the little finger. The right *I* hand is held with its back side toward the viewer. Then, the little finger grazes the left palm as the hand is moved to make the formation of the letter *J*. The right hand is then returned to its original position and repeats the motion.

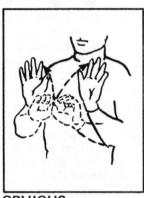

OBVIOUS

Both hands first assume the configuration of the letter *O* and are placed in front of the body so that their thumbnails are touching (the back sides of the *O* hands are facing the signer). Next, both *O* hands open as they are spread upward and apart. The sign ends with the palmar sides of the hands facing the viewer and the fingers pointing upward.
NOTE: The signs for "bright" and "clear" are made similarly, once the hands assume the configuration for the letters *B* and *C*, respectively.

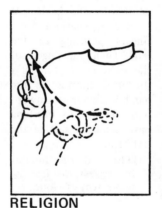

RELIGION

The right hand assumes the configuration of the letter *R*, which first is placed over the region of the heart with the back of the hand facing up. Next, the forearm swings the *R* hand in an upward direction to the right. The sign ends with the *R* hand held in front of the body at shoulder level with the fingertips pointing upward and the back of the hand facing the signer.

PAIR

The right hand, in the configuration of the letter *P*, is held in front of the body with the back of the *P* hand facing up. Next, the right *P* hand is moved to the right.

INTELLIGENT, BRILLIANT

The right hand, with only the middle finger flexed to about a 45-degree angle (remaining fingers and thumb are extended and apart), first touches the forehead with its middle fingertip; then, with the configuration maintained, the hand is rotated as it is moved forward.

EGG

The left hand, in the configuration of the letter *H*, is positioned in front of the body with the fingers pointing to the viewer at a downward angle and the back side of the hand facing to the left. The right hand, in a similar configuration, makes contact with the left *H* hand. (The right second finger touches the top of the left index finger near the middle joint. The right *H* fingers are pointing to the viewer at an angle and the back of the hand is facing to the right.) Next, the *H* hands are separated as their wrists flex them to the right and left, respectively. The sign ends with the *H* fingertips of both hands pointing to the viewer.

NOTE: This sign is imitative of how egg shells are separated.

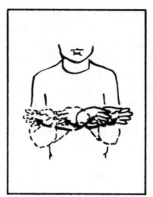

WIND* (noun)

The left hand, with the thumb and fingers extended and slightly apart, is positioned in front and to the left side of the body with the fingers pointing to the viewer at an angle and the palm toward the viewer at about a 45-degree angle. The right hand, with the thumb and fingers extended and slightly apart, is positioned approximately four to five inches from the left hand and parallels it. Both hands have their fingers pointing to the viewer at an angle to the left and their palmar sides are facing each other. Next, with the configuration and parallelism maintained, the arms swing to the right side of the body with the wrists bending the hands so that now their fingers are pointing to the viewer at about a 45-degree angle to the right. The hands then execute the same movement as they are moved from right to left.

NOTE: This motion is suggestive of the effect of air currents on an object.

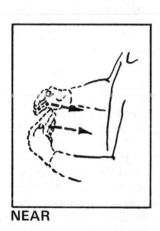

NEAR

The left hand, with the thumb and fingers joined and with its fingers flexed at the base, is positioned in front of the body with the fingers pointing to the right and the back side of the fingers facing the viewer. The right hand, in a similar configuration, but with the fingers pointing to the left, is positioned slightly in front (closer to the viewer) of the left hand. Next, with the configuration and parallelism maintained, both hands are drawn toward the body and stop when they are about four to five inches in front of the signer's body.

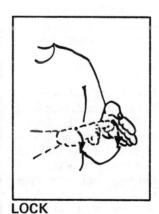

LOCK

The left hand, with the thumb and fingers extended and joined, is held in front and to the left side of the body with the palm facing to the right and the fingers pointing to the viewer. The right hand makes the letter *X*, which is placed on the left palm so that contact is made between the palm and the second joint of the flexed right index finger. Then, the *X* hand is moved to make *one* twisting movement in a clockwise direction against the left palm.

SECRETARY

The left hand, with the thumb and fingers extended and joined, is held in front of the body with the palm facing up and the fingers pointing to the viewer. The right hand first forms the letter *H* and touches the ear (contact is between the ear and the *H* fingertips). Then, the *H* hand is moved toward the left palm, as it changes its configuration so that now only the right thumb and index fingertip are touching (remaining fingers are contracted to the palm), and makes a wavy line across the left palm in the direction of the fingertips. (The latter portion of this sign is the word "write," lesson 9. The sign is imitative of a message heard and then written out.)

SELECT

The right hand assumes the configuration of the letter *G* and is held in front of the body with the *G* fingers pointing to the viewer and the back side of the *G* hand facing the signer. Next, the thumb and index finger are joined as the hand is pulled toward the signer's body.

FAR

Both hands, each with the thumb extended upward and the remaining fingers contracted, are positioned in front of the body so that their knuckles are touching and with their backs facing to the right and left. Next, with the configuration maintained, the right hand is moved forward, following a 45-degree angle to the right.

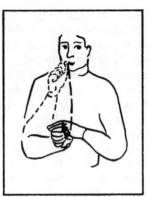

HIDE, CONCEAL

The right hand assumes the configuration of the letter *A*, which is placed over the lips so that contact is made between the back side of the thumb and the lips. Next, the *A* hand is pulled away and placed directly under the left hand which is held in front of the body with the thumb and fingers extended and joined. The left fingers are pointing to the right and the palm is facing down.

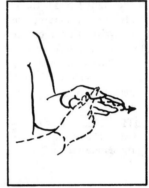

PEN
(writing instrument)

The left hand, with the thumb and fingers extended and joined, is held in front and slightly to the left side of the body with the palm facing up and the fingers pointing to the viewer. The right hand, in the configuration of the letter *P*, first touches the left palm (contact is made between the middle fingertip of the right *P* hand and the left palm). Next, a wavy line is made as the right middle finger grazes the left palm in the direction of the fingertips.

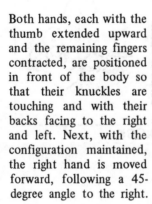

EXCEPT

The left hand, with only its index finger extended (remaining fingers and thumb are contracted), is held in front of the body so that the index finger is pointing upward and with its back side facing the viewer. The right hand, in the configuration of the letter *Q*, first is held approximately an inch above the left index finger. Then, the *Q* hand is moved downward, pinches the left index finger and then pulls the left hand upward.

A) Exercises in Encoding

Encode the following material using signs and fingerspelling. Use fingerspelling for all underlined words.

1. WOULD YOU LIKE MORE JELLY ON YOUR BREAD?
2. SOME PEOPLE DON'T BELIEVE THAT RELIGION IS IMPORTANT.
3. I AGREE THAT HE IS AN INTELLI-GENT STUDENT. ("Student" is signed as "learn" plus "er.")
4. WHY ARE YOU DIVORCING HIM?
5. DON'T BE SO OBVIOUS ABOUT IT.
6. IT WAS A BRIGHT DAY. ("Bright" is signed similarly to "obvious," but with *B* hands.)
7. IT WAS SO CLEAR THAT YOU COULD SEE FOR MILES. ("Clear" is signed similarly to "obvious," but with *C* hands.)
8. I LEFT MY NEW PAIR OF SHOES IN YOUR OFFICE.
9. IF YOU ARE TIRED, STAY HOME AND SLEEP.
10. MY FOSTER PARENTS WERE KILLED DURING THE WAR.
11. YOUR BROTHER HAS THE CAR KEY.
12. EVERY TIME I SEE BLOOD, I FAINT. ("Time" is signed as "time" in the abstract sense—*T* hand which makes a circle over the left palm.)
13. WHY DID YOU SELECT THIS BOX?
14. DON'T FORGET TO BUY SOME EGGS.
15. HE IS HIDING BEHIND THE DOOR.
16. WHO IS YOUR NEW SECRETARY?
17. WHAT SOUND DOES THE WIND MAKE?
18. ALL OF THEM MAY LEAVE THE ROOM EXCEPT HIM.
19. MAY WE USE YOUR PEN FOR A MINUTE?
20. LOCK THE DOOR AFTER I LEAVE.
21. HOW FAR IS IT FROM HERE?
22. DID YOU KNOW THAT YOU LIVE NEAR US?
23. WHY DID HE HIDE IT UNDER THE TABLE?
24. SELECT THE TWO WORDS THAT MEAN THE SAME.

B) Exercises in Decoding

Decode the following illustrated exercises:

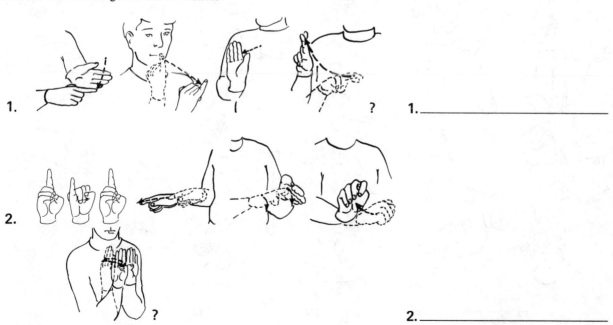

1.

1. _____

2.

2. _____

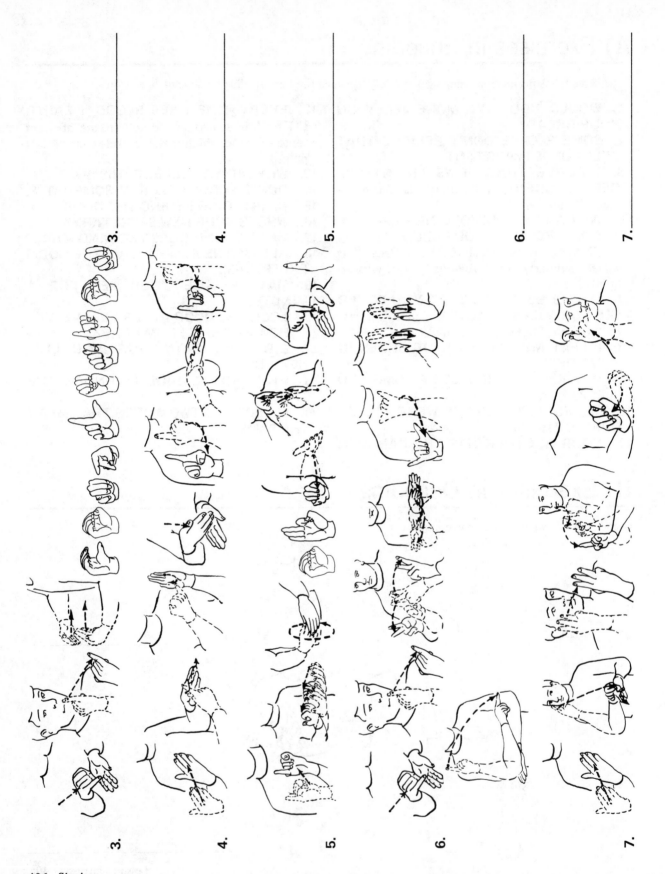

3.

4.

5.

6.

7.

3.

4.

5.

6.

7.

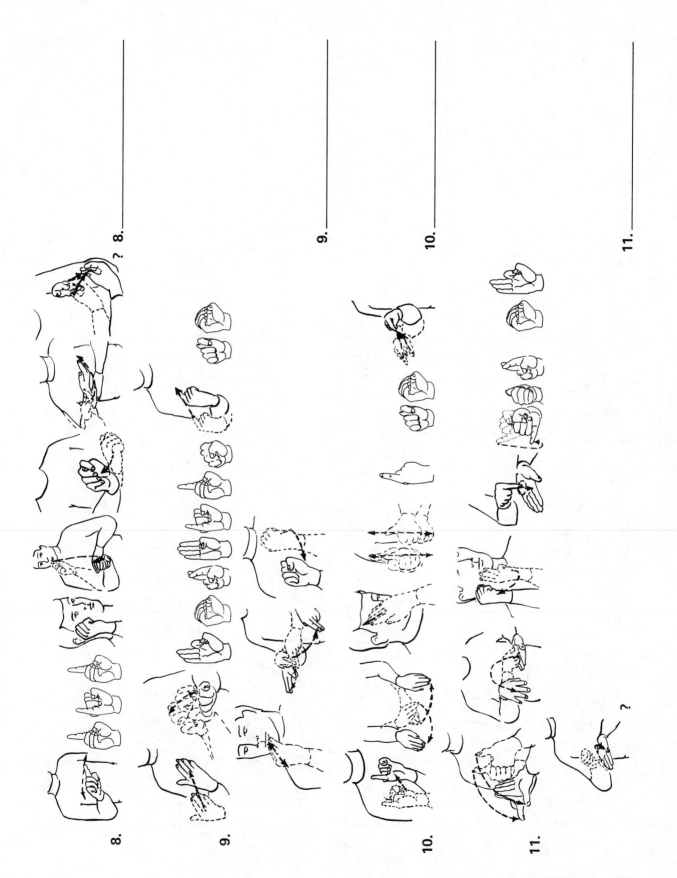

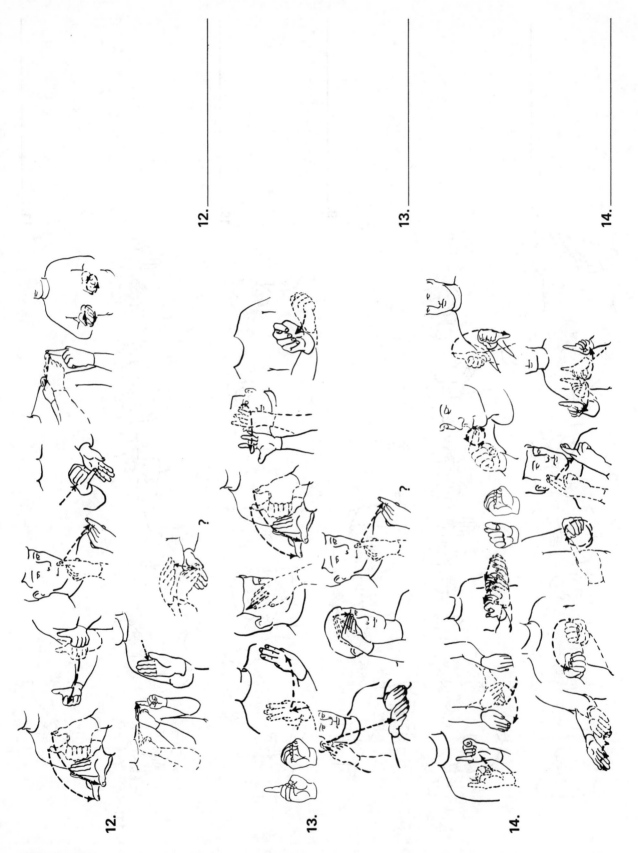

12.

13.

14.

15. _____

16. _____

17. _____

18. _____

15.

16.

17.

18.

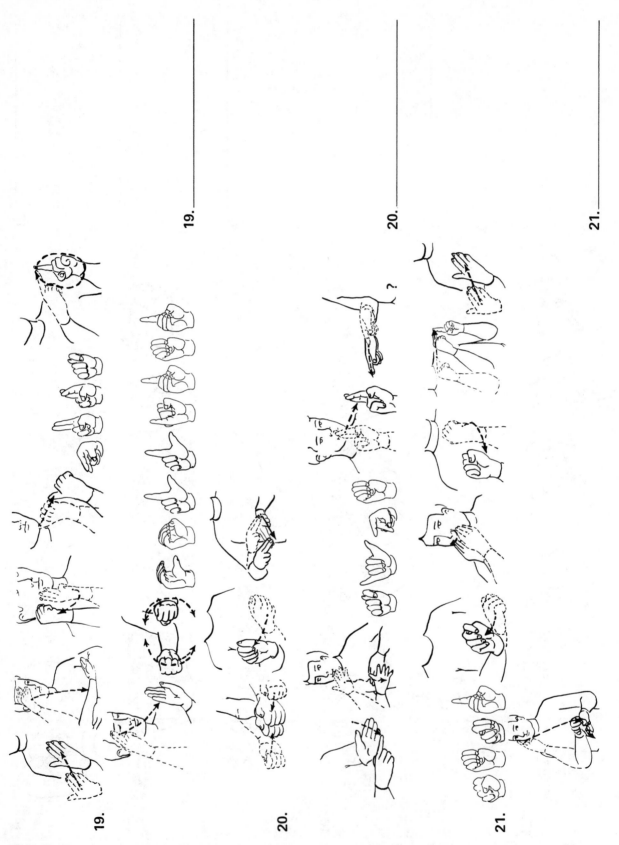

19.

20.

21.

C) Answers for Decoding Part (B), Lesson 36

Underlined words indicate that they should have been fingerspelled.

1. WHAT IS YOUR RELI-GION?
2. <u>DID</u> YOU (singular) LOCK THE DOOR?
3. IT IS NEAR <u>COMPLE-TION</u>.
4. MY PEN JUST STOPPED WRITING.
5. I WANT ALL <u>OF</u> THEM EXCEPT THIS ONE.
6. IT IS VERY WINDY TODAY.
7. MY SECRETARY WILL ANSWER THE TELE-PHONE.
8. WHERE <u>DID</u> SHE HIDE THE NEW MAGAZINE?
9. MY DOCTOR <u>FORBIDS</u> ME <u>TO</u> EAT EGGS.
10. I DON'T KNOW WHICH ONE <u>TO</u> SELECT.
11. HOW EXPENSIVE WAS THIS <u>JAR</u> <u>OF</u> JELLY?
12. HOW <u>FAR</u> IS IT FROM HERE TO YOUR SCHOOL?
13. <u>DO</u> WE KNOW HOW INTELLIGENT THE DEAF BOY IS?
14. I DON'T WANT <u>TO</u> SAY ANYTHING ELSE <u>ABOUT</u> HER DIVORCE.
15. SOME THINGS ARE NOT ALWAYS OBVIOUS.
16. <u>DID</u> YOU (plural) FIND A PAIR <u>OF</u> <u>GLASSES</u> YES-TERDAY?
17. YOU (singular) MAY SLEEP WHILE I DRIVE.
18. I CAN'T FIND MY HOUSE KEY.
19. MY SON WAS NOT <u>HURT</u> WHEN HIS CAR <u>COLLIDED</u> WITH A TRAIN.
20. WHAT BLOOD <u>TYPE</u> ARE YOU (singular)?
21. <u>SEND</u> THE FLOWERS TO MY SECRETARY.
22. IS HER HOUSE NEAR THE UNIVERSITY?
23. WE WANT YOU (singu-lar) <u>TO</u> SELECT THREE THINGS THAT ARE THE SAME COLOR.
24. <u>DID</u> HE WALK VERY FAR?
25. <u>DID</u> I LEAVE MY PEN ON YOUR TABLE?

lesson thirty-seven

Signs presented in this lesson are:

ASSISTANT*	GRAVY*	FAIL	WEALTH
CLASS	PROTECT	HEAD	PURPOSE
PERFECT, PRECISE	BREAKFAST	HAT*	DULL, DRY
GALLAUDET	TELEGRAM	HAIR	UGLY
GLASSES*	BUSINESS	LETTER	RESTAURANT

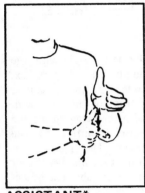

ASSISTANT*

The left hand, with the thumb extended and pointing upward and the remaining fingers extended and joined, is held in front and slightly to the left side of the body with the fingers pointing to the viewer and the back side of the hand facing to the left. The right hand makes the letter *L*; then the thumb of the *L* hand pokes against the bottom edge of the left hand (the index finger of the *L* hand is pointing to the viewer). This motion is repeated several times.

PERFECT, PRECISE

Both hands, each in the configuration of the letter *P*, are held approximately one to two inches from each other in front of the body at an oblique angle, the right nearer the signer and slightly higher than the left (the back side of the right *P* hand is facing the signer, while that of the left *P* hand is facing down at an angle), with the tips of the middle fingers of the *P* hands pointing to each other. Next, the *P* hands are moved toward each other so that their middle fingertips touch.

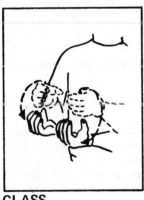

CLASS

Both hands, each in the configuration of the letter *C*, are held side-by-side in a horizontal plane in front of the body with their palmar sides facing each other. Next, the forearms rotate the *C* hands to the right and left as they form downward arc motions. The sign ends with the *C* hands side-by-side and with their palmar sides facing up.

NOTE: The signs for "group," "organization" and "association" are made similarly once the hands assume the configuration for the letters *G* for "group," *O* for "organization," and *A* for "association," respectively.

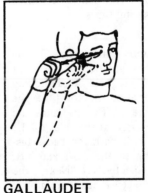

GALLAUDET

The right hand, in the configuration of the letter *G*, is placed near the corner of the right eye with the wrist facing down. Then, the thumb and index finger touch as the *G* hand is pulled to the right.

NOTE: This sign may refer either to Gallaudet College located in Washington, D.C. (the only liberal arts college for the deaf in the world) or to Thomas Hopkins Gallaudet, the man who introduced sign language to the United States in 1817. This became his "name sign" because he wore glasses.

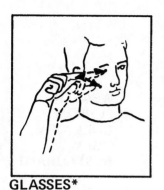

GLASSES*

This sign is made similarly to the previous one ("Gallaudet"), with the only difference being that the motion is repeated *several* times.

BREAKFAST

This sign is made by combining two other signs, "eat," lesson 13, plus "morning," lesson 21. First, make the sign for "eat," followed by the sign for "morning."

NOTE: The sign for lunch is made by combining "eat" plus "noon," lesson 22; the sign for "dinner" is made by combining "eat" plus "night," lesson 22.

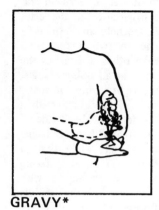

GRAVY*

The left hand, with the thumb and fingers extended and joined, is held in front and slightly to the left side of the body with the fingers pointing to the viewer and the back side of the hand facing to the left. The right thumb and middle finger, from beneath, simultaneously touch the palmar and back sides of the left hand. (The back of the right hand is facing down and the remaining fingers are extended and pointing left.) Next, the hand is pulled downward as the thumb and middle finger touch. This motion is repeated several times.

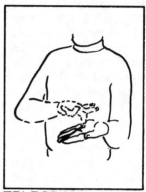

TELEGRAM

The left hand, with the thumb and fingers extended and joined, is held in front of the body with the palm facing up and the fingers pointing to the viewer. The right hand, with the middle finger flexed to about a 45-degree angle (remaining fingers and thumb are extended and apart), first touches the left palm with its middle fingertip. (The right fingers are pointing left with the palm facing down.) Then, the right hand is moved forward (in the direction of the left fingertips), while the middle finger grazes the palm and fingers.

PROTECT

Both hands, each in the configuration of the letter *P*, are held in a crossed position in front of the body. (The *P* hands are crossed at the sides of the wrists with the backs facing to the right and left, respectively.) Next, the crossed *P* hands are moved forward while maintaining their contact.

NOTE: The signs for "guard" and "defend" are made similarly, once the hands assume the configuration of the letter *G* for "guard" and *D* for "defend."

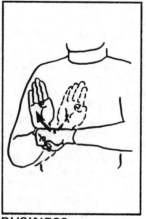

BUSINESS

The left forearm is laid across the front of the body with the hand in a fist position and facing down. The right hand, in the configuration of the letter *B* is held against the side of the left wrist, with the fingers pointing upward and the palm of the *B* hand facing the viewer. Next, the *B* hand swings slightly upward as it is moved front-to-back along the left forearm.

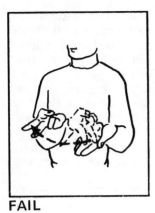

FAIL

The left hand, with the thumb and fingers extended and joined, is held in front of the body with the palm facing up and the fingers pointing to the viewer. The right hand, in the configuration of the letter *V*, first makes contact with the left palm. (The back sides of the fingers of the *V* hand make contact with the left palm.) Next, the *V* hand is moved forward, beyond the left fingertips and curves to the right. The sign ends with the *V* hand in front of the right side of the body (the *V* fingers are pointing to the viewer with the back sides facing down).

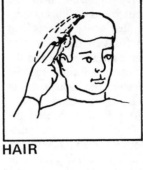

HAIR

The right hand, in the configuration of the letter *H*, first is placed on top of the signer's head so that the palmar side of the *H* hand is touching the hair. Next, the *H* hand brushes the signer's hair as it is moved toward the ear.

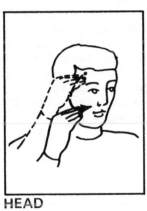

HEAD

The right hand, with the thumb and fingers joined and with the fingers flexed at the base, first touches the right side of the forehead (contact is made between the fingertips and the side of the head) with the hand held so that the back side is facing to the right. Next, with the configuration maintained, the hand is separated from the head, moved downward and touches the cheek with the fingertips.

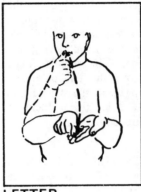

LETTER

The left hand, with the thumb and fingers extended and joined, is held in front of the body with the palm facing up and the fingers pointing to the viewer. The palmar side of the right thumb (remaining fingers are contracted), first touches the lips and then, the hand is turned forward and in a downward direction so that the thumb makes contact with the first and second fingers of the left hand near the fingertips.
NOTE: This sign is imitative of placing a stamp on an envelope.

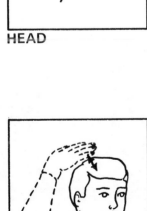

HAT*

The right hand, with the thumb and fingers extended and joined, is held approximately two or three inches above the signer's head with the fingers pointing to the left and the back of the hand facing up. Next, the hand is brought down and pats the head several times.

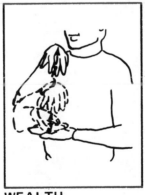

WEALTH

The left hand, with the thumb and fingers extended and joined, is held in front of the body with the fingers pointing to the right and the palm facing up. The right hand, with thumb bending inward to touch the extended and joined fingers, touches the left palm with the back sides of the fingers. (This is the sign for "money," lesson 17, and is repeated several times.) Next, the forearm inverts the hand (the thumb and fingers are now extended, apart, and pointing to the left palm) and pulls it upward. This sign intends to convey the idea of "money piled up."

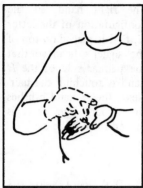

PURPOSE

The left hand, with the thumb and fingers extended and joined, is held in front of the body with the palm facing up and the fingers pointing to the viewer. The right hand, in the configuration of the letter *P*, first touches the left palm (contact is made between the middle fingertip and the left palm) with the *P* hand held so that the index finger is pointing to the left and the back side of the hand facing up. Then, the middle finger grazes the left palm and fingers as the wrist flexes the *P* hand in a clockwise direction.

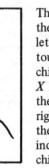

DULL, DRY

The right hand assumes the configuration of the letter *X*, which first touches the left side of the chin. The back side of the *X* hand is facing up. Next, the *X* hand is pulled to the right, across the chin as the side of the flexed index finger grazes the chin.

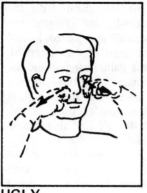

UGLY

Both hands, each in the configuration of the letter *X*, are held under each eye with their index fingertips pointing downward and with the backs of the hands facing up. Next, the *X* hands are pulled downward at oblique angles, while their flexed index fingers graze both sides of the cheeks.

NOTE: This sign may intend to suggest, perhaps, facial asymmetry.

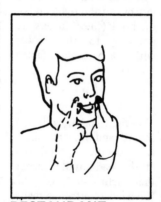

RESTAURANT

The right hand, in the configuration of the letter *R*, first touches the right corner of the mouth with the sides of its *R* fingers. The back of the hand is facing to the right. Next, the forearm twists the *R* hand as it moves from right to left and touches the left corner of the mouth. The *R* hand is held with its back toward the viewer as the sign comes to an end.

A) Exercises in Encoding

Encode the following material using signs and fingerspelling. Use fingerspelling for all underlined words.

1. WOULD YOU LIKE TO COME TO OUR HOUSE FOR BREAKFAST?
2. CAN YOU MEET ME FOR LUNCH? ("Lunch" is signed as "eat" plus "noon.")
3. SHOULD WE SEND OUR BOY TO GALLAUDET COLLEGE?
4. PLEASE WEAR YOUR GLASSES WHEN YOU DRIVE.
5. GIVE THIS PAPER TO YOUR ASSISTANT CLINICIAN.
6. THERE ARE NO PERFECT PROGRAMS. ("No" is signed as "none.")
7. HOW LARGE IS YOUR CLASS?
8. DOES YOUR GROUP HAVE A NAME? ("Group" is signed similarly to "class," but with G hands.)
9. DOES HIS ORGANIZATION SUPPORT THE IDEA? ("Organization" is signed similarly to "class," but with O hands.)
10. WHAT IS THE NAME OF YOUR ASSOCIATION? ("Association" is signed similarly to "class," but with A hands.)
11. DID YOU BUY A NEW HAT?
12. WHAT KIND OF GRAVY IS IT?
13. WHAT KIND OF BUSINESS DID YOUR GRANDFATHER HAVE?
14. IF YOU SHOULD HAPPEN TO NEED MORE MONEY, SEND US A TELEGRAM.
15. WHO WILL PROTECT US WHILE YOU ARE AWAY?
16. WE SHOULD GUARD AGAINST BECOMING SELFISH. ("Guard" is signed similarly to "protect," but with G hands.)
17. WHY DO YOU THINK THAT HE IS UGLY?
18. PLEASE GIVE THIS LETTER TO YOUR MOTHER.
19. YOU FAILED BECAUSE YOU DID NOT STUDY VERY MUCH.
20. THE FOOD IN THIS RESTAURANT IS VERY GOOD.
21. OUR ONLY PURPOSE TODAY IS TO TRY TO EXPLAIN HOW IT STARTED.
22. WE KNOW NOTHING ABOUT HIS WEALTH.
23. HOW DID SHE HURT HER HEAD?
24. WE MEAN PRECISELY WHAT WE SAY!
25. DO YOU HAVE MY AUDIOGRAM?
26. DO YOU LIKE MY NEW GLASSES?
27. WHAT TIME WILL DINNER BE READY? ("Dinner" is signed as "food" plus "night.")

B) Exercises in Decoding

Decode the following illustrated exercises:

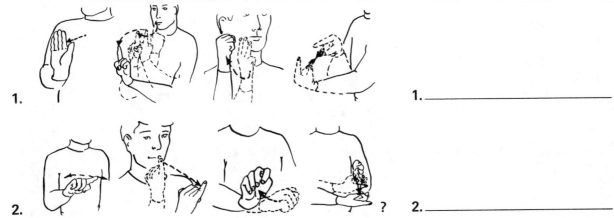

1. _____

1. _____

2. _____

2. _____

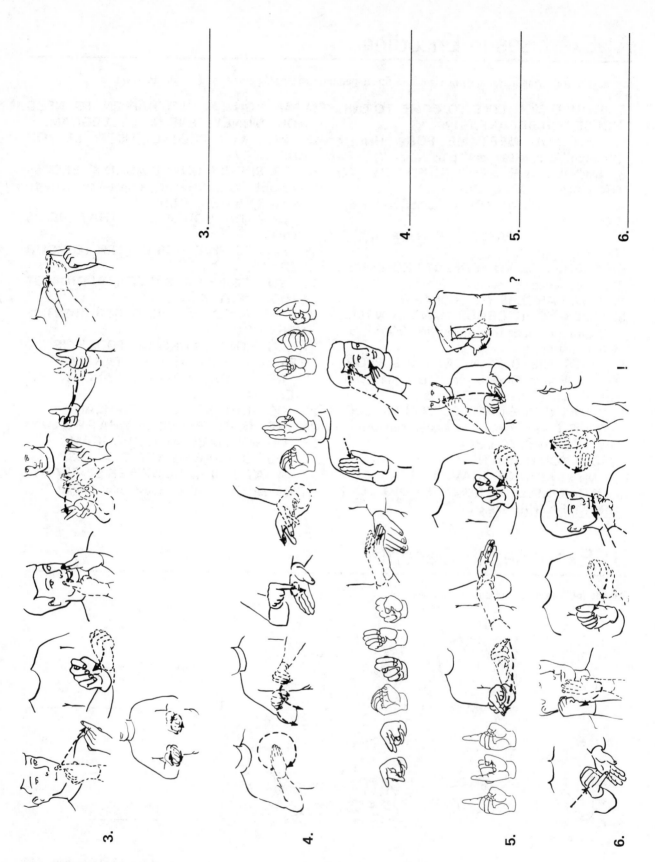

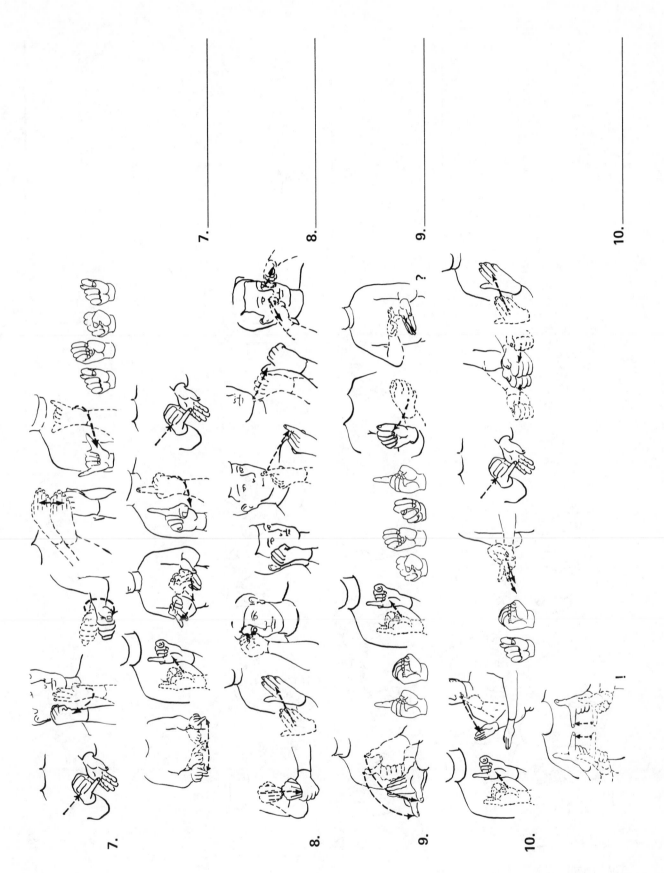

11.

12.

13.

14.

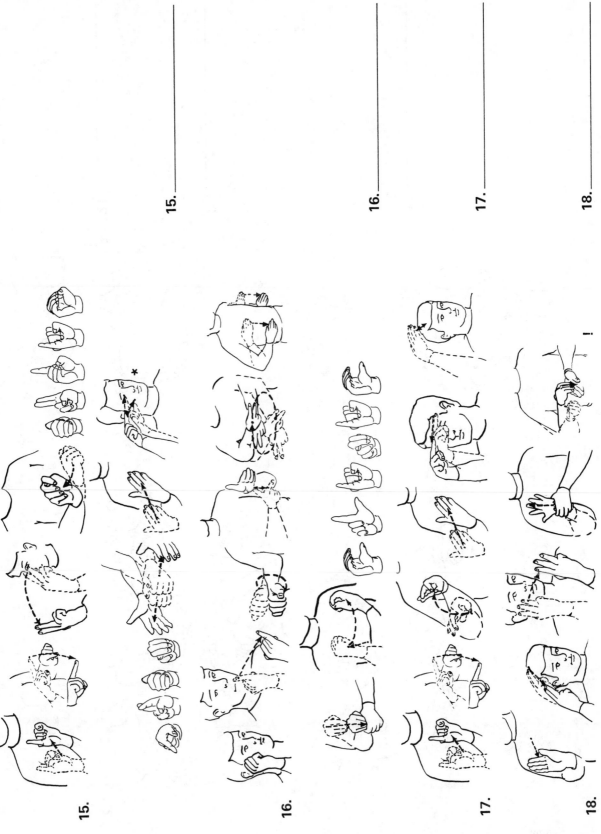

15.

16.

17.

18.

15.

16.

17.

18.

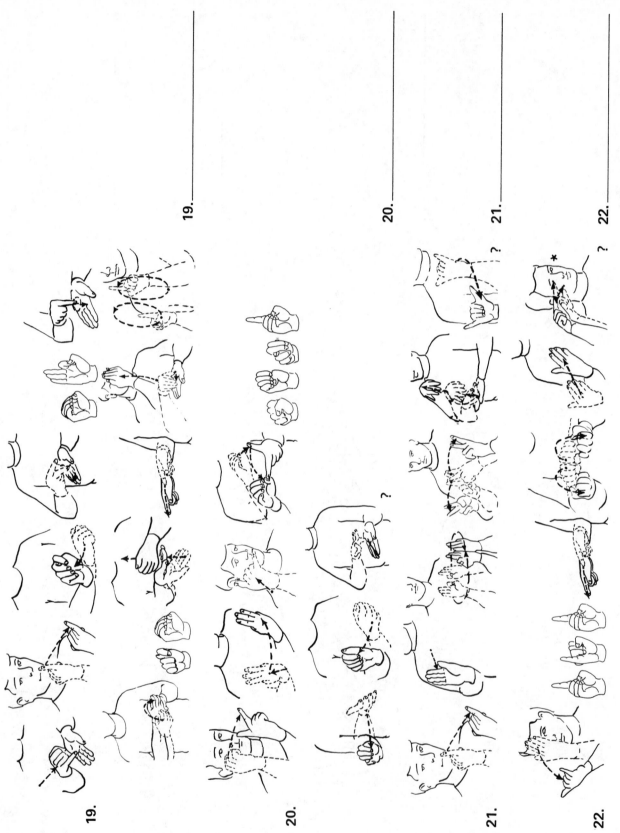

19.

20.

21.

22.

23.

24.

25.

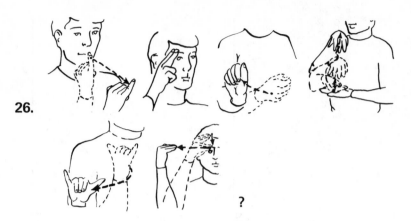

26. ?

26._____

C) Answers for Decoding Part (B), Lesson 37

Underlined words indicate that they should have been fingerspelled.

1. YOUR ANSWER WAS PERFECT.
2. WHERE IS THE GRAVY?
3. IS THE RESTAURANT VERY FAR FROM HERE?
4. PLEASE PUT THIS PAIR _OF_ _EARPHONES_ ON YOUR HEAD.
5. _DID_ YOU (plural) WRITE THE LETTER YET?
6. IT WAS A DULL LECTURE!
7. IT WAS AN EASY _TEST_, BUT I FAILED IT.
8. IN MY OPINION, SHE IS NOT UGLY.
9. HOW _DO_ I _SEND_ A TELEGRAM?
10. I PROMISE _TO_ PROTECT IT WITH MY LIFE!
11. IF I DON'T SEE YOU (singular) TOMORROW, I SHALL TELEPHONE YOU.
12. I AM IN YOUR MORNING CLASS.
13. WHAT IS THE PURPOSE _OF_ THIS MEETING?
14. IS YOUR SISTER AT GALLAUDET NOW?
15. I CAN'T SEE THE _AUDIOGRAM_ WITHOUT MY GLASSES.
16. SHE IS AN ASSISTANT SUPERVISOR IN OUR _CLINIC._
17. I CAN'T FIND MY BLACK HAT.
18. YOUR HAIR WILL GROW AGAIN!
19. IT IS THE PURPOSE _OF_ THIS COURSE _TO_ HELP YOU LEARN SIGN LANGUAGE.
20. SHALL WE CALL OR _SEND_ THEM A TELEGRAM?
21. IS YOUR FAMILY VERY WEALTHY?
22. WHY _DID_ YOU (singular) BREAK MY GLASSES?
23. HE IS THE NEW ASSISTANT MANAGER _OF_ OUR SCHOOL.
24. IS IT NECESSARY FOR ME _TO_ REGISTER FOR THIS CLASS?
25. WHICH BOY IS WEARING THE WHITE HAT?
26. IS HE A WEALTHY MAN?

lesson thirty-eight

Signs presented in this lesson are:

MEAT*	AUDIOGRAM	JUMP	DIE, DEATH
DREAM	AUDIOLOGY	DO (verb)*	PRESIDENT, CHAIRMAN
REVENGE*	RELATIVE	GRANDFATHER	EXERCISE*
COST, CHARGE	WALL	GRANDMOTHER	UMBRELLA
NERVE	CIRCLE (verb)	SAD	FOREVER

MEAT*

The left hand, with the thumb extended and pointing upward (remaining fingers are extended and joined), is positioned in front of the body with the fingers pointing to the right and the back of the hand facing the viewer. The right hand, in the configuration of the letter *G*, but with the remaining three fingers extended and apart, is moved toward the left hand and with its thumb and index finger pinches the fleshy part of the left hand (near the base of the left thumb). Then, with the contact maintained, both hands quickly are moved slightly up and down at an oblique angle. This latter motion is repeated several times.

REVENGE*

The left hand, with the thumb and index finger touching to form a loop (remaining fingers are contracted), is positioned in front of the body with the back of the hand facing to the left. The right hand, in a similar configuration, is positioned parallel to the left hand and its back side is facing to the right. Next, with the configuration maintained, both hands quickly are moved toward the midline and strike their joined thumbs and fingertips. The hands then are returned to their original position and repeat the motion.

DREAM

The right hand, with only the index finger extended (remaining fingers and thumb are contracted), first touches the right side of the signer's forehead with the index fingertip. Then, the hand is pulled to the right and upward at an oblique angle while the index finger quickly bends and extends several times. NOTE: This sign may be suggestive, perhaps, of the mind wandering.

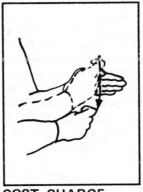

COST, CHARGE

The left hand, with the thumb and fingers extended and joined, is held in front and to the left side of the body with the fingers pointing to the viewer and the palmar side facing to the right. The right hand assumes the configuration of the letter *X* and is held slightly above the top edge of the left hand with its back side facing the viewer. Then, the back side of the crooked right index finger (first and second joints) grazes the left palm as the right hand is moved downward past the left hand.

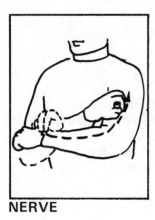

NERVE

The left forearm is laid across the body with the hand in a fist position and facing down. The right hand, in the configuration of the letter *N*, first touches the back side of the left fist hand with its *N* fingertips (index and middle fingers). Then, the right *N* hand grazes the left arm as a line is traced from the wrist to the upper portion of the left arm, suggestive of the course of a peripheral nerve.

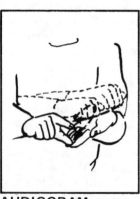

AUDIOGRAM

In this sign the hands attempt to illustrate the vertical (intensity) and horizontal (frequency) co-ordinates of an audiogram. This motion is executed in two steps by the right hand. First, the left hand, with the thumb and fingers extended and joined, is held in front and slightly to the left side of the body with the palm facing up and the fingers pointing to the viewer. *Step one:* The right hand, in the configuration of the letter *A*, first is positioned near the base of the left thumb with its back side facing up. Then, the knuckles of the *A* hand graze the left palm as the *A* hand is drawn across and past the bottom portion of the left hand to the right. *Step two:* The right hand changes its configuration to that of the letter *G* and, first, is positioned on the left palm with the wrist facing down and its *G* fingers pointing to the left. Then, with the configuration maintained, the *G* hand is moved forward toward the viewer.

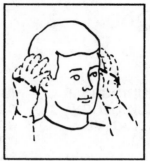

AUDIOLOGY

Both hands, each with the thumb and fingers slightly apart and semi-curved, are placed opposite each ear with their back sides facing sideways. Then, the wrists alternately rock the hands front-to-back. The sign is suggestive of the earphones used in testing one's hearing.

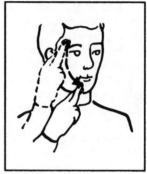

RELATIVE

The right hand, in the configuration of the letter *R*, first touches the right side of the forehead with its *R* fingers. The right hand fingers are pointing upward and the back of the hand is facing the viewer. Next, the *R* hand is moved downward and the fingers touch the right side of the signer's chin.

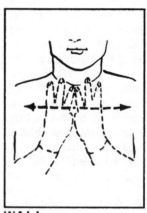

WALL

Both hands, each in the configuration of the letter *W*, are positioned side-by-side in front of the body with the bottom portion of the hands touching. The hands have their *W* fingertips pointing upward and their back sides facing the viewer. Then, with the configuration preserved, the *W* hands are pulled apart to the right and left sides of the body.

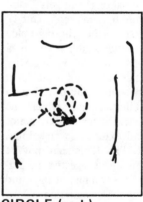

CIRCLE (verb)

The right hand, with only the index finger extended (thumb and remaining fingers are contracted), is held in front of the body with the index fingertip pointing to the viewer and the back side of the hand facing to the right. Next, the right hand is moved to complete a small circle in a clockwise direction in front of the body.

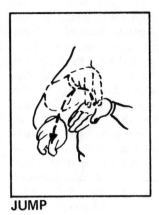

JUMP

The left hand, with the thumb and fingers extended and joined, is held in front of the body with the palm facing up and the fingers pointing to the viewer. The fingertips of the right *V* hand first touch the left palm (the back sides of the right *V* fingers face the viewer). Then, the *V* hand is arched forward off the left palm as the *V* fingers are crooked. The sign comes to an end with the right hand positioned about three or four inches beyond the left hand fingertips and the right crooked *V* fingers pointing downward.

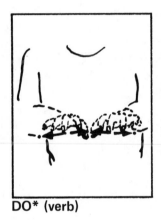

DO* (verb)

Both hands, each with the fingers and thumb slightly apart and bent, are placed approximately four inches from each other in front of the body with their palmar sides facing down. Next, with the configuration preserved, the hands simultaneously are moved to the midline and then are returned to their original position. This motion is repeated several times.

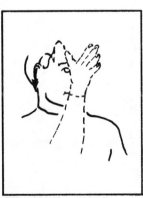

GRANDFATHER

The right hand, with the thumb and fingers extended and slightly apart, first places the thumb on the middle of the signer's forehead (the back side of the hand is facing to the right and the fingers are pointing upward at about a 45-degree angle). Next, with the configuration preserved, the right hand executes two small, upward arc movements while moving to the right side of the body.

GRANDMOTHER

The right hand, with its thumb and fingers extended and slightly apart, first places the thumb on the chin (the back side of the hand is facing to the right and the fingers are pointing upward at about a 45-degree angle). Next, with the configuration preserved, the right hand executes two small upward arc movements while moving to the right side of the body.

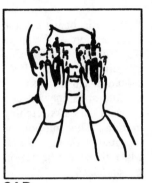

SAD

Both hands, each with the thumb and fingers extended and apart, are positioned side-by-side in front of the signer's face with their fingers pointing upward and their back sides facing the viewer. Next, with the configuration maintained, the hands are pulled slightly downward. NOTE: This motion may be accompanied with an appropriate facial expression.

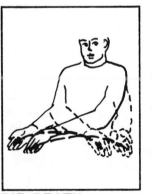

DIE, DEATH

Both hands, each with the thumb and fingers extended and joined, are placed side-by-side in front and to the left side of the body with the palmar side of the left hand facing up, while that of the right hand is facing down. Both hands have their fingertips pointing to the viewer. Next, the hands simultaneously are rotated 180 degrees clockwise as they are moved to the right side of the body so that now the palm of the left hand is facing down, while the right palm is facing up. The distance relationship between the two hands remains the same.

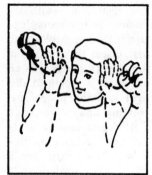

PRESIDENT, CHAIRMAN

Both hands, each with the thumb slightly apart and remaining fingers joined and cupped slightly, are positioned near each side of the head with their palmar sides facing the viewer. Next, the hands clasp into fists as each is moved in a short curve upward and slightly out to the side.

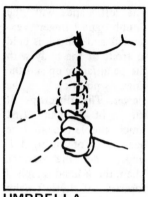

UMBRELLA

The left hand, in the configuration of the letter *A*, is held in front of the body with its back side facing to the left. The right hand, also in the configuration of the letter *A*, first is positioned on the top portion of the left *A* hand with its back side facing to the right. Next, the right *A* hand is moved straight up, as if it were opening an imaginary umbrella.

EXERCISE*

With both hands in the configuration of the letter *A*, pantomime exercising by first touching both shoulders and then extending the arms upward and outward in a stretching motion. This motion is repeated several times, while the *A* configuration is maintained.

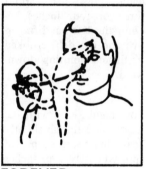

FOREVER

This sign is made by combining two other signs, the sign "For," lesson 8 and the sign "always," lesson 9. First, make the sign "For," followed by "always."

A) Exercises in Encoding

Encode the following material using signs and fingerspelling. Use fingerspelling for all underlined words.

1. THERE ARE PEOPLE WHO DON'T BELIEVE THAT AUDIOLOGY IS A SCIENCE.
2. WHAT <u>KIND</u> <u>OF</u> MEAT <u>DID</u> YOU BUY?
3. <u>DO</u> YOU WANT MORE GRAVY ON YOUR MEAT?
4. HE IS NOT OUR RELATIVE.
5. WHOSE UMBRELLA IS IT?
6. HELP ME <u>HANG</u> THIS PICTURE ON THE WALL.
7. PLEASE DON'T JUMP ON OUR NEW CHAIR.
8. WHICH WORD <u>DO</u> YOU WANT ME <u>TO</u> CIRCLE?
9. I THINK I CAN DO IT BY MYSELF.
10. <u>DO</u> I NEED <u>TO</u> EXERCISE MORE? ("Do" is used here as a helping verb and is different from "do" or "act"; when "do" is used as a helping verb, it is usually fingerspelled.)
11. THE EVALUATION SHOWS THAT YOU HAVE NERVE DEAFNESS.
12. I DREAMED ABOUT YOU AGAIN LAST NIGHT.
13. FOREVER IS A VERY LONG TIME. ("Forever" is signed as "for" plus "always." "Time" is signed as "time" in the abstract sense—*T* hand making a circle over the left palm.)
14. WHEN <u>DID</u> YOUR GRANDMOTHER DIE?
15. HOW MUCH <u>DID</u> THIS MACHINE COST?
16. I SHALL FLY TO <u>WASHINGTON</u> ON WEDNESDAY <u>TO</u> MEET <u>WITH</u> THE PRESIDENT. ("Wednesday" is signed similarly to "Monday," but with a *W* hand.)
17. WHY IS SHE SO SAD TODAY?
18. OUR GRANDFATHER CAME <u>TO</u> VISIT US.
19. I DON'T WANT <u>TO</u> DO IT FOREVER!
20. WHO IS THE CHAIRMAN OF YOUR GROUP? ("Group" is signed similarly to "class," but with *G* hands.)
21. WE HAVE NO DESIRE FOR REVENGE.
22. HE INFORMED US THAT THERE WAS A DEATH IN THE FAMILY.
23. MAY WE BORROW YOUR UMBRELLA?
24. CAN SURGERY HELP NERVE DEAFNESS?
25. SHE IS OUR NEW AUDIOLOGIST. ("Audiologist" is signed as "audiology" plus "-ist.")

B) Exercises in Decoding

Decode the following illustrated exercises:

1. _____

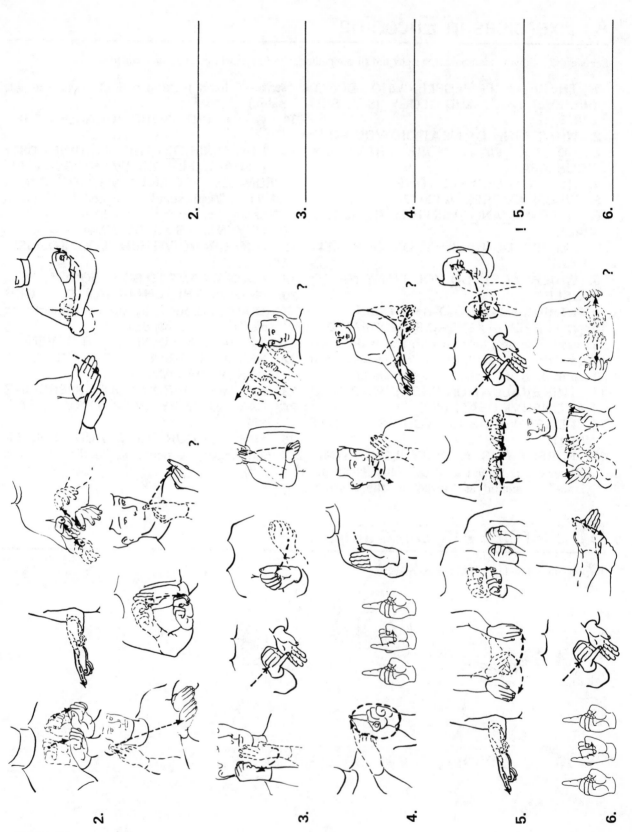

7.

8.

9.

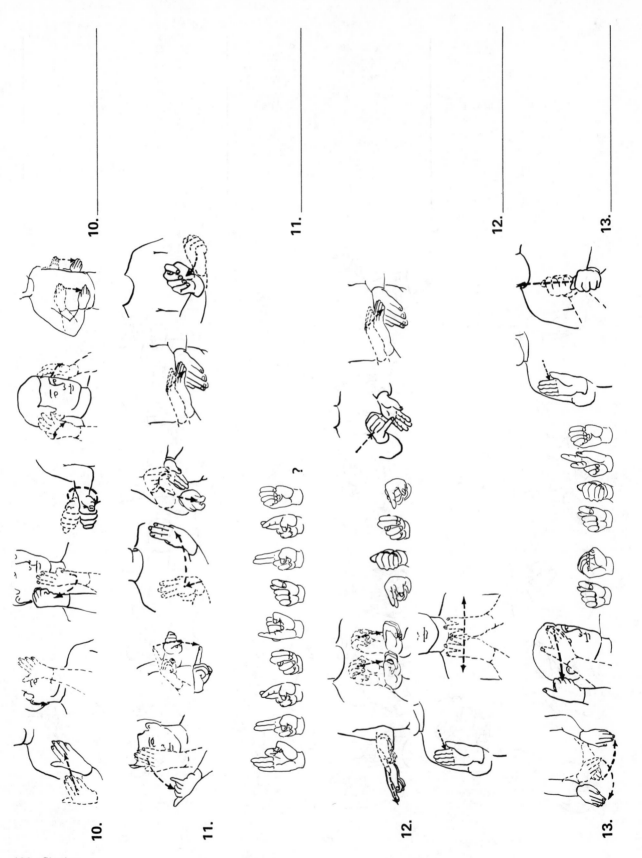

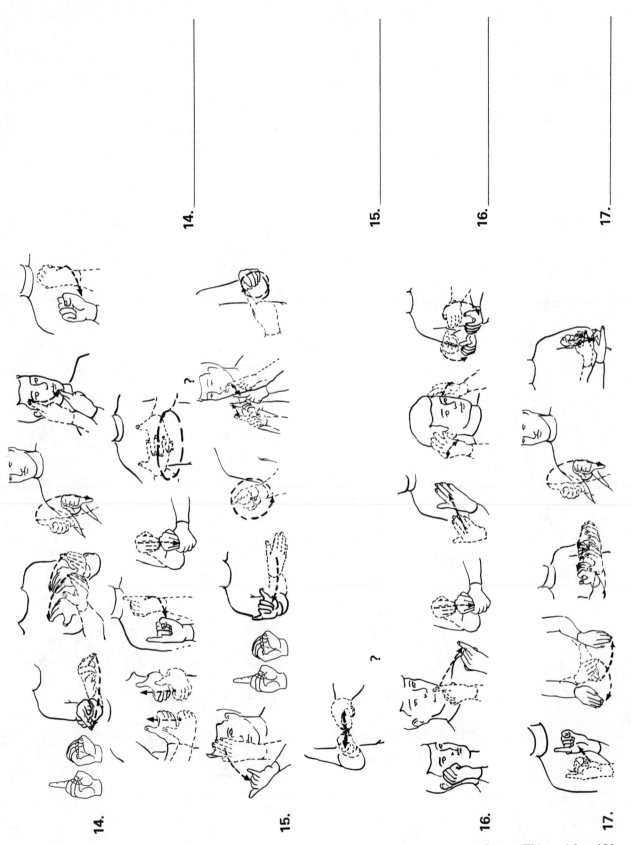

14.

15.

16.

17.

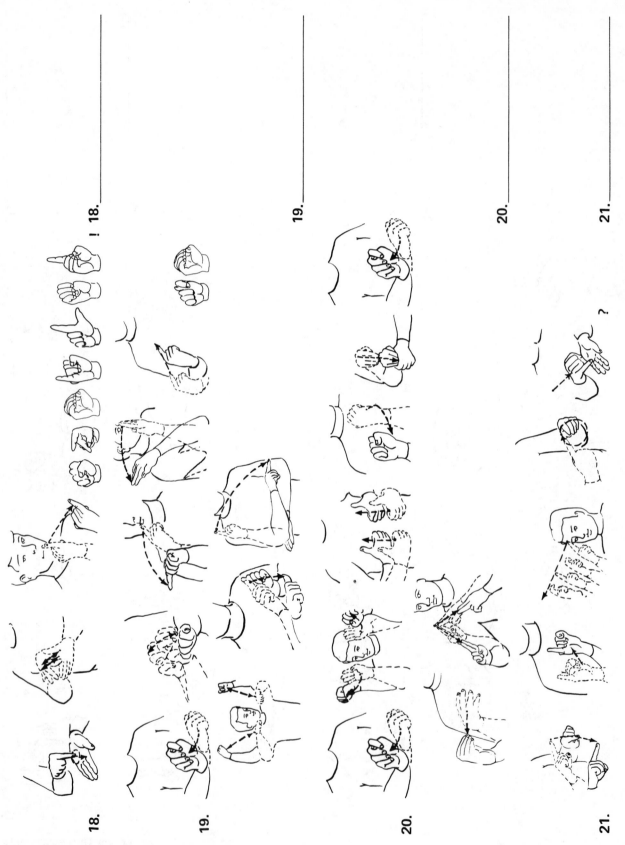

18.

19.

20.

21.

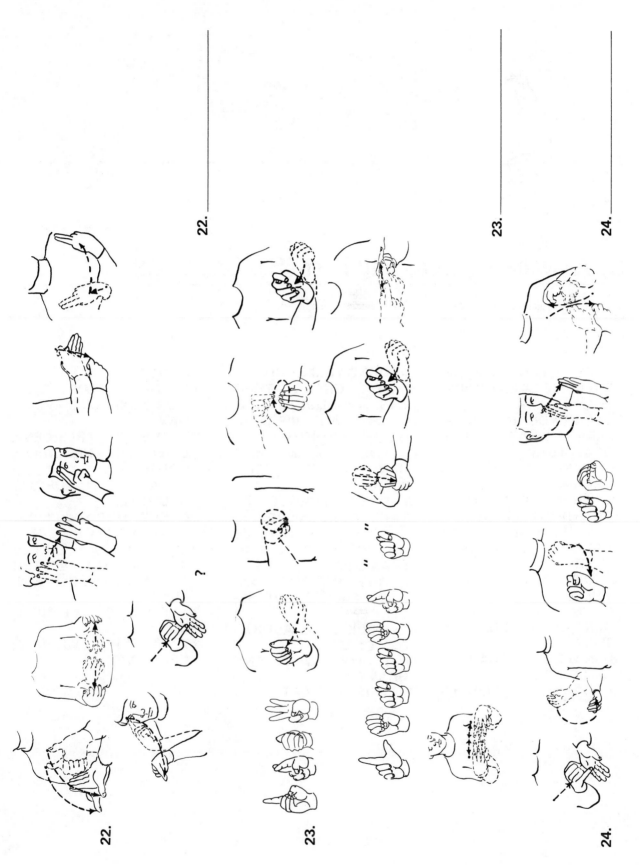

22.

23.

24.

22.

23.

24.

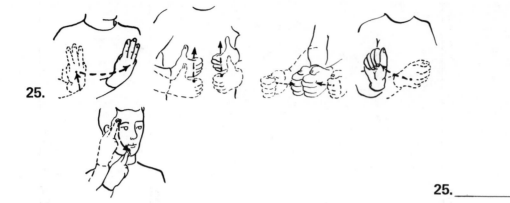

25. 25._____

C) Answers for Decoding Part (B), Lesson 38

Underlined words indicate that they should have been fingerspelled.

1. <u>DO</u> YOU (singular) EXERCISE EVERY MORNING?

2. CAN YOU (singular) EXPLAIN WHAT NERVE DEAFNESS IS?

3. WAS IT A BAD DREAM?

4. WHEN <u>DID</u> YOUR GRANDMOTHER DIE?

5. YOU (singular) DON'T HAVE <u>TO</u> DO IT FOREVER!

6. <u>DID</u> IT COST VERY MUCH?

7. WHO IS THE PRESIDENT <u>OF</u> YOUR UNIVERSITY?

8. I AM SAD BECAUSE I AM LEAVING.

9. <u>DRAW</u> A CIRCLE AROUND THIS WORD.

10. MY GRANDFATHER WAS AN AUDIOLOGIST.

11. WHY CAN'T WE JUMP ON THE <u>FURNITURE</u>?

12. YOU (singular) MAY <u>HANG</u> IT ON YOUR <u>WALL</u>.

13. DON'T FORGET <u>TO</u> <u>TAKE</u> YOUR UMBRELLA.

14. <u>DO</u> YOU (plural) HAVE ANY RELATIVES LIVING IN AMERICA?

15. WHY <u>DO</u> THEY ALWAYS TALK ABOUT REVENGE?

16. SHE IS IN MY AUDIOLOGY CLASS.

17. I DON'T WANT ANY GRAVY.

18. THIS MEAT IS SPOILED!

19. THE DOCTOR TOLD ME <u>TO</u> EXERCISE EVERY DAY.

20. THE PRESIDENT LIVES IN THE WHITE HOUSE.

21. CAN'T I DREAM ABOUT IT?

22. HOW MUCH WILL HE CHARGE US FOR IT?

23. <u>DRAW</u> A CIRCLE <u>AROUND</u> THE <u>LETTER</u> "T" IN THE WORD "WINTER."

24. IT SEEMS <u>TO</u> BE DIFFICULT.

25. WE LIVE WITH A RELATIVE.

lesson thirty-nine

Signs presented in this lesson are:

TEMPERATURE*	FREE	SATISFY	BLOCK (noun)
IRRITATED, CROSS	VINEGAR*	ABBREVIATE, CONDENSE	TURTLE*
COMMUNITY*	FISH (noun)	LET	PUSH
PREPARE, ARRANGE	PLAN	ALLOW	COUNT
BOUNCE*	THROW	PERMIT	PULL

TEMPERATURE*

The left hand, with only the index finger extended (remaining fingers and thumb are contracted), is held in front of the body with the index finger pointing upward and the back side of the hand facing the signer. The right hand, in the configuration of the letter *T*, first touches the side of the left index finger (contact is made between the side of the left index finger and the back side of the first joint of the right index finger). Next, the *T* hand slides downward, stopping near the base of the left index finger. This motion is repeated several times.

NOTE: The sign may intend to suggest, perhaps, the rise and fall of the mercury inside a thermometer.

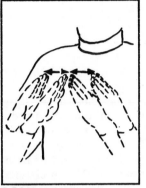

COMMUNITY*

The left hand, with the thumb and fingers extended and joined, is held in front of the body with the fingers, hand, and forearm pointing upward at about a 45-degree angle and the back of the left hand facing to the left at an angle. The right hand, in a similar configuration, is placed in front of the body and approximately four to five inches from the left hand. Then, with the configuration and angularity maintained, both hands are moved toward midline and touch their fingers. The hands then are separated and repeat the motion.

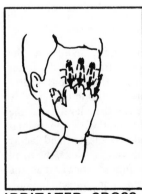

IRRITATED, CROSS

The right hand, with the thumb and fingers extended and apart, is placed in front of the face so that the back side of the hand is facing the viewer and the fingers are pointing upward. Next, the fingers and thumb are rapidly contracted, while the hand remains stationary.

NOTE: An appropriate facial expression may accompany this motion, expressing the degree of irritability.

PREPARE, ARRANGE

This sign is executed similarly to one on the next page ("plan"), except that the hand configuration is different. Both hands, each with the thumb extended vertically and the fingers both extended and joined, are placed about four to six inches apart in front and to the left side of the body. Both hands have their fingertips pointing to the viewer and their palmar surfaces facing each other. Next, with the configuration and parallelism maintained, both hands are moved to the right side of the body

437

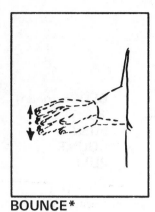

BOUNCE*

The right hand, with the thumb and fingers extended and joined, is held in front and to the right side of the body with the palm facing down and the fingers pointing to the viewer. Then, without bending the wrist, the forearm moves the hand up and down several times, imitative of how an imaginary ball would be bounced.

FISH (noun)

The right hand, with the thumb and fingers extended and joined, is held in front and to the right side of the body with the palm facing to the left and the fingers pointing to the viewer. The left hand, with the thumb and fingers extended and joined, first places its fingertips on the right wrist. Next, with contact maintained, both hands are moved forward as the fingers of the right hand make a waving motion, suggestive of the movement of a fish's tail.
NOTE: The sign for "fish" (verb) is made by imitating first the casting of a line into the water and then a reeling motion suggestive of winding up an imaginary line.

FREE

Both hands, each in the configuration of the letter *F*, are crossed at their wrists in front of the body (the side of the right hand wrist rests on the side of the left hand wrist). Both hands have their back sides facing the viewer, while their *F* fingers are pointing to the left and right. Then, the *F* hands are moved slightly downward and pulled apart laterally (clockwise for the right hand and counter-clockwise for the left one) so that now the *F* fingers are pointing to the viewer.
NOTE: This sign intends to suggest that the bound hands are now unbound.

PLAN

Both hands, each in the configuration of the letter *P*, are placed side-by-side in front and to the left side of the body with the back sides of both hands facing up. Next, with the configuration and parallelism maintained, both *P* hands are moved to the right side of the body.

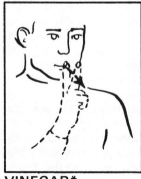

VINEGAR*

The right hand assumes the configuration of the letter *V* and is held approximately two inches in front of the lips with the *V* fingers pointing upward and the back sides of the hand facing to the right. Then, the *V* hand is moved toward and touches the lips. This motion is repeated several times.

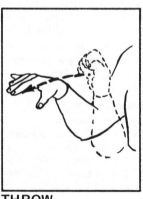

THROW

The right hand, in the configuration of the letter *O*, is held in front and to the right side of the body near the level of the shoulder with the palmar side of the *O* hand facing the viewer. Next, the hand is moved forward as the thumb and fingers fan out. The fingers point to the viewer as the sign comes to an end.

438 Signing

SATISFY

The left hand, with the thumb and fingers joined and with the fingers flexed at the base, is positioned in front of the body at the level of the neck. The fingers are pointing to the right and their palmar sides are facing down. The right hand, in a similar configuration, but with its fingers pointing to the left, is positioned on the level of the left hand and slightly in front of it (closer to the viewer). Then, with the configuration and distance between the hands maintained, both hands are moved toward and stop short of touching the signer's neck.

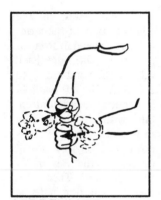

ABBREVIATE, CONDENSE

Both hands, each in the configuration of the letter C, are held about four to five inches apart in front of the body with their palmar sides facing each other; next, the C hands approach each other quickly as they change to an S configuration and finish with the right S hand on top of the left S hand. The backs of both S hands are facing to the right and left, respectively.

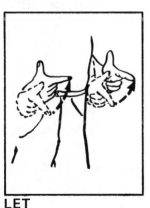

LET

Both hands, each in the configuration of the letter L, are placed on each side of the body near the waistline with the back sides of the hands facing sideways and the index fingers of the L hands pointing downward at an angle. Next, the L hands simultaneously are moved forward as their wrists flex them in a slightly upward direction so that now the index fingers of both L hands are pointing to the viewer.

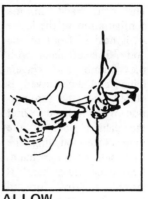

ALLOW

This sign is made similarly to the previous one ("let"), except that the hands first assume the configuration of the letter A, and are placed on each side of the body near the waistline. Next, the A hands simultaneously are moved forward as they change to an L configuration, with the wrists flexing the L hands in a slightly upward direction.

PERMIT

This sign is executed similarly to "let," except that the hands first assume the configuration of the letter P, and are placed on each side of the body near the waistline with the back sides of the P hands facing up. Then, the P hands simultaneously are moved forward as their wrists flex them slightly upward so that their index fingers are pointing at an upward angle as the sign comes to an end.

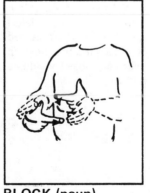

BLOCK (noun)

This sign is imitative of the four sides of a square block. First, the hands make the letter B and are positioned approximately six to eight inches apart in front of the body with their fingers pointing to the viewer and their palmar surfaces facing each other. Next, the hands change to an L configuration while moving so that now the right hand is approximately six to eight inches in front of the left one. Both L hands have their back sides facing the viewer and their thumbs are pointing upward, while their index fingers are pointing to the left and right, respectively.

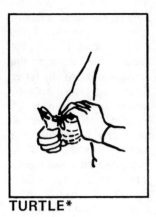

TURTLE*

The right hand, in the configuration of the letter *A*, is held in front of the body. The left hand, with the thumb and fingers joined and semi-curved, is placed over the top portion of the *A* hand so that the palmar sides of the fingers are touching the back side of the *A* hand. Next, the right hand is moved slightly forward from underneath the left hand, with the right thumb curving upward. This motion is repeated several times.

NOTE: This sign imitates how a turtle might first protrude and then withdraw his head back into his shell.

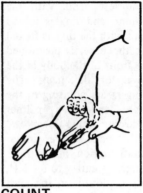

COUNT

The left hand, with the thumb and fingers extended and joined, is placed in front of the body with the palm facing up and the fingers pointing to the viewer. The right hand assumes the configuration of the letter *F*, which is placed on the left palm with the tips of the thumb and index finger touching it (the back side of the *F* hand is facing up). Then, the *F* hand slides across the left palm in the direction of the fingertips and comes to an end about three to four inches beyond the left hand.

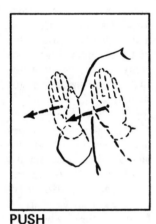

PUSH

Both hands, each with the thumb and fingers extended and joined, are held side-by-side in front of the body with their palmar sides facing the viewer and their fingertips pointing upward. Next, with the configuration maintained, the hands simultaneously are moved forward imitating how an imaginary object would be pushed.

PULL

The right hand, in the configuration of the letter *A*, is positioned in front of the body with the back side of the hand facing to the right. The left hand, in a similar configuration, but with its back side facing to the left, is positioned slightly ahead (closer to the viewer) of the right hand. Then, with the configuration and spatial positioning maintained, both *A* hands are drawn toward the signer.

A) Exercises in Encoding

Encode the following material using signs and fingerspelling. Use fingerspelling for all underlined words.

1. THE BOY IS PULLING HIS RED WAGON.
2. HELP US PUSH THIS TABLE TO THE NEXT ROOM.
3. DO YOU LIKE TURTLE SOUP?
4. THEY DON'T PERMIT US TO SIGN AT SCHOOL.
5. WE DON'T ALLOW HER TO PLAY WITH OTHER CHILDREN BECAUSE SHE IS DEAF.
6. DO YOU EVER LET HER TRY TO DO IT BY HERSELF?
7. THE FOOD HAS TOO MUCH VINEGAR IN IT.
8. PLEASE TRY TO CONDENSE IT FOR US.
9. HE IS ALWAYS COUNTING HIS MONEY!
10. JANE IS THROWING THE BALL.
11. WHO IS BOUNCING THE BALL?
12. DO YOU WANT TO PLAY WITH THE BLOCKS?
13. WHO KNOWS THE NAME OF THIS FISH?
14. WHY CAN'T WE EVER SATISFY THEM?
15. I AM A FREE MAN!
16. DID YOU HELP PREPARE THE PROGRAM?
17. I CAN ARRANGE FOR YOU TO SEE HIM.
18. DID YOU PLAN ANYTHING FOR THERAPY?
19. WHY ARE THEY CROSS WITH US?
20. HOW MANY MEN DID YOU SEE? ("Men" is signed similarly to "man," except that an additional movement is required—see lesson 30.)
21. IS THERE A DEAF COMMUNITY NEAR YOU?
22. AT WHAT TEMPERATURE WILL WATER BEGIN TO BOIL?
23. LET HER COUNT IT BY HERSELF.
24. YOU ARE NOT PERMITTED TO THROW THINGS!
25. YES, YOUR ANSWER DID SATISFY US.

B) Exercises in Decoding

Decode the following illustrated exercises:

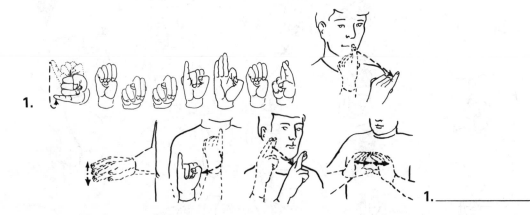

1. _____

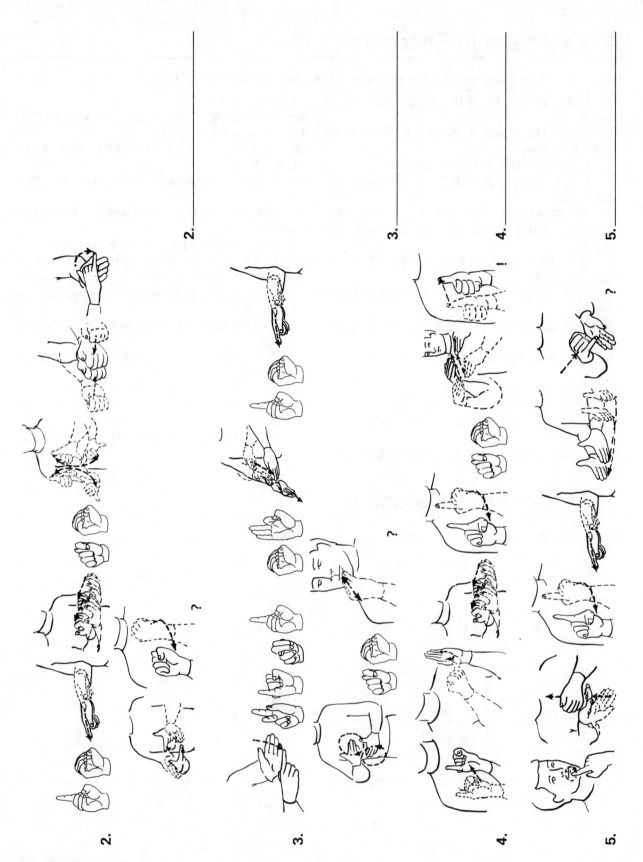

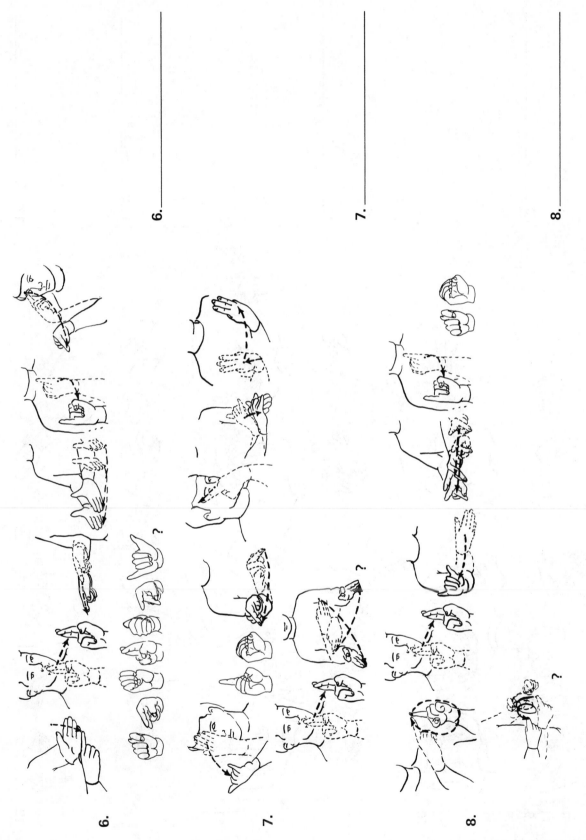

6.

7.

8.

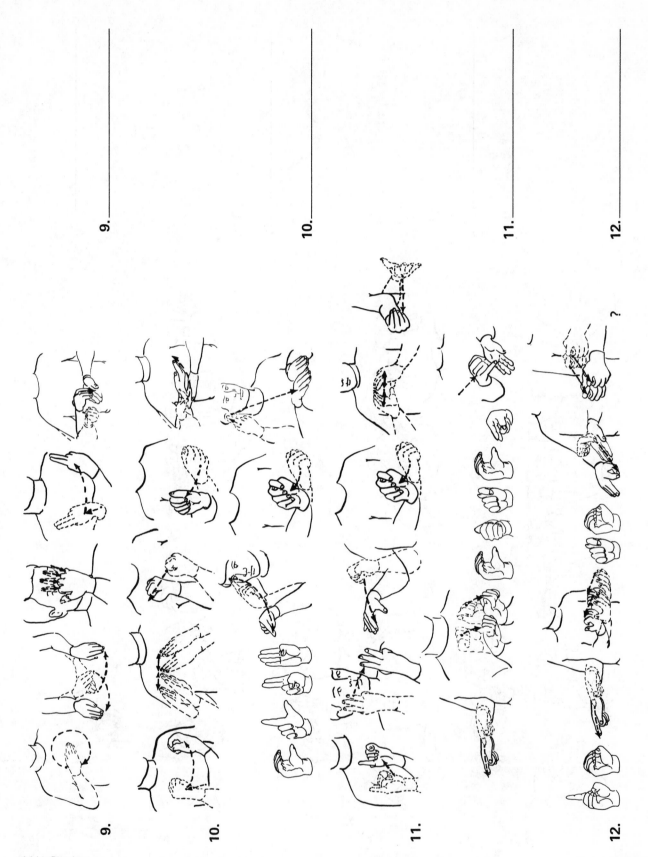

9.

10.

11.

12.

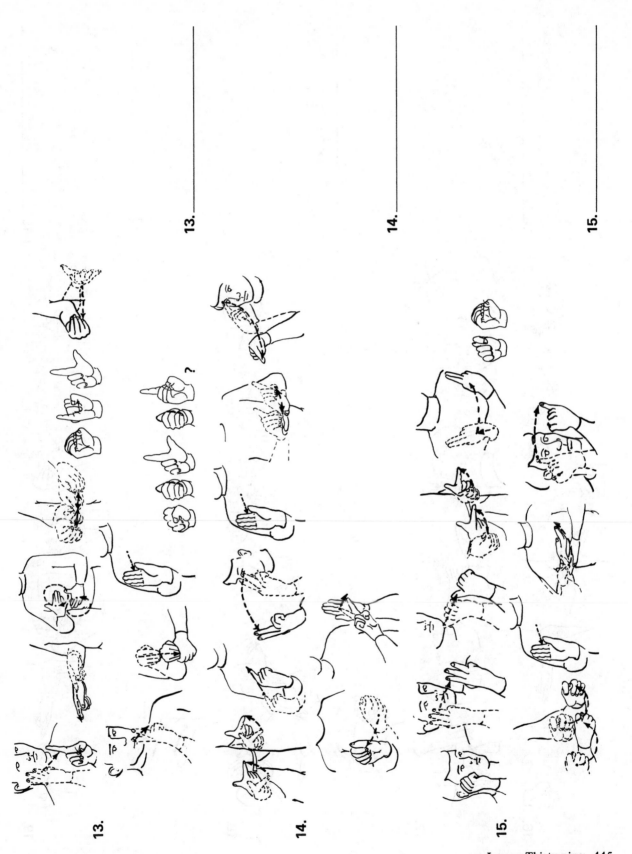

13.

14.

15.

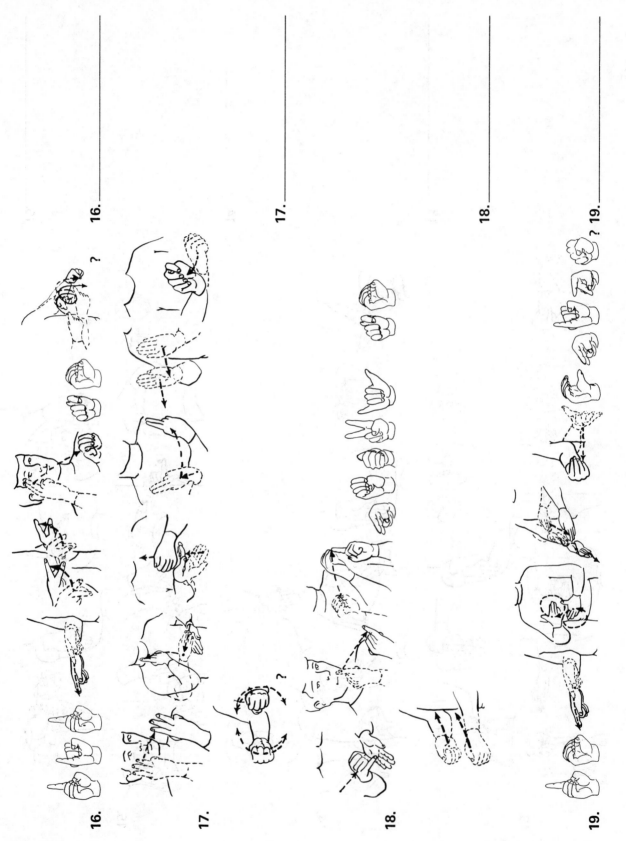

16.

17.

18.

? 19.

16.

17.

18.

19.

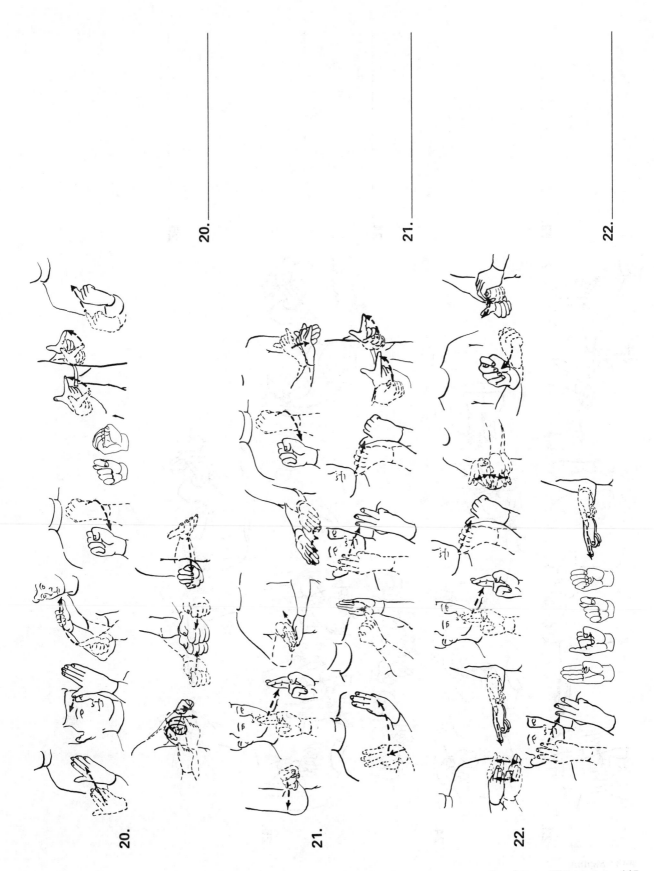

20.

21.

22.

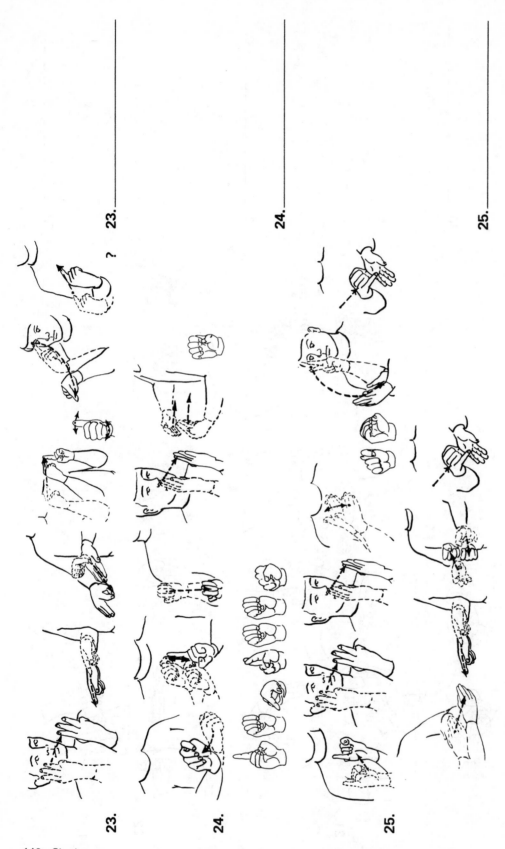

23.

24.

25.

C) Answers for Decoding Part (B), Lesson 39

Underlined words indicate that they should have been fingerspelled.

1. <u>JENNIFER</u> IS BOUNCING HER BALL.
2. <u>DO</u> YOU (singular) WANT <u>TO</u> PLAY WITH THESE BLOCKS?
3. WHAT <u>KIND</u> <u>OF</u> FISH <u>DO</u> YOU LIKE <u>TO</u> EAT?
4. I JUST WANTED <u>TO</u> SATISFY MYSELF!
5. WHO HELPED YOU (singular) ARRANGE IT?
6. WHAT ARE YOU PREPARING FOR <u>THERAPY</u>?
7. WHY <u>DO</u> YOU (plural) THINK THAT WE ARE FREE?
8. WHEN ARE THEY PLANNING <u>TO</u> COME?
9. PLEASE DON'T CROSS US AGAIN.
10. OUR COMMUNITY HAS A NEW <u>CLUB</u> FOR THE DEAF.
11. I WILL THROW THE BALL AND YOU CAN <u>CATCH</u> IT.
12. <u>DO</u> YOU WANT <u>TO</u> COUNT TOGETHER?
13. WOULD YOU LIKE MORE <u>OIL</u> AND VINEGAR IN YOUR <u>SALAD</u>?
14. LET ME SEE YOUR DICTIONARY FOR A MINUTE.
15. SHE WILL NOT ALLOW US <u>TO</u> TRY YOUR NEW IDEA.
16. <u>DID</u> YOU (singular) PERMIT HIM <u>TO</u> GO?
17. WILL SOMEONE HELP US PUSH THE CAR?
18. IT IS TOO <u>HEAVY</u> <u>TO</u> PULL.
19 <u>DO</u> YOU (singular) LIKE FISH AND <u>CHIPS</u>?
20 MY FATHER REFUSES <u>TO</u> LET ME GO WITH THEM.
21. THERE ARE SOME THINGS THAT WE JUST WILL NOT ALLOW.
22. IF YOU (singular) ARE NOT CAREFUL, THE TURTLE WILL <u>BITE</u> YOU (singular).
23. WILL YOU (singular) COUNT TO TEN FOR ME?
24. THE TEMPERATURE MUST BE NEAR ZERO <u>DEGREES</u>.
25. I WILL BE HAPPY <u>TO</u> READ IT AFTER YOU CONDENSE IT.

lesson forty

Signs presented in this lesson are:

ANGER	ROLL (verb)	BICYCLE	DRESS (verb)
TAKE	WARM	ICE	BUTTON (noun)
FOOTBALL*	BATTLE*	KISS	RAIN*
CATCH	WAR*	WELCOME	STRONG
SUCCEED, SUCCESS	BELL*	SCISSORS*	SNOW

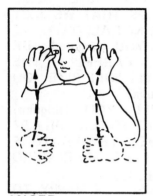

ANGER

Both hands, with their thumbs and fingers apart and curved, are positioned approximately four to five inches from each other in front of the body at the level of the abdomen with their back sides facing the viewer. Next, with the configuration maintained, the hands simultaneously are moved upward as the wrists turn the hands outward. Both hands are positioned in front of the signer's face, with the fingertips pointing to the signer as the sign comes to an end.

NOTE: This sign may be imitative, perhaps, of a "quick flare up." An appropriate facial expression may accompany this sign indicating the degree of anger. Please note that the sign for "angry" may be made by signing "anger" and fingerspelling the letter "Y."

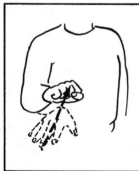

TAKE

The right hand, with the thumb and fingers extended and apart, is positioned in front and slightly to the right side of the body with its back side facing up and the fingers pointing to the viewer at a downward angle; next, the hand is pulled toward the signer, while clenching into a fist.

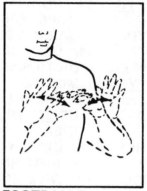

FOOTBALL*

Both hands, each with the thumb and fingers extended and apart, are positioned approximately six inches from each other in front of the body with the fingers pointing upward at about a 45-degree angle toward the midline and their palmar surfaces facing each other at an angle. Next, both hands simultaneously are bent toward each other so that their fingers become interlocked. Then, the hands separate and quickly repeat the motion.

NOTE: This sign is imitative of the contact which is made between the members of the two opposing teams once the ball is snapped.

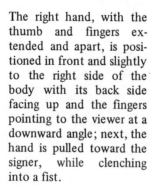

CATCH

The left forearm is stretched across the body and is held about eight to ten inches in front of the body with the hand in a fist position and facing down. The right hand, with the thumb and fingers extended and apart, is held above the left *S* hand with its fingers pointing upward and the palm facing the viewer. Then, the right hand clenches into a fist as it is tilted forward and its knuckles make contact with the back side of the left hand.

450

SUCCEED, SUCCESS

Both hands, each with only the index finger extended (remaining fingers and thumb are contracted), touch both cheeks simultaneously with their index fingertips (the back sides of the index fingers are facing up). Next, with the configuration preserved, both hands simultaneously create two *concave* arcs as they are raised upward.

NOTE: This sign often is confused with "'famous," lesson 34. For "famous" the index fingers touch the cheeks, and then the hands create two *convex* arcs as they are raised upward.

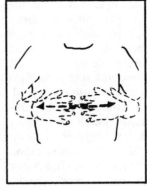

BATTLE*

Both hands, with their thumbs and fingers extended and apart, are held approximately three to four inches apart in front of the body with their back sides facing the viewer and their fingertips pointing at each other. Then, both hands simultaneously are moved toward each other, but do not touch. The hands then are returned to their original position and the motion is repeated.

NOTE: This sign may be imitative, perhaps, of two opposing camps at odds with each other.

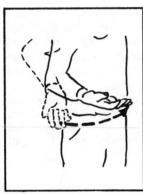

ROLL (verb)

The right hand, with the thumb and fingers apart and slightly cupped, is held near the right side of the body at the level of the waistline with the palmar side facing the viewer. Next, the hand is moved forward and swings slightly upward.

NOTE: This sign is imitative of rolling an imaginary ball.

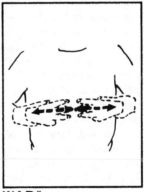

WAR*

This sign is made similarly to the previous one ("battle"), except that the hands are in the configuration of the letter *W*. The *W* hands, with their back sides toward the viewer and their fingertips pointing at each other, are moved toward each other along a horizontal plane. The hands then are returned to their original position and the motion is repeated.

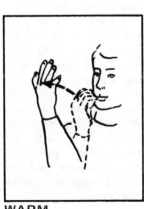

WARM

The right hand, in the configuration of the letter *O*, is placed over the lips so that the fingertips of the *O* hand are touching the lips. Next, the right hand is moved forward and slightly upward as the fingers and thumb are extended, separated and pointing upward, with the back side of the hand facing the viewer.

BELL*

The right hand, with the thumb bending inward to touch the joined and slightly curved fingers, is held in front and to the right side of the body with its back side facing up. Next, with the configuration maintained, the hand is moved to execute several quick side-to-side movements, imitative of ringing an imaginary bell.

BICYCLE

The right hand, in the configuration of the letter *S*, is positioned in front of the body with the wrist facing down. The left hand, in a similar configuration, is positioned parallel with, and farther forward (closer to the viewer) than the right hand. Next, with the configuration maintained, both *S* hands alternately complete circular movements forward, imitative of peddling a bicycle.

WELCOME

The right hand, in the configuration of the letter *W*, is positioned in front and to the right side of the body with the fingers pointing to the viewer and the back side of the *W* hand facing to the right. Next, with the configuration maintained, the hand is rotated clockwise as it is moved toward midline. The sign ends with the back side of the *W* hand facing down and the fingers pointing to the viewer at an angle to the left.

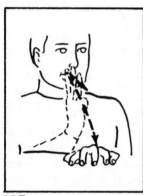

ICE

This sign is executed in two steps. *Step one:* The right hand makes the sign for "water" as described in lesson 13. That is, the right hand, in the configuration of the letter *W*, is moved in and touches the lips several times (contact is made between the lips and the side of the index finger of the *W* hand. *Step two:* The *W* hand twists as it is moved forward and downward with the thumb and fingers assuming a claw-like formation. The back side of the hand is facing up as the sign comes to an end.

SCISSORS*

The right hand, in the configuration of the letter *V*, is held in front and slightly to the right side of the body with the *V* fingers pointing to the right. Next, the index and middle fingers are joined and separated several times as the *V* hand is moved forward.

NOTE: This action may be imitative, perhaps, of the opening and closing of a pair of blades.

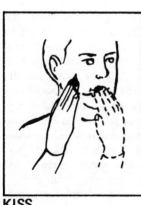

KISS

The right hand, with the thumb and fingers extended, joined and pointing upward, first is moved toward and touches the signer's lips (contact is made between the lips and the palmar sides of the fingers). Then, with the configuration maintained, the right hand is moved to the right and touches the signer's cheek.

DRESS (verb)

Both hands, each with the thumb and fingers extended and apart, are positioned side-by-side on the signer's chest with only the palmar sides of their fingers touching the chest. Both hands have their thumbs pointing upward and the fingers facing midline. Next, with the configuration preserved, the fingers graze the body as both hands are turned downward.

452 Signing

BUTTON (noun)

The right hand, in the configuration of the letter *F*, first is placed against the chest with the fingers pointing upward and the palmar side of the *F* hand facing to the left. Next, with the configuration maintained, the *F* hand makes a small, forward arc motion as it is moved downward and touches the lower portion of the signer's chest.

STRONG

Both hands, each in the configuration of the letter *S*, are held in front of the body at the level of the lower chest with their back sides facing the viewer. Next, with the configuration preserved, both *S* hands simultaneously execute an upward arc movement forward.

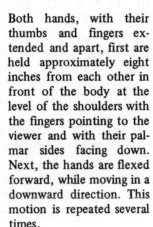

RAIN*

Both hands, with their thumbs and fingers extended and apart, first are held approximately eight inches from each other in front of the body at the level of the shoulders with the fingers pointing to the viewer and with their palmar sides facing down. Next, the hands are flexed forward, while moving in a downward direction. This motion is repeated several times.

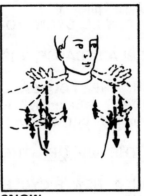

SNOW

Both hands, with their thumbs and fingers extended and apart, first are held approximately eight inches from each other in front of the body at the level of the shoulders with the fingers pointing at the viewer and their palmar sides facing down. Next, without bending their wrists, the hands simultaneously are moved downward as their fingers execute small wiggling motions, imitative of falling snow flakes.

A) Exercises in Encoding

Encode the following material using signs and fingerspelling. Use fingerspelling for all underlined words.

1. CAN YOU HEAR THE BELL WITHOUT YOUR HEARING AID?
2. WE ARE AGAINST WARS.
3. IS IT IMPORTANT <u>TO</u> REMEMBER WHO WON THE BATTLE?
4. WHY ARE YOU TRYING <u>TO</u> ANGER ME AGAIN?
5. IS HE ANGRY WITH ME OR YOU? ("Angry" is signed as "anger" plus "Y.")
6. <u>DO</u> YOU THINK IT WILL SNOW TO-MORROW?
7. USE YOUR UMBRELLA BECAUSE IT IS RAINING.
8. <u>DID</u> YOU WATCH THE FOOTBALL <u>GAME</u> LAST SATURDAY? ("Saturday" is signed similarly to "Monday," but with an *S* hand.)
9. PLEASE <u>SCRAPE</u> THE ICE <u>OFF</u> THE CAR WINDOW.
10. <u>DID</u> HE BUY YOU A NEW BICYCLE FOR YOUR BIRTHDAY?
11. <u>DO</u> YOU HAVE A PAIR <u>OF</u> SCISSORS IN YOUR ROOM?
12. HOW MANY BUTTONS <u>DOES</u> YOUR COAT HAVE?
13. I DON'T FEEL VERY STRONG NOW BECAUSE I HAVE BEEN SICK.
14. IF YOU PRACTICE EVERY DAY, YOU WILL SUCCEED.
15. IS THE WATER WARM YET?
16. TAKE THE <u>TOY</u> OUT <u>OF</u> THE BOX.
17. WATCH HOW HE CATCHES THE BALL.
18. DOES YOUR FRIEND SNOW <u>SKI</u>?
19. IS THE BOY BOUNCING OR ROLLING THE BALL?
20. WE CAN SAY THAT IT WAS A SUCCESS.
21. WHAT <u>DO</u> YOU WANT ME <u>TO</u> DO WITH THE SCISSORS?
22. HE WILL GET ANGRY IF YOU ARE LATE FOR HIS CLASS. ("Get" is signed as "become.")
23. YOU ARE WELCOME <u>TO</u> COME TO OUR HOUSE FOR LUNCH. ("Lunch" is signed as "eat" plus "noon.")
24. MAY I KISS YOUR BABY?
25. YOUR GRANDMOTHER IS WELCOME <u>TO</u> <u>STAY</u> OVERNIGHT.

B) Exercises in Decoding

Decode the following illustrated exercises:

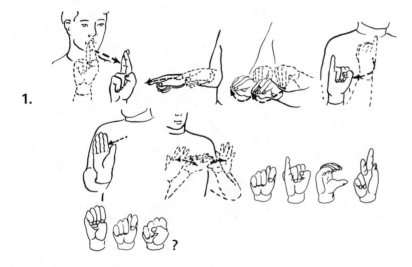

1.

1. _____

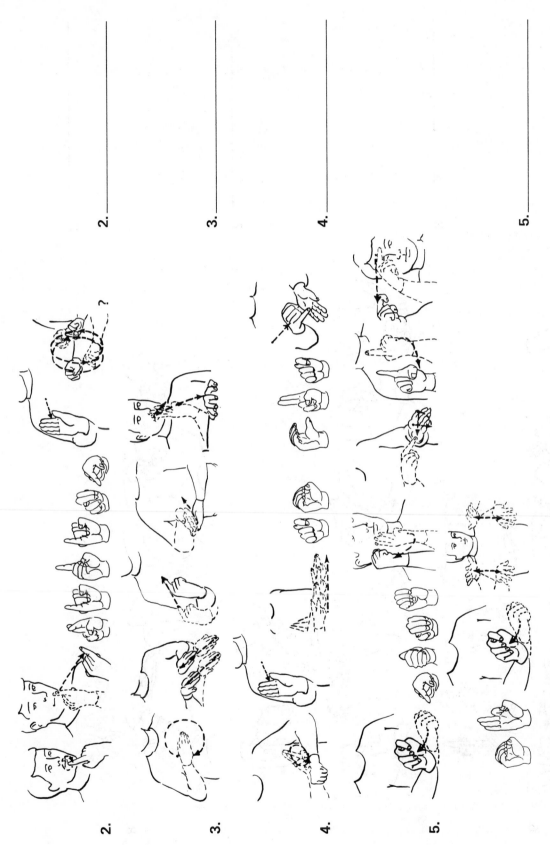

2.

3.

4.

5.

2.

3.

4.

5.

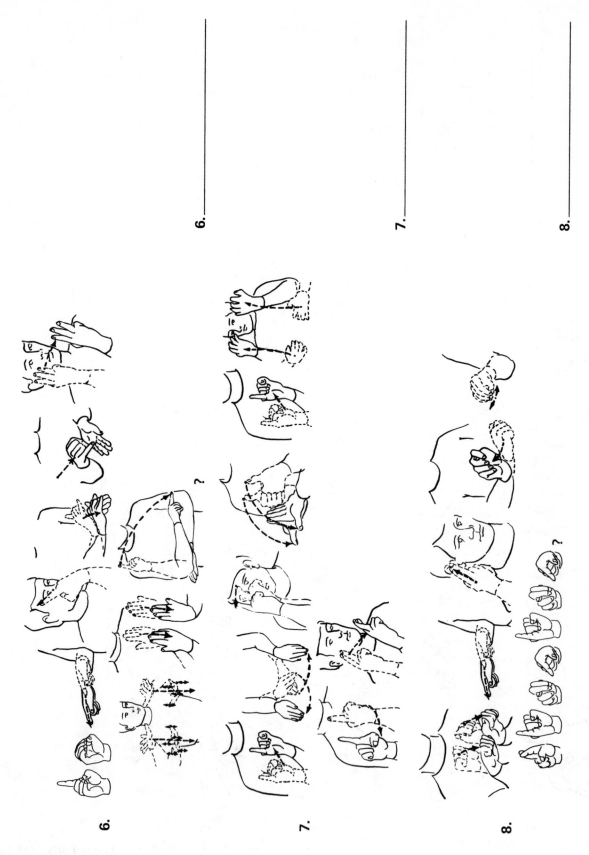

6.

7.

8.

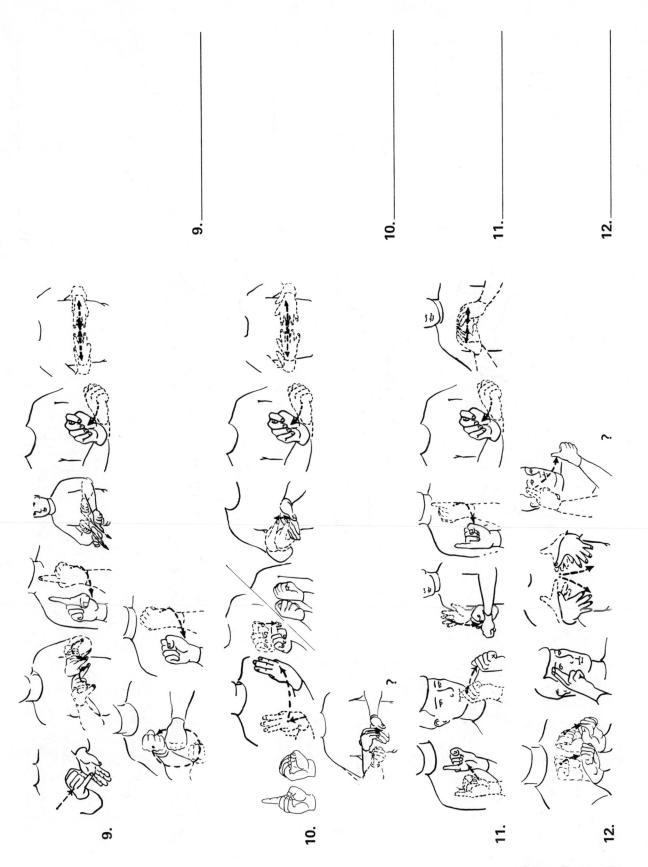

9.

10.

11.

12.

9.

10.

11.

12.

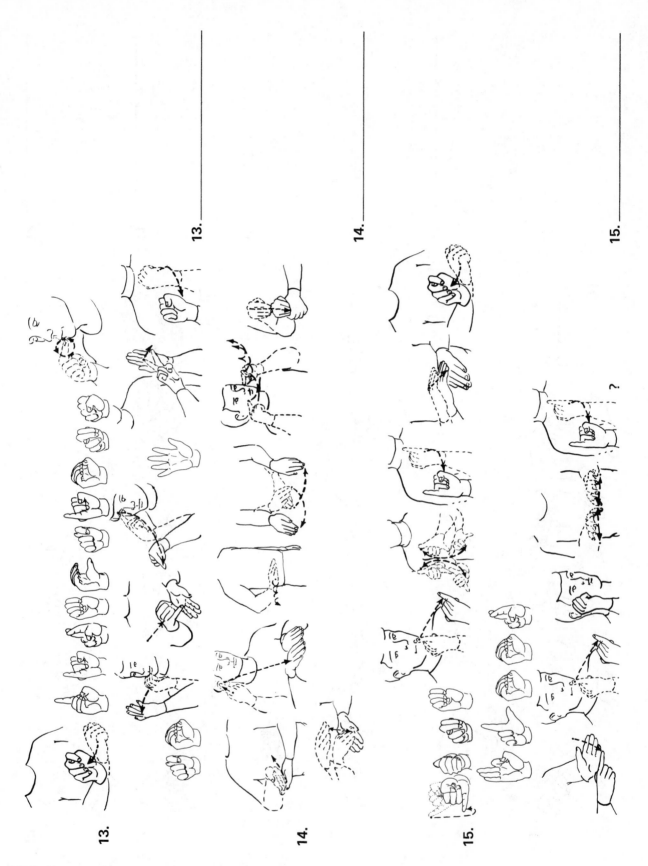

13.

14.

15.

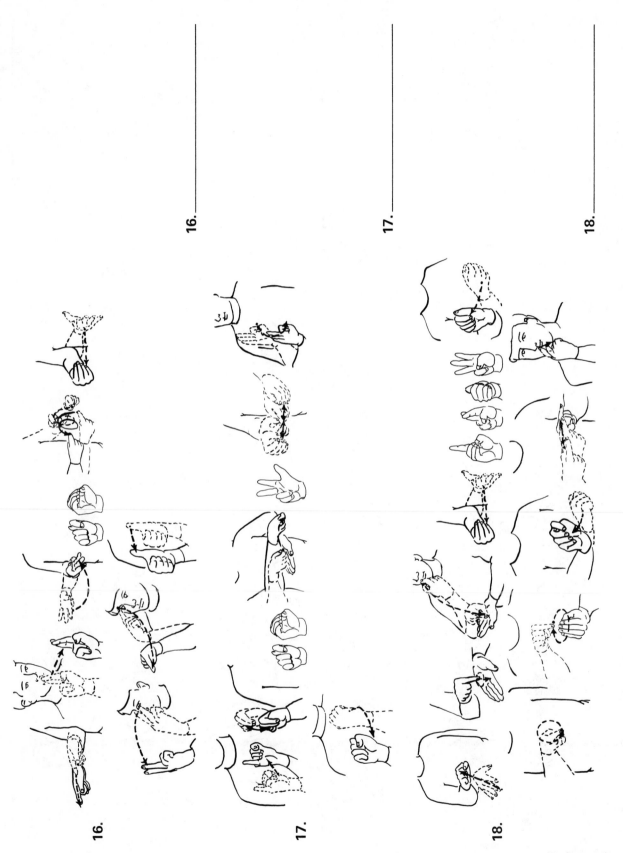

16.

17.

18.

16.

17.

18.

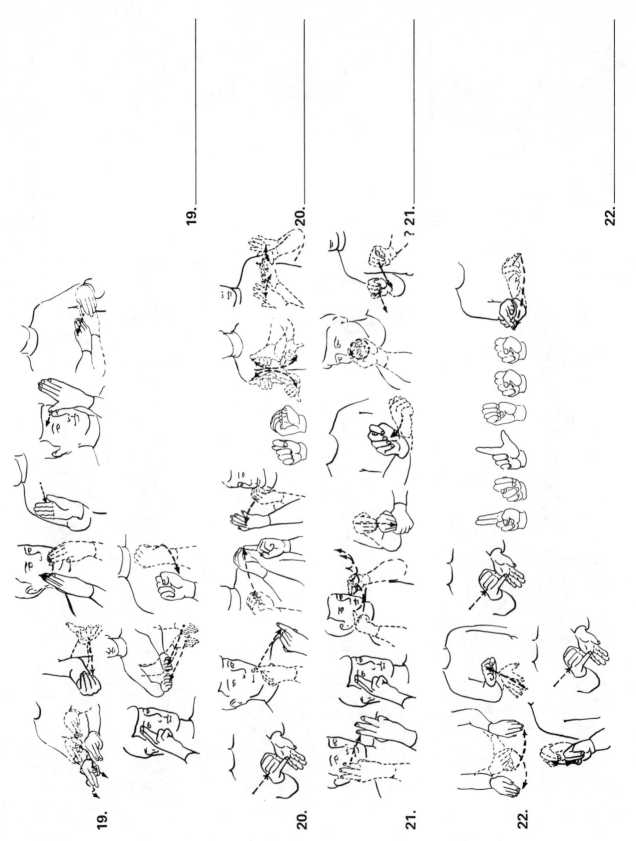

19.

20.

? 21.

22.

19.

20.

21.

22.

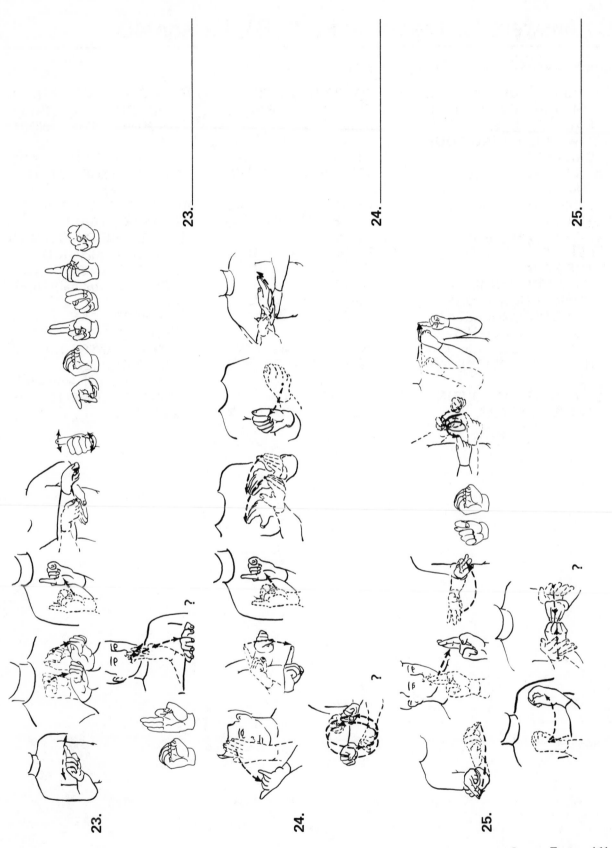

23.

24.

25.

23.

24.

25.

C) Answers for Decoding Part (B), Lesson 40

Underlined words indicate that they should have been fingerspelled.

1. ARE YOU (singular) SELLING YOUR FOOT-BALL <u>TICKETS</u>?

2. WHO IS <u>RIDING</u> YOUR BICYCLE?

3. PLEASE BRING ME SOME ICE.

4. USE YOUR SCISSORS <u>TO CUT</u> IT.

5. THE <u>GAME</u> WAS CAN-CELLED BECAUSE <u>OF</u> THE RAIN.

6. <u>DO</u> YOU THINK THAT IT WILL SNOW TODAY?

7. I DON'T UNDERSTAND HOW I ANGERED HER.

8. CAN YOU (singular) HEAR THE BELL <u>RING-ING</u>?

9. IT HAPPENED DURING THE WAR YEARS.

10. <u>DO</u> WE HAVE TO DIS-CUSS THE BATTLE AGAIN?

11. I AM CATCHING THE BALL.

12. CAN HE DRESS HIM-SELF?

13. THE <u>DIRECTIONS</u> SAY <u>TO</u> WARM IT FOR FIVE MINUTES.

14. SOME DEAF CHIL-DREN DON'T SUCCEED IN SCHOOL.

15. <u>JANE</u> IS PLAYING ON THE <u>FLOOR</u>. WHAT IS SHE DOING?

16. YOU ARE WELCOME <u>TO</u> COME AND SEE FOR YOURSELF.

17. I NEED <u>TO</u> BUY THREE MORE BUTTONS.

18. TAKE THIS PENCIL AND <u>DRAW</u> A CIRCLE AROUND THE WORD "RED."

19. HURRY AND KISS YOUR FATHER BEFORE HE LEAVES.

20. IT IS TOO WARM <u>TO</u> PLAY FOOTBALL.

21. WILL HE SUCCEED IN THE ORAL METHOD?

22. DON'T TAKE IT <u>UN-LESS</u> YOU (plural) NEED IT.

23. WHERE CAN I BUY TEN <u>POUNDS</u> OF ICE?

24. WHY CAN'T I HAVE A NEW BICYCLE?

25. YOU (plural) ARE WEL-COME <u>TO</u> COME TO OUR MEETING.

lesson forty-one

Signs presented in this lesson are:

TROUBLE	HUSBAND	LIST (noun)	RAT
REPRESENT	WIFE	GLOVE	WET*
WORRY	MARRY	DROP	REBEL, REVOLT
CALL, SUMMON	STAY, REMAIN	SOFT*	MOUTH
HUMBLE	SINK (noun)	WED	CURRICULUM

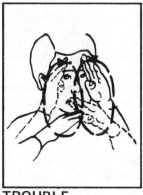

TROUBLE

The left hand, in the configuration of the letter *B*, is positioned in front of the signer's chin with the fingers pointing upward at about a 45-degree angle and the palm facing to the right. The right hand, also in the configuration of the letter *B*, is positioned in front and to the right side of the face with the fingertips pointing upward at an angle while the palm faces to the left. Next, with the configuration preserved and without flexing the hands, both *B* hands alternately complete a circular movement along a vertical plane in front of the face.

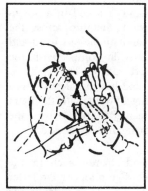

WORRY

The left hand, in the configuration of the letter *W*, is positioned in front of the signer's chin with the fingertips pointing upward at about a 45-degree angle and the palm facing to the right. The right hand, also in the configuration of the letter *W*, is positioned in front and to the right side of the face with the fingertips pointing upward at an angle with the palm facing to the left; next, with the configuration preserved and without flexing the hands, both *W* hands alternately complete a circular movement along a vertical plane in front of the signer's face.

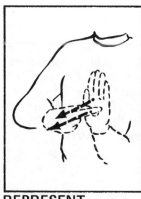

REPRESENT

The left hand, with the thumb and fingers extended and joined, is held in front and slightly to the left side of the body with the fingers pointing upward and the palmar side facing the viewer. The right hand, in the configuration of the letter *R*, touches the left palm with its *R* fingertips (the right hand is held with the fingers pointing left and the back side toward the viewer); next, with the contact maintained, both hands are moved toward the viewer.

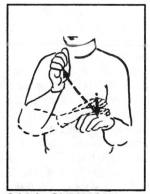

CALL, SUMMON

The left hand, with the thumb and fingers joined, slightly curved and pointing downward at an angle, is held in front and to the left side of the body with the palm side facing down. The right hand, with the thumb and fingers extended and joined, slaps the back side of the left hand with the palmar side of the fingers and then the right hand is pulled upward at an oblique angle in the direction of the right shoulder, while assuming the configuration of the letter *A*.

463

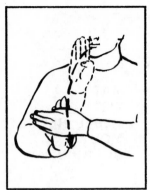

HUMBLE

The left hand, with the thumb and fingers extended and joined, is held in front of the body with the fingers pointing to the right and the back side of the hand facing the viewer. The right hand forms the letter *B*; the index finger edge of the right *B* hand first is touched to the signer's lips, and then the outside edge of the right *B* hand is sliced in a downward direction across the palm of the left hand and rests in contact with the left palm. The right *B* hand has the fingers pointing upward with the palm facing to the left as the sign comes to an end.

MARRY

The left hand, with the thumb extended and pointing upward with the remaining fingers joined and cupped slightly, is positioned in front of the body with the palmar side facing to the right. The right hand, in a similar configuration and in the same plane, is placed approximately six to seven inches from the left hand so that their palmar sides are facing one another. Next, both hands are moved toward midline and clasp one another.

NOTE: This sign intends to suggest the creation of unity between two people.

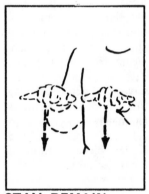

STAY, REMAIN

Both hands, each in the configuration of the letter *Y*, are placed side-by-side in front of the body with the wrists facing down and the little fingers of the *Y* hands pointing to the viewer; next, with the configuration preserved and without flexing the wrists, the hands simultaneously are pulled downward.

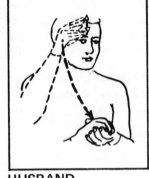

HUSBAND

This sign is made by combining the signs for "boy" (lesson 3) and "marry." First, make the sign for "boy," followed by the sign for "marry."

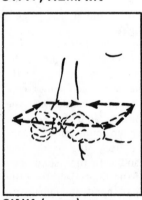

SINK (noun)

In this sign, the hands depict a "sink" by making the outline of a square in front of the body. First, both hands assume the configuration of the letter *S* and are placed in front of the body with the sides of the thumbs touching and with the backs facing right and left. Then, the *S* hands separate sideways (to the right and left). From this position, the *S* hands are moved toward the body, followed by coming together again at the midline.

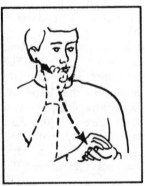

WIFE

This sign is made by combining the signs for "girl" (lesson 5) and "marry." First, make the sign for "girl," followed by the sign for "marry."

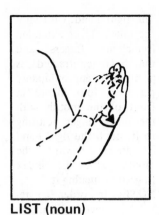

LIST (noun)

The left hand, with the thumb and fingers extended and joined, is held in front and to the left side of the body with the fingers pointing upward and with the palmar side facing to the right. The right hand, with the thumb and fingers extended and joined, first touches the fingertips of the left hand. (The right hand fingers are pointing to the left with the back side facing up.) The right hand makes three to four small skipping movements as it is moved from the fingertips toward the wrist area of the left hand.

SOFT*

The left hand, with the thumb and fingers apart and slightly flexed, is positioned in front of the body with the fingers pointing slightly upward at an angle and the back of the hand facing down. The right hand, in a similar configuration, is positioned parallel to, and several inches apart from the left hand. Next, both hands are moved slightly downward as each hand cups the fingers and flexes the thumb to touch the joined fingers. This motion is repeated several times.

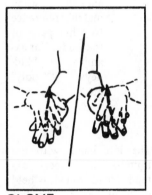

GLOVE

The left hand, with the thumb and fingers extended and apart, is held in front of the body with the fingers pointing downward at about a 45-degree angle with the palm facing down. The right hand, with the thumb and fingers extended and apart, is laid on top of the left hand with the fingers pointing downward in the direction of the left wrist. The hands then exchange spatial positions and repeat the motion.

NOTE: This sign is imitative of putting on a pair of gloves.

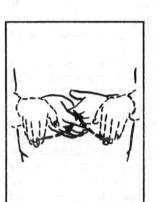

WED

Both hands, with only the thumbs extended and slightly apart (remaining fingers are extended and joined), are placed side-by-side in front of the body with the fingers pointing downward and the palmar sides facing the signer. Next, the wrists tilt both hands toward each other so that the fingers of the left hand are clasped by the thumb and forefingers of the right hand.

NOTE: This sign is used metonymically. That is, the act of joining (hands) is used to represent the wedding (joining) of two people.

DROP

Both hands, in the configuration of the letter *S*, are positioned side-by-side in front of the body with the back sides facing up; next, both hands simultaneously are moved slightly downward as the thumbs and fingers are fanned out.

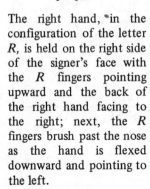

RAT

The right hand, *in the configuration of the letter *R*, is held on the right side of the signer's face with the *R* fingers pointing upward and the back of the right hand facing to the right; next, the *R* fingers brush past the nose as the hand is flexed downward and pointing to the left.

WET*

This sign is made by combining the signs for "water" (lesson 13) and "soft" which is described in this lesson. The left hand, with the thumb and fingers apart and slightly flexed, is positioned in front of the body with the back side of the hand facing down. The right hand, in the configuration of the letter *W*, is positioned in front of the mouth with the fingers pointing upward and the back of the right hand facing to the right; next, the index finger of the *W* hand touches the lips, then the hand is moved forward (with the fingers and thumb now being apart and slightly flexed) and is placed parallel to and about four or five inches from the left hand with the back facing down. Then, the hands simultaneously are moved slightly downward as each hand flexes the thumb and touches the joined fingers. The latter motion is repeated several times.

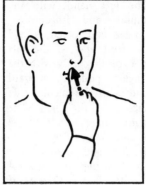

MOUTH

The right hand, with only the index finger extended (remaining fingers and thumb are contracted), is positioned approximately three to four inches in front of the mouth with the index finger pointing to it; next, the right hand is drawn toward the mouth with the index fingertip touching it.

NOTE: In order to reduce misunderstanding, fingerspell "mouth" as soon as you finish pointing to it. This practice of "pointing," followed by fingerspelling may be applied when making reference to other parts of the body. For example, "kidneys," "foot," etc.

REBEL, REVOLT

The right hand assumes the configuration of the letter *S* and is held in front and to the right side of the body at the level of the shoulder with the back side of the *S* hand facing the viewer; next, the wrist is quickly rotated as the *S* hand makes an arc motion upward. The sign ends with the back side of the *S* hand facing the signer.

CURRICULUM

The left hand, with the thumb and fingers extended and joined, is held in front and to the left side of the body with the fingers pointing upward and the palmar side facing to the right. The right hand first makes the letter *C* and touches the left hand near the fingertips (the back side of the *C* hand is facing the signer). Then, the *C* hand is moved downward toward the palm of the left hand while changing its configuration to the letter *M*.

A) Exercises in Encoding

Encode the following material using signs and fingerspelling. Use fingerspelling for all underlined words.

1. WE ARE IN TROUBLE AND NEED YOUR HELP.
2. STOP WORRYING ABOUT IT.
3. <u>DO</u> WE WANT SOMEONE <u>TO</u> REPRESENT OUR GROUP?
4. <u>DID</u> YOU <u>LOOK</u> INTO HER MOUTH?
5. HE WAS <u>MOST</u> HUMBLE ABOUT IT.
6. ARE YOU AFRAID <u>TO</u> MARRY A DEAF PERSON?
7. STAY WITH US UNTIL THIS AFTERNOON.
8. WHERE <u>DOES</u> YOUR HUSBAND WORK?
9. <u>DID</u> YOUR WIFE <u>GRADUATE</u> FROM GALLAUDET?
10. DON'T TOUCH IT BECAUSE IT IS WET.
11. PLEASE BE VERY CAREFUL NOT <u>TO</u> DROP IT.
12. CAN YOU WASH THEM IN THE SINK?
13. WHERE IS THE OTHER GLOVE?
14. THE MEETING WAS ABOUT CURRICU-LUM DEVELOPMENT. ("Development" is signed as "develop" plus "ment.")
15. IS OUR CURRICULUM HELPING DEAF CHILDREN?
16. I JUST SAW A RAT UNDER YOUR DOOR.
17. WHEN <u>DO</u> THEY PLAN <u>TO</u> WED?
18. <u>DO</u> YOU LIKE SOFT BREAD?
19. HE NEVER WEARS HIS GLOVES.
20. WHY <u>DID</u> THE PRISONERS REBEL? ("Prisoners" is signed as "prison" plus "er" plus "s.")
21. I AM AFRAID <u>TO</u> STAY IN THE HOUSE BY MYSELF.
22. I FORGOT <u>TO</u> BRING THE LIST WITH ME.
23. IF IT IS IMPORTANT, WE WILL HAVE <u>TO</u> SUMMON THEM.
24. IF YOU DON'T DO IT, I WILL WORRY ABOUT IT.

B) Exercises in Decoding

Decode the following illustrated exercises:

1.

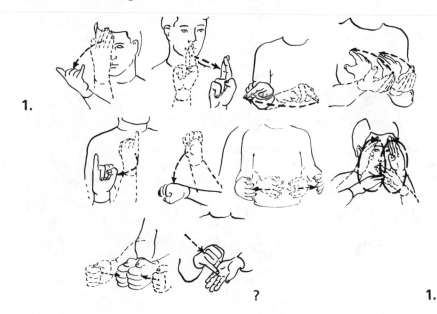

?

1._____

6.

7.

8.

9.

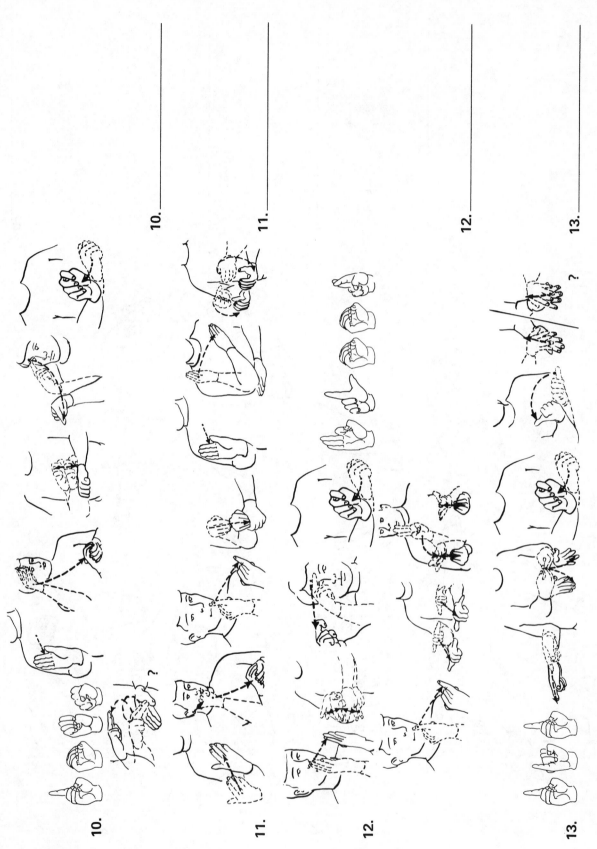

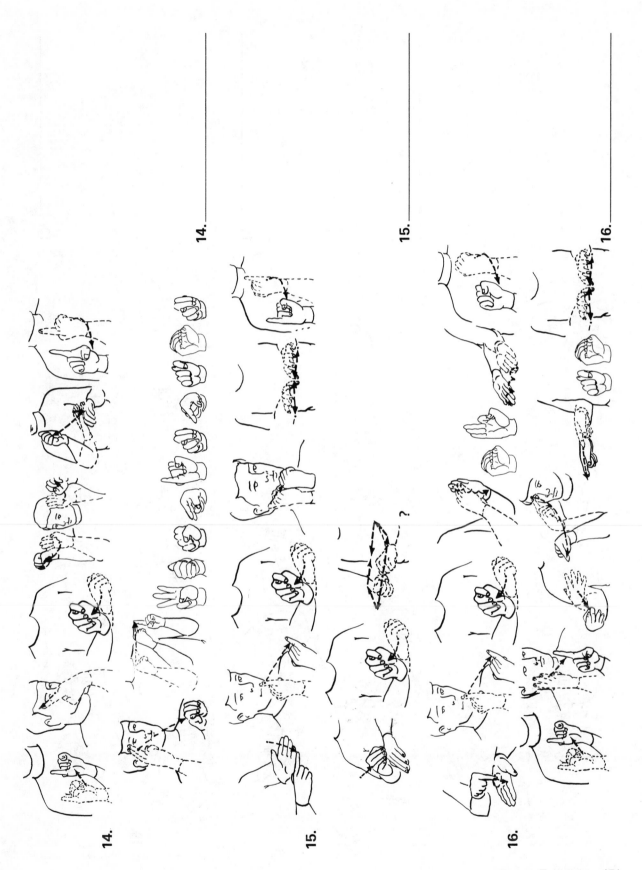

14.

15.

16.

17.

18.

19.

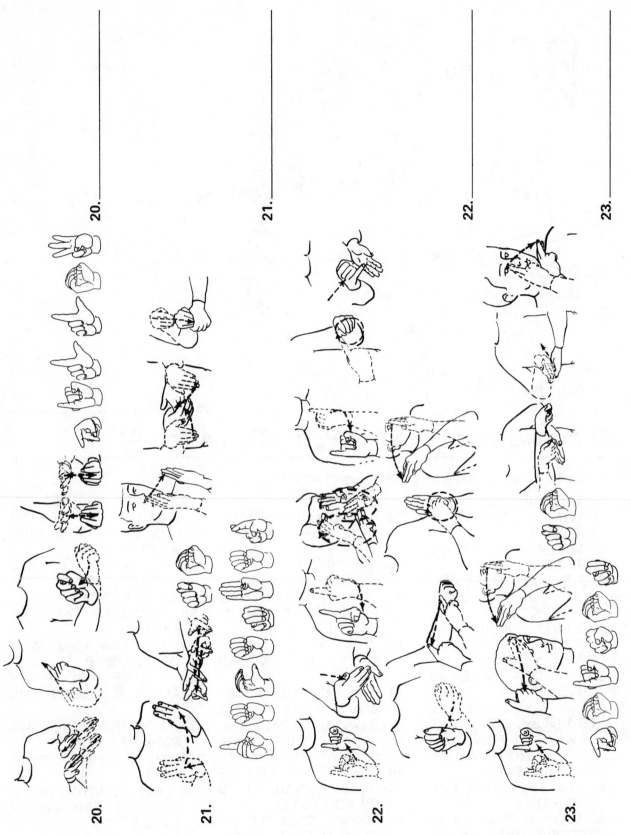

20.

21.

22.

23.

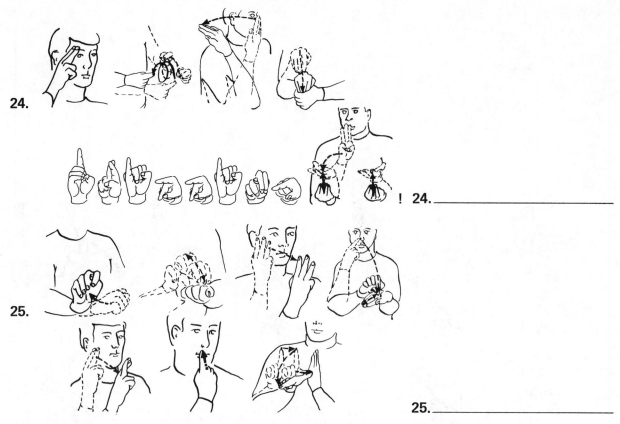

24. _____

25. _____

C) Answers for Decoding Part (B), Lesson 41

Underlined words indicate that they should have been fingerspelled.

1. WHY ARE YOU (plural) HAVING SO MUCH TROUBLE WITH IT?
2. WE WORRY ABOUT OUR DEAF SON.
3. WE WOULD LIKE FOR YOU TO REPRESENT OUR SCHOOL.
4. HAVE YOU (singular) LOOKED INTO HER MOUTH YET?
5. IS HE ALWAYS SO HUMBLE?
6. WE WILL REBEL IF YOU (plural) DON'T GIVE US WHAT WE WANT.
7. DID SHE MARRY YOUR BROTHER?
8. CAN THEY STAY FOR DINNER?
9. MAY I TELL YOU AFTER I THINK ABOUT IT?
10. DOES YOUR HUSBAND WORK FOR THE UNIVERSITY?
11. MY WIFE IS IN YOUR AFTERNOON CLASS.
12. BE CAREFUL BECAUSE THE FLOOR IS STILL WET.
13. DID YOU (singular) LOSE THE OTHER GLOVE?
14. I THINK THE PRESIDENT SUMMONED HIM TO WASHINGTON.
15. WHAT IS THE GIRL DOING AT THE SINK?
16. THIS IS THE LIST OF THINGS I WOULD LIKE FOR YOU TO DO.
17. DON'T DROP IT BECAUSE IT WILL BREAK.
18. WHICH METHOD SHOULD WE USE TO EVALUATE OUR CURRICULUM?
19. WE ARE STUDYING ABOUT RATS IN OUR SCIENCE CLASS.
20. BRING ME THE SOFT PILLOW.
21. WE PLAN TO BE WED IN DECEMBER.
22. I STOPPED WORRYING ABOUT IT A LONG TIME AGO.
23. I FORGOT TO BUY SOME RAT POISON.
24. HE CAME IN DRIPPING WET!
25. THE DOCTOR WILL EXAMINE HER MOUTH LATER.

lesson forty-two

Signs presented in this lesson are:

QUIET	**END**	**EXCHANGE**	**ELECTRIC***
CELEBRATE	**TONGUE**	**BUCKET**	**FINISH**
DEMAND	**COMPLETE**	**EMBARRASS**	**HOP**
ENOUGH*	**STAMP (noun)**	**SEND**	**FULL**
REQUIRE	**MOTORCYCLE***	**BASKETBALL**	**FACE (noun)**

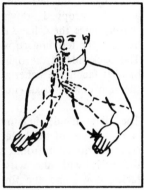

QUIET

The right hand, with the thumb and fingers extended and joined, is held with the top portion of the hand touching the signer's lips. The fingers of the right hand are pointing upward with the back side facing to the right. The left hand, with the thumb and fingers extended and joined, is moved toward and touches the right palm with the left fingertips. (The backs of the left fingers are facing upward at about a 45-degree angle.) Next, both hands simultaneously are moved downward with the wrists turning the hands outward. As the sign ends the fingertips point at about a 45-degree angle downward with the palms down.

NOTE: This sign may be suggestive, perhaps, of sound waves "dying" down.

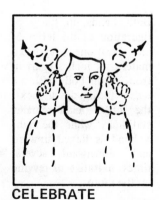

CELEBRATE

Each hand, with the thumb touching the extended index finger (remaining fingers are contracted), is positioned on each side of the body at eye level and with the joined fingertips pointing upward; next, with the configuration maintained, both hands are spiraled upwards.

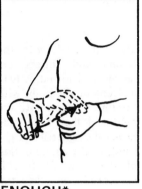

ENOUGH*

The left hand, in the configuration of the letter S, is held in front of the body with the back side facing to the left; the right hand, with the thumb and fingers extended, joined and pointing to the left, first touches the top portion of the left S hand with the palmar side of the fingers; next, with the configuration maintained, the right hand is moved forward and approximately two or three inches past the left hand. This motion is repeated several times.

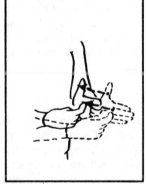

DEMAND

The left hand, with the thumb extended and sticking upward and the remaining fingers extended and joined, is held in front of the body with the fingers pointing to the viewer while the back side of the hand is facing to the left. The right hand, with the index finger bent slightly (remaining fingers and thumb are contracted), touches the left palm with the index fingertip (the back of the hand faces the viewer); next, with the contact maintained, both hands are moved toward the signer.

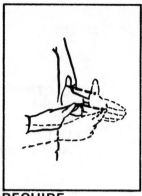

REQUIRE

This sign is made similarly to the previous one ("demand"), except that the right hand assumes the configuration of the letter *R* and touches the left palm with the fingertips (the *R* hand is held with the back side facing the viewer); next, with the contact maintained, both hands are moved toward the signer.

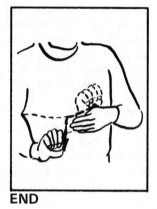

END

The left hand, with the thumb and fingers extended and joined, is held in front of the body with the fingers pointing to the right and the palmar side facing the signer. The right hand, in the configuration of the letter *E*, first is positioned on the top portion of the left hand near the base of the thumb with the back side of the *E* hand facing the signer; next, the *E* hand is moved forward along the top edge of the left hand and is dropped down sharply once the *E* hand is beyond the left fingertips. The back side of the *E* hand continues to face the signer as the sign comes to an end.

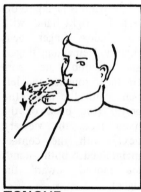

TONGUE

The right hand, in the configuration of the letter *H*, is held with the back side touching the signer's mouth and the *H* fingers pointing to the viewer; next, with the hand maintaining the contact and with the forearm held still, the *H* fingers are raised up and down, imitative of one of the motions associated with this organ.

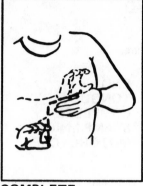

COMPLETE

This sign is made similarly to one in the left column ("end"), except that the right hand assumes the configuration of the letter *C* and is positioned on the top portion of the left hand near the base of the thumb with the back side of the *C* hand facing the signer; next, the *C* hand is moved forward along the top edge of the left hand and is dropped down sharply once the *C* hand is beyond the left fingertips. The back side of the right hand is facing the signer as the sign comes to an end.

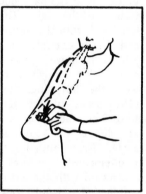

STAMP (noun)

The left hand, in the configuration of the letter *H*, is positioned in front of the body with the wrist facing down and the fingertips pointing to the right. The right hand, also in an *H* configuration, first is brought to the lips with the palmar side of the fingers touching the lips; next, with the configuration maintained, the right hand is rotated over as it is moved forward and downward to touch the back side of the left fingers. The back of the right *H* hand is facing up and the fingers are pointing to the viewer as the sign comes to an end.

MOTORCYCLE

Both hands, in the configuration of the letter *S*, are positioned approximately six inches apart in front of the body with the wrists facing down; next, the left *S* hand remains stationary while the right *S* hand is flexed upward and downward several times, imitative of revving up the motor.

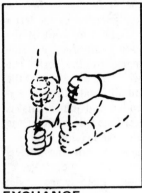

EXCHANGE

The right hand, in the configuration of the letter *E*, is positioned in front of the body with the back side facing to the right; the left hand, also in an *E* configuration, is positioned approximately two inches in front of the right hand (closer to the viewer); next, with the configuration and parallel formation maintained, the *E* hands exchange spatial positions. The left *E* hand makes a small upward arc motion as it is moved toward the signer, while the right *E* hand makes a small downward arc motion as it is moved forward.

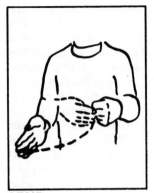

SEND

The left hand, in the configuration of the letter *S*, is held in front of the body with the back side facing the viewer at about a 45-degree angle. The right hand, with the thumb and fingers extended and joined, first touches the back side of the left *S* hand at the third joint with the palmar side of the fingers (the back of the right hand is facing the viewer and the fingers are pointing to the left); next, the right hand is moved forward with a slight curve to the right side of the body. The sign ends with the right hand fingers pointing to the viewer while the back side of the hand is facing to the right.

BUCKET

Both hands, in the configuration of the letter *B*, are positioned side-by-side in front of the body with the palmar sides facing up and the fingers pointing to the viewer; next, both *B* hands are curved upward with the wrists turning the *B* hands inward so that the palmar sides are facing each other and the fingertips point to the viewer.

NOTE: This sign is imitative of the shape of this object.

BASKETBALL

In this sign, the hands pantomime first holding a basketball and then shooting it. Both hands, with the thumbs and fingers apart and slightly bent, are positioned in front of the body with the palmar sides facing each other; next, with the configuration maintained, both hands are moved upward with the wrists curving the hands toward the signer.

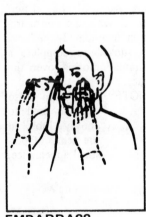

EMBARRASS

Both hands have the thumbs and fingers extended and joined and are positioned so that the palm of the left hand touches the cheek while the right one faces the cheek; next, the hands are moved simultaneously to complete circles over the cheeks, ending with the right palm touching the cheek while the left hand faces it.

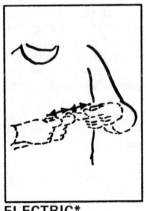

ELECTRIC*

Both hands, in the configuration of the letter *X*, are positioned approximately two to three inches from each other in front of the body with the back sides facing the viewer; next, with the configuration maintained, the *X* hands are drawn to midline, make contact at the second joint, return to their original positions and repeat the motion.

Lesson Forty-two 477

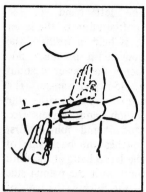

FINISH

This sign is made similarly to "end" and "complete," except that the right hand assumes the configuration of the letter *F*. The left hand, with the thumb and fingers extended and joined, is held in front of the body with the fingers pointing to the right and the palmar side facing the signer. The right hand, in the configuration of the letter *F*, first is positioned on the top portion of the left hand near the base of the thumb with the palmar side of the *F* hand facing the viewer; next, the *F* hand is moved forward along the top edge of the left hand and is dropped down sharply once the *F* hand is beyond the left fingertips. The palmar side of the *F* hand is facing the viewer as the sign comes to an end.

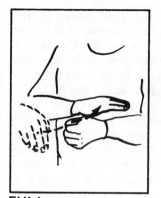

FULL

The left hand, in the configuration of the letter *S*, is held in front of the body with the back side facing to the left. The right hand, with the thumb and fingers extended and joined, first is positioned in front of the left hand (closer to the viewer) with the fingers pointing to the viewer at about a 45-degree angle; next, the palmar side of the right hand grazes past the top portion of the left *S* hand as the right hand is moved toward the signer.

NOTE: This sign often is confused with "enough." However, please remember that for "enough" the right hand is moved *forward,* away from the signer, as well as requiring that the motion be repeated several times.

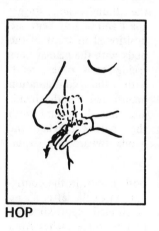

HOP

The left hand, with the thumb and fingers extended and joined, is held in front of the body with the fingers pointing to the viewer and the palmar side facing up. The right hand, in the configuration of the letter *V*, first is inverted so that the *V* fingertips are touching the left palm and the back side of the right *V* fingers is facing the viewer; next, with the configuration maintained, the right hand executes three or four small jumping movements as it is moved toward and past the fingertips of the left hand.

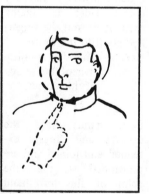

FACE (noun)

The right hand, with only the index finger extended (remaining fingers and thumb are contracted), is held approximately two to three inches in front of the signer's chin and is pointing toward the signer; next, with the configuration maintained, the hand is moved to complete a circular motion over the face.

NOTE: This sign also may be used to convey "look" in the sense of personal appearance.

A) Exercises in Encoding

Encode the following material using signs and fingerspelling. Use fingerspelling for all underlined words.

1. WHAT <u>DID</u> HE REQUIRE YOU <u>TO</u> DO?
2. THEY <u>DEMANDED</u> AN ANSWER FROM US BY NEXT THURSDAY.
3. IS THIS THE END <u>OF</u> THE SENTENCE?
4. HAVE YOU COMPL<u>E</u>TED ALL <u>OF</u> THE REQUIREMENTS?
5. WHEN <u>DID</u> YOU BUY THE MOTOR-CYCLE?
6. WE CAN'T GO BECAUSE WE DON'T HAVE ENOUGH MONEY.
7. ASK MY SECRETARY FOR A STAMP.
8. <u>DOES</u> HE HAVE AN ELECTRIC PENCIL <u>SHARPENER</u>?
9. WE HAVE NOTHING <u>TO</u> CELEBRATE.
10. IF YOU ARE NOT HAP<u>P</u>Y WITH IT, YOU MAY EXCHANGE IT.
11. WHEN YOU HEAR THE SOUND, DROP THE BLOCK IN THE BUCKET.
12. I DON'T KNOW WHY HE EMBAR-RASSED ME.
13. <u>DOES</u> YOUR DEAF SON PLAY BASKET-BALL?
14. I AM NOT SURE WHEN I WILL BE ABLE <u>TO</u> FINISH IT.
15. LET ME SEE YOUR TONGUE AGAIN.
16. WHEN <u>DID</u> YOU SEND US THE MONEY?
17. WHY <u>IS</u> SHE COMPLAINING ABOUT HER FACE?
18. IS IT FULL YET?
19. <u>DID</u> YOU COMPLETE THE EVALUA-<u>TION</u> ON HER?
20. PLEASE DON'T BE SO DEMANDING!
21. WHY <u>DID</u> YOU REQUIRE US <u>TO</u> READ ALL THOSE BOOKS?
22. <u>POINT</u> TO THE BOY'S TONGUE.
23. PUT THE <u>TOYS</u> IN THE GREEN BUCK-ET.
24. ALL <u>OF</u> US BECAME VERY QUIET AFTER THE <u>ANNOUNCEMENT</u>.

B) Exercises in Decoding

Decode the following illustrated exercises:

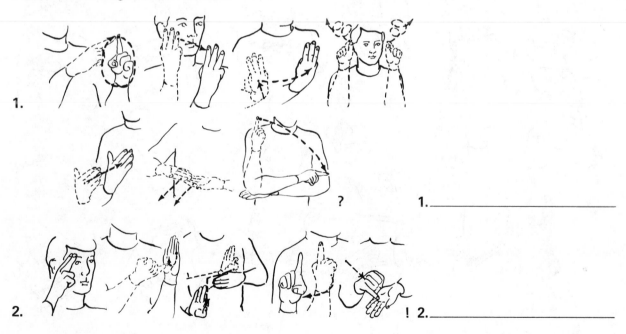

1.

?   1._____

2.   ! 2._____

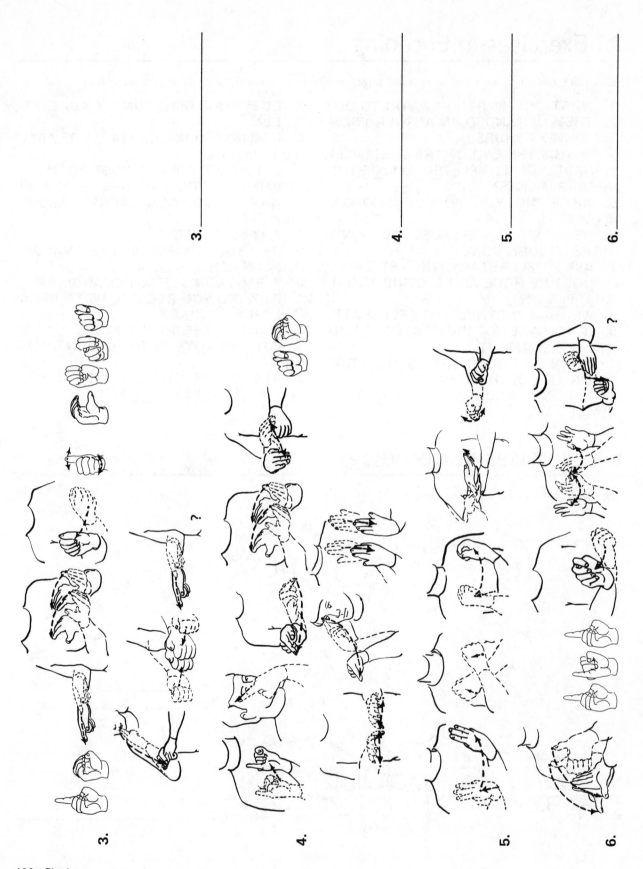

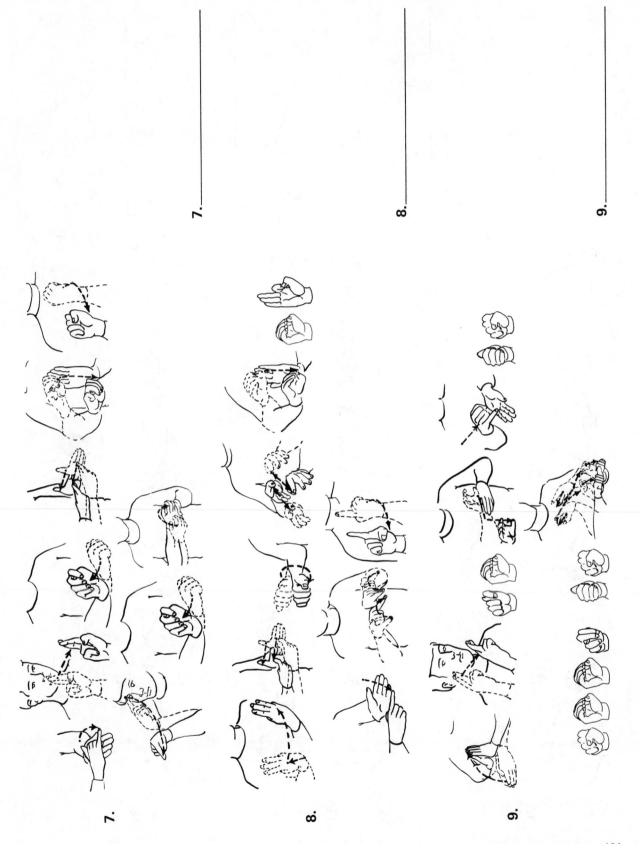

7.

8.

9.

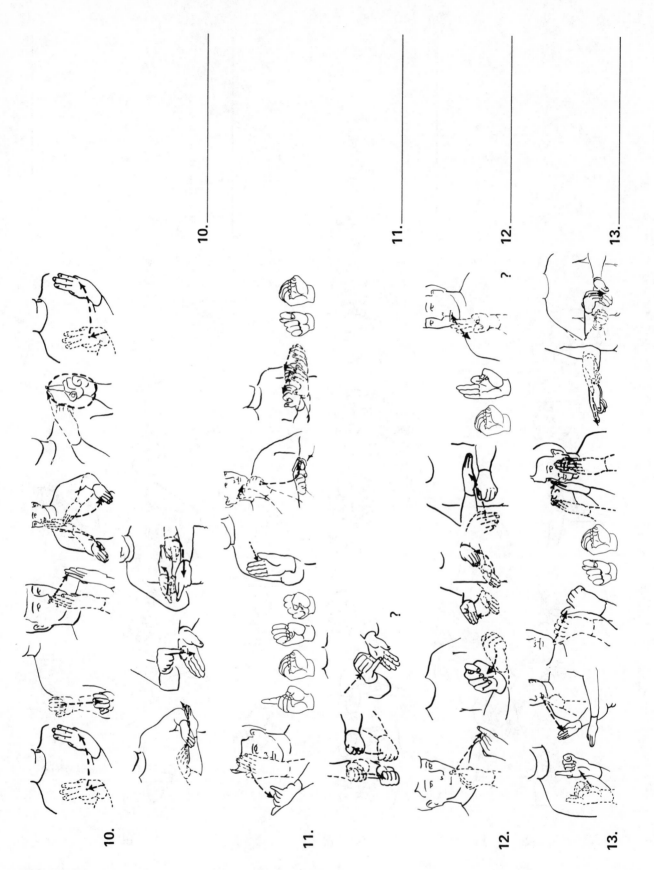

14.

15.

16.

?

?

14.

15.

16.

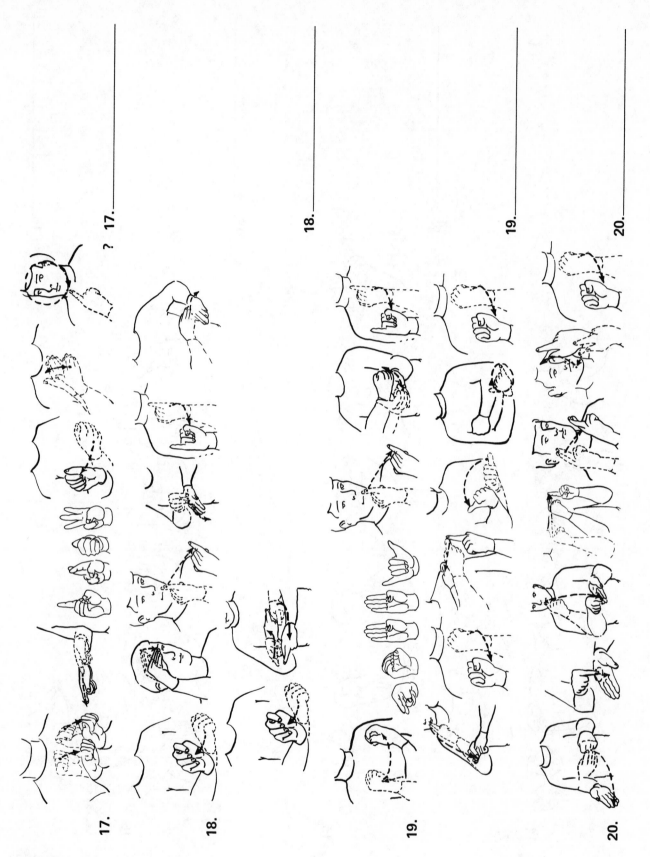

17.

18.

19.

20.

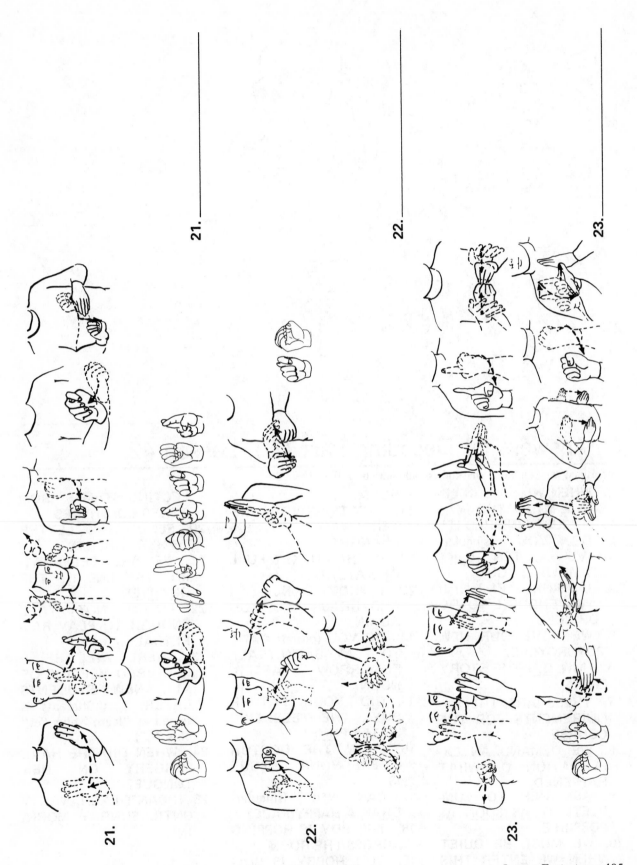

21.

22.

23.

21.

22.

23.

24.

? 24._____

25.

25._____

C) Answers for Decoding Part (B), Lesson 42

Underlined words indicate that they should have been fingerspelled.

1. WHEN WILL WE CELE-BRATE MY BIRTHDAY?
2. HE JUST FINISHED IT!
3. <u>DO</u> YOU (singular) HAVE A TEN <u>CENT</u> STAMP WITH YOU?
4. I THINK YOU (plural) HAVE ENOUGH <u>TO</u> DO FOR NOW.
5. WE LOVE OUR NEW MOTORCYCLE.
6. HOW <u>DID</u> THE STORY END?
7. THESE ARE THE RE-QUIREMENTS FOR THE COURSE.
8. WE DEMAND AN EX-PLANATION <u>OF</u> WHAT HAPPENED.
9. ASK HER <u>TO</u> COM-PLETE IT <u>AS SOON AS</u> POSSIBLE.
10. WE MUST BE QUIET WHEN WE ENTER THIS ROOM.
11. WHY <u>DOES</u> YOUR SIS-TER WANT TO EX-CHANGE IT?
12. IS THE BUCKET FULL <u>OF</u> WATER?
13. I PROMISE NOT <u>TO</u> EMBARRASS YOU AGAIN.
14. <u>DO</u> YOU (plural) WANT <u>TO</u> PLAY BASKETBALL TOMORROW AFTER-NOON?
15. <u>DID</u> YOUR FATHER BUY THE ELECTRIC WATER <u>PUMP</u>?
16. SHOW THE DOCTOR WHERE YOUR TONGUE IS.
17. CAN YOU (singular) <u>DRAW</u> A HAPPY FACE?
18. THE BOY IS HOPPING ACROSS THE ROOM.
19. OUR <u>HOBBY</u> IS COL-LECTING STAMPS FROM OTHER COUNTRIES.
20. SEND THIS LETTER <u>TO</u> HER PARENTS.
21. WE ARE CELEBRAT-ING THE END <u>OF</u> THE <u>QUARTER</u>.
22. I AM NOT TALL ENOUGH <u>TO</u> PLAY BAS-KETBALL.
23. THERE WILL BE A REQUIRED MEETING <u>OF</u> ALL NEW STUDENTS LATER. ("Students" is signed as "learn" plus "er" plus "s.")
24. WHEN <u>DID</u> SHE HAVE SURGERY ON HER TONGUE?
25. I CAN'T EXCHANGE IT UNTIL SUNDAY MORN-ING.

lesson forty-three

Signs presented in this lesson are:

WORSE	LOUSY	SAVE*	IMPRESS
ONCE	SPEECH	HOSPITAL	GRADUATE (verb)
APPOINTMENT	HANDSOME	INFIRMARY	PRETTY
KEEP*	CURIOUS*	CLINIC	DANCE
ROCK (noun)	SUGAR*	PATIENT (noun)	CLIENT

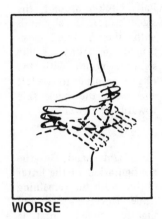

WORSE

Both hands, in the configuration of the letter *W*, are positioned approximately six to seven inches from each other in front of the body with the *W* fingers pointing to the viewer and the back sides facing down; next, with the configuration maintained, the *W* hands are moved toward midline and are crossed at the wrists (with the *W* hands flexed so that the fingers are pointing to the left and right) and are held with the back sides facing the viewer.

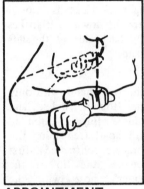

APPOINTMENT

The left forearm is positioned at about a 45-degree angle in front of the body with the hand in the configuration of a letter *S* and the wrist facing down. The right hand, in the configuration of the letter *A*, is held approximately three to four inches above the back of the *A* hand facing up. With the configuration maintained, the right hand makes a small arc motion as it is moved slightly to the left and then upward; next, the hand is brought straight down and with its wrist touches the back side of the left hand wrist.

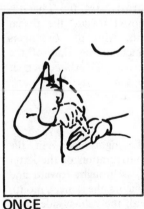

ONCE

The left hand, with the thumb and fingers extended and joined, is held in front of the body with the palm facing up and with the fingers pointing to the viewer; the right hand, with only the index finger extended (remaining fingers and thumb are contracted), is held with the index fingertip touching the left palm and the back side facing up; next, with the configuration maintained, the right hand is curved upward and to the right side with the hand rotating so that the index finger is pointing upward and the back side is facing the viewer as the sign comes to an end.

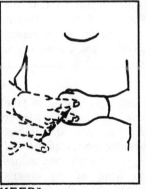

KEEP*

The left hand, in the configuration of the letter *S*, is held in front of the body with the back side facing the viewer. The right hand, in the configuration of the letter *V*, first is positioned approximately six to eight inches in front of the left hand (closer to the viewer) with the *V* fingers pointing to the left and the back side facing the viewer; next, with the configuration maintained, the right hand is moved toward the left *S* hand with the right hand fingers touching the third joint of the fingers of the left *S* hand. This motion is repeated several times.

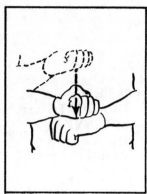

ROCK (noun)

The left forearm is positioned at about a 45-degree angle in front of the body with the hand in the configuration of the letter *S* and with its back side facing up. The right hand, in the configuration of the letter *S*, first is held approximately six to seven inches above the left *S* hand with the back side facing down; next, the right *S* hand is moved straight down as it strikes the back side of the left hand.

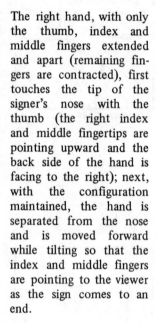

LOUSY

The right hand, with only the thumb, index and middle fingers extended and apart (remaining fingers are contracted), first touches the tip of the signer's nose with the thumb (the right index and middle fingertips are pointing upward and the back side of the hand is facing to the right); next, with the configuration maintained, the hand is separated from the nose and is moved forward while tilting so that the index and middle fingers are pointing to the viewer as the sign comes to an end.

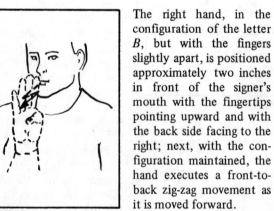

SPEECH

The right hand, in the configuration of the letter *B*, but with the fingers slightly apart, is positioned approximately two inches in front of the signer's mouth with the fingertips pointing upward and with the back side facing to the right; next, with the configuration maintained, the hand executes a front-to-back zig-zag movement as it is moved forward.

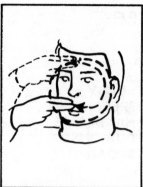

HANDSOME

The right hand, in the configuration of the letter *H*, first is positioned on the middle of the signer's forehead with the fingers pointing to the left and the back side facing the viewer; next, with the configuration maintained, the right hand is moved in a clockwise direction and completes one and one-half circles around the signer's face. The sign ends with the *H* hand positioned in front of the signer's mouth with the fingers pointing to the left and with the back side toward the viewer.

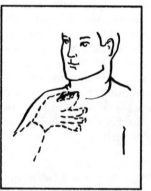

CURIOUS*

The right hand, in the configuration of the letter *G* (but with the remaining three fingers apart and slightly curved), first is positioned four or five inches in front of the signer's neck, with the back side of the hand facing the viewer and the *G* fingers pointing to the throat; next, the *G* hand is moved toward the throat and, with the *G* fingers pinching the skin of the throat, the skin then is tugged outward repeatedly.

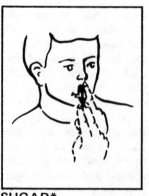

SUGAR*

The right hand, in the configuration of the letter *H*, is brought toward and touches the signer's mouth with the palmar side of its fingers (the back side of the hand is toward the viewer); next, the right hand fingers brush the lips as the hand is drawn slightly downward. This motion is repeated several times.

488 Signing

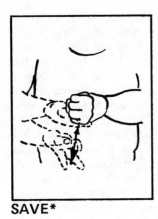

SAVE*

The left hand, in the configuration of the letter *S*, is positioned in front of the body with the back side facing to the left. The left hand, in the configuration of the letter *V*, first is held approximately three to four inches directly beneath the bottom portion of the left *S* hand with the fingers pointing to the viewer and the back side facing down. Next, the right *V* hand is moved up from beneath and, with its fingers, touches the bottom portion of the left *S* hand. This motion is repeated several times.

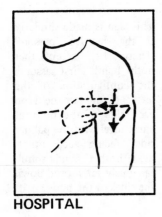

HOSPITAL

In this sign, the right hand executes the sign of a cross on the left arm. The right hand, in the configuration of the letter *H*, first is positioned on the upper portion of the left arm with the fingers pointing to the left and the back side of the hand facing the viewer; next, the right *H* hand is moved about an inch to the right and then the direction is reversed so that the hand is moved the same distance downward, while grazing the arm.

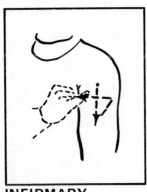

INFIRMARY

This sign is made similarly to the previous one ("hospital"), except that the right hand first assumes the configuration of the letter *I*; then, the *I* hand executes the sign of a cross on the left arm.

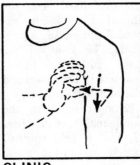

CLINIC

This sign is made similarly to the previous two signs ("hospital," "infirmary"), except that the right hand first assumes the configuration of the letter *C* and is held with the back side facing to the right; next, the *C* hand executes the sign of a cross on the left arm.

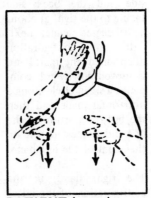

PATIENT (noun)

This sign is made by combining two other signs, "sick" (lesson 15) and "person" (lesson 12). Having made the sign for "sick," the sign for "person" then is executed. Please note that the sign for "sick" is executed with only the right hand involved, whereas, in lesson 15, the sign involved both hands. It is permissible to do the sign both ways.

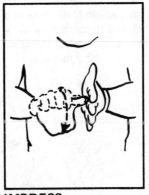

IMPRESS

The left hand, with the thumb extended and sticking up and the remaining fingers extended and joined, is positioned in front of the body with the fingers pointing to the viewer and the back side facing to the left. The right hand, with only the thumb extended and sticking out to the left (remaining fingers are contracted), touches the left palm with the thumb (the back side of the right hand is facing up); next, the right thumb presses against the left palm as the right hand is rotated forward and downward (in a clockwise direction) while the back side is facing the viewer as the sign comes to an end.

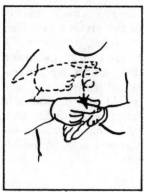

GRADUATE (verb)

The left hand, with the thumb and fingers extended and joined, is positioned in front of the body with the fingers pointing to the viewer and the back side facing down. The right hand, in the configuration of the letter *G*, first is held approximately six inches above the left palm with the fingers pointing to the left side and the back side facing to the right at about a 45-degree angle; next, with the configuration maintained, the right hand is moved downward, completes a small circle along a horizontal plane and then the bottom portion of the *G* hand comes to rest on the palm of the left hand.

DANCE

The left hand, with the thumb and fingers extended and joined, is positioned in front of the body with the fingers pointing to the viewer and the back side facing down. The right hand, in the configuration of the letter *V*, is inverted and held approximately an inch above the left palm with the *V* fingertips pointing to the palm and the back side of the hand facing up. Next, the right *V* hand is swung front-to-back above the left palm. The right arm does not move.

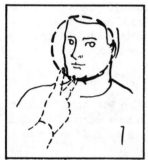

PRETTY

The right hand, in the configuration of the letter *P*, first is positioned on the signer's chin with the middle fingertip touching the chin and the back side of the hand facing the viewer; next, the *P* hand is moved to complete a circle in a clockwise direction around the signer's face.

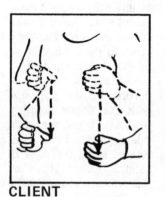

CLIENT

This sign is made similarly to the sign for "person" (lesson 12), except that both hands first assume the configuration of the letter *C* and are held on each side of the body at chest level with the palmar sides facing each other; next, both *C* hands simultaneously are moved down the sides of the body.

A) Exercises in Encoding

Encode the following material using signs and fingerspelling. Use fingerspelling for all underlined words.

1. YOUR APPOINTMENT WITH THE AUDIOLOGIST IS FOR THURSDAY MORNING.
2. IN MY OPINION, IT WAS WORSE.
3. I ONCE WORKED FOR YOUR GRANDFATHER.
4. I WAS IMPRESSED WITH HER ANSWER.
5. WHEN <u>DID</u> SHE GRADUATE FROM THIS INSTITUTION?
6. ARE YOU GOING TO THE DANCE TONIGHT?
7. HOW EXPENSIVE WAS THE <u>MOON</u> ROCK?
8. I JUST FINISHED READING THE NEW BOOK AND I THINK IT IS LOUSY!
9. WE ARE CURIOUS <u>TO</u> KNOW WHY YOU DID IT.
10. WHY IS YOUR FRIEND IN THE HOSPITAL AGAIN?
11. IF YOU ARE SICK, GO TO THE INFIRMARY.
12. WHERE IS THE HEARING AND SPEECH CLINIC?
13. THIS PATIENT NEEDS SPEECH IMPROVEMENT.
14. SHE IS A VERY PRETTY GIRL.
15. HOW MUCH SUGAR <u>DO</u> YOU WANT IN YOUR COFFEE?
16. WHY <u>DID</u> YOUR CLIENT CANCEL HIS APPOINTMENT?
17. IS THE CLINIC OPEN TODAY?
18. I THINK YOU ARE A HANDSOME MAN.
19. HE IS DEAF, BUT YOU CAN UNDERSTAND HIS SPEECH.
20. HOW MANY <u>OF</u> YOUR PATIENTS ARE ON <u>WELFARE</u>?
21. SHALL WE EVALUATE BOTH HER SPEECH AND LANGUAGE?
22. ARE YOU SAVING YOUR MONEY FOR COLLEGE?
23. WE AGREE THAT HER SPEECH IS GETTING WORSE. ("Getting" is signed as "becoming.")
24. HE BELIEVES THAT HIS SPEECH IS LOUSY.
25. MAY WE KEEP IT UNTIL SUNDAY?

B) Exercises in Decoding

Decode the following illustrated exercises:

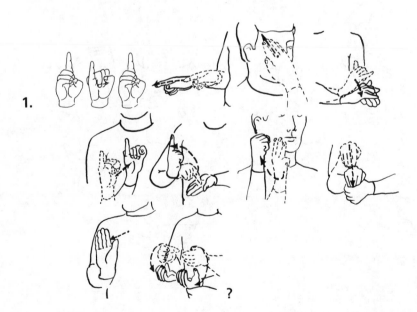

1.

1._____

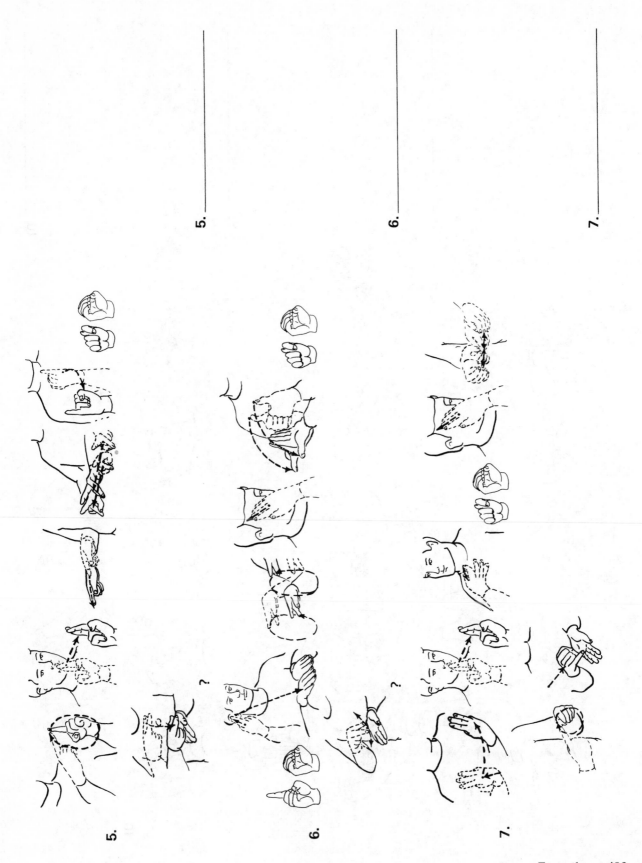

5.

6.

7.

5.

6.

7.

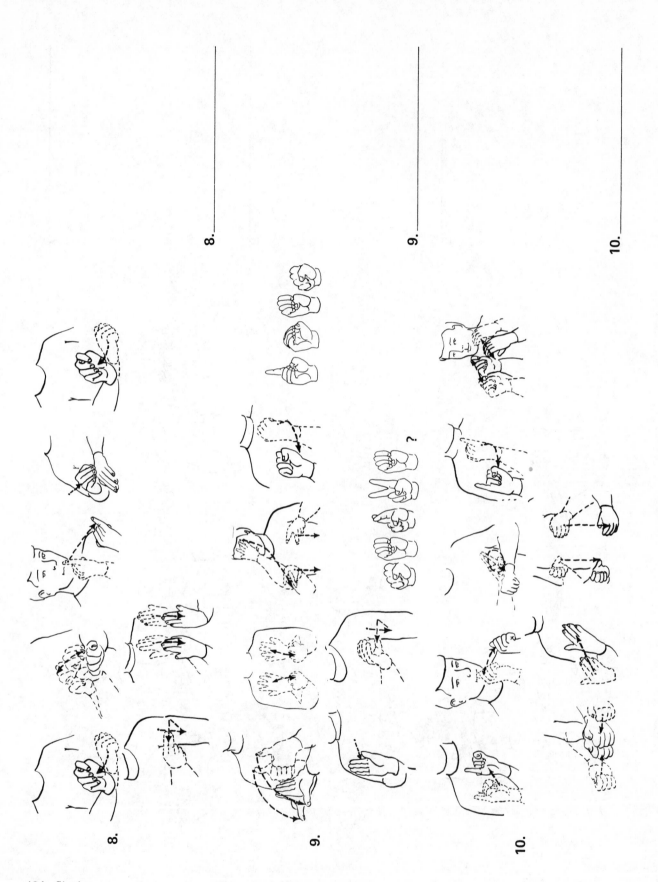

8.

9.

10.

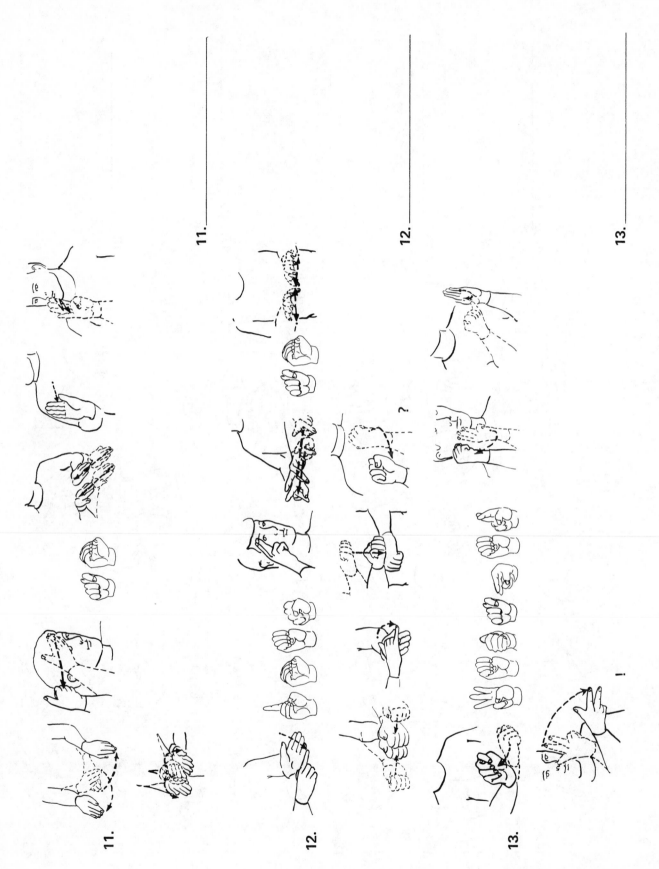

11.

12.

13.

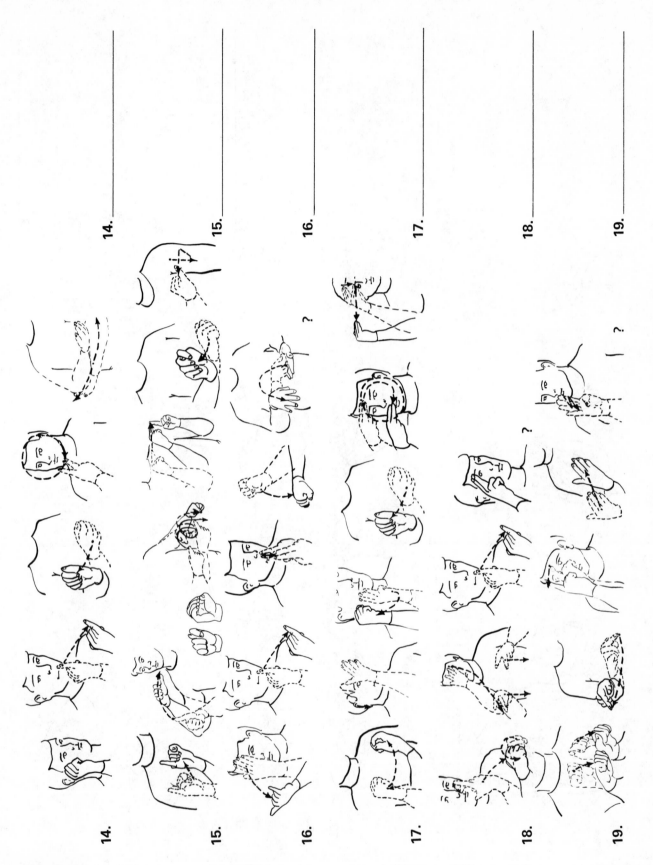

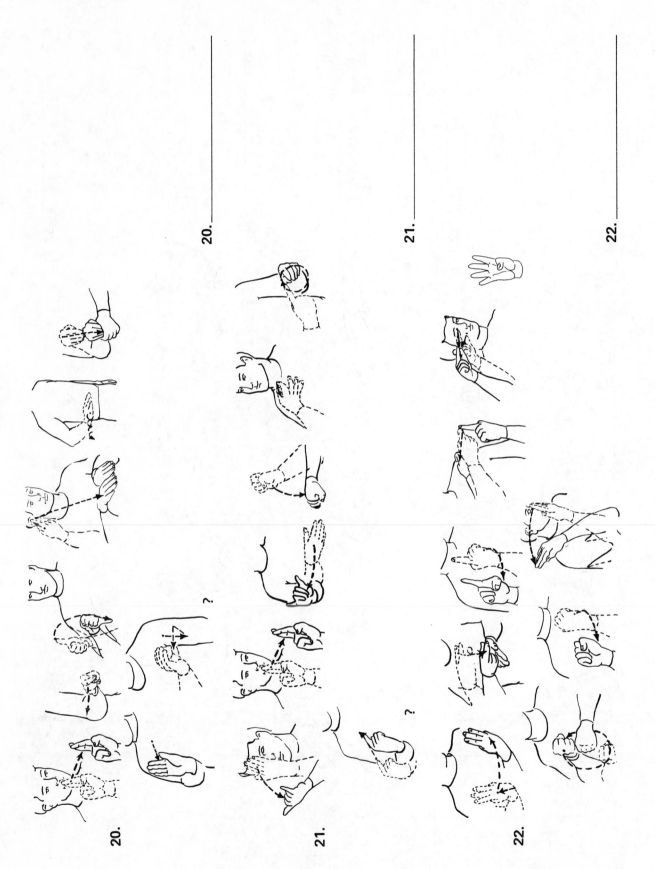

20.

21.

22.

20.

21.

22.

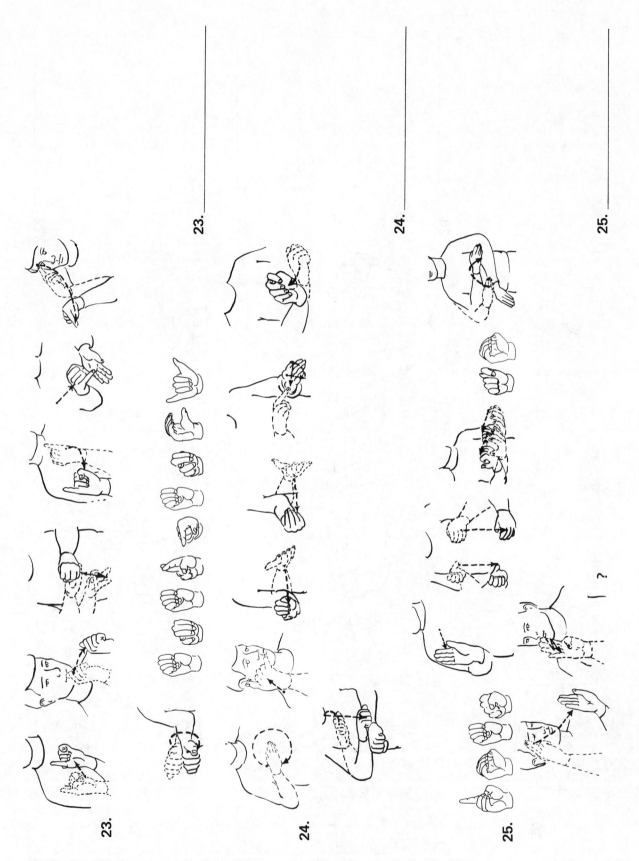

C) Answers for Decoding Part (B), Lesson 43

Underlined words indicate that they should have been fingerspelled.

1. <u>DID</u> YOU (singular) KNOW THAT I ONCE WAS IN YOUR CLASS?
2. WHEN IS YOUR APPOINTMENT WITH YOUR SUPERVISOR?
3. MOST <u>OF</u> US DON'T KNOW HOW <u>TO</u> SAVE MONEY.
4. WHY ARE THEY TRYING <u>TO</u> IMPRESS US?
5. WHEN ARE YOU (singular) PLANNING <u>TO</u> GRADUATE?
6. <u>DO</u> DEAF PEOPLE KNOW HOW <u>TO</u> DANCE?
7. WE ARE CURIOUS <u>TO</u> KNOW MORE ABOUT IT.
8. THE DOCTOR IS AT THE HOSPITAL NOW.
9. HOW MANY PATIENTS <u>DOES</u> YOUR CLINIC <u>SERVE</u>?
10. I AM USING "TOTAL COMMUNICATION" WITH MY CLIENT.
11. DON'T FORGET <u>TO</u> BRING YOUR SPEECH BOOK.
12. WHAT <u>DOES</u> HE PLAN <u>TO</u> DO WITH THESE ROCKS?
13. THE <u>WEATHER</u> WAS JUST LOUSY!
14. SHE IS A PRETTY BABY.
15. I REFUSE <u>TO</u> GO TO THE INFIRMARY.
16. WHY IS SUGAR SO EXPENSIVE?
17. OUR GRANDFATHER WAS A HANDSOME MAN.
18. WHOSE PATIENT IS HE?
19. CAN YOU (plural) UNDERSTAND MY SPEECH?
20. ARE THERE ANY DEAF CHILDREN IN YOUR CLINIC?
21. WHY ARE THEY SO CURIOUS ABOUT ME?
22. WE GRADUATED FROM GALLAUDET FOUR YEARS AGO.
23. I AM SAVING IT FOR AN <u>EMERGENCY</u>.
24. PLEASE CALL THEM AND CANCEL THE APPOINTMENT.
25. <u>DOES</u> YOUR CLIENT WANT <u>TO</u> IMPROVE HIS SPEECH?

lesson forty-four

Signs presented in this lesson are:

WEIGH,* WEIGHT*	DRAW	BUS	LION
CONFUSE	DESIGN (verb)	DECREASE, LESS	APARTMENT
GAME*	BITE	CONSCIENCE,* GUILT*	SUBTRACT
TOY*	LIST (verb)	PIE	TICKET
SOIL (noun)	MUMPS	TRUCK	TEASE*

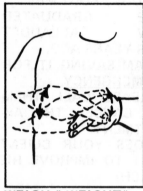

WEIGH,* WEIGHT*

The left hand, in the configuration of the letter *H*, is positioned in front of the body with the fingers pointing to the viewer and the back side facing to the left. The right hand, also in an *H* configuration, is placed on the left hand (contact is made at the second joints of the middle finger of the right *H* hand and the index finger of the left *H* hand); the right hand fingers are pointing to the left with the back side of the right hand facing the viewer; next, with the configuration maintained, the right wrist is raised and lowered *several* times.

GAME*

Both hands, in the configuration of the letter *G*, are positioned approximately six inches from each other in front of the body with the fingers pointing toward each other and the back sides facing right and left, respectively. Next, with the configuration and distance between the hands maintained, the forearms simultaneously turn the *G* hands inward (the fingers are pointing downward at an angle), and then outward (the fingers are now pointing upward at an angle). The wrists do not bend. This motion is quick and is repeated several times.

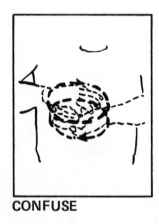

CONFUSE

The left hand, with the thumb and fingers apart and slightly bent, is positioned in front of the body with the palm facing up. The right hand, in a similar configuration, is positioned approximately an inch above the left hand with the palmar sides of the hands facing each other; next, with the configuration maintained, both hands complete a circular movement along a horizontal plane while moving in a clockwise direction with one hand following the other.

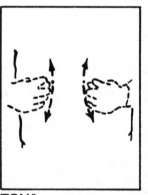

TOY*

This sign is made similarly to the previous one ("game"), except that both hands first assume the configuration of the letter *T*. The *T* hands are positioned approximately six inches from each other in front of the body with the back sides facing the viewer at an angle. Next, with the configuration and distance between the hands maintained, the forearms simultaneously turn the *T* hands inward and then outward. The wrists do not bend. This motion is quick and is repeated several times.

500

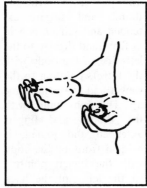

SOIL (noun)

The left hand, with the thumb touching the joined and slightly curved fingers, is positioned in front of the body with the palm facing upward. The right hand, in a similar configuration, first is positioned parallel to and approximately four or five inches from the left hand; next, with the configuration and distance between the hands maintained, each thumb rubs the fingers of each hand, completing several small circular motions.

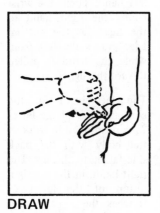

DRAW

The left hand, with the thumb and fingers extended and joined, is held in front and slightly to the left side of the body with the fingers pointing to the viewer and the back side facing down. The right hand, in the configuration of the letter *I*, touches the left palm with the little fingertip as the back side of the right hand faces the viewer; next, with the configuration maintained, the hand is drawn to the right as the little finger makes a wavy line across and past the bottom portion of the left hand.

DESIGN (verb)

This sign is done similarly to the previous one ("draw"), except that the right hand assumes the configuration of the letter *D* and touches the left hand. The *D* hand is held with the index finger pointing upward at an angle as the wrist faces down; next, with the configuration maintained, the *D* hand is drawn to the right, following a wavy motion across and past the bottom portion of the left hand.

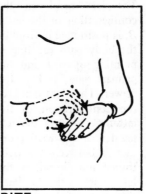

BITE

The left hand, with the thumb and fingers extended and joined, is positioned in front and slightly to the left side of the body with the fingers pointing to the viewer and the palmar side facing down. The right hand, in the configuration of the letter *C*, is held in front of the body approximately two or three inches from the left hand with the back side facing to the right and the fingers pointing to the left; next, the right *C* hand is moved toward and clasps the palm and back side of the left hand with the thumb and fingers.

LIST (verb)

The left hand, with the thumb and fingers extended and joined, is held in front and to the left side of the body with the fingers pointing upward and the back side facing to the left. The right hand, with the thumb bent inward and touching the extended and joined fingers, touches the left hand near the fingertips (the back side of the right hand fingers is facing up); next, with the configuration preserved, the right hand makes four or five small skipping movements over the left palm, while moving downward.

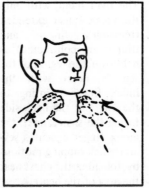
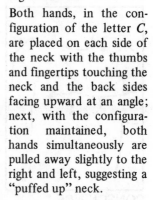

MUMPS

Both hands, in the configuration of the letter *C*, are placed on each side of the neck with the thumbs and fingertips touching the neck and the back sides facing upward at an angle; next, with the configuration maintained, both hands simultaneously are pulled away slightly to the right and left, suggesting a "puffed up" neck.

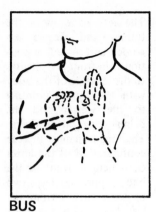

BUS

The left hand, in the configuration of the letter *B*, is positioned in front of the body with the fingers pointing upward and the palmar side facing the viewer. The right hand, in the configuration of the letter *C*, touches the left hand near the wrist (contact is between the right thumb and the side of the left wrist with the back side of the *C* hand facing to the right at an angle); next, with the configuration maintained, both hands are moved forward, while maintaining contact.

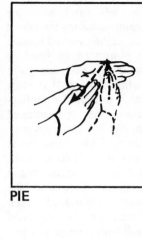

PIE

The left hand, with the thumb and fingers extended and joined, is held in front and slightly to the left side of the body with the fingers pointing to the viewer and the palm facing up. The right hand, with the thumb and fingers extended and joined, is held in front of the body with the fingers pointing to the left and the back side toward the viewer. Next, the bottom edge of the right hand grazes the palm and top edge of the left hand. Then, the wrist bends the right hand to the inside as the bottom edge grazes the left palm while the hand is pulled toward the signer.

The left hand, with the thumb and fingers joined and slightly cupped, is positioned in front of the body with the back side facing down while the fingers face toward the viewer and point at an upward angle. The right hand, in a similar configuration, is positioned approximately four to five inches above the left hand with the back side facing up and the fingers pointing to the left at a downward angle; next, with the configuration maintained, the right hand is moved slightly downward, suggesting that something is being reduced or compressed.

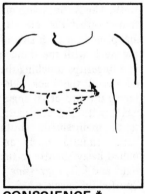

DECREASE, LESS

TRUCK

The left hand, in the configuration of the letter *T*, is positioned in front of the body with the back side facing to the left. The right hand, in the configuration of the letter *C*, touches the *T* hand near the base of the thumb (contact is made between the right thumb and the left hand with the back side of the right *C* hand facing to the right); next, with the configuration maintained, both hands are moved forward, while maintaining contact.

The right hand, with only the index finger extended (remaining fingers and thumb are contracted), is held over the region of the signer's heart with the index finger pointing to the left and the back side facing the signer; next, the index finger executes several quick tapping motions by touching the chest near the area of the heart.

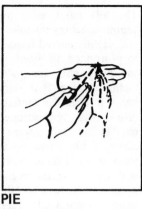

CONSCIENCE,*
GUILT*

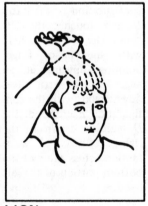

LION

The right hand, with the thumb and fingers bent, first is positioned on the signer's head with the flexed fingers touching the forehead and the back side facing up; next, with the configuration maintained, the hand is flipped backward causing the palmar side to face upward.

NOTE: This sign is imitative of a lion's mane.

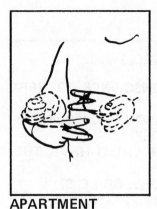

APARTMENT

In this sign, the hands attempt to illustrate the four sides of a room (the sign for "room" was presented in lesson 33). First, both hands assume the configuration of the letter *A* and are positioned in a parallel manner in front of the body approximately to the right and left; next, both hands, while maintaining the distance between them, are moved to complete the remaining two sides of a "room." This is accomplished by the right hand moving to the left (to midline) while the left hand is moving to the right (to midline) with both hands changing their configuration to the letter *P* while executing this latter movement. As the sign comes to an end, both hands are at midline with the right *P* hand directly in front of (closer to the viewer) the left *P* hand with the back sides facing the viewer.

TICKET

The left hand, with the thumb and fingers extended and joined, is positioned in front of the body with the fingers pointing to the viewer and the palm facing up. The right hand, with the index and middle fingers apart and crooked (the thumb and remaining fingers are contracted), is positioned in front of, and slightly to the right side of the body, approximately four to five inches from the left hand with the back side facing the viewer; next, with the configuration maintained, the right hand is moved toward the left hand as the curved index and middle fingers clench both the palmar and back side of the bottom portion of the left hand.

NOTE: This sign is imitative of how a punch may be used to cancel a ticket.

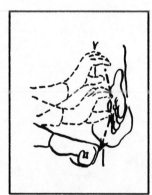

SUBTRACT

The left hand, with the thumb extended and pointing upward while the remaining fingers are extended and joined, is positioned in front and to the left side of the body with the fingers pointing to the viewer and with the back side facing to the left. The right hand, in the configuration of the letter *C*, is held two or three inches above the top edge of the left hand with the back side facing up; next, the back side of the right hand fingers graze the palm and bottom portion of the left hand as the right hand is moved downward, while changing to a fist position which faces downward.

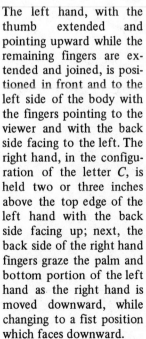

TEASE*

The left hand, with the index finger apart and bent (remaining fingers and thumb are contracted), is positioned in front of the body with the back side facing to the left and the index finger pointing to the right. The right hand, in a similar configuration, is positioned on the top portion of the left hand with the back side facing to the right while the index fingertip points to the left; next, with the configuration maintained, the bottom portion of the right hand brushes the top portion of the left hand as the right hand is moved forward. This motion is repeated several times.

A) Exercises in Encoding

Encode the following material using signs and fingerspelling. Use fingerspelling for all underlined words.

1. WE ARE NOT TRYING <u>TO</u> CONFUSE YOU.
2. THESE FLOWERS WILL NOT GROW IN THIS SOIL.
3. WHO HELPED YOU DRAW IT?
4. WHO DESIGNED YOUR NEW BUILD-ING? ("Building" is signed as "build" plus "house.")
5. <u>DOES</u> SHE KNOW HOW <u>TO</u> SUBTRACT YET?
6. I AM ONLY TEASING YOU!
7. WHEN <u>DOES</u> THE BUS LEAVE FOR <u>NEW</u> <u>YORK</u>?
8. LIST THE THINGS THAT I TOLD YOU <u>TO</u> REMEMBER.
9. <u>DID</u> YOU <u>BAKE</u> THIS PIE YOURSELF?
10. <u>DO</u> YOU KNOW HOW <u>TO</u> DRIVE A TRUCK?
11. THEY LIVE IN A SMALL APARTMENT.
12. <u>DOES</u> YOUR DOG BITE?
13. WHY IS YOUR CONSCIENCE BOTHER-ING YOU?
14. I FEEL GUILTY ABOUT IT. ("Guilty" is signed as "guilt" plus "Y.")
15. WHEN <u>DID</u> YOUR CHILD HAVE THE MUMPS?
16. <u>DO</u> YOU WANT MORE, OR LESS?
17. HE IS PLAYING WITH HIS NEW TOY.
18. WE WILL PLAY A GAME AFTER WE FINISH THIS LESSON.
19. HOW MUCH <u>DOES</u> HE WEIGH?
20. <u>DOES</u> THE <u>ZOO</u> HAVE ANY LIONS?
21. <u>DO</u> YOU WANT <u>TO</u> BUY A FOOTBALL TICKET?
22. DON'T TEASE THE LION BECAUSE HE WILL BITE YOU.
23. I SOLD BOTH <u>OF</u> MY TICKETS FOR TEN DOLLARS.
24. HOW <u>DID</u> HE BREAK HIS NEW TOY?

B) Exercises in Decoding

Decode the following illustrated exercises:

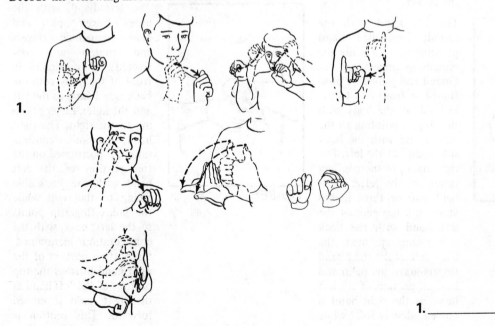

1.

1. _____

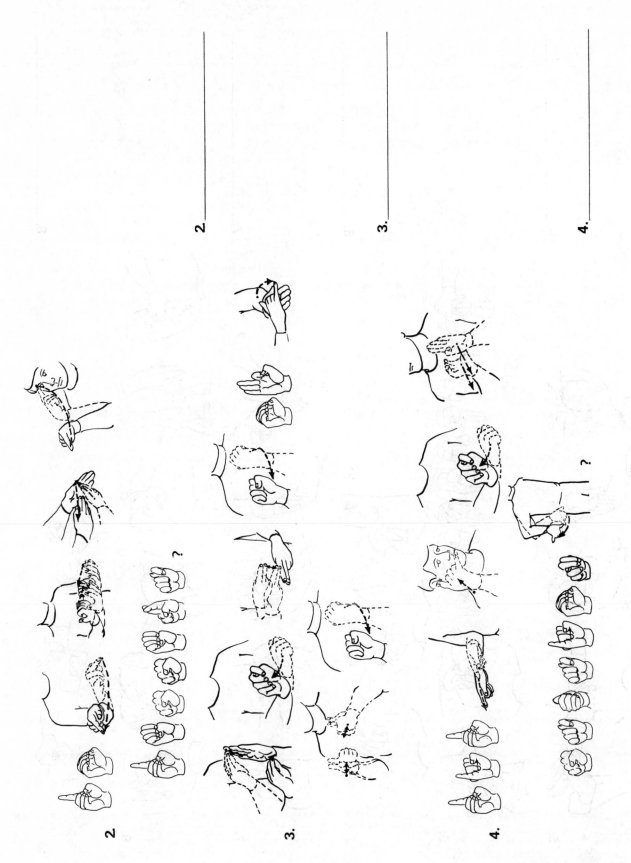

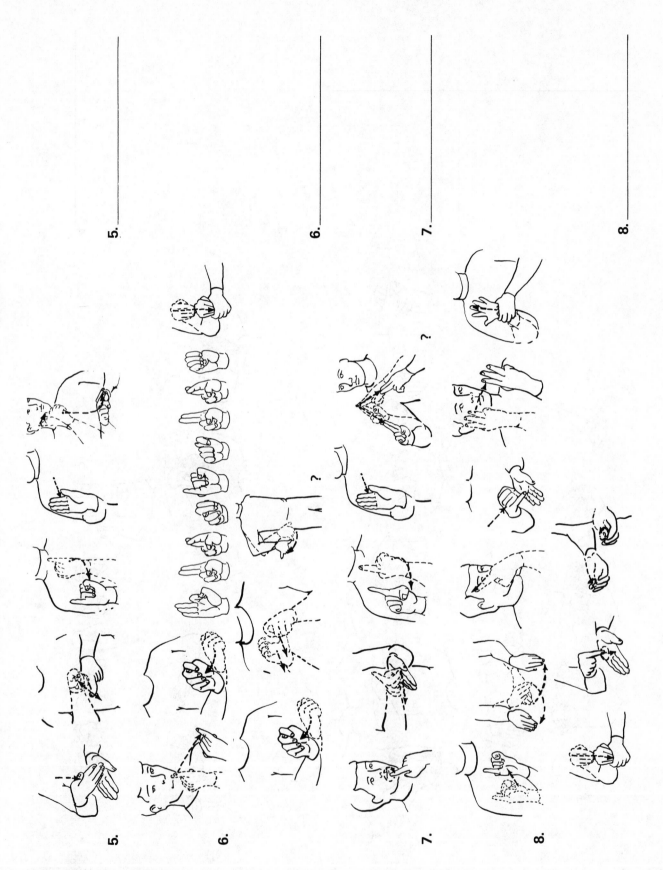

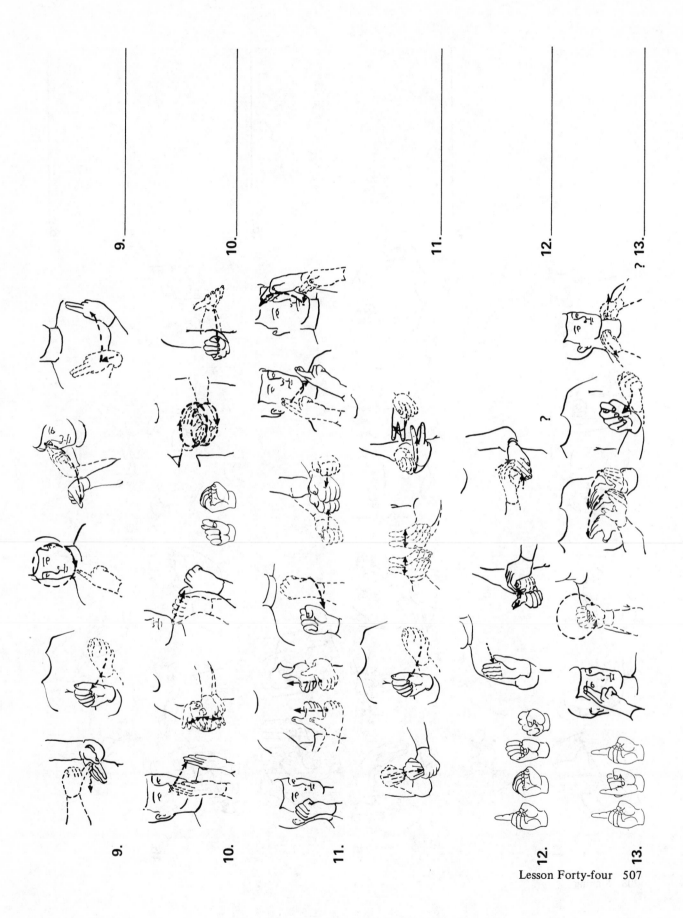

9.

10.

11.

12.

? 13.

9.

10.

11.

12.

13.

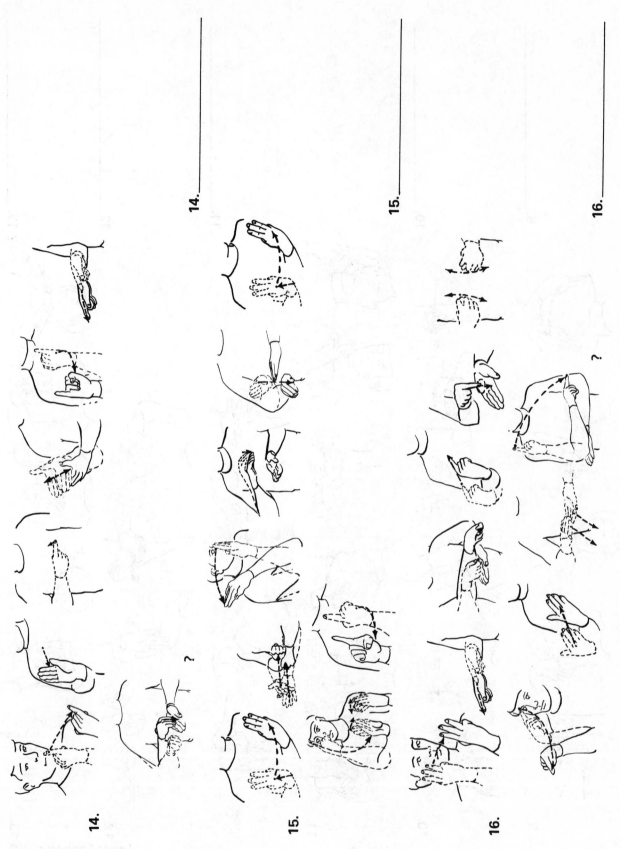

17.

18.

19.

17.

18.

19.

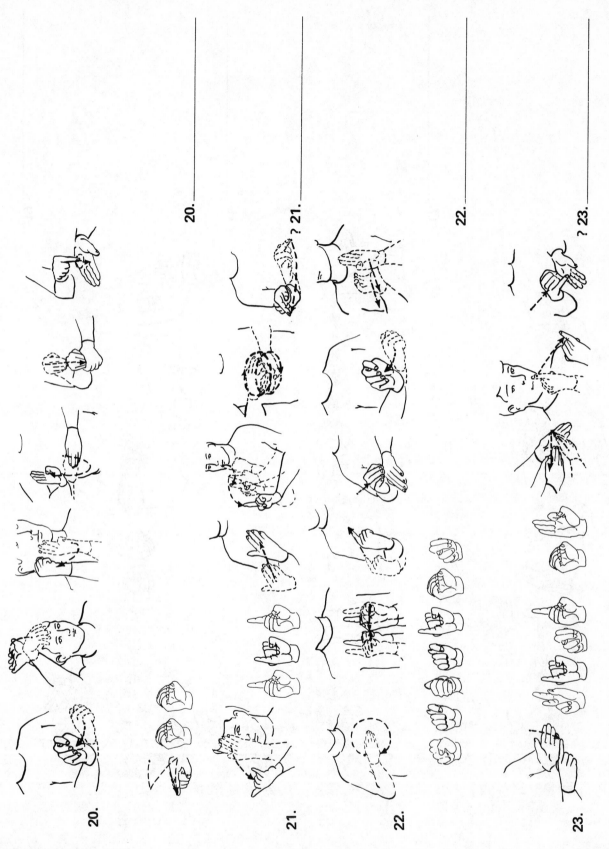

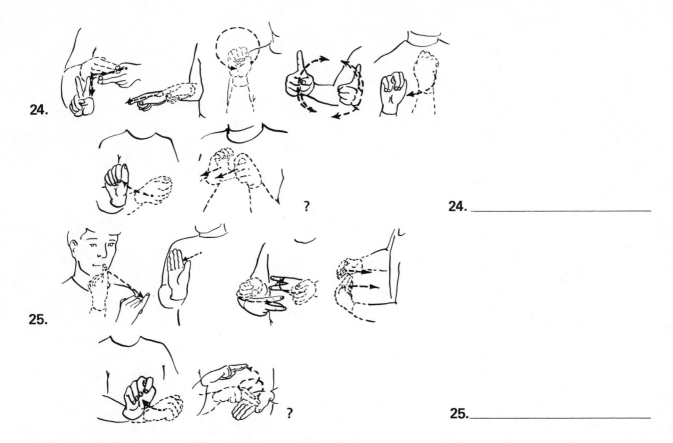

24. _____

25. _____

C) Answers for Decoding Part (B), Lesson 44

Underlined words indicate that they should have been fingerspelled.

1. I AM TEACHING HIM HOW <u>TO</u> SUBTRACT.
2. <u>DO</u> YOU (plural) WANT PIE FOR <u>DESSERT</u>?
3. LIST THE NAMES <u>OF</u> THESE ANIMALS.
4. <u>DID</u> YOU CALL THE BUS <u>STATION</u> YET?
5. STOP TEASING YOUR SISTER.
6. IS THE <u>FURNITURE</u> IN THE TRUCK YET?
7. WHO DESIGNED YOUR HOUSE?
8. I DON'T THINK IT WILL GROW IN THIS SOIL.
9. DRAW A FACE FOR US.
10. BE CAREFUL NOT <u>TO</u> CONFUSE THEM.
11. SHE LIVES WITH HER FOSTER PARENT IN A SMALL APARTMENT.
12. <u>DOES</u> YOUR TURTLE BITE?
13. <u>DID</u> HE EVER HAVE THE MUMPS?
14. IS YOUR CONSCIENCE BOTHERING YOU (singular) AGAIN?
15. WE GOT LESS THAN WE EXPECTED. ("Got" is signed as "get" plus past tense.)
16. WILL YOU (singular) BUY ME THIS TOY FOR MY BIRTHDAY?
17. <u>DID</u> YOU (singular) SEE THE FOOTBALL GAME YESTERDAY?
18. <u>DOES</u> SHE WANT <u>TO</u> SELL HER TICKET?
19. HOW MUCH <u>DO</u> YOU (plural) THINK I WEIGH?
20. THE LION WAS BORN IN THIS <u>ZOO</u>.
21. WHY <u>DID</u> MY ANSWER CONFUSE YOU (plural)?
22. PLEASE MEET ME AT THE BUS <u>STATION</u>.
23. WHAT <u>KIND OF</u> PIE IS IT?
24. HAVE YOU (singular) EVER DRIVEN A TRUCK?
25. IS YOUR APARTMENT NEAR THE UNIVERSITY?

CHAPTER 3

MANUAL COMMUNICATION APPLIED TO HEARING, SPEECH, AND LANGUAGE EVALUATION

The lessons contained in this chapter present the student with an opportunity to apply previously learned signs and fingerspelling to content pertaining to hearing, speech and language evaluation. The lessons present only *sample material* which the student may use for practice purposes. The professional clinician would be the one to judge how best to supplement and/or modify this material to meet a specific need.

Before beginning the evaluation procedures, carefully ascertain the extent to which the patient can decode manual communication, and be equally careful that the patient understands how adept you, the clinician, are with the process. The easiest way to accomplish these aims is either to establish mutual levels indirectly through "ice breaking" social conversation before starting to work where each of you can assess the other, or (fastest) bluntly to identify your proficiency level and ask the patient as to his/her proficiency. A parent or guardian may tell you about a child's ability, but they often are not the best judges.

lesson forty-five / Child's Case History

This lesson presents sample case history questions that a clinician would need to ask a deaf parent or guardian whose child has been referred for a hearing, speech and language evaluation. It is assumed that the parent or guardian both understands and uses one or more (alone or in combination) of the five modes which generally characterize Manual Communication as explained in the foreword. As suggested previously, evaluate the parent or guardian's communicative skills and proceed accordingly.

Using previously learned signs and fingerspelling words for which you may not have learned the sign, encode items 1 through 100 below.

Instructions to the Parent or Guardian:

My name is _____. Before we start testing your child's hearing, speech and language, I would like to ask you some questions. Some of the questions will be easy and some may be difficult to answer. Please try answering them as best you know or can remember. What you tell us may help us decide what the problem is and how we can be of help to you and your child.

To the Clinician:

The following questions are not exhaustive, but are intended to cover basic information categories, and to indicate information areas to be probed. It is assumed that at any appropriate time you will insert "tell me about it," or otherwise request fuller details. The questions listed are useful for practice material, as well as for guides to diagnostic inquiry. The clinician, when interacting with the parent or guardian of a child, should also keep in mind that you can't "whisper" in sign. If the child is around, visual field (even mirrors) can prevent private comments.

1. What is the child's full name?
2. Are you the parent of this child?
3. Has the child been tested before?
   a. Where?
   b. By whom?
   c. What is the name of the center, clinic or hospital?

If previous testing has been done, then the clinician should inform the parent/guardian of the following: It is important for us to know the results of the tests that the child has had. Before we can write to get these results, we need your permission. If you will sign this release form, we can proceed to get the necessary information.

4. What is the month, day and year of the child's birthdate?

5. Where do you live?
6. Does the child live with you?
7. What is your telephone number?
8. What is the father's full name?
9. How old is he?
10. How much education has he had?
11. Where does he live?
12. What is the mother's full name?
13. What is her age?
14. How much education has she had?
15. Where does she live?
16. What is the father's occupation?
17. What is the mother's occupation?
18. Who is your family doctor?
19. What is his/her address?
20. Does your child go to school?
21. What is the name of the school?
    a. What is the address?
22. Are there other children in the family?
    a. How many?
    b. Tell me the name and age of each child.
23. Do any of the children have any hearing, speech or language problems?
24. Does the father have any hearing, speech or language problems?
25. Does the mother have any hearing, speech or language problems?
26. Are there any other adults living in the same house?
    a. How many?
    b. Are they relatives?
    c. How old are they?
    d. Do they have any problems?
27. How many times have you been pregnant before?
    a. How many previous pregnancies miscarried?
28. When you were pregnant with this child, did you have any exceptional problems? For example:

514

a. German measles?

b. Blood problem?

c. Nervous trouble?

d. High fever?

e. Diabetes?

f. Falls or accidents?

g. Other?

29. Where was your baby born?

30. How long were you in labor?

31. What was the length of the baby?

32. Who was your doctor?

33. How much did the baby weigh at birth?

34. Was the baby born blue?

35. Was the baby born with yellow skin?

36. Did the baby have any blue scars?

37. Were any drugs used during labor or birth?

38. Did the doctor have to use surgery to get the baby?

39. Did the doctor have to use forceps?

40. Was the baby born before the nine months time?

41. Did the doctor tell you that the baby was born healthy?

42. Did the baby come out head first?

43. Did the baby have any problems eating after birth?

44. Did the baby seem nervous to you?

45. Did the baby have any swallowing problems?

46. How much weight did the baby lose after birth?

a. How fast?

b. What was the doctor's explanation?

47. When did the child:

a. Hold up his/her head by himself/herself?

b. Start to crawl?

c. Start to walk by himself/herself?

d. Stand by himself/herself?

e. Get the first tooth?

f. Start to eat with a spoon?

48. How old was the child when he/she became toilet trained?

49. Which hand does the child use to do things?

50. Do you think he/she is quick or slow in doing things?

51. Does the child fall easily?

52. Does the child have any difficulty chewing or swallowing?

53. Does the child sleep well at night?

a. How many hours?

b. Does he/she ever have bad dreams?

c. Does he/she wet the bed at night?

d. Does he/she wet the bed during the day?

54. Does the child prefer to play alone or with other children?

55. Does he/she show fear of routine things?

a. Often.

b. Sometimes.

c. Almost never.

56. Does he/she show *exaggerated* fear of fearful things?

a. Often.

b. Sometimes.

c. Almost never.

57. What things does the child fear?

58. Do you feel that the child is nervous?

59. How does he/she show it?

60. What does the child do when he/she meets a person for the first time?

61. What game(s) does the child prefer to play?

62. Does he/she cooperate when you ask him/her to do things?

63. Will the child cooperate with us if you are not in the room?

64. Does the child pay attention when you talk to him/her?

65. Is the child easy to manage?

66. How do you communicate with the child?

a. Speech only?

b. Use of sign language?

c. Speech and sign language?

d. Paper and pencil?

67. Does the child sign?

a. How many signs does he/she know?

68. Does the child seem to enjoy handling things?

69. Does he/she listen for sounds that things make?

70. Does the child watch your face when you are talking to him/her?

71. What does he/she do when he/she wants something?

72. Do you ever play with the child?

73. Does he/she speak?

a. What words does he/she say?

b. How often does he/she say them?

74. Does the child use sentences?

a. Give me an example of a sentence he/she would use?

75. What diseases has the child had?

a. How old was the child when he/she had each disease?

b. How severe was it?

c. Was anything done about it?

d. Were there any special problems?

76. Has the child had any operations or accidents?

77. Does anyone in the family have a health problem?

78. Does the child have any problems with his/her eyes?

79. Does the child wear glasses?

80. How often does he/she visit the dentist?

81. Is there any problem with his/her hearing?

82. Does he/she use a hearing aid?
    a. What kind?
    b. How old is the aid?

83. How old was he/she when he/she started to use the hearing aid?

84. Does he/she use it every day?

85. Does he/she depend on it?

86. Is the hearing aid working all right now?
    a. How long ago was the ear insert now being used made?

87. Did you bring the hearing aid with you today?

88. Does he/she catch colds very often?

89. Does the child ever complain of ear aches?

90. Is he/she on medication now?
    a. What kind of medicine is he/she taking?
    b. What for?
    c. How long has he/she been taking it?
    d. Any special problems connected with the medication?

91. Are there any foods that he/she is not permitted to eat?

92. When did the child start school?

93. Does he/she seem to enjoy school?
    a. If not, why not?
    b. What method is used to teach him/her?

94. Do you think he/she is making progress?

95. What does his/her teacher tell you?

96. What do you think is the problem?

97. Do you receive support money from any organization?
    a. What is the name of the organization?

98. Who will pay for this visit?

99. If we need to see the child again, when can you come?
    a. Do you prefer a morning or afternoon appointment?
    b. Will you drive or do you want us to arrange it for you?
    c. Do you have our telephone number if you need to cancel your appointment?

100. Do you have any questions that you want to ask before we start testing the child?

lesson forty-six / Hearing and Hearing Aid Evaluation

This lesson presents sample material pertaining to an audiological evaluation. The clinician, having carefully ascertained the patient's manual communication skills as previously suggested, may choose to supplement and/or alter what is presented here to meet a specific need.

Using previously learned signs, and fingerspelling words for which you may not have learned the sign, encode the following material.

---

1. Today, we want to evaluate how well you can hear. Before we start testing, we want to ask you some questions.
   a. Do you ever have ear-aches?
   b. Do you have one now?
   c. In which ear?
   d. Have you ever had ear surgery?
   e. When?
   f. Do you seem to understand people better when they are talking in a quiet or noisy place?
   g. What are some of the words that are difficult for you to understand?
   h. Do you wear a hearing aid?
   i. What kind is it?
   j. Do you have it with you today?
   k. Show me where you set the volume.

2. Do you know what a musical tone sounds like? It sounds like this (clinician presents a 500-Hz tone with a tuning fork or by using the bone conduction unit of an audiometer). Now, I will touch your forehead with this instrument and I want you to tell me if you hear it and where you hear the sound. Do you hear it in the middle of your head? Do you hear it better in your left or right ear? Now, tell me if you hear it better when I hold it close to your ear or when I touch the skin behind your ear. Which sounds louder to you?

3. First, we will start testing your right (left) ear. For this test, we would like for you to listen carefully to some musical sounds. These sounds will be similar to the ones you just heard. As soon as you think you heard the tone, we want you to drop a block in the bucket. Remember, drop the block in the bucket as soon as you hear the sound. Don't wait until the sound becomes strong! Now, tell me what I want you to do. Let's practice a little before we start the test.

   Now, we will do the same thing with the other ear. Listen as you did before for the musical sound. As soon as you hear it, drop the block in the bucket.

4. Now, you are going to hear another kind of sound in your right (left) ear. This noise will sound like the wind. We don't want you to pay any attention to it.

Pretend that you don't hear it. As before, we would like for you to listen for the musical sound in your left (right) ear. As soon as you hear the sound, drop the block in the bucket. Do you have any questions? Do you understand what we want you to do?

5. For this test, I am going to say some words to you. For example, you will hear me use the sentence "say the word (*baseball*)," "say the word (*bathtub*)." Sometimes, you will be able to hear these words and sometimes you won't. I want you to drop a block in the bucket each time you think you hear a word. Do you understand what I am asking you to do? Tell me what I want you to do.

6. For this test, I want to evaluate how well you can understand some words that I am going to say to you. Can you hear my voice all right? Am I too loud? Is this loud enough for you? (Do you want my voice to get louder?) Now, I will say some words to you like "dog," "cat," "fish," and "pen." You will have to listen carefully because I will not use signing or fingerspelling and you will *not* be able to watch my lips. I want you to sign or tell me what I said. If you are not sure what I said, you may guess. Do you have any questions? Are you ready?

7. Next, we want to do a hearing aid evaluation. First, we will test you with your own hearing aid to determine how well you can hear with it. Then, we will test you with another hearing aid to determine if it can help you hear any better. As before, I am going to say some words to you. I want you to drop a block in the bucket as soon as you hear the word. Now, I am going to say more words to you, but this time I want you to sign or tell me what I said. As before, I will not sign to you and you will not be able to see my lips. You will have to listen carefully. Tell me when my voice is comfortable for you. Am I loud enough for you? Are you ready?

8. Using one or two different aids, the clinician goes through a similar procedure and tests the patient's speech reception threshold (SRT) and discrimination as well as other types of testing such as establishing tolerance level, discrimination under various signal-to-

517

noise (S/N) conditions, etc.

9. Now that we have finished testing you with these various hearing aids, which one did you like best? Would you like to wear the new hearing aid for a month to see if it really helps you hear better? Do you know how to change the battery? Let me show you how to clean the wax from the ear mold. Do you know how to use the telephone with a hearing aid? Do you have any questions about what we did today?

10. Finally, I want to help you understand some basic ideas about hearing and why you are having difficulty understanding people when they are talking to you. (With the aid of a model or picture of the ear and providing illustrations when necessary, the clinician can help the patient understand some basic concepts concerning hearing.)

This is a picture of the ear. When I speak, the sound comes to this part of your ear, travels through the middle ear and then it goes to what is called the inner ear. Here, there are thousands of nerves which change sounds to electrical signals and send them up to the brain. Sometimes, these nerves become damaged or die. When this happens, the damaged nerves may not be able to hear some sounds well, or if the nerves are dead, you won't be able to hear anything.

A hearing aid may help you depending on how well these nerves are still working. If too many of them are damaged, a hearing aid may not help you very much. We can't be sure until after you have worn the aid for some time. My advice is to try wearing it for awhile. If you think it is helping you, then you can start thinking about buying it. You must remember that a hearing aid rarely gives back normal hearing. Not only will some loudness be lost, but the way things sound can be changed by the aid. This can be annoying, or even discouraging. Just remember that you have to get used to the aid and learn to use it for your best purpose. If you should experience any problems with the aid during these next couple of weeks, call or visit us.

Do you have any questions about anything we did today? If not, thank you for coming and we hope that we have been of some help to you.

lesson forty-seven / Language Evaluation

This lesson presents sample material pertaining to language evaluation. The clinician, having ascertained the patient's manual communication skills as previously suggested, may choose to supplement and/or alter what is presented here to meet a specific need. It is necessary to remember that selection of tests themselves should not have a hearing bias in them, and that you can clearly and completely convey to the patient all instructions necessary for performance of a given test.

Using previously learned signs and fingerspelling words for which you may not have learned the sign, encode the following material.

Instructions to Patient:

Today, I want to evaluate how well you can understand some basic ideas about language. I will sign and fingerspell various things that I want you to show me or do. If you don't understand what I am asking you to do, please feel free to ask me to repeat. Do you have any questions?

1. Here we have four pictures. In each picture, the boy is doing something. Show me the picture of a boy:
   a) eating a pie
   b) looking at his mother's shoes
   c) walking to school
   d) playing with his dog

2. Now, I will give you a dog and a man. Show me how the dog would bite the man.

3. Show me how you would make the man stand up.

4. Show me how you would make the man run.

5. This picture shows the cat is in the box and the dog is out. Which one is not in the box?

6. Show me how a fish would swim in the water.

7. This is a *little* horse and this is a *big* one. Show me how the *little* horse would run.

8. This is a small, red ball and this is a big, blue ball. Show me how you would roll the small, red ball.

9. Which of these two pictures shows that the box is *unopened*?

10. Take this boy and show me how he would wash himself.

11. Which one of these two boys is taller?

12. With your pencil, check (√) the picture that shows a boy pulling a wagon.

13. Give me the picture that shows the girl was pushed by the boy.

14. Which one of these pictures shows the dog is standing on the table?

15. Read these three sentences and check (√) the one that you think is correct.
   a) The boy are playing.
   b) The boys is playing.
   c) The boys are playing.

16. Which one of these sentences is correct?
   a) She know my name.
   b) She knows my name.

17. Which of these sentences is wrong?
   a) They eated the apple.
   b) They ate the apple.

18. Which one of these four words means the same as "man"?
   a) female
   b) male
   c) mail
   d) tree

19. We eat some things with a spoon. What do we do with a cup?

20. I will write some numbers for you and I want you to check (√) the number twelve.
   a) 6
   b) 9
   c) 4
   d) 15
   e) 12
   f) 8

21. Write the number eight for me.

22. Look at these words and check (√) every one that means more than one:
   a) cup
   b) toys
   c) geese
   d) I
   e) us
   f) tables

23. Show me how you would put the ball:
   a) on the box
   b) under the box
   c) beside the box
   d) in the box

24. Tell me which one of these three things you would wear:

519

a) food
b) shoes
c) pencil

25. Look at these four words and circle the word that starts with "P."

    a) ball
    b) cab
    c) pear
    d) cap

26. Circle the *smallest* number:

    a) 12
    b) 8
    c) 11
    d) 3
    e) 9

27. Read this sentence and circle the word that tells "who." John is walking to school.

28. Read this sentence and tell me what the girl is writing. The girl is writing a letter.

29. Circle the word that tells "how many": John borrowed five books from me yesterday.

30. One of these words is different from the other words. Which one is different? Why?

    a) fruit
    b) orange
    c) candy
    d) banana

31. Find the picture that is the *same* as this one.

32. Can you tell me what is happening in this picture?

33. Draw a face for me.

34. How many days are there in one week?

35. Complete this sentence for me:

    a) Today is Tuesday. Yesterday was _____.
    b) If today is Friday, then tomorrow must be _____.

36. Circle the word which is spelled correctly.

    a) Wedesday
    b) televizion
    c) picture
    d) booklit

37. Check (√) the word that means "color" in this sentence.

  a) The purple cat ate the mouse.

38. Draw a circle around the word that means the *opposite* of "close."

    a) closet
    b) lose
    c) open
    d) chose

39. Select the word that should not be in this group of words:

a) refrigerator
b) policeman
c) sink
d) stove

40. What do we call a person who works in a library?

    a) library
    b) libraries
    c) librarian

41. Complete the sentence by selecting the right word from this list. My _____ has been in the hospital for two weeks.

    a) car
    b) father
    c) phone
    d) dinner

42. There are three children in our family. Mary is ten years old, John is five and Bill is twelve. Who is the *youngest* of the three children?

43. Complete these sentences by adding either "ing" or "ed" to the word:

    a) John is walk_____to school.
    b) She play_____with the red ball.
    c) I am eat_____candy.

44. Show me how you would arrange these words to make a complete sentence.

    a) want I you to help.

45. Check (√) the sentence that tells you that it happened *first*.

    a) I ate.
    b) I woke up.
    c) I ran to school.

46. These four pictures tell a story. Look at them carefully and tell me which picture should be first. Which one should be last?

47. Which of these sentences is correct? Why?

    a) "I see he."
    b) "They sees him."
    c) "I see you."

48. Next, I will ask you to do some things. For example, "Stand up, count to four, walk to the door, but don't open it."

49. Select the word that means the *same* as "not happy":

    a) dishappy
    b) ilhappy
    c) unhappy
    d) be happy

50. Roll this ball to me. Now, if you did this yesterday, you would say: "I _____ the ball to you."

lesson forty-eight / Aspects of Speech Evaluation

The speech production-discrimination, oral peripheral examination, and psychometrics aspects of a patient's evaluation are very broad and complex. This book can not attempt to prescribe the elements that should be contained therein, much less to indicate specific tests to be used. Instead, under each heading, some of the more commonly used expressions are used for you to practice. For instance, the phrases and sentences listed under *Speech Evaluation* could be used as a resource for administering any one of the dozens of published tests of articulatory production. Also, it is not intended that the sentences must be used verbatim. They are, as was noted, for practice and to alert you to particular words and signs you may need to use. If you don't know the sign, use fingerspelling.

At all times, it is necessary to remember that these evaluations are being performed with the hearing handicapped. This must remind you that the selection of tests will be guided by the criteria that the tests themselves should not have a hearing bias in them, and that you can clearly and completely convey to the patient all instructions necessary for performance of the test.

Speech:

1. Look at the:
   a) pictures
   b) objects
   c) colors
2. Name the:
   a) pictures
   b) objects
   c) colors
3. Say it again for me.
4. Try speaking slowly.
5. Try to say it the best you can.
6. What are they doing?
7. Say it quickly, several times, without pausing (stopping).
8. Repeat after me.
9. Watch my lips (tongue, teeth, etc).
10. Try to say it as I do.
11. Use this word in a sentence for me.
12. Read these words (sentences, this paragraph) out loud.
13. Tell me about this.
14. Tell me a story about . . .
15. I will show you two pictures. Name them both, saying them as if they were one word. Let's practice it. Good! Now, I will change only one of the pictures each time, and you keep naming the two pictures as if they were one word. Do you understand what I am asking you to do? (If necessary, repeat the directions and demonstrate.)

Discrimination:

1. Now, I want you to tell me which one of these is:
   a) longer?
   b) shorter?
   c) louder?
   d) softer?
   e) higher in pitch?
   f) lower in pitch?
2. Close your eyes and I will make a sound. Then open your eyes and try to tell me which one of these things made the sound.
3. Again, close your eyes and listen. I will make two sounds. I want you to tell me if it was the *same* sound both times, or if it was a *different* sound each time.
4. (Repeat number three, but insert the word "speech" before the word "sounds.")
5. Now, I will say two words. Tell me if the words start (end) with the *same* sound, or a *different* sound.
6. I will say three words. Two of the words start (end) with the same sound. Listen and tell me which word begins (ends) with a *different* sound.

Oral-Peripheral Examination:

1. Watch what I do, and then you do it in the mirror.
2. Smile

(In items three through eight it may be necessary to demonstrate to the patient what you are requesting him/her to do.)

521

3. Frown.
4. Stick out your lower lip.
5. Wrinkle your upper lip.
6. Wrinkle your lower lip.
7. Pucker your lips, as for a whistle.
8. Stick your tongue out flat.
9. Open your mouth so I can see inside.
10. Keep your mouth open.
11. This is a tongue depressor to hold your tongue down out of the way.
12. Take this gauze pad and hold your tongue down like this.
13. Take a deep breath.
14. Say a long "ah" for me.
15. Keep saying "ah-ah" until I tell you to stop.
16. Tilt your head back, like this.
17. Rest your head on your arm, like this.
18. This is an otoscope. It is like a special flashlight to help me look at your ear.
19. I want you to say "buh-buh-buh" as fast as you can.
20. (Repeat number 19, substituting, "duh-duh-duh," "guh-guh-guh," and "la-la-la.")
21. Listen to the pattern or rhythm I use when I say this sentence and then try to imitate it.
22. Watch the pattern or rhythm I tap on the table. Then you imitate it, using the sound _____.

Psychometrics:

1. Point to (show me) the one that _____.
2. Which one of these does *not* belong?
3. Which one of these is not like the others?
4. What is this?
5. When I say a word, point to the picture (object) that goes with the word.
6. You do it now.
7. Make one like mine.
8. Take the pencil and draw one like this.
9. Do not start until I tell you.
10. Now, please stop.
11. Work as fast as you can.
12. Take all the time you need. (You don't have to hurry.)
13. You are correct (right).
14. This is wrong.
15. Draw a picture of a man (woman, yourself) for me. You don't have to hurry. I want you to draw the entire (full) figure. Do the best job you can.
16. Which two things (objects) go together?
17. Start here and come out there, like this. Do not cross any lines, and do not go into any "dead ends." Do not lift your pencil off the paper. Let me show you what I want you to do. Now, you do it.
18. Check (√) each one of these that does not belong.
19. Arrange these to make a complete picture.
20. Arrange these so they tell a story.
21. What does the word _____ mean?
22. Repeat these numbers after me.
23. Tell me the days of the week (months of the year).
24. Count to ____ for me.
25. Don't guess.
26. Think about it carefully before you answer me.

REFERENCES

Guillory, L. M. 1966. *Expressive and Receptive Fingerspelling for Hearing Adults*. Claitor's Book Store, Baton Rouge, Louisiana.

Hoemann, H. W. 1970. *Improved Techniques of Communication: A Training Manual for Use with Severely Handicapped Deaf Clients*. Bowling Green State University.

Kannapell, B., Hamilton, L. and Bornstein, H. 1969. *Signs for Instructional Purposes*. Gallaudet College Press, Washington, D.C.

O'Rourke, T. J., Ed. 1970. *A Basic Course in Manual Communication*. National Association of the Deaf, Communicative Skills Program.

Rush, M. L. 1970. *The Language of Directions - A Programmed Workbook*. Alexander Graham Bell Association for the Deaf.

Stokoe, W., Casterline, D. and Croneberg, C. 1965. *A Dictionary of the American Sign Language*. Gallaudet College Press, Washington, D.C.

Washington State School for the Deaf, The. 1972. *An Introduction to Manual English*. The Washington State School for the Deaf, Vancouver, Washington.

Watson, D. O. 1973. *Talk With Your Hands, Volume I*. George Banta Company, Menasha, Wisconsin.

Index

The page numbers indicate where the signs are first presented.

tell, 45
temperature, 437
than, 156
thank, 124
that (conjunction), 62
the, 37
them, 44
then, 157
there (expletive), 93
these, 62
they, 37
thin, 331
thing, 82
think, thought, 136
thirst, 226
this, 45
those, 62
thrill, 320
throat, 379
through, 238
throw, 438
ticket, 503
time (abstract), 248
time, o'clock, 248
-tion, 71
tired, 190
to, toward, 113
toilet, 180
tomorrow, 178
tongue, 476
together, 81
too, 116
toothbrush, 378
total communication, 156
touch, contact, 237
toy, 500
train (noun), railroad, 389
train (verb), 158
tree, 191
trouble, 463
truck, 502
true, sure, 102
try, 214
turtle, 440

ugly, 416
umbrella, 428
uncle, 192
under, 180
understand, 147
university, 52
until, 114
up, 193
us, 43
use, 125

various, 307
very, 124
vinegar, 438
visit, 190

vocabulary, 146
voice, 169
volunteer, candidate, 306
vote, 365

wait, 260
walk, 82
wall, 426
want, 83
war, 451
warm, 451
warn, 307
was, 60
wash, 294
waste, 181
watch (verb), 368
water, 136
way, 341
we, 37
weak, 354
wealth, 415
wear, 125
wed, 465
week, 179
weigh, weight, 500
welcome, 452
were, 60
wet, 466
what, 45
when, 82
where, 62
whether, 136
which, 135
white, 169
who, 44
whom, 44
whose, 44
why, 52
wife, 464
will (auxillary verb), 45
win, victory, 341
winter, 285
wind (noun), 403
window, 202
wise, 332
wish, 214
with, 51
without, 51
woman, 332
wonderful, 283
word, 146
work, 296
workshop, 392
world, 379
worry, 463
worse, 487
worth, 366
would, 93
write, 92
wrong, mistake, error, 102

-y, 72
year, 179
yellow, 248
yes, 91
yesterday, 179
yet, 391
you (plural), 36
you (singular), 36
young, 285
your (singular), 53
yourself, 53
yourselves, 53

Special Acknowledgment

A special note of gratitude and indebtedness is due Dr. Richard E. Ham, Associate Dean for Administration, College of Osteopathic Medicine, and former Director of the School of Hearing and Speech Sciences at Ohio University, for his constant encouragement and enthusiasm in the implementation of the idea of imparting the skill of Manual Communication to speech and hearing majors as well as to nonmajors.

Additionally, I appreciate his invaluable suggestions and constructive criticisms as well as the length of time he spent in reading the manuscript. His involvement, which could not have been any greater if the project had been his very own, contributed significantly toward making this book possible.

Acknowledgments

I wish to express my gratitude to my administrative assistant, Sherry Edwards, for her dedicated involvement with the development of this manuscript from its inception.

I am grateful to Dr. George D. Davis, Chairman of the Department of Speech Pathology and Audiology at The University of Akron and former Coordinator of Clinical Services in the School of Hearing and Speech Sciences at Ohio University, for his direct and indirect support during the preparation of an earlier draft of this manuscript.

To the students Cindy, Diane, Kelly, Marlene, Pam, Roberta, and Sandy, who volunteered so much of their valuable time to help prepare this book, I should like to express my heartfelt thanks.

I should like to acknowledge the cooperation of the publishing staff at University Park Press, especially Theodore W. Logan, who provided many valuable suggestions in the preparation of this manuscript.

Most of all, I acknowledge my indebtedness to the many students who used and criticized portions of an earlier draft and, in the process, taught me while I attempted to teach them.

Finally, I acknowledge the great population with hearing handicaps who constitute the challenge and the stimulus to all who would attempt to bridge the silent gap in their world of communication.